BIBLICAL AND THEOLOGICAL STUDIES

BENJAMIN BRECKINRIDGE WARFIELD
(1887)

BIBLICAL
AND
THEOLOGICAL STUDIES

BY

BENJAMIN BRECKINRIDGE WARFIELD

*Professor of Didactic and Polemic Theology
in the Theological Seminary of Princeton
New Jersey, 1887-1921*

Edited by

SAMUEL G. CRAIG

*For I am persuaded, that neither death, nor life, nor
angels, nor principalities, nor things present, nor things
to come, nor powers, nor height, nor depth, nor any
other creature, shall be able to separate us from the
love of God, which is in Christ Jesus our Lord.*

Distributed by

BAKER BOOK HOUSE
Grand Rapids, Michigan

PRINTED IN THE UNITED STATES OF AMERICA

FOREWORD

THIS is the third volume of the writings of Benjamin B. Warfield to be published by the Presbyterian and Reformed Publishing Company. The first contained his principal writings dealing with *The Inspiration and Authority of the Bible,* the second with his principal writings dealing with *The Person and Work of Christ.* This third volume contains a more varied assortment but they deal for the most part with the Biblical doctrine of God, the Biblical doctrine of predestination, and the Biblical doctrine of faith and matters related to these themes. In addition it includes articles dealing with such matters as the supernaturalism of Christianity, the antiquity and unity of the human race, mysticism, and the prophecies of Paul.

All the articles included in this volume, with the exception of the one entitled, "Are They Few That Be Saved?," have been taken from the ten volumes of the collected writings of Warfield —all of which have been out of print for some years—published under the auspices of the Oxford University Press subsequent to his death. To be more specific, three have been taken from the volume entitled *Christology and Criticism,* five from the one entitled *Studies in Theology,* and eight from the one entitled *Biblical Doctrines.*

Other Biblical and theological studies, in the form of sermons, may be found in its supplement. These sermons, all of which were preached in the chapel of Princeton Theological Seminary to audiences composed almost exclusively of theological students, have been taken from his published sermons—two from the volume entitled *The Power of God unto Salvation* and two from the one entitled *The Saviour of the World.* Warfield's sermons serve to remind us in a way that some of his more technical writings naturally fail to do that in him a mind of rare power, extraordinary erudition, and a remarkable facility for accurate, concise and telling expression was combined with a deeply religious heart—the primary qualification of a truly Christian theologian.

A special feature of this volume is its sketch of Warfield as a man and theologian. It may seem that this sketch should have appeared in the first of the volumes of his writings published by the Presbyterian and Reformed Publishing Company. However, in view of the fact that this volume contains a more varied assortment of his writings, dealing with more aspects of his teaching, it has been thought that it has an even better claim to this distinction. It is to be hoped that the day is not far distant when some scholar with the requisite knowledge and ability will give the theological world something like a full length portrait of Warfield as a man and theologian. Believing as we do that he labored within the main stream of Christianity as it makes its way across the centuries from the Protevangelium to the Consummation at a time when its progress, humanly speaking, was being seriously impeded—as is still the case—we are confident that such a volume would have more than a passing value.

Thirty years have come and gone since Warfield's death. Certain of the chapters of this volume were written as much as fifty years ago. For those who like the Athenians of Paul's day are interested only in telling or hearing some new thing this will be its sufficient condemnation. It will be found, however, we believe, that it deals with matters of perennial interest in a manner which has rarely, if ever, been surpassed. If many of the names which appear in its pages are unfamiliar to its readers it will nonetheless be found that the Biblical and theological views which they defended or opposed are much under discussion today. What is more, there is every reason to think that this will continue to be the case for years and even centuries to come. If we mistake not, Warfield's contribution to their discussion is, as a whole, among the best available or that is apt to be available for a long time to come.

The three volumes of the writings of Warfield thus far published by the Presbyterian and Reformed Publishing Company contain less than a third of the material included in the ten volumes published by the Oxford University Press—in terms of bulk though hardly in terms of value—not to mention his numerous writings not included in the Oxford edition. A large portion of the material included in the Oxford edition, other than that already republished, consists of studies of Calvin and Calvinism, Augustine and Augustinianism, and Christian Perfectionism. Whether interest in some or all of these writings is sufficiently widespread to warrant their republication in the near future, in view of prevailing high publication costs, is not clear. Most of the interest thus far expressed has been in his more distinctly Biblical and theological writings—two or three more of which would have been included in this volume if the space had been available. It is regrettable that the sponsors of the Oxford Edition so greatly underestimated the demand that would develop for the writings of Warfield. On the other hand, the fact that the writings of Warfield are more in demand today than at the time of his death may indicate a change for the better in the religious and theological atmosphere.

S. G. C.

Princeton, New Jersey

CONTENTS

FOREWORD v

BENJAMIN B. WARFIELD xi

CHAPTER   PAGE

I. CHRISTIAN SUPERNATURALISM 1

II. THE BIBLICAL DOCTRINE OF THE TRINITY 22

III. "GOD OUR FATHER AND THE LORD JESUS CHRIST" .. 60

IV. THE DIVINE MESSIAH IN THE OLD TESTAMENT 79

V. THE SPIRIT OF GOD IN THE OLD TESTAMENT 127

VI. THE SUPERNATURAL BIRTH OF JESUS 157

VII. THE FORESIGHT OF JESUS 169

VIII. MISCONCEPTION OF JESUS, AND BLASPHEMY OF THE SON OF MAN 196

IX. ON THE ANTIQUITY AND THE UNITY OF THE HUMAN RACE 238

X. IMPUTATION 262

XI. PREDESTINATION 270

XII. ARE THEY FEW THAT BE SAVED? 334

XIII. ON THE BIBLICAL NOTION OF "RENEWAL" 351

XIV. ON FAITH IN ITS PSYCHOLOGICAL ASPECTS 375

XV. FAITH 404

XVI. MYSTICISM AND CHRISTIANITY 445

XVII. THE PROPHECIES OF ST. PAUL 463

SUPPLEMENT: SERMONS

I. GOD'S IMMEASURABLE LOVE 505

II. THE PRODIGAL SON 523

III. THE LEADING OF THE SPIRIT 543

IV. FALSE RELIGIONS AND THE TRUE 560

BENJAMIN B. WARFIELD

Benjamin Breckinridge Warfield was born at "Grasmere" near Lexington, Kentucky, November 5, 1851 and died at Princeton, New Jersey, February 17, 1921.

His progenitors of English and Scotch-Irish origin, on both his paternal and maternal sides, were early settlers in this country who like their descendants took an active and often a leading part in the political, educational and religious problems of the day in which they lived.

His father, William Warfield, was a well-to-do farmer, owner of a considerable landed estate, who was a widely recognized authority on the breeding of cattle.[1] His mother was the daughter of the Rev. Robert Jefferson Breckinridge, D.D., LL.D., distinguished as a preacher, Moderator of the 1841 General Assembly of the Presbyterian Church (Old School Branch), president of Jefferson College in Pennsylvania, president and professor of theology as well as founder of the theological Seminary at Danville, Kentucky, advocate of the emancipation of the slaves and the maintenance of the Union, temporary chairman of the Republican Convention of 1864 which renominated Abraham Lincoln, and most permanently known perhaps as the author of two volumes of systematic theology entitled *The Knowledge of God Objectively and Subjectively Considered*.

His early education was received in private schools in nearby Lexington where he was fortunate in having among his teachers Lewis Barbour, afterwards professor of mathematics in Central University, and James K. Patterson, afterwards president of the State College of Kentucky. He entered the College of New Jersey—now Princeton University—as a sophomore and graduated with the highest honors of his class in 1871 at the age of nineteen. He took an active interest in undergraduate activities, won prizes for essay and debate in the American Whig

---

[1] He was the author of *The Theory and Practice of Cattle-Breeding* and *American Short Horn Importations*.

Society and was one of the editors of the *Nassau Literary Magazine*.

His early tastes were strongly scientific. He collected bird's eggs, butterflies and moths, and geological specimens; studied the fauna and flora of his neighborhood; read Darwin's newly published books with enthusiasm; and counted Audubon's works on American birds and mammals his chief treasure. He came to Princeton the same year that James McCosh arrived from Scotland to become one of the most famous of its presidents. That Dr. McCosh did not succeed in making him a Darwinian, as in the case of so many of his fellow-students, finds its explanation in the fact, as he himself has told us,[2] that knowing his *Origin of Species* and *The Variations of Animals and Plants Under Domestication* "almost from A to Izzard" he was already a "Darwinian of the purest water" before coming under McCosh's influence—a position which he later repudiated, not without warrant as even biologists have come more and more to admit.[3] During his college days he took a special interest in mathematics and physics and planned to seek the fellowship in experimental science but was dissuaded from this by his father on the ground that he did not need the money in order to pursue graduate studies and that it would be more profitable for him to spend the time studying in Europe without being bound to any particular course of study.

His departure for Europe was delayed by family illness with

[2] *Princeton Alumni Weekly*, April 19, 1926.

[3] Though Warfield early "outgrew" Darwinism, as he put it, he maintained to the end a keen and informed interest in the theories of evolution that from time to time made their appearance. He never denied that evolution is a method that God has employed in bringing the world to its present stage of development, but he did deny with emphasis that it is the only method He has employed. Its fatal weakness as an all-sufficient explanation, he maintained, is its inability to account not only for the origin of things but for the appearance of anything specifically new since the creation of the original world stuff, such as man and particularly the God-man and all the redemptive deeds that have their center in Him. To account for the specifically new we need, he ever alleged, an act of God analogous to what we know as miracle—a "flash of the will that can." He did not ignore the basic difference between creation and evolution. Since creation is origination and evolution modification it will remain forever true, he insisted, that what is created is not evolved and what is evolved is not created.

the result that it was not until February 1872 that he embarked. He first went to Edinburgh. After spending some time there he transferred to Heidelberg. Writing from the latter place in the mid-summer of that year he announced his decision to enter the Christian ministry—an announcement that came as a surprise to his family and friends as he had given no previous intimation of a serious intention of studying theology, and was especially pleasing to his mother who had often expressed the hope that her sons would become ministers. We have no knowledge as to when or why he made this decision as, like his father, he was ever reticent with regard to personal matters. It may be added that he had made a public profession of faith and united with the Second Presbyterian Church in Lexington in his sixteenth year.

He entered Princeton Theological Seminary in 1873 and was graduated with the class of 1876. Licensed to preach by the Presbytery of Ebenezer of Kentucky in 1875, he was stated supply of the Presbyterian Church of Concord, Kentucky, during that summer. During the summer of 1876 he was stated supply of the First Presbyterian Church of Dayton, Ohio. He received a call to become the pastor of the latter church but declined it in order that he might go abroad for further study. On the third of August of that summer he was married to Miss Annie Pearce Kinkead, daughter of a prominent lawyer, and shortly thereafter they sailed for Europe where he studied at Leipsic. In the course of the year he was offered an appointment in the Old Testament Department of Western Theological Seminary in Pittsburgh but declined the offer because the New Testament had now become his main interest—a marked change from the time when as a school boy he strenuously, though unsuccessfully, objected to studying Greek—so his brother Ethelbert has related[4]—on the ground that since he expected to follow a scientific career he would have no need for Greek.

Following his return to America, late in the summer of 1877,

[4] Large use has been made of the biographical note by Ethelbert D. Warfield in *Revelation and Inspiration* (Oxford edition) as a source of factual information.

he became assistant pastor of the First Presbyterian Church of Baltimore but resigned this position after a short period to accept another call from Western Theological Seminary—this time as instructor in New Testament Language and Literature. Going there in September 1878 as an instructor he was appointed professor the following year. It was not until then (1879) that he was ordained as a minister of the Presbyterian Church in the United States of America.

He remained at Western Theological Seminary for nine years during which he won a reputation as a teacher and Biblical exegete rarely attained by so young a man. He was then forced to make a difficult decision by the fact that following the death of Archibald Alexander Hodge he received a call from Princeton Theological Seminary to occupy the chair of Systematic Theology made famous by Charles Hodge. In view of the exceptional gifts as an exegete he had displayed and the promise they offered for the future along that line, many of his wisest friends and well-wishers questioned the wisdom of his accepting this new call. Years afterwards, if our memory serves us right, William Robertson Nicoll, the distinguished editor of *The British Weekly*, expressed the opinion in that publication that it was a thousand pities that Warfield did not continue to make the New Testament his chief field of study in the belief that such were his qualifications as an exegete that had he done so he might have ranked with Meyer and others as a New Testament commentator. It must have been a difficult decision for him to make. Doubtless he was influenced, as his brother Ethelbert has intimated, by the fact that Charles Hodge, his revered teacher, had begun his career as a theological professor as a student and exegete of the New Testament. Be that as it may, the years spent at Western Theological Seminary were not wasted years from the standpoint of the more than thirty-three years spent at Princeton. Rather they were years of training and preparation apart from which he might not have become the distinctly Biblical theologian he became by way of eminence among recent theologians. It may be added that in 1881 he had declined a call to occupy the Chair of Theology at the Theological Seminary of the Northwest at Chicago—now McCormick Theological Seminary

Warfield was a voluminous writer. During his lifetime he published the following volumes: *Introduction to the Textual Criticism of the New Testament* (1886); *The Gospel of the Incarnation* (1893); *Two Studies in the History of Doctrine* (1893); *The Right of Systematic Theology* (1897); *The Significance of the Westminster Standards* (1898); *Acts and the Pastoral Epistles* (1902); *The Power of God Unto Salvation* (1903); *The Lord of Glory* (1907); *Calvin as a Theologian and Calvinism Today* (1909); *Hymns and Religious Verse* (1910); *The Saviour of the World* (1915); *The Plan of Salvation* (1915); *Faith and Life* (1916); and *Counterfeit Miracles* (1918). The bulk of his writings, however, made their first appearance in Bible dictionaries, encyclopaedias and theological magazines, especially the *Presbyterian and Reformed Review* and its successor the *Princeton Theological Review*. Following his death, sufficient of this material to make ten large volumes was selected by his literary executors, Ethelbert D. Warfield, William Park Armstrong and Caspar Wistar Hodge, and published by the Oxford University Press. It is from these ten volumes that most of the material reproduced in the volumes published by the Presbyterian and Reformed Publishing Company has been taken.

Warfield received the degree of Doctor of Divinity in 1880 and that of Doctor of Laws in 1892 from the College of New Jersey; that of Doctor of Laws from Davidson College in 1892; that of Doctor of Letters from Lafayette College in 1911; and that of Sacrae Theologiae Doctor from the University of Utrecht in 1913.

Perhaps no better description of Warfield as a man and as a writer has been made, or could be made, than that given by Francis Landey Patton, president of Princeton Theological Seminary and ex-president of Princeton University, in the *Memorial Address* he delivered by invitation of the Faculty of Princeton Theological Seminary in the First Presbyterian Church of Princeton, May 2, 1921. "Dr. Warfield," he said, "was a most imposing figure. Tall, erect, with finely moulded features and singular grace and courtesy of demeanor, he bore the marks of a gentleman to his fingertips. There was something remarkable about his voice. It had the liquid softness of the South rather than the metallic resonance which we look for in those who breathe the crisp air of a northern climate. His public utterance took the form of a conversational tone, and his sentences often closed with the suggestion of a rising inflection, as if he invited a hospitable reception from his hearers. He lacked the clarion tones of impassioned oratory, but oratory of this kind was not natural to him. He kept the calm level of deliberate speech, and his words proceeded out of his mouth as if they walked on velvet. But public speaking was not his chosen form of self-expression. He was pre-eminently a scholar and lived among his books. With the activities of the Church he had comparatively little to do. He seldom preached in our neighboring cities, was not prominent in debates of the General Assembly, was not a member of any of the Boards of our Church, did not serve on committees, and wasted no energy in the pleasant but perhaps unprofitable pastime of after-dinner speaking. As was to be expected, therefore, he was too much of a recluse to be what is known as a popular man. His public was small, but it covered a wide area and he reached it with his pen. Through the pages of the *Presbyterian and Reformed Review* and later of the *Princeton Theological Review,* he was speaking regularly to men who waited eagerly to see what he had to say concerning the latest book on New Testament Criticism or the most recent phase of theological opinion. It is difficult, of course, to estimate the influence he exerted in this way, but geographically speaking it was widely extended, and I may be pardoned perhaps for saying somewhat extravagantly that his line has gone out into all the earth and his words to the end of the world. His writings impress me as the fluent, easy, offhand expression of himself. He wrote with a running pen, in simple, unaffected English, but with graceful diction, and only a moderate display of documented erudition. His weapon in controversy was the sword and not the battle-axe. His gleaming blade had a keen edge, but the *quarte* and *tierce* of logical encounter went on without loss of temper or lapse of good behaviour. His mental machinery was in constant use. It never rusted and was always ready for the work it had to do. Something is undoubtedly lost in the transfer of thought to the printed page. We see it through a glass darkly—darkly, sometimes because we look through a cloudy medium, and sometimes the prismatic colors of the lens have a confusing effect upon our vision. But Dr. Warfield's style was the servant of his thoughts and expressed them accurately and clearly. He made no phrases, pointed no epigrams, did not have the habit of putting his own image and superscription on some common coin of speech and sending it forth as his seal and sign-manual of originality."[5]

What most impresses the student of Warfield's writings—apart from his deeply religious spirit, his sense of complete dependence on God for all things including especially his sense of indebtedness as a lost sinner to His free grace—is the breadth of his learning and the exactness of his scholarship. Caspar Wistar Hodge, his immediate successor at Princeton Seminary and long his associate, in his Inaugural Address after referring to the illustrious men who had given the institution fame throughout the world for sound learning and true piety, such as Archibald Alexander, Charles Hodge and Archibald Alexander Hodge, spoke of Warfield as "excelling them all in erudition." John DeWitt, long the professor of Church History in Princeton Seminary and himself a man of no mean scholarship, once told the writer that he had known intimately the three great Reformed theologians of America of the preceding generation—Charles Hodge, W.G.T. Shedd and Henry B. Smith—and that he was not only certain that Warfield knew a great deal more than any one of them but that he was disposed to think that he knew more than all three of them put together. A less sympathetic writer, Otto A. Piper, professor of New Testament Literature and Exegesis at Princeton Seminary, has written: "Aided by an indefatigable study of the New Testament Criti-

[5] *Princeton Theological Review*, July 1921, p. 370 f.

cism and interpretation, patristics, church history and Reformed theology and familiar with all that had been written in foreign languages, he expounded in innumerable articles the truths of the Bible and, based on the Bible, those of the Westminster Confession."[6] The wide range of Warfield's scholarship is intimated even if not fully indicated by Dr. Piper. To do that it is necessary to direct attention to the fact that to a degree that has rarely if ever been equalled, at least in America, Warfield made the whole field of theology—exegetical, historical, doctrinal, polemical and apologetical—the object of thorough-going study. It is safe to say that he was qualified to occupy with rare distinction any of the principal chairs of theological instruction, so that he was one of the few professors who, no matter what the question put to him might be, rarely if ever needed to sidestep it by saying that it did not belong to his department. There have been few if any who have had less need to fear the taunt: "If I knew as little as you do, I too might believe as you do." Moreover, as his brother Ethelbert has pointed out, he "read widely over a wide range of general literature, including poetry, fiction and drama and often drew illustrations from the most unexpected sources." Those who refer to him as a "fundamentalist" (he was in the broad sense in that he held that Christianity has a specific content of its own, factual, doctrinal and ethical, that was given it once and for all by Christ and His apostles and that Christianity exists in the world today only to the extent to which that content is confessed by word and deed), not in order to stress the genuineness of his Christianity but rather in order to disparage him as a scholar, only advertise, in the words of Patton, their "ignorance of his exact scholarship, wide learning, varied writings, and the masterly way in which he did his work."

So much for the biographical part of this sketch. We turn now to the theological part—the more important part since the question who and what Warfield was is less important than the question whether and to what extent he grasped and taught the truth of God. What was the sum and substance of his teach-

[6] *Encyclopedia of Religions*, p. 819.

ing? What is the source and content of that system of thought and life that he so ably and valiantly expounded and defended at a time when it was being everywhere affirmed, especially in academic circles, that its day was done?

We are dealing with the source rather than with the content of his theology when we direct attention in the first place to the fact that he was a Biblical theologian to such an extent that it is hardly too much to say that he was the Biblical theologian of his generation by way of eminence in the English-speaking world. There is no doubt a sense in which all theologians calling themselves Christians are Biblical theologians inasmuch as there are none, as far as we know, who rate the Koran or the Upanishads or other "sacred" books as on a par with, still less as above, the Biblical books as a source of religious knowledge and aspiration. Much as they differ in the significance they attach to the Bible they all ascribe to it a place they do not ascribe to any other book. It is also true that most of the professedly Christian theologians who preceded him, as well as most of those who were his contemporaries, attached a significance to the Bible similar to his own since the view of the inspiration and authority of the Bible expounded and defended by Warfield is essentially that which has been held by the Christian Church in all its main branches throughout its entire history, at least until relatively recent times. That Warfield devoted so much attention to the defense of the Bible as the source and norm of theology finds its explanation not in the fact that those who had preceded him, including for the most part those who were his contemporaries, were not Biblical theologians but rather to the fact that it was not until his day and generation that many, influenced by an anti-supernaturalistic spirit, were led to question the trustworthiness of the Bible or at least to fail to emphasize it. Fully abreast of the critical scholarship of the age and a foe of irrationalism in all its forms, it was inevitable that his active and powerful intellect should face the question whether the Bible is in fact the source of all sound Christian theology as had been all but universally believed by those calling themselves Christians. The results of his studies of this question are embodied in a series of articles which gathered together and published in book form are generally admitted to constitute the ablest defense of the Bible as "the Word of God, the only infallible rule of faith and practice," which has yet appeared in the English language.[7]

To appreciate the value that Warfield attached to the Bible it is imperative that we perceive that he looked upon it as containing not only a record of the great deeds that God has wrought for the salvation of the world—deeds that culminate in the birth, life, death, resurrection and heavenly priesthood of Jesus Christ—but as also containing an *authoritative interpretation* of those deeds. "Give the facts no interpretation, and we cannot find in them what we call Christianity; give them a different interpretation and we shall have something other than Christianity. Christianity is constituted, therefore, not by the facts, but by the 'dogmas,' *i.e.*, by the facts understood in one specific manner." This means that Christianity is constituted by certain great facts plus the true meaning of these facts. The facts without the words are dumb; the words without the facts are empty. Words to which no facts correspond are at best myths and at worst lies. It is also true, however, that uninterpreted facts lack significance. Those who stress revelation-events stress an important part of Christianity—so important that apart from it there could be no such thing as Christianity—but there is another part equally important, viz., revelation-truths, *i.e.*, the interpretation of those events given by Christ and His prophets and apostles. In the Bible the facts or events are inextricably interwoven with the interpretation. If then we cannot trust prophets and apostles for the meaning they ascribe to the events, how can we trust them for our knowledge of the facts or events themselves.[8]

Believing as he did that the Bible contains not only the record of an inspired history but an inspired record of that history—revelation-truths as well as revelation-events—it follows as a matter of course that Warfield was an authoritarian

[7] *The Inspiration and Authority of the Bible.*
[8] Compare what is said on page 17 f. of this volume.

in the field of theology. The deepest cause of that rejection of external authority in religion which is so outstanding a characteristic of present-day religious thinking is the naturalism of thought and sentiment which is so widespread. Apart from a supernatural revelation we may with the rationalist and the mystic have the authority of the human expert but nothing more. Since "external authority" is a correlate of supernatural revelation those who have such a revelation have something more. Warfield has repeatedly given explicit expression to his conviction that the rejection of external authority cannot but lead to the repudiation of Christianity in any adequate sense of the word.[9]

Important as it is, in Warfield's opinion, to maintain the plenary inspiration of the Bible, he was far from maintaining that without such inspiration there could have been no Christianity. "Without any inspiration," he has declared, "we could have had Christianity; yea, and men could still have heard the truth and through it have been awakened, and justified, and sanctified, and glorified." He expressed himself in full harmony with the statement made by one of his contemporaries that "if the authors of the Bible were credible reporters of revelations of God, whether in the form of historical transactions of which they were witnesses, or of divine mysteries that were unveiled to their minds, their testimony would be entitled to belief, even if they were shut up to their unaided faculties in communicating what they had received." This admission clearly did not mean, however, that he thought it a matter of secondary importance whether we believe in the full inspiration of the Old and New Testaments. Apart from such belief we can hardly accept their writers as wholly trustworthy teachers since this belief is among their teachings. On the other supposition, it might have been that their writings contain as much as eighty per cent of well expressed and accurately defined truth but the possibility would exist that the other twenty per cent would be full of errors and mistakes. Thus the reliability of the Bible as the Word of God would be lacking. Only as we maintain this

[9] See, for instance, p. 455 of this volume.

belief can we say with the writers of the New Testament that it is all the same whether we say "Scripture says" or "God says"; and only as we can do that can it be maintained that the individual Christian as he reads the Bible is brought into immediate relation to God in the revelation of truth given through prophets and apostles.[10]

In view of the fact that Emil Brunner among others has accused Warfield, and those who share his view of the Bible, of bibliolatry, it may not be wholly a work of supererogation to mention the fact that for Warfield the Bible was "not the object of theology but only its source." The writer recalls being in Warfield's study on one occasion and having his attention called to a letter which Warfield had received a short time before from a nationally known Bible teacher urging his support of an effort to get Christians together on the basis of their common belief in the Bible. Warfield mentioned certain specific teachings of the Bible which this particular Bible teacher openly rejected and went on to say that what he wanted was that Christians get together on the basis of the contents of the Bible. Much as he prized the Bible as the receptacle of the truth of God it was the truth rather than the receptacle that he most prized. To him it was a matter of little interest that men should more or less loudly proclaim their acceptance of the Bible as the infallible Word of God if they did not at the same time accept the truths enshrined in the Bible. Brunner has frequently cited the saying of Luther, "Scripture is the cradle in which Christ lies," apparently in justification of his own view of the Bible, as if this saying of Luther's means that his view of the Bible was basically different from that of men like Warfield. If so, it would seem that Luther was not aware of it.[11] It is true that Luther was critical of and spoke disparagingly of James, Jude, Hebrews and the Apocalypse but that was because he did not accept these books as Scripture. It was as regards the *extent* of Scripture rather than as regards its *nature* that Luther differed with men like Warfield. Understood as Luther himself must have

---

[10] *Inspiration and Authority of the Bible*, pp. 212 ff. and 299 ff.
[11] M. Reu, *Luther and the Scriptures.*

intended, there is no reason why Warfield should not have cited this saying with approval. Understood as Luther must have meant it, it is in full harmony with a saying of Calvin's, cited by Kuyper, that "the object of saving faith is none other than the Mediator, and invariably in the garments of Sacred Scriptures." Profession of faith in Christ means little or nothing unless it be in Christ as He is set forth in Scripture. Calvin did not worship the "garments" any more than Luther worshipped the "cradle." Both worshipped what both the cradle and the garments, so to speak, contained. Whether we use the figure of the cradle or of the garments it is what the cradle holds and what we perceive in the garments of Scripture that is the priceless jewel. This is not to imply that the cradle and the garments are not also of priceless value since they too are the handiwork of God. It is merely to imply that they are of secondary value in comparison with what they contain or enclose. To accuse Warfield, and those who share his view of the Bible, of bibliolatry is to bring against them what Scripture would call a "railing judgment."

We are still dealing with the source rather than with the content of Warfield's theology when we direct more definite attention to the fact that he was frankly a supernaturalist in his world and life view. He denied the essential oneness of all reality and affirmed the existence of two levels of reality—that of the Creator and His creation—between which there was and is constant inter-relation. In doing this he was, of course, merely doing what practically all theologians calling themselves Christians who had preceded him had done. That few of his immediate predecessors, at least in English speaking circles, had emphasized the place of the supernatural in the Cnristian world and life view to the same degree finds its explanation in the fact that they, for the most part, lived before there was any widespread denial of the supernatural even in non-Christian circles. For it is true, as Herman Bavinck has asserted, that "the religious supernaturalistic world-view has universally prevailed among all people and in all ages down to our own day, and only in the last hundred and fifty years has given way to the empirico-scientific."[12] Nothing is more characteristic, however, of this "empirico-scientific" world and life view than its thorough-going naturalism, the resoluteness with which it turns its back on all supernaturalism and professes to explain all that is, including man and religion and morality, purely from resident forces acting according to unvarying laws. At first its spread was slow as might have been expected but by the time Warfield had appeared upon the scene it had gained such widespread acceptance that he could write: "It has invaded with its solvent every form of thought and every activity of life. It has given us a naturalistic philosophy (in which all being is evaporated into becoming), a naturalistic science (the single-minded zeal of which is to eliminate design from the universe), a naturalistic politics (the first fruits of which was the French Revolution, and its last may well be an atheistic socialism), a naturalistic history (which can scarcely find place for even human personality among the causes of events), and a naturalistic religion, which says 'Hands off!' to God, if indeed it troubles itself to consider whether there be a God, or, if there be a God, whether he be a person, or if he be a person, whether he can or will concern himself with men."[13]

It would have been serious enough if only those who were professedly non-Christians had been influenced by this hostility to the supernatural. Such was not the case. Some who continued to call themselves Christians took the position that, while the supernatural has been associated with Christianity historically, yet that it does not belong to its essence. So they have commended a de-supernaturalized or as it is more frequently called a non-miraculous Christianity. More numerous were those who while not rejecting the supernatural altogether, instead of boldly confessing the full measure of that supernaturalism involved in the Christianity of Christ and His apostles, have yielded to the temptation to confess as little of it as possible while still calling

[12] *Philosophy of Revelation*, 1908, p. 1.
[13] *Calvin as a Theologian and Calvinism Today*, p. 39 f. It may not be out of place to call attention to the fact that this reference to atheistic socialism was uttered in 1909.

themselves Christians. We are spared the need, as far as the
readers of this volume are concerned, of indicating the extent
and degree to which the supernatural, according to Warfield,
belongs to the essence of Christianity by the fact that he has
done this for us in the address entitled "Christian Supernaturalism" which has been reprinted as its opening chapter. At the
risk of undue repetition we quote its concluding statement:
"The core of the Christian profession is the confession of a
supernatural God, who may and does act in a supernatural
mode, and who acting in a supernatural mode has wrought out
for us a supernatural redemption, interpreted in a supernatural
revelation, and applied by the supernatural operations of His
Spirit."

Careful readers of the first chapter of this volume will not
fail to note that for all the stress he places on the supernatural
Warfield's own position lay somewhere between a consistent
naturalism and an exclusive supernaturalism. He was as far
from saying "all is supernatural" as he was from saying that "all
is natural." Moreover while he would not hesitate to say that
a non-miraculous Christianity is just no Christianity at all yet
he was by no means prodigal in his recognition of the strictly
miraculous—apart from the events that enter into the substance
of Christianity such as the Incarnation and the Resurrection—
which he ever defined as events in the external world due to
the immediate rather than the mediate activity of God. That
such was the case is evidenced particularly by his volume entitled *Counterfeit Miracles* in which he dealt at length with
miracles alleged to have taken place since Apostolic times in
Patristic, Medieval, Roman Catholic, Faith Healing, Mind
Healing, Christian Science and other circles, and maintained
that they are all counterfeit. The function of miracles in the
early Church was, he claimed, to authenticate the Apostles as
the authoritative founders of the Church and inasmuch as their
function confined them distinctly to the Apostolic age they
necessarily ceased when that had been accomplished. He did
not allege, of course, that only the Apostles appear in the New
Testament as working miracles but he did not fail to point out

that apart from the two great instances of the descent of the Holy Spirit at Pentecost and the reception of Cornelius into the Church there are no instances of miracles recorded in the New Testament except those wrought by the Apostles and those upon whom the power of working miracles had been conferred by the imposition of their hands. More broadly speaking Warfield held that in the history of mankind miracles have been confined to revelation-periods and thus that miracles have happened only when God was speaking to His people through accredited messengers declaring His gracious purposes for mankind. It would carry us too far afield to consider whether or not Warfield was justified in characterizing all the miracles alleged to have taken place since Apostolic times as counterfeit, but the fact that he has done so at least serves to make clear that he was not prodigal in his recognition of miracles in the strict sense of the word. According to Warfield we are not to expect more of such miracles to take place preceding the return of the Lord.

We enter upon the consideration of the substance of Warfield's theology when we call attention to the fact that he was an evangelical. But what is an evangelical? According to Warfield: "That only is true evangelicalism, therefore, in which sounds clearly the double confession that all the power exerted in saving the soul is from God, and that God in His saving operations acts directly upon the soul."[14] It is undeniable, however, that as widely employed today the word merely designates those who maintain the second part of this confession, particularly those who reject sacerdotalism according to which God saves men not by dealing with them immediately as individuals but only through the church and its ordinances—of which Roman Catholicism is not only the typical but the most conspicuous example. Evidence of this may be found on every hand. In the Church of England the word is widely used to designate the Low-Church or anti-sacerdotal party in distinction from the High-Church or sacerdotal party. In various parts of Europe and South America and to a considerable extent in the United States the word is widely used to designate Protestants in dis-

[14] *Plan of Salvation*, p. 20.

tinction from Roman Catholics with the result that it frequently means little if anything more than that the persons so designated are not Roman Catholics. Another factor that has contributed to a loose and unhistorical understanding of the word is the fact that the Federal Council of the Churches of Christ in America (now merged with the National Council) has limited its membership to evangelical churches which has led many to infer that all those active in that organization were evangelicals. This tendency has been offset to some extent by such organizations as the Evangelical Alliance and United Evangelical Action as both of these organizations make membership contingent on the acceptance of creeds that make clear that in their judgment an evangelical is one who not only denies the existence of any intermediary between the individual soul and God but affirms that the soul is directly dependent on the free grace of God for its salvation. In general, however, it can hardly be maintained that the word evangelical in current religious speech means anything definite. If everything called evangelicalism in these days is evangelical it is hardly too much to say that there is no such thing as evangelicalism, since a word applied to designate diverse sorts of things ends by designating nothing. Hence the need of keeping Warfield's definition of evangelicalism in mind if we are to understand the significance of saying that he was an evangelical.

Warfield, then, did not suppose that a man was an evangelical merely because he was not a sacerdotalist. In stressing the evangelical's opposition to sacerdotalism he did not overlook his even deeper opposition to religious naturalism. Warfield's primary protest, in fact, was against naturalism—the notion that man is or can be his own saviour. This means that he was less opposed to Roman Catholicism, for instance, than to that present-day religion, rooted in naturalism, that goes under the name of "liberalism" or "modernism," in all of its consistent expressions. Important as is the difference between the evangelicals and the sacerdotalists it is by no means as significant as the difference between both of them and the naturalists. Both the evangelicals and the sacerdotalists are supernaturalists and both hold as over against the naturalists that all the power exerted in saving the sinner is ultimately from God. But while Warfield looked upon sacerdotalism as a perversion or corruption of Christianity rather than its falsification as he held any and all forms of naturalistic Christianity to be, yet it should not be supposed for a moment that he regarded it as a matter of small practical importance whether men are sacerdotalists or evangelicals. That would mean that he thought it a matter of small moment whether it is God himself acting directly on the soul who saves us, or whether we are saved through the instrumentality of men acting in the name and clothed with the power of God. "It makes every difference to the religious life," he writes, "and every difference to the comfort and assurance of the religious hope, whether we are consciously dependent upon instrumentalities of grace, or upon God the Lord himself, experienced as personally present to our souls, working salvation in His loving grace. The two types of piety, fostered by dependence on instrumentalities of grace and by conscious communion with God the Holy Spirit as a personal Saviour, are utterly different, and the difference from the point of view of vital religion is not favorable to sacerdotalism. It is in the interest of vital religion, therefore, that the Protestant spirit repudiates sacerdotalism. And it is this repudiation which constitutes the very essence of evangelicalism. Precisely what evangelical religion means is immediate dependence of the soul on God and on God alone for salvation."[15]

Much as Warfield was opposed to sacerdotalism and much as he regarded its influence as baneful he was not at all disposed to make common cause with naturalistic religious liberalism or modernism—call it which you will—in order to combat its influence. That in his opinion would have been to throw out the baby with the bath with a vengeance. He looked upon religious naturalism as the main enemy of evangelical Christianity today because of the degree to which it has seeped into the Protestant churches—all of which, Lutheran, Reformed and Wesleyan alike, are explicitly evangelical in their creeds and

[15] *Ibid.*, p. 81 f.

confessions of faith, according to his understanding of the term —with the result that it threatens where it has not already become controlling within their councils. This is not to imply that he was any more disposed to make common cause with the sacerdotalists against the naturalists. "Sacerdotalism, Evangelicalism, Naturalism," he has written with the Church of England particularly in mind, "are not complementary elements in one whole of truth but stand related as precise contradictions in their fundamental principles. No doubt there is a larger body of truth held in common between Sacerdotalism and Evangelicalism than between either and Naturalism, and these may therefore seem in their common opposition to Naturalism to draw together. Supernaturalism for instance—which is the very breath of life of any operative religion for sinners—is common ground between them. But this agreement in certain fundamental truths does not void their contradiction at vital points, although it does explain how Dr. Headlam, for example, can argue that it is an exaggeration to speak of them as different religious systems. . . . No error could be more fatal than for Evangelicalism, under the sting of the common assault made upon both of them by Sacerdotalism, to make common cause with Naturalism. What is needed above everything else in the Church of England is that Evangelicals—who after all constitute the only legitimate Church of England—should recover their self-consciousness and assert themselves; no longer seeking as 'good churchmen' to conciliate the Sacerdotalists or as 'men of open mind' to conciliate the Liberals, but as faithful stewards of the saving gospel to please the Master. There is an application here too of the saying: 'Be not unequally yoked together with unbelievers.' "[16]

We indicate more precisely the type of theology to which Warfield gave his adherence when we say that he was a Calvinist or, if you prefer, a Reformed theologian. As a Calvinist he held that Christ came into this world to save particular individuals and that the particular individuals He came to save will certainly be saved. "As supernaturalism is the mark of Chris-

[16] *Princeton Theological Review*, October 1914, p. 584 f.

tianity at large, and evangelicalism·the mark of Protestantism,"
he wrote, "so particularism is the mark of Calvinism. The Calvinist is he who holds with full consciousness that God the Lord,
in His saving operations, deals not generally with mankind at
large, but particularly with the individuals who are actually
saved. Thus, and thus only, he contends, can either the supernaturalism of salvation which is the mark of Christianity at
large and which ascribes all salvation to God, or the immediacy
of the operations of saving grace which is the mark of evangelicalism and which ascribes salvation to the direct working of
God upon the soul, come to its rights and have justice accorded it."[17]

It should not be supposed that in his estimation Calvinistic
particularism involves parsimony in salvation. The chapter in
this volume entitled "Are They Few That Be Saved?" is more
than sufficient to make clear that such is not the case. He did
not go as far as some Calvinists have gone, notably William
Hastie and William P. Patterson of Scotland, by maintaining
that it involves universal salvation. That he regarded as for-
bidden by the explicit teaching of Scripture. But if he did not
teach "universalism" in the common meaning of the term he
did teach what he called an "eschatological universalism." Witness the following: "When the Scriptures say that Christ came
to save the world, that He does save the world, and that the
world shall be saved by Him, they do not mean that there is no
human being whom He did not come to save, whom He does
not save, who is not saved by Him. They mean that He came to
save and does save the human race; and that the human race is
being led by God into a racial salvation: that in the age-long
development of the race of men, it will attain at last a complete
salvation, and our eyes will be greeted with the glorious spectacle of a saved world."[18] Moreover he held that it is Calvinism
and Calvinism alone which not only proclaims that particularism which enables the Christian to say, "He loved me and gave
himself for me" but at the same time enables him to see in

[17] *The Plan of Salvation*, p. 111.
[18] *Ibid.*, p. 131.

Christ the Saviour of the World. "If you wish, as you lift your eyes to the far horizon of the future, to see looming on the edge of time the glory of a saved world, you will find warrant for so great a vision in the high principles that it is God and God alone who saves men, that all their salvation is from Him, and that in His own good time and way He will bring the world in its entirety to the feet of Him whom He has not hesitated to present to our adoring love not merely as the Saviour of our own souls, but as the Saviour of the world; and of whom He has Himself declared that He has made propitiation not for our sins only, but for the sins of the world."[19]

Obviously Warfield did not regard himself any less of an evangelical because he was a Calvinist; rather he regarded evangelicalism as finding its purest and most stable expression in Calvinism. Neither did he regard himself as any less of a supernaturalist; rather he did not hesitate to say that "Calvinism is only another name for consistent supernaturalism in religion."[20] Moreover it should not be supposed that he assumed an unfriendly attitude toward other manifestations of Christianity. "I think it important to insist," he wrote, "that Calvinism is not a specific variety of theistic thought, religious experience, evangelical faith. . . . The difference between it and other forms of theism, religion, evangelicalism is a difference not of kind but of degree. There are not many kinds of theism, religion, evangelicalism, each with its own special characteristics, among which men are at liberty to choose, as may suit their individual tastes. There is but one kind of theism, religion, evangelicalism; and if there are several constructions laying claim to these names they differ from one another not as correlative species of a more inclusive genus, but only as more or less good or bad specimens of the same thing differ from one another. Calvinism comes forward simply as pure theism, religion, evangelicalism, as over against less pure theism, religion, evangelicalism. . . . It has no difficulty, then, in recognizing the theistic character of all truly theistic thought, the religious note of all really

19 *Ibid.*, p. 127.
20 *Calvin as a Theologian and Calvinism Today*, p. 37.

religious manifestations, the evangelical quality of all actual evangelical faith. It refuses to be set antagonistically over against any of these things wherever they exist in any degree; it claims them in every instance of their emergence as its own and seeks only to give them their due place in thought and life. Whoever believes in God; whoever recognizes his dependence on God; whoever hears in his heart the echo of the *soli Deo gloria* of the evangelical profession—by whatever name he may call himself, by whatever logical puzzles his understanding may be confused—Calvinism recognizes as its own, and as only requiring to give full validity to these fundamental principles—which underlie and give its body to all true religion—to become explicitly a Calvinist."[21]

This means, if we mistake not, that Warfield held that all Christians are implicit Calvinists however explicit they may be in denying it. In further support of this opinion we cannot refrain from citing a statement made by Abraham Kuyper—a statement that had the hearty approval of Warfield as evidenced by the fact that he once said that even the gifted Kuyper had never written anything better. It reads as follows: "Religion on earth finds its highest expression in the act of prayer. But Calvinism in the Christian Church is simply that tendency which makes a man assume the same attitude toward God in his profession and life which he exhibits in prayer. There is no Christian, be he Lutheran or Baptist, Methodist or Greek, whose prayer is not thoroughly Calvinistic; no child of God, to whatever Church organization he may belong, but in his prayer he gives glory to God above and renders thanks to his Father in heaven for all the grace working in him, and acknowledges that the eternal love of God alone has, in the face of his resistance, drawn him out of darkness into light. On his knees before God everyone that has been saved will recognize the sole efficiency of the Holy Spirit in every good work performed, and will acknowledge that without the atoning grace of Him who is rich in mercies, he would not exist for a moment, but would sink away in guilt and sin. In a word, whoever truly prays ascribes

[21] *Ibid.*, p. 24 f.

nothing to his own will or power except the sin that condemns him before God, and knows of nothing that could endure the judgment of God except it be wrought in him by divine love. But whilst all other tendencies in the Church preserve this attitude as long as the prayer lasts, to lose themselves in radically different conceptions as soon as the Amen has been pronounced, the Calvinist adheres to the truth of his prayer, in his confession, in his theology, in his life, and the Amen that has closed his petition re-echoes in the depth of his consciousness and throughout the whole of his existence."[22]

Warfield recognized that much of the prejudice against Calvinism is due to the false notion that its formative principle is the doctrine of predestination. Rather he affirmed that predestination is "its logical implication. It is not the root from which Calvinism springs; it is one of the branches which it has inevitably thrown out. And so little is it the peculiarity of Calvinism that it underlay and gave form and power to the whole Reformation movement. There was accordingly no difference among the Reformers on this particular point; Luther and Melanchthon and the compromising Bucer were no less zealous for absolute predestination than were Zwingli and Calvin."[23] The same he held to be true of the "five points of Calvinism" as a whole—more accurately called the five points at which the Arminians reacted against Calvinism—total depravity, unconditional election, limited atonement, irresistible grace, and the perseverance of the saints. They too, he affirmed, are logical consequences rather than the point of departure, branches that bear witness to the luxurious growth of the tree of Calvinism rather than the root from which it has grown. The root or formative principle of Calvinism in distinction from its distinctive doctrines he saw "in a profound apprehension of God in His majesty, with the poignant realization which, inevitably accompanies this apprehension, of the relation sustained to God by the creature as such and particularly by the sinful creature." The Calvinist, he continues, "is the man who has seen God, and

---

[22] *Presbyterian and Reformed Review,* 1891, p. 382.
[23] *Calvin as a Theologian and Calvinism Today,* p. 19 f.

who, having seen God in His glory, is filled on the one hand with a sense of his own unworthiness to stand in God's sight, as a creature, and much more as a sinner, and on the other hand with adoring wonder that nevertheless this God is a God who receives sinners. He who believes in God without reserve, and is determined that God shall be God to him, in all his thinking, feeling, willing—in the entire compass of his life-activities, intellectual, moral, spiritual—is, by the force of that strictest of all logic which presides over the outworking of principles into thought and life, by the very necessity of the case, a Calvinist."[24]

If predestination were the root principle from which Calvinism has grown it would have been more or less inevitable that antinomianism would have been widely prevalent in Calvinist circles. History, however, abundantly testifies that such has not been the case; rather that on the whole Calvinists have excelled in moral earnestness and all manner of good works, even exhibiting, in the judgment of many, too Puritanic a zeal in frowning on their moral shortcomings. There must be an explanation of this and he held that the explanation is to be found in the fact that the root principle of Calvinism lies elsewhere than in predestination—that it lies rather in the fact, to cite the words of Kuyper, that "the majesty of God and the authority of God press upon the Calvinist in the whole of human existence. He is a pilgrim, not in the sense that he is marching through a world with which he has no concern, but in the sense that at every step of the long way he must remember his responsibility to that God so full of majesty, who awaits him at his journey's end. In front of the portal which opens for him, on the entrance into eternity, stands the Last Judgment; and that judgment shall be one broad and comprehensive test, to ascertain whether the long pilgrimage has been accomplished with a heart that aimed at God's glory, and in accordance with the ordinances of the Most High."[25] Warfield was indeed a predestinarian. He regarded the idea of predestination as a constitutive idea of Biblical religion to such a degree

[24] *Ibid.*, p. 22 f.
[25] *Calvinism*, Eerdman edition, p. 113.

that he writes: "It is not too much to say that it is fundamental to the whole religious consciousness of the Biblical writers, and is so involved in all their religious conceptions that to eradicate it would transform the entire scriptural representation." One is not, however, a Calvinist merely because he is a predestinarian. If so, every Mohammedan would be a Calvinist. There is much more to Calvinism than its doctrine of predestination and that much more includes what is more central in Calvinism than its doctrine of predestination.

It is a perennial objection to the supernaturalism of salvation taught by Calvinism—the contention that it is God and God alone who saves and that He is at work in every element of the saving process—that it infringes upon our inalienable freedom of the will. Special objection is registered against the doctrine of "irresistible grace" or "effectual calling" which Warfield represents as "the hinge of the Calvinistic soteriology and much more deeply imbedded in the system than many a doctrine more closely connected with it in the popular mind."[26] The reader is referred in this connection to what Warfield has said about the supernaturalness of salvation in Section V of the chapter entitled "Christian Supernaturalism" in this volume (p. 19 f.). No doubt the question of the relation between the sovereignty of God and the freedom of man confronts us with an apparent paradox; but the Scriptures clearly teach both and certainly we are never justified in denying one fact merely because we cannot reconcile it with another fact. And surely Loraine Boettner is right when he says that the true solution of this difficult problem respecting the sovereignty of God and the freedom of man "is not to be found in the denial of either but rather in such a reconciliation as gives due weight to each, yet which assigns a pre-eminence to the divine sovereignty corresponding to the infinite exaltation of the Creator above the sinful creature."[27] Undoubtedly much of the confusion is due to the fact that many of the advocates of a self-salvation operate with the notion that men have a power of contrary choice which as a

26 *Calvin as a Theologian and Calvinism Today*, p. 26.
27 *The Reformed Doctrine of Predestination*, p. 208.

matter of fact no man has. No one can choose contrary to his nature. It is forever true that grapes are not gathered from thorns, nor figs from thistles. It is only the good tree that brings forth good fruit while the evil tree always and everywhere brings forth evil fruit. Those dead in trespasses and sin must, therefore, be enabled as well as persuaded to embrace Christ as He is offered to them in the Gospel. Basically there are but two kinds of religion. The one, whatever its historic form, assumes that man must save himself, that literally he is the architect of his own fortune, the carver of his own destiny: the other, whatever its historic form, assumes that, if man is to be saved at all, he must be saved by a power outside of himself, that in the strict sense of the word there is no such thing as a self-saved man, that the saved man is ever one who says with Paul, "By the grace of God I am what I am." The contrast between these two types of religion is clear and unmistakable. The one calls upon man to save himself; the other brings him into contact with a Power that saves him. The one is a religion replete it may be with moral and spiritual lessons, abounding in wise counsel and good advice, but with no dynamic, no source of energy, save that which inheres in man as man. The other, while equally rich in wise counsel and moral and spiritual teaching, yet finds its distinctive quality in the fact that it pro-claims a completed redemption, by bringing man into contact with a living Redeemer and so with a dynamic, an energy other than that which inheres in man as man. What is too often over-looked is that Christianity is the only religion that even pro-fesses to offer the world a divine redemption in and by the work of another, and so to do more than first instruct and then arouse to activity those powers of intellect, sensibility and will that inhere in man as man. Belief in the supernaturalness of salvation is a doctrine common to universal Christianity. In as far as Calvinists differ from other Christians at this point it is merely in the purity and consistency with which they teach it— at least that was the opinion of Warfield.

Another perennial objection to the supernaturalism of salva-tion as advocated by Calvinists, has to do with the principle of particularism governing God's dealings with man in the matter of salvation. It is alleged that if God saves some He is under obligation to save all provided He has the ability. Clearly the basic presupposition underlying this objection is that sin is misfortune rather than ill-desert. It shuts its eyes to the fact that sinners are guilty criminals rather than merely unfortunates, and so to the fact that God owes no man salvation, that it is a matter of grace and of grace alone that any are saved. Just why the love of God did not lead Him to save all men we can only surmise. It would seem, however, that no better explanation can be given than that given by Warfield: "The love of God is in its exercise necessarily under the control of His righteousness: to plead that His love has suffered an eclipse because He does not do all that He has the bare power to do, is in effect to deny to Him a moral nature. The real solution to the puzzle that is raised with respect to the distribution of the divine grace is, then, not to be sought along the lines either of the denial of the omnipotence of God's grace with the Arminians, or of the denial of the reality of His reprobation with our neo-universalists, but in the affirmation of His righteousness. The old answer is after all the only sufficient one: God in His love saves as many of the guilty race as He can get the consent of His whole nature to save. Being God and all that God is, He will not permit even His ineffable love to betray Him into any action which is not right."[28]

Warfield did not admit for one moment that those who minimize the righteousness of God to the extent of denying the need of an expiatory atonement, have the highest conception of His love. Rather he maintained that they have no adequate conception of the marvelousness of His love. "When we take those blessed words, 'God is love,' upon our lips, are we sure," he asks, "we mean to express much more than that we do not wish to believe that God will hold any man to a real account for his sins? Are we, in a word, in these modern days, so much soaring upwards toward a more adequate apprehension of the transcendent truth that God is love, as passionately protesting

28 *Plan of Salvation*, p. 93.

against being ourselves branded and dealt with as wrath-deserving sinners? Assuredly it is impossible to put anything like their real content into the great words, 'God is love,' save as they are thrown out against the background of those other conceptions of equal loftiness, 'God is Light,' 'God is Righteousness,' 'God is Holiness,' 'God is a consuming fire.' The love of God cannot be apprehended in its length and breadth and height and depth—all of which pass knowledge—save as it is apprehended as the love of a God who turns from the sight of sin with inexpressible abhorrence, and burns against it with unquenchable indignation. The infinitude of His love would be illustrated not by His lavishing His favor on sinners without requiring an expiation for sin, but by His—through such holiness and through such righteousness as cannot but cry out with infinite abhorrence and indignation—still loving sinners so greatly that He provides a satisfaction for their sin adequate to these tremendous demands. It is in fact the distinguishing characteristic of Christianity, after all, not that it preaches a God of love but that it preaches a God of conscience."[29]

Warfield held, rightly or wrongly, that the saving grace of God includes all those dying in infancy whether they be the offspring of believers or unbelievers. We mention this in connection with our consideration of the supernaturalism of salvation as taught by Calvinists partly because of its bearing on Warfield's belief concerning the number of the saved—since there is good reason to believe that the majority of those born of women have died in infancy—but more particularly because of the incontrovertible evidence it offers, if true, as all evangelicals apparently profess to believe, that the majority of the human race have up to the present, at least, been saved after the manner taught by the Calvinists. Naturally Warfield found in this strong confirmation or rather conclusive evidence that the absolutely free and loving election of God and that alone is determinative of the saved. It is a matter to which he paid large attention. One of the most valuable of his historical studies is entitled "The Development of the Doctrine of Infant Salvation"

[29] *The Person and Work of Christ*, p. 385 f.

in which following an exhaustive study of the various views that have been held from patristic to modern times concerning the fate of those dying in infancy he arrives at the following conclusion: "If all infants dying in infancy are saved, it is certain that they are not saved by or through the ordinances of the visible Church; for they have not received them. It is equally certain that they are not saved through their own improvement of a grace common to all men; for, just because they die in infancy, they are incapable of personal activity. It is equally certain that they are not saved through granting to them a bare opportunity of salvation in the next world; for a bare opportunity indubitably falls short of salvation. If all that die in infancy are saved, it can only be through the almighty operation of the Holy Spirit, who works when, and where, and how He pleases, through whose ineffable grace the Father gathers these little ones to the home He has prepared for them. If, then, the salvation of all that die in infancy be held to be a certain or probable fact, this fact will powerfully react on the whole complex of our theological conceptions, and no system of theological thought can live in which it cannot find a natural and logical place. It can find such a place in the Reformed theology. It can find such a place in no other system of theological thought."[30]

Many, perhaps most, Calvinists, not to mention evangelicals other than Reformed, do not share Warfield's post-millennialism. Both of his great Calvinistic contemporaries, Kuyper and Bavinck, for instance, were a-millennialists, as was his esteemed colleague, Geerhardus Vos, perhaps the most erudite advocate of a-millennialism in America. He himself freely admitted that a-millennialism, though not known in those days under that name, is the historic Protestant view, as expressed in the creeds of the Reformation period including the Westminster Standards. The fact that he made little if any use of the terms, "pre-millennial," "post-millennial" and "a-millennial"—he regarded them as unfortunate terms that embodied and so perpetuated a misapprehension of the meaning of the opening verses of the twentieth

[30] *Two Studies in the History of Doctrine*, p. 238 f.

chapter of Revelation—has perhaps contributed to a misconception of his position in some quarters. More particularly the fact that his interpretation of the passage just mentioned[31] readily fits into a-millennialism but not at all into pre-millennialism has more or less inevitably lead those who hold that the only live choice is between pre-millennialism and a-millennialism to class him as an a-millennialist. However, whether or not he ever explicitly called himself a post-millennialist, his position at this point was unquestionably essentially that of the post-millennialists. Possibly the nearest he ever came to explicitly classing himself as a post-millennialist was in an article published in *The Bible Magazine*, April 1945, in response to a request of its editor that he "set forth the post-millennial view." With the pre-millennial view particularly in view he concluded that article with the following: "The assumption that the dispensation in which we live is an indecisive one, and that the Lord waits to conquer the world to Himself until after He returns to earth, employing then new and more effective methods than He has set at work in our own time, is scarcely in harmony with the New Testament point of view. According to the New Testament, this time in which we live is precisely the time in which our Lord is conquering the world to Himself: and it is the completion of this conquest which, as it marks the completion of His redemptive work, so sets the time for His return to earth to consummate His kingdom and establish it in its eternal form." But if Warfield avoided the terms, commonly used to designate the various views concerning the Lord's return, he frequently used language that implied that his view was essentially that of the post-millennialists. It is implied in the words we have already quoted from him affirming that before our race has run its course "our eyes shall be greeted with the spectacle of a saved world." It is all but openly expressed in the closing paragraph of the chapter of this volume entitled "The Prophecies of Paul"—the purpose of which may be said to be to present

[31] *Biblical Doctrines,* p. 643 ff. According to Warfield "the millennium of the Apocalypse is the blessedness of the saints who have gone away from the body to be at home with the Lord."

the exegetical basis for this view as far as Paul is concerned. It is no less openly implied in the conclusion to his article on "The Millennium and the Apocalypse." There we read: "As emphatically as Paul, John teaches that the earthly history of the Church is not a history merely of conflict with evil, but of conquest over evil: and even more richly than Paul, John teaches that this conquest will be decisive and complete."[32] It is no less openly implied in the sermon on "God's Immeasurable Love," which is included in this volume, particularly its closing paragraphs. How far Warfield was from thinking that the Church has almost run its course is indicated with startling clearness by the fact that in the chapter of this volume, entitled "Are They Few That Be Saved?" he speaks of the twentieth century Church as still the primitive Church.[33]

Whatever may be thought of Warfield's post-millennialism, it must not for a moment be identified with the "post-millennialism" of modernism. That is precluded by his thorough-going supernaturalism. No a-millennialist or even pre-millennialist can surpass him in that respect. It may be added that while he regarded the millennial question as highly important he did not believe in making it a divisive issue in the Church. While he agreed with the a-millennialists that the Lord's return will usher in the final consummation, and while his idea of the manner in which the aspirations of the prophets and the dreams of the seers of the Old Testament are to be fulfilled has perhaps greater affinity with that of the pre-millennialists, yet the most extreme evangelical chiliast or millennialist was to him a "brother beloved" as compared with any and all naturalistic "post-millennialists."

Many have wondered, not without regret, why Warfield, born as it were with ink in his blood, who taught Systematic Theology with such distinction for more than thirty-three years did not write a Systematic Theology of his own. It was hardly because the author of *The Right of Systematic Theology* thought it presumptuous to attempt such a task—after the

[32] *Ibid.*, p. 662.
[33] See page 347, particularly footnote 34, of this volume.

manner of certain of the "Neo-Orthodox." It is also difficult to believe that it was because he lacked systematizing ability, being basically a critical and polemical rather than a constructive theologian, though some color is given to this allegation by the fact that he gave the greater part of his attention to the consideration of individual Christian doctrines. That he devoted so much of effort to the exposition and defense of particular doctrines and so little to organizing them into a system finds its explanation largely, if we mistake not, in the times in which he lived and labored. When the writer once asked him why he did not write a Systematic Theology he replied that the time was not ripe for another effort in that direction because of the critical rather than constructive nature of the period in which we were living—a period in which all the principal doctrines of Christianity were being widely called in question if not openly denied. The implication of his reply was that the time would come for a more adequate systematic theology, but that that time had not yet arrived.

Warfield was not at all opposed to the notion that modern Christians should state their beliefs in modern terms. "Every age," he said, "has a language of its own and can speak no other. Mischief comes only when, instead of stating Christian beliefs in terms of modern thought, an effort is made, rather, to state modern thought in terms of Christian belief." This was not, of course, to say that he held that Christianity should be constantly altered, refashioned, even transformed, if necessary, in order to bring it into harmony with the science, philosophy and scholarship of the day—rather the contrary. "Nothing is more certain," he writes, "than that a 'Christianity' and a 'theology' which are closely in harmony with the 'science, philosophy and scholarship' of today will be out of harmony with the 'science, philosophy and scholarship' of tomorrow." "After all," he continues, "is it not enough to ask that 'Christianity' and 'theology' be in harmony with truth? And if it be in harmony with truth, must it not be out of harmony with all the half-truths, and quarter-truths, and no-truths, which pass from time to time for truth, while truth is only in the making?"[34] Back of this attitude toward the science, philosophy and scholarship of the day was, of course, his conviction that Christianity is an historical entity with a definite content of its own—factual, doctrinal and ethical—and that this content remains true as age succeeds age. He fully agreed with John Robinson "that God has more truth yet to break forth from His Holy Word." He had no quarrel, whatever, with the notion that men's understanding of Christianity will advance as their understanding of both natural and special revelation is corrected and enlarged, but at the same time he held that Christianity in its great outlines was already known and that no developments in science and philosophy will result in these lines being radically altered. Because he held that there is explication as well as corruption in the course of Christian history, he held that Christians of the twentieth century may have a more adequate conception of Christianity than the Christians of the second or even the sixteenth century and that it may be anticipated that as the years unroll our generation will be surpassed in this respect. This means that Warfield is rightly classed as an advocate of progressive orthodoxy but distinctly not as one who imagined that progressive orthodoxy and retrogressive heterodoxy are synonymous terms. He realized full well what apparently many do not realize that "construction is not destruction; neither is it the outcome of destruction." He held that the task of the theologian today is to perfect an existing structure rather than construct a wholly new one. This is evident from his comparison of the theologian's task to that of those who completed the great cathedrals of the middle ages. It was not theirs to lay the foundations. If they had begun by destroying what their predecessors had done, he reminds us, none of these cathedrals would ever have been reared; and so, "if the temple of God's truth is ever to be completely built, we must not spend our efforts in digging at the foundations which have been securely laid in the distant past, but must rather give our best efforts to rounding

[34] *Critical Reviews*, p. 322.

the arches, carving the capitals, and fitting in the fretted roof. What if it is not ours to lay foundations? Let us rejoice that that work has been done! Happy are we if our God will permit us to plant a single capstone into place."[35]

If in the work of completing the temple of God's truth in his day Warfield's work was largely like those in the days of Nehemiah who held "the spears, the shields, and the bows and habergeons" rather than that of those who built the walls, we may be sure that this finds its explanation not in the fact that he lacked ability to build but rather in the fact that his unusual ability as a Christian warrior was so sorely needed in the days in which his lot was cast. However, such were his constructive contributions, despite his large attention to critical and polemical matters, that it was not without warrant that Patton did not hesitate to say that when the day comes not for a new theology but for a new systematic theology and God raises up the man with the architectonic gifts needed for this task: "I venture the prediction that some of the choicest stones in that new building will be those which have been hewn and shaped in the Warfield quarry."[36]

It remains to be said that Warfield was a ranking apologete as well as a ranking theologian of his generation. It is significant that it was Warfield, the theologian, who was secured to write the article on "Apologetics" for *The New Schaff-Herzog Encyclopedia of Religious Knowledge*, published in 1908. It is only necessary to read that article (republished in *Studies in Theology*) to be apprised not only of the thoroughness with which he had mastered the literature on the subject throughout the Christian centuries but of the vigor of his thinking in this field. He is about the last man to be found anywhere that could rightly be called a Christian fideist. It is equally obvious that were he living today he would take radical issue with those irrationalists who follow in the footsteps of Kierkegaard, for whom faith and knowledge are "polar opposites."[37] For War-

---

[35] *Studies in Theology*, p. 76.
[36] *Princeton Theological Review*, July 1921, p. 390.
[37] *A Kierkegaard Anthology*, ed. by Robert Bretall, p. xxi.

field, in a broad sense, they are identical, inasmuch as he held that faith in all its forms is conviction grounded on evidence. This is not to say that he did not distinguish between them but merely that he did not do so on the ground that knowledge is conviction based on evidence while faith is an ungrounded conviction. When rightly distinguished, he affirms in the chapter in this volume entitled "On Faith in its Psychological Aspects,"—but not there alone—knowledge is used to designate convictions based on reason while faith is used to designate convictions based on testimony. All convictions of every sort, however, he asserts, are based on evidence—evidence that is at least subjectively valid; and while men may and no doubt do hold convictions on grounds not objectively valid it is psychologically impossible for anyone to hold as indubitably true anything what he consciously recognizes as inadequately grounded. It is more to our immediate purpose to call attention to the fact that he held that the evidence for the truth of Christianity is objectively valid and that "we believe in Christ because it is rational to believe in Him, not though it be irrational." "It is not true," he maintained, "that the Christian cannot soundly prove his position. It is not true that the Christian view of the world is subjective merely, and is incapable of validation in the forum of pure reason. It is not true that the arguments adduced for the support of the foundations of the Christian religion lack objective validity." So fully convinced was he of this that he did not hesitate to say: "Face to face with the tremendous energy of thought and the incredible fertility in assault which characterizes the world in its anti-Christian manifestation, Christianity finds its task in thinking itself thoroughly through, and in organizing, not its defense only, but also its attack."[38] It must at least be confessed that Warfield gave full heed to Paul's exhortation to the Philippians to stand fast "in nothing affrighted by the adversaries" (1:28).

Though Warfield believed in Christianity on the ground that such belief was rational, not irrational, it should not be supposed that he thought that evidence is all that is needed to make a

[38] Introduction to *Apologetics* by Francis R. Beattie, pp. 26 and 30.

man a Christian—not because the evidence is weak but because
dead souls cannot and do not respond to the evidence. Only if
and when the Holy Spirit opens the blind eyes and unstops the
deaf ears, he held, will the soul dead in sin perceive the validity
of the evidence and make the proper response thereto; but that
did not lead him to suppose that Apologetics are without value
in winning the world to Christ. As he puts it: "It certainly is
not in the power of all the demonstration in the world to make a
Christian. Paul may plant and Apollos may water; it is God
alone who gives the increase. But it does not seem to follow
that Paul would as well, therefore, not plant, and Apollos as
well not water. Faith is the gift of God; but it does not in the
least follow that the faith that God gives is an irrational faith,
that is, a faith without grounds in right reason."[39]

It should perhaps be added that Warfield did not think
that the task of the apologete is merely to defend "the minimum of Christianity," the least that we can get along with and
still call ourselves Christians, but rather "to validate the Christian 'view of the world' with all that is contained in the Christian
'view of the world.'" He held that we weaken rather than
strengthen our position when unduly concessive. Like the wise
general he held that if we would save the citadel we should not
surrender the outposts. Defeat, he held, lies in the path of all
half-hearted schemes and compromising constructions. Witness
his unqualified approval of Henry B. Smith's pronouncement:
"One thing is certain—that infidel science will rout everything
excepting thorough-going Christian orthodoxy. All the flabby
theories, and the molluscous formations, and the intermediate
purgatories of speculation will go by the board. The fight will
be between a stiff, thorough-going orthodoxy and a stiff,
thorough-going infidelity. It will be, for example, Augustine or
Comte, Athanasius or Hegel, Luther or Schopenhauer, J. S. Mill
or John Calvin."[40]

[39] *Ibid.*, p. 25. Warfield did not, of course, conceive of saving faith, or
faith of any kind for that matter, as a mere assent of the intellect much as he
insisted that such faith is always present as an element of central importance.
See page 395 ff. and page 422 ff. of this volume.

[40] H. B. Smith, *Apologetics*, p. 194.

We have sought to characterize Warfield as a theologian as far as possible in his own words rather than in paraphrase lest it be supposed or alleged that we have more or less modified or even transformed his position—and that without attempting either to defend or criticize any aspect of his theological position. We have pictured him as a Biblical theologian who believed that the religion of the Bible has found its purest and most adequate expression in Calvinistic circles. He was under no illusions as to the present-day status of Calvinism. He was well aware that its fortunes were not at flood tide; that many circles in which it was once dominant had drifted away from it; and that if hard words broke bones it would soon be ground to powder. The main and for the most part sufficient explanation of this situation he found in the anti-supernatural spirit of the age—a spirit that could not but react unfavorably to the thorough-going supernaturalism of Calvinism. And since he looked upon exclusive naturalism as both inhuman and unphilosophical he was convinced that the time would come when the supernatural would again be given its rights in the thinking of mankind—and that in all probability shortly, at least, according to the divine time-table according to which a thousand years is as one day. In the meantime, the formative principles of Calvinism being what they are, he believed that it "can no more perish out of the earth than the sense of sin can pass out of the heart of sinful humanity; than the perception of God can fade out of the minds of dependent creatures; than God himself can perish out of the heavens." Discouraging as the situation seemed to many who still walked in Calvinistic paths, he, with Calvinism in mind, did not shrink from saying that "as it has supplied the sinews of evangelical Christianity in the past, so is it its strength in the present and its hope for the future." This total lack of an inferiority complex despite the unfriendly faces on every side was due to his confidence in the Lord God Almighty as revealed through prophets and apostles and above all as revealed in Jesus Christ. The plans and purposes of this only God, he was persuaded, will not and cannot fail of realization though all the hosts of earth and hell be gathered together in opposition. We may be sure, therefore, that he died confident that at the end of the years all that is opposed to God will have been conquered and that the day is coming when it will be possible for 'a great multitude which no man could number, out of every nation and all tribes and peoples and tongues'—redeemed humanity in a word—to assemble before the throne of God at whose right hand sits the Lamb that was slain and join in the great jubilation: "Unto Him that loveth us, and loosed us from our sins in His own blood; and He made us to be a kingdom, to be priests unto His God and Father; to Him be the glory and the dominion for ever and ever. Amen."

SAMUEL G. CRAIG

BIBLICAL AND THEOLOGICAL STUDIES

CHAPTER I

CHRISTIAN SUPERNATURALISM[1]

DR. JOHN BASCOM has lately told us afresh and certainly, as we shall all agree, most truly, that "the relation of the natural and supernatural" is the "question of questions which underlies our rational life." "The fact of such a relation," he justly adds, "is the most patent and omnipresent in the history of the human mind." We cannot think at all without facing the great problems which arise out of the perennial pressure of this most persistent of intellectual questions. From the first dawn of intelligence each human mind has busied itself instinctively with their adjustment. The history of human thought in every race from its earliest beginnings is chiefly concerned with the varying relations which men—in this or that stage of culture, or under the influence of this or that dominating conception—have conceived to exist between the natural world in which they lived and that supernatural world which they have ever been prone to conceive to lie above and beyond it. The most elaborate systems of philosophy differ in nothing in this respect from the tentative efforts of untutored thinking. For them, too, the problem of the supernatural is the prime theme of their investigation: and the solutions which have commended themselves to them too have been the most varied possible, running through the entire series from the one-sided assertion of the natural as absolute and complete, with the exclusion of all supernaturalism, to the equally one-sided affirmation of the reality of the supernatural alone with the entire exclusion of all that can properly be called natural. Between these two extremes of atheistic naturalism and superstitious supernaturalism nearly every possible adjustment of the relation of the two factors has found some advocates. So that there is some color to Dr. Bas-

[1] Reprinted from *The Presbyterian and Reformed Review*, viii. 1897, pp. 58-74; also from *Studies in Theology*, pp. 25-46.

com's plaint that, though the proper appreciation of their relation constitutes "the summation of sound philosophy," "its final
conception and statement elude us all."

Some color, but not a thorough justification. For, amid all
the variety and confusion of men's ideas on this great subject,
there are not lacking certain lines of direction leading to one
assured goal, broadly outlined only it may be and seen only
dimly through the mist of innumerable errors of detail, within
which it is demonstrable that the æonian thinking of the race
is always traveling: within which also it is clear that the best
and most vital of that high, conscious thinking which we call
philosophy finds the limits of its conceptions and the pathway
of its advance. We may not fancy that every conceivable conception of the relation of the natural and supernatural has found
equal favor in the unsophisticated mind of man, or has won
equal support from the criticized elaborations of philosophic
contemplation. No one who will permit to pass before his mental
vision the long procession of world-conceptions which have
dominated the human race in its several stages of development
will imagine that humanity at large has ever been tempted to
doubt, much less to deny, the reality or the significance to it of
either the natural or the supernatural. On any adequate survey
of the immanent thought of the world as expressed in its systems of popular belief, atheistic naturalism and exclusive supernaturalism exhibit themselves as alike inhuman. Atheists have
existed, who knew and would know nothing beyond what their
five senses immediately gave them, and naturalistic atheism has
found expression in elaborate systems which have warped the
conceptions of large masses of men: and in like manner a de-
based superstition has fallen like a pall over entire communities
and for ages has darkened their minds and cursed their whole
life. So there have, from time to time, appeared among men
both ascetic solitaries and communistic socialists, though God
has set mankind in families. The band of camp-followers on
either wing of an army confuses no man's judgment as to the
whereabouts of the army itself, but rather points directly to its
position. Similarly a general consideration of the great philo-

sophical systems of the world will leave us in no doubt as to the trend of deliberate pondering upon this subject. Somewhere between the two extremes of a consistent naturalism and an exclusive supernaturalism we shall assuredly find the center of gravity of the thinking of the ages—the point on which philosophy rests all the more stably that on both sides wings stretch themselves far beyond all support and hang over the abyss. Precisely where, between the two extremes, this stable center is to be found, it may be more difficult to determine—our instruments of measurement are not always "implements of precision." Assuredly, however, it will not be found where either the purely supernatural or the purely natural is excluded, and in any case it is much to know that it lies somewhere between the two extremes, and that it is as unphilosophical as it is inhuman to deny or doubt either the natural or the supernatural.

It is not to be gainsaid, of course, that from time to time, strong tendencies of thought set in to this direction or to that; and, for a while, it may seem as if the whole world were rushing to one extreme or the other. A special type of philosophizing becomes temporarily dominant and its conceptions run burning over the whole thinking world. At such times men are likely to fancy that the great problem of the ages is settled, and to felicitate themselves upon the facility with which they see through what to men of other times were clouds of great darkness. Such a period visited European thought in the last century, when English Deism set the supernatural so far off from the world that French Atheism thought it an easy thing to dispense with it altogether. "Down with the infamy!" cried Voltaire, and actually thought the world had hearkened to his commandment. The atheistic naturalism of the eighteenth century has long since taken up its abode with the owls and bats; but the world has not yet learned its lesson. An even more powerful current seems to have seized the modern world, and to be hurling it by a very different pathway to practically the same conclusion. It is to be feared that it cannot be denied that we are today in the midst of a very strong drift away from frank recognition of the supernatural as a factor in human life. To this also Dr. Bascom may be cited as a witness. "The task which the bolder thinking of our time has undertaken," he tells us, is "to curb the supernatural, to bring it into the full service of reason." "To curb the supernatural"—yes, that is the labor with which the thinkers of our day have burdened themselves. The tap-root of this movement is firmly set in a pantheistic philosophy, to which, of course, there is no such distinction possible as that between the natural and supernatural: to it all things are natural, the necessary product of the blind interaction of the forces inherent in what we call matter, but which the pantheist calls "God" and thinks he has thereby given not only due but even sole recognition to the supernatural. But it has reached out and embraced in its ramified network of branches the whole sphere of human thinking through the magic watchword of "evolution," by means of which it strives to break down and obliterate all the lines of demarcation which separate things that differ, and thus to reduce all that exists to but varying forms taken, through natural processes, by the one life that underlies them all. How absolutely determinant the conception of evolution has become in the thinking of our age, there can be no need to remind ourselves. It may not be amiss, however, to recall the anti-supernaturalistic root and the anti-supernaturalistic effects of the dominance of this mode of conceiving things; and thus to identify in it the cause of the persistent anti-supernaturalism which at present characterizes the world's thought. The recognition of the supernatural is too deeply intrenched in human nature ever to be extirpated; man is not a brute, and he differs from the brutes in nothing more markedly or more ineradicably than in his correlation with an unseen world. But probably there never was an era in which the thinking of the more or less educated classes was more deeply tinged with an anti-supernatural stain than at present. Even when we confess the supernatural with our lips and look for it and find it with our reasons, our instincts as modern men lead us unconsciously to neglect and in all practical ways to disallow and even to scout it.

It would be impossible that what we call specifically Christian thought should be unaffected by such a powerful trend in the thinking of the world. Christian men are men first and Christians afterwards: and therefore their Christian thinking is superinduced on a basis of world-thinking. Theology accordingly in each age is stamped with the traits of the philosophy ruling at the time. The supernatural is the very breath of Christianity's nostrils and an anti-supernaturalistic atmosphere is to it the deadliest miasma. An absolutely anti-supernaturalistic Christianity is therefore a contradiction in terms. Nevertheless, immersed in an anti-supernaturalistic world-atmosphere, Christian thinking tends to become as anti-supernaturalistic as is possible to it. And it is indisputable that this is the characteristic of the Christian thought of our day. As Dr. Bascom puts it, the task that has been set themselves by those who would fain be considered the "bolder thinkers of our time" is "to curb the supernatural, to bring it into the full service of reason." The real question with them seems to be, not what kind and measure of supernaturalism does the Christianity of Christ and His apostles recognize and require; but, how little of the supernatural may be admitted and yet men continue to call themselves Christians. The effort is not to Christianize the world-conception of the age, but specifically to desupernaturalize Christianity so as to bring it into accord with the prevailing world-view.

The effects of the adoption of this point of view are all about us. This is the account to give, for example, of that speculative theism which poses under the name of "non-miraculous Christianity" and seeks to convince the world through reasoners like Pfleiderer and to woo it through novels like "Robert Elsmere." This is also the account to give of that odd positivistic religion offered us by the followers of Albrecht Ritschl, who, under color of a phenomenalism which knows nothing of "the thing in itself," profess to hold it not to be a matter of serious importance to Christianity whether God be a person, or Christ be God, or the soul have any persistence, and to find it enough to bask in the sweet impression which is made on the heart by the personality of the man Jesus, dimly seen through the mists of critical history. This is the account again to give of the growing disbelief and denial of the virgin-birth of our Lord; of the increasingly numerous and subtle attempts to explain away His bodily resurrection; and, in far wider circles, of the ever renewed and constantly varying efforts that positively swarm about us to reduce His miracles and those of His predecessors and followers—the God-endowed prophets and apostles of the two Testaments—to natural phenomena, the product of natural forces, though these forces may be held to be as yet undiscovered or even entirely undiscoverable by men. This also is the account to give of the vogue which destructive criticism of the Biblical books has gained in our time; and it is also the reason why detailed refutations of the numerous critical theories of the origin of the Biblical writings, though so repeatedly complete and logically final, have so little effect in abolishing destructive criticism. Its roots are not set in its detailed accounts of the origin of the Biblical writings, but in its anti-supernaturalistic bias: and so long as its two fixed points remain to it—its starting point in unbelief in the supernatural and its goal in a naturalistic development of the religion of Israel and its record—it easily shifts the pathway by which it proceeds from one to the other, according to its varying needs. It is of as little moment to it how it passes from one point to the other, as it is to the electrician what course his wire shall follow after he has secured its end attachments. Therefore theory follows theory with bewildering rapidity and—shall we not say it?—with equally bewildering levity, while the conclusion remains the same. And finally this is the account to give of the endlessly varying schemes of self-salvation offered the world in our day, and of the practical neglect and not infrequent open denial of the personal work of the Holy Spirit on the heart. In every way, in a word, and in every sphere of Christian thought, the Christian thinking of our time is curbed, limited, confined within unnatural bounds by doubt and hesitation before the supernatural. In wide circles the reality of direct supernatural activity in this world is openly rejected: in wider circles still it is doubted: almost everywhere its assertion is timid and chary. It is significant of much that one of the brightest of recent Christian apologists has found it necessary to prefix to his treatment of Christian supernaturalism a section on "the evasion of the supernatural" among Christian thinkers.

It is certainly to be allowed that it is no light task for a Christian man to hold his anchorage in the rush of such a current of anti-supernaturalistic thought. We need not wonder that so many are carried from their moorings. How shall we so firmly brace ourselves that, as the flood of the world's thought beats upon us, it may bring us cleansing and refreshment, but may not sweep us away from our grasp on Christian truth? How, but by constantly reminding ourselves of what Christianity is, and of what as Christian men we must needs believe as to the nature and measure of the supernatural in its impact on the life of the world? For this nature and measure of the supernatural we have all the evidence which gives us Christianity. And surely the mass of that evidence is far too great to be shaken by any current of the world's thought whatever. Christian truth is a rock too securely planted to go down before any storm. Let us attach ourselves to it by such strong cables, and let us know so well its promontories of vantage and secure hiding-places, that though the waters may go over us we shall not be moved. To this end it will not be useless to recall continually the frankness of Christianity's commitment to the absolute supernatural. And it may be that we shall find profit in enumerating at this time a few of the points, at least, at which, as Christian men, we must recognize, with all heartiness, the intrusion of pure supernaturalism into our conception of things.

I. The Christian man, then, must, first of all, give the heartiest and frankest recognition to *the supernatural fact*. "God," we call it. But it is not enough for us to say "God." The pantheist, too, says "God," and means this universal frame: for him accordingly the supernatural is but the more inclusive natural. When the Christian says "God," he means, and if he is to remain Christian he must mean, a *supernatural* God—a God who is not entangled in nature, is not only another name for nature in its coördinated activities, or for that mystery which lies beneath and throbs through the All; but who is above nature and beyond, who existed, the Living God, before nature was, and should nature cease to be would still exist, the Everlasting God, and so long as this universal frame endures exists above and outside of nature as its Lord, its Lawgiver, and its Almighty King.

No Christian man may allow that the universe, material and spiritual combined, call it infinite if you will, in all its operations, be they as myriad as you choose, sums up the being or the activities of God. Before this universe was, God was, the one eternal One, rich in infinite activities: and while this universe persists, outside and beyond and above it God is, the one infinite One, ineffably rich in innumerable activities inconceivable, it may be, to the whole universe of derived being. He is not imprisoned within His works: the laws which He has ordained for them express indeed His character, but do not compass the possibilities of His action. The Apostle Paul has no doubt told us that "in Him we live and move and have our being," but no accredited voice has declared that in the universe He lives and moves and has His being. No, the heaven of heavens cannot contain Him; and what He has made is to what He is only as the smallest moisture-particle of the most attenuated vapor to the mighty expanse of the immeasurable sea.

The divine immanence is a fact to the Christian man. But to the Christian man this fact of the divine immanence is not the ultimate expression of his conception of God. Its recognition does not operate for him as a limitation of God in being or activities; it does not result in enclosing Him within His works and confining the possibilities of His action to the capacities of their laws. It is rather the expression of the Christian's sense of the comparative littleness of the universe—to every part and activity of which God is present because the whole universe is to Him as the mustard seed lying in the palm of a man. An immanent God, yes: but what is His immanence in even this immense universe to a God like ours? God in nature, yes: but what is God in nature to the inconceivable vastness of the God above nature? To the Christian conception, so far is the immanent God from exhausting the idea of God, that it touches but the skirt of His garment. It is only when we rise above the divine immanence to catch some faint glimpse of the God that transcends all the works of His hands—to the truly *supernatural* God—that we begin to know who and what the Christian God is. Let us say, then, with all the emphasis that we are capable of, that the Christian's God is before all else the transcendent God —a God so great that though He be truly the supporter of this whole universe as well as its maker, yet His activity as ground of existence and governor of all that moves, is as nothing to that greater activity which is His apart from and above what is to us the infinite universe but to Him an infinitesimal speck of being that cannot in any way control His life. The Christian's God is no doubt the God of nature and the God in nature: but before and above all this He is the God above nature—the Supernatural Fact. As Christian men we must see to it that we retain a worthy conception of God: and an exclusively immanent God is, after all, a very little and belittling notion to hold of Him the product of whose simple word all this universe is.

II. The Christian man, again, must needs most frankly and heartily believe in *the supernatural act*. Belief in the supernatural act is, indeed, necessarily included in belief in the supernatural fact. If immanence is an inadequate formula for the being of God, it is equally inadequate as a formula for His activities. For where God is, there He must act: and if He exists above and beyond nature He must act also above and beyond nature. The supernatural God cannot but be conceived as a supernatural actor. He who called nature into being by a word cannot possibly be subject to the creature of His will in the mode of His activities. He to whom all nature is but a speck of derived and dependent being cannot be thought of as, in the reach of His operations, bound within the limits of the laws which operate within this granule and hold it together.

Before all that we call nature came into existence God was, in infinite fullness of life and of the innumerable activities which infinite fullness of life implies: and that nature has come into existence is due to an act of His prenatural power. Nature, in other words, has not come into existence at all: it has been made. And if it was made it must have been by a *supernatural* act. The Christian conception of creation involves thus the frankest recognition of the supernatural act. To the Christian man nature cannot be conceived either as self-existent or as self-made or as a necessary emanation from the basal Being which we call God, nor yet as a mere modification in form of the one eternal substance. It is a manufactured article, the product of an act of power. God spoke and it was: and the God that thus spoke nature into being, is necessarily a supernatural God, creating nature by a supernatural act. As Christian men, we must at all hazards preserve this supernaturalistic conception of creation.

There are voices strong and subtle which would woo us from it. One would have us believe that in what we call creation, God did but give form and law to a dark Somewhat, which from all eternity lay beside Him—chaining thus by His almighty power the realm of inimical matter to the divine chariot wheels of order and progress. Or, if that crass dualism seems too gross, the outlying realm of darkness is subtly spoken of as the Nothing, the power it exerts is affirmed to be simply a dull and inert resistance, while yet the character of the product of God's creative power is represented as conditioned by the "Nothing" out of which it is made. Another would have us believe that what we call nature is of the substance of God Himself, and what we call creation is but the modification of form and manifestation which takes place in the eternal systole and diastole of the divine life. Or, if this crass pantheism seems too gross, a subtle ontology is called in, matter is resolved into its atoms, the atoms are conceived as mere centers of force, and this force is asserted to be the pure will of God: so that after all no substance exists except the substance of God. As over against all such speculations, gross and subtle alike, the Christian man is bound to maintain that God created the heavens and the earth— that this great act by which He called into being all that is was in the strictest sense of the words a *creation*, and that in this act of creation He produced in the strictest sense of the words a *somewhat*. It was an act of *creation:* not a mere molding or ordering of a preëxistent substance—not a mere evolution or modification of His own substance. And in it He produced a *somewhat*—not a mere appearance or simulacrum, but being, derived and dependent being, but just as real being as His own infinite essence. In creation, therefore, the Christian man is bound to confess a frankly supernatural act—an act above nature, independent of nature, by which nature itself and all its laws were brought into existence.

Nor can he confine himself to the confession of this one supernatural act. The Christian's God not only existed before nature and is its Creator, but also exists above nature and is its Governor and Lord. It is inconceivable that He should be active only in that speck of being which He Himself has called into existence by an act of His independent power. It exists in Him, not He in it; and just because it is finite and He is infinite, the great sphere of His life and activity lies above it and beyond. It is equally inconceivable that His activities with reference to it, or even within it, should be confined to the operation of the laws which He has ordained for the regulation of *its* activities and not of *His*. What power has this little speck of derived being to exclude the operation upon it and within it of that almighty force to whose energy it owes both its existence and its persistence in being? Have its forces acquired such strength as to neutralize the power which called it into being? Or has it framed for itself a crust so hard as to isolate it from the omnipotence which plays about it and successfully to resist the power that made it, that it may not crush it or pierce it at will through and through? Certainly he who confesses the Christian's God has no ground for denying the supernatural act.

Now nothing is further from the Christian's thought than to doubt the reality and the efficiency of second causes. Just because he believes that in creation God created a *somewhat*—real substance endowed with real powers—he believes that these powers really act and really produce their effects. He thinks of nothing so little, to be sure, as to doubt the immanence of God in these second causes. It is his joy to see the hand of God in all that occurs, and to believe that it is not only by His preserving care, but in accordance with His direction, that every derived cause acts and every effect is produced. But least of all men has the Christian a desire to substitute the immediate energy of God for His mediate activity in His ordinary government of the universe which He has made. Just because he believes that the universe was well made, he believes that the forces with which it was endowed are competent for its ordinary government and he traces in their action the divine purpose unrolling its faultless scroll. The Christian man, then, is frankly ready to accredit to second causes all that second causes are capable of producing. He is free to trace them in all the products of time, and to lend his ear to the poets when they tell him that

> This solid earth whereon we tread,
>   In tracts of fluent heat began,
> And grew to seeming random forms,
> The seeming prey of cyclic storms,
>   Till at the last arose the man.

He only insists that in all this great process by which, he is told, the ordered world was hacked and hewn out by the great forces and convulsions of nature, we shall perceive, also with the poets, that those great artificers, "Hack and Hew, were the sons of God," and stood

> One at His right hand and one at His left,
>   To obey as He taught them how.

Let us open our eyes wide to the grandeur and perfection of God's providential government; and let us not neglect to note that here too is a supernaturalism, and that in the ordered progress of the world towards that one far-off divine event we can trace the very finger of God.

But let us not fancy, on the other hand, that the providence of God any more than the immanence of God is a formula adequate to sum up all His activities. God is the God of providence: but He is much more than the God of providence. The universe is but a speck in His sight: and its providential government is scarcely an incident in the infinite fullness of His life. It is certain that He acts in infinitely varied modes, otherwise and beyond providence, and there is no reason we can give why He should not act otherwise and beyond providence even in relation to the universe which He has made. In our conception of a supernatural God, we dare not erect His providential activity into an exclusive law of action for Him, and refuse to allow of any other mode of operation. Who can say, for example, whether creation itself, in the purity and absoluteness of that conception, may not be progressive, and may not correlate itself with and follow the process of the providential development of the world, in the plan of such a God—so that the works of creation and providence may interlace through all time in the production of this completed universe? What warrant, then, can there be to assume beforehand that some way must be found for "evolution" to spring the chasms in the creative process over which even divinely led second causes appear insufficient to build a bridge? And if for any reason—certainly not unforeseen by God, or in contradiction to His ordering—there should a "rift appear in the lute," who dare assert that the supernatural God may not directly intervene for its mending, but must needs beat out His music on the broken strings or let their discord jar down the ages to all eternity? The laws of nature are not bonds by which God is tied so that He cannot move save within their limits: they are not in His sight such great and holy things that it would be sacrilege for Him not to honor them in all His activities. His real life is above and beyond them: there is no reason why He may not at will act independently of them even in dealing with nature itself: and if there be reason why He should act apart from them we may be sure that the supernatural God will so act. The frank recognition of the possibility of the supernatural act, and of its probable reality on adequate occasion, is in any event a part of the Christian man's heritage.

III. And this leads us to recognize next that the Christian man must cherish a frank and hearty faith in a *supernatural redemption*. As certainly as the recognition of the great fact of sin is an element in the Christian's world-conception, the need and therefore the actuality of the direct corrective act of God—

of miracle, in a word—enters ineradicably into his belief. We cannot confess ourselves sinners—radically at breach with God and broken and deformed in our moral and spiritual being—and look to purely natural causes or to simply providential agencies, which act only through natural causes and therefore never beyond their reach, for our recovery to God and to moral and spiritual health. And in proportion as we realize what sin is— what, in the Christian conception, is the nature of that bottom-less gulf which it has opened between the sinning soul and the all-holy and faultlessly just God, the single source of the soul's life, and what is the consequent mortal character of the wound which sin has inflicted on the soul—in that proportion will it become more and more plain to us that there is no ability in what we fondly call the remedial forces of nature, no capacity in growth, however skillfully led by even an all-wise providence, to heal this hurt. A seed of life may indeed be developed into abounding life: but no wise leading can direct a seed of death into the ways of life. Dead things do not climb. As well expect dead and decaying Lazarus through the action of natural forces, however wisely directed, to put on the fresh firmness of youth-ful flesh and stand forth a sound and living man, as a soul dead in sin to rise by natural powers into newness of life. No, the world knows that dead men do not live again: and the world's singers, on the plane of nature, rightly declare,

> One thing is certain, and the rest is lies;
> The flower that once has blown, forever dies.

If no supernatural voice had cried at the door of Lazarus' tomb, "Lazarus, come forth!" it would have been true of him, too, what the rebellious poet shouts in the ears of the rest of men,

> Once dead, you never shall return.

And if there be no voice of supernatural power to call dead souls back unto life, those who are dead in sin must needs fester in their corruption to the eternity of eternities.

One might suppose the supernaturalness of redemption to be too obviously the very heart of the whole Christian system, and to constitute too fundamentally the very essence of the Christian proclamation, for it to be possible for any one claiming the Christian name to lose sight of it for a moment. Assuredly the note of the whole history of redemption is the supernatural. To see this we do but need to focus our eyes on the supernatural man who came to redeem sinners—the "man from heaven," as Paul calls Him, who was indeed of the seed of David according to the flesh but at the same time was God over all, blessed forever, and became thus poor only that by His poverty we might be made rich—the Word who was in the beginning with God and was God, as John calls Him, who became flesh and dwelt among men, exhibiting to their astonished eyes the glory of an only-begotten of the Father— the One sent of the Father, whom to have seen was to see the Father also, as He Himself witnessed, who *is* before Abraham was, and while on earth abides still in Heaven—who came to earth by an obviously supernatural pathway, breaking His way through a virgin's womb, and lived on earth an obviously supernatural life, with the forces of nature and powers of disease and death subject to His simple word, and left the earth in an obviously supernatural ascension after having burst the bonds of the grave and led captivity captive. The whole course of preparation for His coming, extending through centuries, is just as clearly a supernatural history—sown with miracle and prophecy, and itself the greatest miracle and prophecy of them all: and the whole course of garnering the fruits of His coming in the establishment of a Church through the apostles He had chosen for the task, is supernatural to the core. Assuredly, if the redemptive process is not a supernatural operation, the entire proclamation of Christianity is a lie: as Paul declared with specific reference to one of its supernatural items, we, as Christians, "are found false-witnesses of God," "our preaching is vain," and "our faith is also vain."

Nevertheless, inconceivable as it would appear, there are many voices raised about us which would fain persuade us, in the professed interest of Christianity itself, to attenuate or evacuate the supernatural even in redemption. That supernatural history of preparation for the Redeemer, we are asked, did it indeed all happen as it is there recorded by the simple-minded writers? Are we not at liberty to read it merely as the record of what pious hearts, meditating on the great past, fancied ought to have occurred, when God was with the fathers; and to dig out from beneath the strata of its devout imaginations, as veritable history, only a sober narrative of how Israel walked in the felt presence of God and was led by His providence to ever clearer and higher conceptions of His Holy Being and of its mission as His chosen people? And that supernatural figure which the evangelists and apostles have limned for us, did it indeed ever walk this sin-stricken earth of ours? Are we not bound to see in it, we are asked, merely the projection of the hopes and fears swallowed up in hope of His devoted followers, clothing with all imaginable heavenly virtues the dead form of their Master snatched from their sight—of whom they had "hoped that it was He who should deliver Israel"? And are we not bound reverently to draw aside the veil laid by such tender hands over the dead face, that we may see beneath it the real Jesus, dead indeed, but a man of infinite sweetness of temper and depth of faith, from whose holy life we may even yet catch an inspiration and receive an impulse for good? And Peter and Paul and John and the rest of those whose hearts were set on fire by the spectacle of that great and noble life, are we really to take their enthusiasm as the rule of our thought? Are we not bound, we are asked, though honoring the purity of their fine hero-worship, to curb the extravagance of their assertions; and to follow the faith quickened in them by the Master's example while we correct the exuberance of their fancy in attributing to Him superhuman qualities and performances? In a word—for let us put it at length plainly—are we not at liberty, are we not bound, to eviscerate Christianity of all that makes it a redemptive scheme, of all that has given it power in the earth, of all that has made it a message of hope and joy to lost men, of all that belongs to its very heart's blood and essence, as witnessed by all history and all experience alike, and yet claim still to remain Christians? No, let our answer be: as Christian men, a thousand times, no! When the anti-supernaturalistic bias of this age attacks the supernatural in the very process of redemption, and seeks to evaporate it into a set of platitudes about the guiding hand of God in history, the power of the man Jesus' pure faith over His followers' imaginations, and the imitation by us of the religion of Jesus—it has assaulted Christianity in the very citadel of its life. As Christian men we must assert with all vigor the purity and the absoluteness of the supernatural in redemption.

IV. And let us add at once, further, that as Christian men we must retain a frank and hearty faith in a *supernatural revelation*. For how should we be advantaged by a supernatural redemption of which we knew nothing? Who is competent to uncover to us the meaning of this great series of redemptive acts but God Himself? It is easy to talk of revelation by deed. But how little is capable of being revealed by even the mightiest deeds, unaccompanied by the explanatory word? Two thousand years ago a child was born in Bethlehem, who throve and grew up nobly, lived a life of poverty and beneficence, was cruelly slain and rose from the dead. What is that to us? After a little, as His followers sat waiting in Jerusalem, there was a rush as of a mighty wind, and an appearance of tongues of fire descending upon their heads. Strange: but what concern have we in it all? We require the revealing word to tell us who and what this goodly child was, why He lived and what He wrought by His death, what it meant that He could not be holden of the grave, and what those cloven tongues of flame signified—before they can avail as redemptive facts to us. No earthly person knew, or could know, their import. No earthly insight was capable of divining it. No earthly authority could assure the world of any presumed meaning attached to them. None but God was in a position to know or assert their real significance. Only, then, as God spake through His servants, the prophets and apostles, could the mighty deeds by which He would save the world be given a voice and a message—be transformed into a gospel. And so the supernatural word receives its necessary position among the redemptive acts as their interpretation and their complement.

We cannot miss the fact that from the beginning the word of God took its honorable place among the redemptive deeds of God. "God spake," declares the record as significantly and as constantly as it declares that "God did." And we cannot miss the fact that God's word, giving their meaning, their force, and their value to His great redemptive acts, enters as vitally into our Christian faith and hope as the acts themselves. As Christian men we cannot let slip our faith in the one without losing also our grasp upon the other. And this is the explanation both, on the one hand, of the constancy of the hold which Christianity has kept upon the Word of God, and, on the other, of the persistency of the assault which has been made upon it in the interests of an anti-supernaturalistic world-view. It is no idle task which has been set itself by naturalistic criticism, when it has undertaken to explain away the supernaturalism of this record of God's redemptive work, which we call the Bible. This is the rock upon which all its efforts to desupernaturalize Christianity break. It is no otiose traditionalism which leads the Christian man to cling to this Word of the living God which has come down to him through the ages. It is his sole assurance that there has been a redemptive activity exercised by God in the world—the single Ariadne's thread by which he is enabled to trace the course of redemption through the ages. If God did not so speak of old to the fathers by the prophets, if He has not in the end of these days so spoken to us in His Son—He may indeed have intervened redemptively in the world, but to us it would be as if He had not. Only as His voice has pierced to us to declare His purpose, can we read the riddle of His operations: only as He interprets to us their significance can we learn the wonder of His ways. And just in proportion as our confidence in this interpretative word shall wane, in just that proportion shall we lose our hold upon the fact of a redemptive work of God in the world. That we may believe in a supernatural redemption, we must believe in a supernatural revelation, by which alone we can be assured that this and not something else was what occurred, and that this and not something other was what it meant. The Christian man cannot afford to relax in the least degree his entire confidence in a supernatural revelation.

V. And finally, we need to remind ourselves that as Christian men we must cherish a frank and hearty faith in a *supernatural salvation*. It is not enough to believe that God has intervened in this natural world of ours and wrought a supernatural redemption: and that He has Himself made known to men His mighty acts and unveiled to them the significance of His working. It is upon a field of the dead that the Sun of righteousness has risen, and the shouts that announce His advent fall on deaf ears: yea, even though the morning stars should again sing for joy and the air be palpitant with the echo of the great proclamation, their voice could not penetrate the ears of the dead. As we sweep our eyes over the world lying in its wickedness, it is the valley of the prophet's vision which we see before us: a valley that is filled with bones, and lo! they are very dry. What benefit is there in proclaiming to dry bones even the greatest of redemptions? How shall we stand and cry. "O ye dry bones, hear ye the word of the Lord!" In vain the redemption, in vain its proclamation, unless there come a breath from heaven to breathe upon these slain that they may live. The redemption of Christ is therefore no more central to the Christian hope than the creative operations of the Holy Spirit upon the heart: and the supernatural redemption itself would remain a mere name outside of us and beyond our reach, were it not realized in the subjective life by an equally supernatural application.

Yet how easy it is, immersed in an anti-supernaturalistic world, to forget this our sound confession! Are we not men? we are asked: and is not the individuality of every human being a sacred thing? Must not each be the architect of his own fortunes, the creator of his own future—not indeed apart from the influence of the Holy Spirit, but certainly without His compulsion? Is it not mere fanaticism to dream that the very penetralium of our personality is invaded by an alien power, and the whole trend of our lives reversed in an instant of time, independently of our previous choice? Led, led certainly we may be by the Holy Spirit: but assuredly our manhood is respected and no non-ethical cataclysms are wrought in our lives by intrusive powers, not first sought and then yielded to at our own proper motion. But alas! alas! dead things are not led! Of course, the Christian is led by the Holy Spirit—and let us see to it that we heartily acknowledge it and fully recognize this directive supernaturalism throughout the Christian life. But that it may become Christian, and so come under the leading of the Spirit, the dead soul needs something more than leading. It needs re-animation, resurrection, regeneration, re-creation. So the Scriptures unwearyingly teach us. And so the Christian must, with all frankness and emphasis, constantly maintain.

The Christian man is not the product of the regenerative forces of nature under however divine a direction; he is not an "evolution" out of the natural man: he is a new creation. He has not made himself by however wary a walk, letting the ape and tiger die and cherishing his higher ideals until they become dominant in his life; he is not merely the old man improved: he is a new man, recreated in Christ Jesus by the almighty power of the Holy Spirit—by a power comparable only to that by which God raised Jesus Christ from the dead. As well might it be contended that Lazarus, not only came forth from the tomb, but rose from the dead by his own will and at his own motion, as that the Christian man not only of his own desire works out his salvation with fear and trembling, in the knowledge that it is God who is working in him both the willing and the doing according to His own good pleasure, but has even initiated that salvation in his soul by an act of his own will and accord. He lives by virtue of the life that has been given him, and prior to the inception of that life, of course, he has no power of action: and it is of the utmost importance that as Christian men we should not lower our testimony to this true supernaturalness of our salvation. We confess that it was God who made us men: let us confess with equal heartiness that it is God who makes us Christians.

Of such sort, then, is the supernaturalism which is involved in the confession of Christians. We have made it no part of our present task to enumerate all the ways in which the frank recognition of the supernatural enters into the very essence of Christianity. Much less do we essay here to discriminate between the several modes of supernatural action which Christian thought is bound to admit. We have fancied it well, however, to bring together a few of the instances in which the maintenance of the occurrence of the absolute supernatural is incumbent on every Christian man. Thus we may fortify ourselves against that unconscious yielding of the citadel of our faith to which every one is exposed who breathes the atmosphere of our unbelieving and encroaching world. The confession of a supernatural God, who may and does act in a supernatural mode, and who acting in a supernatural mode has wrought out for us a supernatural redemption, interpreted in a supernatural revelation, and applied by the supernatural operations of His Spirit—this confession constitutes the core of the Christian profession. Only he who holds this faith whole and entire has a full right to the Christian name: only he can hope to conserve the fullness of Christian truth. Let us see to it that under whatever pressure and amid whatever difficulties, we make it heartily and frankly our confession, and think and live alike in its strength and by its light. So doing, we shall find ourselves intrenched against the assaults of the world's anti-supernaturalism, and able by God's grace to witness a good confession in the midst of its most insidious attacks.

Chapter II

THE BIBLICAL DOCTRINE OF THE TRINITY[1]

THE term "Trinity" is not a Biblical term, and we are not using Biblical language when we define what is expressed by it as the doctrine that there is one only and true God, but in the unity of the Godhead there are three coeternal and coequal Persons, the same in substance but distinct in subsistence. A doctrine so defined can be spoken of as a Biblical doctrine only on the principle that the sense of Scripture is Scripture. And the definition of a Biblical doctrine in such un-Biblical language can be justified only on the principle that it is better to preserve the truth of Scripture than the words of Scripture. The doctrine of the Trinity lies in Scripture in solution; when it is crystallized from its solvent it does not cease to be Scriptural, but only comes into clearer view. Or, to speak without figure, the doctrine of the Trinity is given to us in Scripture, not in formulated definition, but in fragmentary allusions; when we assembled the *disjecta membra* into their organic unity, we are not passing from Scripture, but entering more thoroughly into the meaning of Scripture. We may state the doctrine in technical terms, supplied by philosophical reflection; but the doctrine stated is a genuinely Scriptural doctrine.

In point of fact, the doctrine of the Trinity is purely a revealed doctrine. That is to say, it embodies a truth which has never been discovered, and is indiscoverable, by natural reason. With all his searching, man has not been able to find out for himself the deepest things of God. Accordingly, ethnic thought has never attained a Trinitarian conception of God, nor does any ethnic religion present in its representations of the Divine Being any analogy to the doctrine of the Trinity.

[1] Article "Trinity" from *The International Standard Bible Encyclopaedia*, James Orr, General Editor, v. v, pp. 3012-3022. Pub. Chicago, The Howard-Severance Co. 1915; also from *Biblical Doctrines*, pp. 133-171.

Triads of divinities, no doubt, occur in nearly all polytheistic religions, formed under very various influences. Sometimes, as in the Egyptian triad of Osiris, Isis and Horus, it is the analogy of the human family with its father, mother and son which lies at their basis. Sometimes they are the effect of mere syncretism, three deities worshipped in different localities being brought together in the common worship of all. Sometimes, as in the ,Hindu triad of Brahma, Vishnu and Shiva, they represent the cyclic movement of a pantheistic evolution, and symbolize the three stages of Being, Becoming and Dissolution. Sometimes they are the result apparently of nothing more than an odd human tendency to think in threes, which has given the number three widespread standing as a sacred number (so H. Usener). It is no more than was to be anticipated, that one or another of these triads should now and again be pointed to as the replica (or even the original) of the Christian doctrine of the Trinity. Gladstone found the Trinity in the Homeric mythology, the trident of Poseidon being its symbol. Hegel very naturally found it in the Hindu Trimurti, which indeed is very like his pantheising notion of what the Trinity is. Others have perceived it in the Buddhist Triratna (Söderblom); or (despite their crass dualism) in some speculations of Parseeism; or, more frequently, in the notional triad of Platonism (e.g., Knapp); while Jules Martin is quite sure that it is present in Philo's neo-Stoical doctrine of the "powers," especially when applied to the explanation of Abraham's three visitors. Of late years, eyes have been turned rather to Babylonia; and H. Zimmern finds a possible forerunner of the Trinity in a Father, Son, and Intercessor, which he discovers in its mythology. It should be needless to say that none of these triads has the slightest resemblance to the Christian doctrine of the Trinity. The Christian doctrine of the Trinity embodies much more than the notion of "threeness," and beyond their "threeness" these triads have nothing in common with it.

As the doctrine of the Trinity is indiscoverable by reason, so it is incapable of proof from reason. There are no analogies to it in Nature, not even in the spiritual nature of man, who is made in the image of God. In His trinitarian mode of being, God is unique; and, as there is nothing in the universe like Him in this respect, so there is nothing which can help us to comprehend Him. Many attempts have, nevertheless, been made to construct a rational proof of the Trinity of the Godhead. Among these there are two which are particularly attractive, and have therefore been put forward again and again by speculative thinkers through all the Christian ages. These are derived from the implications, in the one case, of self-consciousness; in the other, of love. Both self-consciousness and love, it is said, demand for their very existence an object over against which the self stands as subject. If we conceive of God as self-conscious and loving, therefore, we cannot help conceiving of Him as embracing in His unity some form of plurality. From this general position both arguments have been elaborated, however, by various thinkers in very varied forms.

The former of them, for example, is developed by a great seventeenth century theologian—Bartholomew Keckermann (1614)—as follows: God is self-conscious thought: and God's thought must have a perfect object, existing eternally before it; this object to be perfect must be itself God; and as God is one, this object which is God must be the God that is one. It is essentially the same argument which is popularized in a famous paragraph (§73) of Lessing's "The Education of the Human Race." Must not God have an absolutely perfect representation of Himself—that is, a representation in which everything that is in Him is found? And would everything that is in God be found in this representation if His necessary reality were not found in it? If everything, everything without exception, that is in God is to be found in this representation, it cannot, therefore, remain a mere empty image, but must be an actual duplication of God. It is obvious that arguments like this prove too much. If God's representation of Himself, to be perfect, must possess the same kind of reality that He Himself possesses, it does not seem easy to deny that His representations of everything else must possess objective reality. And this would be as much as to say that the eternal objective co-existence of all that God can conceive is given in the very idea of God; and that is open pantheism. The logical flaw lies in including in the perfection of a representation qualities which are not proper to representations, however perfect. A perfect representation must, of course, have all the reality proper to a representation; but objective reality is so little proper to a representation that a representation acquiring it would cease to be a representation. This fatal flaw is not transcended, but only covered up, when the argument is compressed, as it is in most of its modern presentations, in effect to the mere assertion that the condition of self-consciousness is a real distinction between the thinking subject and the thought object, which, in God's case, would be between the subject ego and the object ego. Why, however, we should deny to God the power of self-contemplation enjoyed by every finite spirit, save at the cost of the distinct hypostatizing of the contemplant and the contemplated self, it is hard to understand. Nor is it always clear that what we get is a distinct hypostatization rather than a distinct substantializing of the contemplant and contemplated ego: not two persons in the Godhead so much as two Gods. The discovery of the third hypostasis—the Holy Spirit—remains meanwhile, to all these attempts rationally to construct a Trinity in the Divine Being, a standing puzzle which finds only a very artificial solution.

The case is much the same with the argument derived from the nature of love. Our sympathies go out to that old Valentinian writer—possibly it was Valentinus himself—who reasoned—perhaps he was the first so to reason—that "God is all love," "but love is not love unless there be an object of love." And they go out more richly still to Augustine, when, seeking a basis, not for a theory of emanations, but for the doctrine of the Trinity, he analyzes this love which God is into the triple implication of the "lover," "the loved" and "the love itself," and sees in this trinary of love an analogue of the Triune God. It requires, however, only that the argument thus broadly suggested should be developed into its details for its artificiality to become apparent. Richard of St. Victor works it out as follows: It belongs to the nature of *amor* that it should turn to another as *caritas*. This other, in God's case, cannot be the world; since such love of the world would be inordinate. It can only be a person; and a person who is God's equal in eternity, power and wisdom. Since, however, there cannot be two Divine substances, these two Divine persons must form one and the same substance. The best love cannot, however, confine itself to these two persons; it must become *condilectio* by the desire that a third should be equally loved as they love one another. Thus love, when perfectly conceived, leads necessarily to the Trinity, and since God is all He can be, this Trinity must be real. Modern writers (Sartorius, Schöberlein, J. Müller, Liebner, most lately R. H. Grützmacher) do not seem to have essentially improved upon such a statement as this. And after all is said, it does not appear clear that God's own all-perfect Being could not supply a satisfying object of His all-perfect love. To say that in its very nature love is self-communicative, and therefore implies an object other than self, seems an abuse of figurative language.

Perhaps the ontological proof of the Trinity is nowhere more attractively put than by Jonathan Edwards. The peculiarity of his presentation of it lies in an attempt to add plausibility to it by a doctrine of the nature of spiritual ideas or ideas of spiritual things, such as thought, love, fear, in general. Ideas of such things, he urges, are just repetitions of them, so that he who has an idea of any act of love, fear, anger or any other act or motion of the mind, simply so far repeats the motion in question; and if the idea be perfect and complete, the original motion of the mind is absolutely reduplicated. Edwards presses this so far that he is ready to contend that if a man could have an absolutely perfect idea of all that was in his mind at any past moment, he would really, to all intents and purposes, be over again what he was at that moment. And if he could perfectly contemplate all that is in his mind at any given moment, as it is and at the same time that it is there in its first and direct existence, he would really be two at that time, he would be twice at once: "The idea he has of himself would be himself again." This now is the case with the Divine Being. "God's idea of Himself is absolutely perfect, and therefore is an express and perfect image of Him, exactly like Him in every respect. . . . But that which is the express, perfect image of God and in every respect like him is God, to all intents and purposes, because there is nothing wanting: there is nothing in the Deity that renders it the Deity but what has something exactly answering to it in this image, which will therefore also render that the Deity." The Second Person of the Trinity being thus attained, the argument advances. "The Godhead being thus begotten of God's loving [having?] an idea of Himself and showing forth in a distinct Subsistence or Person in that idea, there proceeds a most pure act, and an infinitely holy and sacred energy arises between the Father and the Son in mutually loving and delighting in each other. . . . The Deity becomes all act, the Divine essence itself flows out and is as it were breathed forth in love and joy. So that the Godhead therein stands forth in yet another manner of Subsistence, and there proceeds the Third Person in the Trinity, the Holy Spirit, viz., the Deity in act, for there is no other act but the act of the will." The inconclusiveness of the reasoning lies on the surface. The mind does not consist in its states, and the repetition of its states would not, therefore, duplicate or triplicate it. If it did, we should have a plurality of Beings, not of Persons in one Being. Neither God's perfect idea of Himself nor His perfect love of Himself reproduces Himself. He differs from His idea and His love of Himself precisely by that which distinguishes His Being from His acts. When it is said, then, that there is nothing in the Deity which renders it the Deity but what has something answering to it in its image of itself, it is enough to respond—except the Deity itself. What is wanting to the image to make it a second Deity is just objective reality.

Inconclusive as all such reasoning is, however, considered as rational demonstration of the reality of the Trinity, it is very far from possessing no value. It carries home to us in a very suggestive way the superiority of the Trinitarian conception of God to the conception of Him as an abstract monad, and thus brings important rational support to the doctrine of the Trinity, when once that doctrine has been given us by revelation. If it is not quite possible to say that we cannot conceive of God as eternal self-consciousness and eternal love, without conceiving Him as a Trinity, it does seem quite necessary to say that when we conceive Him as a Trinity, new fulness, richness, force are given to our conception of Him as a self-conscious, loving Being, and therefore we conceive Him more adequately than as a monad, and no one who has ever once conceived Him as a Trinity can ever again satisfy himself with a monadistic conception of God. Reason thus not only performs the important negative service to faith in the Trinity, of showing the self-consistency of the doctrine and its consistency with other known truth, but brings this positive rational support to it of discovering in it the only adequate conception of God as self-conscious spirit and living love. Difficult, therefore, as the idea of the Trinity in itself is, it does not come to us as an added burden upon our intelligence; it brings us rather the solution of the deepest and most persistent difficulties in our conception of God as infinite moral Being, and illuminates, enriches and elevates all our thought of God. It has accordingly become a commonplace to say that Christian theism is the only stable theism. That is as much as to say that theism requires the enriching conception of the Trinity to give it a permanent hold upon the human mind—the mind finds it difficult to rest in the idea of an abstract unity for its God; and that the human heart cries out for the living God in whose Being there is that fulness of life for which the conception of the Trinity alone provides.

So strongly is it felt in wide circles that a Trinitarian conception is essential to a worthy idea of God, that there is abroad a deep-seated unwillingness to allow that God could ever have made Himself known otherwise than as a Trinity. From this point of view it is inconceivable that the Old Testament revelation should know nothing of the Trinity. Accordingly, I. A. Dorner, for example, reasons thus: "If, however—and this is the faith of universal Christendom—a living idea of God must be thought in some way after a Trinitarian fashion, it must be antecedently probable that traces of the Trinity cannot be lacking in the Old Testament, since its idea of God is a living or historical one." Whether there really exist traces of the idea of the Trinity in the Old Testament, however, is a nice question. Certainly we cannot speak broadly of the revelation of the doctrine of the Trinity in the Old Testament. It is a plain matter of fact that none who have depended on the revelation embodied in the Old Testament alone have ever attained to the doctrine of the Trinity. It is another question, however, whether there may not exist in the pages of the Old Testament turns of expression or records of occurrences in which one already acquainted with the doctrine of the Trinity may fairly see indications of an underlying implication of it. The older writers discovered intimations of the Trinity in such phenomena as the plural form of the Divine name *Ĕlōhīm*, the occasional employment with reference to God of plural pronouns ("Let us make man in our image," Gen. i. 26; iii. 22; xi. 7; Isa. vi. 8), or of plural verbs (Gen. xx. 13; xxxv. 7), certain repetitions of the name of God which seem to distinguish between God and God (Ps. xlv. 6, 7; cx. 1; Hos. i. 7), threefold liturgical formulas (Num. vi. 24, 26; Isa. vi. 3), a certain tendency to hypostatize the conception of Wisdom (Prov. viii.), and especially the remarkable phenomena connected with the appearances of the Angel of Jehovah (Gen. xvi. 2-13, xxii. 11, 16; xxxi. 11, 13; xlviii. 15, 16; Ex. iii. 2, 4, 5; Jgs. xiii. 20-22). The tendency of more recent authors is to appeal, not so much to specific texts of the Old Testament, as to the very "organism of revelation" in the Old Testament in which there is perceived an underlying suggestion "that all things owe their existence and persistence to a threefold cause," both with reference to the first creation, and, more plainly, with reference to the second creation. Passages like Ps. xxxiii. 6; Isa. lxi. 1; lxiii. 9-12; Hag. ii. 5, 6, in which God and His Word and His Spirit are brought together, co-causes of effects, are adduced. A tendency is pointed out to hypostatize the Word of God on the one hand (e.g., Gen. i. 3; Ps. xxxiii. 6; cvii. 20; cxlvii. 15-18; Isa. lv. 11); and, especially in Ezek. and the later Prophets, the Spirit of God, on the other (e.g., Gen. i. 2; Isa. xlviii. 16;

lxiii. 10; Ezek. ii. 2; viii. 3; Zec. vii. 12). Suggestions—in Isa.
for instance (vii. 14; ix. 6)—of the Deity of the Messiah are appealed to. And if the occasional occurrence of plural verbs and
pronouns referring to God, and the plural form of the name
Ĕlōhīm, are not insisted upon as in themselves evidence of a
multiplicity in the Godhead, yet a certain weight is lent them as
witnesses that "the God of revelation is no abstract unity, but
the living, true God, who in the fulness of His life embraces the
highest variety" (Bavinck). The upshot of it all is that it is very
generally felt that, somehow, in the Old Testament development
of the idea of God there is a suggestion that the Deity is not a
simple monad, and that thus a preparation is made for the revelation of the Trinity yet to come. It would seem clear that we
must recognize in the Old Testament doctrine of the relation
of God to His revelation by the creative Word and the Spirit,
at least the germ of the distinctions in the Godhead afterward
fully made known in the Christian revelation. And we can
scarcely stop there. After all is said, in the light of the later revelation, the Trinitarian interpretation remains the most natural
one of the phenomena which the older writers frankly interpreted as intimations of the Trinity; especially of those connected with the descriptions of the Angel of Jehovah no doubt,
but also even of such a form of expression as meets us in the
"Let us make man in our image" of Gen. i. 26—for surely verse
27: "And God created man in his own image," does not encourage us to take the preceding verse as announcing that man
was to be created in the image of the angels. This is not an illegitimate reading of New Testament ideas back into the text
of the Old Testament; it is only reading the text of the Old
Testament under the illumination of the New Testament revelation. The Old Testament may be likened to a chamber richly
furnished but dimly lighted; the introduction of light brings
into it nothing which was not in it before; but it brings out into
clearer view much of what is in it but was only dimly or even
not at all perceived before. The mystery of the Trinity is not
revealed in the Old Testament; but the mystery of the Trinity
underlies the Old Testament revelation, and here and there

almost comes into view. Thus the Old Testament revelation of God is not corrected by the fuller revelation which follows it, but only perfected, extended and enlarged.

It is an old saying that what becomes patent in the New Testament was latent in the Old Testament. And it is important that the continuity of the revelation of God contained in the two Testaments should not be overlooked or obscured. If we find some difficulty in perceiving for ourselves, in the Old Testament, definite points of attachment for the revelation of the Trinity, we cannot help perceiving with great clearness in the New Testament abundant evidence that its writers felt no incongruity whatever between their doctrine of the Trinity and the Old Testament conception of God. The New Testament writers certainly were not conscious of being "setters forth of strange gods." To their own apprehension they worshipped and proclaimed just the God of Israel; and they laid no less stress than the Old Testament itself upon His unity (Jn. xvii. 3; I Cor. viii. 4; I Tim. ii. 5). They do not, then, place two new gods by the side of Jehovah as alike with Him to be served and worshipped; they conceive Jehovah as Himself at once Father, Son and Spirit. In presenting this one Jehovah as Father, Son and Spirit, they do not even betray any lurking feeling that they are making innovations. Without apparent misgiving they take over Old Testament passages and apply them to Father, Son and Spirit indifferently. Obviously they understand themselves, and wish to be understood, as setting forth in the Father, Son and Spirit just the one God that the God of the Old Testament revelation is; and they are as far as possible from recognizing any breach between themselves and the Fathers in presenting their enlarged conception of the Divine Being. This may not amount to saying that they saw the doctrine of the Trinity everywhere taught in the Old Testament. It certainly amounts to saying that they saw the Triune God whom they worshipped in the God of the Old Testament revelation, and felt no incongruity in speaking of their Triune God in the terms of the Old Testament revelation. The God of the Old Testament was their God, and their God was a Trinity, and their sense of the identity of the two was so complete that no question as to it was raised in their minds.

The simplicity and assurance with which the New Testament writers speak of God as a Trinity have, however, a further implication. If they betray no sense of novelty in so speaking of Him, this is undoubtedly in part because it was no longer a novelty so to speak of Him. It is clear, in other words, that, as we read the New Testament, we are not witnessing the birth of a new conception of God. What we meet with in its pages is a firmly established conception of God underlying and giving its tone to the whole fabric. It is not in a text here and there that the New Testament bears its testimony to the doctrine of the Trinity. The whole book is Trinitarian to the core; all its teaching is built on the assumption of the Trinity; and its allusions to the Trinity are frequent, cursory, easy and confident. It is with a view to the cursoriness of the allusions to it in the New Testament that it has been remarked that "the doctrine of the Trinity is not so much heard as overheard in the statements of Scripture." It would be more exact to say that it is not so much inculcated as presupposed. The doctrine of the Trinity does not appear in the New Testament in the making, but as already made. It takes its place in its pages, as Gunkel phrases it, with an air almost of complaint, already "in full completeness" (*völlig fertig*), leaving no trace of its growth. "There is nothing more wonderful in the history of human thought," says Sanday, with his eye on the appearance of the doctrine of the Trinity in the New Testament, "than the silent and imperceptible way in which this doctrine, to us so difficult, took its place without struggle—and without controversy—among accepted Christian truths." The explanation of this remarkable phenomenon is, however, simple. Our New Testament is not a record of the development of the doctrine or of its assimilation. It everywhere presupposes the doctrine as the fixed possession of the Christian community; and the process by which it became the possession of the Christian community lies behind the New Testament.

We cannot speak of the doctrine of the Trinity, therefore, if we study exactness of speech, as revealed in the New Testament, any more than we can speak of it as revealed in the Old Testament. The Old Testament was written before its revelation; the New Testament after it. The revelation itself was made not in word but in deed. It was made in the incarnation of God the Son, and the outpouring of God the Holy Spirit. The relation of the two Testaments to this revelation is in the one case that of preparation for it, and in the other that of product of it. The revelation itself is embodied just in Christ and the Holy Spirit. This is as much as to say that the revelation of the Trinity was incidental to, and the inevitable effect of, the accomplishment of redemption. It was in the coming of the Son of God in the likeness of sinful flesh to offer Himself a sacrifice for sin; and in the coming of the Holy Spirit to convict the world of sin, of righteousness and of judgment, that the Trinity of Persons in the Unity of the Godhead was once for all revealed to men. Those who knew God the Father, who loved them and gave His own Son to die for them; and the Lord Jesus Christ, who loved them and delivered Himself up an offering and sacrifice for them; and the Spirit of Grace, who loved them and dwelt within them a power not themselves, making for righteousness, knew the Triune God and could not think or speak of God otherwise than as triune. The doctrine of the Trinity, in other words, is simply the modification wrought in the conception of the one only God by His complete revelation of Himself in the redemptive process. It necessarily waited, therefore, upon the completion of the redemptive process for its revelation, and its revelation, as necessarily, lay complete in the redemptive process.

From this central fact we may understand more fully several circumstances connected with the revelation of the Trinity to which allusion has been made. We may from it understand, for example, why the Trinity was not revealed in the Old Testament. It may carry us a little way to remark, as it has been customary to remark since the time of Gregory of Nazianzus, that it was the task of the Old Testament revelation to fix firmly in the minds and hearts of the people of God the great fundamental truth of the unity of the Godhead; and it would have been dangerous to speak to them of the plurality within this unity until this task had been fully accomplished. The real reason for the delay in the revelation of the Trinity, however, is grounded in the secular development of the redemptive purpose of God: the times were not ripe for the revelation of the Trinity in the unity of the Godhead until the fulness of the time had come for God to send forth His Son unto redemption, and His Spirit unto sanctification. The revelation in word must needs wait upon the revelation in fact, to which it brings its necessary explanation, no doubt, but from which also it derives its own entire significance and value. The revelation of a Trinity in the Divine unity as a mere abstract truth without relation to manifested fact, and without significance to the development of the kingdom of God, would have been foreign to the whole method of the Divine procedure as it lies exposed to us in the pages of Scripture. Here the working out of the Divine purpose supplies the fundamental principle to which all else, even the progressive stages of revelation itself, is subsidiary; and advances in revelation are ever closely connected with the advancing accomplishment of the redemptive purpose. We may understand also, however, from the same central fact, why it is that the doctrine of the Trinity lies in the New Testament rather in the form of allusions than in express teaching, why it is rather everywhere presupposed, coming only here and there into incidental expression, than formally inculcated. It is because the revelation, having been made in the actual occurrences of redemption, was already the common property of all Christian hearts. In speaking and writing to one another, Christians, therefore, rather spoke out of their common Trinitarian consciousness, and reminded one another of their common fund of belief, than instructed one another in what was already the common property of all. We are to look for, and we shall find, in the New Testament allusions to the Trinity, evidence of how the Trinity, believed in by all, was conceived by the authoritative teachers of the church, rather than formal attempts, on their part, by authoritative declarations, to bring the church into the understanding that God is a Trinity.

The fundamental proof that God is a Trinity is supplied thus by the fundamental revelation of the Trinity in fact: that is to say, in the incarnation of God the Son and the outpouring of God the Holy Spirit. In a word, Jesus Christ and the Holy Spirit are the fundamental proof of the doctrine of the Trinity. This is as much as to say that all the evidence of whatever kind, and from whatever source derived, that Jesus Christ is God manifested in the flesh, and that the Holy Spirit is a Divine Person, is just so much evidence for the doctrine of the Trinity; and that when we go to the New Testament for evidence of the Trinity we are to seek it, not merely in the scattered allusions to the Trinity as such, numerous and instructive as they are, but primarily in the whole mass of evidence which the New Testament provides of the Deity of Christ and the Divine personality of the Holy Spirit. When we have said this, we have said in effect that the whole mass of the New Testament is evidence for the Trinity. For the New Testament is saturated with evidence of the Deity of Christ and the Divine personality of the Holy Spirit. Precisely what the New Testament is, is the documentation of the religion of the incarnate Son and of the outpoured Spirit, that is to say, of the religion of the Trinity, and what we mean by the doctrine of the Trinity is nothing but the formulation in exact language of the conception of God presupposed in the religion of the incarnate Son and outpoured Spirit. We may analyze this conception and adduce proof for every constituent element of it from the New Testament declarations. We may show that the New Testament everywhere insists on the unity of the Godhead; that it constantly recognizes the Father as God, the Son as God and the Spirit as God; and that it cursorily presents these three to us as distinct Persons. It is not necessary, however, to enlarge here on facts so obvious. We may content ourselves with simply observing that to the New Testament there is but one only living and true God; but that to it Jesus Christ and the Holy Spirit are each God in the fullest sense of the term; and yet Father, Son and Spirit stand over against each other as I, and Thou, and He. In this composite fact the New Testament gives us the doctrine of the

Trinity. For the doctrine of the Trinity is but the statement in well-guarded language of this composite fact. Throughout the whole course of the many efforts to formulate the doctrine exactly, which have followed one another during the entire history of the church, indeed, the principle which has ever determined the result has always been determination to do justice in conceiving the relations of God the Father, God the Son and God the Spirit, on the one hand to the unity of God, and, on the other, to the true Deity of the Son and Spirit and their distinct personalities. When we have said these three things, then—that there is but one God, that the Father and the Son and the Spirit is each God, that the Father and the Son and the Spirit is each a distinct person—we have enunciated the doctrine of the Trinity in its completeness.

That this doctrine underlies the whole New Testament as its constant presupposition and determines everywhere its forms of expression is the primary fact to be noted. We must not omit explicitly to note, however, that it now and again also, as occasion arises for its incidental enunciation, comes itself to expression in more or less completeness of statement. The passages in which the three Persons of the Trinity are brought together are much more numerous than, perhaps, is generally supposed; but it should be recognized that the formal collocation of the elements of the doctrine naturally is relatively rare in writings which are occasional in their origin and practical rather than doctrinal in their immediate purpose. The three Persons already come into view as Divine Persons in the annunciation of the birth of Our Lord: 'The Holy Ghost shall come upon thee,' said the angel to Mary, 'and the power of the Most High shall overshadow thee: wherefore also the holy thing which is to be born shall be called the Son of God'; (Lk. i. 35 m; cf. Mt. i. 18 ff.). Here the Holy Ghost is the active agent in the production of an effect which is also ascribed to the power of the Most High, and the child thus brought into the world is given the great designation of "Son of God." The three Persons are just as clearly brought before us in the account of Mt. (i. 18 ff), though the allusions to them are dispersed through a

longer stretch of narrative, in the course of which the Deity of
the child is twice intimated (ver. 21: 'It is He that shall save
His people from their sins'; ver. 23: 'They shall call His name
Immanuel; which is, being interpreted, *God-with-us*'). In the
baptismal scene which finds record by all the evangelists at
the opening of Jesus' ministry (Mt. iii. 16, 17; Mk. i. 10, 11;
Lk. iii. 21, 22; Jn. i. 32-34), the three Persons are thrown up
to sight in a dramatic picture in which the Deity of each is
strongly emphasized. From the open heavens the Spirit de-
scends in visible form, and 'a voice came out of the heavens,
Thou art my Son, the Beloved, in whom I am well pleased.'
Thus care seems to have been taken to make the advent of the
Son of God into the world the revelation also of the Triune
God, that the minds of men might as smoothly as possible
adjust themselves to the preconditions of the Divine redemption which was in process of being wrought out.

With this as a starting-point, the teaching of Jesus is Trini-
tarianly conditioned throughout. He has much to say of God
His Father, from whom as His Son He is in some true sense
distinct, and with whom He is in some equally true sense one.
And He has much to say of the Spirit, who represents Him as
He represents the Father, and by whom He works as the Father
works by Him. It is not merely in the Gospel of John that such
representations occur in the teaching of Jesus. In the Synoptics,
too, Jesus claims a Sonship to God which is unique (Mt. xi. 27;
xxiv. 36; Mk. xiii. 32; Lk. x. 22; in the following passages the
title of "Son of God" is attributed to Him and accepted by Him:
Mt. iv. 6; viii. 29; xiv. 33; xxvii. 40, 43, 54; Mk. iii. 11; xv. 39;
Lk. iv. 41; xxii. 70; cf. Jn. i. 34, 49; ix. 35; xi. 27), and which
involves an absolute community between the two in knowledge,
say, and power: both Mt. (xi. 27) and Lk. (x. 22) record His
great declaration that He knows the Father and the Father
knows Him with perfect mutual knowledge: "No one knoweth
the Son, save the Father; neither doth any know the Father,
save the Son." In the Synoptics, too, Jesus speaks of employing
the Spirit of God Himself for the performance of His works,
as if the activities of God were at His disposal: "I by the Spirit

of God"—or as Luke has it, "by the finger of God"—"cast out demons" (Mt. xii. 28; Lk. xi. 20; cf. the promise of the Spirit in Mk. xiii. 11; Lk. xii. 12).

It is in the discourses recorded in John, however, that Jesus most copiously refers to the unity of Himself, as the Son, with the Father, and to the mission of the Spirit from Himself as the dispenser of the Divine activities. Here He not only with great directness declares that He and the Father are one (x. 30; cf. xvii. 11, 21, 22, 25) with a unity of interpenetration ("The Father is in me, and I in the Father," x. 38; cf. xvi. 10, 11), so that to have seen Him was to have seen the Father (xiv. 9; cf. xv. 21); but He removes all doubt as to the essential nature of His oneness with the Father by explicitly asserting His eternity ("Before Abraham was born, I am," Jn. viii. 58), His co-eternity with God ("had with thee before the world was," xvii. 5; cf. xvii. 18; vi. 62), His eternal participation in the Divine glory itself ("the glory which I had with thee," in fellowship, community with Thee "before the world was," xvii. 5). So clear is it that in speaking currently of Himself as God's Son (v. 25; ix. 35; xi. 4; cf. x. 36), He meant, in accordance with the underlying significance of the idea of sonship in Semitic speech (founded on the natural implication that whatever the father is that the son is also; cf. xvi. 15; xvii. 10), to make Himself, as the Jews with exact appreciation of His meaning perceived, "equal with God" (v. 18), or, to put it brusquely, just "God" (x. 33). How He, being thus equal or rather identical with God, was in the world, He explains as involving a coming forth (ἐξῆλθον, exelthon) on His part, not merely from the presence of God (ἀπό, apó, xvi. 30; cf. xiii. 3) or from fellowship with God (παρά, pará, xvi. 27; xvii. 8), but from out of God Himself (ἐκ, ek, viii. 42; xvi. 28). And in the very act of thus asserting that His eternal home is in the depths of the Divine Being, He throws up, into as strong an emphasis as stressed pronouns can convey, His personal distinctness from the Father. 'If God were your Father,' says He (viii. 42), 'ye would love *me:* for *I* came forth and am come out of God; for neither have I come of *myself,* but it was *He* that sent *me.*' Again, He says (xvi. 26, 27):

'In that day ye shall ask in my name: and I say not unto you that *I* will make request of the Father for you; for *the Father Himself* loveth you, because ye have loved *me*, and have believed that it was *from fellowship with the Father* that *I* came forth; I came from out of the Father, and have come into the world.' Less pointedly, but still distinctly, He says again (xvii. 8): 'They know of a truth that it was *from fellowship with Thee* that I came forth, and they believed that it was Thou that didst send me.' It is not necessary to illustrate more at large a form of expression so characteristic of the discourses of Our Lord recorded by John that it meets us on every page: a form of expression which combines a clear implication of a unity of Father and Son which is identity of Being, and an equally clear implication of a distinction of Person between them such as allows not merely for the play of emotions between them, as, for instance, of love (xvii. 24; cf. xv. 9 [iii. 35]; xiv. 31), but also of an action and reaction upon one another which argues a high measure, if not of exteriority, yet certainly of exteriorization. Thus, to instance only one of the most outstanding facts of Our Lord's discourses (not indeed confined to those in John's Gospel, but found also in His sayings recorded in the Synoptists, as e.g., Lk. iv. 43 [cf. || Mk. i. 38]; ix. 48; x. 16; iv. 34; v. 32; vii. 19; xix. 10), He continually represents Himself as on the one hand sent by God, and as, on the other, having come forth from the Father (e.g., Jn. viii. 42; x. 36; xvii. 3; v. 23, *et saepe*).

It is more important to point out that these phenomena of interrelationship are not confined to the Father and Son, but are extended also to the Spirit. Thus, for example, in a context in which Our Lord had emphasized in the strongest manner His own essential unity and continued interpenetration with the Father ("If ye had known me, ye would have known my Father also"; "He that hath seen me hath seen the Father"; "I am in the Father, and the Father in me"; "The Father abiding in me doeth his works," Jn. xiv. 7, 9, 10), we read as follows (Jn. xiv. 16-26): 'And *I* will make request of the *Father*, and He shall give you *another* [thus sharply distinguished from Our Lord as a distinct Person] Advocate, that *He* may be with you for-

ever, the Spirit of Truth . . . He abideth with you and shall
be in you. I will not leave you orphans; I come unto you. . . .
In that day ye shall know that I am in the Father. . . . If a
man love me, he will keep my word; and my Father will love
him and we [that is, both Father and Son] will come unto him
and make our abode with him. . . . These things have I spoken
unto you while abiding with you. But the Advocate, the Holy
Spirit, whom the Father will send in my name, *He* shall teach
you all things, and bring to your remembrance all that *I* said
unto you.' It would be impossible to speak more distinctly of
three who were yet one. The Father, Son and Spirit are constantly distinguished from one another—the Son makes request
of the Father, and the Father in response to this request gives
an Advocate, "another" than the Son, who is sent in the Son's
name. And yet the oneness of these three is so kept in sight that
the coming of this "another Advocate" is spoken of without
embarrassment as the coming of the Son Himself (vs. 18, 19,
20, 21), and indeed as the coming of the Father and the Son
(ver. 23). There is a sense, then, in which, when Christ goes
away, the Spirit comes in His stead; there is also a sense in
which, when the Spirit comes, Christ comes in Him; and with
Christ's coming the Father comes too. There is a distinction
between the Persons brought into view; and with it an identity
among them; for both of which allowance must be made. The
same phenomena meet us in other passages. Thus, we read
again (xv. 26): 'But when there is come the Advocate whom
I will send unto you from [fellowship with] the Father, the
Spirit of Truth, which goeth forth from [fellowship with] the
Father, *He* shall bear witness of *me*.' In the compass of this
single verse, it is intimated that the Spirit is personally distinct
from the Son, and yet, like Him, has His eternal home (in fellowship) with the Father, from whom He, like the Son, comes
forth for His saving work, being sent thereunto, however, not
in this instance by the Father, but by the Son.

This last feature is even more strongly emphasized in yet
another passage in which the work of the Spirit in relation to
the Son is presented as closely parallel with the work of the

Son in relation to the Father (xvi. 5 ff.). 'But now I go unto Him that sent me. . . . Nevertheless *I* tell you the truth: it is expedient for you that *I* go away; for, if I go not away the Advocate will not come unto you; but if I go I will send Him unto you. And *He*, after He is come, will convict the world . . . of righteousness because I go to the Father and ye behold me no more. . . . I have yet many things to say unto you, but ye cannot bear them now. Howbeit when *He*, the Spirit of truth is come, He shall guide you into all the truth; for He shall not speak from Himself; but what things soever He shall hear, He shall speak, and He shall declare unto you the things that are to come. *He* shall glorify *me*: for He shall take of mine and shall show it unto you. All things whatsoever *the Father* hath are *mine*: therefore said I that He taketh of mine, and shall declare it unto you.' Here the Spirit is sent by the Son, and comes in order to complete and apply the Son's work, receiving His whole commission from the Son—not, however, in derogation of the Father, because when we speak of the things of the Son, that is to speak of the things of the Father.

It is not to be said, of course, that the doctrine of the Trinity is formulated in passages like these, with which the whole mass of Our Lord's discourses in John are strewn; but it certainly is presupposed in them, and that is, considered from the point of view of their probative force, even better. As we read we are kept in continual contact with three Persons who act, each as a distinct person, and yet who are in a deep, underlying sense, one. There is but one God—there is never any question of that—and yet this Son who has been sent into the world by God not only represents God but is God, and this Spirit whom the Son has in turn sent unto the world is also Himself God. Nothing could be clearer than that the Son and Spirit are distinct Persons, unless indeed it be that the Son of God is just God the Son and the Spirit of God just God the Spirit.

Meanwhile, the nearest approach to a formal announcement of the doctrine of the Trinity which is recorded from Our Lord's lips, or, perhaps we may say, which is to be found in the whole compass of the New Testament, has been preserved for us, not by John, but by one of the synoptists. It too, however, is only incidentally introduced, and has for its main object something very different from formulating the doctrine of the Trinity. It is embodied in the great commission which the resurrected Lord gave His disciples to be their "marching orders" "even unto the end of the world": "Go ye therefore, and make disciples of all the nations, baptizing them into the name of the Father and of the Son and of the Holy Spirit" (Mt. xxviii. 19). In seeking to estimate the significance of this great declaration, we must bear in mind the high solemnity of the utterance, by which we are required to give its full value to every word of it. Its phrasing is in any event, however, remarkable. It does not say, "In the names [plural] of the Father and of the Son and of the Holy Ghost"; nor yet (what might be taken to be equivalent to that), "In the name of the Father, and in the name of the Son, and in the name of the Holy Ghost," as if we had to deal with three separate Beings. Nor, on the other hand, does it say, "In the name of the Father, Son and Holy Ghost," as if "the Father, Son and Holy Ghost" might be taken as merely three designations of a single person. With stately impressiveness it asserts the unity of the three by combining them all within the bounds of the single Name; and then throws up into emphasis the distinctness of each by introducing them in turn with the repeated article: "In the name of the Father, and of the Son, and of the Holy Ghost" (Authorized Version). These three, the Father, and the Son, and the Holy Ghost, each stand in some clear sense over against the others in distinct personality: these three, the Father, and the Son, and the Holy Ghost, all unite in some profound sense in the common participation of the one Name. Fully to comprehend the implication of this mode of statement, we must bear in mind, further, the significance of the term, "the name," and the associations laden with which it came to the recipients of this commission. For the Hebrew did not think of the name, as we are accustomed to do, as a mere external symbol; but rather as the adequate expression of the innermost being of its bearer. In His name the Being of God finds expression; and the Name of God—"this glorious and fearful name,

Jehovah thy God" (Deut. xxviii. 58)—was accordingly a most sacred thing, being indeed virtually equivalent to God Himself. It is no solecism, therefore, when we read (Isa. xxx. 27), "Behold, the name of Jehovah cometh"; and the parallelisms are most instructive when we read (Isa. lix. 19): 'So shall they fear the Name of Jehovah from the west, and His glory from the rising of the sun; for He shall come as a stream pent in which the Spirit of Jehovah driveth.' So pregnant was the implication of the Name, that it was possible for the term to stand absolutely, without adjunction of the name itself, as the sufficient representative of the majesty of Jehovah: it was a terrible thing to 'blaspheme the Name' (Lev. xxiv. 11). All those over whom Jehovah's Name was called were His, His possession to whom He owed protection. It is for His Name's sake, therefore, that afflicted Judah cries to the Hope of Israel, the Saviour thereof in time of trouble: 'O Jehovah, Thou art in the midst of us, and Thy Name is called upon us; leave us not' (Jer. xiv. 9); and His people find the appropriate expression of their deepest shame in the lament, 'We have become as they over whom Thou never barest rule; as they upon whom Thy Name was not called' (Isa. lxiii. 19); while the height of joy is attained in the cry, 'Thy Name, Jehovah, God of Hosts, is called upon me' (Jer. xv. 16; cf. II Chron. vii. 14; Dan. ix. 18, 19). When, therefore, Our Lord commanded His disciples to baptize those whom they brought to His obedience "into the name of . . . ," He was using language charged to them with high meaning. He could not have been understood otherwise than as substituting for the Name of Jehovah this other Name "of the Father, and of the Son, and of the Holy Ghost"; and this could not possibly have meant to His disciples anything else than that Jehovah was now to be known to them by the new Name, of the Father, and the Son, and the Holy Ghost. The only alternative would have been that, for the community which He was founding, Jesus was supplanting Jehovah by a new God; and this alternative is no less than monstrous. There is no alternative, therefore, to understanding Jesus here to be giving for His community a new Name to Jehovah and that new Name to be the threefold Name of "the Father, and the Son, and the Holy Ghost." Nor is there room for doubt that by "the Son" in this threefold Name, He meant just Himself with all the implications of distinct personality which this carries with it; and, of course, that further carries with it the equally distinct personality of "the Father" and "the Holy Ghost," with whom "the Son" is here associated, and from whom alike "the Son" is here distinguished. This is a direct ascription to Jehovah the God of Israel, of a threefold personality, and is therewith the direct enunciation of the doctrine of the Trinity. We are not witnessing here the birth of the doctrine of the Trinity; that is presupposed. What we are witnessing is the authoritative announcement of the Trinity as the God of Christianity by its Founder, in one of the most solemn of His recorded declarations. Israel had worshipped the one only true God under the Name of Jehovah; Christians are to worship the same one only and true God under the Name of "the Father, and the Son, and the Holy Ghost." This is the distinguishing characteristic of Christians; and that is as much as to say that the doctrine of the Trinity is, according to Our Lord's own apprehension of it, the distinctive mark of the religion which He founded.

A passage of such range of implication has, of course, not escaped criticism and challenge. An attempt which cannot be characterized as other than frivolous has even been made to dismiss it from the text of Matthew's Gospel. Against this, the whole body of external evidence cries out; and the internal evidence is of itself not less decisive to the same effect. When the "universalism," "ecclesiasticism," and "high theology" of the passage are pleaded against its genuineness, it is forgotten that to the Jesus of Matthew there are attributed not only such parables as those of the Leaven and the Mustard Seed, but such declarations as those contained in viii. 11, 12; xxi. 43; xxiv. 14; that in this Gospel alone is Jesus recorded as speaking familiarly about His church (xvi. 18; xviii. 17); and that, after the great declaration of xi. 27 ff., nothing remained in lofty attribution to be assigned to Him. When these same objections are urged against recognizing the passage as an authentic saying of Jesus' own, it is quite obvious that the Jesus of the evangelists cannot be in mind. The declaration here recorded is quite in character with the Jesus of Matthew's Gospel, as has just been intimated; and no less with the Jesus of the whole New Testament transmission. It will scarcely do, first to construct *a priori* a Jesus to our own liking, and then to discard as "unhistorical" all in the New Testament transmission which would be unnatural to such a Jesus. It is not these discarded passages but our *a priori* Jesus which is unhistorical. In the present instance, moreover, the historicity of the assailed saying is protected by an important historical relation in which it stands. It is not merely Jesus who speaks out of a Trinitarian consciousness, but all the New Testament writers as well. The universal possession by His followers of so firm a hold on such a doctrine requires the assumption that some such teaching as is here attributed to Him was actually contained in Jesus' instructions to His followers. Even had it not been attributed to Him in so many words by the record, we should have had to assume that some such declaration had been made by Him. In these circumstances, there can be no good reason to doubt that it was made by Him, when it is expressly attributed to Him by the record.

When we turn from the discourses of Jesus to the writings of His followers with a view to observing how the assumption of the doctrine of the Trinity underlies their whole fabric also, we naturally go first of all to the letters of Paul. Their very mass is impressive; and the definiteness with which their composition within a generation of the death of Jesus may be fixed adds importance to them as historical witnesses. Certainly they leave nothing to be desired in the richness of their testimony to the Trinitarian conception of God which underlies them. Throughout the whole series, from I Thess., which comes from about 52 A.D., to II Tim., which was written about 68 A.D., the redemption, which it is their one business to proclaim and commend, and all the blessings which enter into it or accompany it are referred consistently to a threefold Divine causation. Everywhere, throughout their pages, God the Father, the Lord Jesus Christ, and the Holy Spirit appear as the joint objects of all

religious adoration, and the conjunct source of all Divine operations. In the freedom of the allusions which are made to them,
now and again one alone of the three is thrown up into prominent view; but more often two of them are conjoined in thanksgiving or prayer; and not infrequently all three are brought
together as the apostle strives to give some adequate expression
to his sense of indebtedness to the Divine source of all good for
blessings received, or to his longing on behalf of himself or of
his readers for further communion with the God of grace. It is
regular for him to begin his Epistles with a prayer for "grace
and peace" for his readers, "from God our Father, and the
Lord Jesus Christ," as the joint source of these Divine blessings
by way of eminence (Rom. i. 7; I Cor. i. 3; II Cor. i. 2; Gal. i. 3;
Eph. i. 2; Phil. i. 2; II Thess. i. 2; I Tim. i. 2; II Tim. i. 2; Philem.
ver. 3; cf. I Thess. i. 1). It is obviously no departure from this
habit in the essence of the matter, but only in relative fulness
of expression, when in the opening words of the Epistle to the
Colossians the clause "and the Lord Jesus Christ" is omitted,
and we read merely: "Grace to you and peace from God our
Father." So also it would have been no departure from it in the
essence of the matter, but only in relative fulness of expression,
if in any instance the name of the Holy Spirit had chanced to
be adjoined to the other two, as in the single instance of II Cor.
xiii. 14 it is adjoined to them in the closing prayer for grace
with which Paul ends his letters, and which ordinarily takes the
simple form of, "the grace of our Lord Jesus Christ be with you"
(Rom. xvi. 20; I Cor. xvi. 23; Gal. vi. 18; Phil. iv. 23; I Thess.
v. 28; II Thess. iii. 18; Philem. ver. 25; more expanded form,
Eph. vi. 23, 24; more compressed, Col. iv. 18; I Tim. vi. 21;
II Tim. iv. 22; Tit. iii. 15). Between these opening and closing
passages the allusions to God the Father, the Lord Jesus Christ,
and the Holy Spirit are constant and most intricately interlaced.
Paul's monotheism is intense: the first premise of all his thought
on Divine things is the unity of God (Rom. iii. 30; I Cor. viii. 4;
Gal. iii. 20; Eph. iv. 6; I Tim. ii. 5; cf. Rom. xvi. 22; I Tim. i. 17).
Yet to him God the Father is no more God than the Lord Jesus
Christ is God, or the Holy Spirit is God. The Spirit of God is to

him related to God as the spirit of man is to man (I Cor. ii. 11),
and therefore if the Spirit of God dwells in us, that is God dwelling in us (Rom. viii. 10 ff.), and we are by that fact constituted
temples of God (I Cor. iii. 16). And no expression is too strong
for him to use in order to assert the Godhead of Christ: He is
"our great God" (Tit. ii. 13); He is "God over all" (Rom. ix. 5);
and indeed it is expressly declared of Him that the "fulness of
the Godhead," that is, everything that enters into Godhead and
constitutes it Godhead, dwells in Him. In the very act of asserting his monotheism Paul takes Our Lord up into this unique
Godhead. "There is no God but one," he roundly asserts, and
then illustrates and proves this assertion by remarking that the
heathen may have "gods many, and lords many," but "to us
there is one God, the Father, of whom are all things, and we
unto him; and one Lord, Jesus Christ, through whom are all
things, and we through him" (I Cor. viii. 6). Obviously, this
"one God, the Father," and "one Lord, Jesus Christ," are embraced together in the one God who alone is. Paul's conception
of the one God, whom alone he worships, includes, in other
words, a recognition that within the unity of His Being, there
exists such a distinction of Persons as is given us in the "one
God, the Father" and the "one Lord, Jesus Christ."

In numerous passages scattered through Paul's Epistles,
from the earliest of them (I Thess. i. 2-5; II Thess. ii. 13, 14)
to the latest (Tit. iii. 4-6; II Tim. i. 3, 13, 14), all three Persons,
God the Father, the Lord Jesus Christ and the Holy Spirit, are
brought together, in the most incidental manner, as co-sources
of all the saving blessings which come to believers in Christ.
A typical series of such passages may be found in Eph. ii. 18;
iii. 2-5, 14, 17; iv. 4-6; v. 18-20. But the most interesting instances are offered to us perhaps by the Epistles to the Corinthians. In I Cor. xii. 4-6 Paul presents the abounding spiritual
gifts with which the church was blessed in a threefold aspect,
and connects these aspects with the three Divine Persons. "Now
there are diversities of gifts, but the same Spirit. And there are
diversities of ministrations, and the same Lord. And there are
diversities of workings, but the same God, who worketh all

things in all." It may be thought that there is a measure of what might almost be called artificiality in assigning the endowments of the church, as they are graces to the Spirit, as they are services to Christ, and as they are energizing to God. But thus there is only the more strikingly revealed the underlying Trinitarian conception as dominating the structure of the clauses: Paul clearly so writes, not because "gifts," "workings," "operations" stand out in his thought as greatly diverse things, but because God, the Lord, and the Spirit lie in the back of his mind constantly suggesting a threefold causality behind every manifestation of grace. The Trinity is alluded to rather than asserted; but it is so alluded to as to show that it constitutes the determining basis of all Paul's thought of the God of redemption. Even more instructive is II Cor. xiii. 14, which has passed into general liturgical use in the churches as a benediction: "The grace of the Lord Jesus Christ, and the love of God, and the communion of the Holy Spirit, be with you all." Here the three highest redemptive blessings are brought together, and attached distributively to the three Persons of the Triune God. There is again no formal teaching of the doctrine of the Trinity; there is only another instance of natural speaking out of a Trinitarian consciousness. Paul is simply thinking of the Divine source of these great blessings; but he habitually thinks of this Divine source of redemptive blessings after a trinal fashion. He therefore does not say, as he might just as well have said, "The grace and love and communion of God be with you all," but "The grace of the Lord Jesus Christ, and the love of God, and the communion of the Holy Spirit, be with you all." Thus he bears, almost unconsciously but most richly, witness to the trinal composition of the Godhead as conceived by Him.

The phenomena of Paul's Epistles are repeated in the other writings of the New Testament. In these other writings also it is everywhere assumed that the redemptive activities of God rest on a threefold source in God the Father, the Lord Jesus Christ, and the Holy Spirit; and these three Persons repeatedly come forward together in the expressions of Christian hope or the aspirations of Christian devotion (e.g., Heb. ii. 3, 4; vi. 4-6;

x. 29-31; I Pet. i. 2; ii. 3-12; iv. 13-19; I Jn. v. 4-8; Jude vs. 20, 21; Rev. i. 4-6). Perhaps as typical instances as any are supplied by the two following: "According to the foreknowledge of God the Father, in sanctification of the Spirit, unto obedience and sprinkling of the blood of Jesus Christ" (I Pet. i. 2); "Praying in the Holy Spirit, keep yourselves in the love of God, looking for the mercy of our Lord Jesus Christ unto eternal life" (Jude vs. 20, 21). To these may be added the highly symbolical instance from the Apocalypse: 'Grace to you and peace from Him which is and was and which is to come; and from the Seven Spirits which are before His throne; and from Jesus Christ, who is the faithful witness, the firstborn of the dead, and the ruler of the kings of the earth' (Rev. i. 4, 5). Clearly these writers, too, write out of a fixed Trinitarian consciousness and bear their testimony to the universal understanding current in apostolical circles. Everywhere and by all it was fully understood that the one God whom Christians worshipped and from whom alone they expected redemption and all that redemption brought with it, included within His undiminished unity the three: God the Father, the Lord Jesus Christ, and the Holy Spirit, whose activities relatively to one another are conceived as distinctly personal. This is the uniform and pervasive testimony of the New Testament, and it is the more impressive that it is given with such unstudied naturalness and simplicity, with no effort to distinguish between what have come to be called the ontological and the economical aspects of the Trinitarian distinctions, and indeed without apparent consciousness of the existence of such a distinction of aspects. Whether God is thought of in Himself or in His operations, the underlying conception runs unaffectedly into trinal forms.

It will not have escaped observation that the Trinitarian terminology of Paul and the other writers of the New Testament is not precisely identical with that of Our Lord as recorded for us in His discourses. Paul, for example—and the same is true of the other New Testament writers (except John)—does not speak, as Our Lord is recorded as speaking, of the Father, the Son, and the Holy Spirit, so much as of God, the Lord Jesus

Christ, and the Holy Spirit. This difference of terminology finds
its account in large measure in the different relations in which
the speakers stand to the Trinity. Our Lord could not naturally
speak of Himself, as one of the Trinitarian Persons, by the
designation of "the Lord," while the designation of "the Son,"
expressing as it does His consciousness of close relation, and
indeed of exact similarity, to God, came naturally to His lips.
But He was Paul's Lord; and Paul naturally thought and spoke
of Him as such. In point of fact, "Lord" is one of Paul's favorite
designations of Christ, and indeed has become with him practically a proper name for Christ, and in point of fact, his Divine
Name for Christ. It is naturally, therefore, his Trinitarian
name for Christ. Because when he thinks of Christ as Divine
he calls Him "Lord," he naturally, when he thinks of the three
Persons together as the Triune God, sets Him as "Lord" by the
side of God—Paul's constant name for "the Father"—and the
Holy Spirit. Question may no doubt be raised whether it would
have been possible for Paul to have done this, especially with
the constancy with which he has done it, if, in his conception of
it, the very essence of the Trinity were enshrined in the terms
"Father" and "Son." Paul is thinking of the Trinity, to be sure,
from the point of view of a worshipper, rather than from that
of a systematizer. He designates the Persons of the Trinity
therefore rather from his relations to them than from their
relations to one another. He sees in the Trinity his God, his
Lord, and the Holy Spirit who dwells in him; and naturally he
so speaks currently of the three Persons. It remains remarkable,
nevertheless, if the very essence of the Trinity were thought of
by him as resident in the terms "Father," "Son," that in his
numerous allusions to the Trinity in the Godhead, he never betrays any sense of this. It is noticeable also that in their allusions
to the Trinity, there is preserved, neither in Paul nor in the
other writers of the New Testament, the order of the names as
they stand in Our Lord's great declaration (Mt. xxviii. 19).
The reverse order occurs, indeed, occasionally, as, for example,
in I Cor. xii. 4-6 (cf. Eph. iv. 4-6); and this may be understood
as a climactic arrangement and so far a testimony to the order

of Mt. xxviii. 19. But the order is very variable; and in the most
formal enumeration of the three Persons, that of II Cor. xiii. 14,
it stands thus: Lord, God, Spirit. The question naturally suggests itself whether the order Father, Son, Spirit was especially
significant to Paul and his fellow-writers of the New Testament.
If in their conviction the very essence of the doctrine of the
Trinity was embodied in this order, should we not anticipate
that there should appear in their numerous allusions to the
Trinity some suggestion of this conviction?

Such facts as these have a bearing upon the testimony of
the New Testament to the interrelations of the Persons of the
Trinity. To the fact of the Trinity—to the fact, that is, that in the
unity of the Godhead there subsist three Persons, each of whom
has his particular part in the working out of salvation—the New
Testament testimony is clear, consistent, pervasive and conclusive. There is included in this testimony constant and decisive
witness to the complete and undiminished Deity of each of
these Persons; no language is too exalted to apply to each of
them in turn in the effort to give expression to the writer's sense
of His Deity: the name that is given to each is fully understood
to be "the name that is above every name." When we attempt to
press the inquiry behind the broad fact, however, with a view
to ascertaining exactly how the New Testament writers conceive the three Persons to be related, the one to the other, we
meet with great difficulties. Nothing could seem more natural,
for example, than to assume that the mutual relations of the
Persons of the Trinity are revealed in the designations, "the
Father, the Son, and the Holy Spirit," which are given them by
Our Lord in the solemn formula of Mt. xxviii. 19. Our confidence in this assumption is somewhat shaken, however, when
we observe, as we have just observed, that these designations
are not carefully preserved in their allusions to the Trinity by
the writers of the New Testament at large, but are characteristic
only of Our Lord's allusions and those of John, whose modes of
speech in general very closely resemble those of Our Lord. Our
confidence is still further shaken when we observe that the
implications with respect to the mutual relations of the Trini-

tarian Persons, which are ordinarily derived from these designations, do not so certainly lie in them as is commonly supposed.

It may be very natural to see in the designation "Son" an
intimation of subordination and derivation of Being, and it may
not be difficult to ascribe a similar connotation to the term
"Spirit." But it is quite certain that this was not the denotation
of either term in the Semitic consciousness, which underlies the
phraseology of Scripture; and it may even be thought doubtful
whether it was included even in their remoter suggestions.
What underlies the conception of sonship in Scriptural speech
is just "likeness"; whatever the father is that the son is also.
The emphatic application of the term "Son" to one of the Trinitarian Persons, accordingly, asserts rather His equality with the
Father than His subordination to the Father; and if there is any
implication of derivation in it, it would appear to be very distant. The adjunction of the adjective "only begotten" (Jn. i. 14;
iii. 16-18; I Jn. iv. 9) need add only the idea of uniqueness, not
of derivation (Ps. xxii. 20; xxv. 16; xxxv. 17; Wisd. vii. 22 m.);
and even such a phrase as "God only begotten" (Jn. i. 18 m.)
may contain no implication of derivation, but only of absolutely
unique consubstantiality; as also such a phrase as "the first-
begotten of all creation" (Col. i. 15) may convey no intimation
of coming into being, but merely assert priority of existence. In
like manner, the designation "Spirit of God" or "Spirit of
Jehovah," which meets us frequently in the Old Testament,
certainly does not convey the idea there either of derivation or
of subordination, but is just the executive name of God—the
designation of God from the point of view of His activity—and
imports accordingly identity with God; and there is no reason
to suppose that, in passing from the Old Testament to the New
Testament, the term has taken on an essentially different meaning. It happens, oddly enough, moreover, that we have in the
New Testament itself what amounts almost to formal definitions of the two terms "Son" and "Spirit," and in both cases the
stress is laid on the notion of equality or sameness. In Jn. v. 18
we read: 'On this account, therefore, the Jews sought the more
to kill him, because, not only did he break the Sabbath, but also

called God his own Father, making himself equal to God.' The point lies, of course, in the adjective "own." Jesus was, rightly, understood to call God "his *own* Father," that is, to use the terms "Father" and "Son" not in a merely figurative sense, as when Israel was called God's son, but in the real sense. And this was understood to be claiming to be all that God is. To be the Son of God in any sense was to be like God in that sense; to be God's *own* Son was to be exactly like God, to be "equal with God." Similarly, we read in I Cor. ii. 10, 11: 'For the Spirit searcheth all things, yea, the deep things of God. For who of men knoweth the things of a man, save the spirit of man which is in him? Even so the things of God none knoweth, save the Spirit of God.' Here the Spirit appears as the substrate of the Divine self-consciousness, the principle of God's knowledge of Himself: He is, in a word, just God Himself in the innermost essence of His Being. As the spirit of man is the seat of human life, the very life of man itself, so the Spirit of God is His very life-element. How can He be supposed, then, to be subordinate to God, or to derive His Being from God? If, however, the sub-ordination of the Son and Spirit to the Father in modes of subsistence and their derivation from the Father are not impli-cates of their designation as Son and Spirit, it will be hard to find in the New Testament compelling evidence of their sub-ordination and derivation.

There is, of course, no question that in "modes of operation," as it is technically called—that is to say, in the functions ascribed to the several persons of the Trinity in the redemptive process, and, more broadly, in the entire dealing of God with the world —the principle of subordination is clearly expressed. The Father is first, the Son is second, and the Spirit is third, in the opera-tions of God as revealed to us in general, and very especially in those operations by which redemption is accomplished. What-ever the Father does, He does through the Son (Rom. ii. 16; iii. 22; v. 1, 11, 17, 21; Eph. i. 5; I Thess. v. 9; Tit. iii. 5) by the Spirit. The Son is sent by the Father and does His Father's will (Jn. vi. 38); the Spirit is sent by the Son and does not speak from Himself, but only takes of Christ's and shows it unto His people (Jn. xvii. 7 ff.); and we have Our Lord's own word for it that 'one that is sent is not greater than he that sent him' (Jn. xiii. 16). In crisp decisiveness, Our Lord even declares, indeed: 'My Father is greater than I' (Jn. xiv. 28); and Paul tells us that Christ is God's, even as we are Christ's (I Cor. iii. 23), and that as Christ is "the head of every man," so God is "the head of Christ" (I Cor. xi. 3). But it is not so clear that the principle of subordination rules also in "modes of subsistence," as it is technically phrased; that is to say, in the necessary relation of the Persons of the Trinity to one another. The very richness and variety of the expression of their subordination, the one to the other, in modes of operation, create a difficulty in attaining certainty whether they are represented as also subordinate the one to the other in modes of subsistence. Question is raised in each case of apparent intimation of subordination in modes of subsistence, whether it may not, after all, be explicable as only another expression of subordination in modes of operation. It may be natural to assume that a subordination in modes of operation rests on a subordination in modes of subsistence; that the reason why it is the Father that sends the Son and the Son that sends the Spirit is that the Son is subordinate to the Father, and the Spirit to the Son. But we are bound to bear in mind that these relations of subordination in modes of operation may just as well be due to a convention, an agreement, between the Persons of the Trinity—a "Covenant" as it is technically called—by virtue of which a distinct function in the work of redemption is voluntarily assumed by each. It is eminently desirable, therefore, at the least, that some definite evidence of subordination in modes of subsistence should be discoverable before it is assumed. In the case of the relation of the Son to the Father, there is the added difficulty of the incarnation, in which the Son, by the assumption of a creaturely nature into union with Himself, enters into new relations with the Father of a definitely subordinate character. Question has even been raised whether the very designations of Father and Son may not be expressive of these new relations, and therefore without significance with respect to the eternal relations of the

Persons so designated. This question must certainly be answered in the negative. Although, no doubt, in many of the instances in which the terms "Father" and "Son" occur, it would be possible to take them of merely economical relations, there ever remain some which are intractable to this treatment, and we may be sure that "Father" and "Son" are applied to their eternal and necessary relations. But these terms, as we have seen, do not appear to imply relations of first and second, superiority and subordination, in modes of subsistence; and the fact of the humiliation of the Son of God for His earthly work does introduce a factor into the interpretation of the passages which import His subordination to the Father, which throws doubt upon the inference from them of an eternal relation of subordination in the Trinity itself. It must at least be said that in the presence of the great New Testament doctrines of the Covenant of Redemption on the one hand, and of the Humiliation of the Son of God for His work's sake and of the Two Natures in the constitution of His Person as incarnated, on the other, the difficulty of interpreting subordinationist passages of eternal relations between the Father and Son becomes extreme. The question continually obtrudes itself, whether they do not rather find their full explanation in the facts embodied in the doctrines of the Covenant, the Humiliation of Christ, and the Two Natures of His incarnated Person. Certainly in such circumstances it were thoroughly illegitimate to press such passages to suggest any subordination for the Son or the Spirit which would in any manner impair that complete identity with the Father in Being and that complete equality with the Father in powers which are constantly presupposed, and frequently emphatically, though only incidentally, asserted for them throughout the whole fabric of the New Testament.

The Trinity of the Persons of the Godhead, shown in the incarnation and the redemptive work of God the Son, and the descent and saving work of God the Spirit, is thus everywhere assumed in the New Testament, and comes to repeated fragmentary but none the less emphatic and illuminating expression in its pages. As the roots of its revelation are set in the threefold

Divine causality of the saving process, it naturally finds an echo also in the consciousness of everyone who has experienced this salvation. Every redeemed soul, knowing himself reconciled with God through His Son, and quickened into newness of life by His Spirit, turns alike to Father, Son and Spirit with the exclamation of reverent gratitude upon his lips, "My Lord and my God!" If he could not construct the doctrine of the Trinity out of his consciousness of salvation, yet the elements of his consciousness of salvation are interpreted to him and reduced to order only by the doctrine of the Trinity which he finds underlying and giving their significance and consistency to the teaching of the Scriptures as to the processes of salvation. By means of this doctrine he is able to think clearly and consequently of his threefold relation to the saving God, experienced by Him as Fatherly love sending a Redeemer, as redeeming love executing redemption, as saving love applying redemption: all manifestations in distinct methods and by distinct agencies of the one seeking and saving love of God. Without the doctrine of the Trinity, his conscious Christian life would be thrown into confusion and left in disorganization if not, indeed, given an air of unreality; with the doctrine of the Trinity, order, significance and reality are brought to every element of it. Accordingly, the doctrine of the Trinity and the doctrine of redemption, historically, stand or fall together. A Unitarian theology is commonly associated with a Pelagian anthropology and a Socinian soteriology. It is a striking testimony which is borne by F. E. Koenig ("Offenbarungsbegriff des AT," 1882, I, 125): "I have learned that many cast off the whole history of redemption for no other reason than because they have not attained to a conception of the Triune God." It is in this intimacy of relation between the doctrines of the Trinity and redemption that the ultimate reason lies why the Christian church could not rest until it had attained a definite and well-compacted doctrine of the Trinity. Nothing else could be accepted as an adequate foundation for the experience of the Christian salvation. Neither the Sabellian nor the Arian construction could meet and satisfy the data of the consciousness of salvation, any more than either could meet and satisfy the data of the Scriptural revelation. The data of the Scriptural revelation might, to be sure, have been left unsatisfied: men might have found a *modus vivendi* with neglected, or even with perverted Scriptural teaching. But perverted or neglected elements of Christian experience are more clamant in their demands for attention and correction. The dissatisfied Christian consciousness necessarily searched the Scriptures, on the emergence of every new attempt to state the doctrine of the nature and relations of God, to see whether these things were true, and never reached contentment until the Scriptural data were given their consistent formulation in a valid doctrine of the Trinity. Here too the heart of man was restless until it found its rest in the Triune God, the author, procurer and applier of salvation.

The determining impulse to the formulation of the doctrine of the Trinity in the church was the church's profound conviction of the absolute Deity of Christ, on which as on a pivot the whole Christian conception of God from the first origins of Christianity turned. The guiding principle in the formulation of the doctrine was supplied by the Baptismal Formula announced by Jesus (Mt. xxviii. 19), from which was derived the ground-plan of the baptismal confessions and "rules of faith" which very soon began to be framed all over the church. It was by these two fundamental *principia*—the true Deity of Christ and the Baptismal Formula—that all attempts to formulate the Christian doctrine of God were tested, and by their molding power that the church at length found itself in possession of a form of statement which did full justice to the data of the redemptive revelation as reflected in the New Testament and the demands of the Christian heart under the experience of salvation.

In the nature of the case the formulated doctrine was of slow attainment. The influence of inherited conceptions and of current philosophies inevitably showed itself in the efforts to construe to the intellect the immanent faith of Christians. In the second century the dominant neo-Stoic and neo-Platonic ideas deflected Christian thought into subordinationist channels, and produced what is known as the Logos-Christology, which looks upon the Son as a prolation of Deity reduced to such dimensions as comported with relations with a world of time and space; meanwhile, to a great extent, the Spirit was neglected altogether. A reaction which, under the name of Monarchianism, identified the Father, Son, and Spirit so completely that they were thought of only as different aspects or different moments in the life of the one Divine Person, called now Father, now Son, now Spirit, as His several activities came successively into view, almost succeeded in establishing itself in the third century as the doctrine of the church at large. In the conflict between these two opposite tendencies the church gradually found its way, under the guidance of the Baptismal Formula elaborated into a "Rule of Faith," to a better and more well-balanced conception, until a real doctrine of the Trinity at length came to expression, particularly in the West, through the brilliant dialectic of Tertullian. It was thus ready at hand, when, in the early years of the fourth century, the Logos-Christology, in opposition to dominant Sabellian tendencies, ran to seed in what is known as Arianism, to which the Son was a creature, though exalted above all other creatures as their Creator and Lord; and the church was thus prepared to assert its settled faith in a Triune God, one in being, but in whose unity there subsisted three consubstantial Persons. Under the leadership of Athanasius this doctrine was proclaimed as the faith of the church at the Council of Nice in 325 A.D., and by his strenuous labors and those of "the three great Cappadocians," the two Gregories and Basil, it gradually won its way to the actual acceptance of the entire church. It was at the hands of Augustine, however, a century later, that the doctrine thus become the church doctrine in fact as well as in theory, received its most complete elaboration and most carefully grounded statement. In the form which he gave it, and which is embodied in that "battle-hymn of the early church," the so-called Athanasian Creed, it has retained its place as the fit expression of the faith of the church as to the nature of its God until today. The language in which it is couched, even in this final declaration, still retains elements of speech which owe their origin to the modes of thought characteristic of the Logos-Christology of the second century, fixed in the nomenclature of the church by the Nicene Creed of 325 A.D., though carefully guarded there against the subordinationism inherent in the Logos-Christology, and made the vehicle rather of the Nicene doctrines of the eternal generation of the Son and procession of the Spirit, with the consequent subordination of the Son and Spirit to the Father in modes of subsistence as well as of operation. In the Athanasian Creed, however, the principle of the equalization of the three Persons, which was already the dominant motive of the Nicene Creed—the *homooúsia*—is so strongly emphasized as practically to push out of sight, if not quite out of existence, these remanent suggestions of derivation and subordination. It has been found necessary, nevertheless, from time to time, vigorously to reassert the principle of equalization, over against a tendency unduly to emphasize the elements of subordinationism which still hold a place thus in the traditional language in which the church states its doctrine of the Trinity. In particular, it fell to Calvin, in the interests of the true Deity of Christ—the constant motive of the whole body of Trinitarian thought—to reassert and make good the attribute of self-existence *(autotheotós)* for the Son. Thus Calvin takes his place, alongside of Tertullian, Athanasius and Augustine, as one of the chief contributors to the exact and vital statement of the Christian doctrine of the Triune God.

[NOTE.—In this article the author has usually given his own renderings of original passages, and not those of any particular VS.—EDITOR.]

CHAPTER III

"GOD OUR FATHER AND THE LORD JESUS CHRIST"[1]

IN THE opening sentence of the very first of Paul's letters which have come down to us—and that is as much as to say, in the very first sentence which, so far as we know, he ever wrote, —he makes use of a phrase in speaking of the Christians' God, which at once attracts our interested attention. According to the generous way he had of thinking and speaking of his readers at the height of their professions, he describes the church at Thessalonica as living and moving and having its being in God. But, as it was a Christian church which he was addressing, he does not content himself, in this description, with the simple term "God." He uses the compound phrase, "God the Father and the Lord Jesus Christ." The Thessalonians, he says, because they were Christians, lived and moved and had their being "in God the Father and the Lord Jesus Christ."

It is quite clear that this compound phrase was not new on Paul's lips, coined for this occasion. It bears on its face the evidence of a long and familiar use, by which it had been worn down to its bare bones. All the articles have been rubbed off, and with them all other accessories; and it stands out in its baldest elements as just "God Father and Lord Jesus Christ." Plainly we have here a mode of speaking of the Christians' God which was customary with Paul.

We are not surprised, therefore, to find this phrase repeated in precisely the same connection in the opening verses of the next letter which Paul wrote—II Thessalonians—with only the slight variation that an "our" is inserted with "God the Father," —"in God our Father and the Lord Jesus Christ." The significance of this variation is, probably, that, although it is a cus-

---

[1] From *The Princeton Theological Review*, v. xv, 1917, pp. 1-20; also from *Biblical Doctrines*, pp. 213-231.

tomary formula which is being employed, it has not hardened
into a mechanically repeated series of mere words. It is used
with lively consciousness of its full meaning, and with such
slight variations of wording from time to time as the circumstances of each case, or perhaps the mere emotional movement
of the moment, suggested.

This free handling of what is, nevertheless, clearly in essence
a fixed formula, is sharply illustrated by a third instance of its
occurrence. Paul uses it again in the opening sentence of the
third letter which he wrote,—that to the Galatians. Here it is
turned, however, end to end, while yet preserving all its essential elements; and is set in such a context as to throw its fundamental meaning into very strong emphasis. Paul was called
upon to defend to the Galatians the validity of his apostleship,
and he characteristically takes occasion to assert, in the very
first words which he wrote to them, that he received it from
no human source,—no, nor even through any human intermedi-
ation,—but directly from God. The way he does this is to announce himself as "an apostle not from men, neither through
man, but through Jesus Christ and God the Father"—"who,"
he adds, "raised Him from the dead." The effect of the addition
of these last words is to throw the whole emphasis of the clause
on "Jesus Christ"; even "God the Father" is defined in relation
to Him. Yet the whole purpose of the sentence is to assert the
divine origin of Paul's apostleship in strong contrast with any
possible human derivation of it. Clearly, the phrase "Jesus Christ
and God the Father" denotes something purely Divine. It is in
effect a Christian periphrasis for "God." And in this Christian
periphrasis for "God" the name of Jesus Christ takes no subordinate place.

It will conduce to our better apprehension of the nature and
implications of this Christian periphrasis for "God" which Paul
employs in the opening words of each of the first three of his
epistles, if we will set side by side the actual words in which it
is phrased in these three instances.

I Thess. i. 1: ἐν θεῷ πατρὶ καὶ κυρίῳ Ἰησοῦ Χριστῷ.

II Thess. i. 1: ἐν θεῷ πατρὶ ἡμῶν καὶ κυρίῳ Ἰησοῦ Χριστῷ.

Gal. i. 1: διὰ Ἰησοῦ Χριστοῦ καὶ θεοῦ πατρὸς τοῦ ἐγείραντος αὐτὸν ἐκ νεκρῶν.

It is not, however, merely or chiefly in these three instances that Paul uses this Christian periphrasis for God. It is the apostle's custom to bring the address which he prefixes to each of his letters to a close in a formal prayer that the fundamental Christian blessings of grace and peace (or, in the letters to Timothy, grace, mercy and peace) may be granted to his readers. In this prayer he regularly employs this periphrasis to designate the Divine Being to whom the prayer is offered. It fails to appear in this opening prayer in two only of his thirteen letters; and its failure to appear in these two is useful in fixing its meaning in the other eleven. It is quite clear that Paul intends to say the same thing in all thirteen instances: they differ only in the fulness with which he expresses his identical meaning. When he says in I Thess. i. 1 only "Grace to you and peace," he is not expressing a mere wish; he is invoking the Divine Being in prayer; and his mind is as fully on Him as if he had formally named Him. And when he names this Divine Being whom he is invoking in this prayer, in Col. i. 2, "God our Father,"—"Grace to you and peace from God our Father"—his meaning is precisely the same as when he names Him in the companion letter, Eph. i. 2, "God our Father and the Lord Jesus Christ"—"Grace to you and peace from God our Father and the Lord Jesus Christ"—or in a similar prayer at the end of the same letter, Eph. vi. 23, "God the Father and the Lord Jesus Christ"—"Peace to the brethren and love along with faith from God the Father and the Lord Jesus Christ." In every instance Paul is invoking the Divine Being and only the Divine Being. Once he leaves that to be understood from the nature of the case. Once he names this Being simply "God the Father." In the other eleven instances he gives Him the conjunct name, which ordinarily takes the form of "God our Father and the Lord Jesus Christ,"—obviously employing a formula which had become habitual with him in such formal prayers.

That we may see at a glance how clear it is that Paul is making use here of a fixed formula in his designation of the

Christians' God, and may observe at the same time the amount of freedom which he allows himself in repeating it in these very formal prayers, we bring together the series of these opening prayers, in the chronological order of the epistles in which they occur.

I Thess. i. 1:   χάρις ὑμῖν καὶ εἰρήνη.

II Thess. i. 2:   χάρις ὑμῖν καὶ εἰρήνη ἀπὸ θεοῦ πατρὸς καὶ κυρίου Ἰησοῦ Χριστοῦ.

Gal. i. 3:   χάρις ὑμῖν καὶ εἰρήνη ἀπὸ θεοῦ πατρὸς ἡμῶν καὶ κυρίου Ἰησοῦ Χριστοῦ.

I Cor. i. 3:   χάρις ὑμῖν καὶ εἰρήνη ἀπὸ θεοῦ πατρὸς ἡμῶν καὶ κυρίου Ἰησοῦ Χριστοῦ.

II Cor. i. 2:   χάρις ὑμῖν καὶ εἰρήνη ἀπὸ Θεοῦ πατρὸς ἡμῶν καὶ κυρίου Ἰησοῦ Χριστοῦ.

Rom. i. 7:   χάρις ὑμῖν καὶ εἰρήνη ἀπὸ θεοῦ πατρὸς ἡμῶν καὶ κυρίου Ἰησοῦ Χριστοῦ.

Eph. i. 2: χάρις ὑμῖν καὶ εἰρήνη ἀπὸ θεοῦ πατρὸς ἡμῶν καὶ κυρίου Ἰησοῦ Χριστοῦ.

[Eph. vi. 23:   εἰρήνη τοῖς ἀδελφοῖς καὶ ἀγάπη μετὰ πίστεως ἀπὸ θεοῦ πατρὸς καὶ κυρίου Ἰησοῦ Χριστοῦ.]

Col. i. 2:   χάρις ὑμῖν καὶ εἰρήνη ἀπὸ θεοῦ πατρὸς ἡμῶν.

Phile. 3: χάρις ὑμῖν καὶ εἰρήνη ἀπὸ θεοῦ πατρὸς ἡμῶν καὶ κυρίου Ἰησοῦ Χριστοῦ.

Phil. i. 2: χάρις ὑμῖν καὶ εἰρήνη ἀπὸ θεοῦ πατρὸς ἡμῶν καὶ κυρίου Ἰησοῦ Χριστοῦ.

I Tim. i. 2:   χάρις ἔλεος εἰρήνη ἀπὸ θεοῦ πατρὸς καὶ Χριστοῦ Ἰησοῦ τοῦ κυρίου ἡμῶν.

Tit. i. 4:   χάρις καὶ εἰρήνη ἀπὸ θεοῦ πατρὸς καὶ Χριστοῦ Ἰησοῦ τοῦ σωτῆρος ἡμῶν.

II Tim. i. 2:   χάρις ἔλεος εἰρήνη ἀπὸ θεοῦ πατρὸς καὶ Χριστοῦ Ἰησοῦ τοῦ κυρίου ἡμῶν.

Alfred Seeberg, seeking evidence of the survival of old Christian formulas in the literature of the New Testament, very naturally fixes on these passages, and argues that we have here a combination of the names of God the Father and the Lord Jesus Christ in prayer which Paul found already in use in the

Christian community when he attached himself to it, and which he took over from it. It is a hard saying when Ernst von Dobschütz professes himself ready to concede that Paul received this combination of names from his predecessors, but sharply denies that he received it as a "fixed formula." One would have supposed it to lie on the face of Paul's use of it that he was repeating a formula; while it might be disputed whether it was a formula of his own making or he had adopted it from others. It goes to show that it was not invented by Paul, that it is found not only in other connections in Paul's writings, as we have seen, but also in other New Testament books besides his.

Jas. i. 1:   θεοῦ καὶ κυρίου Ἰησοῦ Χριστοῦ δοῦλος.
II Pet. i. 2:   ἐν ἐπιγνώσει τοῦ θεοῦ καὶ Ἰησοῦ τοῦ κυρίου ἡμῶν.
II Jno. 3:   ἔσται μεθ' ἡμῶν χάρις ἔλεος εἰρήνη παρὰ θεοῦ πατρὸς καὶ παρὰ Ἰησοῦ Χριστοῦ τοῦ υἱοῦ τοῦ πατρός.

In the presence of these passages it is difficult to deny that we have in the closely knit conjunction of these two Divine names part of the established phraseology of primitive Christian religious speech.

It would not be easy to exaggerate the closeness with which the two names are knit together in this formula. The two persons brought together are not, to be sure, absolutely identified. They remain two persons, to each of whom severally there may be ascribed activities in which the other does not share. In Gal. i. 1 we read of "Jesus Christ and God the Father who raised Him from the dead." In Gal. i. 3, we read of "God the Father and our Lord Jesus Christ who gave Himself for our sins." The epithets by which they are described, moreover, are distinctive, —the Father, our Father, the Lord, our Lord, our Saviour. There is no obscuration, then, of the peculiarities of the personalities brought together. But their equalization is absolute. And short of thoroughgoing identification of persons the unity expressed by their conjunction seems to be complete.

How complete this unity is may be illustrated by another series of passages. J. B. Lightfoot has called attention to the symmetrical structure of the two Epistles to the Thessalonians.

Each is divided into two parts ("the first part being chiefly narrative and explanatory, and the second hortatory"), and each of these parts closes with a prayer introduced by αὐτὸς δέ followed by the Divine name,—a construction not found elsewhere in these epistles. Clearly there is formal art at work here; and it will repay us to bring together the opening words of the four prayers, including the designations by which God is invoked in each.

I Thess. iii. 11: αὐτὸς δὲ ὁ θεὸς καὶ πατὴρ ἡμῶν καὶ ὁ κύριος ἡμῶν Ἰησοῦς.

I Thess. v. 23: αὐτὸς δὲ ὁ θεὸς τῆς εἰρήνης.

II Thess. ii. 16: αὐτὸς δὲ ὁ κύριος ἡμῶν Ἰησοῦς Χριστὸς καὶ ὁ θεὸς ὁ πατὴρ ἡμῶν ὁ ἀγαπήσας ἡμᾶς καὶ δοὺς παράκλησιν αἰωνίαν καὶ ἐλπίδα ἀγαθὴν ἐν χάριτι.

II Thess. iii. 16: αὐτὸς δὲ ὁ κύριος τῆς εἰρήνης.

It is remarkable how illuminating the mere conjunction of these passages is. Taking I Thess. iii. 11 in isolation, we might wonder whether we ought to read it, "God Himself, even our Father and our Lord Jesus," or "Our God and Father Himself, and our Lord Jesus," or "Our God and Father and our Lord Jesus, Himself." So, taking it in isolation, we might hesitate whether we should construe II Thess. ii. 16, "Our Lord Jesus Christ Himself, and God our Father," or "Our Lord Jesus Christ and God our Father, Himself." The commentators accordingly divide themselves among these views, each urging reasons which scarcely seem convincing for his choice. But so soon as we bring the passages together it becomes clear that the αὐτός is to be construed with the whole subject following it in every case, and thus a solid foundation is put beneath the opinion arrived at on other grounds by Martin Dibelius, Ernst von Dobschütz and J. E. Frame, that in I Thess. iii. 11 and II Thess. ii. 16, the αὐτός binds together the two subjects, God and the Lord, as the conjunct object of Paul's prayer.

The four prayers are in every sense of the word parallel. The petition is substantially the same in all. It cannot be imagined that the Being to whom the several prayers are addressed was consciously envisaged as different. Paul is in every case simply bringing his heart's desire for his converts before his God. Yet, in describing the God before whom he lays his petition, he fairly exhausts the possibilities of variety of designation which the case affords. As a result, God the Father and the Lord Jesus Christ could not be more indissolubly knit together as essentially one. Both are mentioned in two of the addresses, but the order in which they are mentioned is reversed from one to the other, and all the predicates in both instances are cast in the singular number. In the other two addresses only one is named, but it is a different one in each case, although an identical epithet is attributed to them both. We learn thus not only that Paul prays indifferently to God and to the Lord—in precisely the same way, for precisely the same things, and with precisely the same attitude of mind and heart, expressed in identical epithets,—but also that he prays thus indifferently to God or the Lord separately and to God and the Lord together. And when he prays to the two together, he does all that it is humanly possible to do to make it clear that he is thinking of them not as two but as one. Interchanging the names, so that they stand indifferently in the order "God and the Lord," or "the Lord and God," he binds them together in a single "self"; and then, proceeding with his prayer, he construes this double subject, thus bound together in a single "self," in both cases alike with a singular verb,—"Now our Lord Jesus Christ and God our Father who loved us . . . Himself," he prays, "may He comfort your hearts and establish them in every good work and word." "Now our God and Father and our Lord Jesus, Himself," he prays again, "may He direct our way unto you": and then he proceeds immediately, continuing the prayer, but now with only one name, though obviously with no change in the Being addressed, —"and may the Lord make you to increase and abound in love toward one another and toward all men." If it was with any difference of consciousness that Paul addressed God or the Lord, or God and the Lord together, in his prayers, he certainly has taken great pains to obscure that fact. If he had intended to show plainly that to him God and the Lord were so one that

God and the Lord conjoined were still one to his consciousness, he could scarcely have found more effective means of doing so. There is probably no instance in all Paul's epistles where God and the Lord are mentioned together, that they are construed with a plural adjective or verb.

We should not pass without notice that it is in the passages from II Thessalonians that ὁ κύριος is given relative prominence. In the two passages from I Thessalonians ὁ θεός comes forward, while in those from II Thessalonians it is ὁ κύριος. That is in accordance with the general character of II Thessalonians, which is distinctively a κύριος epistle. Proportionately to the lengths of the two epistles, while θεός occurs about equally often in each, κύριος occurs about twice as often in the second as in the first. We do not pause to inquire into the causes of this superior prominence of κύριος in II Thessalonians, although it may be worth remarking in passing that in both epistles it is relatively prominent in the hortatory portions. Whatever, however, may have been the particular causes which brought about the result in this case, the result is in itself one which could not have been brought about if θεός and κύριος had not stood in the consciousness of Paul in virtual equality as designations of Deity. For the phenomenon amounts at its apex, — as we see in the four passages more particularly before us — to the simple replacement of θεός by κύριος as the designation of Deity. And that means at bottom that Paul knows no difference between θεός and κύριος in point of rank; they are both to him designations of Deity and the discrimination by which the one is applied to the Father and the other to Christ is (so far) merely a convention by which two that are God are supplied with differentiating appellations by means of which they may be intelligibly spoken of severally. With respect to the substance of the matter there seems no reason why the Father might not just as well be called κύριος and Christ θεός.

Whether the convention by which the two appellations are assigned respectively to the Father as θεός and to Christ as κύριος is ever broken by Paul, is a question of little intrinsic importance, but nevertheless of some natural interest. It is probable that Paul never,—not only in these epistles to the Thessalonians, but throughout his epistles,—employs κύριος of the Father. The term seems to appear uniformly in his writings, except in a few (not all) quotations from the Old Testament, as a designation of Christ. Thus the Old Testament divine name κύριος (Jehovah) is appropriated exclusively to Christ; and that in repeated instances even when the language of the Old Testament is adduced,—which Paul carries over to and applies to Christ as the Lord there spoken of. The question whether Paul ever applies the term θεός to Christ is brought sharply before us by the form in which the formula, the use of which we are particularly investigating, occurs in II Thess. i. 12. There we read of Paul's constant prayer that "our God" should count his readers worthy of their calling and fulfil with reference to them every good pleasure of goodness and work of faith with power, to the end that "the name of our Lord Jesus" might be glorified in them, and they in Him, κατὰ τήν χάριν τοῦ θεοῦ ἡμῶν καὶ κυρίου Ἰησοῦ Χριστοῦ.

It will probably be allowed that in strictness of grammatical rule, rigidly applied, this should mean, "according to the grace of our God and Lord Jesus Christ," or, if we choose so to phrase it, "according to the grace of our God, even the Lord Jesus Christ." All sorts of reasons are advanced, however, why the strict grammatical rule should not be rigidly applied here. Most of them are ineffective enough and testify only to the reluctance of expositors to acknowledge that Paul can speak of Christ as "God." This reluctance is ordinarily given expression either in the simple empirical remark that it is not in accordance with the usage of Paul to call Christ God, or in the more far-reaching assertion that it is contrary to Paul's doctrinal system to represent Christ as God. Thus, for example, W. Bornemann comments briefly: "In themselves, these words might be so taken as to call Jesus here both God and Lord. That is, however, improbable, according to the Pauline usage elsewhere." This mild statement is particularly interesting as a recession from the strong ground taken by G. Lünemann, whose commentary on the Thessalonian epistles in the Meyer series Bornemann's superseded. Lünemann argues the question at some length and one might almost say with some heat. "According to Hofmann and Riggenbach," he writes, "Christ is here named both our God and our Lord,—an interpretation which, indeed, grammatically is no less allowable than the interpretation of the doxology ὁ ὤν ἐπὶ πάντων θεὸς εὐλογητὸς εἰς τοὺς αἰῶνας, Rom. ix. 5, as an apposition to Χριστός; but is equally inadmissible as it would contain an un-Pauline thought: on account of which also Hilgenfeld, "Zeitschr.f.d. wiss. Theol.," Halle, 1862, p. 264, in the interest of the supposed spuriousness of the Epistle, has forthwith appropriated to himself this discovery of Hofmann." Ernst von Dobschütz, who has superseded Bornemann as Bornemann superseded Lünemann, is as sure as Lünemann that it is un-Pauline to call Christ God; but as he is equally sure that this passage does call Christ God, he has no alternative but to deny the passage to Paul,—though he prefers to deny to him only this passage and not, like Hilgenfeld, the whole Epistle. "But an entirely un-Pauline trait meets us here," he writes, "that to τοῦ θεοῦ ἡμῶν there is added καὶ κυρίου Ἰησοῦ Χριστοῦ. Not that the combination, God our Father and the Lord Jesus Christ, is not original-Pauline (see on I Thess. i. 1), but that what stands here must be translated, 'Of our God and Lord Jesus Christ' as Hofmann and Wohlenberg rightly maintain. This, however, is in very fact in the highest degree un-Pauline (Lünemann) in spite of Rom. ix. 5, and has its parallel only in Tit. ii. 13, 'Of our Great God and Saviour, Christ Jesus,' or II Pet. i. 1, 11, 'Of our God (Lord) and Saviour, Jesus Christ.'" H. J. Holtzmann, as is his wont, sums up the whole contention crisply: "In the entire compass of the Pauline literature, only II Thess. i. 12 and Tit. ii. 13 supply two equally exegetically uncertain parallels" to Rom. ix. 5 "while, in Eph. iv. 6, God the Father is ὁ ἐπὶ πάντων."

It is manifest that reasoning of this sort runs great risk of merely begging the question. The precise point under discussion is whether Paul does ever. or could ever, speak of Christ as God. This passage is offered in evidence that he both can and does. It is admitted that there are other passages which may be adduced in the same sense. There is Rom. ix. 5 which everybody allows to be Paul's own. There is Tit. ii. 13 which occurs in confessedly distinctively "Pauline literature." There is Acts xx. 28, credibly attributed to Paul by one of his pupils. There is II Pet. i. 1 to show that the usage was not unknown to other of the New Testament letter-writers. It is scarcely satisfactory to say that all these passages are as "exegetically uncertain" as II Thess. i. 12 itself. This "exegetical uncertainty" is in each case imposed upon the passage by reluctance to take it in the sense which it most naturally bears, and which is exegetically immediately given. It is as exegetically certain, for example, as any thing can be purely exegetically certain, that in Rom. ix. 5 Paul calls Christ roundly "God over all." It is scarcely to be doubted that this would be universally recognized if Romans could with any plausibility be denied to Paul, or even could be assigned to a date subsequent to that of, say, Colossians. The equivalent may be said of each of the other passages *mutatis mutandis*. The reasoning is distinctly circular which denies to each of these passages in turn its natural meaning on the ground of lack of supporting usage, when this lack of supporting usage is created by a similar denial on the same ground of its natural meaning to each of the other passages. The ground of the denial in each case is merely the denial in the other cases. Meanwhile the usage is there, and is not thus to be denied away. If it may be, any usage whatever may be destroyed in the same manner.

In these circumstances there seems no reason why the ordinary laws of grammar should not determine our understanding of II Thess. i. 12. We may set it down here, therefore, with its parallels in Tit. ii. 13 and II Pet. i. 1 in which the same general phrasing even more clearly carries this sense.

II Thess. i. 12: τὴν χάριν τοῦ θεοῦ ἡμῶν καὶ κυρίου Ἰησοῦ Χριστοῦ.

Tit. ii. 13: καὶ ἐπιφάνειαν τῆς δόξης τοῦ μεγάλου θεοῦ καὶ σωτῆρος ἡμῶν Χριστοῦ Ἰησοῦ.

II Pet. i. 1: πίστιν ἐν δικαιοσύνῃ τοῦ θεοῦ ἡμῶν καὶ σωτῆρος Ἰησοῦ Χριστοῦ.

In these passages the conjunction, in which God and Christ are brought together in the general formula which we are investigating, reaches its culmination in an express identification of them. We have seen that the two are not only united in this formula on terms of complete equality, but are treated as in some sense one. Grammatically at least, they constitute one "self" (αὐτός); and they are presented in nearly every phraseology possible as the common source of Christian blessing and the unitary object of Christian prayer. Their formal identification would seem after this to be a matter of course, and we may be a little surprised that the recognition of it should be so strenuously resisted. The explanation is no doubt to be sought in the consideration that so long as this formal identification is not acknowledged to be expressly made, those who find difficulty in believing that Christ is included by Paul in the actual Godhead may feel the way more or less open to explain away by one expedient or another the identity of the two, manifoldly implied in the general representation indeed, but not formally announced.

Expositor after expositor, at any rate, may be observed introducing into his reproduction of Paul's simple equalization, or rather, unification, of God and the Lord, qualifying phrases of his own which tend to adjust them to his personal way of thinking of the relations subsisting between the two. C. J. Ellicott already found occasion to rebuke this practice in G. Lünemann and A. Koch. The former explains that Paul conjoins Christ with God in his prayers, because, according to Paul's conception—"see Usteri, 'Lehrb.' ii. 2. 4, p. 315"—Christ, as sitting at the right hand of God, has a part in the government of the world. The latter, going further, asserts that Paul brings the two together only because he regards Christ "as the wisdom and power of God." Few expositors entirely escape the temptation to go thus beyond what is written. It is most common, perhaps, to follow the path in which Lünemann walks, and to declare that Paul unites the two persons because Christ by His exaltation has been made for the time co-regnant with God over the universe, or perhaps only over the Church. Quite frequently, however, it is asserted, more like Koch, that the unity instituted between them amounts merely to a unity of will, or even only to a harmony of operation. At the best it is explained that our Lord is placed by the side of God only because it is through Him as intermediary that the blessings which have their source in God are received or are to be sought. An especially flagrant example of the substitution of quite alien phraseology for Paul's, in a professed restatement of his conception, is afforded by David Somerville in his Cunningham Lectures on "St. Paul's Conception of Christ." He tells us that Paul's "conjunction of God and Christ in his stated greetings to the churches indicated his belief that a co-partnership of Divine power and honor was included in the exaltation of Christ to be Lord." It obviously smacks, however, less of Paul than of Socinus to speak of the relation of Christ to God as a "co-partnership of Divine power and honor," and of this co-partnership of Divine power and honor between them as resulting from Christ becoming Lord by His exaltation.

Benjamin Jowett, with that fine condescension frequently exhibited by the "emancipated," remarks on Chrysostom's comment on Gal. i. 3: "This is the mind not of the Apostolic but of the Nicene age." He does not stay to consider that the mind of his own age and coterie may in such a matter be as much further removed than that of the Nicene age from the mind of the Apostolic age in substance as it is in time. Nevertheless it may be admitted that even the Nicene commentators were prone to read their own conceptions of the relations of Christ to God explanatorily into Paul's simple equalization of them. Athanasius appeals,—as he was thoroughly entitled to do,—to Paul's conjunction of God the Father and the Lord Jesus Christ as the common source of grace and the common object of prayer, against the Arian contention that the Father and the Son are concordant, indeed, in will but not one in being. In the eleventh section of the third of his Orations against the Arians he gives expression to this appeal thus: "Therefore also, as we said just now, when the Father gives grace and peace, the Son also gives it, as Paul signifies in every epistle, writing,

'Grace to you and peace, from God our Father and the Lord Jesus Christ.' For one and the same grace is from the Father in the Son, as the light of the sun and of the radiance is one, and as the sun's illumination is effective through the radiance; and so, when he prays for the Thessalonians, in saying, 'Now God even the Father and the Lord Jesus Christ Himself, may He direct our way unto you,' he has guarded the unity of the Father and of the Son. For he has not said, 'May they direct,' as of a double grace given from two, from This and That, but, 'May he direct,' to show that the Father gives it through the Son." This is not to emphasize the unity of the Father and the Son more strongly than Paul does: it is only to repeat Paul's testimony to their unity. But Athanasius cannot repeat Paul's testimony to their unity without interpolating his own conception of the manner in which this unity is to be conceived. One and the same grace comes to us from the Father and the Son, he gives us to understand, because the grace of the Father comes to us in the Son; one and the same prayer is addressed to the Father and the Son, because whatever the Father gives He gives through the Son. This explanation is interpolated into Paul's language. Paul places God and the Lord absolutely side by side, as joint source of the blessings he seeks for his readers; addresses his prayers for benefits he desires for his readers to them in common; treats them, in a word, as one. Athanasius' explanations are, of course, not as gross interpolations into the text as Arius'; but they are no less real interpolations. The outstanding fact governing Paul's collocation of God and the Lord, is that he makes no discrimination between them whatever, but treats them as a unity.

This is well brought out in the remarks of Chrysostom on which Jowett had his eye when he accused him of intruding a Nicene meaning on the text. These remarks are on the prepositions in Gal. i. 1 and Rom. i. 7. Had Paul written in the former of these passages, says Chrysostom, either "through Jesus Christ," or "through God the Father," alone, the Arians would have had their explanation of his having done so, in the interests of some essential distinction between the Father and the

Son. But Paul "leaves no opening for such a cavil, by mention-
ing at once both the Son and the Father, and making the
language apply to both." "This he does," he adds, "not as
referring the acts of the Son to the Father, but to show that the
expression implies no distinction of essence." On Rom. i. 7 he
remarks similarly on the use of "from" with both the Father
and the Son. "For he did not say, 'Grace be unto you and
peace, from God the Father, through the Lord Jesus Christ,'
but 'from God the Father and the Lord Jesus Christ.'" There
is no imposing of a Nicene sense on Paul's language here. There
is a simple reflection, as in a clear mirror, of the exact sense of
the texts in hand, with an emphasis on their underlying implication of oneness between God and our Lord.

We are constantly pointed to I Cor. viii. 6, to be sure, as
in some way supplying a warrant for supposing an unexpressed
subordinationism to be hidden beneath the surface of all of
Paul's equalizations of God the Father and the Lord Jesus
Christ. It is exceedingly difficult, however, to see how this
passage can be made to supply such a warrant. It lies open to
the sight of all, of course, that in it the one God the Father
and the one Lord Jesus Christ,—who are included in the one
only God that, it is understood by all, alone exists,—are differentiated by the particular relations in which the first and
the second creations alike are said to stand to them severally.
All things are said to be "of" God the Father and "through"
the Lord Jesus Christ; Christians are said to be "unto" the
one and "by means of" the other. These characterizations are,
of course, not made at random; and it is right to seek diligently
for their significance. It would doubtless be easy, however, to
press such prepositional distinctions too far, as such passages
as Rom. xi. 36 and Col. i. 16 may advise us. Perhaps it would
not be wrong to say that they are to be taken rather eminently
than exclusively. What it is at the moment especially important
that we observe, however, is that they concern the relations of
God the Father and the Lord Jesus Christ *ad extra* and say
nothing whatever of their relations to one another. With respect to their relations to one another, what the passage tells

us is that they are both embraced in that one God which, it is declared with great emphasis, alone exists. We must not permit to fall out of sight that the whole passage is dominated by the clear-cut assertion that "there is no God but one" (verse 4, at the end). Of this assertion the words now particularly before us (verse 6b) are the positive side of an explication and proof (verse 5, γάρ). And the thing for us distinctly to note is that Paul explicates the assertion that there is no God but one by declaring, as if that was quite *ad rem*, that Christians know but one God the Father and one Lord Jesus Christ. There meets us here again, we perceive,—as underlying and giving its force to this assertion,—the precise formula we have been having under consideration. And it·meets us after a fashion which brings very strikingly to our attention once more that, when Paul says "God the Father and the Lord Jesus Christ," he has in mind not two Gods, much less two beings of unequal dignity, a God and a Demi-god, or a God and a mere creature, —but just one God. Though Christians have one God the Father and one Lord Jesus Christ, they know but one only God.

The essential meaning of the passage is wholly unaffected by the question whether in the words, "There is no God but one" at the end of verse 4, we have Paul's own language or that of his Corinthian correspondents repeated by him. We may read the verse, if we choose,—perhaps we ought to,— "Concerning the meats offered to idols, then, we are perfectly well aware that, as you say, there is no idol in the world, and there is no God but one." Still, the assertion that there is no God but one rules the succeeding verses, which, introduced as its justification, become in effect a reiteration of it. "There is no God but one, *for*—for, although there are indeed so-called Gods, whether in heaven or on earth,—as there are Gods a-plenty and Lords a-plenty!—yet for us there is one God the Father . . . and one Lord Jesus Christ. . . ." Obviously this can mean nothing else than that the "one God the Father and one Lord Jesus Christ" of the Christians is just the one only God which exists. To attempt to make it mean anything else is to stultify the whole argument. You cannot prove that only one God exists by pointing out that you yourself have two.

We are referred, it is true, to the declaration that the heathen have not only many Gods, but also many Lords, and we are bidden to see in their one God the Father and one Lord Jesus Christ a parallel among the Christians to this state of affairs among the heathen. And then we are further instructed that it is only fair to suppose that Paul felt some difference in grade between the Gods and the Lords of the heathen and, in paralleling the two objects of Christian worship with them respectively, intended to intimate a discrimination in rank between God the Father and the Lord Jesus Christ. On this ground, we are then asked to conclude that Paul does not range the Lord Jesus Christ here along with God the Father within the Godhead, but adjoins Him to God the Father as an additional and inferior object of reverence, placed distinctly as "Lord" outside the category of "God." This whole construction, however, is purely artificial and has no standing ground in the world of realities. There is no evidence that the heathen discriminated between the designations "God" and "Lord" in point of dignity to the disadvantage of the latter; this, at the end of the day, has to be admitted by both Johannes Weiss and W. Bousset, who yet urge that Paul must be supposed to presuppose such a distinction here. Paul, however, intimates in no way at all that he felt any such distinction on his part; on the contrary he includes the "Gods many" and "Lords many" of the heathen without question in their "so-called Gods" on equal terms. Least of all is it possible to separate off "one God the Father" from its fellow "one Lord Jesus Christ," linked to it immediately by the simple "and," and make the former alone refer back to the "There is no God but one." Paul obviously includes both "God the Father" and "the Lord Jesus Christ" within this one only God whom alone he and his readers alike recognize as existing. It would void his whole argument if Jesus Christ were conceived of as a second and inferior object of worship outside the limits of the one only God. The thing which above all others the passage says plainly, is that the acknowledgment by Christians of "one God the Father and one Lord Jesus Christ" accords with the fundamental postulate that "there is no God but one." And that can mean nothing else than that God the Father and the Lord Jesus Christ together make but one God. So far from this passage throwing itself athwart the implications of the repeated employment by Paul, as by others of the writers of the New Testament, of the formula in which God the Father and the Lord Jesus Christ are conjoined as the one object of Christian prayer and source of Christian blessings, it brings a notable support to them. It supplies what is in effect an explicit assertion of the fact on which this formula implicitly proceeds. It declares that the one God of the Christians includes in His Being both "God the Father" and "the Lord Jesus Christ." Christians acknowledge but one God; and these are the one God which Christians acknowledge.

Something of the same things that Paul expresses by this conjunction of God the Father and the Lord Jesus Christ, John expresses in his own phraseology by the conjunction of the Father and the Son,—as in I Jno. ii. 24: "If what you heard from the beginning abide in you, you also shall abide in the Son and the Father"; or II Jno. 9, in the reverse order: "He that abideth in the teaching, the same hath the Father and the Son"; as well as in II Jno. 3, already quoted: "Grace, mercy, peace shall be with us, from God the Father, and from Jesus Christ, the Son of the Father." It is true, but not adequate, to say that John never thinks of Christ apart from God and never thinks of God apart from Christ. With him, to have the Son is to have the Father also, and to have the Father is to have the Son also. The two are as inseparable in fact as in thought. The terminology is different, but the idea is the same as that which underlies Paul's unification of God the Father and the Lord Jesus Christ.

Clearly the suggestions of this formula carry us into the midst not only of Paul's Christology but of his conception of God—which obviously is not simple. Short of this, they bring us face to face with two matters of great preliminary importance to the correct apprehension of Paul's doctrines of Christ and of God, which have been much discussed of late, not always very illuminatingly. We mean the matters of the significance of the title "Lord" which is so richly applied to Christ in the New Testament writings, and of the meaning of the adoration of Christ which is everywhere reflected in these writings. We must deny ourselves the pleasure of following out these suggestions here. It must content us for the moment to have pointed out a line of approach to the correct understanding of these great matters which, surely, cannot be neglected in any earnest attempt to reach the truth concerning them, and which, if not neglected, will certainly conduct us to very high conclusions in regard to them.

CHAPTER IV

THE DIVINE MESSIAH IN THE OLD TESTAMENT[1]

THE question whether the Old Testament has any testimony to give as to the Deity of our Lord, when strictly taken, resolves itself into the question whether the Old Testament holds out the promise of a Divine Messiah. To gather the intimation of a multiplicity in the Divine unity which may be thought to be discoverable in the Old Testament,[2] has an important indeed, but, in the first instance at least,[3] only an indirect bearing on this precise question. It may render, it is true, the primary service of removing any antecedent presumption against the witness of the Old Testament to the Deity of the Messiah, which may be supposed to arise from the strict monadism of Old Testament monotheism. It is quite conceivable, however, that the Messiah might be thought to be Divine, and yet God not be conceived pluralistically. And certainly there is no reason why, in the delivery of doctrine, the Deity of the Messiah might not be taught before the multiplicity in the unity of the Godhead had been revealed. In the history of Christian doctrine the

1 From *The Princeton Theological Review*, xiv. 1916, pp. 379-416; also from *Christology and Criticism*, pp. 3-49.

2 As H. P. Liddon does in the former portion of the lecture in which he deals with the "Anticipations of Christ's Divinity in the Old Testament" ("The Divinity of our Lord and Saviour, Jesus Christ." Bampton Lectures for 1866. Ed. 4, 1869, pp. 44 ff.). Similarly E. W. Hengstenberg gives by far the greater part of his essay on "The Divinity of the Messiah in the Old Testament" ("Christology of the Old Testament," 1829, E. T. of ed. 2, 1865, pp. 282-331),—namely from p. 284 on—to a discussion of the Angel of Jehovah.

3 For such questions remain as, for example, whether the Angel of Jehovah be not identified in the Old Testament itself with the Messiah (Daniel, Malachi). So G. F. Oehler (art. "Messias" in Herzog's "Realencyc.," p. 417; "Teol. des A. T.," ii. pp. 144, 265; "The Theology of the Old Testament," E. T. American ed., pp. 446, 528), A. Hilgenfeld, "Die jüdische Apokolyptik," pp. 47 ff. Cf. E. Riehm, "Messianic Prophecy," E. T.[2] pp. 195, 282, who cites these references in order to oppose them.

conviction of the Deity of Christ was the condition, not the result, of the formulation of the doctrine of the Trinity.

It cannot be said in any case, therefore, that the discovery of a Divine Messiah in the Old Testament is dependent on the discovery also in the Old Testament of intimations of multiplicity in the unity of the Godhead. The two things go together in the sense that the discovery of either would be a natural preparation for the discovery of the other; that it would supply a matrix into which the other would nicely fit; and would set over against it a correlative doctrine with which it would readily unite to form a rational system. The two doctrines, though interdependent and mutually supporting one another in the system of which they form parts, are nevertheless not so dependent on one another that one of them might not conceivably be true without the other, and certainly not so that one could not conceivably be taught before the other. It seems in every way best, therefore, when inquiring after Old Testament intimations of the Deity of Christ, to keep this inquiry distinct from the parallel inquiry into possible Old Testament intimations of the multiplex constitution of the Godhead.

It is quite clear, at the outset, that the writers of the New Testament and Christ Himself understood the Old Testament to recognize and to teach that the Messiah was to be of divine nature. For example, they without hesitation support their own assertions of the Deity of Christ by appeals to Old Testament passages in which they find the Deity of the Messiah afore-proclaimed. This habit may be observed, as well as anywhere else perhaps, in the first chapter of the Epistle to the Hebrews. There, the author, after having announced the exalted nature of the Son, as the effulgence of the glory and the very image of the substance of God, illustrates His superiority to the angels, the highest of creatures, by appealing to a series of Old Testament passages, in which a "more excellent name" than is given to angels is shown to belong of right to Him. The exaltation of the Son to the right hand of the majesty on high, he says, is in accordance with the intrinsic dignity of His person as manifested in this "more excellent name." The "more excellent name" which he cites from the Old Testament is in the first instance none other than that of Son itself, whence we learn that when the Old Testament gives to the Messiah the designation of Son of God—or we would better say, when it ascribes Sonship to God to Him (for it is after this broader fashion that the author develops his theme)—it ascribes to Him, in the view of the author of this Epistle, a super-angelic dignity of person.[4] Of this Son, now, he goes on to say that, in contrast with the names of mere ministry given to the angels, there are ascribed to Him the supreme names of "God" and "Lord"; and with the names all the dignities and functions which they naturally connote. These great names of "God" and "Lord" are apparently not adduced as new names, additional to that of "Son," but as explications of the contents of that one "more excellent name"; and thus we are advised of the loftiness of the name of "Son" in the mind of this writer.[5] From this catena of passages we perceive, then, that in the view of this writer the Old Testament presents to our contemplation a Messiah who is not merely transcendent but sheerly Divine; to whom the great names of "Son of God," "God," "Lord" belong of right, and to whom are ascribed all the dignities, powers and functions which these great names suggest.

The passages of Scripture relied upon by the author of the Epistle to the Hebrews to make his point are, broadly speaking, derived from what we know as the Messianic Psalms. More particularly, his argument depends especially on citations from the Second, Forty-fifth, and Hundred-and-tenth Psalms. Except for an allusion in Rev. xix. 8 the Forty-fifth Psalm is not else-

[4] This representation of the author, embodied in the sharp demand: "Unto which of the angels said he at any time, Thou art my son?" has given the commentators some trouble in view of the designation of the angels in the Old Testament as "Sons of God." The notes of A. B. Davidson and Franz Delitzsch may be profitably consulted. When G. Hollmann, *in loc.*, pp. 204-205, remarks: "There is meant not the mere name of son, which is used in the Old Testament, as of the people, the king, and others, so also of angels but *the* name of Son, which is described in verses 2 and 3, according to its contents and its peculiarity," he is right in the substance of the matter but hardly in form.

[5] Cf. Lünemann (in Meyer, E. T. p. 83) on the passage.

where cited in the New Testament. But the Second and Hundred-and-tenth seem to have been much in the minds, and passages from them much on the lips, of its writers. To the Second, the very term Messiah, Christ, as applied to our Lord, goes back, as well as His loftier designation of Son of God; and it is adduced with great reverence as the Old Testament basis of these titles not only by the author of the Epistle to the Hebrews (i. 5; v. 5), but by the original apostles (Acts iv. 24-26) and by Paul (Acts xiii. 33) as reported in the Acts, while its language has supplied to the Book of Revelations its standing phrases for describing the completeness of our Lord's conquest of the world (Rev. ii. 27; xii. 5; xix. 15). It was the Hundred-and-tenth Psalm which first gave expression to the Session of the Messiah at the right-hand of God, and not only is it repeatedly referred to with reference to this great fact by the Epistle to the Hebrews (i. 13; v. 6; vii. 17-21; x. 13), but Paul adopts its language when speaking of the exaltation of Christ (I Cor. xv. 25) and Peter, in his initial proclamation of the Gospel at Pentecost, employs it in proof that Jesus has been raised to the right-hand of God and made Lord of Salvation (Acts ii. 32-36). Even more to the point, Jesus Himself adduces it to confound His opponents, who, harping on the title "Son of David," had forgotten that David himself recognized this, his greater Son as also his Lord. "And Jesus answered and said, we read in Mark's narrative (xii. 35-37; cf. Mt. xxii. 45-46; Lk. xx. 41-44), How say the Scribes that the Christ is the Son of David? David himself said in the Holy Spirit, The Lord said unto my Lord, Sit thou on my right hand, till I make thine enemies the footstool of thy feet. David himself calleth Him Lord; and whence then is He his Son?" We shall let Johannes Weiss tells us what this means. The Scribes, says he,[6] had built up a whole system of doctrine about the Messiah, and an important caption in it ran that He (according to the prophesy, for example, of Is. xi. 1) is (the present is timeless: He must be it: that is required by the doctrine) a descendant of David.

[6] "Die Schriften des Neuen Testaments,[1] 1906, i. p. 175.

"This declaration Jesus proves untenable, since David in his Psalm cx, inspired by the Holy Spirit, calls the Messiah his 'Lord,' and, therefore, to put it bluntly, looks up to Him with religious veneration. . . . It follows from this that He must be a higher being than David himself. . . . Jesus accordingly shows here that his conception of the Messiah was different from the current political one. According to the Book of Daniel, and according to the convictions of the pious circle out of which the so-called Apocalypses came the Messiah comes down from heaven, 'the man on the clouds.' That Jesus also thought thus we have already seen." Johannes Weiss writes, of course, from his own point of view, which we do not share in many of its implications—as, for example, in the assumption that Jesus repudiates descent from David. He makes, however, the main matter perfectly clear. Jesus saw in the Hundred-and-tenth Psalm a reference to the transcendent Messiah in which He Himself believed.[7] In Jesus' view, therefore, the transcendent Messiah is already an object of Old Testament revelation.

What Jesus and the writers of the New Testament saw in the Messianic references of the Psalms, it is natural that those who share their view-point should also see in them. How the matter looks to one of the most searching expounders of the Scriptures that God has as yet given His church—we mean E. W. Hengstenberg—he sums up himself for us in a passage brief enough to quote in its entirety.[8] He has no difficulty in speaking directly of passages in the Psalms "which contain a reference to the superhuman nature of the Messiah;—passages," he adds,

on which we must the less think of forcing another meaning as in the prophets (for example, in Is. ix. where even Hitzig is obliged to recognize it) there is found something unquestionably similar. Such indications [he continues] pervade all the Messianic Psalms;

[7] Cf. the discussion of the meaning of Jesus' question and comment, F. Godet *in loc.* Luke (E. T. ii. pp. 251-254): and also J. A. Alexander on Mk. xii. p. 37.

[8] "Commentary on the Psalms," E. T. iii. appendix, p. lvi. in the essay "On the Doctrinal Matter of the Psalms," near the beginning.

and quite naturally. For the more deeply the knowledge of human sinfulness, impotence and nothingness sunk into Israel (compare, for example, Ps. ciii. 14-16), the less could men remain satisfied with the thought of a merely human redeemer, who, according to the Israelitish manner of contemplation, could do extremely little. A human king (and all the strictly Messianic Psalms have to do with Messiah as king), even of the most glorious description, could never accomplish what the idea of the kingdom of God imperiously required, and what had been promised even in the first announcement respecting the Messiah, namely, the bringing the nations into obedience, blessing all the families of the earth, and acquiring the sovereignty of the world. In Psalm ii. 12, the Messiah is presented *simpliciter* as the Son of God, as He, confidence in whom brings salvation, whose wrath is perdition. In Psalm xlv. 6-7 He is named God, Elohim. In Psalm lxxii. 5, 7, 17, eternity of dominion is ascribed to Him. In Psalm cx. 1, He at last appears as the Lord of the community of saints and of David himself, sitting at the right hand of the Almighty, and installed in the full enjoyment of Divine authority over heaven and earth.

That the state of the case may be fully before us, it will be useful to place by the side of this brief statement a somewhat more lengthy one, the tone of which very fairly represents the spirit of devout students of Scripture of the middle of last century. For a reason which will appear later, it seems to us to be an unusually instructive statement, to the entire compass of which it will repay us to give attention. We draw it from William Binnie's work on the Psalms:[9]

Respecting the Person of Christ, the testimony of the Psalms is copious and sufficiently distinct. For one thing, it is everywhere assumed that He is the Kinsman of His people. The Christ of the Old Testament is one who is to be born of the seed of *Abraham* and *family of David*. The modern Rationalists, in common with the unbelieving Jews of all ages, refuse to go further. They will not recognize in Him more than man, maintaining with great confidence that superhuman dignity is never attributed to the Messiah, either in the law, or the prophets, or the psalms. It would be strange indeed if the fact were so. The disciples were slow of heart to receive any

[9] "The Psalms: Their History, Teachings and Use," 1870, pp. 200 ff.

truth that happened to lie out of the line of their prior expectations, —any truth of which the faithful who lived before the incarnation had had no presentiment; yet we know that they readily accepted the truth that Jesus was more than man. The Cross of Christ was long an offence to them. It was not without a long struggle that they were constrained to acknowledge the abrogation of the Mosaic law and the opening of the door of faith to the Gentiles. But there is no trace of any similar struggle in regard to Christ's *superhuman dignity*. The moment Nathaniel recognized in Jesus of Nazareth the expected Redeemer, he cried out, "Rabbi, thou art the Son of God"; and, long before the close of the public ministry, Peter, in the name of all the rest, made the articulate profession of faith, "Thou art the Christ, the Son of the living God." They believed Him to be the Son of God, in a sense in which it would have been blasphemy to affirm the same of any mere man. Instead, therefore, of deeming it a thing incredible, or highly improbable, that intimations of Christ's superhuman dignity should be found in the psalms, we think it in every way likely that they will be discoverable on a diligent search. In truth they are neither few nor recondite. Take these three verses:

"Thy throne, O God, is for ever and ever:
    A scepter of equity is the scepter of Thy kingdom" (xlv. 6).
"Jehovah hath said unto me, Thou art my Son;
    This day have I begotten Thee" (ii. 7).
"Thus saith Jehovah to my Lord,
    Sit Thou at my right hand,
Until I lay Thy foes as a footstool at Thy feet" (cx. 1).

I do not forget the attempts that have been made to put a lower sense on each of these passages. I do not think they are successful. But suppose it were admitted to be just possible to put on each of them separately, a meaning that should come short of the ascription of superhuman dignity to the Son of David, we should still be entitled to deduce an argument in favor of our interpretation from the fact that in so many separate places, He is spoken of in terms which most naturally suggest the thought of a superhuman person. From the exclamation of Nathaniel it is evident that the thought did suggest itself to the Jews, before the veil of unbelief settled down upon their hearts in the reading of the Old Testament. The truth is that, if a man reject the eternal Godhead of Christ, he must either lay

the Psalms aside or sing them with bated breath. The Messiah whom
they celebrate is fairer than the sons of men, one whom the peoples
shall praise for ever and ever (Ps. xlv. 2, 17). The ancient Jews understood the particular psalms now quoted to refer to the Messiah;
and no one who heartily believes in the inspiration of the Psalter
will be at a loss to discern in it more testimonies to the proper Divinity of the Hope of Israel than could well have been discovered before His incarnation and death lighted up so many dark places of
the ancient Scriptures. It will be sufficient for our purpose to indicate a single example. The coming of Jehovah to establish a
reign of righteousness in all the earth is exultingly announced in
several lofty psalms. It may be doubted, indeed, whether the ancient
Jews were able to link these to the person of the Messiah; but we
are enabled to do it, and have good ground to know that it was of
Him that the Spirit spoke in them from the first. The announcement
is thus made in the Ninety-sixth Psalm:

11. "Let the heavens rejoice and let the earth be glad;
    Let the sea roar, and the fulness thereof;
12. Let the field be joyful, and all that is therein:
    Then shall all the trees of the wood shout for joy
13. Before Jehovah: for He cometh, for He cometh to judge the earth:
    He shall judge the world with righteousness,
    And the peoples with His faithfulness."

We know whose advent this is. No Christian can doubt that the
proper response to the announcement is that furnished by the Book
of Revelation, "Amen. Even so, come Lord Jesus."

The circumstance which lends peculiar instructiveness to
this statement is that, although conceived in a popular vein,
and addressed rather to instruct the popular mind than to meet
the difficulties raised by sceptical criticism; although written
with absolutely no fear of sceptical criticism before the eye,
—witness the unhesitating employment of John's Gospel as
testimony to historical fact—and of course without knowledge
of the phases of criticism which belong particularly to the
twentieth century: it yet in all its main assertions fits so nicely
into the present state of critical opinion that it might well have

been written yesterday instead of fifty years ago. For example, it was rather bold fifty years ago to declare that it was the cross purely and simply, and not the assertion of a super-human dignity for Christ, which was an offence to our Lord's Jewish contemporaries. Such a declaration is a commonplace today. There are few things which are more vigorously asserted by the latest phase of sceptical criticism than that the doctrine of a superhuman Messiah was native to pre-Christian Judaism. "The house was already prepared," declares W. Bousset;[10] "the faith in Jesus only needed to enter it." The whole secret of the Christology of the New Testament, explains Hermann Gunkel,[11] lies in the fact that it was the Christology of pre-Christian Judaism before it was the Christology of Christianity. It came from afar—this picture of the heavenly King, he intimates; but it had taken such hold of men that they could not free themselves from it.

Nothing could lie further from the purpose of writers of this tendency, of course, than to justify faith in the superhuman nature of Jesus. Of nothing are they more firmly convinced than that Jesus was merely a man. The whole object of their particular reading of the history of the Jewish Messianic ideal is, indeed, to smooth the way for a credible account of the immediate acceptance of Jesus by His followers as a superhuman being, although He was really only human. The pre-Christian conception of the Messiah, they say, involved the ascription to Him of a superhuman nature, and the acceptance of Jesus as Messiah, therefore, necessarily carried with it the ascription to Him of a superhuman nature.[12] But one of the results of this point of view is, naturally, that the mind is released from the prepossessions which formerly hindered recognition of traces of belief in a superhuman Messiah in the earlier Jewish litera-

10 "Die jüdische Apokalyptik," p. 59.

11 "Zum religionsgeschichtlichen Verständnis des Neuen Testaments," 1903, p. 93.

12 Cf. W. Wrede, "Paul," E. T. 1907, pp. 151 ff.; H. Weinel, "Saint Paul," E. T. 1906, p. 313.

ture. Hermann Gunkel, for example, having concluded that the conception of the heavenly Christ must have arisen somewhere before the New Testament, and having found traces of it in the Jewish Apocalypses, is able to see something like it also, centuries earlier, in the prophets.[13] Traits of a mythical God-King shine through the picture which the Prophets draw of the Messiah. "He receives already in Isaiah names which belong literally to no man—God-Hero, Father of Eternity (Is. ix. 5); He is the King of the Golden Age, in which sheep and wolf lie down together (Is. xi.); especially striking is it that His birth is celebrated with various mysterious statements (Is. ix. 5, Mic. v. 2)—for a just-born human child cannot aid His people, though perhaps a Divine child can. It is observable that other prophets and many Psalmists speak of a God, who is to be King of the whole world; that is, Jahveh, whose coronation and ascension (Ps. xlvii. 6, 9; lvii. 12) in the End-time are sung especially by many Psalmists." And so, he adds, we can feel no sort of wonder "when we meet in the later Apocalypses with a heavenly figure who is sometime to descend from heaven and establish a blessed kingdom on earth. This figure of the divine king is no new creation of Apocalyptic Judaism. It is the same figure which already lies at the basis of the prophetic hope."[14] The appeal to such passages as Ps. xlv. 6; ii. 7; cx. 1; xcvi. 11-13, as indications that the Messiah was thought of by the Psalmists as a superhuman being may now, then, hope for a more sympathetic hearing, in critical circles, than could be expected for it fifty years ago.

It undoubtedly does not make for edification to observe the expedients which have been resorted to by expositors to escape recognizing that these Psalms do ascribe a superhuman nature and superhuman powers to the Messiah. What they have done with Ps. xlv. 6—to take it as an example[15]—"in order to avoid the addressing of the king with the word *Elohim*," as Franz

[13] *Op. cit.*, p. 93.

[14] *Op. cit.*, pp. 24-25.

[15] The helplessness with which they face the passage is illustrated by the note of G. S. Goodspeed, "Israel's Messianic Hope," 1900, p. 69.

Delitzsch puts it,[16] may be conveniently glanced at in the summary statement given by J. A. Selbie.[17] Rather than take it as it stands, they would prefer, it seems, to translate vilely, "Thy throne is God," "Thy throne of God," "Thy throne is of God," or to rewrite the text and make it say something else,—"Thy throne [its foundation is firmly fixed], God [has established it]," or "Thy throne [shall be] for ever."[18] Even Franz Delitzsch who turns away from such violent avoidances,[19] can permit the Psalmist his own word, only if he may be allowed an equally violent reduction of its meaning. Because, immediately after addressing the King by the great name of "God,"—a name which in this class of Psalms confessedly means just God and nothing else[20]—the Psalmist refers the King to "God, thy God," Delitzsch supposes that the Psalmist must use "God" when applied to the King in some lowered sense. "Since elsewhere earthly authorities," he reasons,

are also called *Elohim* (Ex. xxi. 6; xxii. 7 ff.; Ps. lxxxii, cf. cxxxviii, 1) because they are God's representatives and the bearers of His image upon earth, so the king who is celebrated in this Psalm may be all the more readily styled *Elohim*, when in his heavenly beauty, his irresistible doxa or glory, and his divine holiness, he seems to the Psalmist to be the perfected realization of the close relationship in

16 "Psalms," E. T. ii. p. 82. The spirit in which expositors approach the matter is illustrated by the remark of J. H. Kurtz, "Zur Theologie der Psalmen," 1865, pp. 52 f.: if "God" *can* be taken in a lower sense here, it *must*. Kurtz wishes to translate, "Thy throne of God."

17 Hastings' *B.D.* iv. pp. 756-757.

18 T. K. Cheyne, "The Origin and Religious Contents of the Psalter," 1891, pp. 181-182, while adopting the penultimate of these expedients, makes himself somewhat merry over the rest. In his "The Book of Psalms," 1904, i. p. 198, he has eliminated the verse and no longer considers the (mutilated) Psalm to be addressed to an earthly king. "It has now," he says, "become superfluous to look for a contemporary king as the hero of the poem. . . ." It is "really a Messianic poem; the King, as the Targum says, is 'King Messiah.'" It is a "description of the ideal King."

19 That is to say in his "Commentary on the Psalms." In his later "Messianic Prophecy," 1891, E. T. p. 115, he appears to accept the rendering, "Thy throne of God," as probable.

20 Delitzsch himself says: "It is certainly true that the custom with the Elohim Psalms of using *Elohim* as of equal dignity with Jahve is not favorable to this supposition."

which God has set David and his seed to Himself. He calls Him *Elohim* just as Isaiah calls the exalted royal child, whom he exultingly salutes in Ch. ix. 1-6, *'El Gibbōr*. He gives Him this name, because in the transparent exterior of His fair humanity, he sees the glory and holiness of God as having attained a salutary or merciful conspicuousness among men. At the same time, however, he guards this calling of the king by the name of *Elohim* against being misapprehended, by immediately distinguishing the God, who stands above him, from the divine king, by the words "*Elohim*, Thy God," which, in the Korahitic Psalms, and in the Elohimic Psalms in general, is equivalent to "Jahve, thy God" (xliii. 4; xlviii. 15; l. 7), and the two words are accordingly united by *Munach*.

Delitzsch does not believe, indeed, that when this is said, all has been said. According to his view, this was all that the writer of the Psalm meant; he was as far as possible from assigning Deity in any sense to the King he was addressing; he applies the term "God" to Him only in a lower sense of the word. But "the Church," in adopting this Psalm into its sacred use, attached another meaning to it, referring a song "which took its origin from some passing occasion, as a song for all ages, to the great King of the future, the goal of its hope." Its prophetically Messianic sense was "therefore not the original sense of the Psalm," though it was very ancient,[21] and was, indeed, conferred upon it by its admission into the Psalter.[22]

It is a refreshing return to common sense when the new critical school renounces these artificialities of interpretation, and begins by recognizing that the Psalmist in calling the King "God," means precisely what he says, namely, to ascribe the Divine name to the King he is addressing. The sense is quite clear, says Hermann Gunkel,[23] and we must not follow the multitude in explaining it away, and much less in altering the

---

[21] How ancient we may learn from the remark: "Just as Ezek. xxi. 32 refers back to שׁילה, Gen. xlix. 10, *'El Gibbōr*, among the names of the Messiah in Is. ix. 6 (cf. Zech. xii. 8) refers back in a similar manner to Ps. xlv. 5."

[22] "Psalms," E. T. ii. pp. 73-74; cf. i. p. 67 and especially p. 70; also "Hebrews," E. T. i. p. 77, "Messianic Prophecy," E. T. p. 114.

[23] "Ausgewählte Psalmen,"² 1911, pp. 106 f. Similarly H. Gressmann, "Der Ursprung der israelitisch-jüdischen Eschatologie," 1905, pp. 255-256.

text. But, having recognized so much, Gunkel stops right there. The Messianic understanding of the Psalm (although that not only of the New Testament but of Judaism as well, from at least the time of the LXX), cannot come into consideration "for our scientific interpretation." Just an Israelitish king is meant, very likely Jeroboam II. That he is called "God" by the Psalmist is merely a solitary survival of a habit of speech common in the nations surrounding Israel, and, as we see here, not without its examples in Israel. "Veneration of kings as Gods was not rare in the ancient East; we are not surprised, therefore, that such a declaration meets us just once on the lips of an Israelitish singer. There was, no doubt, in ancient Israel a strong opposing current against such deification of the ruler; the genuine Jahve-religion, as it was advocated by the prophets, wishes that Jahve alone shall be God, and speaks with horror of everything human that would place itself by His side." We may learn from a passage like this, however,

that the distinction between the Divine and the human was not always and everywhere in Israel perfectly strictly conceived. There are many other passages also in which God and king are spoken of in the same breath; in which the king is compared with God or His angel; or in which he is called God's Son; and when Solomon built himself a throne, which stood on six steps flanked by lions, he imitated in it the throne of the highest God of heaven who sits high aloft above the seven heavenly stages, guarded by demons. Such a declaration as the singer's shows us, then, that there were tendencies approaching heathenism in ancient Israel, especially in the palace. In Israel, as elsewhere, it belonged to the court-style to promise an eternal dominion to the king, or eternal life to his house.

Hugo Gressmann[24] so far agrees with this, that he supposes that, in Ps. xlv. 6, we have a solitary "survival from a period when it was more customary in Israel to call the king God"; "although," he adds, "the usage had perhaps never been very common." But he improves upon it by thinking of this custom as really little more than an instance of an inflated court-style, which had become acclimated in Israel, too, on the basis of

[24] Op. cit., pp. ff.

general oriental models. The language which is employed of
the king in such Psalms as the Second, Forty-fifth, Seventy-
second and Hundred-and-tenth, cannot be taken literally, of
course, of any earthly monarch. But, says Gressmann, it was
never intended to be taken literally. It is merely the language of
court-flattery and was fully understood to mean nothing. This
was the language in which kings had been spoken of and to,
say in Babylon, from of old. It had found its way, no doubt
indirectly, possibly through Phoenicia, into Israel; and had been
popularized there merely as a matter of court-form. Of course,
it was gradually modified, in its Israelitish use, in the direction
of an ever closer assimilation of it to the Israelitish point of
view. The deification of the king, for example, regular in the
case of the Babylonian-Assyrian kings and a dogma in Egypt,
was more and more eliminated from the court-style as it was
employed in Israel. "In the whole Old Testament, the (reigning) King is addressed only a single time by the title of God:
'Thy throne, O God, stands for ever and ever'" (Ps. xlv. 6).
Other remnants of similarly inflated flattery have, however,
better maintained their place. World-wide dominion is promised
to the king; eternal life and power are ascribed to him; he is
presented as the (adopted) Son of God. All such modes of
speech are merely relics of a court-style which originated elsewhere, and which, as used in Israel, was without meaning.
"From the technical designation of the king as Son of God
(II Sam. vii. 14, Ps. ii. 7) no inferences can be drawn as to the
deification of the king. For it was merely the style to speak thus
of the king, and, when it is the style to speak thus, nobody asks
whether it has any meaning or not."[25] "The style permits the
court-poet to praise any and every king as a world-ruler, even
though the world which he really rules be no bigger than
Israel."[26] What we learn from such language is not how Israel
thought of its king, and much less how Israel thought of its
Messiah. There is no reference to the Messiah in this language;

[25] P. 256.
[26] P. 262.

and Israel did not think thus of its king. What we learn is only where Israel got its court-style, and how that court-style was slowly modified in its use in Israel, to suit Israelitish modes of conception, until it was at last almost cleansed of its assimilation of the monarch to God.

The parallel between Delitzsch's and Gressmann's treatments of Ps. xlv. 6 should not be missed. Both start with the recognition that the Psalmist addresses the king as "God." Both set themselves at once to empty that fact of its significance. Delitzsch pursues a philological method, and concludes that, in such a connection, "God" does not mean God, but rather something which is not God. Gressmann follows the religio-historical method, and concludes that, in such instances, "God" means just nothing at all; it is mere bombast. That the view taken of the Psalm by either was not the view taken of it by those who gave it a place in the Psalter, at least, each is compelled to allow. It owes its place in the Psalter in fact, as neither would deny, precisely to its not having been understood to speak meaninglessly, or even moderately, of any earthly king, but, in the loftiest of ascriptions, of King Messiah. The question which presses for answer is whether it is possible thus to evacuate the language of the Psalm of its meaning. That Gressmann's method of evacuating it has some tactical advantage over that of the "psychological school" may be admitted. He is at least relieved from the necessity of accounting for the language employed from the Psalmist's own experience. He avoids so far, therefore, the impact of the pointed questions of Ernst Sellin:[27] "When did an Anointed of Juda ever have dominion over the peoples of the earth, against which they could rebel? When were the ends of the earth really promised by God to such an one, for his possession (Ps. ii.)? When and how could a king of Israel be called 'God,' and his sons be constituted princes over the whole world, as is done in Ps. xlv. 7, 17; when did such an one rule from the Euphrates to the end of the earth, like the

[27] "Der alttestamentliche Prophetismus," 1912, p. 169.

king of lxxii. 8; and finally when did such an one lead a host out of the dew of the morning and hold judgment among the peoples like him of cx. 6?" But what advantage is it to escape these questions, only to fall into the way of the still more pointed one, When was it possible in Israel to ascribe to its kings *simpliciter* such Divine qualities and functions? Or, as Sellin sharply puts it, How could a king in Israel be directly addressed as God, as in Ps. xlv. 6?[28]

Is it adequate to say that it was natural for Israel to imitate the court-style of its neighbors, and that this court-style in its Israelitish employment had worn itself down, through long years of use, into a mere set of meaningless words? Kings had not existed in Israel for ever and ever; and Israel differed from the surrounding nations precisely in this—that there was but one God in Israel, and the king was not this God. "The deification of princes is everywhere else directly perhorrescent in Israel," remarks Sellin, and declares that there is but one solution possible: "a hymn which celebrated the Divine World-Savior is taken as the basis of a wedding-song addressed to an earthly king, and he is lauded as the introducer of the new age, which this world-savior is expected sometime to introduce."[29] That is to say, on the foundation of the new religio-historical point of view, Sellin returns in effect (although not altogether without defect, it must be allowed) to the old typical-messianic method

---

[28] Cf. T. K. Cheyne, "The Origin and Religious Contents of the Psalter," 1891, p. 181: "But from the severely monotheistic Jewish point of view, to represent this king as God, was impossible (Zech. xii. 8 is no proof to the contrary)." Also Gunkel, when speaking of Ps. xx. writes ("Ansgewählte Psalmen,"[3] p. 41 f.): "The piety is accordingly clear, which guards the singer from glorifying the king too much. This tone dominates also the other Royal Songs (xx. xxi. lxxii. cx. ii.) contained in the Psalter; they do not, or at least not in the first rank, glorify the king, but the God who protects and blesses him; a somewhat different 'more heathenish' note sounds, on the other hand, in the very ancient song, Ps. xlv. The deification of the King which was at home in the ancient orient from primitive times, was certainly an abomination to these pious people."

[29] "Die israelitisch-jüdische Heilandserwartung," 1909, p. 16 (the second and third parts of the fifth volume of the "Biblische Zeit- und Streitfragen").

of interpreting these Psalms.[30] They speak of the contemporary kings, but through them they speak of the Great King yet to come. And their language can receive its full meaning only when it is read with reference to Him.

In order that we may apprehend Sellin's point of view, we shall need to have it before us in a somewhat broadened statement.[31] What we are particularly indebted to him for is the clearness with which he throws up to observation the main fact, that the center of Israel's eschatology lay in the settled expectation of the universal establishment of the reign of Jehovah. The way he puts it is, "Jahve is to come and simply be manifested as Lord—that is the kernel of the whole eschatology."[32] But alongside of this expectation there runs, he tells us, throughout the literature, the hope of the coming of a world-savior, the coming of whom is described in much the same language as the coming of Jehovah Himself. We may be tempted to identify the two after a fashion which will eliminate Jehovah's coming in favor of that of this savior: Jehovah comes only in His representative. The difficulty is that, in the documents, the identification goes beyond the coming to the figures themselves. Nor will it quite meet the case to say that Jehovah's representative is clothed with the attributes of Jehovah. The epithets given to Him pass beyond official identification and imply personal identity. And

---

[30] "Prophetismus," p. 129: "The right way to solve the riddle has been pointed out by Gunkel, though only by a modernization of what used to be contended for by Franz Delitzsch and others, when they said that David was here always the type of the Messiah. Hymns were written by court-poets to actual Israelitish or Jewish kings, on the occasion of their coronation or marriage, which transferred to them the long existent hope of the divine world-savior, and these songs became also prophecies."

[31] An admirable account of Sellin's views in their historical setting has been given to the readers of The Princeton Theological Review (October, 1913, xi. pp. 630-649) by J. Oscar Boyd under the title of "The Source of Israel's Eschatology." W. Nowack's criticisms of the "Heilandserwartung" in the Theologische Rundschau for 1912, xv. pp. 91-96, and of the "Prophetismus" in the same Journal for 1914, xvii. pp. 65-68, are also worth consulting.

[32] "Prophetismus," p. 174. Cf. p. 172: "The coming of God as Lord and King, we have already presented as the kernel of the Old-Israelitish Eschatology of woe and weal."

yet not such personal identity as excludes all distinction, or
even all subordination. We are confronted in this figure with a
problem very similar to that which meets us in the mysterious
figure of the Angel of Jehovah and similar methods of solving
it will naturally occur to us. Now, as Sellin makes clear, this
figure of a world-savior is both original and aboriginal in Israel.
It was not, as Gunkel and Gressmann imagine, derived at a
comparatively late date from the myths of Israel's oriental
neighbors. The myths of Israel's oriental neighbors, in point of
fact, knew nothing of such a figure. "The old-oriental literature," writes Sellin,[33] "has been searched with the greatest zeal,
especially during the last decade for traces of a hope of a Divine
Savior, of a new era of salvation to be brought in by him, and a
return of Paradise. . . . But I hold it to be my duty to say at
once without reserve, that not the slightest trace of proof has
been adduced, that this era is to be introduced by a great and
miraculous Divine-human ruler of the End-time. Absolutely all
that has been said, up to today, of an old-oriental 'expectation
of a redeemer-king' is merely construction,—or, where is there
a Babylonian or Egyptian text which speaks of such a future
redeemer as Jacob's blessing speaks of Shiloh,—and the like? . . .
The eschatological king is not known by the ancient orient."[34]
It is quite possible that in expounding and adorning its expectation, Israel may have employed figures and conceptions derived
from without. But the expectation itself is certainly its own.
"The specifically Israelitish character and the original parentage
of its kernel are firmly established; and its roots are not set in
mythology but in the religion of Israel, in Israel's belief in the
God of Sinai, to whom in the end the world must belong."[35]

Throughout the whole course of the history of Israel, we
may trace this expectation of a Savior running parallel with the

[33] P. 175 f.

[34] We observe that even Meinhold thanks Sellin for saying this: "I am glad
that Sellin declares strongly and clearly that 'the eschatological king is not
known to the ancient orient'—naturally Israel excepted" ("Theolog. Litera-
turzeitung," 1913, 19, 580).

[35] P. 183.

fundamental expectation of the coming of God as Ruler and King. The parallel is very complete.

"He too is the ruler over the peoples (Gen. xlix. 10; Ps. lxxii. 11), to the ends of the earth (Deut. xxxiii. 17; Mic. v. 3; Zech. ix. 10 f.), the scepter-bearer over the nations (Num. xxiv. 17-19; Ps. xlv. 17) to whose dominion there are no limits (Is. ix. 6), etc.; he too bears sometimes but not often the title of "King" (Ps. xlv. 2; lxxii. 1; Zech. ix. 9; Jer. xxiii. 5), elsewhere those of "Judge" (Mic. v. 1), "Father" (Is. ix. 5), "Anointed" or "Son of Jehovah" (Ps. ii. 2, 7). Precisely as the activity of the one, so that of the other is three-fold: it is his to destroy the enemies (Num. xxiv. 17 b; Deut. xxxiii. 17; Ps. ii. 9; xlv. 6; cx. 1, 2, 5); he has to judge (Is. ix. 6 b; xi. 3; Jer. xxiii. 5 b; Ps. lxxii. 6); and finally he has to "save" (Zech. ix. 9; Jer. xxiii. 6; Ps. lxxii. 4, 12), above all by bringing social betterment, Paradise, and universal peace (Gen. xlix. 11, 12; Is. vii. 15; xi. 4, 6-9; Mic. iv. 4 a, 5 b; Zech. iii. 9 b, 10; ix. 10; Ps. lxxii. 12, 16).[36] . . . Moreover he is given a name, "Immanuel," by which his appearance is notified as the fulfilment of Balaam's prophecy of the end of the days, "Jahve, his God, is with him"; and he is further designated as "Star" (Num. xxiv. 17), as "God-Hero" (Is. ix. 5), as "God's Son" (Ps. ii. 7); . . . [and] exegesis is continually bringing us back to the idea that Is. vii. 14, Mic. v. 2 assume thoroughly a miraculous birth for him without the aid of a man; . . . [and] there is promised to him when scarcely born, the dominion of the world (Gen. xlix. 10; Is. ix. 5; Mic. v. 3).[37]

The kernel of the whole matter is this:[38] "Israel's savior is, throughout the whole course of the Old Testament history the counterpart of the World-God who is sometime to bring woe and weal; precisely as of the one, so of the other there sounds out—from the oldest to the latest sources—although, no doubt with external differences, the mighty 'He comes' (cf. Gen. xlix. 10), 'He appears' (Num. xxiv. 17), 'He cometh' (Zech. ix. 9), 'He is born' (Is. vii. 14, ix. 4), 'He comes forth' (xi. 1), 'He comes forth' (Mic. v. 1), 'He is raised up' (Jer. xxiii. 5), 'until He comes' (Ez. xxi. 32), 'I will raise up' (xxxiv. 23), 'I bring' (Zech. iii. 8), 'I saw, there come' (Dan. vii. 13)." This con-

[36] Pp. 172-173.
[37] P. 173.
[38] P. 181.

tinually recurring assurance that the Paradise-prince will come
to destroy all enemies and judge even to the ends of the earth,
forms the deepest core of the mystery—it is expressed by a
single word in Hebrew, יָבֹא, in English, "He comes."[39] It
stamps the religion of the Old Testament as specifically a religion of hope. "Yes, for us the Old Testament religion, from the
very beginning is a religion of hope, prepared from the very
beginning sometime to become the world-religion; the Old
Testament God from the beginning the God of heaven and
earth; who, it is true, first of all chose only that one people, but
looked forward to the day when He should destroy all other
Gods and bring all other peoples to His feet."[40] It is from Sinai,
and from the revelation-act at Sinai alone that this religion of
hope can have derived. "Here, and only here, can a foundation
be laid for viewing the whole history from the point of sight of
waiting for the appearance of the world-God, who is to fill the
universe with His glory."[41] But as no man could look upon this
His glory and live, an organ for its manifestation was necessary,
and a type of this organ was given in the Paradisiacal man, who,
though a creature of God, was made in the image of the Divine
glory and destined for communion with Him and the enjoyment
of dominion over the world. Back to this figure, the old-oriental
directed his eyes. "But in the old-Israelitish eschatology, this
backwards directed longing became suddenly something wholly
different—a clear, distinct, religiously oriented, historical expectation directed to the future: Jahve, the God of Sinai, will Himself, in this man, who, no doubt, is a creature, but who was
with Him before the mountains were,—in this, His Chosen-One,
His Servant, His Son—Himself come to establish the world-
dominion, to judge Israel, and the peoples, to bring Paradise
and the world-peace. There is no parallel to this assured confidence in the ancient orient."[42]

There are elements in this brilliant piece of constructive

[39] P. 193.
[40] P. 192.
[41] P. 182.
[42] P. 182.

work which will require correction. The use made of the Paradisiacal man in the account given of the origin of Israel's expectation of a Savior, and the apparently defective Christology in part founded upon this, attract dissenting attention. But this ought not to blind us to the value of the broad presentation given us here of the eschatological hope of Israel, including, as it does, the correlation of the hope of the coming Savior, with the hope of what we have been accustomed to speak of as "the advent of Jehovah." It has been usual to separate these two things mechanically and to set them over against one another as quite independent, and indeed never even osculating, items of Israel's belief.[43] Gunkel even represents them as mutually exclusive. "In the whole eschatology," he says,[44] "we can distinguish two tendencies, both of which speak of a coming King; whereas the one calls the king David or David's Son, in the other Jahve Himself is the Ruler of the future; everywhere where God's kingdom is spoken of, the human king is lacking, for a 'Messiah' has no place in 'God's kingdom.'" Charles A. Briggs, while he does not go so far as to represent these two elements of Old Testament eschatology as mutually contradictory, yet thinks, equally extremely, of the whole body of Old Testament Messianic hopes as a congeries of unharmonized items standing off in isolation from one another. "There are in the Old Testament," he says,[45] "two distinct lines of Messianic idea—the one predicting the advent of God for redemption and judgment, the other predicting the advent of a redemptive man. The redemptive man is conceived sometimes as the Seed of the Woman or Seed of Abraham, as the Lion of Judah, as the Second Moses, as the Son of David, the Son of God, the Messiah, as the Martyr Servant, as the Priest King, as the Martyr Shepherd, as the Son of Man. It is impossible to combine these in any unity, so far as the Old

[43] E.g. E. Riehm, "Messianic Prophecy," E. T.[2] 1891, p. 282, supporting himself on Oehler, "Prolegomena zur Theologie des A. T.," pp. 67 f. and art. "Messias," in Herzog's "Realencyklopädie," pp. 408 f. So also Ottley, Hastings' B.D. ii. p. 459a, repeating Riehm.

[44] "Ausgewählte-Psalmen,"[3] pp. 191 f.

[45] "The Incarnation of the Word," 1902, p. 173.

Testament is concerned. And there is not the slightest indication that there is any coincidence of the line of the divine advent with the line of the advent of any of these human Messiahs." The effect of a comprehensive presentation of the material like Sellin's is thoroughly to do away with such impressions. The complete synthesis of the various representations waits, of course, for the fulfilment of them all in one Person. But it becomes clear at least that the hope of the coming of the world-savior, which includes in it the more specifically defined "Messianic" hope, is but another aspect of the hope of the coming of Jehovah to judge the world and to introduce the eternal kingdom of peace. One of the results of this is that the testimony of the Old Testament to "the transcendent Messiah" becomes pervasive. We no longer look for it in a text here and there which we are tempted to explain away as unexpected, perhaps intolerable, exaggerations, but rather see it involved in the entire drift of the eschatological expectations of the Old Testament, and view the special texts in which it finds particularly poignant expression as only the natural high lights thrown up upon the surface of the general picture.

This underlying coalescence of the advent of Messiah and the advent of Jehovah is perhaps more commonly vaguely felt than is generally recognized. It seems to be thus felt—in his own way and from his own point of view, of course,—by Gressmann.[46]

In the Israelitish eschatology [he writes] the Messiah and Jahve alternate. That is already intelligible, because the Messiah is ultimately a Divine figure, a God-king, and is thus elevated into the sphere of Deity. It becomes more intelligible when we observe a second parallel fact. Almost everywhere where Jahve meets us in the eschatology of weal, He is presented in a quite distinctive way. We can refer the descriptions which are given of Him and the functions which are ascribed to Him to the conception of the eschatological king. With respect to the thing, not to the person, the Jahve here described and the Messiah were originally as it seems counterparts: the functions of the two are still almost identical. The Messiah is

[46] "Der Ursprung," etc., p. 294.

described more as a King exalted into God, Jahve more as God exalted into the King. It is no doubt possible that in the eschatology
which influenced the Israelitish religion, a single figure which united
in itself the traits of both, occupied a middle ground. In its passage
to Israel this figure was divided, and the one, the more divine, side
of its being was assigned to Jahve, the other, the more human side
of its being to the Messiah. The eschatological hero, which originally
bore rich mythical traits, that are still perceptible in the older
prophecy, up to Isaiah and Micah, is in the course of time ever more
degraded into an earthly king, and acquired a purely national
character. Jahve, however, was inhibited from this development,
since He could not lose the Divine type. Accordingly we may perhaps again ascribe to the *original* eschatalogical figure the things
which in the *present* tradition are no longer said of the Messiah, but
only now of Jahve.[47]

Such a speculation cannot commend itself to sober thought;
but the fact that it suggests itself to Gressmann hints of what
he finds in the Old Testament descriptions of the Messiah, and
of the relation which the hope of His coming bore to the hope of
the advent of Jehovah, and indeed which His person bore to the
person of Jehovah. He who reads the Old Testament, however
cursorily, will not escape a sense, however dim, that he is
brought into contact in it with a Messiah who is more than
human in the fundamental basis of His being, and in whose
coming Jehovah visits His people in some more than representative sense.

It is naturally the customary representation of Franz Delitzsch that the two lines of prediction never meet in the pages
of the Old Testament, but wait for their conjunction until He
to whom they both point had come. Says he:[48]

For the announcement of salvation in the Old Testament runs on
two parallel lines: the one has for its termination the Anointed of
Jahve, who rules all nations out of Zion; the other the Lord Himself,
sitting above the Cherubim, to whom all the earth does homage.
These two lines do not meet in the Old Testament; it is only the ful-

[47] P. 301.
[48] "Psalms," E. T. i. p. 67 f., cf. p. 70.

filment that makes it plain, that the advent of the Anointed One and
the advent of Jahve is one and the same. . . . An allegory may serve
to illustrate the way in which the Old Testament proclamation of
salvation unfolds itself. The Old Testament in relation to the Day of
the New Testament is Night. In this Night there rise in opposite
directions, two stars of Promise. The one describes its path from
above downwards; it is the promise of Jahve who is about to come.
The other describes its path from below upwards: it is the hope
which rests on the seed of David, the prophecy of the Son of David,
which at the outset assumes a thoroughly human and merely earthly
character. These two stars meet at last, they blend together into
one star: the Night vanishes and it is Day. This one Star is Jesus
Christ, Jahve and the Son of David in one person, the King of
Israel and at the same time the Redeemer of the world—in a word,
the God-man![49]

Elsewhere, however, he speaks with a juster divination:[50]

We find indeed undeniable traces in the Old Testament of a prophetic *presentiment* that the great Messias of the future, who was
destined to accomplish what had been vainly looked for in David
and Solomon, etc., should also present in His own person an unexampled union of human and divine. The mystery of the incarnation is still veiled under the Old Testament, and yet the two great
lines of prophecy running through it—one leading on to a final
manifestation of Jehovah, the other to the advent of a Son of David
—do so meet and coalesce at certain points, as by the light thus
generated, to burst through the veil. This is as clear as day in the
one passage, Is. ix. 5, where the Messias is plainly called אל גבור
(the Mighty God), an ancient traditional appellation for the Most
High (Deut. x. 17; cf. Jer. xxxii. 8; Neh. ix. 32; Ps. xxiv. 8). And
so (Jer. xxiii. 6) He is entitled "Jehovah our righteousness," following which, as Biesenthal has shown (p. 7), the ancient synagogue
recognized Jehovah (יהוה) as one of the names of the Messiah.[51]

[49] "Psalms," E. T. ii. p. 300 (on Ps. lxxii). Cf. the similar statement of
W. T. Davidson, in Hastings' *B.D.* iv. p. 151. Delitzsch seems to imply that it is
only to Jehovah and not to the Messiah that the function of Savior is ascribed
(cf. G. Dalman, "Words of Jesus," p. 295); this can be sustained only if we
take the term "the Messiah" in too narrow a sense.

[50] "Hebrews," E. T. i. p. 79.

[51] Cf. on this Messianic title, A. Edersheim, "The Life and Times of Jesus
the Messiah,"[1] 1883, i. p. 178, who gives the references.

That the New Testament writers throughout proceed on the assumption that all those Old Testament passages in which the Advent of Jehovah is spoken of refer to the coming of the Messiah, Delitzsch himself is led to tell us when commenting on the catena of passages adduced in the first chapter of Hebrews in support of the Deity of Christ, among which are some of this kind.[52] Their consciousness of the identity of the two comings "finds an utterance," as Delitzsch reminds us, "at the very threshold of the evangelical history." (Lk. i. 17, 26) when Malachi's prediction of the coming of Elijah "before the day of Jehovah" to prepare His way, is adduced as fulfilled in John the Baptist the forerunner of Jesus.[53] We shall at once recall also the similar appeal of all three of the Synoptic Gospels to Is. xliii. 3, as fulfilled in John the Baptist. In Jesus they saw all the lines of Messianic prediction converge; and they declare Him no less the Jehovah who was expected to come to save His people, than the Son of David or the Suffering Servant of God. "When St. Mark tells us," remarks Charles A. Briggs justly, "that St. John the Baptist was the herald of the advent of Yahweh, at the beginning of the Gospel, what else can he mean than that Jesus Christ whose redemptive life is the theme of his Gospel was the very Yahweh?" And, we add, what can he mean except that, in predicting this advent of Jehovah, Isaiah was proclaiming the Deity of the Messiah in whose coming it was to be fulfilled? The same is true also, of course, of Matthew and Luke in their parallel passages, so that Briggs is thoroughly justified[54] in summing up "with confidence" in the remark that "the three Synoptic Evangelists agree in thinking of Jesus Christ as the Yahweh of the Old Testament, and that His advent, as heralded by St. John the Baptist, was the Divine advent of the Second Isaiah, as well as the human advent of the Servant of Yahweh; in other words that they saw in Jesus Christ the Messiah of history, the coincidence of the line of the divine

[52] "Hebrews," E. T. i. pp. 71-72.
[53] Cf. A. B. Davidson, "Old Testament Prophecy," 1913, p. 412. Cf. also pp. 311 and 147.
[54] P. 182.

redeemer with the line of the human Messiah; that they saw all
the Messianic ideals combine in Him." The only difference between John and the other Evangelists here is that the identification of the Baptist with the voice crying in the wilderness,
"Prepare ye the way of Jehovah," which the others make on
their own account, John quotes from the lips of the Baptist.
Briggs thinks the identification can scarcely have been made
by the Baptist.[55] Such a judgment is certainly rash in view of
the exalted conception which the Baptist in any event expresses
of Him whose mere forerunner he undoubtedly recognizes
himself as being. His shoe-latchets he declares himself unworthy to unloose; he calls Him the Lamb of God which taketh
away the sin of the world; he even gives Him the great name
of the Son of God—a name which in this context must surely
bear its metaphysical sense (cf. verses 7 and 25). Beginning
on this note, the New Testament proceeds throughout its whole
extent on the unchanging supposition that in the coming of
Jesus Christ there is fulfilled the repeated Old Testament promise, made in Psalm and Prophet alike, that God is to visit His
people, in His own good time, to save them. It is therefore,
indeed, so we are told, that He is called Jesus,—precisely because "it is He that shall save His people from their sins"—He,
that is, Jesus, shall save His people, that is, Jesus' people,—in
fulfilment of the promise of the Saving Jehovah.

Among the high lights thrown up on the surface of the general picture of the Divine Messiah, as it lies on the pages of the
Old Testament, such a passage as Is. ix. 6 challenges attention
with the same insistency as Ps. xlv. 6, and has met with much
the same treatment at the hands of the expositors. There have
always been some, of course, who have not shrunk from reading
the passage as it stands, and giving it its obvious meaning. Outstanding instances are supplied by E. W. Hengstenberg and
J. A. Alexander. Alexander, speaking of the hypothesis that by
the child mentioned by the prophet, Hezekiah is meant—an
hypothesis once much in vogue, but now out of date—and the

[55] P. 171.

unnatural explanations of particular terms which it compelled, writes:[56]

The necessity of such explanations is sufficient to condemn the exegetical hypothesis involving it, and shows that this hypothesis has only been adopted to avoid the natural and striking application of the words to Jesus Christ, as the promised *child,* emphatically *born for us* and *given to us,* as the *Son* of God, and the *Son* of man, as being *wonderful* in his person, works, and *sufferings*—a *counsellor,* prophet, and authoritative teacher of the truth, a wise administrator of the Church, and confidential adviser of the individual believer —a real man and yet the *mighty God*—eternal in his own existence, and the *giver of eternal life* to others—the great *peacemaker* between God and man, between Jew and Gentile, the umpire between nations, the abolisher of war, and the giver of internal peace to all who *being justified by faith have peace with God through our Lord Jesus Christ* (Rom. v. 1). The doctrine that this prophecy relates to the Messiah was not disputed even by the Jews, until the virulence of the anti-Christian controversy drove them from the ground which their own progenitors had steadfastly maintained. In this departure from the truth they have been followed by some learned writers who are Christians only in the name, and to whom may be applied with little alteration, what one of them (Gesenius) has said with respect to the ancient versions of this very text, viz., that the general meaning put upon it may be viewed as the criterion of a Christian and an anti-Christian writer.

Hengstenberg's remarks we prefer to give through the medium of T. K. Cheyne, who, in one of the stages of his ever-shifting opinion, adopts the core of them as his own. In an essay on "The Christian Element in the Book of Isaiah," Cheyne remarks:[57]

Both parts of Isaiah give us to understand clearly (and not as a mere ὑπόνοια) that the agent of Jehovah in the work of government and redemption is himself divine. Not indeed the much vexed passage in iv. 2, where, even if the date of this prophecy allowed us to suppose an allusion to the Messiah, "sprout of Jehovah" is much too vague a phrase to be a synonym of "God's Only-begotten Son." But the not less famous 'El Gibbōr in ix. 6 may and must still be

[56] "Commentary on the Prophecies of Isaiah," 1874, i. p. 204.
[57] "The Prophecies of Isaiah,"[3] 1884, ii. p. 209.

quoted. As Hengstenberg remarks it "can only signify God-Hero, a Hero who is infinitely exalted above all human heroes by the circumstance that he is *God*. To the attempts at weakening the import of the name, the passage x. 21, [where 'El Gibbōr is used of Jehovah] appears a very inconvenient obstacle."[58] And who can doubt that, granting the subject of chap. liii. to be an individual, he must be the incarnation of the Divine?

Cheyne's direct comment on the passage itself in this work needs to be read in the light of these remarks to preserve it from ambiguity; but he doubtless means it to be taken in much the same sense which he unambiguously expresses here. "The meaning of the phrase," he declares,[59] "is defined by x. 21, where it occurs again of Jehovah"; that is to say, the Messiah is declared to be God in the same sense in which Jehovah is God. When he proceeds to say, "It would be uncritical to infer that Isaiah held the metaphysical oneness of the Messiah and Jehovah," he does not require to mean more than that Isaiah is not to be inferred to have as yet clearly formulated in his mind the doctrine of the Trinity,—and need not be supposed to have adjusted in his thinking the Deity of the Messiah to the fundamental doctrine of the unity of the Godhead. But when he goes on to say, "But he evidently does conceive the Messiah, somewhat as the Egyptians, Assyrians and Babylonians regarded their kings, as an earthly representation of Divinity (see on xiv. 13-14)," the comparison, although probably inevitable, yet tends to lower the conception of 'El Gibbōr beyond its power to stretch. Accordingly Cheyne continues: "No doubt this development of the Messianic doctrine was accelerated by contact with foreign nations; still it is in harmony with fundamental Biblical ideas and expressions. This particular title of the Messiah is, no doubt, unique. But if even a Davidic king may be described as 'sitting upon the throne of Jehovah' (I Chr. xxix. 23), and the Davidic family be said, in a predictive passage it is true, to be 'as God (ēlohīm), as the (or, an) angel of Jehovah' (Zech. xii. 8), much more may similar titles be applied to the

[58] "Christology of the Old Testament," Edinburgh ed., ii. p. 88.
[59] *Op. cit.*, i. p. 61 f.

Messiah. The last comparison would, indeed, be especially suitable to the Messiah, and it is a little strange that we do not find it." So far the tendency seems to be to lower the implication of the title,[60] but the lost ground is now recovered: "But we do find the Messiah, in a well-known Psalm, invited to sit at the right hand of Jehovah (Ps. cx. 1), and it is only a step further to give him the express title, 'God the Mighty One.' It is no doubt a very great title. The word selected for 'God' is not *ēlohīm*, which is applied to the judicial authority (Ex. xxi. 6, xxii. 8), to Moses (Ex. vii. 1), and to the apparition of Samuel (I Sam. xxviii. 13); but *el* which, whenever it denotes (as it generally does; and in Isaiah always) Divinity, does so in an absolute sense;—it is never used hyperbolically or metaphorically."[61]

The thing most insisted upon by Cheyne in these remarks is that *'El Gibbōr* can mean nothing but "Mighty God"; as Is. x. 21 shows. It illustrates the uncertainty of touch which characterizes the "Liberal" criticism of this type, that, in his later book on Isaiah, he simply deserts this ground and explains *'El Gibbōr* as describing the ideal king as indued from on high with might, and comments somewhat blindly: "x. 21, which shows that we are not to render *divine hero;* the king seems to Isaiah in his lofty enthusiasm, like one of those *angels* (as we moderns call them), who, in old time were said to mix with men, and even contend with them, and who, as superhuman beings, were called by the name of *'el* (Gen. xxxii. 22-32)." If Is. x. 21, where Cheyne himself renders *'El Gibbōr*, "the Mighty God" (p. 23), shows that this term cannot be rendered "divine hero," but at least, as he himself renders it, "Mighty Divinity,"—which seems synonymous with "Mighty God"—it is difficult to see how Isaiah by its use designates the ideal king

---

[60] In his later work: "The Book of the Prophet Isaiah: A New English Translation," 1898, p. 145, Cheyne actually lowers his view of the meaning of *'El Gibbōr.*

[61] Cf. Hengstenberg, "Christology," ii. p. 85 on the meaning of *'El* and the impossibility of rendering it (as Gesenius does) by "hero"; cf. also the citations given by J. D. Davis, in the "Princeton Biblical and Theological Studies," 1912, p. 99.

(not now the Messiah) an angel and not a God. By reducing the person spoken of from the Messiah to the king, and the dignity ascribed to him from the Divine to the angelic rank, Cheyne has, no doubt, effectually removed the passage from the category of Old Testament testimonies to the Deity of the Messiah. But he appears to have done so only at the cost not only of some violence, but also of some confusion.

It is to attain this end that the exegesis of the "Old Liberal school" is particularly directed, and the exegesis seems patient of nearly any conclusion which falls short of ascribing Deity to the Messiah.[62] E. Kautzsch can lay it down dogmatically as a principle of exegesis, which must govern the rendering of '*El Gibbōr*, that "an absolute predication of Godhead, even in the case of the Messiah, would be inconceivable in the Old Testament."[63] He therefore denies that it is possible to take the term as "hero God," and insists on translating it "God of a hero," that is "Godlike hero." And George Adam Smith can actually permit himself to write such sentences as these:[64]

In any case the application of these prophecies to Jesus Christ must be made with discrimination. They have been too hastily used as predictions of the Godhead of the Messiah. But not even do the names in Chapter ix. 6, f. imply Deity; while all the functions attributed to the promised King are human. Isaiah's Messiah is an earthly monarch of the stock of David, and with offices that are political, both military and judicial. He is not the mediator of spiritual gifts to his people: forgiveness, a new knowledge of God and the like. It is only in this, that he saves the people of God from destruction and reigns over them with justice in the fear of God, that he can be regarded as a type of Jesus Christ.

We have only to place by the side of this an equally brief statement emanating from a newer school, for its marvellousness to strike the eye. Martin Brückner writes:[65]

[62] The various senses which have been put upon the words '*El Gibbōr* have been collected and discussed by J. D. Davis, as cited, pp. 93-105.

[63] Hastings' *B.D.*, extra volume, 1904, p. 695b.

[64] "Modern Criticism and the Preaching of the Old Testament," 1901, p. 161; cf. Hastings' *B.D.*, ii. p. 491.

[65] "Die Entstehung der paulinischen Christologie," 1903, p. 97, note.

In any case "the old-prophetic Messiah-consciousness," for example, of Isaiah, would not be, on the assumption of the genuineness of his Christology, that of a "purely human King of David's line" but that of the Apocalyptic introducer of the blessed end-time. For a Messiah who reigns "without end" (ix. 6), who is called the God-Hero and the Eternal One, who is the personal concentration of the spirit (xi. 2 ff.), and destroys the wicked with the breath of his mouth (xi. 4), is not "purely human" but superhuman, wholly apart from this—that the kingdom over which he reigns is the miraculous kingdom of peace and blessedness, the splendor of which is the light of the benighted peoples (ix. 1 ff.; xi. 7 ff.).

The several representatives of the "Old Liberal school" differ very much among themselves, of course, in details of interpretation. The thing which they are agreed upon is that the Messiah is called 'El Gibbōr—whatever that may be made to mean—not because he is himself Divine, but because he is the representative of Jehovah on earth. It is allowed that the description given of him scales all the heights permissible to such a representative. "In the brilliant picture of chapter ix.," writes G. S. Goodspeed,[66] "the child who occupies the throne of David is to overthrow the enemy and to rule for ever and ever. The names which are given to him describe a personage more glorious than any prophet has hitherto mentioned, except perhaps the writer of Psalm xlv." But, however glorious, they fall short of declaring him divine. "These divine titles," writes James Crichton,[67] "do not necessarily"—what is the function of this "necessarily" here?—"imply that in the mind of the prophet the Messianic king is God in the metaphysical sense—the essence of the divine nature is not a dogmatic conception in the Old Testament"—surely a blind remark!—"but only that Jehovah is present in Him in perfect wisdom and power, so that He exercises over His people for ever a fatherly and peaceful rule." Perhaps, however, Eduard Riehm may still stand as the typical

[66] "Israel's Messianic Hope," 1900, p. 120.
[67] Orr's, "International Standard Bible Encyclopaedia," 1915, p. 2040.

representative of this system of interpretation. The Messiah, says he,[68] is represented in Old Testament prophecy

as a human king, an offspring from the stem of David, whose eminence is far above the position of all other men, and whose personality has about it something wonderful and mysterious. Although it is nowhere indicated that he is to enter the world in an extraordinary and wonderful manner,[69] he yet, as the earthly representative of the Divine King, and his instrument in establishing His kingdom, and exercising His government, stands in an absolutely unique and intimate relationship to God, Whose Spirit rests upon him as upon no other, and Whose almighty power, wisdom, righteousness and helpful grace work through him in such full measure that in and through his government God's great name, that is, His revealed glory is made known. In other words, God makes him the organ of His self-revelation, just as elsewhere He uses the "angel of Jehovah." Hence, even the divine designation *'El Gibbōr* (God-hero) is one of the names ascribed to him; and hence also, even in a more general announcement applied to the house of David, there occurs the expression: "it shall be as *God* and the *angel of Jehovah* before" the inhabitants of Jerusalem. Both in the kingdom of God and in humanity, the Messiah assumes thus a central position, not only as their "head" but also as the mediating organ whence proceed the judicial and saving operations and the self-revelation of the Divine King.

It is no more than this that A. F. Kirkpatrick says when he expounds the Isaian declaration as follows:[70]

The fourfold name of this prince declares his marvellous nature and proclaims him to be, in an extraordinary and mysterious way, the representative of Jehovah. The title, *Wonderful Counsellor*, conveys the idea of his endowment with supernatural wisdom in that counsel which was peculiarly the function of a king. *Mighty God* expresses his divine greatness and power, as the unique representative of Jehovah, who is Himself the *Mighty God* (x. 21). *Eternal Father* describes his paternal tenderness and unending care for his people.

---

[68] "Messianic Prophecy,"2 1884, E. T. 1891, p. 280; cf. p. 182.

[69] This means, of course, that Riehm does not regard Is. vii. 14, Mic. v. 1 as involving this for the Messiah.

[70] "The Doctrine of the Prophets,"2 1897, p. 193.

Prince of Peace denotes the character and end of his government. His advent is still future but it is assured. *The zeal of Jehovah of hosts will perform this.*

To the exposition of the term "the Mighty God" Kirkpatrick attaches a footnote, which without comment adduces the following words from C. Orelli: "In such passages the Old Testament revelation falls into a self-contradiction, from which only a miracle has been able to deliver us, the Incarnation of the Son of God." Thus, and thus only, does he intimate that he is aware that the treatment of the epithet "Mighty God" as a suitable one for a merely human representative of Jehovah, however unique, does violence to all linguistic propriety.

Orelli, from whom the quotation is taken, it is needless to say, did not write the words taken over from him on any such hypothesis. In his opinion the prophet has in view a truly superhuman figure and one gets the impression, as he reads Orelli's exposition of the passage, that, so far as he fails to give its full meaning, the failure is due to a defect in his Christological thought, rather than to unwillingness to take the prophet at the height of his meaning. He writes:[71]

When in the first name a miraculous, divine character is ascribed to the ruler in his capacity of counsellor, planning for his people's good, this is saying more than that his wisdom far exceeds that usual among rulers; it is affirmed that his wisdom is related to the human as divine. Just so, the second predicate attributes to him energy in action. He is called *strong God*, not merely a divine hero: *a God of a hero*, for גִּבּוֹר is an adjective, and the phrase cannot be understood differently than in x. 21, where it is used of the Lord Himself. In this second name, also, doubtless, a definite expression of his dignity, one side of his working, is taken into view, namely, his divine energy in action, as in the first the superhuman grandeur of his counsel; but his person itself is thereby raised to divine greatness. He is called *strong God* in a way that would be inapplicable to a man, unless the one God who rightly bears the name *strong God* were perfectly set forth in this His Anointed One. In such passages, the Old Testament revelation falls into a self-contradiction, from which only

[71] "Old Testament Prophecy," E. T. 1885, p. 274 f.

a miracle has been able to deliver us, the Incarnation of the Son of God. Elsewhere it draws the sharpest limit between the holy God and the sinful child of man, and its superiority to heathen religions depends in great part on this limit. Prophecy gradually lets this limit drop, in proof that the aim of God's action is to transcend it and to unite Himself most closely with humanity. In such oracles we Christians find no deification of the human, such as is the order of the day on heathen soil. Otherwise prophecy would be a retrogression from the teaching of the law into naturalism and heathen idealism. But in such oracles we find a clear proof that even in the time of the old covenant the Spirit of God was consciously striving after the goal that we see reached in the new.

"Divine wisdom," he continues after a page or two,[72] "divine strength, paternal love faithful as God's, divine righteousness and peace are ascribed to him, in such a way, indeed, that his person also appears divine: he perfectly exhibits God to the world; consequently his dominion is really God's dominion on earth. Every Judaizing and rationalizing attempt to adapt the insignia conferred on the Messiah here to a man of our nature, degrades them, and with them the Spirit who framed them." After this there is nothing left to say except what V. H. Stanton says with the simplicity of truth:[73] "Language is used" in this passage "to which only the person of a truly Divine Messiah could adequately correspond." This appears to be recognized, after his own fashion, even by G. B. Gray, when he comments:[74]

Some of the names singly and even more in combination, are, as applied to men, unparalleled in the Old Testament, and on this account are regarded by Gressmann (p. 280 ff.) as mythological and traditional; cf. also Rosenmüller, *Scholia*. . . . The Child is to be more than mighty . . . more than a mighty man . . . more than a mighty king; he is to be a mighty אל, God. This attribution of divinity, implying that the Messiah is to be a kind of demi-God, is without clear analogy in the Old Testament, for Ps. xlv. 7 (6) is ambiguous.

[72] P. 277.
[73] "Jewish and Christian Messiah," p. 104.
[74] "Isaiah" (International Critical Commentary), 1912, i. p. 173.

The language in which this comment is couched, as well as the direct reference to him, recalls us to the effect on the interpretation of the passage of the new point of view introduced by Gressmann and his fellow-workers in the field of the history of religion.[75] The essence of this new point of view lies in the contention that the religious development and the religious language of Israel are to be explained after the analogy of the religious development and the religious language of the neighboring peoples; and on the assumption of a common body of old-oriental mythical ideas underlying them all alike. How this applies to the Messianic conceptions of Israel Gunkel briefly explains to us. He says:[76]

The figure of the Messiah, too, belongs to this originally mythological material. It is true that the new David or sprout of David whom the prophets expect, is only a man, though endowed with divine powers, and the hope that such a king should arise and bless Israel is primarily a purely natural one. But there are traits in this figure of a king, nevertheless, which intimate to us that this expected king was originally a God-king. Already in Isaiah he receives names which literally belong to no man: God-hero, Father of Eternity; he is the king of the Golden Age when sheep and wolf lie down together; particularly striking is it that his birth is celebrated repeatedly with mysterious statements, and that the salvation of Israel is hoped for from it: for a fresh-born human child cannot help his people, though no doubt a divine child could. We notice also that other prophets and many psalmists speak of a God who is to be King of the whole world; that is, Jahveh whose enthronement and ascension in the last times the Psalmists particularly sing. The whole material falls most beautifully into order if we assume that the Israelitish hope of a king was preceded by an alien mythical one, according to which a new God ascends as King the throne of the world. And it therefore does not surprise us when we meet in the later Apocalypses with a heavenly figure who is to come from heaven and establish a blessed kingdom on earth. This figure of a

[75] Cf. for example Julius Boehmer, "Reichgottesspuren in der Völkerwelt" in Schlatter and Lütgert's "Beiträge zur Fördering christlicher Theologie," 1906, x.-i. p. 87.

[76] "Zum religionsgeschichtlichen Verständnis," p. 24 f.

divine king is, therefore, no new creation of Apocalyptic Judaism: but it is the same figure which already lies at the foundation of the prophetic hopes.

This ingenious construction has been worked out into greater detail by Gressmann and set forth by him in perhaps as attractive a form as it is capable of receiving.[77] The difficulty with it is that it requires too many assumptions, and that these assumptions receive no support from the facts. As we have already seen, the ancient orient knows nothing of an eschatological king.[78] Israel knows as little of a deified King.[79] The whole mythological framework of the edifice thus breaks down. E. Sellin has solidly shown, moreover, that the entire development, which it is here sought to explain on the basis of an alien mythology taken over by Israel from its neighbors, is purely native to Israel and has its roots set in the revelation-act at Sinai.[80]

The promulgation of this new view, however, has focussed attention on the prophetic language to which it seeks to assign a mythological significance,—with the effect of rendering the current attempts to explain that language away absurd. It has become quite clear in the course of the discussion that the prophets do attribute a divine nature and do ascribe divine functions to the Messiah. Indeed, the entire body of "results"

[77] "Der Ursprung," pp. 250-301. Arthur Drews, of course, makes the most of it, in his fashion: "Christusmythe,"[1] pp. 8-9.

[78] See above.

[79] Gressmann writes, op. cit., p. 285: "The general religious presupposition, under which alone a figure like that of the God-King could be formed, is the king-deification, which, to be sure, cannot be proved for Israel, but certainly may be for its neighboring nations."

[80] "Der alttestament. Prophetismus," p. 183: "The specifically Israelitish character and the original grounding of its kernel is certain. And its roots are set not in mythology but in the religion of Israel, in Israel's belief in the God of Sinai, to whom in the end the world must belong." So, p. 182: "The real root of the expectation of a Savior lies also here in the revelation act of Sinai. Here and here only could a foundation be laid for viewing the whole history under the point of sight of waiting for the appearance of the world-God, who is to fill the universe with His glory."

of the "Old Liberal" criticism concerning the development of
the Messianic hope—which it tended to relegate more and more
completely to post-exilic times—has been hopelessly broken
up.[81] It has again been made plain that the Messianic hope was
aboriginal in Israel, and formed, indeed, in all ages the heart
of Israelitish religion. In sequence to this, much of the disintegrating criticism of the documents which had been indulged
in for the purpose of giving a semblance of verisimilitude to the
hypothesis of the late origin of the Messianic development, has
become antiquated; the integrity and early date of sections and
passages hitherto removed to a late period have been restored;
and the unity of the Messianic hope in Israel, throughout all
ages, has been vindicated,—so that, from the beginning down
through the Apocalypses of the later Judaism and the songs of
the earlier chapters of the Gospel of Luke, we see exhibited
essentially a single unitary hope. In a passage written with great
restraint, Herman Bavinck describes the effect produced by the
introduction of the new view, thus:[82]

In place of the feverish efforts which were more and more ruling
in the dominant school of literary criticism to remove all Messianic
prediction to post-exilic times, it is now acknowledged that the pre-
exilic prophets, not only themselves cherished such Messianic expectations, but also presuppose them among the people; nor have
they themselves excogitated them and proclaimed them as novelties
to the people; but they have received them from the past and are
building on expectations which have existed from ancient times and
have been current in Israel. Accordingly this new tendency among
Old Testament scholars, as good as altogether discards the earlier
interpolation hypothesis and recognizes a high antiquity for all
eschatological ideas concerning the day of the Lord, the destruction
of enemies, the deliverance of the people, the appearance of the
Messiah, the consummation of the kingdom of God, and the like,
and in the figure of the Messiah, as presented in the Old Testament,
permits to come again fully to their rights even the supernatural

81 Cf. what Sellin says, "Der alttestament. Prophetismus," pp. 167-168.
82 "Gereformeerde Dogmatiek,"3 1910, p. 249.

traits, such as the miraculous birth (Is. vii. 14; Mic. v. 1), the divine names (Is. ix. 5) and so forth. Numerous texts and pericopes, which were considered post-exilic by the earlier critics, now again rank as genuine, and the so-called Christology of the Old Testament finds itself thus once more restored more or less fully to its rights and its value.

Perhaps there is no passage which more immediately suggests itself, when we ask after Old Testament testimonies to the transcendence of the Messiah than Daniel's account of his great vision of one like unto a Son of Man coming with the clouds of heaven (vii. 13, 14). So far as appears no doubt was felt as to the Messianic reference of this vision until modern times.[83] Even the Rationalists, as Hengstenberg points out,[84] though with strong temptations to reject it, yet for the most part recognized its Messianic character. And even up to the present day, when it has become the "Liberal" tradition[85] that, by the "one like unto a son of man," not the Messiah but the Israelitish people is intended, not only does the original Messianic interpretation still hold its own, but can be spoken of still by S. R. Driver, for example, as "the current interpretation."[86] Perhaps Hermann Schultz and Eduard Riehm may be taken as fair examples of how those "Liberals" who still cling to the interpretation of the vision of an individual, wish it to be understood. Schultz, who decides for this personal application only as probable, supposes[87] that Daniel conceived of the Messiah as a being dwelling with God in the heavens, like one of the angel-princes of whom he also speaks as like sons of

[83] The solitary exceptions of Ephraem Syrus among the Church Fathers and of Abenezra among the Jews may be left out of account.

[84] "Christology," iii. p. 88. He mentions De Wette, Bertholdt, Gesenius, van Lengerke, Maurer.

[85] It is this that Sellin means when he says that the figure is "according to the dominant exposition simply a representation of the people of God" ("Der israelitisch-jüdische Heilandserwartung," p. 70).

[86] "The Book of Daniel" ("The Cambridge Bible for Schools and Colleges"), 1900, p. 102; cf. list of supporters of the two views on p. 108, note 4.

[87] "Alttestamentliche Theologie,"[5] 1896, pp. 635 f.

men.[88] Riehm[89] will not allow even so much. He will not agree that there is in the vision any hint that the "one like unto a son of man" is of Divine or of angelic, or even in any sense of heavenly (as in Beyschlag's "heavenly man") nature. The prophet, he insists, gives no intimation of the origin of this Being, beyond the constant presupposition that he belongs with "the saints of the Most High." He is represented as being in heaven and coming thence *only because* he is the representative and organ of the God of heaven," and a "superhuman character and a divine position and dignity" are thus "lent, as it were, to Him." That is to say we can learn from this passage only that this Being comes from God, in the sense that he is sent by God to do God's work in the world.

The element of truth in this reasoning lies in its refusal to separate the "one like unto a son of man" completely from humanity, as if he were presented as a purely heavenly Being, and thus dissevered wholly from the entire course of Messianic expectation heretofore, in which the Messiah uniformly appears in close connection with Israel from whom He springs. It is the more important to point out the inconsequence of the total transcendentalizing of the Messiah on the basis of this vision, that the novelty of the vision in the history of the Messianic expectation lies precisely in its throwing up the transcendental element of the Messianic figure into such a strong light as apparently to neglect, if not quite to obscure, its human side. "Now," writes Sellin,[90] "the expectation here presented to us is new in so far as this Future Ruler appears in Daniel absolutely as a heavenly Being, borne on clouds, stand-

---

[88] This is probably the ruling view among those "Liberals" who allow the personal interpretation. For example, A. Schweitzer writes (*The Expositor*, Nov. 1913, p. 444): "In the Book of Daniel the view is taken that there is no longer a ruling Davidic family from which a ruler could be raised up to be Messiah. The author, therefore, expects that God will confer the supreme power in the coming world-age on an angelic Being who possesses human form and has the appearance of a 'son of man' (Dan. vii. 13-14)."

[89] "Messianic Prophecy," p. 196.

[90] "Der israelitisch-jüdische Heilandserwartung," p. 72 f.

ing before the heavenly throne of God; that there is complete
silence as to His human derivation; that He, although He also
has human traits, is a heavenly Being; that, on the other hand,
all actual earthly traits such as are always attributed by the
prophets to the Savior, because He is born into this world, are
stripped off. In this expectation of Daniel's all and every earthly
human being is transcended; the Savior comes no longer from
this world, no matter how miraculously given by God, but
wholly and exclusively from the transcendental world." This
side of the matter may be capable thus of exaggeration, but it is
clearly hopeless to represent a figure in any measure so presented to us, as wholly human, as Riehm would fain do. If it
must be held that room is left for human traits not here insisted
upon, the traits which are insisted upon are obviously distinctly
superhuman, or, we should rather say, distinctly divine. This is
already apparent from his representation as coming with (or
on) the clouds. It is always the Lord, as Hengstenberg already
pointed out,[91] who appears with, or on, the clouds of heaven;
none but the Lord of nature can ride on the clouds of heaven;
and the clouds, as Michaelis says, "are characteristic of divine
majesty." Julius Grill is quite right when he throws into emphasis[92] that "majesty" is the one characteristic which is insisted
upon in the "one like unto a son of man." He is not represented
as coming from heaven to earth (Holsten, Appel), or as going
from earth to heaven, or as coming out of obscurity into manifestation (H. Holtzmann). What he is represented as doing is
simply drawing nigh to the throne. "What is emphasized in
Daniel vii. 13 is the immediate vicinity of God into which the
'one like unto a son of man' is brought," says Grill, and compares Ps. cx. 1, and Jer. xxx. 21. "It is," he says again,[93] "a veritable coronation act which the author has seen and wishes to
describe."

[91] "Christology," iii. 83: so also Pusey, "Daniel the Prophet,"2 1868, p. 85 f.
Cf. Driver, in *loc.*: "*with the clouds of heaven:* in superhuman majesty and
state."

[92] "Untersuchungen über die Entstehung des vierten Evangeliums," i. 1902,
p. 52.

[93] P. 54.

The investigation of the passage by Grill has apparently become the starting-point for a new movement of "Liberal" authors towards recognizing its reference to an individual figure. This does not appear to be due to any peculiar strength or special novelty in Grill's manner of prosecuting the discussion; the reasons which he presents for understanding the passage thus, are very much the same that have been repeatedly urged before. But he approaches the question from a new angle and his readers have been prepared to follow his suggestion by their participation in his general presuppositions. Grill himself thinks of a purely heavenly being as presented to us here, an angel, perhaps Michael, perhaps a higher Being still, "a most exalted personal intermediary between God and the world; and," he somewhat unexpectedly adds, "a transcendent prototype of the God-pleasing humanity ultimately to be realized in the people of the Most High." Nathaniel Schmidt had already[94] expressed a similar view, interpreting the man-like Being as an angel and more particularly as Michael, the guardian angel of Israel; and his view had attracted to itself Frank C. Porter.[95] In a later article[96] Schmidt restates his view, citing Grill in support of it in general, but declining to accept the somewhat incongruous addition by which Grill attempts to combine the two main interpretations of the passage—that the man-like Being is an exalted heavenly personage and that he is the type of the saints of God. "Whether Michael or any other angel was ever thought of as the ideal Israelite," he declares to be doubtful. T. K. Cheyne[97] follows in Schmidt's steps, and, as was his wont, seeks to improve on him. Schmidt strongly repels the idea that Daniel's figure is the Messiah; to him this figure is distinctively a heavenly being,—angelic or more probably superangelic, Michael or one higher still than Michael. To Cheyne,[98] he is both the Messiah, and "an angel, presumably Michael, the

---

[94] *Journal of Biblical Literature*, xix, 1900.
[95] "Hastings' B.D.," iv. p. 260.
[96] "Encyclopaedia Biblica," iv. 1903, p. 4710 f.
[97] "Bible Problems," 1904, pp. 213 ff.
[98] Pp. 73, 214 ff.

great prince-angel who defends the interests of the people of Israel,"—or rather Michael, the somewhat obscured representative of Marduk who was no angel but a God; in a word "a degraded (but an honorably degraded) deity," a "great superhuman (and originally divine) personage," "the heavenly Messiah" who, having played a great rôle in the creation of the world and the deliverance from Egypt (as the Angel of Jehovah) is in the last days to "redeem the world and mankind." In sharp contrast with Cheyne, Paul Volz,[99] while following Grill in rejecting the symbolical interpretation and seeing in the one "like unto a son of man" an individual being, is clear that Michael is not meant, nor any angelic being, but a simple man, the Lord-Messiah, the Lord of the new world, to whom is to be given the dominion of the world, and all the peoples and all the times. "He is certainly not the symbolical representative of the Kingdom of God, but the prince of his Kingdom. He is the representative (Stellvertreter) of God, to whom the power and honor and dominion belong; he stands, however, also in direct relation to the people of the seer, to the people Israel, his dominion is their dominion"—in short, he is the Messiah. Though he thus belongs to the category of man, he is not, however, forthwith to be assigned to the earthly sphere. He comes from heaven. The old myth of a primitive man comes into view here: a primitive man created as the opponent of the primitive beasts, the demonic monsters, who is to deliver the cosmos from them and secure the heavenly beings from their assaults. "This primitive Savior was brought forward, now, by the Apocalyptists for their eschatological purposes: Daniel recalls that man of whom the myth speaks and sees him in the vision; the Savior of the primitive age becomes the Savior of the last age, and the one as the other has to do with the beasts; the Apocalypse of Daniel, nevertheless, pays no further attention to the primitive existence of this man." According to Volz, then, Daniel's "one like unto a son of man" is, indeed, a transcendent being, but yet only a man, though a heavenly man: conceived on the lines of the primitive man and so far a repro-

[99] "Jüdische Eschatologie," 1903, pp. 101 f., 214 ff.

duction of him; but not precisely that primitive man and therefore not necessarily preëxistent.

All this, now, Gressmann turns right as its head.[100] All investigators are agreed, says he with fine neglect of his colleagues, that in the text as it lies before us, the Man stands as a symbol of Israel, as the beasts do of the heathen kingdoms. But this is only a use to which Daniel has put a borrowed figure: "the originality of the reworker consists only in this—that he has reinterpreted the Man of Israel." Whatever else there is in the passage, we may safely employ for the reconstruction of the old myth, and adventuring on this path we find in the Man a parallel figure to the Messiah, who, according to the old Israelitish conception, was to stand at the beginning of the new age and all the peoples be subject to Him. He is, no doubt, an angel, but no common angel, the highest angel rather, the Being who is the greatest of all, next after only the Ancient of Days; hence He is not Gabriel or Michael—they are not high enough. We cannot give Him a name; we must be modest and say merely that this angel means that eschatological figure, whom everybody knows as the eschatological man which in the end of the days is to be made the Lord of the world. In the heathen form of this myth, which lies behind the Jewish one, He was, of course, a God; and this God has only been degraded into an angel in consequence of Jewish monotheism. It was as an angel therefore that He came to Daniel; and Daniel turned Him into a symbol of Israel. The development thus proceeded in directly the opposite direction from what is commonly thought. Israel is not here represented as one like unto a son of man; but the man is represented as Israel.

Sellin[101] makes it his primary task to draw the teeth of

100 "Der Ursprung," usw. p. 340.

101 In Sellin's view, Dan. vii. 13, in the original Biography of Daniel, "referred to the proclamation of the Saviour as the Second Adam, as a heavenly man, free from all that is earthly, and to His kingdom"; but the later author of the Apocalypse of Daniel—that is, our Daniel—has transferred this to the whole people of God. So he explains in "Prophetismus," p. 97, note 1. In the discussion in "Heilandserwartung," pp. 70 ff., he deals with Daniel's presentation of "one like unto a son of man" as an individual figure without raising question of the composition of the passage.

Gressmann's mythology. He takes his start frankly from Gressmann's findings. It is true enough, he says, that the Messianic conception is wider than that of the Son of David; wider and older. We may see proofs of this all through the prophets. Witness what we are told in them of the birth of Immanuel from the Almah who was with child, of the travail of the Yoledhah, of the seven shepherds and eight princes of the fifth chapter of Micah, of the "Mighty God" and other great names of the ninth chapter of Isaiah, above all of the eating of milk and honey, the picture of the King of Paradise riding on the ass, and the like.[102] But why represent these things as borrowed goods? Why, above all, think of Daniel's Man, who certainly was not invented by Daniel, but was already known to his readers, as a recent importation from heathendom? Rather, Daniel throws himself back on the prophets before him where we may find these things fragmentarily alluded to; as, for example, in Isaiah, and everywhere in the Old Israelitish expectations of a Being coming out of the Divine sphere. What we have in Daniel is not something new to Israel, but the primaeval Jewish expectation of a Savior newborn, stripped of this-world traits, and transformed into the sphere of the transcendental world.[103]

So, the discussion goes on. But it does not remain without results. And the main result of it is, that assurance is rendered doubly sure that in the "one like unto a son of man" of Dan. vii. 13, we have a superhuman figure, a figure to whose superhuman character justice is not done until it is recognized as expressly divine. It was understood to be a superhuman figure by everyone who appealed to it and built his Messianic hopes upon its basis throughout the whole subsequent development of the Jewish Church.[104] Wherever, in the Apocalyptic litera-

---

[102] "Die alttestamentliche Religion im Rahmen der andern altorientalischen," 1908, p. 45.

[103] "Der israelitisch-jüdische Heilandserwartung," pp. 70 ff.

[104] Cf. A. Dillmann, "Handb. der alttest. Theologie," p. 538: "Finally the whole exegetical tradition from the Book of Enoch (which is directly depend-

ture we meet with the figure of the Son of Man, it is transcendentally conceived.[105] When our Lord Himself derived from it His favorite self-designation of Son of Man,[106] He too took it over in a transcendental sense; and meant by applying it to Himself to present Himself as a heavenly Being who had come forth from heaven and descended to earth on a mission of mercy to lost men. On every occasion on which our Lord called Himself the Son of Man thus, He bears His witness to the transcendental character of the figure presented to Daniel. There is no reason apparent today why His judgment of the seer's meaning should be revised. If by his "one like to a son of man" Daniel meant to bring before us the figure of an individual being, and that seems to us to be beyond question,—it is very certain that the individual the figure of whom he brings before us is superhuman, or rather Divine.

In attempting to illustrate the testimony of the Old Testament to the deity of the Messiah we have laid particular stress on the great declarations in Ps. xlv. 6, Is. ix. 6 and Dan. vii. 13. These are, as we have said, high lights shining out brightly on the surface of a pervasive implication. They are not the only points which shine out on its surface with special brilliancy. We might just as well have chosen to dwell, instead, on Ps. ii. or Ps. cx. or Mic. v. 2, or Jer. xxiii. 6 or Zech. xiii. 7 or Mal. iii. 1,

ent on Daniel) on, has even understood by this title the king of the kingdom. I cannot help holding that this interpretation is right. In this case we have not only the beginning of the development of the earthly kingdom of God into a βασιλεία τῶν οὐρανῶν here, but also its head is designated as like an angelic being (for these are elsewhere in Daniel also designated כְּבַר אֱנָשׁ), a preëxistent Being present already in heaven who in the fulness of the times will come and establish the eternal kingdom of heaven."

105 Cf. W. Bousset, "Religion des Jüdentums,"[1] p. 24 ff. (In ed. 2, pp. 301 f. the more relevant part of this statement is eliminated).

106 Cf. H. J. Holtzmann, "Lehrbuch der Neutestament. Theologie,"[1] i. p. 247: "The reference of the term back to Dan. vii. 13 (already essayed by expositors of the Reformation period like Chemnitz and recommended by Ewald and Hitzig) is today the, at all events, most recognized and most assured result of the discussions of the 'Son of Man,' vexed in so many points."

and the like.[107] A selection, however, had to be made and we have endeavored to select those particular points on which the light seemed to shine with the purest illumination. We should be sorry to leave the impression, however, that the testimony of the Old Testament to the Deity of the Messiah is dependent upon these particular passages, and their fellows. The salient fact regarding it is that it is an essential element in the eschatological system of the Old Testament and is inseparably imbedded in the hope of the coming of God to His kingdom which formed the heart of Israelitish religion from its origin. We have only to free ourselves from the notion that the Messianic hope was the product of the monarchy and to realize that, however closely it becomes attached to the Davidic dynasty in one of its modes of expression, it was an aboriginal element in the religion of Israel, to understand how little it can be summed up in the expectation of the coming of an earthly king. It is one of the chief merits of the new school of research that it is making this ever more and more clear.

Meanwhile, it is an unhappy fact that we may search in vain through many of the current treatises on the Messianic hope for intimations that it included the promise of a Divine Redeemer. It is much, indeed, if we find a hearty recognition that a Messianic figure occupied an essential place in it; at least during the larger space of the history of Israelitish religion. Even devout-minded students have been sometimes tempted to represent Messianic prophecy as fulfilled "not so much in the personality and work of Christ as in the religion of Christ."[108] When the person of the Messiah is given its rights, however, as the center of Messianic prophecy, it is still often insisted that He was conceived purely as a human being,—as Trypho, Justin Martyr's collocutor in the famous dialogue, contended in the second century. At the best, we get such a

[107] F. E. König, "Offenbarungsbegriff," ii. p. 398, illustrating how the light of salvation breaks now and again through the veil of Old Testament conceptions, by which it is covered in the Old Testament announcements, observes (among other things) that "the superhumanness of the mediator grows ever clearer (Is. ix. 6 ff., xi. 1 ff.; Mat. v. 1)." Cf. Ottley, Hastings' *B.D.*, ii. p. 459 f.

[108] Cf. F. H. Woods, "The Hope of Israel," 1896, p. 184.

concession as A. Dillmann's. "We have then," says he,[109] "in this whole series of Messianic prophecies certainly the portrait of a sovereign of the kingdom, endowed with Divine attributes and powers, but nowhere a God or God-man; on the other hand, however, the Book of Daniel advances to a still higher, metaphysical or mystical view of His nature . . . an already existing being preëxisting in the heavens, who in the fulness of the times comes and establishes the kingdom of the saints."[110] On this A. B. Davidson makes less than no advance, when he declares[111]—shall we not say, evidently not without some misgivings?—"In Is. ix. xi. it is not taught that Messiah is God, but that Jehovah is fully present in Him. The general eschatological idea was that the presence of Jehovah in person among men would be their salvation. The prophet gives a particular turn to this general idea, representing that Jehovah shall be present in the Davidic king. The two are not identified but Jehovah is fully manifested in the Messiah." The sufficient answer to such comments is that they are obviously minifying in intention; they are endeavors not to concede too much where concession is seen to be nevertheless necessary. We do not wonder that Davidson feels constrained to add: "The passage goes very far." Pity it is that he could not see his way to go the whole length that it goes.

Happily, however, there have always been some who, standing less under the blight of the current critical theories, have been able to see more clearly. Thus, for example, F. Godet has seen his way to declare[112] that "the idea of the Divinity of the Messiah" is "the soul of the entire Old Testament"; and, after adducing Isaiah's designation of Him as "Wonderful," "Mighty God," and Micah's discrimination of His historical birth at Bethlehem from His prehistoric birth "from everlasting," and Malachi's calling Him "Adonai coming to His temple," to sum

---

[109] "Handbuch der Alttestament. Theologie," pp. 538-539.

[110] The schematization of the Messianic hope worked out from this point of view is very clearly presented by C. F. Kent, "The Sermons, etc., of Israel's Prophets," 1910, pp. 45-47.

[111] Hastings' *B.D.*, iv. p. 124 f.; similarly, "Old Testament Prophecy," 1903, pp. 367-368.

[112] "Commentary on Luke," E. T. ii. p. 251.

up in these sentences: "There was in the whole of the Old Testament from the patriarchal theophanies down to the latest prophetic visions, a constant current towards the incarnation as the goal of all these revelations. The appearance of the Messiah presents itself more and more clearly to the view of the prophets as the perfect theophany, the final coming of Jehovah." It is upon this thread of Old Testament teaching, he goes on to remark—broken off in the Rabbinical development—that Jesus laid hold in His assertion of the dignity of His person as Messiah. These words might well have been written today; they express admirably the new insight which we have obtained unto the nature and development of Old Testament eschatology.

CHAPTER V

THE SPIRIT OF GOD IN THE OLD TESTAMENT[1]

THE doctrine of the Spirit of God is an exclusively Biblical doctrine. Rückert tells us that the idea connoted by the term is entirely foreign to Hellenism, and first came into the world through Christianity.[2] And Kleinert, in quoting this remark, adds that what is peculiarly anti-heathenish in the conception is already present in the Old Testament.[3] It would seem, then, that what is most fundamental in the Biblical doctrine of the Spirit of God is common to both Testaments.

The name meets us in the very opening verses of the Old Testament, and it appears there as unannounced and unexplained as in the opening verses of the New Testament. It is plain that it was no more a novelty in the mouth of the author of Genesis than in the mouth of the author of Matthew. But though it is common to both Testaments, it is not equally common in all parts of the Bible. It does not occur as frequently in the Old Testament as in the New. It is found as often in the Epistles of Paul as in the whole Old Testament. It is not as pervasive in the Old Testament as in the New. It fails in no New Testament book, except the three brief personal letters Philemon and II and III John. On the other hand, in only some half of the thirty-nine Old Testament books is it clearly mentioned,[4] while in as many as sixteen all definite allusion to it

[1] From *The Presbyterian and Reformed Review*, v. vi, 1895, pp. 665-687; also from *Biblical Doctrines*, pp. 101-129.

[2] "Korinthierbriefe" i, p. 80.

[3] Article, "Zur altest. Lehre vom Geiste Gottes," in the "Jahrbb. für deutsch. Theologie" for 1867, i, p. 9.

[4] These are Genesis, Exodus, Numbers, Judges, I and II Samuel, I and II Kings, II Chronicles, Nehemiah, Job, Psalms, Isaiah, Ezekiel, Joel, Micah, Haggai, Zechariah. Deuteronomy and I Chronicles may be added, although they do not contain the explicit phrase, "the Spirit of God" or "the Spirit of Jehovah."

seems to be lacking.[5] The principle which governs the use or disuse of it does not lie on the surface. Sometimes it may, perhaps, be partly due to the nature of the subject treated. But if mention of the Spirit of God fails in Leviticus, it is made in Numbers; if it fails in Joshua and Ruth, it is made in Judges and Samuel; if it fails in Ezra, it is made in Nehemiah; if it fails in Jeremiah, it is made in Isaiah and Ezekiel; if it fails in seven or eight of the minor prophets, it is made in the remaining four or five. Whether it occurs in an Old Testament book seems to depend on a number of circumstances which have little or no bearing on the history of the doctrine. We need only note that the name "Spirit of God" meets us at the very opening of revelation, and it, or its equivalents, accompanies us sporadically throughout the volume. The Pentateuch and historical books provide us with the outline of the doctrine; its richest depositories among the prophets are Isaiah and Ezekiel, from each of which alone probably the whole doctrine could be derived.[6]

In passing from the Old Testament to the New, the reader is conscious of no violent discontinuity in the conception of the Spirit which he finds in the two volumes. He may note the increased frequency with which the name appears on the printed page. But he would note this much the same in passing from the earlier to the later chapters of the *Epistle to the Romans*. He may note an increased definiteness and fulness in the conception itself. But something similar to this he would note in passing from the Pentateuch to Isaiah, or from Matthew to

[5] These are Leviticus, Joshua, Ruth, Ezra, Esther, Ecclesiastes, Song of Songs, Jeremiah, Lamentations, Hosea, Amos, Obadiah, Jonah, Nahum, Habakkuk and Zephaniah. Proverbs, Daniel and Malachi may, for one reason or another, remain unclassified.

[6] "There is one writer of the Old Testament, in whom all lines and rays of this development come together, and who so stood in the matter of time and of inner manner that they had to come together in this point of unity, if the Old Testament had otherwise found such. This is Ezekiel" (Kleinert, *op. cit.* p. 45). "Isaiah has scattered throughout his prophecies allusions to the Spirit so manifold and various in express descriptions and in brief turns of phrase, that it might not be difficult to put together from his words, the complete doctrine of the Spirit" (Smeaton, "Doctrine of the Holy Spirit," p. 35).

John or Paul. The late Professor Smeaton may have overstated the matter in his interesting Cunningham Lectures on "The Doctrine of the Holy Spirit." "We find," he says, "that the doctrine of the Spirit taught by the Baptist, by Christ and by the Apostles, was in every respect the same as that with which the Old Testament church was familiar. We nowhere find that their Jewish hearers on any occasion took exception to it. The teaching of our Lord and His Apostles never called forth a question or an opposition from any quarter—a plain proof that on this question nothing was taught by them which came into collision with the sentiments and opinions which up to that time had been accepted, and still continued to be current among the Jews." Some such change in the conception of God doubtless needs to be recognized as that which Dr. Denney describes in the following words: "The Apostles were all Jews,—men, as it has been said, with monotheism as a passion in their blood.[7] They did not cease to be monotheists when they became preachers of Christ, but they instinctively conceived God in a way in which the old revelation had not taught them to conceive him. . . . Distinctions were recognized in what had once been the bare simplicity of the Divine nature. The distinction of Father and Son was the most obvious, and it was enriched, on the basis of Christ's own teaching, and of the actual experience of the Church, by the further distinction of the Holy Spirit."[8] But if there be any fundamental difference between the Old and the New Testament conceptions of the Spirit of God, it escapes us in our ordinary reading of the Bible, and we naturally and without conscious straining read our New Testament conceptions into the Old Testament passages.

We are, indeed, bidden to do this by the New Testament itself. The New Testament writers identify their "Holy Spirit" with the "Spirit of God" of the older books. All that is attributed to the Spirit of God in the Old Testament, is attributed by them to their personal Holy Ghost. It was their own Holy Ghost who was Israel's guide and director and whom Israel re-

[7] Fairbairn, "Christ in Modern Theology," p. 377.
[8] James Denney, "Studies in Theology," p. 70.

jected when they resisted the leading of God (Acts vii. 51).
It was in Him that Christ (doubtless in the person of Noah)
preached to the antediluvians (I Pet. iii. 18). It was He who
was the author of faith of old as well as now (II Cor. iv. 13).
It was He who gave Israel its ritual service (Heb. ix. 8). It was
He who spoke in and through David and Isaiah and all the
prophets (Matt. xxii. 43, Mark xii. 36, Acts i. 16, xxviii. 25,
Heb. iii. 7, x. 15). If Zechariah (vii. 12) or Nehemiah (ix. 20)
tells us that Jehovah of Hosts sent His word by His Spirit by
the hands of the prophets, Peter tells us that these men from
God were moved by the Holy Ghost to speak these words
(II Pet. i. 21), and even that it was specifically the Spirit of
Christ that was in the prophets (I Pet. i. 11). We are assured
that it was in Jesus upon whom the Holy Ghost had visibly
descended, that Isaiah's predictions were fulfilled that Jehovah
would put His Spirit upon his righteous servant (Isa. xlii. 1)
and that (Isa. lxi. 1) the Spirit of the Lord Jehovah should be
upon Him (Matt. xii. 18, Luke iv. 18, 19). And Peter bids us
look upon the descent of the Holy Spirit at Pentecost as the
accomplished promise of Joel that God would pour out His
Spirit upon all flesh (Joel ii. 27, 28, Acts ii. 16).[9] There can
be no doubt that the New Testament writers identify the Holy
Ghost of the New Testament with the Spirit of God of the Old.

This fact, of course, abundantly justifies the instinctive
Christian identification. We are sure, with the surety of a divine
revelation, that the Spirit of God of the Old Testament is the
personal Holy Spirit of the New. But this assurance does not
forestall the inquiry whether this personal Spirit was so fully
revealed in the Old Testament that those who were dependent
on that revelation alone, without the inspired commentary of
the New, were able to know Him as He is known to us who
enjoy the fuller light. The principle of the progressive delivery
of doctrine in the age-long process of God's self-revelation, is
not only a reasonable one in itself and one which is justified by
the results of investigation, but it is one which is assumed in the

[9] Cf. also the promise of Ezek. xxxvi. 27 and I Thess. iv. 8 (see Toy, "Quotations in the New Testament," p. 202). Cf. also Luke i. 17.

Scriptures themselves as God's method of revealing Himself, and which received the practical endorsement of our Saviour in His manner of communicating His saving truth to men. The question is still an open one, therefore, how much of the doctrine of the Holy Spirit as it lies in its completeness in the pages of the New Testament had already been made the property of the men of the old dispensation; in other words, what the Old Testament doctrine of the Spirit of God is. We may not find this inconsistent with the fuller New Testament teaching, but we may find it fall short of the whole truth revealed in the latter days in God's Son.

The deep unity between the New and Old Testament conceptions lies, in one broad circumstance, so upon the surface of the two Testaments that our attention is attracted to it at the outset of any investigation of the material. In both Testaments the Spirit of God appears distinctly as *the executive of the Godhead.* If in the New Testament God works all that He does by the Spirit, so in the Old Testament the Spirit is the name of God working. The Spirit of God is in the Old Testament the executive name of God—"the divine principle of activity everywhere at work in the world."[10] In this common conception lies doubtless the primary reason why we pass from one Testament to the other without sense of discontinuity in the doctrine of the Spirit. The further extent in which this unity may be traced will depend on the nature of the activities which are ascribed to the Spirit in both Testaments.

The Old Testament does not give us, of course, an exhaustive record of all God's activities. It is primarily an account of God's redemptive work prior to the coming of the Messiah—of the progress, in a word, so far, of the new creation of grace built upon the ruins of the first creation, a short account of which is prefixed as background and basis. In the nature of the case, we learn from the Old Testament of those activities of God

[10] These words are C. F. Schmid's ("Biblical Theology of the New Testament," Div. ii. § 24, p. 145, E. T.). Cf. Smeaton, *op. cit.* p. 36: "Events occurring in the moral government of God are (in the Old Testament) also ascribed to the Spirit as the Executive of all the divine purposes."

only which naturally emerge in these accounts; and accordingly the doctrine of the Spirit of God as the divine principle of activity, as taught in the Old Testament, is necessarily confined to the course of divine activities in the first and the initial stages of the second creation. In other words, it is subsumable under the two broad captions of God in the world, and God in His people. It is from this that the circumstance arises which has been frequently noted, that, after the entrance of sin into the world, the work of the Spirit of God on men's spirits is always set forth in the Old Testament in the interests and in the spirit of the kingdom of God.[11] The Old Testament is concerned after the sin of man only with the recovery of man; it traces the preparatory stages of the kingdom of God, as God laid its foundations in a chosen nation in whom all the nations of the earth were to be blessed. The segregation of Israel and the establishment of the theocracy thus mark the first steps in the new creation; and following this course of divine working, the doctrine of the Spirit in the new creation as taught in the Old Testament naturally concerns especially the activities of God in the establishment and development of the theocracy and in the preparation of a people to enjoy its blessings. In other words, it falls under the two captions of His national, or rather churchly, and of His individual work. Thus the Old Testament teaching concerning the Spirit, brings before us three spheres of His activity, which will correspond broadly to the conceptions of God in the world, God in the theocracy, and God in the soul.

Broadly speaking, these three spheres of the Spirit's activity appear successively in the pages of the Old Testament. In these pages the Spirit of God is introduced to us primarily in His cosmical, next in His theocratic, and lastly in His indi-

---

[11] Kleinert, *op. cit.*, p. 30: "The Old Testament everywhere knows only of an influence of the Divine Spirit upon the human Spirit in the interest and sphere of the Kingdom of God, which is in Israel and is to come through Israel." Hävernick, "Theologie des alten Testaments," p. 77: "Of a communication of the Spirit in the narrower sense, after the entrance of sin, there can be question only in the Theocracy." Oehler, "Biblical Theology of the Old Testament," § 65: "But the Spirit as רוּחַ יְהוָה, or to express it more definitely רוּחַ קֹרֶשׁ יְהוָה only acts within the sphere of revelation. It rules within the Theocracy."

vidual relations.[12] This is, of course, due chiefly to the natural correspondence of the aspects of His activity which are presented with the course of history, and is not to be taken so strictly as to imply that the revelations relative to each sphere of His working occur exclusively in a single portion of the Old Testament. It supplies us, however, not only with the broad outlines of the historical development of the doctrine of the Spirit in the Old Testament, but also with a logical order of presentation for the material. Perhaps we may also say, in passing, that it suggests a course of development of the doctrine of the Spirit which is at once most natural and, indeed, rationally inevitable, and, as Dr. Dale points out,[13] closely correspondent with what have come to be spoken of as the "traditional" dates attributed to the books of the Old Testament. These books, standing as they stand in this dating, are in the most natural order for the development of this doctrine.

THE COSMICAL SPIRIT

I. The Spirit of God is first brought before us in the Old Testament, then, in His relations to the first creation, or in what may be called His cosmical relations. In this connection He is represented as the source of all order, life and light in the universe. He is the divine principle of all movement, of all life and of all thought in the world. The basis of this conception is already firmly laid in the first passage in which the Spirit of God is mentioned (Gen. i. 2). In the beginning, we are told, God created the heavens and the earth. And then the process is detailed by which the created earth, at first waste and void, with darkness resting upon the face of the deep, was transformed by successive fiats into the ordered and populous world in which we live. As the ground of the whole process, we are informed that "the Spirit of God was brooding upon the face

---

[12] For example, in the Pentateuch His working is perhaps exclusively cosmical and theocratic-official, (Oehler, *op. cit.* § 65); while His ethical work in individuals is, throughout the Old Testament, more a matter of prophecy than of present enjoyment (Dale, "Christian Doctrine," p. 317).

[13] Dale, "Christian Doctrine," p. 318. A striking passage both for its presentation of this fact and for its unwillingness to accept its implications.

of the waters," as much as to say that the obedience, and the precedent power of obedience, of the waste of waters to the successive creative words—as God said, Let there be light; Let there be a firmament; Let the waters be gathered together; Let the waters and the earth bring forth—depended upon the fact that the Spirit of God was already brooding upon the formless void. To the voice of God in heaven saying, Let there be light! the energy of the Spirit of God brooding upon the face of the waters responded, and lo! there was light. Over against the transcendent God, above creation, there seems to be postulated here God brooding upon creation, and the suggestion seems to be that it is only by virtue of God brooding upon creation that the created thing moves and acts and works out the will of God. The Spirit of God, in a word, appears at the very opening of the Bible as God immanent; and, as such, is set over against God transcendent. And it is certainly very instructive to observe that God is conceived as immanent already in what may be called the formless world-stuff which by His immanence in it alone it constituted a stuff from which on the divine command an ordered world may emerge.[14] The Spirit of God thus appears from the outset of the Old Testament as the principle of the very existence and persistence of all things, and as the source and originating cause of all movement and order and life. God's thought and will and word take effect in the world, because God is not only over the world, thinking and willing and commanding, but also in the world, as the principle of all activity, *executing*: this seems the thought of the author of the Biblical cosmogony.[15]

[14] Cf. Schultz, "Old Testament Theology," E. T. ii, 184: "Over the lifeless and formless mass of the world-matter this Spirit broods like a bird on its nest, and thus transmits to it the seeds of life, so that afterwards by the word of God it can produce whatever God wills."

[15] Compare some very instructive words as to this account of creation, by the Rev. John Robson, D.D. of Aberdeen (*The Expository Times*, July, 1894, vol. v. No. 10, pp. 467, *sq.*): "The divine agents in creation are brought before us in the opening of the Book of Genesis, and in the opening of the Gospel of John. The object of John in his Gospel is to speak of Jesus Christ, the Word of God; and so he refers only to His agency in the work of creation. The object of Moses in Genesis is to tell the whole divine agency in that work; so in his

A series of Old Testament passages range themselves under this conception and carry it forward. It is by the Spirit of God, says Job, that the heavens are garnished (xxvi. 13). Isaiah compares the coming of the God of vengeance, repaying fury to His adversaries and recompense to His enemies, to the bursting forth "of a pent-in stream which the Spirit of Jehovah driveth" (lix. 19); and represents the perishing of flesh as like the withering of the grass and the fading of the flower when "the Spirit of Jehovah bloweth upon it" (xl. 7). In such passages the Spirit appears as the principle of cosmical processes. He is also the source of all life, and, as such, the executor of Him with whom, as the Psalmist says, is the fountain of life (Ps. xxxvi. 10 [9]). The Psalmist accordingly ascribes the being of all creatures to Him: "Thou sendest forth thy Spirit, they are created" (Ps. civ. 30). "The Spirit of God hath made me," declares Job, "and the breath of the Almighty giveth me life" (xxxiii. 4). Accordingly he represents life to be due to the persistence of the Spirit of God in his nostrils (xxvii. 3), and therefore its continuance to be dependent upon the continuance of the Spirit with man: "If He set His heart upon man, if He gather unto Himself His Spirit and His breath all flesh shall perish together, and man shall turn again unto dust" (xxxiv. 14, 15, cf. xii. 10). He is also the source of all intellectual life. Elihu tells us that it is not greatness, nor years, but the Spirit of God that gives understanding: "There is a Spirit in man, and the breath of the Almighty giveth them understanding" (Job xxxii. 8)—a thought which is probably only expressed in another way in Prov. xx. 27, which declares that the spirit of man is "the lamp

narrative we have the work of the Spirit recognized. But he does not ignore the Word of God; he begins his account of each epoch or each day of creation with the words, 'And God said.' We do not find in Genesis the theological fulness that we do in subsequent writers in the Bible; but we do find in it the elements of all that we subsequently learn or deduce regarding the divine agency in creation. . . . Two agents are mentioned: 'The Spirit of God brooding on the surface of the waters,' and at each new stage of creative development, the Word of God expressed in the words 'God said.' . . . There is thus the Spirit of God present as a constant energy, and there is the Word of God giving form to that energy, and at each new epoch calling new forms into being."

of the Lord, searching all the innermost parts of the belly."
That the Spirit is the source also of all ethical life seems to
follow from the obscure passage, Genesis vi. 3: "And the Lord
said, My Spirit shall not strive with man for ever, for that he
also is flesh." Apparently there is here either a direct threat
from Jehovah to withdraw that Spirit by virtue of which alone
morality could exist in the world, or else a threat that He will,
on account of their sin, withdraw the Spirit whose presence
gives life so that men may no longer be upheld in their wicked
existence, but may sink back into nothingness. In either case
ethical considerations come forward prominently,—the occasion
of the destruction of mankind is an ethical one, and the gift of
life appears as for ethical ends. This, however, is an element in
the conception of the Spirit's work which comes to clear enunciation only in another connection.

It would not be easy to overestimate the importance of the
early emergence of this doctrine of the immanent Spirit of God,
side by side with the high doctrine of the transcendence of God
which pervades the Old Testament. Whatever tendency the
emphasis on the transcendence of God might engender towards
Deistic conceptions would be corrected at once by such teaching as to the immanent Spirit; while in turn any tendencies to
Pantheistic or Cosmotheistic conceptions which it might itself
arouse would be corrected not only by the prevailing stress upon
the divine transcendence, but also by the manner in which the
immanence of God is itself presented. For we cannot sufficiently
admire the perfection with which, in delivering the doctrine of
the immanent Spirit, all possibility is excluded of conceiving
of God as entangled in creation—as if the Spirit of God were
merely the physical world-spirit, the proper ground rather than
effecting cause of cosmical activities. In the very phraseology
of Genesis i. 2, for example, the moving Spirit is kept separate
from the matter to which He gives movement; He *broods over*
rather than is merged in the waste of waters; He acts upon them
and cannot be confounded with them as but another name for
their own blind surging. So in the 104th Psalm (verses 29, 30)
the creative Spirit is *sent forth* by God, and is not merely an

alternative name for the unconscious life-ground of nature. It is a thing which is *given* by God and so produces life (Isa. xlii. 5). Though penetrating all things (Ps. cxxxix. 7) and the immanent source of all life-activities (Ps. civ. 30), it is nevertheless always the *personal* cause of physical, psychical and ethical activities. It exercises choice. It is not merely the *general* ground of all such activities; it is the determiner as well of all the *differences* that exist among men. So, for example, Elihu appeals to the Spirit of understanding that is in him (Job xxxii. 8). It is not merely the ground of the *presence* of these powers; it is also to it that their *withdrawal* is to be ascribed (Isa. xl. 7, Gen. vi. 3). Nor are its manifestations confined altogether to what may be called *natural* modes of action; room is left among them for what we may call truly *supernatural* activity (I Kgs. xviii. 12, II Kgs. ii. 16, cf. II Kgs. xix. 7, Isa. xxxvii. 7). All nature worship is further excluded by the clearness of the identification of the Spirit of God with the God over all. Thus the unity of God was not only preserved but emphasized, and men were taught to look upon the emergence of divine powers and effects in nature as the work of His hands. "Whither shall I go," asks the Psalmist, "from thy Spirit? or whither shall I flee from thy presence" (Ps. cxxxix. 7)? Here the spiritual presence of God is obviously the presence of the God over all in His Spirit. "Who hath . . . meted out heaven with a span? . . . Who hath meted out the Spirit of Jehovah, or being his counsellor hath taught him?" asks Isaiah (xl. 12, 13) in the same spirit. Obviously the Spirit of God was not conceived as the impersonal ground of life and understanding, but as the personal source of all that was of being, life and light in the world, not as apart from but as one with the great God Almighty in the heavens. And yet, as immanent in the world, He is set over against God transcendent in a manner which prepares the way for His hypostatizing and so for the Christian doctrine of the Trinity.

It requires little consideration to realize how greatly the Old Testament conception of God is enriched by this teaching. In particular, it behooves us to note how, side by side with the emphasis that is laid upon God as the maker of all things, this doctrine lays an equal emphasis on God as the upholder and governor of all things. Side by side with the emphasis which is laid on the unapproachable majesty of God as the transcendent Person, it lays an equal emphasis on God as the immanent agent in all world changes and all world movements. It thus lays firmly the foundation of the Christian doctrine of Providence— God in the world and in history, leading all things to their destined goal. If without God there was not anything made that has been made, so without God's Spirit there has not anything occurred that has occurred.

The Theocratic Spirit

II. All this is still further emphasized in the second and pre-dominant aspect in which the Spirit of God is brought before us in the Old Testament, viz., in His relations to the second creation.

1. Here, primarily, He is presented as the source of all the supernatural powers and activities which are directed to the foundation and preservation and development of the kingdom of God in the midst of the wicked world. He is thus represented as the theocratic Spirit as pointedly as He is represented as the world-spirit. We are moving here in a distinctly supernatural atmosphere and the activities which come under review belong to an entirely supernatural order. There are a great variety of these activities, but they have this in common: they are all endowments of the theocratic organs with the gifts requisite for the fulfilment of their functions.[16]

There are, for example, the supernatural gifts of strength,

---

[16] Oehler, "Old Testament Theology," § 65: "But the Spirit as רוּחַ יְהוָה, or to express it more definitely רוּחַ קֹדֶשׁ יְהוָה, only acts within *the sphere of revelation*. It rules within the theocracy (Isa. lxiii. 11, Hag. ii. 5, Neh. ix. 20) but not as if all citizens of the Old Testament Theocracy as such participated in this Spirit, which Moses expresses as a wish (Num. xi. 29), but which is reserved for the future community of salvation (John iii. 1). In the Old Testament the Spirit's work in the divine kingdom is rather that of *endowing the organs of the theocracy with the gifts required for their calling*, and those gifts of office in the Old Testament are similar to the gifts of grace in the New Testament, I Cor. xii. ff."

resolution, energy, courage in battle which were awakened in chosen leaders for the service of God's people. Thus we are told that the Spirit of Jehovah came upon Othniel to fit him for his work as judge of Israel (Judg. iii. 10), and clothed itself with Gideon (vi. 34), and came upon Jephthah (xi. 29), and, most remarkably of all, came mightily upon and moved Samson, endowing him with superhuman strength (xiii. 25, xiv. 6, 19, xv. 14). Similarly the Spirit of God came mightily upon Saul (I Sam. xi. 6) and upon David (I Sam. xvi. 13), and clothed Amasai (I Chron. xii. 18). Then, there are the supernatural gifts of skill by which artificers were fitted to serve the kingdom of God in preparing a worthy sanctuary for the worship of the King. There were, for instance, those whom Jehovah had filled with the spirit of wisdom and who were, therefore, wise-hearted to make Aaron's sacred garments (Ex. xxviii. 3). And especially we are told that Jehovah had filled Bezalel "with the Spirit of God, in wisdom and in understanding, and in knowledge, and in all manner of workmanship, to devise cunning works, to work in gold, and in silver, and in brass, and in cutting of stones for setting, and in carving of wood, to work in all manner of workmanship" (Ex. xxxi. 3 f. cf. xxxv. 31):—and that he should therefore preside over the work of the wise-hearted, in whom the Lord had put wisdom, for the making of the tabernacle and its furniture. Similarly when the temple came to be built, the pattern of it, we are told, was given of Jehovah "by his Spirit" to David (I Chron. xxviii. 12). Quite near to these gifts, but on a higher plane, lies the supernatural gift of wisdom for the administration of judgment and government. Moses was so endowed. And, therefore, the seventy elders were also endowed with it, to fit them to share his cares: "And I will take of the Spirit which is upon thee," said Jehovah, "and will put it upon them; and they shall bear the burden of the people with thee" (Num. xi. 17, 25).[17] It is in this sense also, doubtless, that Joshua

[17] The idea of communicating to others the Spirit already resting on one occurs again in II Kings ii. 9, 15, of the communication of Elijah's Spirit (of Prophecy) to Elisha. Cf. Oehler, "Biblical Theology of the Old Testament," § 65.

is said to have been full of the Spirit of wisdom (Num. xxvii. 18, Deut. xxxiv. 9).[18] In these aspects, the gift of the Spirit, appearing as it does as an endowment for office, is sometimes sacramentally connected with symbols of conference: in the case of Joshua with the laying on of hands (Deut. xxxiv. 9), in the cases of Saul and David with anointing (I Sam. x. 1, xvi. 13). Possibly its symbolical connection in Samson's case with Nazaritic length of hair may be classed in the same general category.

Prominent above all other theocratic gifts of the Spirit, however, are the gifts of supernatural knowledge and insight, culminating in the great gift of Prophecy. This greatest of gifts in the service of the Kingdom of God is sometimes very closely connected with the other gifts which have been mentioned. Thus the presence of the Spirit in the seventy elders in the wilderness, endowing them to share the burden of judgment with Moses, was manifested by prophetic utterance (Num. xi. 25). The descent of the Spirit upon Saul was likewise manifested by his prophesying (I Sam. x. 6, 10). Sometimes the Spirit's presence in the prophet even manifests itself in the production in others of what may be called sympathetic prophecy accompanied with ecstasy. Instances occur in the cases of the messengers sent by Saul and of Saul himself, when they went to apprehend David (I Sam. xix. 20, 23); and in these cases the phenomenon served the ulterior purpose of a protection for the prophets.[19] In the visions of Ezekiel the presence of the inspiring Spirit is manifested in physical as well as in mental effects (Ezek. iii. 12, 14, 24, viii. 3, xi. 1, 5, 24, xxxvii. 1). Thus clear it is that all these are the work of one and the same Spirit.

In all cases, however, Prophecy is the free gift of the Spirit of God to special organs chosen for the purpose of the revelation of His will. It is so represented in the cases of Balaam (Num. xxiv. 2), of Saul (I Sam. x. 6), of David (I Sam. xvi. 13), of Azariah the son of Oded (II Chron. xv. 1), of Jahaziel

---

[18] Cf. the prayer and endowment of Solomon, in I Kgs. iii.

[19] Compare the cases of the communication of the Spirit, in a different way, in Num. xi. 17, 25, 26 and II Kgs. ii. 9, 15—already mentioned.

the son of Zechariah (II Chron. xx. 14), of Zechariah the son
of Jehoiada (II Chron. xxiv. 20). To Hosea, "the man that hath
the Spirit" was a synonym for "prophet" (ix. 7). Isaiah (xlviii.
16) in a somewhat puzzling sentence declares, "The Lord God
hath sent me and His Spirit," which seems to conjoin the Spirit
either with Jehovah as the source of the mission, or else with
the prophet as the bearer of the message; and, in either case,
refers the prophetic inspiration to the Spirit. A very full insight
into the nature of the Spirit's work in prophetic inspiration is
provided by the details which Ezekiel gives of the Spirit's mode
of dealing with him in communicating his visions. While the
richness of the prophetic endowment is indicated to us by
Micah (iii. 8): "But I truly am full of power by the Spirit of
the Lord, and of judgment, and of might, to declare unto Jacob
his transgression, and to Israel his sin." There are, however,
two passages that speak quite generally of the whole body of
prophets as Spirit-led men, which, in their brief explicitness,
deserve to be called the classical passages as to prophetic inspiration. In one of these,—the great psalm-prayer of the Levites
recorded in the ninth chapter of Nehemiah,—God is first lauded
for "giving His good Spirit to instruct" His people, by the mouth
of Moses; and then further praised for enduring this people
through so many years and "testifying against them by His
Spirit through His prophets" (Neh. ix. 20, 30). Here the prophets are conceived as a body of official messengers, through
whom the Spirit of God made known His will to His people
through all the ages. In exactly similar wise, Zechariah testifies
that the Lord of Hosts had sent His words "by His Spirit by
the hand of the former prophets" (Zech. vii. 12). These are
quite comprehensive statements. They include the whole series
of the prophets, and they represent them as the official mouth-
pieces of the Spirit of God, serving the people of God as His
organs.[20]

[20] In such passages as Gen. xli. 38, Dan. iv. 8, ix. 18 and v. 11, 14, we have
"the Spirit of the Gods" as the equivalent of "the Spirit of God" on the lips of
heathen.

It is sufficiently clear that an official character attaches to all the manifestations of what we have called the theocratic Spirit. The theocratic Spirit appears to be represented as the executive of the Godhead within the sacred nation, the divine power working in the nation for the protection, governing, instruction and leading of the people to its destined goal. The Levitic prayer in the ninth chapter of Nehemiah traces the history of God's people with great fulness; and all through this history represents God as not only looking down from heaven upon His people, leading them, but, as it were, working within them, inspiring organs for their government and instruction,— "clothing Himself with these" organs as the media of His working, as the expressive Hebrew sometimes suggests (Judges vi. 34, I Chron. xii. 18, II Chron. xxiv. 20). The aspect in which the theocratic Spirit seems to be conceived is as God in His people, manifesting Himself through inspired instruments in supernatural leading and teaching. Very illuminating as to the mode of His working are the instructions given to Zerubbabel through the prophets Zechariah and Haggai. He—and, with him, all the people of the land—is counseled to be strong and of good courage, "for I am with you, saith the Lord of Hosts, according to the word that I covenanted with you when you came out of Egypt, and my Spirit abideth among you: fear ye not" (Hag. ii. 5). "This is the word of the Lord unto Zerubbabel, saying, Not by might, nor by power, but by my Spirit, saith the Lord of Hosts" (Zech. iv. 6). The mountains of opposition are to be reduced to a plain; but not by armed force. The symbol of the source of strength is the seven lamps burning brightly by virtue of perennial supplies from the living olives growing by their side; thus, by a hidden, divine supply of deathless life, the Church of God lives and prospers in the world. Not indeed as if God so inhabited Israel, that all that the house of Israel does is of the Lord. "Shall it be said, O house of Israel, Is the Spirit of the Lord straitened?—are these his doings? Do not my words do good to him that walketh uprightly?" (Micah ii. 7). The gift of the Spirit is only for good.

But there is very clearly brought before us here the fact and the mode of God's official inspiration. The theocratic Spirit represents, in a word, the presence of God with His people. And in the Old Testament teaching concerning it, is firmly laid the foundation of the Christian doctrine of God in the Church, leading and guiding it, and supplying it with all needed instruction, powers and graces for its preservation in the world.

We must not omit to observe that in this higher sphere of the theocratic Spirit, the freedom and, so to speak, detachment of the informing Spirit is even more thoroughly guarded than in the case of His cosmical relations. If in the lower sphere the Spirit hovered over rather than was submerged in matter, so here He acts upon His chosen organs in the same sense from without, so that it is impossible to confound His official gifts with their native powers, however exalted. The Spirit here, too, is given by God (Num. xi. 29, Isa. xlii. 1). God puts it on men or fills men with it (Num. xi. 25, Ex. xxviii. 3, xxxi. 3); or the Spirit comes (Judg. iii. 10, xi. 29), comes mightily (xiv. 6, 19, etc., I Sam. xi. 6) upon men, falls on them (Ezek. xi. 5), breaks in upon them, seizes them violently, as it were, and puts them on as a garment (Judg. vi. 34). And this is no less true of the prophets than of the other organs of the Spirit's theocratic work: they are all the instruments of a mighty power, which, though in one sense it is conceived as the endowment of the theocratic people, in another sense is conceived as seizing upon its organs from without and above. And "because it is thus fundamentally a power seizing man powerfully, often violently," it is often replaced by the locution, "the hand of Jehovah,"[21] which is, in this usage, the equivalent of the Spirit of Jehovah (II Kgs. iii. 15, Ezek. i. 3, iii. 14, 22, xxxiii. 22, xxxvii. 1, xl. 1). The intermittent character of the theocratic gifts still further emphasized their gift by a personal Spirit working purposively. They were not permanent possessions of the theocratic organs, to be used according to their own will, but came and went according

21 Cf. Orelli, "The Old Testament Prophecy," etc., E. T. p. 11, and also Oehler, "Biblical Theology of Old Testament," § 65 *ad fin.*

to the divine gift.[22] The theocratic gifts of the Spirit are, in a word, everywhere emphatically gifts *from* God as well as *of* God; and every tendency to conceive of them as formally the result of a general inspiration of the nation instead of a special inspiration of the chosen organs is rebuked by every allusion to them. God working in and through man, by whatever variety of inspiration, works divinely and from above. He is no more merged in His church than in the creation, but is, in all His operations alike, the free, transcendent Spirit, dividing to each man severally as He will.

The representations concerning the official theocratic Spirit culminate in Isaiah's prophetic descriptions of the Spirit-endowed Messiah:

"And there shall come forth a shoot out of the stock of Jesse, and a branch out of his roots shall bear fruit: and the Spirit of the Lord shall rest upon him, the Spirit of wisdom and understanding, the Spirit of counsel and might, the Spirit of knowledge and of the fear of the Lord; and his delight shall be in the fear of the Lord: and he shall not judge after the sight of his eyes, neither reprove after the hearing of his ears: but with righteousness shall he judge the poor, and reprove with equity for the meek of the earth: and he shall smite the earth with the rod of his mouth, and with the breath of his lips shall he slay the wicked. And righteousness shall be the girdle of his loins, and faithfulness the girdle of his reins" (Isa. xi. 1 *sq.*).

"Behold my servant whom I uphold; my chosen in whom my soul delighteth: I have put my Spirit upon him; he shall bring forth judgment to the Gentiles. . . . He shall bring forth judgment in truth. He shall not fail nor be discouraged, till he have set judgment in the earth; and the isles shall wait for his law. Thus saith God the Lord, he that created the heavens, and stretched them forth; he that spread abroad the earth and that which cometh out of it; he that giveth breath unto the people upon it and Spirit to them that walk therein;

---

[22] Cf. A. B. Davidson (*The Expositor*, July, 1895, p. 1): "The view that prevailed among the people—and it seems the view of the Old Testament writers themselves—appears to have been this: the prophet did not speak out of a general inspiration of Jehovah, bestowed upon him once for all, as, say, at his call; each particular word that he spoke, whether a prediction or a practical counsel, was due to a special inspiration, exerted on him for the occasion." The statement might well have been stronger.

I the LORD have called thee in righteousness, and will hold thine hand and will keep thee, and give thee for a covenant of the people, for a light of the Gentiles; to open the blind eyes, to bring out the prisoners from the dungeon, and them that sit in darkness out of the prison-house. I am the Lord: that is my name: and my glory will I not give to another, neither my praise unto graven images" (Isa. xlii. 1 *sq.*).

"The Spirit of the Lord God is upon me"—this is the response of the Messiah to such gracious promises—"because the Lord hath anointed me to preach good-tidings unto the meek; he hath sent me to bind up the broken hearted, to proclaim liberty to the captives, and the opening of the prison to them that are bound; to proclaim the acceptable year of the Lord, and the day of vengeance of our God; to comfort all that mourn; to appoint unto them that mourn in Zion, to give unto them a garland for ashes, the oil of gladness for mourning, the garment of praise for the spirit of heaviness; that they might be called trees of righteousness, the planting of the Lord, that he might be glorified" (Isa. lxi. 1 *sq.*).

No one will fail to observe in these beautiful descriptions of the endowments of the Messiah, how all the theocratic endowments which had been given separately to others unite upon Him; so that all previous organs of the Spirit appear but as partial types of Him to whom as we are told in the New Testament, God "giveth not the Spirit by measure" (John iii. 34). Here we perceive the difference between the Messiah and other recipients of the Spirit. To them the Spirit had been "meted out" (Isa. xl. 13), according to their place and function in the development of the kingdom of God; upon Him it was poured out without measure. By Him, accordingly, the kingdom of God is consummated. The descriptions of the spiritual endowments of the Messiah are descriptions also, as will no doubt have been noted, of the consummated kingdom of God. His endowment also was not for himself but for the kingdom; it, too, was official. Nevertheless, it was the source in Him of all personal graces also, the opulence and perfection of which are fully described. And thus He becomes the type not only of the theocratic work of the Spirit, but also of His work upon the individual soul, perfecting it after the image of God.

THE INDIVIDUAL SPIRIT

2. And this brings us naturally to the second aspect in which the Spirit is presented to us in relation to the new creation—His relation to the individual soul, working inwardly in the spirits of men, fitting the children of God for the kingdom of God, even as, working in the nation as such, He, as theocratic Spirit, was preparing God's kingdom for His people. In this aspect He appears specifically as the Spirit of grace. As He is the source of all cosmical life, and of all theocratic life, so is He also the source of all spiritual life. He upholds the soul in being and governs it as part of the great world He has created; He makes it sharer in the theocratic blessings which He brings to His people; but He deals with it, too, within, conforming it to its ideal. In a word, the Spirit of God, in the Old Testament, is not merely the immanent Spirit, the source of all the world's life and all the world's movement; and not merely the inspiring Spirit, the source of His church's strength and safety and of its development in accordance with its special mission; He is as well the indwelling Spirit of holiness in the hearts of God's children. As Hermann Schultz puts it: "The mysterious impulses which enable a man to lead a life well-pleasing to God, are not regarded as a development of human environment, but are nothing else than 'the Spirit of God,' which is also called as being the Spirit peculiarly God's—His Holy Spirit."[23]

We have already had occasion to note that these personal effects of the Spirit's work are sometimes very closely connected with others of His operations. Already as the immanent Spirit of life, indeed, as we saw, there did not lack a connection of His activity with ethical considerations (Gen. vi. 3). We will remember, too, that Nehemiah recalls the goodness—*i.e.*, possibly the graciousness—of the Spirit, when He came to instruct Israel in the person of Moses in the wilderness: "Thou gavest

[23] *Op. cit.* ii, p. 203. The passage is cited for its main idea: we demur, of course, to some of its implications.

also thy good Spirit to instruct them" (Neh. ix. 20).[24] When the Spirit came upon Saul, endowing him for his theocratic work, it is represented as having also a very far-reaching personal effect upon him. "The Spirit of the Lord will come mightly upon thee," says Samuel, "and thou shalt prophesy with them, and shalt be turned into another man" (I Sam. x. 6). "And it was so," adds the narrative, "that when he had turned his back to go from Samuel, God gave him a new heart," or, as the Hebrew has it, "turned him a new heart." Possibly such revolutionary ethical consequences ordinarily attended the official gift of the Spirit, so that the gloss may be a true one which makes II Peter i. 21 declare that they were "holy men of God" who spake as they were moved by the Holy Ghost.[25]

At all events this conception of a thorough ethical change characterises the Old Testament idea of the inner work of the Spirit of Holiness, as He first comes to be called in the Psalms and Isaiah (Ps. li. 11; Isa. lxiii. 10, 11 only).[26] The classical passage in this connection is the Fifty-first Psalm—David's cry of penitence and prayer for mercy after Nathan's probing of his sin with Bathsheba. He prays for the creation within him of a new heart and the renewal of a right spirit within him; and he represents that all his hopes of continued power of new life rest on the continuance of God's holy Spirit, or of the Spirit

24 In Num. xiv. 24 we are told that Caleb followed the Lord fully, "because he had another spirit in him," from that which animated his rebellious fellows. Possibly the Spirit of the Lord may be intended.

25 Exceptions are found, of course; such as the cases of Balaam, Samson, etc. Cf. H. G. Mitchell, "Inspiration in the Old Testament," in Christian Thought for December 1893, p. 190.

26 Cf. F. H. Woods, in The Expository Times, July, 1895, pp. 462-463: "It may be extremely difficult to say what was the precise meaning which prophet or psalmist attached to the phrases, 'the Spirit of God' and 'the Spirit of Holiness.' But such language, at any rate, shows that they realised the divine character of that inward power which makes for holiness and truth. 'Cast me not away from Thy presence, and take not the Spirit of Thy holiness from me' (Ps. li. 11). 'And now the Lord God hath sent me, and His Spirit' (Isa. xlviii. 16). 'Not by might, nor by power, but by My Spirit, saith Jehovah of Hosts' (Zech. iv. 6). In such passages as these we can see the germ of the fuller Christian thought."

of God's holiness, with him. Possibly the Spirit is here called holy, primarily, because He is one who cannot dwell in a wicked heart; but it seems also to be implicated that David looks upon Him as the author within him of that holiness without which he cannot hope to see the Lord. A like conception meets us in another Psalm ascribed to David, the One Hundred and Forty-third "Teach me to do thy will; for thou art my God: thy Spirit is good; lead me in the land of uprightness." The two conceptions of the divine grace and holiness are also combined by Isaiah in an account of how Israel had been, since the days of Moses, dealing ungratefully with God, and, by their rebellion, grieving "the Holy Spirit whom He had graciously put in the midst of them" (Isa. lxiii. 10, 11).[27] The conception may primarily be that the Spirit given to guide Israel was a Spirit of holiness in the sense that He could not brook sin in those with whom He dealt, but the conception that He would guide them in ways of holiness underlies that.

This aspect of the work of the Spirit of God is most richly developed, however, in prophecies of the future. In the Messianic times, Isaiah tells us, the Spirit shall be poured out from on high with the effect that judgment shall dwell in the wilderness and righteousness shall abide in the peaceful field (Isa. xxxii. 15). It is in such descriptions of the Messianic era as a time of the reign of the Spirit in the hearts of the people, that the opulence of His saving influences is developed. It is He who shall gather the children of God into the kingdom, so that no one shall be missing (Isa. xxxiv. 16). It is He who, as the source of all blessings, shall be poured out on the seed with the result that it shall spring up in the luxuriant growth and bear such rich fruitage that one shall cry 'I am the Lord's,' and another shall call himself by the name of Jacob, and another shall write on his hand, 'Unto the Lord,' and shall surname himself by the name of Israel (Isa. xliv. 3 *sq.*). It is His abiding presence which constitutes the preëminent blessing of the new covenant which Jehovah makes with His people in the day of

[27] Cf. Psalm cvi. 13.

redemption: "And as for me, this is my covenant with them, saith the Lord: my Spirit that is upon thee, and my words which I have put in thy mouth, shall not depart out of thy mouth, nor out of the mouth of thy seed, nor out of the mouth of thy seed's seed, saith the Lord, from henceforth and for ever" (Isa. lix. 21). The gift of the Spirit as an abiding presence in the heart of the individual is the crowning Messianic blessing. To precisely the same effect is the teaching of Ezekiel. The new heart and new spirit is one of the burdens of his message (xi. 19, xviii. 31, xxxvi. 26): and these are the Messianic gifts of God to His people through the Spirit. God's people are dead; but He will open their graves and cause them to come up out of their graves: "And I will put my Spirit in you, and ye shall live" (xxxvii. 14). They are in captivity; he will bring them out of captivity: "Neither will I hide my face any more from them: for I have poured out my Spirit upon the house of Israel, saith the Lord God" (xxxix. 29). Like promises appear in Zechariah: "And I will pour upon the house of David, and upon the inhabitants of Jerusalem, the Spirit of grace and supplication; and they shall look upon me whom they have pierced" (xii. 10). It is the converting Spirit of God that is spoken of. One thing only is left to complete the picture,—the clear declaration that, in these coming days of blessing, the Spirit hitherto given only to Israel shall be poured out upon the whole world. This Joel gives us in that wonderful passage which is applied by Peter to the out-pouring begun at Pentecost: "And it shall come to pass afterward," says the Lord God through His prophet, "that I will pour out my Spirit upon all flesh; . . . and also upon the servants and upon the handmaids in those days will I pour out my Spirit. . . . And it shall come to pass, that whosoever shall call on the name of the Lord shall be delivered" (ii. 28-32).

In this series of passages, the indwelling Spirit of the New Testament is obviously brought before us—the indwelling God, author of all holiness and of all salvation. Thus there are firmly laid by them the foundations of the Christian doctrine of Regeneration and Sanctification,—of God in the soul quickening its powers of spiritual life and developing it in holiness. Nor can it be a ground of wonder that this aspect of His work is less frequently dwelt upon than His theocratic activities; nor that it is chiefly in prophecies of the future that the richer references to it occur.[28] This was the time of theocratic development; the old dispensation was a time of preparation for the fulness of spiritual graces. It is rather a ground of wonder that even in few and scattered hints and in prophecies of the times of the Spirit yet to come, such a deep and thorough grasp upon His individual work should be exhibited.

By its presentation of this work of the Spirit in the heart, the Old Testament completes its conception of the Spirit of God—the great conception of the inmanent, inspiring, indwelling God. In it the three great ideas are thrown prominently forward, of God in the world, God in the Church, God in the soul: the God of Providence, the immanent source of all that comes to pass, the director and governor of the world of matter and spirit alike; the God of the Church, the inspiring source of all Church life and of all Church gifts, through which the Church is instructed, governed, preserved and extended; and the God of grace, the indwelling source of all holiness and of all religious aspirations, emotions and activities. Attention has already been called to the great enrichment which was brought to the general conception of God by this doctrine of the Spirit of God in its first aspect. The additional aspects in which He is presented in the pages of the Old Testament of course still further enrich and elevate the conception. By throwing a still stronger emphasis on the personality of the Spirit they made even wider the great gulf that already yawned between all Pantheising notions and the Biblical doctrine of the Personal God, the immanent source of all that comes to pass. And they bring out with great force and clearness the conceptions of grace and holiness as inherent in the idea of God working, and thus operate to deepen the ethical conception of the Divine Being. It is only as a personal, choosing, gracious and holy God,

[28] See such wonder, nevertheless, expressed by Dr. Dale, in a striking passage in his "Christian Doctrine," p. 317.

who bears His people on His heart for good, and who seeks to conform them in life and character to His own holiness—that we can conceive the God of the Old Testament, if we will attend to its doctrine of the Spirit. Thus the fundamental unity of the conception with that of the Holy Ghost of the New Testament grows ever more obvious, the more attentively it is considered. The Spirit of God of the Old Testament performs all the functions which are ascribed to the Holy Ghost of the New Testament, and bears all the same characteristics. They are conceived alike both in their nature and in their operations. We cannot help identifying them.

Such an identification need not involve, however, the assertion that the Spirit of God was conceived in the Old Testament as the Holy Ghost is in the New, as a distinct hypostasis in the divine nature. Whether this be so, or, if so in some measure, how far it may be true, is a matter for separate investigation. The Spirit of God certainly acts as a person and is presented to us as a person, throughout the Old Testament. In no passage is He conceived otherwise than personally—as a free, willing, intelligent being. This is, however, in itself only the pervasive testimony of the Scriptures to the personality of God. For it is equally true that the Spirit of God is everywhere in the Old Testament identified with God. This is only its pervasive testimony to the divine unity. The question for examination is, how far the one personal God was conceived of as embracing in His unity hypostatical distinctions. This question is a very complicated one and needs very delicate treatment. There are, indeed, three questions included in the general one, which for the sake of clearness we ought to keep apart. We may ask, May the Christian properly see in the Spirit of God of the Old Testament the personal Holy Spirit of the New? This we may answer at once in the affirmative. We may ask again, Are there any hints in the Old Testament anticipating and adumbrating the revelation of the hypostatic Spirit of the New? This also, it seems, we ought to answer in the affirmative. We may ask again, Are these hints of such clearness as actually to reveal this doctrine, apart from the revelation of the New Testament? This should be doubtless answered in the negative. There are hints, and they serve for points of attachment for the fuller New Testament teaching. But they are only hints, and, apart from the New Testament teaching, would be readily explained as personifications or ideal objectivations of the power of God. Undoubtedly, side by side with the stress put upon the unity of God and the identity of the Spirit with the God who gives it, there is a distinction recognized between God and His Spirit—in the sense at least of a discrimination between God over all and God in all, between the Giver and the Given, between the Source and the Executor of the moral law. This distinction already emerges in Genesis i. 2; and it does not grow less observable as we advance through the Old Testament. It is prominent in the standing phrases by which, on the one hand, God is spoken of as sending, putting, placing, pouring, emptying His Spirit upon man, and on the other the Spirit is spoken of as coming, resting, falling, springing upon man. There is a sort of objectifying of the Spirit over against God in both cases; in the former case, by sending Him from Himself God, as it were, separates Him from Himself; in the latter, He appears almost as a distinct person, acting *sua sponte*. Schultz does not hesitate to speak of the Spirit even in Genesis i. 2 as appearing "as very independent, just like a hypostasis or person."[29] Kleinert finds in this passage at least a tendency towards hypostatizing—though he thinks this tendency was not subsequently worked out.[30] Perhaps we are warranted in saying as much as this—that there is observable in the Old Testament, not, indeed, an hypostatizing of the Spirit of God, but a tendency towards it—that, in Hofmann's cautious language, the Spirit appears in the Old Testament "as somewhat distinct from the 'I' of God which God makes the principle of life in the world."[31] A preparation, at least, for the full revelation of the

[29] *Op. cit.* ii. p. 184.
[30] *Op. cit.* pp. 55-56.
[31] "Schriftbeweis," i. p. 187.

Trinity in the New Testament is observable;[32] points of connection with it are discoverable; and so Christians are able to read the Old Testament without offence, and to find without confusion their own Holy Spirit in its Spirit of God.[33]

More than this could scarcely be looked for. The elements in the doctrine of God which above all others needed emphasis in Old Testament times were naturally His unity and His personality. The great thing to be taught the ancient people of God was that the God of all the earth is one person. Over against the varying idolatries about them, this was the truth of truths for which Israel was primarily to stand; and not until this great truth was ineffaceably stamped upon their souls could the personal distinctions in the Triune-God be safely made known to them. A premature revelation of the Spirit as a distinct hypostasis could have wrought nothing but harm to the people of God. We shall all no doubt agree with Kleinert[34] that it is pragmatic in Isidore of Pelusium to say that Moses knew the doctrine of the Trinity well enough, but concealed it through fear that Polytheism would profit by it. But we may

[32] Cf. Oehler, op. cit. § 65, note 5. He looks on Isa. xliii. 16 as implying personality and reminds us that the Old Testament prepared the way for the economic Trinity of the new. Cf. also Dale, "Christian Doctrine," p. 317.

[33] Cf. Dr. Hodge's admirable summary statement: "Even in the first chapter of Genesis, the Spirit of God is represented as the source of all intelligence, order and life in the created universe; and in the following books of the Old Testament He is represented as inspiring the prophets, giving wisdom, strength and goodness to statesmen and warriors, and to the people of God. This Spirit is not an agency but an agent, who teaches and selects; who can be sinned against and grieved; and who in the New Testament is unmistakably revealed as a distinct person. When John the Baptist appeared, we find him speaking of the Holy Spirit as of a person with whom his countrymen were familiar, as an object of Divine worship and the giver of saving blessings. Our divine Lord also takes this truth for granted, and promised to send the Spirit as a Paraclete, to take his place, to instruct, comfort and strengthen them; whom they were to receive and obey. Thus, without any violent transition, the earliest revelations of this mystery were gradually unfolded, until the Triune God, Father, Son and Spirit, appears in the New Testament as the universally recognized God of all believers" (Charles Hodge, "Systematic Theology," i. p. 447).

[34] Op. cit. p. 56.

safely affirm this of God the Revealer, in the gradual delivery of the truth concerning Himself to men. He reveals the whole truth, but in divers portions and in divers manners: and it was incident to the progressive delivery of doctrine that the unity of the Godhead should first be made the firm possession of men, and the Trinity in that unity should be unveiled to them only afterwards, when the times were ripe for it. What we need wonder over is not that the hypostatical distinctness of the Spirit is not more clearly revealed in the Old Testament but that the approaches to it are laid so skillfully that the doctrine of the hypostatical Holy Spirit of the New Testament finds so many and such striking points of attachment in the Old Testament, and yet no Israelite had ever been disturbed in repeating with hearty faith his great Sch'ma, "Hear O Israel, the Lord our God is one Lord" (Deut. vi. 4). Not until the whole doctrine of the Trinity was ready to be manifested in such visible form as at the baptism of Christ—God in heaven, God on earth and God descending from heaven to earth—could any part of the mystery be safely uncovered.

There yet remains an important query which we cannot pass wholly by. We have seen the rich development of the doctrine of the Spirit in the Old Testament. We have seen the testimony the Old Testament bears to the activity of the Spirit of God throughout the old dispensation. What then is meant by calling the new dispensation the dispensation of the Spirit? What does John (vii. 39) means by saying that the Spirit was not yet given because Jesus was not yet glorified? What our Lord Himself, when He promised the Comforter, by saying that the Comforter would not come until He went away and sent Him (John xvi. 7); and by breathing on His disciples, saying, "Receive ye the Holy Spirit" (John xx. 22)? What did the descent of the Spirit at Pentecost mean, when He came to inaugurate the dispensation of the Spirit? It cannot be meant that the Spirit was not active in the old dispensation. We have already seen that the New Testament writers themselves represent Him to have been active in the old dispensation in all the varieties of activity with which He is active in the new.

Such passages seem to have diverse references. Some of them may refer to the specifically miraculous endowments which characterized the apostles and the churches which they founded.[35] Others refer to the world-wide mission of the Spirit, promised, indeed, in the Old Testament, but only now to be realized. But there is a more fundamental idea to be reckoned with still. This is the idea of the preparatory nature of the Old Testament dispensation. The old dispensation was a preparatory one and must be strictly conceived as such. What spiritual blessings came to it were by way of prelibation.[36] They were many and various. The Spirit worked in Providence no less universally then than now. He abode in the Church not less really then than now. He wrought in the hearts of God's people not less prevalently then than now. All the good that was in the world was then as now due to Him. All the hope of God's Church then as now depended on Him. Every grace of the godly life then as now was a fruit of His working. But the object of the whole dispensation was only to prepare for the outpouring of the Spirit upon all flesh. He kept the remnant safe and pure; but it was primarily only in order that the seed might be preserved. This was the fundamental end of His activity, then. The dispensation of the Spirit, properly so-called, did not dawn until the period of preparation was over and the day of out pouring had come. The mustard seed had been preserved through all the ages only by the Spirit's brooding care. Now it is planted, and it is by His operation that it is growing up into a great tree which shades the whole earth, and to the branches of which all the fowls of heaven come for shelter. It is

[35] Cf. Redford, "Vox. Dei.," p. 236.

[36] Smeaton (*Op. cit.* p. 49) comments on John vii. 37 *sq.* thus: "But the apostle adds that 'the Spirit was not yet' because Christ's glorification had not yet arrived. He does not mean that the Spirit did not yet exist—for all Scripture attests His eternal preëxistence—nor that His regenerative efficacy was still unknown—for countless millions had been regenerated by His power since the first promise in Eden—but that these operations of the Spirit had been but an anticipation of the atoning gift of Christ rather than a GIVING. The apostle speaks comparatively, not absolutely." Compare further the eloquent words on page 53 with the quotation there from Goodwin.

not that His work is more real in the new dispensation than in the old. It is not merely that it is more universal. It is that it is directed to a different end—that it is no longer for the mere preserving of the seed unto the day of planting, but for the perfecting of the fruitage and the gathering of the harvest. The Church, to use a figure of Isaiah's, was then like a pent-in stream; it is now like that pent-in stream with the barriers broken down and the Spirit of the Lord driving it. It was He who preserved it in being when it was pent in. It is He who is now driving on its gathered floods till it shall cover the earth as the waters cover the sea. In one word, that was a day in which the Spirit restrained His power. Now the great day of the Spirit is come.

CHAPTER VI

THE SUPERNATURAL BIRTH OF JESUS[1]

I HAVE promised the editors of the *American Journal of Theology* to indicate to their readers the answer I think must be given to the question, "Is the doctrine of the supernatural birth of Jesus essential to Christianity?" In addressing myself to fulfil this promise, however, I find myself laboring under a good deal of embarrassment. I am naturally embarrassed, for example, by the narrowness of the space at my disposal. Within the limits allowed me, I can hope to do nothing more than suggest a few of the considerations which weigh with me, and these only in the most cursory manner. I am much more embarrassed, however, by the infelicity of discussing the relation to Christianity, considered as a system of doctrine (that is to say, as a consistent body of truth), of a fact, the historicity of which I am to leave to others to discuss, who may perhaps reach conclusions to which I could by no means assent, whether in kind or merely in degree. I can only say that I have myself no doubt whatever of the fact of the supernatural birth of Jesus, as that fact is recorded in the opening chapters of the gospels of Matthew and Luke. I certainly make no question that additional evidence of tremendous weight is brought to this fact by its place in the system of Christianity, commended as this system as a whole is by the entire body of proof which we call the "Christian evidences." But I do not believe that it needs this additional evidence for its establishment. And I prefer my readers to understand that I proceed to the consideration of its place in the Christian system with it in my hands, not as a hypothesis of more or less probability (or improbability), but as a duly authenticated actual occurrence, recognized as such

[1] From *The American Journal of Theology*, x. 1906, pp. 21-30; also from *Christology and Criticism*, pp. 447-458.

on its own direct evidence, and bringing as such its own quota of support to the Christian system of which it forms a part.

I am embarrassed most of all, however, by the ambiguity of the language in which the question I am to discuss is stated. What is "the doctrine of the supernatural birth of Jesus"? What exactly, indeed, is intended by the main term employed? What is a "supernatural birth"? Were the births of Isaac and of John the Baptist "supernatural births"? Or those of Samson and of Samuel? Or those of Jeremiah and of Paul, whom, we are told, the Lord had selected for his own in or from the womb? Is not, indeed, the birth of every good man whom God prepares for some special work for him—certainly by influences beginning in the loins of his ancestors—in some sense supernatural? Nay, no one who believes in Providence can doubt that there is a supernatural element in the birth of every man that comes into the world. It may easily come about, therefore, that one may be found contending earnestly that the "supernatural birth" of Jesus is essential to Christianity, and yet sharply denying that that birth was "supernatural" in the only sense in which it is important to contend for its supernaturalness. What sense, further, we need to ask, is to be attached to the word "essential" here? Is the inquiry, perchance, whether the supernatural birth of Jesus constitutes the very essence of Christianity, so that in this doctrine Christianity is summed up? Or merely whether it enters so into the substance of Christianity that Christianity is not fully stated without it? The crowning ambiguity attaches, however, to the term "Christianity" itself. Is it to be taken subjectively or objectively? Are we asking whether it is possible for a man to commit his soul to Christ as his Savior without a clear knowledge and firm conviction of his Lord's virgin birth? Or are we asking whether any statement of Christianity can be thought complete which omits or ignores this doctrine? Or if it be supposed that this question is already settled by the use of the word "doctrine," we still have to ask what objective "Christianity" it is that we are to have in mind? The Christianity of the New Testament, or of some fragment of the New Testament, arbitrarily torn from its context and interpreted in isolation?

The Christianity of the churches—the historical Christianity embodied in the authoritative creeds of Christendom; or the Christianity of a certain school of recent critical speculations—the Christianity of Auguste Sabatier, say, or of Paul Lobstein, or of Otto Pfleiderer, or of Adolf Harnack?

Were the inquiry a purely historical one, it might no doubt be soon settled. It admits of no doubt, for example, that, historically speaking, the "supernatural birth of Jesus" forms a substantial element in the Christianity as well of the New Testament, taken in its entirety, as of the creeds of the church. There it stands plainly written in both, and even he who runs may read it.[2] Of course, it does not stand written on every page of the New Testament or of the creeds—why should it? And, of course, it may be thought a debatable question whether it has been logically or practically as important to historical Christianity as its prominent confession in the documents might seem to imply.[3] That it holds no essential place in much of the "Christianity" current at the opening of the twentieth century is certainly too obvious for discussion. To the late Auguste Sabatier, for example, "Christianity" had come to mean just the altruistic temper; and nobody will imagine the "supernatural birth of Jesus"—or any kind of birth of Jesus, for that matter, natural or supernatural or unnatural—essential to the altruistic temper. Must not much the same be said also of the "Christianity" of Otto Pfleiderer, or of any form of that at present very fashionable "Christianity" which supposes the parable of the Prodigal Son, say, to contain a complete statement of the Christian religion? As there is no atonement, and no expiation, and no satisfaction, so there is no mediator, no Jesus of any kind

[2] "The church assigns the highest value to the doctrine of the virgin birth" (Schmiedel, "Encyclopaedia Biblica," col. 2964). It is "a constant and, we may truly say, universally recognized element in the doctrinal tradition of the post-apostolic period, for of any important or fruitful opposition to it the history of doctrine knows nothing" (Hering, "Zeitschrift für Theologie und Kirche," v. p. 67).

[3] This is the gist of Hering's assault on it; cf. as above, and p. 74: "The denial of the fact (of the virgin birth) has in all ages been adjudged heresy, but its positive utilization has been very slight."

in the parable of the Prodigal Son. And the "Christianity" which refuses to know anything but the love of God which is there revealed to us, as it has no need of a Jesus, can have no need of a "supernatural birth" for the Jesus whom it totally ignores, or for whom it makes at best but an unessential place.

It is very evident, then, that if we are to ask whether "the doctrine of the supernatural birth of Jesus is essential to Christianity," we must settle it in our minds very clearly at the outset what "Christianity" it is we are talking about. Our answer will be one thing if we are thinking of what many about us are vaguely and vainly calling "Christianity," and perhaps quite another thing if we are thinking of the Christianity of Christ and his apostles, recorded in the New Testament, and drawn from the New Testament by the historical church through all ages. This latter is the only Christianity in which I can personally have more than a historical interest. I shall, therefore, confine myself to it. For the same reason I shall take "the supernatural birth of Jesus" in its highest sense—that of the truly miraculous birth of Jesus from a virgin mother, without intervention of man. It is in this sense that the "supernatural birth of Jesus" was actual; and this is the only sense, therefore, in which a discussion of it can have a real, as distinguished from a merely academic, interest. Defining thus my terms, the specific question which I shall seek to answer is whether the doctrine of the miraculous birth of Jesus from a virgin mother, taught in the opening chapters of the gospels of Matthew and Luke, forms an element in the Christianity of the New Testament, indispensable in the sense that without it that Christianity would be incompletely stated and left in one important matter defective, and, therefore, liable to misconception, if not open to dangerous assault.

Were I asked to name the three pillars on which the structure of Christianity, as taught in the New Testament in its entirety, especially rests, I do not know that I could do better than point to these three things: the supernatural, the incarnation, redemption. In an important sense, these three things constitute the Christianity of the New Testament; proceeding from the more general to the more specific, they sum up in themselves its essence. What interests us particularly at the moment is that the virgin birth of Jesus takes its significant place and has its significant part to play with respect to each one of them. Without it each one of them would be sheared of some portion of its meaning and value, and would take on a different and weakened aspect.

No one can doubt that the Christianity of the New Testament is supernaturalistic through and through. Whether we have regard to the person of Jesus or to the salvation he brought to men, the primary note of this Christianity certainly is supernaturalism. He who walked the earth as its Lord, and whom the very winds and waves obeyed; who could not be holden of the grave, but burst the bonds of death and ascended into the heavens in the sight of man: he who now sits at the right hand of God and sheds down his gift of salvation through his Spirit upon the men of his choice—it were impossible that such a one should have entered the world undistinguished among common men. His supernatural birth is given already, in a word, in his supernatural life and his supernatural work, and forms an indispensable element in the supernatural religion which he founded.

It would no doubt be difficult—or impossible, if you will —to believe that a natural Jesus had a supernatural origin; or, going at once to the root of the matter, that a natural "salvation" requires a supernatural Redeemer. Much of the Christianity about us today is distinctively, and even polemically, to use von Hartmann's term, "autosoteric"; and he who feels entirely competent to save himself finds a natural difficulty in believing that God must intervene to save him. I fully agree with the adherents of this "autosoteric" Christianity, that from their point of view a supernatural birth for Jesus would be devoid of significance, and therefore incredible. They should with similar frankness allow to me, I think, that to the Christianity of the New Testament, on the other hand, just because it stands as the opposite pole to their "autosoteric Christianity," the supernatural birth of Jesus is a necessity.

This, indeed, they in effect do when they argue that the

virgin birth of Jesus is the invention of the Christianity of the
New Testament on the basis of the extreme supernaturalism of
its conception of Christianity. Thinking of Jesus as they did, we
are told, the early Christians could not but postulate for him
an origin consonant with what they conceived to be his nature,
his powers, his career, the work he came to do, did do, is doing.[4]
Nothing could be more true. The supernatural Christ and the
supernatural salvation carry with them by an inevitable consequence the supernatural birth. In other words, the supernatural birth of Jesus is an implication of the Christian consciousness
—that is, of course, of the supernaturalistic Christian consciousness.[5] And the Christian consciousness in this judgment receives
the support of the universal human consciousness. Men have
always and everywhere judged that a supernatural man, doing
a supernatural work, must needs have sprung from a supernatural source.[6] If there had been nothing extraordinary in the
coming of the Saviour into the world, a discordant note would
have been struck at this point in the "heterosoteric" Christianity

[4] "The conception that our Savior was a son of God born from a virgin was
the involuntary, yea the inevitable, reflection of the divinity of Christ in the
souls of converted Greeks" (Usener, "Das Weihnachtsfest," p. 75; cf. p. 76:
"There could not fail the birth as visible sign that something divine had entered
the world"). Cf. Soltau, "The Birth of Jesus Christ," p. 44.

[5] Lobstein, "The Virgin Birth of Christ," 1903, p. 33, argues that the consciousness of the gulf which separates the believer from "the One in whom he
has found his Master," leads him instinctively to infer a difference in origin,
and thus "the tradition of the miraculous birth of Jesus seems to anticipate the
conviction of the believer, merely transferring into the realm of history a truth
of which he finds in himself the most conclusive confirmation"; cf. p. 35. What
is this but to say that in the logic of the heart the supernatural Redeemer demands for himself a supernatural origin?

[6] "Stories of supernatural birth may be said to have a currency as wide as
the world. Heroes of extraordinary achievement or extraordinary qualities were
necessarily of extraordinary birth. The wonder or the veneration they inspired
seemed to demand that their entrance upon life, and their departure from it,
should correspond with the impression left by their total career" (Hartland,
"The Legend of Perseus," i. pp. 71, 72). So Origen ("Contra Celsum," i. 37),
speaking of the story of Plato's supernatural birth, says: "But this is really a
myth, and the simple incitement to imagine this of Plato was that man believes
that a man of wisdom and power greater than those of the multitude must have
had a higher and more divine origin than they." The point of importance is
whether the truly supernatural *life and work* are real.

of the New Testament, which would have thrown it in all its elements out of tune. To it, it would have been unnatural if the birth of the Savior had been natural, just because it itself in none of its elements is natural, but is everywhere and through all its structure, not, indeed, unnatural or contra-natural, but distinctively supernatural.

The cardinal point upon which the whole of this super-naturalistic Christianity, commended to us by the New Testament, turns, is formed by its doctrine of incarnation. The supernatural Savior, who has come into the world to work a supernatural salvation, could not possibly be conceived by it as of this world. If it would be to "annul Jesus," to imagine that he had not come in the flesh, or that he who had come in the flesh was not the Word of God who in the beginning was with God and was God—God only-begotten who was in the bosom of the Father—it would no less be to "annul him" to imagine that he could owe his coming to earthly causes or collocations. Born into our race he might be and was; but born of our race, never—whether really or only apparently.

There has been a very odd attempt made, to be sure, to set over against one another the doctrines of the pre-existence and of the supernatural birth of our Lord, as if they were mutually exclusive, or at least parallel rather than complementary conceptions. In speaking of such a thing as birth, however, it is obvious that when we say pre-existence we have already said supernatural, and as soon as we have said Deity we have said miraculous. So far as appears, it required the Socinians to teach us that one of these things could be taken and the other left—that any rational mind could suppose a non-supernatural being to be the product of a supernatural birth; while surely only a pronounced pantheist could so confound things that differ as to imagine that for bringing a supernatural being into the world those causes may be thought to suffice by which commonly mere men are produced. Ordinary people may be trusted to continue to judge that, as incarnation means precisely the entrance into the human race of a being not in any sense the product of the forces working in that race, but introduced from without and above, it is in its very essence a supernatural occurrence, and will necessarily bear in its mode of occurrence its credentials as such. It is, indeed, obviously not enough to say that it behooved the Divine Person who became incarnate in Jesus Christ, in entering into a new phase of existence, not to seem then first to begin to be; although to say that is no doubt to say something to the point. Would we do justice to the case, we must go on and affirm that, when the Life itself (which is also the Truth itself) entered into the conditions of human existence, it could not but come, according to its nature, creatively—bringing its own self-existing Life with it, and not making a round-about way so as to appear only now to begin, by way of derivation, to exist. When the Word was made flesh and tabernacled among men, it could not be but that men should behold his glory—a glory as of an only-begotten of the Father, full of grace and truth.

In point of fact, accordingly, it is just in proportion as men lose their sense of the Divine personality of the messianic king who is Immanuel, God with us, that they are found to doubt the necessity of the virgin birth; while in proportion as the realization of this fundamental fact of the Christianity of the New Testament remains vivid and vital with them, do they instinctively feel that it is alone consonant with it that this Being should acknowledge none other father than that Father which is in heaven, from whom alone he came forth to save the world. Accordingly, the adherents of the modern kenosis doctrine of the person of Christ, seeing in Jesus Christ nothing but God (though God shrunk to man's estate), have become the especial defenders of the doctrine of the virgin birth, and at this point the especial opponents of the modern rationalists, with whom otherwise they have so much in common. In contradistinction to both, the Christianity of the New Testament, remembering the two natures—which nowadays nearly everybody forgets—offers us in our Lord's person, not a mere man (perhaps in some sense made God), nor a mere God (perhaps in some sense made man), but a true God-man, who, being all that God is and at the same time all that man is, has come into the world in a fashion suitable to his dual nature, conceived indeed in a virgin's womb, and born of a woman and under the law, but not by the will of the flesh, nor by the will of man, but solely by the will of God who he is.[7]

Not even in the incarnation, however, is the Christianity of the New Testament summed up. Rather, the incarnation appears in it, not for its own sake, but as a means to a farther end—redemption. And it is only in its relation to the New Testament doctrine of redemption that the necessity of the virgin birth of Jesus comes to its complete manifestation. For in this Christianity the redemption that is provided is distinctively redemption from sin; and that he might redeem men from sin it certainly was imperative that the Redeemer himself should not be involved in sin. He would be a bold man, indeed, who would affirm that the incarnation of the Holy One in sinful flesh presents no difficulties to his thought. The sinlessness of Jesus, in the sense of freedom from subjective corruption as well as from overt acts of sin, seems to be involved in the incarnation itself, purely and simply; and, in point of fact, those who imagine it was in principle sinful flesh which was assumed by the Son of God are prone to represent this flesh as actually cleansed of its sinfulness, either by the act of incarnation itself or by the almighty operation of the Spirit of God as a condition precedent to incarnation. But something more than sinlessness in this subjective sense was requisite for the redemption up to which the incarnation leads. Assuredly no one, resting for himself

[7] Such criticisms as that of Réville, "Histoire du dogme de la divinité de Jésus-Christ" (1869, p. 30; 1904, p. 27), miss the mark and would apply only to the Kenotic perversion: "A pre-existent being who becomes man reduces himself, if you will, to the condition of a human embryo; but he is not conceived by virtue of an act external to himself in the womb of a woman, etc." In the New Testament view of the God-man, as there is no reduction of the Godhead to the level of a human embryo, so there is a true conception of a complete human embryo by an act external to itself. Only, the cause external to this embryo, by virtue of which it is conceived, is the power of the Most High, and not natural fertilization.

under the curse of sin, could atone for the sin of others; no one owing the law its extreme penalty for himself could pay this penalty for others. And certainly in the Christianity of the New Testament every natural member of the race of Adam rests under the curse of Adam's sin, and is held under the penalty that hangs over it. If the Son of God came into the world therefore—as that Christianity asserts to be a "faithful saying"—specifically in order to save sinners, it was imperatively necessary that he should become incarnate after a fashion which would leave him standing, so far as his own responsibility is concerned, outside that fatal entail of sin in which the whole natural race of Adam is involved. And that is as much as to say that the redemptive work of the Son of God depends upon his supernatural birth.

I am, of course, well aware that this doctrine of redemption, and as well the doctrine of sin which underlies it, is nowadays scouted in wide circles. With that, however, I have no present concern. I cheerfully admit that to a "Christianity" which knows nothing of race-sin and atonement, the necessity of the supernatural birth of the "Redeemer," if it be recognized at all, must rest on other, and perhaps on less stringent, grounds. But I have not undertaken to investigate the possible place of the supernatural birth of Jesus in the varied forms of so-called "Christianity" prevalent in the modern world, many of which stand in no other relation to the Christianity of the New Testament than that of contradiction. Nor am I to be deterred from recognizing the doctrines of "original sin" and of "satisfaction" as fundamental elements in the Christianity of the New Testament, by the habit which has grown up among those who do not like them, of speaking of them scornfully as "Augustinian" and "Anselmic." What rather attracts my attention is that it seems to be universally allowed that, on these "Augustinian" and "Anselmic" presuppositions, the doctrine of the virgin birth of Jesus is an absolutely essential element of Christianity. In so far, then, as it is admitted that the doctrines of "original sin" and of "satisfaction" are constituent elements of the Christianity of the New Testament, it may be taken as acknowledged that the virgin birth of our Lord is confessedly essential to it.[8]

If, then, it cannot be denied that the supernatural birth of Jesus enters constitutively into the substance of that system which is taught in the New Testament as Christianity—that it is the expression of its supernaturalism, the safeguard of its doctrine of incarnation, the condition of its doctrine of redemption—are we to go on and say that no one can be saved who does not hold this faith whole and entire? The question is thoroughly impertinent. We are discussing, not the terms of salvation, but the essential content of the Christian system; not what we must do to be saved, but what it behooved Jesus Christ to be and to do that he might save us. Say that faith is the instrument by which salvation is laid hold upon; the instrument by which the prerequisites of the salvation laid hold of by faith are investigated is the intellect. As it is certain that the only Jesus, faith in whom can save, is the Jesus who was conceived by the Holy Ghost, and born of the virgin Mary, according to the Scriptures, it is equally certain that the act of faith by which he is savingly apprehended involves these presuppositions, were its implicates soundly developed. But our logical capacity can scarcely be made the condition of our salvation.[9] The Scriptures do not encourage us to believe that only the wise are called. They even graciously assure us that blasphemy itself against the Son may be forgiven. It would surely be unfortunate if weakness of intellect were more fatal than wickedness of heart. On the whole, we may congratulate ourselves that it was more imperative that Jesus, by whom the salvation has been wrought, should know what it behooved him to be and to do that he might save us, than it is that we

[8] Cf. Lobstein, op. cit., p. 84; Cheyne, "Bible Problems," p. 95; etc.

[9] I have the unwonted felicity of being thoroughly at one in this with Professor Paul Schwartzkopff, who remarks: "The faith which lays hold of the living God in Christ is not necessarily conditioned by the thoroughness with which the intellect grasps its content" ("The Prophecies of Jesus Christ," E. T. p. 3).

should fully understand it. But, on the other hand, it will scarcely do to represent ignorance or error as advantageous to salvation. It certainly is worth while to put our trust in Jesus as intelligently as it may be given to us to do so. And it certainly will over and over again be verified in experience that he who casts himself upon Jesus as his divine Redeemer, will find the fact of the virgin birth of this Saviour not only consonant with his faith and an aid to it, but a postulate of it without which he would be puzzled and distressed.

Chapter VII

THE FORESIGHT OF JESUS[1]

The interest of the student of the Gospels, and of the life of Jesus which forms their substance, in the topic of this article, is two-fold. Jesus is represented in the Gospels as at once the object and the subject of the most detailed foresight. The work which He came to do was a work ordained in the counsels of eternity, and in all its items prepared for beforehand with the most perfect prevision. In addressing Himself to the accomplishment of this work Jesus proceeded from the beginning in the fullest knowledge of the end, and with the most absolute adjustment of every step to its attainment. It is from this double viewpoint that each of the Evangelists depicts the course of our Lord's life on earth. They consentiently represent Him as having come to perform a specific task, all the elements of which were not only determined beforehand in the plan of God, but adumbrated, if somewhat sporadically, yet with sufficient fulness for the end in view, in the prophecies of the Old Testament. And they represent Him as coming to perform this task with a clear consciousness of its nature and a competent control of all the means for its discharge, so that His whole life was a conscientious fulfilment of a programme, and moved straight to its mark. The conception of foresight thus dominates the whole Evangelical narrative.

It is not necessary to dwell at length upon the Evangelists' conception of our Lord's life and work as *the fulfilment of a plan Divinely predetermined for Him.* It lies on the face of their narratives that the authors of the Gospels had no reservation with respect to the all-embracing predestination of God (see pages 295-302), and least of all could they exclude

[1] Article "Foresight" from A *Dictionary of Christ and the Gospels,* ed. by James Hastings, D.D., v. i, pp. 608-615. Pub. N. Y. 1908, by Charles Scribner's Sons; also from *Biblical Doctrines,* pp. 71-97.

from it this life and work which was to them the hinge upon which all history turns. To them accordingly our Lord is by way of eminence 'the man of destiny,' and His whole life (Lk. ii. 49, iv. 43) was governed by 'the δεῖ of the Divine counsel.' Every step of His pathway was a 'necessity' to Him, in the fulfilment of the mission for which He had 'come forth' (Mk. i. 38, cf. Swete), or as St. Luke (iv. 43) in quite Johannine wise (v. 23, 24, 30, 36, 38, vi. 29, 38, 39, 40 et passim) expresses it, 'was sent' (cf. Mt. x. 40, Mk. ix. 37, Lk. ix. 48, x. 16; Mt. xv. 24, xxi. 37, Mk. xii. 6, Lk. xx. 13, cf. Swete on Mk. ix. 37). Especially was all that concerned His departure, the accomplishment of which (Lk. ix. 31, cf. v. 51) was His particular task, under the government of this 'Divine necessity' (Mt. xvi. 21, xxvi. 54, Mk. viii. 31, Lk. ix. 22, xvii. 25, xxii. 22, 37, xxiv. 7, 44, Jn. iii. 14, xx. 9, cf. Acts ii. 23, iii. 18, iv. 28, and Westcott on Jn. xx. 9). His final journey to Jerusalem (Mt. xvi. 21), His rejection by the rulers (Mk. viii. 31, Lk. ix. 22, xvii. 25), His betrayal (Lk. xxiv. 7), arrest (Mt. xxvi. 54), sufferings (Mt. xxvi. 54, Mk. viii. 31, Lk. ix. 22, xvii. 25), and death (Mt. xvi. 21, Mk. viii. 31, Lk. ix. 22) by crucifixion (Lk. xxiv. 7, Jn. iii. 14), His rising again (Jn. xx. 9) on the third day (Mt. xvi. 21, Mk. viii. 31, Lk. ix. 22, xxiv. 7, 46)—each item alike is declared to have been 'a matter of necessity in pursuance of the Divine purpose' (Meyer, Mt. xxiv. 6), 'a necessary part of the destiny assigned our Lord' (Meyer, Mt. xxvi. 54). 'The death of our Lord' thus appears 'not as the accidental work of hostile caprice, but (cf. Acts ii. 23, iii. 18) the necessary result of the Divine predestination (Lk. xxii. 22), to which Divine δεῖ (Lk. xxiv. 26) the personal free action of man had to serve as an instrument' (Meyer, Acts iv. 28).

How far the several events which entered into this life had been prophetically announced is obviously, in this view of it, a mere matter of detail. All of them lay open before the eyes of God; and the only limit to pre-announcement was the extent to which God had chosen to reveal what was to come to pass, through His servants the prophets. In some instances, however, the prophetic announcement is particularly adduced as the ground on which recognition of the necessity of occurrence rests. The fulfilment of Scripture thus becomes regulative of the life of Jesus. Whatever stood written of Him in the Law or the Prophets or the Psalms (Lk. xxiv. 44) must needs (δεῖ) be accomplished (Mt. xxvi. 54, Lk. xxii. 37, xxiv. 26, Jn. xx. 9). Or, in another form of statement, particularly frequent in Mt. (i. 22, ii. 15, 23, iv. 14, viii. 17, xii. 17, xiii. 35, xxi. 4, xxvi. 56) and Jn. (xii. 38, xiii. 18, xv. 25, xvii. 12, xix. 24, 36), but found also in the other Evangelists (Mk. xiv. 49, Lk. iv. 21), the several occurrences of His life fell out as they did, 'in order that what was spoken by the Lord' through the prophets or in Scripture, 'might be fulfilled' (cf. Mt. ii. 17, xxvi. 54, xxvii. 9, Lk. xxiv. 44; in Jn. xviii. 9, 32, Lk. xxiv. 44 declarations of Jesus are treated precisely similarly). That is to say, 'what was done stood . . . in the connexion of the Divine necessity, as an actual fact, by which prophecy was destined to be fulfilled. The Divine decree expressed in the latter *must* be accomplished, and *to that end this . . . came to pass*, and that, *according to the whole of its contents*' (Meyer, Mt. i. 22). The meaning is, not that there lies in the Old Testament Scriptures a complete predictive account of all the details of the life of Jesus, which those skilled in the interpretation of Scripture might read off from its pages at will. This programme in its detailed completeness lies only in the Divine purpose; and in Scripture only so far forth as God has chosen to place it there for the guidance or the assurance of His people. The meaning is rather that all that stands written of Jesus in the Old Testament Scriptures has its certain fulfilment in Him; and that enough stands written of Him there to assure His followers that in the course of His life, and in its, to them, strange and unexpected ending, He was not the prey of chance or the victim of the hatred of men, to the marring of His work or perhaps even the defeat of His mission, but was following step by step, straight to its goal, the predestined pathway marked out for Him in the counsels of eternity, and sufficiently revealed from of old in the Scriptures to enable all who were not 'foolish and slow of heart to believe in all that the prophets have spoken,' to perceive that the Christ must needs have lived just this life and fulfilled just this destiny.

That the whole course of the life of Jesus, and especially its culmination in the death which He died, was foreseen and afore-prepared by God, enters, thus, into the very substance of the Evangelical narrative. It enters equally into its very substance that *this life was from the beginning lived out by Jesus Himself in full view of its drift and its issue.* The Evangelists are as far from representing Jesus as driven blindly onwards by a Divine destiny unknown to Himself, along courses not of His own choosing, to an unanticipated end, as they are from representing Him as thwarted in His purposes, or limited in His achievement, or determined or modified in His aims or methods, by the conditions which from time to time emerged in His way. The very essence of their representation is that Jesus came into the world with a definite mission to execute, of the nature of which He was perfectly aware, and according to which He ordered the whole course of His life as it advanced under His competent control unswervingly to its preconceived mark. In their view His life was lived out, not in ignorance of its issues, or in the form of a series of trials and corrections, least of all in a more or less unavailing effort to wring success out of failure; but in complete knowledge of the counsels of God for Him, in perfect acquiescence in them, and in careful and voluntary fulfilment of them. The 'Divine δεῖ' which governed His life is represented as fully recognized by Himself (Mt. xvi. 21, Mk. viii. 31, Lk. iv. 43, ix. 22, xvii. 25, xxiv. 7, Jn. iii. 14, xii. 34), and the fulfilment of the intimations of prophecy in His life as accepted by Him as a rule for His voluntary action (Mt. xxvi. 54, Lk. xxii. 37, xxiv. 26, 44, Jn. xx. 9, Mk. xiv. 49, Lk. iv. 21, Jn. xiii. 18, xv. 25, xvii. 12; cf. Mt. xiii. 14, xv. 7, xxiv. 15, xxvi. 56, Mk. vii. 6). Determining all things, determined by none, the life He actually lived, leading up to the death He actually died, is in their view precisely the life which from the beginning He intended to live, ending in precisely the death in which, from the beginning, He intended this life to issue, undeflected by so much as a hair's-breadth from the straight path He had from the start marked out for Himself in the fullest prevision and provision of all the so-called chances and changes which might befall Him. Not only were there no surprises in life for Jesus and no compulsions; there were not even 'influences,' as we speak of 'influences' in a merely human career. The mark of this life, as the Evangelists depict it, is its calm and quiet superiority to all circumstance and condition, and to all the varied forces which sway other lives; its prime characteristics are voluntariness and independence. Neither His mother, nor His brethren, nor His disciples, nor the people He came to serve, nor His enemies bent upon His destruction, nor Satan himself with his temptations, could move Him one step from His chosen path. When men seemed to prevail over Him they were but working His will; the great 'No one has taken my life away from me; I have power to lay it down, and I have power to take it again' (Jn. x. 18), is but the enunciation, for the supreme act, of the principle that governs all His movements. His own chosen pathway ever lay fully displayed before His feet; on it His feet fell quietly, but they found the way always unblocked. What He did, He came to do; and He carried out His programme with unwavering purpose and indefectible certitude. So at least the Evangelists represent Him.

The signature of this supernatural life which the Evangelists depict Jesus as living, lies thus in the perfection of the foresight by which it was governed. Of the reality of this foresight they leave their readers in no doubt, nor yet of its completeness. They suggest it by the general picture they draw of the self-directed life which Jesus lived in view of His mission. They record repeated instances in which He mentions beforehand events yet to occur, or foreshadows the end from the beginning. They connect these manifestations of foresight with the possession by Him of knowledge in general, in comprehension and penetration alike, far beyond what is native to man. It may perhaps be natural to surmise in the first instance that they intend to convey merely the conviction that in Jesus was manifested a prophet of supreme greatness, in whom, as the culminating example of prophecy (cf. Acts iii. 22, 23), resided beyond precedent the gifts proper to prophets. There can be no question that to the writers of the Gospels Jesus was 'the incarnate ideal of the prophet, who, as such, forms a class by Himself, and is more than a prophet' (this is what Schwartz-kopff thinks Him, "The Prophecies of Jesus Christ," p. 7). They record with evident sympathy the impression made by Him at the outset of His ministry, that God had at last in Him visited His people (Mk. vi. 15, Lk. vii. 16, Jn. iv. 19, ix. 17); they trace the ripening of this impression into a well-settled belief in His prophetic character (Mt. xxi. 11, Lk. xxiv. 19, Mt. xxi. 46, Lk. vii. 39, Jn. vii. 40); and they remark upon the widespread suspicion which accompanied this belief, that He was something more than *a* prophet—possibly one of the old prophets returned, certainly a very special prophet charged with a very special mission for the introduction of the Messianic times (Mt. xvi. 14, Mk. vi. 15, viii. 28, Lk. ix. 8, 19, Jn. vi. 14, vii. 40). They represent Jesus as not only calling out and accepting this estimate of Him, but frankly assuming a prophet's place and title (Mt. xiii. 57, Mk. vi. 4, Lk. iv. 24, Jn. iv. 44, Lk. xiii. 33), exercising a prophet's functions, and delivering prophetic discourses, in which He unveils the future (Mt. xxiv. 21, Mk. xiii. 23, Jn. xiv. 29; cf. Mt. xxviii. 6, Lk. xxiv. 44, and such passages as Mt. xxvi. 32, 34, Mk. xvi. 7). Nevertheless it is very clear that in their allusions to the supernatural knowledge of Jesus, the Evangelists suppose themselves to be illustrating something very much greater than merely prophetic inspiration. The specific difference between Jesus and a prophet, in their view, was that while a prophet's human knowledge is increased by many things revealed to him by God (Amos iii. 7), Jesus participated in all the fulness of the Divine knowledge (Mt. xi. 27, Lk. x. 22, Jn. xvi. 15, xviii. 4, xvi. 30, xxi. 17), so that all that is knowable lay open before Him (Jn. xvii. 10). The Evangelists, in a word, obviously intend to attribute Divine omniscience to Jesus, and in their adduction of instances of His supernatural knowledge, whether with respect to hidden things or to those yet buried in the future, are illustrating His possession of this Divine omniscience.

That this is the case with St. John's Gospel is very commonly recognized (for a plain statement of the evidence see Karl Müller, "Göttliches Wissen und göttliche Macht des johann. Christus," 1882, § 4, pp. 29-47: "Zeugnisse des vierten Evangeliums für Jesu göttliches Wissen"). It is not too much to say, indeed, that one of the chief objects which the author of that Gospel set before himself was to make clear to its readers the superhuman knowledge of Jesus, with especial reference, of course, to His own career. It therefore records direct ascriptions of omniscience to Jesus, and represents them as favourably received by Him (Jn. xvi. 30, xxi. 17; cf. Liddon, "The Divinity of our Lord," ed. 4, 1869, p. 466). It makes it almost the business of its opening chapters to exhibit this omniscience at work in the especially Divine form (Lk. xvi. 15, Acts i. 24, Heb. iv. 12, Ps. cxxxviii (cxxxix). 2, Jer. xvii. 10, xx. 12; cf. Swete on Mk. ii. 8) of immediate, universal, and complete knowledge of the thoughts and intents of the human heart (cf. Westcott on Jn. ii. 25), laying down the general thesis in ii. 24, 25 (cf. vi. 64, 70, xxi. 17), and illustrating it in detail in the cases of all with whom Jesus came into contact in the opening days of His ministry (cf. Westcott on Jn. i. 47), Peter (i. 42), Philip (i. 43), Nathanael (i. 47), Mary (ii. 4), Nicodemus (iii.), the woman of Samaria (iv.). In the especially striking case of the choice of Judas Iscariot as one of the Apostles, it expressly explains that this was due to no ignorance of Judas' character or of his future action (vi. 64, 70, xiii. 11), but was done as part of our Lord's voluntary execution of His own well-laid plans. It pictures Jesus with great explicitness as prosecuting His whole work in full knowledge of all the things that were coming upon Him (Jn. xviii. 4, cf. Westcott), and with a view to subjecting them all to His governing hand, so that His life from the beginning should run steadily onward on the lines of a thoroughly wrought-out plan (Jn. i. 47, ii. 19, 24, iii. 14, vi. 51, 64, 70, vii. 6, viii. 28, x. 15, 18, xii. 7, 23, xiii. 1, 11, 21, 38, xiv. 29, xvi. 5, 32, xviii. 4, 9).

It is difficult to see, however, why St. John's Gospel should be separated from its companions in this matter (Schenkel says frankly that it is only because there is no such passage in St. John's Gospel as Mk. xiii. 32, on which see below. Whatever else must be said of W. Wrede's "Das Messiasgeheimnis," etc., 1901, it must be admitted that it has broke down this artificial distinction between the Gospel of John and the Synoptics). If they do not, like St. John (xvi. 30, xxi. 17), record direct ascriptions of precise omniscience to Jesus by His followers, they do, like St. John, represent Him as Himself claiming to be the depository and distributor of the Father's knowledge (Mt. xi. 21-30, Lk. x. 22-24). Nor do they lag behind St. John in attributing to Jesus the Divine prerogative of reading the heart (Mt. ix. 4, Meyer; Mk. ii. 5, 8, viii. 17, xii. 15, 44, Swete, p. lxxxviii; Lk. v. 22, vii. 39) or the manifestation, in other forms, of God-like omniscience (Mt. xvii. 27, xxi. 2, Mk. xi. 2, xiv. 13, Lk. v. 4, xix. 30, xxii. 10; cf. O. Holtzmann, "War Jesus Ekstatiker?" p. 14 and p. 15, note). Least of all do they fall behind St. John in insisting upon the perfection of the foresight of Jesus in all matters connected with His own life and death (Mt. ix. 15, xii. 40, xvi. 21, xx. 18, 22, 28, xxvi. 2, 21, 34, 50, Mk. 1i. 19, viii. 31, ix. 31, x. 33, 39, 45, xi. 2, xiv. 8, 13, 18, 30, Lk. v. 34, ix. 22, 44, 51, xii. 50, xiii. 35, xvii. 25, xviii. 31, xix. 30, xxii. 10, 21, 34, 37, xxiv. 44). Nothing could exceed the detailed precision of these announcements,—a characteristic which has been turned, of course, to their discredit as genuine utterances of Jesus by writers who find difficulty with detailed prediction. 'The form and contents of these texts,' remarks Wrede ("Messiasgeheimnis," etc. p. 88), 'speak a language which cannot be misunderstood. They are nothing but a short summary of the Passion history—"cast, of course, in the future tense."' ' "The Passion-history," ' he proceeds, quoting Eichhorn, ' "could certainly not be more exactly related in few words." ' In very fact, it is perfectly clear—whether they did it by placing upon His lips predictions He never uttered and never could have uttered, is another question—that the Evangelists designed to represent Jesus as endowed with the absolute and unlimited foresight consonant with His Divine nature (see Liddon, "The Divinity of our Lord," ed. 4, p. 464 ff.; and cf. A. J. Mason, "The Conditions of our Lord's Life on Earth," pp. 155-194).

The force of this representation cannot be broken, of course, by raising the question afresh whether the supernatural knowledge attributed by the Evangelists to our Lord may not, in many of its items at least, if not in its whole extent, find its analogues, after all, in human powers, or be explained as not different in kind from that of the prophets (cf. e.g., Westcott, "Additional Note on Jn. ii. 24"; A. J. Mason, "Conditions," etc. pp. 162-163). The question more immediately before us does not concern our own view of the nature and origin of this knowledge, but that of the Evangelists. If we will keep these two questions separate we shall scarcely be able to doubt that the Evangelists mean to present this knowledge as one of the marks of our Lord's Divine dignity. In interpreting them we are not entitled to parcel out the mass of the illustrations of His supernormal knowledge which they record to differing sources, as may fall in with our own conceptions of the inherent possibilities of each case; finding indications in some instances merely of His fine human instinct, in others of His prophetic inspiration, while reserving others—if such others are left to us in our analysis—as products of His Divine intuition. The Evangelists suggest no such lines of cleavage in the mass; and they must be interpreted from their own standpoint. This finds its centre in their expressed conviction that in Jesus Christ dwelt the fulness of the knowledge of God (Mt. xi. 27, Lk. x. 22, Jn. viii. 38, xvi. 15, xvii. 10). To them His knowledge of God and of Divine things, of Himself in His Person and mission, of the course of His life and the events which would befall Him in the prosecution of the work whereunto He had been sent, of the men around Him,—His followers and friends, the people and their rulers,—down to the most hidden depths of their natures and the most intimate processes of their secret thoughts, and of all the things forming the environment in which the drama He was enacting was cast, however widely that environment be conceived, or however minutely it be contemplated,—was but the manifestation, in the ever-widening circles of our human modes of conception, of the perfect apprehension and understanding that dwelt changelessly in His Divine intelligence. He who knew God perfectly,—it were little that He should know man and the world perfectly too; all that affected His own work and career, of course, and with it, equally of course, all that lay outside of this (cf. Mason, "Conditions," etc. p. 168): in a word, unlimitedly, all things. Even if nothing but the Law of Parsimony stood in the way, it might well be understood that the Evangelists would be deterred from seeking, in the case of such a Being, other sources of information besides His Divine intelligence to account for all His far-reaching and varied knowledge. At all events, it is clearly their conviction that all He knew—the scope of which was unbounded and its depth unfathomed, though their record suggests rather than fully illustrates it—found its explanation in the dignity of His person as God manifest in the flesh.

Nor can the effect of their representation of Jesus as the subject of this all-embracing Divine knowledge be destroyed by the discovery in their narratives of another line of representation in which our Lord is set forth as living His life out under the conditions which belong naturally to the humanity He had assumed. These representations are certainly to be neglected as little as those others in which His Divine omniscience is suggested. They bring to our observation another side of the complex personality that is depicted, which, if it cannot be said to be as emphatically insisted upon by the Evangelists, is nevertheless, perhaps, equally pervasively illustrated. This is the true humanity of our Lord, within the scope of which He willed to live out His life upon earth, that He might accomplish the mission for which He had been sent. The suggestion that He might break over the bounds of His mission, in order that He might escape from the ruggedness of His chosen path, by the exercise whether of His almighty power (Mt. iv. 3 f., Lk. iv. 3 f.) or of His unerring foresight (Mt. xvi. 22 ||), He treated first and last as a temptation of the Evil One—for 'how then should the Scriptures be fulfilled that thus it must be' (Mt.

xxvi. 54 ||)? It is very easy, to be sure, to exaggerate the indi-
cations in the Evangelists of the confinement of our Lord's
activities within the limits of human powers. It is an exaggeration, for example, to speak as if the Evangelists represent
Him as frequently surprised by the events which befell Him:
they never predicate surprise of Him, and it is only by a very
precarious inference from the events recorded that they can
ever be supposed even to suggest or allow place for such an
emotion in our Lord. It is an exaggeration again to adduce our
Lord's questions as attempts to elicit information for His own
guidance: His questions are often plainly dialectical or rhetorical, or, like some of His actions, solely for the benefit of
those 'that stood around.' It is once more an exaggeration to
adduce the employment in many cases of the term γινώσκω,
when the Evangelists speak of our Lord's knowledge, as if it
were thereby implied that this knowledge was freshly born in
His mind: the assumed distinction, but faintly marked in Greek
literature, cannot be traced in the usage of the terms γνῶναι
and εἰδέναι in their application to our Lord's knowledge; these
terms even replace one another in parallel accounts of the same
instance (Mt. xxii. 18||Mk. xii. 15; [Mt. ix. 4]||Mk. ii. 8, Lk. v.
22; cf. Mt. xii. 25, Lk. vi. 8, ix. 47, xi. 17, Jn. vi. 61); γνῶναι is
used of the undoubted Divine knowledge of our Lord ([Mt. xi.
25] Lk. x. 22, Jn. x. 15, xvii. 25, Mt. vii. 23; cf. Jn. ii. 24, 25,
v. 42, x. 14, 27); and indeed of the knowledge of God Himself
(Lk. x. 22, xvi. 15, Jn. x. 15 [Mt. xi. 27]): and, in any event,
there is a distinction which in such nice inquiries should not
be neglected, between saying that the occurrence of an event,
being perceived, was the occasion of an action, and saying that
knowledge of the event, perceived as occurring, waited on its
occurrence. Gravely vitiated by such exaggerations as most discussions of the subject are, enough remains, however, after all
exaggeration is pruned away, to assure us, not indeed that our
Lord's life on earth was, in the view of the Evangelists, an
exclusively human one; or that, apart from the constant exercise
of His will to make it such, it was controlled by the limitations
of humanity; but certainly that it was, in their view, lived out,

so far as was consistent with the fulfilment of the mission for which He came—and as an indispensable condition of the fulfilment of that mission—under the limitations belonging to a purely human life. The classical passages in this reference are those striking statements in the second chapter of Luke (ii. 40, 52) in which is summed up our Lord's growth from infancy to manhood, including, of course, His intellectual development and His own remarkable declaration recorded in Mt. xxiv. 36, Mk. xiii. 32, in which He affirms His ignorance of the day and hour of His return to earth. Supplemented by their general dramatization of His life within the range of the purely human, these passages are enough to assure us that in the view of the Evangelists there was in our Lord a purely human soul, which bore its own proper part in His life, and which, as human souls do, grew in knowledge as it grew in wisdom and grace, and remained to the end, as human souls must, ignorant of many things,—nay, which, because human souls are finite, must ever be ignorant of much embraced in the universal vision of the Divine Spirit. We may wonder why the 'day and hour' of His own return should remain among the things of which our Lord's human soul continued ignorant throughout His earthly life. But this is a matter about which surely we need not much concern ourselves. We can never do more than vaguely guess at the law which governs the inclusions and exclusions which characterize the knowledge-contents of any human mind, limited as human minds are not only qualitatively but quantitatively; and least of all could we hope to penetrate the principle of selection in the case of the perfect human intelligence of our Lord; nor have the Evangelists hinted their view of the matter. We must just be content to recognize that we are face to face here with the mystery of the Two Natures, which, although they do not, of course, formally enunciate the doctrine in so many words, the Evangelists yet effectively teach, since by it alone can consistency be induced between the two classes of facts which they present unhesitatingly in their narratives. Only, if we would do justice to their presentation, we must take clear note of two of its characteristics. They do not simply, in separated portions of their narratives, adduce the facts which manifest our Lord's Divine powers and His human characteristics, but interlace them inextricably in the same sections of the narratives. And they do not subject the Divine that is in Christ to the limitations of the human, but quite decisively present the Divine as dominating all, and as giving play to the human only by a constant, voluntary withholding of its full manifestation in the interests of the task undertaken. Observe the story, for example, in Jn. xi, which Dr. Mason ("Conditions," etc. p. 143) justly speaks of as 'indeed a marvellous weaving together of that which is natural and that which is above nature.' 'Jesus learns from others that Lazarus is sick, but knows without any further message that Lazarus is dead; He weeps and groans at the sight of the sorrow which surrounds Him, yet calmly gives thanks for the accomplishment of the miracle before it has been accomplished.' This conjunction of the two elements is typical of the whole Evangelical narrative. As portrayed in it our Lord's life is distinctly duplex; and can be consistently construed only by the help of the conception of the Two Natures. And just as distinctly is this life portrayed in these narratives as receiving its determination not from the human, but from the Divine side. If what John undertakes to depict is what was said and done by the incarnated Word, no less what the Synoptics essay is to present the Gospel (as Mark puts it) of Jesus Christ the Son of God. It is distinctly a supernatural life that He is represented by them all as living; and the human aspect of it is treated by each alike as an incident in something more exalted, by which it is permitted, rather than on which it imposes itself. Though passed as far as was befitting within the limits of humanity, this life remains at all times the life of God manifest in the flesh, and, as depicted by the Evangelists, never escapes beyond the boundaries set by what was suitable to it as such.

The actual instances of our Lord's foresight which are recorded by the Evangelists are not very numerous outside of those which concern the establishment of the Kingdom of God, with which alone, of course, their narratives are particularly engaged. Even the few instances of specific exhibitions of fore-knowledge of what we may call trivial events owe their record to some connexion with this great work. Examples are afforded by the foresight that the casting of the nets at the exact time and place indicated by our Lord would secure a draught of fishes (Lk. v. 4, cf. Jn. xxi. 6); that the first fish that Peter would take when he threw his hook into the sea would be one which had swallowed a stater (Mt. xvii. 27); that on entering a given village the disciples should find an ass tied, and a colt with it, whose owners would be obedient to our Lord's request (Mt. xxi. 2 ||); and that on entering Jerusalem to make ready for the final passover-feast they should meet a man bearing a pitcher, prepared to serve the Master's needs (Mk. xiv. 13). In instances like these the interlacing of prevision and pro-vision is very intimate, and doubt arises whether they illustrate most distinctly our Lord's Divine foresight or His control of events. In other instances the element of foresight comes, per-haps, more purely forward: such are possibly the predictions of the offence of the disciples (Mt. xxvi. 31||), the denial of Peter (xxvi. 34||), and the treachery of Judas (xxvi. 21||). There may be added the whole series of utterances in which our Lord shows a comprehensive foresight of the career of those whom He called to His service (Mt. iv. 19, x. 17, 21, xx. 22, xxiv. 9 f., Jn. xvi. 1 f.); and also that other series in which He exhibits a like full foreknowledge of the entire history of the Kingdom of God in the world (cf. especially the parables of the Kingdom, and such passages as Mt. xvi. 18, xxiv. 5, 24, xxi. 43, xxiv. 14, xxvi. 13, Lk. xix. 11, Jn. xiv. 18, 19). It is, however, particularly with reference to His own work in establishing the Kingdom, and in regard to the nature of that work, that stress is particularly laid upon the completeness of His foreknowl-edge. His entire career, as we have seen, is represented by all the Evangelists as lying plainly before Him from the beginning, with every detail clearly marked and provided for. It is espe-cially, however, with reference to the three great events in which His work in establishing His Kingdom is summed up—His death, His resurrection, His return—that the predictions become numerous, if we may not even say constant. Each of the Evangelists represents Him, for example, as foreseeing His death from the start (Jn. ii. 19, iii. 14, Mt. xii. 40, ix. 15, Mk. ii. 19, Lk. xii. 49, v. 34; cf. Meyer on Mt. ix. 15, xvi. 21; Weiss on Mk. viii. 31; Denney, "Death of Christ," p. 18; Wrede, "Messiasgeheimnis," p. 19, etc.), and as so ordering His life as to march steadfastly forward to it as its chosen climax (cf. e.g., Wrede, p. 84: 'It is accordingly the meaning of Mark that Jesus journeys to Jerusalem because it is His will to die there'). He is represented, therefore, as avoiding all that could lead up to it for a time, and then, when He was ready for it, as setting Himself steadfastly to bring it about as He would; as speaking of it only guardedly at first, and afterwards, when the time was ripe for it, as setting about assiduously to prepare His disciples for it. Similarly with respect to His resurrection, He is reported as having it in mind, indeed, from the earliest days of His ministry (Jn. ii. 19, Mt. xii. 40, xvi. 21, Mk. viii. 31, Lk. ix. 22), but adverting to it with pædagogical care, so as to prepare rather than confuse the minds of His disciples. The same in substance may be said with reference to His return (Mt. x. 23, xvi. 27, Mk. viii. 38, ix. 1, Lk. ix. 26, 27).

A survey in chronological order of the passages in which He is reported as speaking of these three great events of the future, cannot fail to leave a distinct impression on the mind not only of the large space they occupy in the Evangelical narrative, but of the great place they take as foreseen, according to that narrative, in the life and work of our Lord. In the following list the passages in which He adverts to His death stand in the order given them in Robinson's "Harmony of the Gospels": Jn. ii. 19, iii. 14, Mt. xii. 40 (cf. xvi. 4, Lk. xi. 32), Lk. xii. 49, 50, Mt. ix. 15 (Mk. ii. 19, Lk. v. 34), Jn. vi. 51, vii. 6-8, Mt. xvi. 21 (Mk. viii. 31, Lk. ix. 22), Lk. ix. 31, Mt. xvii. 17 (Mk. ix. 12), Mt. xvii. 22, 23 (Mk. ix. 31, Lk. ix. 44), Lk. ix. 51, Jn. vii. 34, viii. 21, 25, ix. 5, x. 11, 15, Lk. xiii. 32, xvii. 25, Mt. xx. 18, 19 (Mk. x. 33, Lk. xviii. 31), Jn. xii. 28, Mt. xx. 22 (Mk. x. 38), Mt. xx. 28 (Mk. x. 45), Mt. xxi. 39 (Mk. xii. 8, Lk. xx. 14), Jn. xii. 23, Mt. xxvi. 2, Jn. xiii. 1, 33, Mt. xxvi.

28 (Mk. xiv. 24, Lk. xxii. 20), Mt. xxvi. 31 (Mk. xiv. 27, Jn.
xiv. 28), Jn. xv. 13, xvi. 5, xvi. 16, xviii. 11, Mt. xxvi. 54 (Jn.
xviii. 11), Lk. xxiv. 26, 46.

The following allusions to His resurrection are in the same
order: Jn. ii. 19, Mt. xii. 40 (Lk. xi. 30), Mt. xvi. 21 (Mk. viii. 31,
Lk. ix. 22), Mt. xvii. 9 (Mk. ix. 9), Mt. xvii. 23 (Mk. ix. 31),
Jn. x. 18 [xvi. 16], Mt. xx. 19 (Mk. x. 34, Lk. xviii. 33), Mt.
xxvi. 32 (Mk. xiv. 28) [Mt. xxviii. 6‖Lk. xxiv. 8], Lk. xxiv. 46.

The following are, in like order, the allusions to His return:
Mt. x. 23, xvi. 27 (Mk. viii. 38, ix. 1, Lk. ix. 26, 27), Mk. x. 40,
Lk. xvii. 22, Mt. xix. 28, xxiii. 39, xxiv. 3 (Mk. xiii. 4, Lk. xxi. 7),
Mt. xxiv. 34-37 (Mk. xiii. 30, Lk. xxi. 32), Mt. xxiv. 44, xxv. 31,
xxvi. 64 (Mk. xiv. 62, Lk. xxii. 69).

The most cursory examination of these series of passages
in their setting, and especially in their distribution through the
Evangelical narrative, will evince the cardinal place which the
eschatological element takes in the life of the Lord as depicted
in the Gospels. In particular, it will be impossible to escape the
conviction that it is distinctly the teaching of the Evangelists
that Jesus came into the world specifically to die, and ordered
His whole life wittingly to that end. As Dr. Denney puts it
(expounding Jn. x. 17, on which see also Westcott's note),
'Christ's death is not an incident of His life, it is the aim of it.
The laying down of His life is not an accident in His career,
it is His vocation; it is that in which the Divine purpose of His
life is revealed.' 'If there was a period in His life during which
He had other thoughts, it is antecedent to that at which we
have any knowledge of Him' ("Death of Christ," pp. 259 and
18). Nothing could therefore be more at odds with the consentient and constant representations of the Evangelists than to
speak of the 'shadow of the cross' as only somewhat late in
His history beginning to fall athwart our Lord's pathway; of
the idea that His earthly career should close in gloom as 'distinctly emerging in the teaching of Jesus only at a comparatively late period,' and as therefore presumably not earlier
'clear in His mind': unless, indeed, it be the accompanying
more general judgment that 'there was nothing extraordinary

or supernatural in Jesus' foreknowledge of His death,' and that 'His prophecy was but the expression of a mind which knew that it could not cease to be obedient while His enemies would not cease to be hostile' (A. M. Fairbairn, "The Expositor," 1897, i.; vol. iv. [1896] 283, 285). It is not less unwarranted to speak of Him as bowing to His fate only 'as the will of God, to which He yielded Himself up to the very end only with difficulty, and at best against His will' (Wernle, "Synopt. Frage," 200).

Such expressions as these, however, advise us that a very different conception from that presented by the Evangelists has found widespread acceptance among a class of modern scholars, whose efforts have been devoted to giving to our Lord's life on earth a character more normally human than it seems to possess as it lies on the pages of the Evangelists. The negative principle of the new constructions offered of the course and springs of our Lord's career being rejection of the account given by the Evangelists, these scholars are thrown back for guidance very much upon their own subjective estimate of probabilities. The Gospels are, however, the sole sources of information for the events of our Lord's life, and it is impossible to decline their aid altogether. Few, accordingly, have been able to discard entirely the general framework of the life of Christ they present (for those who are inclined to represent Jesus as making no claim even to be the Messiah, see H. J. Holtzmann, "Lehrbuch der neutestamentlichen Theologie" i. 280, note; Meinhold as there referred to; and Wrede, "Das Messiasgeheimnis," especially Appendix vii.). Most have derived enough from the Gospels to assume that a crisis of some sort occurred at Cæsarea Philippi, where the Evangelists represent our Lord as beginning formally and frankly to prepare His disciples for His death (Mt. xvi. 21||).

Great differences arise at once, however, over what this crisis was. Schenkel supposes that it was only at this point in His ministry that Jesus began to think Himself the Messiah; Strauss is willing to believe He suspected Himself to be the Messiah earlier, and supposes that He now first began to proclaim Himself such; P. W. Schmidt and Lobstein imagine that on this day He both put the Messianic crown upon His head and faced death looming in His path; Weizsäcker and Keim allow that He thought and proclaimed Himself the Messiah from the beginning, and suppose that what is new here is that only now did He come to see with clearness that His ministry would end in His death,—and as death for the Messiah means return, they added that here He begins His proclamation of His return in glory. To this Schenkel and Hase find difficulty in assenting, feeling it impossible that the Founder of a spiritual kingdom should look forward to its consummation in a physical one, and insisting, therefore, that though Jesus may well have predicted the destruction of His enemies, He can scarcely have foretold His own coming in glory. On the other hand, Strauss and Baur judge that a prediction of the destruction of Jerusalem too closely resembles what actually occurred not to be *post eventum,* but see no reason why Jesus should not have dreamed of coming back on the clouds of heaven. As to His death, Strauss thinks He began to anticipate it only shortly before His last journey to Jerusalem; while Holsten cannot believe that He realized what was before Him until He actually arrived at Jerusalem, and even then did not acquiesce in it (so Spitta). That He went to Jerusalem for the purpose of dying, neither Weizsäcker, nor Brandt, nor H. Holtzmann, nor Schultzen will admit, though the two last named allow that He foresaw that the journey would end in His death; or at least that it possibly would, adds Pünjer, since, of course, a possibility of success lay open to Him (cf. H. J. Holtzmann, "Lehrb. der neutestamentlichen Theologie," i. 285-286, note). As many men, so many opinions. As the positive principle of construction in all these schemes of life for Jesus is desupernaturalization, they differ, so far as the prophetic element in His teaching as reported by the Evangelists is concerned, chiefly in the measure in which they explain it as due more or less entirely to the Evangelists carrying their own ideas, or the ideas of the community in which they lived, back into Jesus' mouth; or allow it more or less fully to Jesus, indeed, but only in a form

which can be thought of as not rising above the natural prog-
nostications of a man in His position. A few deny to Jesus the
entire series of predictions reported in the Gospels, and assign
them in mass to the thought of the later community (e.g., Eichhorn, Wrede). A few, on the other hand, allow the whole, or
nearly the whole, series to Jesus, and explain them all naturalis-
tically. Most take an intermediate position, determined by the
principle that all which seems to each critic incapable of naturalistic explanation as utterances of Jesus shall be assigned to
later origin. Accordingly, the concrete details in the alleged
predictions are quite generally denied to Jesus, and represented
as easily explicable modifications, in accordance with the actual
course of events, of what Jesus really said. The prediction of
resurrection on the third day, for example, is held by many
(e.g., Schwartzkopff) to be too precise a determination, and is
therefore excluded from the prophecy, or explained as only a
periphrasis for an indefinite short time, after the analogy of
Hos. vi. 2 (so even B. Weiss). To others a prediction of a resurrection at all seems incredible (Strauss, Schenkel, Weizsäcker,
Keim, Brandt), and it is transmuted into, at most, a premoni-
tion of future victory. By yet others (as Holsten) even the anticipation of death is doubted, and nothing of forecast is left
to Jesus except, possibly, a vague anticipation of difficulty and
suffering; while with others even this gives way, and Jesus is
represented as passing either the greater part of His life (Fairbairn), or the whole of it, in joyful expectation of more or less
unbroken success, or at least, however thickly the clouds gathered over His head, in inextinguishable hope in God and His
interposition in His behalf (cf. the brief general sketch of
opinions in Wrede, "Messiasgeheimnis," p. 85).

Thus, over against the 'dogmatic' view of the life of Christ,
set forth in the Evangelists, according to which Jesus came into
the world to die, and which is dominated, therefore, by foresight, is set, in polar opposition to it, a new view, calling itself
'historical,' the principle of which is the denial to Jesus of any
foresight whatever beyond the most limited human forecast.
No pretence is ordinarily made that this new view is given

support by the Evangelical records; it is put forward on *a priori* or general grounds—as, for example, the only psychologically possible view (e.g., Schwartzkopff, "Prophecies of Christ," p. 28; cf. Denney, "Death of Christ," p. 11, and especially the just strictures of Wrede, "Messiasgeheimnis," pp. 2, 3). It professes to find it incredible that Jesus entered upon His ministry with any other expectation than success. Contact with men, however, it allows, brought gradually the discovery of the hopelessness of drawing them to His spiritual ideals; the growing enmity of the rulers opened before Him the prospect of disaster; and thus there came to Him the slow recognition, first of the possibility, and then of the certainty, of failure; or, at least, since failure was impossible for the mission He had come to perform, of the necessity of passing through suffering to the ultimate success. So slowly was the readjustment to this new point of view made, that even at the end—as the prayer at Gethsemane shows—there remained a lingering hope that the extremity of death might be avoided. So far as a general sketch can be made of a view presented by its several adherents with great variety of detail, this is the essential fabric of the new view (cf. the general statements of Kähler, "Zur Lehre von der Versöhnung," 159; Denney, "Death of Christ," 11; Wrede, "Messiasgeheimnis," 86). Only such parts of the predictive element of the teaching attributed to Jesus in the Gospels as are thought capable of naturalistic interpretation are incorporated into this new construction. By those who wish to bring in as much as possible, it is said, for example, that our Lord was too firmly persuaded of His Messianic appointment and function, and was too clear that this function centered in the establishment of the Kingdom, to accept death itself as failure. When He perceived death impending, that meant to Him, therefore, return; and return to bring in the Messianic glory meant resurrection. When He thought and spoke of death, therefore, He necessarily thought and spoke also of resurrection and return; the three went inevitably together; and if He anticipated the one, He must have anticipated the others also. Under this general scheme all sorts of opinions are held as to when, how, and under what impulses Jesus formed and taught this eschatological programme. As notable a construction as any holds that He first became certain of His Messiahship in an ecstatic vision which accompanied His baptism; that the Messiah must suffer was already borne in upon His conviction in the course of His temptation; but it was not until the scene at Cæsarea Philippi that He attained the happy assurance that the Messianic glory lay behind the dreadful death impending over Him. This great conviction, attained in principle in the ecstasy of that moment, was, nevertheless, only gradually assimilated. When Jesus was labouring with His disciples, He was labouring also with Himself. In this particular construction (it is O. Holtzmann's) an element of 'ecstasy' is introduced; more commonly the advances Jesus is supposed to make in His anticipations are thought to rest on processes of formal reasoning. In either case, He is pictured as only slowly, under the stress of compelling circumstances, reaching convictions of what awaited Him in the future; and thus He is conceived distinctly as the victim rather than as the Lord of His destiny. So far from entering the world to die, and by His death to save the world, and in His own good time and way accomplishing this great mission, He enters life set upon living, and only yields step by step reluctantly to the hard fate which inexorably closes upon Him. That He clings through all to His conviction of His Messiahship, and adjusts His hope of accomplishing His Messianic mission to the overmastering pressure of circumstances,—is that not a pathetic trait of human nature? Do not all enthusiasts the like? Is it not precisely the mark of their fanaticism? The plain fact is, if we may express it in the brutal frankness of common speech, in this view of Jesus' career He miscalculated and failed; and then naturally sought (or His followers sought for Him) to save the failure (or the appearance of failure) by inventing a new *dénouement* for the career He had hoped for in vain, a new dénouement which—has it failed too? Most of our modern theorizers are impelled to recognize that it too has failed. When Jesus so painfully adjusted Himself to the hard destiny which more and more obtruded itself upon

His recognition, He taught that death was but an incident in His career, and after death would come the victory. Can we believe that He foresaw that thousands of years would intervene between what He represented as but an apparent catastrophe and the glorious reversal to which He directed His own and His followers' eyes? On the contrary, He expected and He taught that He would come back soon—certainly before the generation which had witnessed His apparent defeat had passed away; and that He would then establish that Messianic Kingdom which from the beginning of His ministry He had unvaryingly taught was at hand. He did not do so. Is there any reason to believe that He ever will return? Can the 'foresight' which has repeatedly failed so miserably be trusted still,—for what we choose to separate out from the mass of His expectations as the core of the matter? On what grounds shall we adjust the discredited 'foresight' to the course of events, obviously unforeseen by Him, since His death? Where is the end of these 'adjustments'? Have we not already with 'adjustment' after 'adjustment' transformed beyond recognition the expectations of Jesus, even the latest and fullest to which He attained, and transmuted them into something fundamentally different,—passed, in a word, so far beyond Him, that we retain only an artificial connexion with Him and His real teaching, a connexion mediated by little more than a word?

That in this modern construction we have the precise contradictory of the conception of Jesus and of the course of His life on earth given us by the Evangelists, it needs no argument to establish. In the Gospel presentation, foresight is made the principle of our Lord's career. In the modern view He is credited with no foresight whatever. At best, He was possessed by a fixed conviction of His Messianic mission, whether gained in ecstatic vision (as, e.g., O. Holtzmann) or acquired in deep religious experiences (as, e.g., Schwartzkopff); and He felt an assurance, based on this ineradicable conviction, that in His own good time and way God would work that mission out for Him; and in this assurance He went faithfully onward fulfilling His daily task, bungling meanwhile egregiously in His reading of the scroll of destiny which was unrolling for Him. It is an intensely, even an exaggeratedly, human Christ which is here offered us: and He stands, therefore, in the strongest contrast with the frankly Divine Christ which the Gospels present to us. On what grounds can we be expected to substitute this for that? Certainly not on grounds of historical record. We have no historical record of the self-consciousness of Jesus except that embodied in the Gospel dramatization of His life and the Gospel report of His teaching; and that record expressly contradicts at every step this modern reconstruction of its contents and development. The very principle of the modern construction is reversal of the Gospel delineation. Its peculiarity is that, though it calls itself the 'historical' view, it has behind it no single scrap of historical testimony; the entirety of historical evidence contradicts it flatly. Are we to accept it, then, on the general grounds of inherent probability and rational construction? It is historically impossible that the great religious movement which we call Christianity could have taken its origin and derived its inspiration—an inspiration far from spent after two thousand years—from such a figure as this Jesus. The plain fact is that in these modern reconstructions we have nothing but a sustained attempt to construct a naturalistic Jesus; and their chief interest is that they bring before us with unwonted clearness the kind of being the man must have been who at that time and in those circumstances could have come forward making the claims which Jesus made without supernatural nature, endowment, or aid to sustain Him. The value of the speculation is that it makes superabundantly clear that no such being could have occupied the place which the historical Jesus occupied; could have made the impression on His followers which the historical Jesus made; could have become the source of the stream of religious influence which we call Christianity, as the historical Jesus became. The clear formulation of the naturalistic hypothesis, in the construction of a naturalistic Jesus, in other words, throws us violently back upon the Divine Jesus of the Evangelists as the only Jesus that is historically possible. From this point of view, the labours of the scholars who have with infinite pains built up this construction of Jesus' life and development have not been in vain.

What, then, is to be said of the predictions of Jesus, and especially of the three great series of prophecies of His death, resurrection, and return, with respect to their contents and fulfilment? This is not the place to discuss the eschatology of Jesus. But a few general remarks seem not uncalled for. The topic has received of late much renewed attention with very varied results, the number and variety of constructions proposed having been greatly increased above what the inherent difficulty of the subject will account for, by the freedom with which the Scripture data have been modified or set aside on so-called critical grounds by the several investigators. Nevertheless, most of the new interpretations also may be classified under the old categories of futuristic, preteristic, and spiritualistic.

The spiritualistic interpretation—whose method of dealing with our Lord's predictions readily falls in with a widespread theory that it is 'contrary to the spirit and manner of genuine prophecy to predict actual circumstances like a soothsayer' (Muirhead, "Eschatology of Jesus," p. 10; Schwartzkopff, "Prophecies of Jesus Christ," 78, 250, 258, 275, 312, etc.)—has received a new impulse through its attractive presentation by Erich Haupt ("Eschatolog. Aussagen Jesu," etc., 1895). Christ's eschatology, says Haupt, is infinitely simple, and all that He predicts is to be accomplished in a heavenly way which passes our comprehension; there is no soothsaying in His utterances— 'nowhere any predictions of external occurrences, everywhere only great moral religious laws which must operate everywhere and always, while nothing is said of the form in which they must act' (p. 157). A considerable stir has been created also by the revival (Schleiermacher, Weisse) by Weiffenbach ("Der Wiederkunftsgedanke Jesu," 1873, "Die Frage der Wiederkunft Jesu," 1901) of the identification of the return of Christ with His resurrection, although this view has retained few adherents since its refutation by Schwartzkopff ("The Prophecies of Jesus Christ," 1895), whose own view is its exact contradictory, viz., that by His resurrection Jesus meant just His return. The general conception, however, that 'for Jesus the hope of resurrection and the thought of return fell together,' so that 'when Jesus spoke of His resurrection He was thinking of His return, and *vice versa*' (O. Holtzmann, "War Jesus Ekstatiker?" 67, note), is very widely held. The subsidiary hypothesis (first suggested by Colani) of the inclusion in the great eschatological discourse attributed by the Evangelists to our Lord of a 'little Apocalypse' of Jewish or Jewish Christian origin, by which Weiffenbach eased his task, has in more or less modified form received the widest acceptance (cf. H. J. Holtzmann, "Lehrbuch der neutestamentlichen Theologie," i. 327, note), but rests on no solid grounds (cf. Weiss, Beyschlag, Haupt, Clemen). Most adherents of the modern school are clear that Jesus expected and asserted that He would return in Messianic glory for the consummation of the Kingdom; and most of them are equally clear that in this expectation and assertion, Jesus was mistaken (cf. H. J. Holtzmann, "Lehrbuch der neutestamentlichen Theologie," i. 312 f.). 'In the expectation that the kingdom was soon to come,' says Oscar Holtzmann in a passage typical enough of this whole school of exposition ("War Jesus Ekstatiker?" p. 133), 'Jesus erred in a human way'; and in such passages as Mk. ix. 1, xiii. 30, Mt. x. 23 he considers that the error is obvious. He adds, 'That such an error on the part of Jesus concerning not a side-issue but a fundamental point of His faith,—His first proclamation began, according to Mk. i. 15, with the πεπλή-ρωται ὁ καιρὸς καὶ ἤγγικεν ἡ βασιλεία τοῦ θεοῦ,— does not facilitate faith in Jesus is self-evident; but this error of Jesus is for His Church a highly instructive and therefore highly valuable warning to distinguish between the temporary and the permanent in the work of Jesus.' Not every one even of this school can go, however, quite this length. Even Schwartzkopff, while allowing that Jesus erred in this matter, wishes on that very account to think of the mere definition of times and seasons as belonging to the form rather than to the essence of His teaching ("The Prophecies of Jesus Christ," 1895, Eng. tr. 1897, p. 319; "Konnte Jesus irren?" 1896, p. 3); and in that Baldensperger is in substantial agreement with him ("Selbstbewusstsein Jesu[1], p. 148, ed.[2], p. 205). From the other side, E. Haupt ("Eschatolog. Aussagen Jesu," 1895, p. 138 f.) urges that Jesus must be supposed to have been able to avoid all errors, at least in the religious sphere, even if they concern nothing but the form; while Weiffenbach ("Die Frage," etc. p. 9) thinks we should hesitate to suppose Jesus could have erred in too close a definition of the time of His advent, when He expressly confesses that He was ignorant of its time (cf. Muirhead, "Eschat. of Jesus," 48-50, and especially 117). Probably Fritz Barth ("Die Hauptprobleme des Lebens Jesu," 1899, pp. 167-170) stands alone in cutting the knot by appealing to the conditionality of all prophecy. According to him, Jesus did, indeed, predict His return as coincident with the destruction of Jerusalem; but all genuine prophecy is conditioned upon the conduct of the human agents involved—'between prediction and fulfilment the conduct of man intrudes as a codetermining factor on which the fulfilment depends.' Thus this prediction has not failed, but its fulfilment has only been postponed—in accordance, it must be confessed, not with the will of God, but with that of man. It is difficult to see how Jesus is thus shielded from the imputation of defective foresight; but at least Barth is able on this view still to look for a return of the Lord.

The difficulty which the passages in our Saviour's teaching under discussion present to the reverent expositor is, of course, not to be denied or minimized. But surely this difficulty would need to be much more hopeless than it is before it could compel or justify the assumption of error 'in One who has never been convicted of error in anything else' (Sanday in Hastings' DB ii. 635—the whole passage should be read). The problem that faces us in this matter, it is apparent, in the meantime, is not one which can find its solution as a corollary to a speculative general view of our Lord's self-consciousness, its contents, and development. It is distinctly a problem of exegesis. We should be very sure that we know fully and precisely all that our Lord has declared about His return—its what and how and when—before we venture to suggest, even to our most intimate thought, that He has committed so gross an error as to its what and how and when as is so often assumed; especially as He has in the most solemn manner declared concerning precisely the words under consideration that heaven and earth shall pass away, but not His words. It would be sad if the passage of time has shown this declaration also to be mistaken. Meanwhile, the perfect foresight of our Lord, asserted and illustrated by all the Evangelists, certainly cannot be set aside by the facile assumption of an error on His part in a matter in which it is so difficult to demonstrate an error, and in which assumptions of all sorts are so little justified. For the detailed discussion of our Lord's eschatology, including the determination of His meaning in these utterances, reference must, however, be made to works treating expressly of this subject.

CHAPTER VIII

MISCONCEPTION OF JESUS, AND BLAS-PHEMY OF THE SON OF MAN[1]

IT IS, perhaps, not always appreciated how great a popular excitement was roused when, as Mark puts it, "after that John was delivered up, Jesus came into Galilee, preaching the Gospel of God, and saying, The time is fulfilled, and the Kingdom of God is at hand" (Mk. i. 14, 15). It is not the fault of the Evangelists if it is not fully understood. Mark, for example, adverts no less than eight times before he reaches the middle of his third chapter to the enthusiasm which attended Jesus wherever He appeared. We shall perceive how nearly this constitutes the main subject of these opening chapters of his Gospel, if we will but read consecutively the passages in which it is spoken of. "And the report of Him went out straightway everywhere into all the region of Galilee round about" (i. 28). "And at even when the sun did set they brought unto Him all that were sick, and them that were possessed with devils. And all the city were gathered together at the door" (i. 32, 33). "And they found Him and say unto Him, All are seeking Thee" (i. 37). "Insomuch that Jesus could no more openly enter into a city, and was without in desert places; and they came to Him from every quarter" (i. 45). "And when He entered again into Capernaum after some days it was noised that He was in the house. And many were gathered together so that there was no longer room for them, no, not even about the door . . . and when they could not come nigh Him for the crowd, they uncovered the roof where He was" (ii. 1, 2, 4). "And He went forth again by the seaside, and all the multitude resorted unto Him" (ii. 13). "And Jesus with His disciples withdrew to the sea; and a great multitude from Galilee followed: and from Judea, and from Jeru-

[1] From *The Princeton Theological Review*, xii. 1914, pp. 367-410; also from *Christology and Criticism*, pp. 53-94.

salem, and from Idumea, and beyond Jordan, a great multitude
hearing what great things He did, came unto Him. And He
spoke to His disciples that a little boat should wait on Him
because of the crowd, lest they should throng Him" (iii. 7-9).
"And He cometh into a house, and the multitude cometh together again, so that they could not so much as eat bread"
(iii. 20).[2] We may almost fancy that we can observe the crowds
which thronged Jesus ever increasing in number and persistency under our eyes: they gather at the door (i. 32-34); there
is no longer room even at the door (ii. 2); they are so continually with Him that He has no opportunity even to eat
(iii. 20). But we note that, already at i. 45 (cf. i. 37), they had
not only made the city inaccessible to Him, but had populated
the very desert to which He withdrew; and at iii. 9 (cf. iv. 1)
they so thronged Him even on the open sea-shore as to compel
Him to take refuge in a boat and speak to them thence. The
agency by which this great public agitation was created was
not merely the proclamation that the Kingdom of God was at
hand, but the manifestation of its actual presence in the abounding miracles of healing which were performed (Mat. xii. 28,
Lk. xi. 20).[3] Disease and death must have been almost eliminated for a brief season from Capernaum and the region which
lay immediately around Capernaum as a center. No wonder
the public mind was thrown into a state of profound perturba-
tion, and, the enthusiasm spreading, men flocked from every
quarter to see this great thing, questioning with one another
what it all meant.

Meanwhile, there were necessarily many who were not
drawn into the movement but remained rather, whether mo-
mentarily or permanently, merely spectators of it. Of these
there were in particular two classes who nevertheless could

[2] So, consecutively, iv. 1, v. 21, 24, 27, 31, vi. 34, vii. 24, 33, viii. 1, ix.
14, 25, x. 1, 46.

[3] Cf. E. von Dobschütz, *The Expositor*, VII. ix. (1910), p. 334: "This
'is come' (ἔφθασε) must mean something more than the usual 'is at hand'
(ἤγγικεν); it is the solemn declaration that the Kingdom is present in Jesus'
acting; His casting out of devils proves that the powers of the Kingdom are at
work." Cf. also H. J. Holtzmann, "Synoptiker,"[3] p. 243.

not look with indifference upon the wave of popular excitement sweeping through the land as it rose to its crest. These were those who felt responsible for Jesus Himself on the one hand, and on the other those who felt responsible for the religion of the community,—for we must bear in mind that the movement was from first to last a distinctly and intensely religious one. The circle of Jesus' relations (perhaps we may take the word for the moment in a rather broader sense than that of its current usage) and the body of the constituted religious guides of the people must each have been compelled to form at once a preliminary judgment upon the movement, and to act upon it. Nor was it likely that in either case this judgment would be favorable. Inevitably, in each case alike, it would be the expression of anxiety not to say of irritation. It is this natural judgment of what we may call the two interested classes that Mark records for us when, as he tells of the concourse of the crowd again to Jesus on His return to Capernaum after His second circuit in Galilee (Mk. iii. 20), he adds: "And when His relations heard it, they came forth to take charge of Him, for they said, He is out of His mind. And the scribes who came down from Jerusalem said, He hath Beelzebul, and it is by the prince of the demons that He casteth out the demons" (Mk. iii. 21, 22). The two judgments are as opposed as are the springs of emotion out of which they rise. It is pity that we hear the echoes of in the one; anger in the other. Jesus' relations, who, it must be observed, had a mere hearsay knowledge of the movement which was sweeping over Galilee in His train—He had not yet been to Nazareth (Mk. vi. 1),[4]—judged from the reports of His conduct which had reached them that He was not altogether Himself, and were prepared to take the responsibility of restraining Him. The scribes, who had heard His words and witnessed His works, could not deny that a supernatural power was operative among them; but, being unwilling to accredit this to a divine, ascribed it rather to a demoniac

---

[4] Lk. iv. 16 ff. seems to be a different visit (implied also in Mt. iv. 12, 13) which took place before His Galilean ministry had fairly begun (cf. Meyer, on Mt. xiii. 53).

source, and thus sought to break the influence of Jesus with the people. The two have in common only that they pass an unfavorable judgment upon the movement as a whole.

The naturalness of this unfavorable judgment in each case,[5] in the circumstances in which it was formed, has not prevented its being appealed to, in each instance, in disproof of the supernaturalness of Jesus' person and ministry. It is urged that, if Jesus was really a divine person and His ministry was accompanied by obviously supernatural effects, such as are narrated in the Gospels, it would be inconceivable that those who stood nearest to Him and knew Him best, should have pronounced Him out of His mind. And it is urged again that, in His defence of Himself from the charge of the scribes that He was possessed of a demon and wrought His wonders by the power of the evil one, Jesus so far from asserting that He was a divine person actually contrasts Himself with the divine Spirit as one to speak against whom were a venial sin while to speak against the Spirit is unpardonable blasphemy—obviously because the Spirit is divine. That we may form a right estimate of these representations, we should look a little closely at the relevant passages.

I

It is Mark alone who tells us of the judgment passed upon Jesus by His relations. The words in which he does it are these: "And He cometh home, and the crowd cometh together again, so that they were not able even to eat bread. And when His relations heard it they came forth to take charge of Him; for they said, He is out of His mind."

The opening words, which we have rendered: "And He cometh home," are translated by many rather: "And He

[5] Cf. A. Schweitzer, *The Expositor*, November 1913, p. 449, who remarks of them: "This only means, however, that the former [the scribes] wished at all costs to discredit Him with the people, and that His relatives noticed a change in Him and could not understand how He could come forward as a teacher and prophet."

cometh into a house."[6] This statement is then explained as the fundamental statement of the passage, preparing the way, and setting the scene, for the whole remainder of the chapter. Thus a certain emphasis is made to fall on Jesus' actual entrance into a house. We certainly should not in this case, however, expect the ambiguous simple $\ἔρχομαι$ to be used,—the $\εἰς$ following which might indeed be ordinarily best rendered "to" (compare "unto," Mt. ii. 11, viii. 14, ix. 23, 28, Mk. i. 29, etc.). His actual entrance into the house may thus even be left in some doubt (compare Mk. v. 38, 39: "and they come to the house . . . and entering it . . ."). The more precise $\εἰσέρχομαι$ we may feel sure would have been employed had this been the meaning which was intended to be conveyed, especially if the emphasis which is assumed in the interpretation in question falls upon it (compare Mt. x. 12, xii. 4, 29, Mk. ii. 26, iii. 27, vi. 10, vii. 17, 24, ix. 28, Lk. ix. 4). Moreover it is not easy to find an adequate reason in the immediate context for so formal a statement that Jesus did so simple a thing as to "come into a house." We may say[7] that Jesus went into a house obviously to seek rest and to take food (verse 20): but his need of these things seems to supply no sufficient reason for so formal a record of so slender a circumstance as His going into a house. It is customary, therefore, to go further afield and to seek the real reason of the record in the preparation it gives for the subsequent narrative, the eye being particularly fixed on the statement of verse 31, that His mother and brothers "stood without."[8] Thus, however,

---

[6] James Moffat, who in 1901 ("The Historical New Testament" p. 280), had correctly rendered: "Then He comes home," has substituted for this in 1913 ("The New Testament: A New Translation"): "They went indoors." This would exactly render the words in a different context: and the implication of "home" is in it. But it misses the point here.

[7] With B. Weiss (1878).

[8] B. Weiss *in loc.*: "He goes into a house, because it was in a house that the incident took place which the narrative has in mind (cf. verse 31)" (Meyer on Mark, ed. 6, 1878); "Emphasized in contrast to His sojourn at the sea-side or on the mountain-top (verses 7, 13), because the scene, iii. 31 ff. takes place in a house and Mark wishes to prepare for this," (Meyer on Mark, ed. 8, 1892; ed. 9, 1901); "Prepares for the narrative of iii. 31 ff., which what immediately follows, therefore, only introduces," ("Die vier Evangelien," 1900, p. 186).

an extraordinary method of composition is ascribed to the evangelist. We are to suppose that, having begun an account of Jesus' relations to His family with iii. 20, 21, Mark suddenly breaks off and thrusts in a long account of His relations with the scribes, only to return without warning again to His family at iii. 31, leaving all the sutures unclosed. We are to treat the whole narrative enclosed in verses 22-30, in other words, as a parenthesis, and to expound verses 20, 21 immediately in connection with verses 31 ff., as if the intermediate section were not there—although it grows naturally out of, and forms a natural whole with, verses 20, 21.[9]

Such results as these would seem to be a sufficient indication that a false start has been taken when we render the opening clause: "And He cometh into a house." In point of fact the phrase may in itself just as well mean: "And He cometh home" (compare viii. 3, 26 with defining pronouns and ii. 1, v. r. pregnantly with verb of rest: vii. 17, ix. 28 where εἰς οἶκον is connected with εἰσέρχομαι, are different—render "indoors"); and this sense is strongly recommended by the context. Jesus had been at the seaside (verse 7) and on the mountain (verse 13): He now returns "home," that is to say, to Capernaum (compare i. 21, ii. 1). The narrative is composed of circuits out

[9] The difficulties arising from this construction become flagrantly apparent in the course of A. Loisy's skilful efforts to overcome them ("Les Synoptiques," i. pp. 696 ff.): "To consider only the present order of the texts, it might be said that Mark, having deliberately neglected (not been ignorant of) a fact which did not have in itself any particular prominence, substituted for it, in preparation for an incident which he intended to recount after the discourse of the Saviour [to the scribes], the mention of a judgment passed upon Jesus by His own family, which, though less unfavorable than that of the Pharisees, does not fail to exhibit in a sufficiently startling light, the relations of the new preacher with His own people. The *mise en scène* is the sufficiently natural preamble of the incident concerning the family of Jesus: what is secondary is the connection of the disputation with this incident and the artifice which has permitted Mark to neglect the teaching of the possessed man which in the common source of the Synoptics served as the introduction to the disputation. . . . What is said of the family does not attach itself without some embarrassment to the context: but this is a piece of unskilfulness which belongs to the redaction, arising possibly from the fact that the preamble, though conceived with a view to the anecdote, does not belong to the traditional basis of the narrative."

from Capernaum and returns to Capernaum, as the center of
Jesus' active work: this is one of the points at which His return
to His base of operations is intimated, and, as on the former
occasions (i. 32, ii. 3; compare i. 45 where R.V.mg. questions
whether εἰςπόλιν may not be "*the city*," as indeed A.V. had
boldly translated it[10]), the crowd immediately gathers. In this
case, the close connection which has been assumed between
iii. 20 and iii. 31 falls away; the misleading prominence into
which the simple opening statement of verse 20 has been
thrown is removed; and that statement resumes its natural
place as only one of the numerous intimations in this narrative
of Jesus' alternating excursions from Capernaum and returns to
it (i. 21-35; ii. 1-13; iii. 1-7; iii. 20; iv. 1).

The chief interest of this determination lies in its bearing
on the interpretation of the phrase in verse 21 which we have
translated "His relations." If verses 20, 21 were not written
specifically in preparation for verses 31 ff.; verses 22-30 are not
a parenthesis; and verses 31-35 record a new incident: then
the phrase "His relations" in verse 21 does not find its explanation in "His mother and His brothers" of verse 31—as is very
commonly represented—but must be independently interpreted.
This phrase,[11] in Greek writers generally, bears ordinarily the
meaning of "legates," "representatives," and it still commonly
occurs in the papyri in the sense of "agents," "representatives."
By the side of this usage, however, there is found another, less
common but nevertheless constant, in which it bears the sense,
either broadly of "adherents," "followers," or more narrowly of

10 Render "into town."

11 For discussions of the meaning of the phrase, see especially Fritzsche *in
loc.* and F. Field, "Notes on the Translation of the N. T.," p. 25 (he argues for
the meaning "household"). For the usage of the phrase in the papyri, see J. H.
Moulton, *The Expositor,* VI. vii. p. 118, viii. p. 436; "Prolegomena," etc., pp.
106-107; *The Expository Times,* xx, p. 476. At "Prolegomena," pp. 106-107, he
says: "Οἱ παρ' αὐτοῦ is exceedingly common [in the papyri] to denote 'his agents'
or 'representatives.' It has hitherto been less easy to find parallels for Mk. iii.
21, where it must mean 'his family'; see Swete and Field *in loc.* We can now
cite GH 36 (ii./B.C.) οἱ παρ' ἡμῶν πάντες BU 998 (ii./B.C.) and Par. P. 36
(ii./B.C.)."

"household," "family," or "kindred." It is obvious that it is in this latter general sense that it is employed in our passage, but it is not easy to fix the exact limits of its connotation. That Jesus' disciples—His adherents, followers—are not intended, is clear, since a contrast is drawn with them (verse 20, αὐτούς). Our English versions—Authorized and Revised,—render the term "friends," not badly if it be taken, as it obviously is intended to be, in a personal, rather than an official sense.[12] The margin of the Authorized Version proposes instead the narrower "kinsmen," following in this the Wycliffite "kynnesmen" and the Genevan "kynesfolkes." The modern versions continue the same line: George R. Noyes, "relations"; James Moffat, 1901, "relatives"; *Twentieth Century New Testament*, "relations"; Samuel Lloyd, "kinsmen"; James Moffat, 1913, "family."[13] It can scarcely be doubted that this is practically what is meant, though too restricted a sense should not be insisted upon.[14] Obviously those are intended who bore such a relation to Jesus that they felt themselves responsible for Him, and that they would naturally be looked to by others to take charge of Him in the contingency of His needing to be kept under some restraint. We might think, in the varying circumstances which would render each natural, of His clansmen, of His fellow-townsmen, of His responsible friends, of His blood-kinsmen, of His household, of His family, of His parents, of His brothers.[15] In the absence of closer contextual definition, only the known circumstances of Jesus' case could supply us with confident guidance in fixing upon the precise persons intended. All that is inti-

---

[12] F.·C. Conybeare, "Myth, Magic and Morals," 1909, p. 72, insists *suo more* that the rendering "friends" is a "falsification of the text" with the intention of "deceiving English readers who cannot read Greek." The rebuke administered to him by J. H. Moulton, *The Expository Times*, xx. p. 476, is richly deserved.

[13] But Weymouth, "The Modern Speech New Testament," retains the A. V., "friends." Weizsäcker renders "die Seinigen"; Th. Zahn, "Forschungen," etc., iv. p. 332, "die Angehörigen," as also P. W. Schmiedel, cf. note 41 below.

[14] Cf. Swete's note.

[15] Theophylact defines: οἱ οἰκεῖοι αὐτοῦ, with οἱ ἀπὸ τῆς αὐτῆς πατρίδος and οἱ ἀδελφοὶ αὐτοῦ as alternatives.

mated here is that His natural guardians were inclined to judge Him to be out of His mind, and were prepared to take measures to put Him under the restraint required by His sad condition. Who these natural guardians were we can only conjecturally supply from our further knowledge. There are some who feel quite sure that His mother could not be included among them, because they find it difficult or impossible to believe that she should have so cruelly misjudged Him.[16] There are others, on the contrary,[17] who are prepared to assert confidently, if not even violently, that His mother was included among them; sometimes, apparently, for no other reason than that thus the passage may be exploited as inconsistent, say, with the representations of the Infancy-chapters of Matthew and Luke or in general with the doctrine of the supernatural origin of Jesus. Too great confidence on either part seems misplaced. The passage itself gives us no guidance; and general considerations appear indecisive.

It is important to observe, however, that the judgment informed as to His condition by Jesus' friends or kinsfolk—according to our broader or narrower understanding of the phrase—was founded on hearsay evidence only. "When His relations *heard* . . . ," we read. The meaning can hardly be, merely, that as soon as they heard that He had come home, they went forth to lay hands on Him. Nor does it seem likely that the meaning is merely that they went forth to lay hands on Him when they heard that, on His coming home, a multitude had gathered about Him. The article before "multitude" is probably genuine; and, if genuine, should not be neglected. And, in any event, the "again" has its rights. What appears to be meant is that His relations were moved to their action by the reports which reached them of the great excitement that had been raised by His ministry throughout Galilee, a culminating manifestation of which was seen in this renewed

16 Th. Zahn, "Forschungen," etc., vi. p. 332: "We are scarcely to think of Mary among them . . . the word, ἐξέστη is not suitable in the mouth of the mother, and the intention to use physical force against the madman is attributable only to the men not to the women."

17 Conybeare, as above.

gathering of the crowd at His house.[18] The reports which had reached them of the thronging multitudes that attended His whole work in Galilee and of the popular enthusiasm which followed His movements, led them to suppose Him to be laboring under over-excitement and to undertake the duty of putting Him under restraint.

If His friends, however, had not themselves witnessed His work and knew of its effects only from hearsay, it is not likely that they were living in Capernaum which was the center of His activity and the seat of the most constant popular enthusiasm. On the other hand, in His circuits out from Capernaum He had not yet visited Nazareth (Mk. vi. 1, Mt. xiii. 54).[19] If Nazareth was the home of His friends here mentioned, therefore, their dependence on rumor for knowledge of His work and its effects, is in harmony with what we read in Lk. iv. 23 ff.,[20] Mk. vi. 5, Mt. xiii. 58. It is, indeed, frequently supposed that not Jesus alone, but His family also, had removed from Nazareth to Capernaum at the very beginning of His ministry (Jno. ii. 12).[21] This, however, is little likely in itself;[22] and it would compel us to suppose either that their settlement at Capernaum was quickly abandoned ("and they remained there not many days"[23]), or that by Jesus' friends in our present passage, not "His mother and His brethren and His disciples" are intended, but some broader circle of those responsible for

18 Cf. A. B. Bruce, *in loc.*: "not to be restricted to what is mentioned in verse 20; refers to the whole Galilean ministry with its cures, and crowds, and constant strain."

19 We have already noted (note 4) that Luke iv. 16 ff. seems to record an earlier visit to Nazareth before His systematic Galilean ministry had begun. Besides Meyer's note at Mt. xiii. 53-58 (E. T. p. 372) cf. Godet's notes on Lk. iv. 23 (E. T. i. p. 238), and John ii. 12 (E. T. ii. p. 19). Luke iv. 23 of course offers a difficulty for this view.

20 Cf. Godet, i. p. 237: "This speech betrays an ironical doubt respecting those marvellous things which were attributed to Him."

21 So Wieseler, De Wette, Tholuck, Ewald: cf. esp. Th. Zahn, *in loc.* (p. 163 and note 3) and "Forschungen," vi. p. 331.

22 Cf. Meyer's note on Jno. ii. 12 (E. T. i. p. 149).

23 Cf. Westcott's note on Jno. ii. 12: "This is perhaps mentioned to show that at present Capernaum was not made the permanent residence of the Lord, as it became afterwards."

Him. If Jesus' "friends" in the responsible sense of our passage were dwelling in Capernaum—especially if these "friends" be understood as precisely His mother and brothers, constituting His "household"—it would be inexplicable that His returning "home" should not have been to their house; and not only would their personal lack of acquaintance with His work or movements ("when they heard") be inexplicable, but the action ascribed to them ("they went forth") would be inappropriate. It would seem that we must think of the "friends" in question as living somewhere out of the path of His work hitherto, and away from the "home" to which He returned from the sea-side and mountain-top. The elimination of His disciples—who belonged to the party which returned from Cana—from the "friends" of our present passage is not only required by the situation in our passage itself, but is in harmony with the statement of Jno. ii. 11, that they already believed in Him. For, a certain measure of unbelief is, of course, implied in the judgment passed on Him by His "friends" here. If His brothers are meant, as seems intrinsically probable, this is in harmony with Jno. vii. 5, from which we learn that they remained unbelieving until the end.[24] The phrases of Jno. vii. 3-5 form, indeed, a very pungent commentary on our passage.

The measure of the unbelief—we designedly use the milder term, instead of the stronger, "disbelief"—which is implied in the judgment and action of Jesus' "friends" recorded in our passage is deserving of some consideration. That we may form an estimate of it it would be well to ascertain with some exactness what is really meant by the term, "He is beside Himself." Many insist that there is no real difference between this judgment upon Jesus and that expressed by the scribes in the words, "He hath Beelzebul" (verse 22).[25] Madness, it is urged, was explained as demoniacal possession, and to say that one was

[24] Cf. Swete's note: "The family of Jesus was doubtless inspired by a desire for His safety, but their interpretation of His enthusiasm implied want of faith in Him, cf. Jno. vii. 5; the Mother perhaps was overpersuaded by the brethren."

[25] E.g. H. J. Holtzmann (p. 127), who remarks that Theophylact already explains correctly: δαίμονα ἔχει.

mad was all one with saying that he was possessed.[26] On the face of it, however, this view is untenable. Possession and insanity are not clearly identified in the Evangelical narratives. It is not even intimated that they were constantly associated.[27] In our present passage they even seem to be expressly distinguished. Mark clearly desires to contrast the judgments passed on Jesus by His friends and His enemies, as, though both uncomprehending, yet the pitying and the condemnatory judgment. Even, however, should we identify all mental alienation with possession, the degree of alienation implied in any given instance would still remain undetermined; the effects of the possession would naturally be very varied, and might on occasion involve only the slightest, perhaps the most temporary unbalancing. In any case, therefore, we are thrown back upon what is actually said.

[26] Cf. E. Renan, "Vie de Jesus"[2] 1863, p. 263, note 4 (E. T. of the twenty-third and final ed. 1913, p. 273, note 3): "This phrase 'Thou hast a demon' (Mt. xi. 18, Lk. vii. 33, Jno. vii. 20, viii. 48 ff., x. 20 ff.) should be rendered by 'Thou art insane,' as it is said in Arabic medjnoun enté. This verb, δαιμονᾶν has also in the whole of classical antiquity the sense of 'to be insane.'" In the text, however, it is said: "But here again the difficulties must not be exaggerated. The disorders explained by possessions were often very slight. In our day, in Syria, people are regarded as insane or possessed by a demon (the two notions are the same, medjnoun) who have only some little eccentricity (bizarrerie)."

[27] The physical accompaniment of possession mentioned in Mt. ix. 32, Lk. xi. 14 is only dumbness, in Mt. xii. 22, blindness and dumbness, in Lk. xiii. 10-17, curvature of the spine; Cf. also Mt. xv. 22, Mk. vii. 26, xvi. 9, Lk. iv. 33, viii. 2 in none of which cases is insanity indicated. Only in a single instance is mania expressly intimated, and that only by its contrasting state (Mk. v. 15, Lk. viii. 35; cf. 2 Cor. v. 13). W. M. Alexander, "Demonic Possession in the New Testament," 1902, upholding the thesis that "all cases designated 'demoniac' belong to the category 'Lunacy or Idiocy'" (p. 147), establishes his diagnosis in only three cases (Mk. i. 21-26 = Lk. iv. 31-37; Mt. viii. 28-34 = Mk. v. 1-17, Lk. viii. 26-37; Mt. xvii. 14-20 = Mk. ix. 14-29, Lk. ix. 37-43); and in two of these only with difficulty and at the cost of the enlargement of the category of "lunacy" by the addition of "and idiocy." He then applies this diagnosis, without express warrant from the text, to all other cases of possession. John x. 20 need not be read as identifying all possession with lunacy, but may only identify this particular case of lunacy with possession as its cause: cf. Jno. vii. 20, viii. 48.

The term employed[28] in the present passage is not a strong one and need not imply a serious state of mental disturbance. The fundamental implication of the word is no more than that the subject is thrown out of his normal state into a condition of strong, perhaps ungovernable, emotion. The emotion in question may be of the most varied kind, but commonly in the New Testament usage of the word (uniformly except for our present passage and II Cor. v. 13) it is that of amazement, perhaps with a suggestion of bewilderment.[29] In the special usage illustrated by our present passage (cf. II Cor. v. 13), in which it expresses that state of mental aberration which we also describe as "not one's self," it need not import more than an overwrought condition in which it might be thought that the prudent conduct of life would be unlikely and could become impossible. In this general sense, it occurs nowhere else in the New Testament except in II Cor. v. 13, where (to say nothing of demoniacal possession) it certainly does not suggest either raving madness or irrational insanity, but describes on the contrary an ecstatic state in which the Apostle saw a ground for much glorying (xii. 1).[30] We need not imagine, then, that Jesus' friends saw

[28] J. H. Heinrich Schmidt in § 174 of his *Synonymik der Griechischen Sprache* deals with the terms which designate a perverted state of mind (he had dealt in § 147 with these which express a mental deficiency, especially ἄφρων and ἄνους). He divides them into three groups: (1) Words which in the first instance designate the violent utterances of a disturbed mind; (2) words which express more the inward disorder by which the soul is carried away by senseless passions; (3) words which rather describe the soul which thinks and feels in a disturbed manner. Ἐξίστημι (ἔκστασις) is not included in his lists; but this may be in part because he leaves to one side such terms as require the addition of a φρενός or φρενῶν, or some contextual indication, to define the meaning; and confines himself to such as bear in themselves their significance.

[29] Mt. xii. 23; Mk. ii. 12, v. 42, vi. 51; Lk. ii. 47, viii. 56, xxiv. 22; Acts ii. 7-12, viii. 9, 11, 13, ix. 21, x. 45, xii. 16 = "amazed"; Mk. iii. 21, II Cor. v. 13 = "demented." Cf. ἔκστασις: Mk. v. 42, xvi. 8; Lk. v. 26; Acts iii. 10 = "amazement"; Acts x. 10, xi. 5, xxii. 17 = "trance." Cf. Art. "Amazement" in Hastings' *DCG*.

[30] Cf. C. F. G. Heinrici, "Das zweite Sendschreiben des Apostel Paulus an die Korinthier," 1887, pp. 277 f.: "The fundamental sense of ἐξίστημι *to be*

in Him a maniac; we need only understand,—what surely would not be unnatural in men who had as yet at least no sense of the nature of His mission—that they were led by the reports which had come to them to believe that He was in a state of exaltation which endangered His health and safety and needed some soothing hand to guard Him from Himself.[31]

That they felt His condition to be serious, may be inferred from the fact that they were prepared "to lay hold upon Him." Yet exaggeration must be shunned here too. The term, no doubt emphasizes in its ground-idea the thought of force, even of violence; but, beginning thus with the notion of taking forcible possession of, it came to be employed also of simply taking possession of, with the idea of force quite out of sight, and ended by meaning merely to obtain, to get (Acts xxvii. 13), and, indeed, merely to cling to (Mt. xxviii. 9, Acts iii. 11), to retain, to hold (Mt. vii. 3, 4, 8, 9, 10). There is no need in our present passage to emphasize the idea of violence, as if His

out of oneself, as this is brought about through the experience of an over-mastering impression, makes the word equally suitable for describing conditions of very high emotions, like amazement, joy, terror; and emotions which lie beyond the limits of sound mental life (ἐν ἑαυτῷ εἶναι . . . ἐντὸς ἑαυτοῦ γίνεσθαι), whether of the nature of insanity or of rapture. In the latter sense σωφρονεῖν is the technical contrast to ἐκστῆναι, and it is accordingly introduced here for the purpose of indicating experiences which had for the Apostle a significance similar to that of the rapture which is described later. In this connection the expression then suggests that ecstatic conditions which remain, in their content and source, obscure for the estimate of all others, cannot be the subject of boasting before others. . . . The key to the full understanding of the contrast of ἐκστῆναι and σωφρονεῖν is supplied, however, only by the detailed description of the ecstasy in the polemic concluding sections, which has been mentioned. (xii. 1 f.) . . ."

[31] Cf. A. Loisy, "Evang. Synopt," i. p. 698: "They do not say that Jesus had lost His mind, the word which the Evangelist employs not having this precise meaning in the usage of the New Testament, but being used to designate every transport of astonishment, of admiration, of stupor, of enthusiasm; but they believed Him to be in a state of mystical exaltation, which made Him lose the real sense of life and of His own condition." A. B. Bruce, *in loc.*, goes to an extreme when he says: "In the opinion of His friends, He was in a state of excitement bordering on insanity." Perhaps the English word "transport" presents as fair a rendering of the term here as can be found.

kinsmen wished "to seize" Jesus.[32] Even "to lay hold upon Him"
is too strong a rendering. "To get Him" is nearer to what it
intended; and the idea is not so much to put Him in ward as to
take Him in charge. Of course the idea of compulsion underlies
everything: His relations were acting under the impression that
He was in need of kindly control and were prepared to protect
Him from Himself. But it is the idea of protection which dominates the statement, rather than that of compulsion.

Such a judgment upon Jesus' activities, and such an attitude
towards His person, were inevitable for those of His kindred
who, feeling responsible for Him, were yet ill-informed concerning His person and work. There were some of His kindred,
no doubt, to whom such a judgment and attitude would have
been at this stage impossible. James and John were of His
kindred,[33] and there may have been others of those closest to
Him who, with them, already, in the full sense of Jno. ii. 11,
"believed on Him." But it is not necessary to pronounce this
judgment of His work and attitude toward His person incom-
patible with any measure of faith in Him; or even with a high
degree of faith in Him if imperfectly informed whether of what
was to be expected of Him or of what He was actually doing.
There is no compelling reason for insisting that His mother was
of the number of those of whom it is said here that they were
led to believe that He was "beside Himself" and in need of some
protective care. But neither does there seem to be any compelling reason for assuming that she could not possibly be of their

[32] H. J. Holtzmann: "Their purpose is *to apprehend Him*; to possess
themselves of Him, κρατ . αὐτ., like vi. 17, xii. 12, xiv. 1; they would seek out
the morbidly overstrained member of the family who had become strange and
incomprehensible to them, and, no doubt for His own advantage, but still
forcibly, withdraw Him from public life." Wohlenberg: "In order to seize
Jesus (κρατῆσαι), to possess themselves of Him, if not to take Him into
custody, yet in some sense forcibly to apprehend Him; cf. xii. 12, xiv. 1, 46."
B. Weiss: "In order to apprehend Him, possess themselves of Him. . . . In
spite of the strongly colored expression of Mk. we are by no means to think of
a hostile act (Klostermann), but at the most of a kindly compulsion, which
they thought to exercise in His own interest to protect Him in the keeping
of the family from further crowding."

[33] As Wohlenberg reminds us.

number.[34] Mary too (like John the Baptist, Mt. xi. 2 ff.), may have had searchings of heart before she adjusted herself to the Great Reality; and, in the meantime, as she had exercised control over her son in His infancy (Lk. ii. 51), so in the first days of His ministry she may have fancied that she saw indications that He still required her motherly care. There would be implied in this, not "a total unbelief in His pretensions, but only an imperfect view of them."[35] Where no belief in His pretensions existed such an attitude towards Him as is here intimated, was, as we have said, not only natural but inevitable. His unbelieving brothers, however kindly, must have thought Him in some sense out of His mind, and must have faced the duty of casting around Him some protection.[36]

Natural, however, as the judgment of Jesus and the attitude towards His person which are here recorded, are in the circumstances and to the persons to which they are ascribed, the critics have laid hold upon them as representing a point of view regarding Jesus, or at least regarding Mary, which is inconsistent with the supernaturalistic tradition of Jesus. On this ground they seek to account for the fact that this section appears in

[34] So, e.g., Wohlenberg: "From all that we otherwise know of Mary, His Mother, it must be taken as absolutely excluded that she should come forward in any way antagonistically to Jesus."

[35] The words we have quoted are from the excellent comment of J. A. Alexander on Mk. iii. 21, where, however, he is speaking not of Mary but of Jesus' friends in general, to whom is to be attributed also absence or deficiency of faith. "This," says Alexander, was "a very natural and intelligible state of mind at this stage of the history, and on the part of those whose spiritual or religious feelings were less strong and well-defined than their natural affections or humanity." With Mary also in mind, he repeats in his comment on verse 31, that "nothing could be more natural and pardonable than precisely such solicitude, which is perfectly compatible with true faith and affection, but imperfect views both of His person and mission."

[36] Cf. G. Salmon, "The Human Element in the Gospels," 1907, p. 203: "To the Christan reader it is shocking that any one should be able to suppose that our Lord was out of His mind; yet, if we consider the circumstances, we perceive that the idea was one most likely to occur as it often has done since, when followers of His who were afterwards venerated as saints, had judgments passed on them by sensible men of the world. It is in itself perfectly credible that our Lord should have made the impression commonly produced by one who steps completely out of the beaten track."

Mark's Gospel only. It was omitted by Matthew and Luke, they tell us, because not consonant with their point of view. In what respect Mark's point of view as to the person of Jesus, or his reverence for Jesus, differs from that of Matthew and Luke, it is meanwhile difficult to perceive. The mere presence of this passage in one of the Evangelists is proof enough that it contains nothing contradictory to the reverence for Jesus' person which is common to them all.[37] Nevertheless P. W. Schmiedel gives this passage a place among his nine "pillar-passages" which he pronounces absolutely credible, as preserving traditions of the real Jesus, precisely on the ground that they make assertions about Jesus which could not have been invented by His worshipping followers, and must therefore have thrust themselves upon this or that Evangelist merely by the force of their undeniable authenticity. This is evidenced, he declares, by the fact that they have been omitted by others of the Evangelists as offensive to their reverence for Jesus.[38] On this view, Matthew and Luke are supposed to have had this statement before them and to have omitted it, because it seemed to them derogatory to Jesus' dignity that those nearest to Him should, even at the outset of His ministry, have been led to fear that He might be beside Himself; and Schmiedel labors[39] to show that Matthew's narrative, for example, retains signs of having been consciously adapted from Mark's. It is more usual, however, to suppose that Mark's statement has been omitted by the other Gospels (presumed to be later than Mark and to be in large part based on it) in the interests of growing reverence for Mary as the mother of our Lord, rather than directly of reverence for Jesus.[40] And, indeed, Schmiedel himself when

[37] Cf. *The Princeton Theological Review*, xi. 2 (April, 1913), pp. 252 ff.

[38] "Encyclopaedia Biblica," col. 1881; cf. *The Princeton Theological Review*, xi. 2 (April, 1913), pp. 204 ff.

[39] Coll. 1847-1848.

[40] H. J. Holtzmann may serve as a typical instance ("Synoptiker"[3] p. 68): "Mark in the most significant way stands alone with the notice in verse 21, since Matthew and Luke already are unable to reconcile themselves to this conception of Mary, and therefore the reparation to be spoken of at Lk. ii. 48." Accordingly at p. 323, he follows Pfleiderer in supposing that the "Behold thy

dealing with the passage at large lapses into this point of view.[41]
In a passage like this, it is suggested, Mark accordingly preserves an earlier and truer tradition of the attitude of Jesus'
kinsfolk to His person and work than can be found in the later
Gospels, whether John or Matthew and Luke. It must be borne
in mind, however, that, according to John also, the brothers of
Jesus did not believe in Him (Jno. vii. 5), and must therefore
have held much the view of Him which is placed on the lips of
Jesus' kinsmen in our present passage. The attitude of Mary
towards Him alone, can come into question; and it is upon it,
accordingly, that the contrast between Matthew and Luke, with
their "Infancy chapters" in which Mary's supernatural information as to her son is exploited, and Mark, which has nothing
of this kind, is insisted upon.

The whole case hangs on the suppositions that Mary was
included among the kinsmen of Jesus mentioned in Mk. iii. 21,
and that the judgment upon Jesus there ascribed to His kinsmen
would be impossible to the Mary of the opening chapters of
Matthew and Luke. We have seen that neither supposition is
necessary, or, indeed, in the presence of any good reasons to
the contrary, even reasonable. We may accept the statement of
Mk. iii. 20, 21 as intrinsically self-evidencing and therefore
"absolutely credible" as a genuine historical fact, without any

father and I have sought thee" of Lk. ii. 48 is a reminiscence of Mk. iii. 32,
"Behold thy Mother and thy brothers seek thee," and serves the further purpose
of counteracting what is said in Mk. iii. 21 (not in Luke) together with its
consequences in iii. 31-35 (Lk. xviii. 19-21) and to soften the shadow thrown
by it on Mary.

[41] "Das vierte Evangelium gegenüber den drei ersten," 1906, p. 18:
"We must observe moreover the rôle which *Jesus' Mother* plays in the miracle
at Cana. Although Jesus had never before worked a miracle (Jno. ii. 11) she
knows beforehand that He is going to work one and says to the servants,
although she is rebuffed by Him, 'Whatever He bids you, do.' How entirely
different it is in Mark! Here (iii. 21) Jesus' kinsmen (*Angehörigen*) go out to
lay hold of Him because they said, 'He is beside Himself.' Who these kinsmen
were we very soon learn (iii. 31-35): His mother and His brothers come to
Him and call Him out of the house. And it is only from their purpose to put
a stop to His work and to confine Him to His home that His rude answer finds
its explanation: 'Who is my mother and my brothers? He who does the will of
God, the same is my brother and sister and mother.'"

fear of discrediting thereby either the Infancy chapters of Matthew and Luke or the historical tradition of the supernatural Jesus which constitutes the substance of all the Evangelical records. The attempts to account for the absence of this statement from Matthew and Luke as deliberate omission on dogmatic grounds are accordingly altogether ineffective and the endeavor to discover in the narratives of Matthew and Luke hidden signs of acquaintance with[42] and conscious alteration of Mark's text are too flimsy to justify notice. The entire fact is that we are indebted to Mark for a piece of information altogether natural in itself and consonant with the entire body of facts recorded in the other Evangelists, which nevertheless they do not also preserve for us. This might be inexplicable if we were compelled to suppose that each Evangelist has told us all he knew, or all he knew which he thought "fit to print." But it is just what we should expect on the supposition—which is the only tenable one—that each Evangelist, though serving himself, to a very great extent, with common sources of information, has yet set down in his Gospel from the general store, only what commended itself to him as suitable for his purpose and adapted to advance his particular object in writing.

The naturalness and, indeed, inevitableness of the judgment that Jesus was out of His mind on the part of men not ill-disposed towards Him but yet unable to accept His claims for Himself at their face value, is illustrated by the return to this judgment by a type of modern unbelief. A large literature has in recent years grown up around the suggestion that Jesus was more or less of unsound mind. Whether He is explained as a paranoiac lunatic or merely as a visionary ecstatic, it is inevitable that those who cannot see in Him the Divine Being He proclaimed Himself to be, should think His lofty estimate of Himself too lofty and should seek the account of His too lofty estimate of Himself in some—greater or less—mental derangement. We can scarcely look upon a like judgment among His

---

[42] We do not doubt that the incident recorded in Mark iii. 20-21 was known to the authors of both Matthew and Luke, as was much else which they (as writing freely, each for his own particular end) do not record.

contemporaries as strange when we are so familiar with it today; or urge its existence among His contemporaries as evidence of anything more than it witnesses to today. In simple fact, Jesus' career was not that of an ordinary man: and the dilemma is inevitable that He was either something more than a normal man or something less. We, like His contemporaries,—and His contemporaries like us—have only the alternatives: either supernatural or subnormal, either Divine or else "out of His mind."[43]

II

It is again Mark alone who records the extreme expression of the hatred of the scribes towards Jesus in their ascription to Him of demoniacal possession.[44] All three of the Synoptics, however, report the charge made by His enemies that it was by the aid of Beelzebul, the prince of the demons, that He cast out demons.[45] The solemn warning against blasphemy against the Holy Spirit which Jesus founded upon this charge, occurs —in one form or another—in all three Gospels, though in this connection only in Matthew and Mark,[46] while in Luke it appears in another context.[47] As it is solely with this warning that we are now concerned, we transcribe it in its three forms. "Verily, I say unto you, All things shall be forgiven unto the sons of men, their sins, and their blasphemies wherewithsoever they shall blaspheme; but whosoever shall blaspheme against the Holy Spirit hath never forgiveness, but is guilty of an eternal sin. Because they said, He hath an unclean Spirit" (Mk. iii. 28-30). "And everyone who shall speak a word against the Son of Man, it shall be forgiven unto him; but unto him that blasphemeth against the Holy Spirit, it shall not be forgiven" (Lk. xii. 10). "Therefore I say unto you, every sin and blas-

[43] Cf. what is said with respect to W. Heitmüller's hesitations and difficulties in The Princeton Theological Review, xii. 2 (April, 1914), pp. 315 ff.

[44] Mk. iii. 22-30; cf. Jno. x. 20, vii. 20, viii. 48.

[45] Mt. xii. 22-27; Mk. iii. 22-30; Lk. xi. 14-23; the parallel, Mt. ix. 34 is not genuine.

[46] Mt. xii. 31, 32; Mk. iii. 28-30.

[47] Lk. xii. 10.

phemy shall be forgiven unto men, but the blasphemy against
the Spirit shall not be forgiven. And whosoever shall speak a
word against the Son of Man, it shall be forgiven unto him;
but whosoever shall speak against the Holy Spirit, it shall not
be forgiven unto him, neither in this world nor in that which
is to come" (Mat. xii. 31, 32).

Let us begin by looking at Mark's account.

Mark alone, as we have said, records the opprobrious judgment of the scribes upon Jesus and His work, that He was
possessed by Beelzebul. This is formally due, probably, to the
circumstance that Mark alone introduces his account of this
incident in contrast with the judgment passed upon Jesus by
His friends: here is the judgment passed upon Him by His
enemies. It is intimated, however, that there is a closer connection between this opprobrious judgment of His enemies and
Jesus' warning concerning blasphemy against the Spirit than
merely that it formed the formal occasion of the discourse of
which the warning is a part. Mark expressly tells us that it was
precisely because the scribes attributed demoniacal possession
to Him that Jesus was led to give His solemn warning (verse
30). That is to say, it was precisely in this ascription that their
blasphemous words against the Holy Spirit culminated, or, at
least, that their words approached most dangerously the unpardonable sin of blasphemy against the Spirit. It might infer
a dangerous approach to blasphemy against the Spirit by whom
He wrought His mighty works to say that He wrought them by
means of Beelzebul. But He was able to argue that question.
The assertion that He in whom the Holy Spirit dwelt beyond
measure was possessed (instead) by an unclean Spirit, advanced so far beyond this, however, that not argument but
quick warning was demanded.

The solemnity with which Mark represents Jesus as introducing the declaration regarding blasphemy is marked by its
opening formula: "Verily, I say unto you . . ." And the weight
given to it by this solemn opening formula is sustained throughout in the stately march of its words. The declaration begins
with an impressive proclamation of the forgivableness, in the

wide mercy of God, of all human sin. The words are so arranged as to throw the emphasis upon the universality of this forgivableness:[48] "Verily, I say unto you, that *all things* shall be forgiven to the sons of men"—a solemn periphrasis for the mere "to men." Then this universal "all things" is more closely defined according to its nature, all "acts of sin"; and then the specific sins now more particularly in mind are brought to sight, —all "the blasphemies wherewithsoever they may blaspheme." The effect is to create a most moving sense of the amplitude of the divine forgiveness. All the acts of sin which the sons of men may commit; all the blasphemies wherewith they may blaspheme: all these may be forgiven. It is with the force of a great contrast that the single exception is then brought in: all, all is forgivable except this one thing: "But whosoever shall blaspheme against the Holy Ghost"—the particular form of the designation is chosen which throws the emphasis on His quality of *holiness*[49]—"hath not forgiveness." This was startling enough: but it is rendered even more so by the addition emphatically at the end, of the awful words—"for ever": "hath not forgiveness—for ever." And then the already strained emphasis is still further enhanced by a repetition of the declaration of the hopelessness of this sin, in the negative form: "But is guilty of an eternal sin,"—a sin, that is, which can never in all eternity be expiated or remitted. At the end, the Evangelist adds under the influence of the dread solemnity of the whole, the justification of this terrible warning. "Because," he says, "they said, He hath an unclean spirit." Because they accused Him of being possessed by an unclean spirit, He thus in awe-inspiring words warns them that blasphemy against that Spirit which is holiness itself, by whom He was really informed, is an eternally unforgivable sin.

The terms "blaspheme," "blasphemy," are obviously employed in this passage in their highest sense of irreverent and

---

[48] Meyer: "The order of the words places them so far apart as to place a great emphasis on πάντα." So also Weiss, Holtzmann and others.

[49] Τὸ πνεῦμα τὸ ἅγιον; cf. Swete *in loc.*: "The repeated article brings the holiness of the Spirit into prominence."

impious speech with respect to the Divine Being. The words, no doubt, are capable of employment in a more general sense, to express any reviling or calumniating speech against men. They are actually used in this general sense in the New Testament, including (though with Jesus only as their object) the Synoptic Gospels (Mt. xxvii. 39, Mk. xv. 29, Lk. xxii. 65, xxiii. 39). As the discourse of which it forms the climax has its start in a defamatory speech concerning Jesus, it might be colorably contended that they bear this more general sense in our passage.[50] But the extreme elevation of the language scarcely admits of this lower interpretation of the terms on which the whole turns as on its hinge. Why should such solemn assurance be given that among all the sins which will be forgiven the sons of men shall be included even (the "and" has a slight ascensive force) "the railings wherewith they may rail"—unless those "railings" possessed some special heinousness, as, for example, sins against the majesty of God? Otherwise, this sentence, in other respects so impressive in diction, would end on a sad anti-climax. It would be equivalent to saying: All their robberies and adulteries and murders shall be forgiven to men, yea even whatever bad language they may use. A similar incongruity would be created with the succeeding context, were the general sense of the terms insisted upon here. The heightening of the sin of blasphemy against the Holy Spirit would lose its force if the contrast against which it is thrown up were nothing more than detraction of our neighbors. The full effect of the passage becomes apparent only when we recognize that blasphemy against the Holy Spirit is set as unforgivable over against other—not merely slanders but—veritable blasphemies, described as capable of being pardoned. Moreover the terms "to blaspheme," "blasphemy," when used absolutely, had acquired a technical meaning practically equivalent to these terms in our current English,[51] and they cannot be taken in a lower sense

---

[50] They are so explained, for example, by Wellhausen *in loc.* A parallel to the passage so understood is found in I Sam. ii. 25.

[51] The verb: Mt. ix. 3, xxvi. 65; Mk. ii. 7; Jno. x. 36, but cf. Lk. xxii. 65; and the noun: Mt. xii. 31, xxvi. 65; Lk. v. 21; Jno. x. 33, but cf. Mt. xv. 19; Mk. xii. 22.

here without violence. No simple reader could possibly understand them in any other sense than that of insults to the Divine Being.

It is, no doubt, a startling result of distinguishing blasphemy against the Holy Spirit from blasphemies against God in general, that thus the Holy Spirit is set over against God in general and blasphemy against the Holy Spirit is declared more unpardonable than general blasphemy against God. Startling as this result is, however, it must just be accepted; it is impossible to believe that the contrast in our passage lies only between blasphemy against God and slander against fellow-men—as if what were said were, You can calumniate your fellow-men and it may be forgiven, but if you blaspheme God there is no forgiveness—for ever. We must not be stumbled by the indications of a Trinitarian background in Jesus' speech. Such indications pervade His speech in much greater measure than is commonly recognized. They are present, indeed, in all the expressions of His divine self-consciousness, and we should not forget that it is in His words that the Trinitarian formula finds its most precise enunciation in the New Testament (Mt. xxviii. 19). Meanwhile, what is necessary to recognize at the moment is only that Jesus here declares that blasphemy against the Holy Spirit specifically, not blasphemy in general, is unforgivable; and that He declares this with an emphasis which can only be understood as singling this sin out among all sins as a sin of very singular heinousness. The reason of this seems to reside in the fact that the holiness of God is especially manifested in the Holy Spirit. His designation here is accordingly so phrased as to throw His holiness particularly into prominence: "But whosoever shall blaspheme against the Spirit, that Holy One."[52] Because the holiness of God is peculiarly manifested in the Spirit, whose very name is Holy,[53] insulting

[52] Τὸ πνεῦμα τὸ ἅγιον not τὸ ἅγιον πνεῦμα as in Lk. xii. 10 or the simple τὸ πνεῦμα of Mt. xii. 31 (but in the more emphatic repetition of verse 32 τὸ πνεῦμα τὸ ἅγιον as in Mk. iii. 29).

[53] Cf. Is. lvii. 15.

words spoken against this Holy Spirit are a peculiarly heinous sin.

Mark reports only the contrast which Jesus drew between blasphemy of specifically the Holy Spirit and blasphemy in general. He communicates no specific declaration with respect to the pardonableness of blasphemy against Jesus' own person. The inference to be drawn from this omission may be variously conceived. It may be said that Jesus (according to Mark's conception) never thought of injurious words spoken against His person as "blasphemy." Conscious of His (mere, perhaps sinful) humanity, and setting Himself in all His thought in contrast with God, as a humble creature of His hands, He cannot speak of "blasphemy" with reference to Himself, but only with reference to God, inclusive of course of the Holy Spirit. He can contrast blasphemy against the Holy Ghost and blasphemy against God in general, but not "blasphemy" against Himself and blasphemy against God, the Holy Spirit. Or, more subtly seeking the same end—the presentation of Jesus as in His own estimate of Himself, merely a human being—it may be said that Jesus identifies here opprobrious words against Himself with blasphemy against the Holy Spirit and means to declare that they are the unpardonable sin.[54] The occasion of His remarks was the ascription to Him of demoniacal possession, and the attribution of His miracles to Satanic agency. This He declares to be unpardonable blasphemy, because He really has within Him the Divine Spirit and works His miracles by the Spirit, that is to say, by "the finger" of God. To vilify Him is unpardonably to blaspheme the Holy Spirit within Him by whom all His

[54] Cf. H. J. Holtzmann, "Synoptiker"[3] 1901, p. 128: "Here, therefore in contrast with Mt. xii. 32; Lk. xii. 10 the unforgivable sin consists precisely in blasphemy of Jesus, who, no doubt, possesses His power of exorcism through the Spirit, Mt. xii. 28." Similarly cf. P. W. Schmiedel, "Protestantische Monatshefte," ii. (1898) p. 304: "With Mark, blasphemy of the Messiah is thought to be by no means forgivable, since he expressly indicates (verse 30) as the occasion of the declaration, the contention of the opponents from verse 22 that Jesus was in collusion with Beelzebul or even possessed by him, and therefore wishes to say that there lies in this a blasphemy of the Holy Spirit working in Jesus."

works are wrought. That the injurious words spoken against Him when it was declared that He was possessed of a demon are represented by Him as blasphemy (or as coming very near to blasphemy) of the Holy Spirit is indeed clear: that is precisely what Mark affirms in verse 30. But this does not identify all opprobrious words against His person with blasphemy against the Holy Spirit: it rather distinguishes between His person and that of the Spirit, the point of warning being that such words against Him as these particular words approached to the unpardonable sin because they expressly assailed not Him but the Spirit working in Him. In Mark's report, therefore, there is no express reference to blasphemy against the Son of Man and if it is included at all it must be included in the general reference to "the blasphemies wherewithsoever the sons of men blaspheme"; and these all, with the sole exception of blasphemy against the Holy Spirit, are expressly declared to be forgivable. Since only blasphemy against the Holy Spirit is unpardonable, then, of course blasphemy against His own person is already declared to be pardonable and there is no clamant need of explicating further so obvious a fact. With this understanding of the implications of the passage it stands in harmony with the conception of Jesus' person which underlies the whole of Mark's Gospel (cf. e.g., xiii. 32) and with the more explicated assertion of his companion Evangelists in this place, both of whom speak of a blasphemy of the Son of Man which—like these undefined blasphemies spoken of by Mark— is pardonable. Unless there is some decisive reason why this should not be included in these, it is only reasonable to see it in them.[55] Mark in that case does not explicitly adduce blasphemy against the Son of Man as pardonable only because its pardonableness is already sufficiently asserted in the emphasized declaration that all blasphemies, with the sole exception of that against the Holy Spirit, are pardonable.

[55] Cf. Meyer (E. T. i. p. 59): "The less is it to be said that Mark places on a par the blasphemy against the Person of Jesus (Mt. xii. 31 f.) and that against the Holy Spirit (Köstlin, p. 318), or that he has 'already given up' the former blasphemy (Hilgenfeld). It is included in fact, in verse 28." This note is retained by Weiss.

Let us now look somewhat closely at the reports of the other Evangelists.

Luke gives the declaration its most compressed form, and places it in a wholly different connection from that in which it appears in Mark and Matthew. It may well be, indeed, that he is recording a different utterance of Jesus' of the same general purport. There is no intrinsic reason why Jesus may not have made such a declaration more than once. In any event, however, the declaration given by Luke is of the same general contents as that given by Mark and Matthew.

It is not a little difficult to be quite sure of the exact reference of the blasphemy against the Holy Ghost which is spoken of in Luke's report. On the face of it the declaration is quite general, that blasphemy against the Holy Spirit shall not be forgiven; and no closer definition is supplied by the context. We may conjecture that the reference is to blasphemy of the Holy Spirit speaking in the disciples when put upon their trial (verses 11, 12),[56] or that the denial of the Son (verse 9) is here declared to be, when the act not of His enemies, but of His disciples, not merely "speaking a word against the Son of Man," but actually the unpardonable sin of blasphemy against the Holy Spirit, operative in them.[57] But such conjectures have little to support them.

There is a certain parallelism between the two clauses of verse 10 and those of verses 8, 9, which may warrant us in taking the two pairs of antitheses together as alike under the influence of the solemn opening phrase: "But I say unto you" (verse 8). In that case, we have here two combined encouragements and warnings:

(1a) "Every one who shall confess Me before men, him shall the Son of Man also confess before the angels of God:

(1b) But he that denieth Me in the presence of

---

[56] So J. Weiss. Cf. Th. Zahn who broadens it to include the whole witnessing work of the disciples.

[57] So Hofmann, "Schriftbeweis" ii. 2, p. 342 Cf. especially G. L. Hahn's note.

> men, shall be denied in the presence of the
> angels of God.
>
> (2a) And every one who shall speak a word against the
> Son of Man, it shall be forgiven him:
>
> > (2b) But unto him that blasphemeth against the
> > Holy Spirit, it shall not be forgiven."

Thus a gnomic character attaches to these twin declarations
which lends them great impressiveness and gives to each member of each of them almost equal force. We must, it seems,
assume, then, that our Lord advancing, in verse 10, to the
climax of His combined encouragement and warning, makes
two declarations of generally equal importance,—that to wit,
blasphemy against His own person will be forgiven, and
blasphemy against the Holy Spirit will not be forgiven. Closer
definition wherein either blasphemy against His person or
blasphemy against the Spirit consists is lacking, and would
perhaps be out of place in such crisp, proverbial utterances.

We have spoken of "blasphemy" in both clauses, because
it seems quite clear that the variation in their language, from
"every one who *shall speak a word* against the Son of Man"
in the former, to "to him who *blasphemeth* the Holy Ghost"
in the latter, is without significance (cf. Mt. xii. 32, where
"speak against" is common to both clauses).[58] Obviously the
contrast between the two cases consists not in any difference
in the nature of the offence committed, but in some difference
in the persons against whom the offence is committed. What
is in effect declared is that an offence will be forgiven when
committed against the Son of Man which will not be forgiven
when committed against the Holy Spirit. There is undoubtedly
suggested here a certain subordination of the Son of Man to the
Holy Spirit,—if we cannot say exactly in dignity of person, yet
in the heinousness of the sin of blasphemy when committed
against the two respectively. The ground of this distinction is
in no way intimated unless it be hinted by the designations by

---

[58] Godet (E. T. ii. p. 93) on the contrary emphasizes the difference, as if
the forgivableness of the "speaking a word against" the Son of Man depended
on the precise point that this was not a "blasphemous" word.

which the two persons are described—"the Son of Man" and "the Holy Spirit." It is difficult to discover, however, in these designations, the desired implications of lowliness on the one hand and of exaltation on the other. "The Son of Man" is an exalted title and is employed to suggest the humiliation rather than the humility of Jesus' life on earth; the form of the title "the Holy Spirit" here is not (as in Mk. iii. 29) that which most strongly emphasizes His holiness and consequently His exaltation. Perhaps it would be wise to read the two designations, therefore, so far as simply denotative and not to seek in them for subtle contrasting connotations.

It is meanwhile easy also to misinterpret the contrast in dignity between the two persons involved in the differing treatment of blasphemy against them. It is of immense significance that Jesus should have thought it important to assure His followers that blasphemy against His person could be forgiven.[59] It would be bathos to say that every one who spoke a word against a man could be forgiven but not he who blasphemed the Holy Ghost. A high sense of the dignity of His person underlies the mere adduction of the case of blasphemy against Himself as a sin that might be forgiven. Otherwise that might go without saying. No doubt the immediately preceding declaration that those who denied Him would be denied before the angels of God (verse 9) somewhat prepares the way for such a further declaration. But that cannot empty of its significance the setting side by side of the Son of Man and Holy Spirit as if they had something in common which required that any difference in dealing with sins against them should be expressly notified. The title "Son of Man" moreover is taken up from verse 8 where it is a title of dignity. The effect of its repetition in verse 10 is clearly to aggravate the sin of speaking against Him: the reason why this sin is forgivable cannot be, therefore, that it is a little sin. It is the greatness of the grace of Jesus which is celebrated in this promise of forgiveness as truly as it is the heinousness of the sin of blasphemy against the Holy

[59] And if we consider to "speak a word against" something less than to "blaspheme" the implication is even more striking.

Spirit which is emphasized in the refusal of forgiveness for it in the succeeding clause. We cannot say, then, that the difference in the treatment of blasphemy against the Son of Man and against the Holy Spirit is rooted in an intrinsic difference between the two persons. It must rest on some other ground, and those seem to be led by a right instinct who seek it in the humiliation of the Son of Man in His servant-form on earth,[60] and the culminating manifestation of the holiness of God in the Holy Spirit,—though these things rather underlie the compressed statement before us than find expression in it. It is abundantly clear at all events that there is no depreciation of the dignity of the person of Jesus in the contrast that is drawn between blasphemy against Him as forgivable and blasphemy against the Holy Ghost as unforgivable. That it is possible to blaspheme the Son of Man, itself means that the Son of Man is divine.[61]

All the more clear is it that it is not intended to declare that it is only blasphemy against the Son of Man among blasphemies which is capable of forgiveness. The gist of the declaration is not that only blasphemy against the Son of Man is forgivable, but that only blasphemy against the Holy Spirit is unforgivable. It is the latter, not the former, which is singled out as unique in its treatment. Blasphemy against the Son of Man takes its place, therefore, as one of a class,—the class of forgivable blasphemies. Wherever it may rank within this class, it has its place in this class. In substance of meaning, accordingly, the declaration of Jesus reported by Luke is identical with that reported by Mark. When Mark makes Jesus declare that "all the blasphemies wherewithsoever the sons of men blaspheme," except that against the Holy Spirit, are forgivable, blasphemy against Jesus' own person is naturally included among forgivable blasphemies. When Luke reports Jesus as declaring that blasphemy against the Holy Spirit alone is unforgivable and even blasphemy against the Son of Man may be forgiven, it is necessarily implied that all other blasphemies are forgivable. The essence

60 Mt. xx. 28; Mk. x. 45.
61 Cf. A. B. Bruce in loc.

of both statements is that there is no blasphemy that is unforgivable except that against the Holy Spirit. One explicitly contrasts with this as forgivable, all other blasphemies; the other, even blasphemy against the Son of Man. The ultimate content of both contrasts is the same.

The most notable characteristic of Matthew's report of our Lord's declaration is its comprehensiveness, by which it is markedly distinguished from the compressed report of Luke. In substance, it combines the reports of Mark and Luke; but it does this in language so different from theirs that it is impossible to suppose that one Evangelist is directly dependent upon another. Matthew is obviously giving us an independent report of the substance of what was said by Jesus.

Matthew alone introduces the declaration by an illative particle, connecting it with the preceding discourse. The connection appears to be with the entire preceding discourse. It was because the Pharisees accused Him of casting out demons by Beelzebul, and because this was obviously absurd, and it was clear to every single eye that it was by the Spirit of God that He was casting out the demons (and therefore in Him the Kingdom of God had come upon them), that He solemnly ("I say unto you") warns them against blasphemy of the Spirit. This warning is couched in language of intense impressiveness, and is so ordered as to throw the heinousness of blasphemy against the Spirit into the most poignant emphasis. It contains a double declaration of the unforgivableness of this sin. The former of these is more general in character and contrasts this blasphemy with other blasphemies in general (verse 31). The latter advances to a more pungent assertion and contrasts it specifically with blasphemy against the Son of Man, as more heinous than even it. The effect of the whole is to isolate the sin of blasphemy against the Holy Spirit with even startling distinctness and energy as the only sin which is entirely and forever incapable of pardon.

The former member of this striking declaration is clothed in language of extreme and impressive simplicity. "Every sin and blasphemy," we read—the addition "and blasphemy" de-

scending from the genus to the particular species under discussion, and the combination of the terms focussing attention
on the sinfulness of blasphemy: "Every sin and blasphemy
shall be forgiven to man, but the blasphemy"—"*the* blasphemy,"
isolating the particular blasphemy under discussion—"the blasphemy of the Spirit shall not be forgiven." "Blasphemy" in the
first clause is evidently used in its technical sense and imports
insult to the Divine majesty: and "the blasphemy of the Spirit"
is separated from this only as a particular from the general.
Every term employed is the simplest and most direct attainable,
and the construction is wholly free from rhetorical heightening.
The simple abstract "sin" is used, instead of the more unusual
derivative "acts of sin" of Mark; the simple "blasphemy" instead of Mark's emphasized "the blasphemies wherewithsoever
the sons of men blaspheme." The universal "every" is attached
simply to its substantives instead of separated from them for
increased emphasis. We have the simple "to men" instead of
the solemn "to the sons of men" of Mark. Even the simplest
designation of the Holy Spirit possible is employed—the mere
"the Spirit." The statement takes on, indeed, something of the
baldness of a legislative enactment: there is not a superfluous
particle in it, and not a single rhetorical flourish. It just simply
states a fact of tremendous significance, and leaves it at that:
"Every sin (including blasphemy) shall be forgiven to men;
but blasphemy of the Spirit shall not be forgiven."

To this naked statement of fact, there is adjoined, now, a
repetition which is something more than a repetition. It adds
nothing in substance to what was said in the preceding statement. But it adds a great deal to it in tone and effect. It has
the nature of a startling specific application of a general doctrine, with the effect of carrying the general doctrine home with
tremendous force. All is said when it is said, "Every blasphemy
shall be forgiven except blasphemy of the Spirit." But this all
is said with quite new energy when it is added: "Even if any
one blasphemes the Son of Man, he shall be forgiven, but not
if he blasphemes the very Spirit of holiness—no, not for ever."
The "and" by which this second member of the declaration is

connected with the first, is not merely copulative, nor merely consecutive ("and so"). What follows is not merely an illustration of the general principle or a consequence drawn from it. The "and" has an ascensive force and introduces what is in effect a climax. Perhaps its force may be brought out by rendering it by some such term as "yea": "Every blasphemy shall be forgiven; yea if one blaspheme the Son of Man. . . ." It is not merely *an* instance which is adduced; but *the* instance, which will illustrate above every other instance the incredible reach of the forgiveness that is extended, and which will therefore supply the best background up against which may be thrown the heinousness of blasphemy of the Spirit which cannot be forgiven. The blasphemy which cannot be forgiven when even blasphemy of the Son of Man is forgiven, must be heinous indeed.

That "whosoever shall speak a word against the Son of Man" is just a periphrasis for "whosoever shall blaspheme against the Son of Man" is obvious. There would be an anticlimax if it were made to mean anything less than blasphemy. To declare that every blasphemy shall be forgiven and then add in climacteric illustration of this declaration that even the speaking a word against the Son of Man—which is something less than blasphemy—shall be forgiven would yield only bathos. The progress of the argument requires us, therefore, to take this "speaking a word against the Son of Man" as itself blasphemy in the sense of the preceding declaration. We rise here, not sink, in the definition of the sin. The progress consists in a change, not in the matter of the sin, but in the adduction of an object by which its heinousness is heightened. And, we must add, the heightening is, in the nature of the case, to the extreme limit. Blasphemy against the Son of Man is the extremity of blasphemy which can be forgiven. Beyond that limit, it becomes unforgivable. It is not a little sin, then, which is adduced; it is the greatest of forgivable sins. And therefore the title of dignity, "Son of Man," is employed to designate the object on which it terminates. To blaspheme the Son of Man is a sin so dreadful that it might be thought unforgivable; and the heinousness of the unforgivable sin may be estimated when it is perceived that it is more heinous than this. Clearly the Son of Man is not mere man: it is only because He is not mere man, indeed, that "speaking a word against Him" is blasphemy.

That by "speaking a word against Him" just blasphemy is meant is clear also from the employment of this same phrase in the next clause of blasphemy of the Spirit. For, that this clause must repeat the last clause of the first member of the declaration is beyond dispute: and we do not rise to our climaxes by weakening our expressions. And in this second member all the other expressions are heightened: Jesus designates Himself "the Son of Man" here for the first time in this context; the simple "Spirit" of the former member of the declaration gives place here to the solemnly emphatic "the Spirit, the Holy One"; the simple negative, "shall not be forgiven" of the former member is expanded here to the awe-inspiring, "shall not be forgiven, neither in this world, nor in that which is to come." It would seem, then, that the periphrasis, "to speak a word against," is treated as a more, rather than a less, impressive way of saying "to blaspheme" than the word itself: it is the thing, not the term, that is condemned, and apparently it is felt that the thing is more precisely, and therefore more forcibly, expressed by the periphrasis than by the simple word, which, after all, is very fairly defined by the periphrasis.

By the employment of this periphrasis in this passage with respect to blasphemy against the Holy Spirit we are aided in determining the precise nature of the sin which our Lord pronounced unforgivable. It would seem that it is just speaking injurious or insulting words against the Holy Spirit; such words as are illustrated,—or at least approached—by the opprobrious attribution of acts of the Holy Spirit to Beelzebul. Matthew does not say, as Mark says, that our Lord has particular reference to the ascription to Him of demoniacal possession. What he says is that our Lord was led to give this tremendous warning to the Pharisees, because they declared that it was by Beelzebul, the prince of the demons, that He was casting out demons, this being in effect an identification of the Holy Spirit by whom

He wrought His cures with the foul spirit. He bids them, therefore, to beware. The mercy of God is very wide; every sin and
blasphemy may be forgiven to men—except only blasphemy of
the Spirit; yea, though one speak a word against the Son of
Man it may be forgiven; but if one speak against the Spirit,
that Holy One, it shall not be forgiven—to all eternity.

The comprehensiveness of Matthew's report of Jesus' declaration, embracing as it does the substance of both what Mark
and what Luke reports, affords a temptation to look upon
Matthew's report as artificially made up from a combination
of what is reported by the other evangelists. We have already
pointed out, however, that the divergence of the language in
Matthew's report from that of Mark's and Luke's respectively,
renders this hypothesis untenable. If there ever were three
reports purporting to give the substance of a single utterance—
and actually giving it in complete harmony—which bore decisive marks of literary independence of one another, these
three reports do. Nevertheless the temptation to explain the
three as two divergent reports in Mark and Luke, and a con-
flation of them in Matthew, has proved too strong for the
Synoptical critics to resist.

Which of the two brief divergent reports is to be held the
more original, the critics are less agreed. Wellhausen is sure
that Mark, along with Mt. xii. 31, has preserved in substance
the original form, and that what was meant by it is that railing
against men may be forgiven but not blasphemy against God.
According to this view Jesus did not declare blasphemy against
His own person to be pardonable, the version of Luke and Mt.
xii. 32 resting upon a misunderstanding of the underlying
Aramaic phrase for "man" which transmuted it into a title of
the Messiah, "the Son of Man," used as a personal self-designation by Jesus.[62] The fundamental assumption here is, of course,
that the reason why Jesus did not declare blasphemy against
His person to be pardonable is that He never could have con-

[62] Cf. Arnold Meyer and Lietzmann as cited by P. W. Schmiedel, "Protestantische Monatshefte," ii. 1898, p. 304; also "Encyclopaedia Biblica,"
col. 1848, note 1.

nected the idea of blasphemy with that of "speaking a word against" Himself, conceiving of Himself, as He did, as merely a human being.[63] P. W. Schmiedel, on the other hand, is equally sure that the original form has been preserved by Luke, or rather by the fuller Mt. xii. 31, 32, while Mark represents a dogmatic alteration of this in the interests of the dignity of Jesus' person, men having come to entertain so high an opinion of Jesus' person that it offended them to have it said that blasphemy of even the Holy Spirit would be more unpardonable than blasphemy of Him.[64] According to this view Jesus declares speaking a word against Him to be pardonable because He conceives Himself to be only human, while the Holy Spirit is a periphrasis for God: the upshot of His teaching being just that we may speak against men and be forgiven but we cannot blaspheme God and expect pardon. The pathways over which the two interpretations would travel are different; the goal which they reach is the same; Jesus was only human and spoke out of a purely human consciousness.[65]

[63] N. Schmidt, "The Prophet of Nazareth," p. 112, has a similar view, although he takes Mt. xii. 32 as preserving the original saying, in which, he supposes, *bar nasha*, in the sense of "man," stood in the place now occupied by "the Son of Man," in the sense of Jesus, the Messiah: "He was careful to distinguish between an attack upon a fellow-man and a denunciation of the Spirit that operated in Him, saying: 'If any one speaks against *bar nasha*,— i.e. man—that may be pardoned him, but he that speaks against the Holy Spirit can have no pardon.' No one in the audience could have understood him to say, 'you may blaspheme the Messiah with impunity, but not the Holy Ghost.' The distinction is clearly between the divine spirit and the human instrumentality." C. G. Montefiore, "Synopt. Gospels" ii. p. 624, says quite impartially that this interpretation seems "very strained."

[64] "Encyclopaedia Biblica," col. 1848: "In their worship of Jesus it must have appeared to them in itself the greatest possible blasphemy to say that blasphemy against Jesus could be forgiven."

[65] Cf. the discussion of the opposing views in Schmiedel's article in the "Protestantische Monatshefte," ii. 1908, pp. 303-307: an excellent brief account of them is given by S. R. Driver in Hastings' BD iv. p. 588, at the close of his article on the "Son of Man." E. von Dobschütz, "Theologische Studien und Kritiken" 85 (1912) p. 340, is sure that we have two reports here, but will not decide which is the more original, contenting himself with remarking that the double attestation gives us peculiar surety that something of the sort was said by Jesus: "When we read in the Mark-tradition (Mk. iii. 28 f.;

So sure is Schmiedel that Mt. xii. 31, 32 presents to our view a purely human Jesus, that he includes this passage among those "pillar passages" which he announces as the foundation stones of a truly scientific knowledge of Jesus,—on the precise ground that they could never have been invented by worshippers of Jesus (as all the Evangelists were) but must have come to them as part of an authentic tradition of a human Jesus. This true tradition, he contends, was altered by one or another of the Evangelists in accordance with their later worship of Jesus.[66] Jesus here, he tells us, is represented as frankly ranging Himself with men, speaking against whom is pardonable; and as separating Himself from the Spirit of God to speak against whom is unpardonable.[67] That the passage in Matthew will not bear the meaning which Schmiedel puts upon it, we have already seen. Jesus does not place Himself there among men,

Mt. xii. 31), 'All sins are forgiven to the sons of men and the blasphemies wherewithsoever they blaspheme, but he who blasphemes the Holy Ghost has no forgiveness forever'; but on the other hand in the Q-tradition (Lk. xii. 10; Mt. xii. 32), 'He who speaketh anything against the Son of Man, that will be forgiven him, but he who speaketh against the Holy Spirit, to him it will not be forgiven (neither in this nor in the future world)'; it is clear that we have before us two conceptions and also two translations: *bar nasa* is in one taken collectively, "sons of men," in the other as the well-known personal self-designation of Jesus. The one is a modification of the other, although it is not altogether easy to say in what direction the theology of the community has worked here; it is clear, however, that through this double attestation a declaration of Jesus to His Pharisaic opponents as to unpardonable sin is assured."

[66] "Encyclopaedia Biblica," col. 1881; cf. col. 1848 (d and note 1). See *The Princeton Theological Review*, April, 1913, pp. 204, 252.

[67] The following is Schmiedel's most lucid statement of his view of the bearing of the passage ("Das vierte Evangelium," etc., p. 33): "In John Jesus knows, then, nothing higher than Himself, the bliss or misery of men for time and eternity is determined by whether they believe or do not believe in His divine origin. In the Synoptics, He knows something higher than Himself. He says in Mt. xii. 31, 32: 'Every sin and blasphemy will be forgiven to men, but blasphemy against the Spirit will not be forgiven. And whosoever speaks a word against the Son of Man, it will be forgiven him; but whosoever speaks a word against the Holy Ghost, it will not be forgiven him, either in this world or in the next.' Therefore He places His person below the Holy Spirit, i.e. below the holy work which He advocates." Cf. Karl Thieme, "Die christliche Demut," i. 1906, p. 139.

and subordinate Himself to God in His essential nature. He does not say there that calumniation of men may be forgiven but never blasphemy against God. What He says may be forgiven is precisely blasphemy, in its strict sense. He declares that speaking a word against His person is blasphemy in the strict sense; and that this may be forgiven only because blasphemy may be forgiven.[68] And though He subordinates Himself to the Holy Spirit, at least in manifestation, to this extent, that blasphemy against Him may be forgiven but blasphemy against the Holy Spirit not, it is illegitimate to interpret this as implying a subordination of Himself to the Spirit in intrinsic dignity of person: blasphemy against God may also be forgiven but blasphemy against the Holy Spirit not. It may be difficult to determine precisely why blasphemy against the Spirit is made unpardonable and blasphemy against the Son of Man not: no doubt the reason lies in some discrimination in the modes of divine manifestation in the two persons. But this difficulty

[68] W. Beyschlag, "Die Christologie des Neuen Testaments," 1866, p. 24, had written—no doubt with wrong suggestions, but for the final matter very justly, as we think—as follows (we use Bruce's rendering): "Let us consider the relation here indicated between the Son of Man and the Holy Ghost. It is a relation of distinction; and yet of close connection. The distinction is that in the Son of Man the revelation of God to men is made in mediated, and, so far, veiled form; therefore may be misunderstood, so that the blasphemer may always have the benefit of the prayer, 'Forgive them, they know not what they do'; but in the Holy Ghost the revelation is made immediately, inwardly, therefore unmistakably; therefore there is no excuse for the blasphemer. At the same time the Holy Ghost is not thought of as above the Son of Man but in Him. The Son of Man is the man who has the Spirit of God in His entire fulness, whose inmost though unrecognized essence is the Holy Spirit, the man whose human appearance is the absolute revelation of God. To this corresponds the fact, obvious in the text, that the blasphemy of the Son of Man is represented as the most heinous of pardonable sins." A. B. Bruce, "The Humiliation of Christ,"[2] 1881, p. 227, quotes these statements only unsuccessfully to contravert the view that the passage teaches that "offences against the Son of Man are pardonable, but that is all; such sins form the extreme limit of the forgivable." He supposes that Jesus rather means to say "with characteristic magnanimity" that sins against Himself are easily forgivable, because not more heinous than sins against any other good man, and due to the same general cause; and he adopts the view that Jesus' warning turns precisely on this,—that the Pharisees in their injurious imputations were "not sinning against Him, but against the Holy Ghost."

affords no reason for cutting the knot by representing Jesus as definitely subordinating Himself—and God also—in dignity of person to the Holy Spirit.

It has been frequently remarked that it is only in the two passages, Mt. xii. 32 and Lk. xii. 10, that (as, for example, H. J. Holtzmann expresses it), "a distinction is made between the Spirit as the higher power *(Instanz)* and Jesus as the human vehicle of the Spirit." A somewhat bizarre writer, on that ground, insists that these passages—which, he considers, represent the original form of the declaration—are a Montanistic interpolation into the Gospels, since (as he is reported) "only Montanism places the revelation of the Spirit, the Paraclete, above that of the Apostles of Christ." We cite this extraordinary opinion, not, as we well might, as an example of the lengths to which this kind of criticism can go,—in principle, it is just as sound criticism as that of many who seem to be pillars,—but in order to introduce Schmiedel's, as it seems to us, instructive rejoinder to it. "Certainly," Schmiedel replies, "Montanism was the first to place the Holy Spirit above Jesus—after Jesus Himself. Some effort is made to form an appropriate idea of Montanism: but of what Jesus thought of Himself, none at all. 'Where elsewhere in the Synoptic tradition can anything similar be found?' I should have thought we would have been thankful to find it only once. A pearl does not cease to be genuine merely because it exists in only one example. . . ."[69] Possibly. But meanwhile, it is thus allowed that in this interpretation a meaning is assigned to the passage which is unexampled elsewhere in the Synoptic Gospels, and indeed in the entirety of the Christian literature of the first age; a meaning, that is, so unexpected that surely it cannot be entertained unless it is unassailably shown to be the real meaning of the passage. How little that is the case we have already seen. What Schmiedel is actually doing in his interpretation of the passage is, therefore, importing into the Gospels a conception which is wholly alien to them; and also which, as he expressly admits (for this is the very principle of his criticism), stands in direct contradiction

[69] "Protestantische Monatshefte," ii. (1898) p. 305.

to their whole drift. A human Jesus must be found at all hazards, and if violence is required to find Him in the Evangelical tradition, then violence must be used.[70]

Meanwhile it is unquestionable that the passage contains difficulties. It is not easy to separate clearly blasphemy of the Son of Man from blasphemy of that Holy Spirit by which He wrought His great works of healing upon the possessed. It is not easy to understand in what blasphemy of the Son of Man is a less heinous sin than blasphemy against the Holy Ghost, or why the one is more pardonable than the other. It is not easy indeed to be perfectly sure precisely in what the unpardonable blasphemy of the Holy Spirit consists, or whether our Lord means to convict His opponents of having committed it. We may, of course, form conjectures on these matters; and these conjectures will, no doubt, be more or less plausible; and they may seem to be supported with more or less convincingness by this or that assertion or suggestion of the text or context. The passage itself, however, scarcely gives us decisive instruction on these matters; and on most of them opinions may lawfully differ. They are in any event subjects of perpetual investigation and most of them continue to be zealously debated by the commentators.[71] Many commentators, for example, are eager to make it clear that our Lord does not charge His opponents with having committed the unpardonable sin of blasphemy against the Holy Spirit, but only warns them against committing it.[72] This carries with it, of course, denial that merely to

[70] Into the detailed attempts to account for the divergent forms of the whole passage as given by the three Synoptics, on the Two-Document hypothesis, in its mechanical interpretation, we do not enter. We cannot look upon a discussion like that of Burton Scott Easton, "The Beelzebul Sections," *The Journal of Biblical Literature*, xxxii. (1913) pp. 57-73 as anything more than highly refined speculation without any possibility of attaining valid results.

[71] A good brief *résumé* of the main discussion may be read in Carl Clemen's "Die christliche Lehre von der Sünde," 1897, pp. 89 ff.

[72] For example, Th. Zahn, "Das Evangelium des Matthäus," 1903, pp. 460-466, closing with the statement (p. 466): "Jesus does not yet treat the Pharisees here as such as have already committed the sin against the Holy Spirit, but as such as need to be warned of this ultimate step which they have it in mind to take." Compare the statement on p. 461: "No doubt the Phari-

accuse Jesus of working His healings of demoniacs by the aid of Beelzebul, or even of being possessed by Beelzebul, constitutes the unpardonable sin. And the way having thus been opened, a wide field lies open for conjecture as to what does constitute that sin. Despite these deeper mysteries, however, the main implications of the passage are sufficiently clear, and among these implications this one must rank among the clearest —that He who authoritatively makes this great declaration of the relative heinousness of sins, and calmly announces what sins shall and what sins shall not be forgiven, whether in this world or in that which is to come, does not mean to proclaim Himself a mere man, when He declares that he who speaks a word against Him may be forgiven, but not he who speaks a word against the Holy Spirit. Whatever may be the reason for treating blasphemy of the Son of Man as more pardonable than blasphemy of the Holy Spirit, that reason cannot be found in a sheer difference in the intrinsic dignity of the two persons.

The judgment of unbelief on Jesus, we have found occasion to remark, is inevitably that He was mad. As inevitably the judgment of active disbelief on Him must be that He was wicked. Not only in His own day but throughout all time the

sees called the Power by which Jesus healed the possessed, an evil spirit, whereas that Power was in fact the Spirit of God; but they did not blaspheme the Spirit for they did not recognize Him in the Power which worked through Jesus. They rather concluded from the behavior of Jesus, which in their judgment was godless, lawless, and immoral (ix. 3-11, xii. 2-10) that this man wrought these, in themselves, beneficent and praiseworthy miracles by the aid of evil spirits, and thus they blasphemed the Son of Man. This blasphemy would become a blasphemy of the Holy Spirit, however, if they persisted in it, after Jesus had shown them the irrationality of their inference. When and in the measure in which they must recognize that the Power by which Jesus heals is a holy Power, every inimical word against Him becomes a sin against the Holy Spirit." So also G. Wohlenberg, "Das Evangelium des Markus," 1910, p. 115: "That the scribes have committed such blasphemy the Lord does not say. It may even be judged that even their accusation that Jesus had Beelzebul and cast out the demons through the prince of the demons, or as it is said in verse 30, that He had an unclean spirit, does not yet necessarily involve that terrible sin. For the question continually presents itself, how far uncomprehending but well-meant zeal has coöperated here; how far the conscience has been unpricked, unconcerned, when they so dreadfully accused the Lord." For earlier writers to the same effect, see C. Clemen, as cited, p. 91 note.

alternatives constantly stare us in the face—*aut Deus aut non sanus; aut Deus aut non bonus.* If in our own time the latter alternative has retired somewhat into the background, and that which imposes itself upon the consciousness of contemporary criticism in that between a Divine Jesus and an "ecstatic" Jesus, as it is euphemistically called,—a paranoiac Jesus, as it really would amount to—that is doubtless in part because, in the languid sceptical temper of our times, and their preoccupation with abstract questions of pure history, little occasion or place has been left for the play of the more violent emotions about our historical findings. At bottom, however, disbelief, when it works itself out, must not merely neglect Jesus but condemn Him: and the ravings of a Nietzsche may serve to keep us in mind that the ultimate alternative is always that of the Pharisees and Scribes. Either Jesus has come forth from God, or we can scarcely avoid declaring Him possessed of the Evil One. He makes or mars the world.[73]

[73] Compare the striking closing pages of the fourth of Liddon's Bampton Lectures on "*The Divinity of our Lord, etc.*"

CHAPTER IX

ON THE ANTIQUITY AND THE UNITY
OF THE HUMAN RACE[1]

THE fundamental assertion of the Biblical doctrine of the origin of man is that he owes his being to a creative act of God. Subsidiary questions growing out of this fundamental assertion, however, have been thrown from time to time into great prominence, as the changing forms of current anthropological speculation have seemed to press on this or that element in, or corollary from, the Biblical teaching. The most important of these subsidiary questions has concerned the method of the divine procedure in creating man. Discussion of this question became acute on the publication of Charles Darwin's treatise on the "Origin of Species" in 1859, and can never sink again into rest until it is thoroughly understood in all quarters that "evolution" cannot act as a substitute for creation, but at best can supply only a theory of the method of the divine providence. Closely connected with this discussion of the mode of origination of man, has been the discussion of two further questions, both older than the Darwinian theory, to one of which it gave, however, a new impulse, while it has well-nigh destroyed all interest in the other. These are the questions of the Antiquity of Man and the Unity of the Human Race, to both of which a large historical interest attaches, though neither of them can be said to be burning questions of today.

The question of the antiquity of man has of itself no theological significance. It is to theology, as such, a matter of entire indifference how long man has existed on earth. It is only because of the contrast which has been drawn between the short period which seems to be allotted to human history in the Biblical narrative, and the tremendously long period which

[1] Reprinted from *The Princeton Theological Review*, ix. 1911, pp. 1-25; also from *Studies in Theology*, pp. 235-258.

certain schools of scientific speculation have assigned to the duration of human life on earth, that theology has become interested in the topic at all. There was thus created the appearance of a conflict between the Biblical statements and the findings of scientific investigators, and it became the duty of theologians to investigate the matter. The asserted conflict proves, however, to be entirely factitious. The Bible does not assign a brief span to human history: this is done only by a particular mode of interpreting the Biblical data, which is found on examination to rest on no solid basis. Science does not demand an inordinate period for the life of human beings on earth: this is done only by a particular school of speculative theorizers, the validity of whose demands on time exact investigators are more and more chary of allowing. As the real state of the case has become better understood the problem has therefore tended to disappear from theological discussion, till now it is pretty well understood that theology as such has no interest in it.

It must be confessed, indeed, that the impression is readily taken from a *prima facie* view of the Biblical record of the course of human history, that the human race is of comparatively recent origin. It has been the usual supposition of simple Bible readers, therefore, that the Biblical data allow for the duration of the life of the human race on earth only a paltry six thousand years or so: and this supposition has become fixed in formal chronological schemes which have become traditional and have even been given a place in the margins of our Bibles to supply the chronological framework of the Scriptural narrative. The most influential of these chronological schemes is that which was worked out by Archbishop Usher in his "Annales Veteri et Novi Testamenti" (1650-1654), and it is this scheme which has found a place in the margin of the Authorized English Version of the Bible since 1701. According to it the creation of the world is assigned to the year 4004 B.C. (Usher's own dating was 4138 B.C.); while according to the calculation of Petau (in his "Rationarium temporum"), the most influential rival scheme, it is assigned to the year 3983 B.C.

On a more careful scrutiny of the data on which these calculations rest, however, they are found not to supply a satisfactory basis for the constitution of a definite chronological scheme. These data consist largely, and at the crucial points solely, of genealogical tables; and nothing can be clearer than that it is precarious in the highest degree to draw chronological inferences from genealogical tables.

For the period from Abraham down we have, indeed, in addition to somewhat minute genealogical records, the combined evidence of such so-called "long-dates" as those of I Kings vi. 1, Gal. iii. 17, and several precise statements concerning the duration of definite shorter periods, together with whatever aid it may be possible to derive from a certain amount of contemporary extra-Biblical data. For the length of this period there is no difficulty, therefore, in reaching an entirely satisfactory general estimate. But for the whole space of time before Abraham, we are dependent entirely on inferences drawn from the genealogies recorded in the fifth and eleventh chapters of Genesis. And if the Scriptural genealogies supply no solid basis for chronological inferences, it is clear that we are left without Scriptural data for forming an estimate of the duration of these ages. For aught we know they may have been of immense length.

The general fact that the genealogies of Scripture were not constructed for a chronological purpose and lend themselves ill to employment as a basis for chronological calculations has been repeatedly shown very fully; but perhaps by no one more thoroughly than by Dr. William Henry Green in an illuminating article published in the *Bibliotheca Sacra* for April, 1890. These genealogies must be esteemed trustworthy for the purposes for which they are recorded; but they cannot safely be pressed into use for other purposes for which they were not intended, and for which they are not adapted. In particular, it is clear that the genealogical purposes for which the genealogies were given, did not require a complete record of all the generations through which the descent of the persons to whom they are assigned runs; but only an adequate indication of the particular line through which the descent in question comes. Accordingly it is found on examination that the genealogies of Scripture are freely compressed for all sorts of purposes; and that it can seldom be confidently affirmed that they contain a complete record of the whole series of generations, while it is often obvious that a very large number are omitted. There is no reason inherent in the nature of the Scriptural genealogies why a genealogy of ten recorded links, as each of those in Genesis v. and xi. is, may not represent an actual descent of a hundred or a thousand or ten thousand links. The point established by the table is not that these are all the links which intervened between the beginning and the closing names, but that this is the line of descent through which one traces back to or down to the other.

A sufficient illustration of the freedom with which the links in the genealogies are dealt with in the Biblical usage is afforded by the two genealogies of our Lord which are given in the first chapter of the Gospel of Matthew. For it is to be noted that there are two genealogies of Jesus given in this chapter, differing greatly from one another in fullness of record, no doubt, but in no respect either in trustworthiness or in principle of record. The one is found in the first verse, and traces Jesus back to Abraham in just two steps: "Jesus Christ, the son of David, the son of Abraham." The other is found in verses 2-17, and expands this same genealogy into forty-two links, divided for purposes of symmetrical record and easy memorizing into a threefold scheme of fourteen generations each. And not even is this longer record a complete one. A comparison with the parallel records in the Old Testament will quickly reveal the fact that the three kings, Ahaziah, Joash, and Amaziah are passed over and Joram is said to have begotten Uzziah, his great-great-grandson. The other genealogies of Scripture present similar phenomena; and as they are carefully scrutinized, it becomes ever clearer that as they do not pretend to give complete lists of generations, they cannot be intended to supply a basis for chronological calculation, and it is illegitimate and misleading to attempt to use them for that purpose. The reduction for extraneous reasons of the genealogy of Christ in the first chapter of Matthew into three tables of fourteen generations each, may warn us that the reduction of the patriarchal genealogies in Genesis v. and xi. into two tables of ten generations each may equally be due to extraneous considerations; and that there may be represented by each of these ten generations—adequately for the purposes for which the genealogy is recorded—a very much longer actual series of links.

It must not be permitted to drop out of sight, to be sure, that the appearance of supplying data for a chronological calculation is in these particular genealogies not due entirely to the mere fact that these lists are genealogies. It is due to a peculiarity of these special genealogies by which they are differentiated from all other genealogies in Scripture. We refer to the regular attachment, to each name in the lists, of the age of the father at the birth of his son. The effect of this is to provide what seems to be a continuous series of precisely measured generations, the numbers having only to be added together to supply an exact measure of the time consumed in their sequence. We do not read merely that "Adam begat Seth; and Seth begat Enosh; and Enosh begat Kenan." We read rather that "Adam lived an hundred and thirty years and begat Seth; and Seth lived an hundred and five years and begat Enosh; and Enosh lived ninety years an begat Kenan." It certainly looks, at first sight, as if we needed only to add these one hundred and thirty, one hundred and five, and ninety years together in order to obtain the whole time which elapsed from the creation of Adam to the birth of Kenan; and, accordingly, as if we needed only to add together the similar numbers throughout the lists in order to obtain an accurate measure of the whole period from the Creation to the Deluge. Plausible as this procedure seems, however, it appears on a closer scrutiny unjustified; and it is the especial service which Dr. William Henry Green in the article already mentioned has rendered to the cause of truth in this matter that he has shown this clearly.

For, if we will look at these lists again, we shall find that we have not yet got them in their entirety before us. Not only is there attached to each name in them a statement of the age at which the father begot his son, but also a statement of how long the father lived after he had begotten his son, and how many years his life-span counted up altogether. If we do not read merely, "Adam begat Seth; and Seth begat Enosh; and Enosh begat Kenan"; neither do we read merely, "Adam lived one hundred and thirty years and begat Seth; and Seth lived one hundred and five years and begat Enosh; and Enosh lived ninety years and begat Kenan." What we read is: "Adam lived an hundred and thirty years, and begat a son in his own likeness, after his image; and called his name Seth: and the days of Adam after he begat Seth were eight hundred years: and he begat sons and daughters: and all the days that Adam lived were nine hundred and thirty years: and he died. And Seth lived an hundred and five years, and begat Enosh: and Seth lived after he begat Enosh eight hundred and seven years, and begat sons and daughters: and all the days of Seth were nine hundred and twelve years: and he died. And Enosh lived ninety years, and begat Kenan: and Enosh lived after he begat Kenan eight hundred and fifteen years and begat sons and daughters: and all the days of Enosh were nine hundred and five years: and he died." There is, in a word, much more information furnished with respect to each link in the chain than merely the age to which each father had attained when his son was begotten; and all this information is of the same order and obviously belongs together. It is clear that a single motive has determined the insertion of all of it; and we must seek a reason for its insertion which will account for all of it. This reason cannot have been a chronological one: for all the items of information furnished do not serve a chronological purpose. Only the first item in each case can be made to yield a chronological result; and therefore not even it was intended to yield a chronological result, since all these items of information are too closely bound together in their common character to be separated in their intention. They too readily explain themselves, moreover, as serving an obvious common end which was clearly in the mind of the writer, to justify the ascription of a different end to any one of them. When we are told of any man that he was a hundred and thirty years old when he begat his heir, and lived after that eight hundred years begetting sons and daughters, dying only at the age of nine hundred and thirty years, all these items coöperate to make a vivid impression upon us of the vigor and grandeur of humanity in those old days of the world's prime. In a sense different indeed from that which the words bear in Genesis vi., but full of meaning to us, we exclaim, "Surely there were giants in those days!" This is the impression which the items of information inevitably make on us; and it is the impression they were intended to make on us, as is proved by the simple fact that they are adapted in all their items to make this impression, while only a small portion of them can be utilized for the purpose of chronological calculation. Having thus found a reason which will account for the insertion of all the items of information which are given us, we have no right to assume another reason to account for the insertion of some of them. And that means that we must decline to look upon the first item of information given in each instance as intended to give us chronological information.

The conclusion which we thus reach is greatly strengthened when we observe another fact with regard to these items of information. This is that the appearance that we have in them of a chronological scheme does not reside in the nature of the items themselves, but purely in their sequence. If we read the items of information attached to each name, apart from their fellows attached to the succeeding names, we shall have simply a set of facts about each name, which in their combination make a strong impression of the vigor and greatness of humanity in those days, and which suggest no chronological inference. It is only when the names, with the accompanying comments, are put together, one after the other, that a chronological inference is suggested. The chronological suggestion is thus purely the effect of the arrangement of the names in immediate sequence; and is not intrinsically resident in the items of information themselves.

And now we must call attention to a characteristic of Scripture genealogies in general which seems to find a specially striking illustration in these comments. This is the habit of interposing into the structure of the genealogies, here and there, a short note, attached to this name or that, telling some important or interesting fact about the person represented by it. A simple genealogy would run thus: "Adam begat Seth; and Seth begat Enosh; and Enosh begat Kenan"; and the like. But it would be quite in the Biblical manner if there were attached to some, or even to each of these names, parenthetical remarks, calling attention to something of interest regarding the several persons. For example, it would be quite after the Biblical fashion should we have rather had this: "Adam, who was the first man, begat Seth; and Seth, he it was who was appointed as another seed in the stead of Abel whom Cain slew, begat Enosh; and Enosh, at his birth men began to call on the name of Jehovah, begat Kenan." The insertion of such items of information does not in the least change the character of the genealogy as in itself a simple genealogy, subject to all the laws which governed the formation and record of the Scriptural genealogies, including the right of free compression, with the omission of any number of links. It is strictly parenthetical in nature.

Several examples of such parenthetical insertions occur in the genealogy of Jesus recorded in the first chapter of Matthew, to which we have already referred for illustration. Thus in verse 2, the fact that Judah had "brethren" is interposed in the genealogy, a fact which is noted also with respect to two others of the names which occur in the list (verses 3 and 11): it is noted here doubtless because of the significance of the twelve sons of Jacob as tribe-fathers of Israel. Again we find in four instances a notification of the mother interposed (Tamar, verse 3; Rahab, verse 5; Ruth, verse 5; her of Uriah, verse 6). The introduction of the names of these notable women, which prepares the way for the introduction of that of Mary in verse 16, constitutes a very remarkable feature of this particular genealogy. Another feature of it is suggested by the attachment to the name of David (verse 6) the statement that he was "the

King"; and to the name of Jechoniah (verse 11) the statement that his life-span fell at the time of the carrying away to Babylon: the account of these insertions being found, doubtless, in the artificial arrangement of the genealogy in three symmetrical tables. The habit of inserting parenthetical notes giving items of interest connected with the names which enter into the genealogies is doubtless sufficiently illustrated by these instances. The only point in which the genealogies of Genesis v. and xi. differ in this respect from this one in Matthew i. is that such items of information are inserted with reference to every name in those genealogies, while they are inserted only occasionally in the genealogy of our Lord. This is, however, a difference of detail, not of principle. Clearly if these notes had been constant in the genealogy in Matthew i. instead of merely occasional, its nature as a genealogy would not have been affected: it would still have remained a simple genealogy subject to all the customary laws of simple genealogies. That they are constant in the genealogies of Genesis v. and xi. does not, then, alter their character as simple genealogies. These additions are in their nature parenthetical, and are to be read in each instance strictly as such and with sole reference to the names to which they are attached, and cannot determine whether or not links have been omitted in these genealogies as they are freely omitted in other genealogies.

It is quite true that, when brought together in sequence, name after name, these notes assume the appearance of a concatenated chronological scheme. But this is pure illusion, due wholly to the nature of the parenthetical insertions which are made. When placed one after the other they seem to play into one another, whereas they are set down here for an entirely different purpose and cannot without violence be read with reference to one another. If the items of information were of a different character we should never think of reading them otherwise than each with sole reference to its own name. Thus, if they were given to show us how nobly developed primitive men were in their physical frames and read something as follows: "Adam was eight cubits in height and begat Seth; and

Seth was seven cubits in height and begat Enosh; and Enosh was six cubits in height and began Kenan"; we should have no difficulty in understanding that these remarks are purely parenthetical and in no way argue that no links have been omitted. The case is not altered by the mere fact that other items than these are chosen for notice, with the same general intent, and we actually read: "Adam lived an hundred and thirty years and begat Seth; and Seth lived an hundred and five years and begat Enosh; and Enosh lived ninety years and begat Kenan." The circumstance that the actual items chosen for parenthetical notice are such that when the names are arranged one after the other they produce the illusion of a chronological scheme is a mere accident, arising from the nature of the items chosen, and must not blind us to the fact that we have before us here nothing but ordinary genealogies, accompanied by parenthetical notes which are inserted for other than chronological purposes; and that therefore these genealogies must be treated like other genealogies, and interpreted on the same principles. But if this be so, then these genealogies too not only may be, but probably are, much compressed, and merely record the line of descent of Noah from Adam and of Abraham from Noah. Their symmetrical arrangement in groups of ten is indicative of their compression; and for aught we know instead of twenty generations and some two thousand years measuring the interval between the creation and the birth of Abraham, two hundred generations, and something like twenty thousand years, or even two thousand generations and something like two hundred thousand years may have intervened. In a word, the Scriptural data leave us wholly without guidance in estimating the time which elapsed between the creation of the world and the deluge and between the deluge and the call of Abraham. So far as the Scripture assertions are concerned, we may suppose any length of time to have intervened between these events which may otherwise appear reasonable.

The question of the antiquity of man is accordingly a purely scientific one, in which the theologian as such has no concern. As an interested spectator, however, he looks on as the various schools of scientific speculation debate the question among themselves; and he can scarcely fail to take away as the result of his observation two well-grounded convictions. The first is that science has as yet in its hands no solid data for a definite estimate of the time during which the human race has existed on earth. The second is that the tremendous drafts on time which were accustomed to be made by the geologists about the middle of the last century and which continue to be made by one school of speculative biology today have been definitively set aside, and it is becoming very generally understood that man cannot have existed on the earth more than some ten thousand to twenty thousand years.

It was a result of the manner of looking at things inculcated by the Huttonian geology, that speculation during the first three quarters of the nineteenth century estimated the age of the habitable globe in terms of hundreds of millions of years. It was under the influence of this teaching, for example, that Charles Darwin, in 1859, supposed that three hundred million years were an underestimate for the period which has elapsed since the latter part of the Secondary Age.[2] In reviewing Mr. Darwin's argument in his "Student's Manual of Geology," Professor Jukes remarked on the vagueness of the data on which his estimates were formed, and suggested that the sum of years asserted might with equal reasonableness be reduced or multiplied a hundredfold: he proposed therefore three million and thirty billion years as the minimum and maximum limits of the period in question. From the same fundamental standpoint, Professor Poulton in his address as President of the Zoölogical Section of the British Association for the Advancement of Science (Liverpool, September, 1896) treats as too short from his biological point of view the longest time asked by the geologists for the duration of the habitable earth—say some four hundred millions of years. Dwelling on the number of distinct types of animal existence already found in the Lower Cambrian deposits, and on the necessarily (as he thinks) slow progress of evolution, he stretches out the time required for the advance

[2] "Origin of Species," ed. 1, p. 287.

of life to its present manifestation practically illimitably. Taking up the cudgels for his biological friends, Sir Archibald Geikie[3] chivalrously offers them all the time they desire, speaking on his own behalf, however, of one hundred million years as possibly sufficient for the period of the existence of life on the globe. These general estimates imply, of course, a very generous allowance for the duration of human life on earth; but many anthropologists demand for this period even more than they allow. Thus, for example, Professor Gabriel de Mortillet[4] reiterates his conviction that the appearance of man on earth cannot be dated less than two hundred and thirty thousand years ago, and Professor A. Penck[5] would agree with this estimate, while Dr. A. R. Wallace has been accustomed to ask more than double that period.[6]

These tremendously long estimates of the duration of life on earth and particularly of the duration of human life are, however, speculative, and, indeed, largely the creation of a special type of evolutionary speculation—a type which is rapidly losing ground among recent scientific workers. This type is that which owes its origin to the brooding mind of Charles Darwin; and up to recent times it has been the regnant type of evolutionary philosophy. Its characteristic contention is that the entire development of animate forms has been the product of selection, by the pressure of the environment, of infinitesimal variations in an almost infinite series of successive generations; or to put it rather brusquely, but not unfairly, that chance plus time are the true causes which account for the whole body of differentiated forms which animate nature presents to our observation. Naturally, therefore, heavy drafts have been made on time to account for whatever it seemed hard to attribute to brute chance, as if you could admit the issuing of any effect out of any conditions, if you only conceived the process of production

[3] Address as President of the Geological Section of the British Association, Dover meeting, September, 1899: *Science* for October 13, 1899.

[4] *Revue Mensuelle* of the Paris School of Anthropology, for January 15, 1897.

[5] Silliman Lectures at Yale, for 1908.

[6] *Nature*, October 2, 1873, pp. 462-463; cf. "Darwinism," 1889, p. 456.

as slow enough. James Hutton had duly warned his followers against the temptation to appeal to time as if it were itself an efficient cause of effects. "With regard to the effect of time," he said,[7] "though the continuance of time may do much in those operations which are extremely slow, where no change, to our observation, had appeared to take place, yet, where it is not in the nature of things to produce the change in question, the unlimited course of time would be no more effectual than the moment by which we measure events in our observations." The warning was not heeded: men seemed to imagine that, if only time enough were given for it, effects, for which no adequate cause could be assigned, might be supposed to come gradually of themselves. Aimless movement was supposed, if time enough were allowed for it, to produce an ordered world. It might as well be supposed that if a box full of printers' types were stirred up long enough with a stick, they could be counted on to arrange themselves in time in the order in which they stand, say, in Kant's "Critique of Pure Reason." They will never do so, though they be stirred to eternity. Dr. J. W. Dawson[8] points out the exact difficulty, when he remarks that "the necessity for indefinitely protracted time does not arise from the facts, but from the attempt to explain the facts without any adequate cause, and to appeal to an infinite series of chance interactions apart from a designed plan, and without regard to the consideration, that we know of no way in which, with any conceivable amount of time, the first living and organized beings could be spontaneously produced from dead matter." Nothing could be more certain than that what chance cannot begin the production of in a moment, chance cannot complete the production of in an eternity. The analysis of the complete effect into an infinite series of parts, and the distribution of these parts over an infinite series of years, leaves the effect as unaccounted for as ever. What is needed to account for it is not time in any extension, but an adequate cause. A mass of iron is made no more self-supporting by being forged into an

[7] "Theory of the earth," ii. p. 205.
[8] "Relics of Primeval Life," 1897, p. 323.

illimitable chain formed of innumerable infinitesimal links. We may cast our dice to all eternity with no more likelihood than at the first throw of ever turning up double-sevens.

It is not, however, the force of such reasoning but the pressure of hard facts which is revolutionizing the conceptions of biologists today as to the length of the period during which man has existed on earth. It is not possible to enumerate here all the facts which are coöperating to produce a revised and greatly reduced estimate of this period. First among them may doubtless be placed the calculations of the life-period of the globe itself which have been made by the physicists with ever increasing confidence. Led by such investigators as Lord Kelvin, they have become ever more and more insistent that the time demanded by the old uniformitarian and new biological speculator is not at their disposal. The publication in the seventh decade of the past century of Lord Kelvin's calculations, going to show that the sun had not been shining sixty millions of years, already gave pause to the reckless drafts which had been accustomed to be made on time; and the situation was rendered more and more acute by subsequent revisions of Lord Kelvin's work, progressively diminishing this estimate. Sir Archibald Geikie complains that "he [Lord Kelvin] has cut off slice after slice from the allowance of time which at first he was prepared to grant for the evolution of geological history," until he has reduced it from forty to twenty millions of years, "and probably much nearer twenty than forty."[9] This estimate of the period of the sun's light would allow only something like six millions of years for geological time, only some one-sixteenth of which would be available for the cænozoic period, of which only about one-eighth or forty thousand years or so could be allotted to the pleistocene age, in the course of which the remains of man first appear.[10] Even this meager allowance is cut in half by the

[9] *Loc. cit.*, p. 519.

[10] Cf. the estimates of G. F. Wright, "Records of the Past," vii. 1908, p. 24. He suggests for post-Tertiary time, say 50,000 years; and adds that, even if this be doubled, there could be assigned to the post-glacial period only some 10,000 years.

calculation of Professor Tait;[11] while the general conclusions of these investigators have received the support of independent calculations by Dr. George H. Darwin and Professor Newcomb; and more recently still Mr. T. J. J. See of the Naval Observatory at Washington has published a very pretty speculation in which he determines the total longevity of the sun to be only thirty-six millions of years, thirty-two of which belong to its past history.[12]

It is not merely the physicists, however, with whom the biological speculators have to do: the geologists themselves have turned against them. Recent investigations may be taken as putting pre-Quaternary man out of the question (the evidence was reviewed by Sir John Evans, in his address at the Toronto meeting of the British Association, August 18, 1897). And revised estimates of the rate of denudation, erosion, deposition of alluvial matter in deltas, or of stalagmitic matter on the floors of caves have greatly reduced the exaggerated conception of its slowness, from which support was sought for the immensely long periods of time demanded. The post-glacial period, which will roughly estimate the age of man, it is now pretty generally agreed, "cannot be more than ten thousand years, or probably not more than seven thousand" in length.[13] In this estimate both Professor Winchell[14] and Professor Salisbury[15] agree, and to its establishment a great body of evidence derived from a variety of calculations concur. If man is of post-glacial origin, then, his advent upon earth need not be dated more than five or six thousand years ago; or

[11] "Recent Advances in Physical Science," 1876, pp. 167-168.

[12] On the so-called "Planetesimal Hypothesis" of Professors Chamberlin and Moulton, which does not presuppose a molten sun and earth, these calculations which proceed on the basis of the "cooling-globe hypothesis" are of course without validity. And in recent years a somewhat despairing appeal has been made to the behavior of radium to suggest that all calculations based on rate of waste are valueless.

[13] Cf. especially articles in the Bibliotheca Sacra for July, 1903 (lx. pp. 572-582).

[14] American Geologist, September, 1902, p. 193.

[15] "The Glacial Geology of New Jersey" (Volume V of the Final Report of the State Geologist), 1902, p. 194.

if we suppose him to have appeared at some point in the later glacial period, as Professor G. F. Wright does, then certainly Professor Wright's estimate of sixteen thousand to twenty thousand years is an ample one.

The effect of these revised estimates of geological time has been greatly increased by growing uncertainty among biologists themselves, as to the soundness of the assumptions upon which was founded their demand for long periods of time. These assumptions were briefly those which underlie the doctrine of evolution in its specifically Darwinian form; in the form, that is to say, in which the evolution is supposed to be accomplished by the fixing through the pressure of the environment of minute favorable variations, arising accidentally in the midst of minute variations in every direction indifferently. But in the progress of biological research, the sufficiency of this "natural selection" to account for the development of organic forms has come first to be questioned, and then in large circles to be denied.[16] In proportion, however, as evolution is conceived as advancing in determined directions, come the determination from whatever source you choose;[17] and in proportion as it is conceived as advancing onwards by large increments instead of by insensible changes;[18] in that proportion the demand on time is lessened and even the evolutionary speculator feels that he can get along with less of it. He is no longer impelled to assume behind the high type of man whose remains in the post-glacial deposits are the first intimation of the presence of man on earth, an almost illimitable series of lower and ever lower types of man through which gradually the brute struggled up to the high humanity, records of whose existence

[16] Cf. V. L. Kellogg, "Darwinism To-day," 1907; R. Otto, "Naturalism and Religion," 1907; E. Wasmann, "Die moderne Biologie und die Entwicklungstheorie," ed. 3, 1906; James Orr, "God's Image in Man," 1905; E. Dennert, "Vom Sterbelager des Darwinismus," 1903.

[17] That "orthogenesis" is a fact is much more widely recognized than is the validity of Eimer's special mode of accounting for it.

[18] The recognition of the reality of these saltations—or "mutations," as De Vries inadequately terms them—is again largely independent of any particular theory with reference to them.

alone have been preserved to us.[19] And he no longer requires to postulate immense stretches of time for the progress of this man through paleolithic, neolithic and metal-using periods, for the differentiation of the strongly marked characteristics of the several races of man, for the slow humanizing of human nature and the slower development of those powers within it from which at length what we call civilization emerged. Once allow the principle of modification by leaps, and the question of the length of time required for a given evolution passes out of the sphere of practical interest. The height of the leaps becomes a matter of detail, and there is readily transferred to the estimation of it the importance which was formerly attached to the estimation of the time involved. Thus it has come about, that, in the progress of scientific investigation, the motive for demanding illimitable stretches of time for the duration of life, and specifically for the duration of human life on earth, has gradually been passing away, and there seems now a very general tendency among scientific investigators to acquiesce in a moderate estimate—in an estimate which demands for the life of man on earth not more than, say, ten or twenty thousand years.

If the controversy upon the antiquity of man is thus rapidly losing all but a historical interest, that which once so violently raged upon the unity of the race may be said already to have reached this stage. The question of the unity of the human race differs from the question of its antiquity in that it is of indubitable theological importance. It is not merely that the Bible

19 Cf. Hubrecht in *De Gids* for June, 1896; Otto, "Naturalism and Religion," 1907, p. 110; Orr, "God's Image in Man," 1905, p. 134. E. D. Cope, "The Primary Factors of Organic Evolution," 1896, thinks there is evidence enough to constitute two species of the genus *homo—Homo sapiens* and *Homo neanderthalensis*, to the latter of which he assigns a greater number of simian characteristics than exist in any of the known races of the *Homo sapiens*. But he requires to add (p. 170): "There is still, to use the language of Fraipont and Lohest, 'an abyss' between the man of Spy and the highest ape"—although, on his own account he adds, surely unwarrantably, "though, from a zoölogical point of view, it is not a wide one." In point of fact the earliest relics of man are relics of *men*, with all that is included in that, and there lies between them and all other known beings a hitherto unbridged "abyss."

certainly teaches it, while, as we have sought to show, it has
no teaching upon the antiquity of the race. It is also the postulate of the entire body of the Bible's teaching—of its doctrine
of Sin and Redemption alike: so that the whole structure of
the Bible's teaching, including all that we know as its doctrine
of salvation, rests on it and implicates it. There have been
times, nevertheless, when it has been vigorously assailed, from
various motives, from within as well as from without the
Church, and the resources of Christian reasoning have been
taxed to support it. These times have now, however, definitely
passed away. The prevalence of the evolutionary hypotheses
has removed all motive for denying a common origin to the
human race, and rendered it natural to look upon the differences which exist among the various types of man as differentiations of a common stock. The motive for denying their con-
clusiveness having been thus removed, the convincing evidences of the unity of the race have had opportunity to assert
their force. The result is that the unity of the race, in the sense
of its common origin, is no longer a matter of debate; and
although actually some erratic writers may still speak of it as
open to discussion, they are not taken seriously, and practically
it is universally treated as a fixed fact that mankind in all its
varieties is one, as in fundamental characteristics, so also in
origin.

In our natural satisfaction over this agreement between
Scripture and modern science with respect to the unity of
humanity, we must not permit ourselves to forget that there
has always nevertheless existed among men a strong tendency
to deny this unity in the interests of racial pride. Outside of the
influence of the Biblical revelation, indeed, the sense of human
unity has never been strong and has ordinarily been non-
existent.[20] The Stoics seem to have been the first among the
classical peoples to preach the unity of mankind and the duty
of universal justice and philanthropy founded upon it. With
the revival of classical ideas which came in with what we call
the Renaissance, there came in also a tendency to revive

[20] Cf. H. Bavinck, "The Philosophy of Revelation," 1909, pp. 137 ff.

heathen polygenism, which was characteristically reproduced in the writings of Blount and others of the Deists. A more definite co-Adamitism, that is to say the attribution of the descent of the several chief racial types to separate original ancestors, has also been taught by occasional individuals such, for example, as Paracelsus. And the still more definite pre-Adamitism, which conceives man indeed as a single species, derived from one stock, but represents Adam not as the root of this stock, but as one of its products, the ancestor of the Jews and white races alone, has always found teachers, such as, for example, Zanini. The advocacy of this pre-Adamitic theory by Isaac de la Peyrère in the middle of the seventeenth century roused a great debate which, however, soon died out, although leaving echoes behind it in Bayle, Arnold, Swedenborg. A sort of pre-Adamitism has continued to be taught by a series of philosophical speculators from Schelling down, which looks upon Adam as the first real man, rising in developed humanity above the low, beastlike condition of his ancestors. In our own day George Catlin[21] and especially Alexander Winchell[22] have revived in its essentials the teaching of de la Peyrère. "Adam," says Professor Winchell, "is descended from a black race, not the black race from Adam." The advancing knowledge of the varied races of man produced in the latter part of the eighteenth and the earlier nineteenth century a revival of co-Adamitism (Sullivan, Crueger, Ballenstedt, Cordonière, Gobineau) which was even perverted into a defense of slavery (Dobbs, Morton, Nott, and Gliddon). It was in connection with Nott and Gliddon's "Types of Mankind" that Agassiz first published his theory of the diverse origin of the several types of man, the only one of these theories of abiding interest because the only one arising from a genuinely scientific impulse and possessing a really scientific basis. Agassiz's theory was the product of a serious study of the geographical distribution of animate life, and one of the results of Agassiz's classification of the whole of animate creation

[21] "O-kee-pa," London, 1867: he referred the North American Indians to an antediluvian species, which he called *Anthropus Americanus*.

[22] "Preadamites," Chicago, 1880.

into eight well-marked types of fauna involving, so he thought, eight separate centers of origin. Pursuant to this classification he sought to distribute mankind also into eight types, to each of which he ascribed a separate origin, corresponding with the type of fauna with which each is associated. But even Agassiz could not deny that men are, despite their eightfold separate creation, all of one kind: he could not erect specific differences between the several types of man.[23] The evidence which compelled him to recognize the oneness of man in kind remains in its full validity, after advancing knowledge of the animal kingdom and its geographical distribution[24] has rendered Agassiz's assumption of eight centers of origination (not merely distribution) a violent hypothesis; and the entrance into the field of the evolutionary hypothesis has consigned all theories formed without reference to it to oblivion. Even some early evolutionists, it is true, played for a time with theories of multiplex times and places where similar lines of development culminated alike in man (Haeckel, Schaffhausen, Caspari, Vogt, Büchner), and perhaps there is now some sign of the revival of this view; but it is now agreed with practical unanimity that the unity of the human race, in the sense of its common origin, is a necessary corollary of the evolutionary hypothesis, and no voice raised in contradiction of it stands much chance to be heard.[25]

It is, however, only for its universal allowance at the hands of speculative science that the fact of the unity of the human race has to thank the evolutionary hypothesis. The evidence by which it is solidly established is of course independent of all such hypotheses. This evidence is drawn almost equally from every department of human manifestation, physiological, psychological, philological, and even historical. The physio-

[23] Similarly Heinrich Schurtz, while leaving the descent of men from a single pair an open question, affirms that it is a fact that "humanity forms one great unity."

[24] It was Wallace's "Geographical Distribution of Animals" which struck the first crushing blow.

[25] Klaatsch wishes to postulate two distinct stems for man (now mingled together): see on his views, Keith in *Nature*, December 15, 1910.

logical unity of the race is illustrated by the nice gradations by which the several so-called races into which it is divided pass into one another; and by their undiminished natural fertility when intercrossed; by which Professor Owen was led to remark that "man forms one species, and . . . differences are but indicative of varieties" which "merge into each other by easy gradations."[26] It is emphasized by the contrast which exists between the structural characteristics, osteological, cranial, dental, common to the entire race of human beings of every variety and those of the nearest animal types; which led Professor Huxley to assert that "every bone of a Gorilla bears marks by which it might be distinguished from the corresponding bones of a Man; and that, in the present creation, at any rate, no intermediate link bridges over the gap between *Homo* and *Troglodytes*."[27] The psychological unity of the race is still more manifest. All men of all varieties are psychologically men and prove themselves possessors of the same mental nature and furniture. Under the same influences they function mentally and spiritually in the same fashion, and prove capable of the same mental reactions. They, they all, and they alone, in the whole realm of animal existences manifest themselves as rational and moral natures; so that Mr. Fiske was fully justified when he declared that though for zoölogical man the erection of a distinct family from the chimpanzee and orang might suffice, "on the other hand, for psychological man you must erect a distinct kingdom; nay, you must even dichotomize the universe, putting Man on one side and all things else on the other."[28] Among the manifestations of the psychological peculiarities of mankind, as distinguished from all other animate existences, is the great gift of speech which he shares with no other being: if all human languages cannot be reduced to a single root, they all exhibit a uniquely human faculty working under similar laws, and bear the most striking testi-

[26] E. Burgess, "What is Truth? An Enquiry concerning the Antiquity and Unity of the Human Race," Boston [1871], p. 185.

[27] "Evidence as to Man's Place in Nature," 1864, p. 104.

[28] "Through Nature to God," 1899, p. 82.

mony to the unity of the race which alone has language at its command. The possession of common traditions by numerous widely separated peoples is only a single one of many indications of a historical intercommunion between the several peoples through which their essential unity is evinced, and by which the Biblical account of the origination of the various families of man in a single center from which they have spread out in all directions is powerfuly supported.[29]

The assertion of the unity of the human race is imbedded in the very structure of the Biblical narrative. The Biblical account of the origin of man (Gen. i. 26-28) is an account of his origination in a single pair, who constituted humanity in its germ, and from whose fruitfulness and multiplication all the earth has been replenished. Therefore the first man was called Adam, Man, and the first woman, Eve, "because she was the mother of all living" (Gen. iii. 20); and all men are currently spoken of as the "sons of Adam" or "Man" (Deut. xxxii. 8; Ps. xi. 4; I Sam. xxvi. 19; I Kings viii. 39; Ps. cxlv. 12; etc.). The absolute restriction of the human race within the descendants of this single pair is emphasized by the history of the Flood in which all flesh is destroyed, and the race given a new beginning in its second father, Noah, by whose descendants again "the whole earth was overspread" (Gen. ix. 19), as is illustrated in detail by the table of nations recorded in Genesis x. A profound religious-ethical significance is given to the differentiations of the peoples, in the story of the tower of Babel in the eleventh chapter of Genesis, in which the divergences and separations which divide mankind are represented as the product of sin: what God had joined together men themselves pulled asunder. Throughout the Scriptures therefore all mankind is treated as, from the divine point of view, a unit, and shares not only in a common nature but in a common sinfulness, not only in a common need but in a common redemption.

Accordingly, although Israel was taught to glory in its ex-

[29] Cf. the discussion in the seventh lecture of Bavinck's "Philosophy of Revelation," 1909.

altation by the choice of the Lord to be His peculiar people, Israel was not permitted to believe there was anything in itself which differentiated it from other peoples; and by the laws concerning aliens and slaves was required to recognize the common humanity of all sorts and conditions of men; what they had to distinguish them from others was not of nature but of the free gift of God, in the mysterious working out of His purpose of good not only to Israel but to the whole world. This universalism in the divine purposes of mercy, already inherent in the Old Covenant and often proclaimed in it, and made the very keynote of the New—for which the Old was the preparation—is the most emphatic possible assertion of the unity of the race. Accordingly, not only do we find our Lord Himself setting His seal upon the origination of the race in a single pair, and drawing from that fact the law of life for men at large (Matt. xix. 4); and Paul explicitly declaring that "God has made of one every nation of men" and having for His own good ends appointed to each its separate habitation, is now dealing with them all alike in offering them a common salvation (Acts xvii. 26 ff.); but the whole New Testament is instinct with the brotherhood of mankind as one in origin and in nature, one in need and one in the provision of redemption. The fact of racial sin is basal to the whole Pauline system (Rom. v. 12 ff.; I Cor. xv. 21 f.), and beneath the fact of racial sin lies the fact of racial unity. It is only because all men were in Adam as their first head that all men share in Adam's sin and with his sin in his punishment. And it is only because the sin of man is thus one in origin and therefore of the same nature and quality, that the redemption which is suitable and may be made available for one is equally suitable and may be made available for all. It is because the race is one and its need one, Jew and Gentile are alike under sin, that there is no difference between Jew and Gentile in the matter of salvation either, but as the same God is Lord of all, so He is rich in Christ Jesus unto all that call upon Him, and will justify the uncircumcision through faith alone, even as He justifies the circumcision only by faith (Rom. ix. 22-24, 28 ff.; x. 12).

Jesus Christ therefore, as the last Adam, is the Saviour not of the Jews only but of the world (John iv. 42; I Tim. iv. 10; I John iv. 14), having been given to this His great work only by the love of the Father for the world (John iii. 16). The unity of the human race is therefore made in Scripture not merely the basis of a demand that we shall recognize the dignity of humanity in all its representatives, of however lowly estate or family, since all bear alike the image of God in which man was created and the image of God is deeper than sin and cannot be eradicated by sin (Gen. v. 3; ix. 6; I Cor. xi. 7; Heb. ii. 5 ff.); but the basis also of the entire scheme of restoration devised by the divine love for the salvation of a lost race.

So far is it from being of no concern to theology, therefore, that it would be truer to say that the whole doctrinal structure of the Bible account of redemption is founded on its assumption that the race of man is one organic whole, and may be dealt with as such. It is because all are one in Adam that in the matter of sin there is no difference, but all have fallen short of the glory of God (Rom. iii. 22 f.), and as well that in the new man there cannot be Greek and Jew, circumcision and uncircumcision, barbarian, Scythian, bondman, freeman; but Christ is all and in all (Col. iii. 11). The unity of the old man in Adam is the postulate of the unity of the new man in Christ.

Chapter X

IMPUTATION[1]

I. Origin and Meaning of the Term

THE theological use of the term "imputation" is probably rooted ultimately in the employment of the verb *imputo* in the Vulgate to translate the Greek verb *logizesthai* in Ps. xxxii. 2. This passage is quoted by Paul in Rom. iv. 8 and made one of the foundations of his argument that, in saving man, God sets to his credit a righteousness without works. It is only in these two passages, and in the two axiomatic statements of Rom. iv. 4 and v. 13 that the Vulgate uses *imputo* in this connection (cf., with special application, II Tim. iv. 16; Philemon 18). There are other passages, however, where it might just as well have been employed, but where we have instead *reputo*, under the influence of the mistaken rendering of the Hebrew *hashabh* in Gen. xv. 6. In these passages the Authorized English Version improves on the Latin by rendering a number of them (Rom. iv. 11, 22, 23, 24; II Cor. v. 19; James ii. 23) by "impute," and employing for the rest synonymous terms, all of which preserve the "metaphor from accounts" inherent in *logizesthai* (and *ellogein*) in this usage (cf. W. Sanday and A. C. Headlam, "Commentary on the Epistle to the Romans," iv. 3), such as "count" (Rom. iv. 3, 5), "account" (Gal. iii. 6), and "reckon" (Rom. iv. 4, 9, 10); the last of which the Revised English Version makes its uniform rendering of *logizesthai*. Even the meager employment of *imputo* in the Latin version, however, supplied occasion enough for the adoption of that word in the precise language of theology as the technical term for that which is expressed

[1] Reprinted from "The New Schaff-Herzog Encyclopedia of Religious Knowledge," edited by Samuel Macauley Jackson, D.D., LL.D., v. pp. 465-467 (copyright by Funk and Wagnalls Company, New York, 1909); also from *Studies in Theology*, pp. 301-308.

by the Greek words in their so-called "commercial" sense, or what may, more correctly, be called their forensic or "judicial" sense, "that is, putting to one's account," or, in its twofold reference to the credit and debit sides, "setting to one's credit" or "laying to one's charge."

II. Three Acts of Imputation

From the time of Augustine (early fifth century), at least, the term "imputation" is found firmly fixed in theological terminology in this sense. But the applications and relations of the doctrine expressed by it were thoroughly worked out only in the discussions which accompanied and succeeded the Reformation. In the developed theology thus brought into the possession of the Church, three several acts of imputation were established and expounded. These are the imputation of Adam's sin to his posterity; the imputation of the sins of His people to the Redeemer; the imputation of the righteousness of Christ to His people. Though, of course, with more or less purity of conception and precision of application, these three great doctrines became the property of the whole Church, and found a place in the classical theology of the Roman, Lutheran, and Reformed alike. In the proper understanding of the conception, it is important to bear in mind that the divine act called "imputation" is in itself precisely the same in each of the three great transactions into which it enters as a constituent part. The grounds on which it proceeds may differ; the things imputed may be different; and the consequent treatment of the person or persons to which the imputation is made may and will differ as the things imputed to them differ. But in each and every case alike imputation itself is simply the act of setting to one's account; and the act of setting to one's account is in itself the same act whether the thing set to his account stands on the credit or debit side of the account, and whatever may be the ground in equity on which it is set to his account. That the sin of Adam was so set to the account of his descendants that they have actually shared in the penalty which was threatened to it; and that the sins of His people were so set to the account of our Lord that He bore them in His own body on the tree, and His merits are so set to their account that by His stripes they are healed, the entirety of historical orthodox Christianity unites in affirming.

III. PELAGIAN OPPOSITION TO THE DOCTRINE

Opposition to these doctrines has, of course, not been lacking in the history of Christian thought. The first instance of important contradiction of the fundamental principle involved is presented by the Pelagian movement which arose at the beginning of the fifth century. The Pelagians denied the equity and, therefore, under the government of God, the possibility of the involvement of one free agent in the acts of another; they utterly denied, therefore, that men either suffer harm from Adam's sin or profit by Christ's merits. By their examples only, they said, can either Adam or Christ affect us; and by free imitation of them alone can we share in their merits or demerits. It is not apparent why Pelagius permitted himself such extremity of denial. What he had at heart to assert was the inamissibility by the human subject of plenary ability of will to do all righteousness. To safeguard this he had necessarily to deny all subjective injury to men from Adam's sin (and from their own sins too, for that matter), and the need or actuality of subjective grace for their perfecting. But there was no reason growing out of this point of sight why he might not allow that the guilt of Adam's sin had been imputed to his posterity, and had supplied the ground for the infliction upon them of external penalties temporal or eternal; or that the merits of Christ might be imputed to His people as the meritorious ground of their relief from these penalties, as well as of the forgiveness of their own actual sins and of their reception into the favor of God and the heavenly blessedness. Later Pelagianizers found this out; and it became not uncommon (especially after Duns Scotus' strong assertion of the doctrine of "immediate imputation") for the imputation of Adam's sin to be exploited precisely in the interest of denial or weakening of the idea of the derivation of inherent corruption from Adam.

A very good example of this tendency of thought is supplied by the Roman Catholic theologian Ambrosius Catharinus, whose admirable speech to this effect at the Council of Trent is reported by Father Paul ("History of the Council of Trent," E. T. London, 1676, p. 165). Even Zwingli was not unaffected by it. He was indeed free from the Pelagianizing attenuation of the corruption of nature which is the subjective effect on his posterity of Adam's sin. With him, "original sin" was both extensively and intensively a total depravity, the fertile source of all evil action. But he looked upon it rather as a misfortune than a fault, a disease than a sin; and he hung the whole weight of our ruin on our direct participation in Adam's guilt. As a slave can beget only a slave, says he, so all the progeny of man under the curse are born under the curse.

IV. IMPORTANCE OF THE DOCTRINE

In sharp contradiction to the current tendency to reduce to the vanishing-point the subjective injury wrought by Adam's sin on his posterity, the churches gave themselves to emphasizing the depth of the injury and especially its sinfulness. Even the Council of Trent acknowledged the transfusion into the entire human race of "sin, which is the death of the soul." The Protestants, who, as convinced Augustinians, were free from the Pelagianizing bias of Rome, were naturally even more strenuous in asserting the evil and guilt of native depravity. Accordingly they constantly remark that men's native guilt in the sight of God rests not merely upon the imputation to them of Adam's first sin, but also upon the corruption which they derive from him—a mode of statement which meets us, indeed, as early as Peter Lombard ("Sentences," II. xxx.) and for the same reason. The polemic turn given to these statements has been the occasion of a remarkable misapprehension, as if it were intended to subordinate the imputation of Adam's transgression to the transmission of his corrupted nature as the source of human guilt. Precisely the contrary is the fact. The imputation of Adam's transgression was not in dispute; all parties to the great debate of the age fully recognized it;

and it is treated therefore as a matter of course. What was important was to make it clear that native depravity was along with it the ground of our guilt before God. Thus it was sought to hold the balance true, and to do justice to both elements in a complete doctrine of original sin. Meanwhile the recovery of the great doctrine of justification by faith threw back its light upon the doctrine of the satisfaction of Christ which had been in the possession of the Church since Anselm; and the better understanding of this doctrine, thus induced, in turn illuminated the doctrine of sin, whose correlative it is, Thus it came about that in the hands of the great Protestant leaders of the sixteenth century, and of their successors, the Protestant systematizers of the seventeenth century, the three-fold doctrine of imputation—of Adam's sin to his posterity, of the sins of His people to the Redeemer, and of the righteousness of Christ to His people—at last came to its rights as the core of the three constitutive doctrines of Christianity—the sinfulness of the human race, the satisfaction of Jesus Christ, and justification by faith. The importance of the doctrine of imputation is that it is the hinge on which these three gre t doctrines turn, and the guardian of their purity.

V. Socinian, Arminian, and Rationalistic Opposition

Of course the Church was not permitted to enjoy in quiet its new understanding of its treasures of doctrine. Radical opponents arose in the Reformation age itself, the most important of whom were the Socinians. By them it was pronounced an inanity to speak of the transference of either merit or demerit from one person to another: we can be bad with another's badness, or good with another's goodness, they said, as little as we can be white with another's whiteness. The center of the Socinian assault was upon the doctrine of the satisfaction of Christ: it is not possible, they affirmed, for one person to bear the punishment due to another. But their criticism cut equally deeply into the Protestant doctrines of original sin and justification by faith. The influence of their type of thought, very great from the first, increased as time went on and became a factor

of importance both in the Arminian revolt at the beginning
of the seventeenth century and in the rationalistic defection
a hundred years later. Neither the Arminians (e.g. Limborch,
Curcellæus) nor the Rationalists (e.g. Wegscheider) would
hear of an imputation of Adam's sin, and both attacked with
arguments very similar to those of the Socinians also the imputation of our sins to Christ or of His righteousness to us.
Rationalism almost ate the heart out of the Lutheran Churches;
and the Reformed Churches were saved from the same fate only
by the prompt extrusion of the Arminian party and the strengthening of their position by conflict with it. In particular, about
the middle of the seventeenth century the "covenant" or "federal" method of exhibiting the plan of the Lord's dealings with
men began to find great acceptance among the Reformed
Churches. There was nothing novel in this mode of conceiving truth. The idea was present to the minds of the
Church Fathers and the Schoolmen; and it underlay Protestant thought, both Lutheran and Reformed, from the beginning, and in the latter had come to clear expression, first
in Ursinus. But now it quickly became dominant as the preferable manner of conceiving the method of the divine dealing
with men. The effect was to throw into the highest relief the
threefold doctrine of imputation, and to make manifest as
never before the dependency of the great doctrines of sin,
satisfaction, and justification upon it.

VI. La Place and Later Theologians and Schools

About the same time a brilliant French professor, Josué de
la Place, of the Reformed school at Saumur, reduced all that
could be called the imputation of Adam's sin to his posterity
simply to this—that because of the sin inherent in us from our
origin we are deserving of being treated in the same way as if
we had committed that offense. This confinement of the effect
of Adam's sin upon his posterity to the transmission to them of
a sinful disposition—inherent sin—was certainly new in the
history of Reformed thought: Andreas Rivetus had no difficulty in collecting a long line of "testimonies" from the con-

fessions and representative theologians explicitly declaring that men are accounted guilty in God's sight, both because of Adam's act of transgression imputed to them and of their own sinful disposition derived from him. The conflict of views was no doubt rendered sharper, however, by the prevalence at the time of the "Covenant theology" in which the immediate imputation of Adam's transgression is particularly clearly emphasized. Thus "immediate" and "mediate" imputation (for by the latter name La Place came subsequently to call his view) were pitted against each other as mutually exclusive doctrines: as if the question at issue were whether man stood condemned in the sight of God solely on account of his "adherent" sin, or solely on account of his "inherent" sin. The former of these doctrines had never been held in the Reformed Churches, since Zwingli, and the latter had never been held in them before La Place. From the first both "adherent" and "inherent" sin had been confessed as the double ground of human guilt; and the advocates of the "Covenant theology" were as far as possible from denying the guilt of "inherent" sin. La Place's innovation was as a matter of course condemned by the Reformed world, formally at the Synod of Charenton (1644-1645) and in the Helvetic Consensus (1675) and by argument at the hands of the leading theologians— Rivetus, Turretin, Maresius, Driessen, Leydecker, and Marck. But the tendencies of the time were in its favor and it made its way. It was adopted by theologians like Wyttenbach, Endemann, Stapfer, Roell, Vitringa, Venema; and after a while it found its way through Britain to America, where it has had an interesting history—forming one of the stages through which the New England Theology passed on its way to its ultimate denial of the quality of sin involving guilt to anything but the voluntary acts of a free agent; and finally becoming one of the characteristic tenets of the so-called "New School Theology" of the Presbyterian Churches. Thus it has come about that there has been much debate in America upon "imputation," in the sense of the imputation of Adam's sin, and diverse types of theology have been framed, especially among the Congregationalists and Presbyterians, centering in differences of conception of this doctrine. Among the Presbyterians, for example, four such types are well marked, each of which has been taught by theologians of distinction. These are (1) the "Federalistic," characterized by its adherence to the doctrine of "immediate imputation," represented, for example, by Dr. Charles Hodge; (2) the "New School," characterized by its adherence to the doctrine of "mediate imputation," represented, for example, by Dr. Henry B. Smith; (3) the "Realistic," which teaches that all mankind were present in Adam as generic humanity, and sinned in him, and are therefore guilty of his and their common sin, represented, for example, by Dr. W. G. T. Shedd; and (4) one which may be called the "Agnostic," characterized by an attempt to accept the fact of the transmission of both guilt and depravity from Adam without framing a theory of the mode of their transmission or of their relations one to the other, represented, for example, by Dr. R. W. Landis.

Chapter XI

PREDESTINATION[1]

I. Predestination in the Old Testament

No survey of the terms[2] used to express it can convey an adequate sense of the place occupied by the idea of predestination in the religious system of the Bible. It is not too much to say that it is fundamental to the whole religious consciousness of the Biblical writers, and is so involved in all their religious conceptions that to eradicate it would transform the entire scriptural representation. This is as true of the Old Testament as of the New Testament, as will become sufficiently manifest by attending briefly to the nature and implications of such formative elements in the Old Testament system as its doctrines of God, Providence, Faith, and the Kingdom of God.

Old Testament Doctrine of God

Whencesoever Israel obtained it, it is quite certain that Israel entered upon its national existence with the most vivid consciousness of an almighty personal Creator and Governor of heaven and earth. Israel's own account of the clearness and the firmness of its apprehension of this mighty Author and Ruler of all that is, refers it to His own initiative: God chose to make Himself known to the fathers. At all events, throughout the whole of Old Testament literature, and for every period of history recorded in it, the fundamental conception of God remains the same, and the two most persistently emphasized elements in it are just those of might and personality: before everything else, the God of Israel is the Omnipotent Person.

[1] Article "Predestination," from *A Dictionary of the Bible*, ed. by James Hastings, v. 4, pp. 47-63. Pub. N. Y. 1909, by Charles Scribner's Sons; also from *Biblical Doctrines*, pp. 3-66.

[2] For such a survey see appendix to this chapter.

Possibly the keen sense of the exaltation and illimitable power of God which forms the very core of the Old Testament idea of God belongs rather to the general Semitic than to the specifically Israelitish element in its religion; certainly it was already prominent in the patriarchal God-consciousness, as is sufficiently evinced by the names of God current from the beginning of the Old Testament revelation,—*El, Eloah, Elohim, El Shaddai,*—and as is illustrated endlessly in the Biblical narrative. But it is equally clear that God was never conceived by the Old Testament saints as abstract power, but was ever thought of concretely as the all-powerful Person, and that, moreover, as clothed with all the attributes of moral personality,—pre-eminently with holiness, as the very summit of His exaltation, but along with holiness, also with all the characteristics that belong to spiritual personality as it exhibits itself familiarly in man. In a word, God is pictured in the Old Testament, and that from the beginning, purely after the pattern of human personality,—as an intelligent, feeling, willing Being, like the man who is created in His image in all in which the life of a free spirit consists. The anthropomorphisms to which this mode of conceiving God led were sometimes startling enough, and might have become grossly misleading had not the corrective lain ever at hand in the accompanying sense of the immeasurable exaltation of God, by which He was removed above all the weaknesses of humanity. The result accordingly was nothing other than a peculiarly pure form of Theism. The grosser anthropomorphisms were fully understood to be figurative, and the residuary conception was that of an infinite Spirit, not indeed expressed in abstract terms nor from the first fully brought out in all its implications, but certainly in all ages of the Old Testament development grasped in all its essential elements.

Old Testament Doctrine of Providence

Such a God could not be thought of otherwise than as the free determiner of all that comes to pass in the world which is the product of His creative act; and the doctrine of Providence

(פְּקֻדָּה) which is spread over the pages of the Old Testament fully bears out this expectation. The almighty Maker of all that is is represented equally as the irresistible Ruler of all that He has made: Jehovah sits as King for ever (Ps. xxix. 10). Even the common language of life was affected by this pervasive point of view, so that, for example, it is rare to meet with such a phrase as 'it rains' (Amos iv. 7), and men by preference spoke of God sending rain (Ps. lxv. 9 f., Job xxxvi. 27, xxxviii. 26). The vivid sense of dependence on God thus witnessed extended throughout every relation of life. Accident or chance was excluded. If we read here and there of a מִקְרֶה it is not thought of as happening apart from God's direction (Ruth ii. 3, I Sam. vi. 9, xx. 26, Eccl. ii. 14, cf. I Kings xxii. 34, II Chron. xviii. 33), and accordingly the lot was an accepted means of obtaining the decision of God (Jos. vii. 16, xiv. 2, xviii. 6, I Sam. x. 19, Jon. i. 7), and is didactically recognized as under His control (Prov. xvi. 33). All things without exception, indeed, are disposed by Him, and His will is the ultimate account of all that occurs. Heaven and earth and all that is in them are the instruments through which He works His ends. Nature, nations, and the fortunes of the individual alike present in all their changes the transcript of His purpose. The winds are His messengers, the flaming fire His servant: every natural occurrence is His act: prosperity is His gift, and if calamity falls upon man it is the Lord that has done it (Amos iii. 5, 6, Lam. iii. 33-38, Isa. xlvii. 7, Eccl. vii. 14, Isa. liv. 16). It is He that leads the feet of men, wit they whither or not; He that raises up and casts down; opens and hardens the heart; and creates the very thoughts and intents of the soul. So poignant is the sense of His activity in all that occurs, that an appearance is sometimes created as if everything that comes to pass were so ascribed to His immediate production as to exclude the real activity of second causes. It is a grave mistake, nevertheless, to suppose that He is conceived as an unseen power, throwing up, in a quasi-Pantheistic sense, all changes on the face of the world and history. The virile sense of the free personality of God which dominates all the thought of the Old Testament would alone

have precluded such a conception. Nor is there really any lack
of recognition of 'second causes,' as we call them. They are
certainly not conceived as independent of God: they are rather
the mere expression of His stated will. But they are from the
beginning fully recognized, both in nature—with respect to
which Jehovah has made covenant (Gen. viii. 21, 22, Jer. xxxi.
35, 36, xxxiii. 20, 25, Ps. cxlviii. 6, cf. Jer. v. 22, Ps. civ. 9, Job
xxxviii. 10, 33, xiv. 5), establishing its laws (חֻקּוֹת Job xxviii. 25,
28, Isa. xl. 12, Job xxxviii. 8-11, Prov. viii. 29, Jer. v. 22, Ps. civ. 9,
xxxiii. 7, Isa. xl. 26)—and equally in the higher sphere of free
spirits, who are ever conceived as the true authors of all their
acts (hence God's proving of man, Gen. xxii. 1, Ex. xvi. 4, xx.
20, Deut. viii. 2, 16, xiii. 3, Judg. iii. 1, 4, II Chron. xxxii. 31).
There is no question here of the substitution of Jehovah's operation for that of the proximate causes of events. There is only the
liveliest perception of the governing hand of God behind the
proximate causes, acting through them for the working out of
His will in every detail. Such a conception obviously looks upon
the universe teleologically: an almighty moral Person cannot be
supposed to govern His universe, thus in every detail, either
unconsciously or capriciously. In His government there is necessarily implied a plan; in the all-pervasiveness and perfection
of His government is inevitably implied an all-inclusive and
perfect plan: and this conception is not seldom explicitly
developed.

OLD TESTAMENT RELIGIOUS CONSCIOUSNESS

It is abundantly clear on the face of it, of course, that this
whole mode of thought is the natural expression of the deep
religious consciousness of the Old Testament writers, though
surely it is not therefore to be set aside as 'merely' the religious
view of things, or as having no other rooting save in the imagination of religiously-minded men. In any event, however, it is
altogether natural that in the more distinctive sphere of the
religious life its informing principle of absolute dependence on
God should be found to repeat itself. This appears particularly
in the Old Testament doctrine of faith, in which there sounds

the keynote of Old Testament piety,—for the religion of the Old Testament, so far from being, as Hegel, for example, would affirm, the religion of fear, is rather by way of eminence the religion of trust. Standing over against God, not merely as creatures, but as sinners, the Old Testament saints found no ground of hope save in the free initiative of the Divine love. At no period of the development of Old Testament religion was it permitted to be imagined that blessings might be wrung from the hands of an unwilling God, or gained in the strength of man's own arm. Rather it was ever inculcated that in this sphere, too, it is God alone that lifts up and makes rich, He alone that keeps the feet of His holy ones; while by strength, it is affirmed, no man shall prevail (I Sam. ii. 9). 'I am not worthy of the least of all thy mercies' is the constant refrain of the Old Testament saints (Gen. xxxii. 10); and from the very beginning, in narrative, precept and prophetic declaration alike, it is in trust in the unmerited love of Jehovah alone that the hearts of men are represented as finding peace. Self-sufficiency is the characteristic mark of the wicked, whose doom treads on his heels; while the mark of the righteous is that he lives by his faith (Hab. ii. 4). In the entire self-commitment to God, humble dependence on Him for all blessings, which is the very core of Old Testament religion, no element is more central than the profound conviction embodied in it of the free sovereignty of God, the God of the spirits of all flesh, in the distribution of His mercies. The whole training of Israel was directed to impressing upon it the great lesson enunciated to Zerubbabel, 'Not by might, nor by power, but by my Spirit, saith the Lord of hosts' (Zech. iv. 6)—that all that comes to man in the spiritual sphere, too, is the free gift of Jehovah.

Nowhere is this lesson more persistently emphasized than in the history of the establishment and development of the kingdom of God, which may well be called the cardinal theme of the Old Testament. For the kingdom of God is consistently represented, not as the product of man's efforts in seeking after God, but as the gracious creation of God Himself. Its inception and development are the crowning manifestation of the free grace of the Living God working in history in pursuance of His loving purpose to recover fallen man to Himself. To this end He preserves the race in existence after its sin, saves a seed from the destruction of the Flood, separates to Himself a family in Abraham, sifts it in Isaac and Jacob, nurses and trains it through the weakness of its infancy, and gradually moulds it to be the vehicle of His revelation of redemption, and the channel of Messianic blessings to the world. At every step it is God, and God alone, to whom is ascribed the initiative; and the most extreme care is taken to preserve the recipients of the blessings consequent on His choice from fancying that these blessings come as their due, or as reward for aught done by themselves, or to be found in themselves. They were rather in every respect emphatically not a people of their own making, but a people that God had formed that they might set forth His praise (Isa. xliii. 21). The strongest language, the most astonishing figures, were employed to emphasize the pure sovereignty of the Divine action at every stage. It was not because Israel was numerous, or strong, or righteous, that He chose it, but only because it pleased Him to make of it a people for Himself. He was as the potter, it as the clay which the potter moulds as he will; it was but as the helpless babe in its blood cast out to die, abhorred of man, which Jehovah strangely gathers to His bosom in unmerited love (Gen. xii. 1, 3, Deut. vii. 6-8, ix. 4-6, x. 15, 16, I Sam. xii. 22, Isa. xli. 8, 9, xliii. 20, xlviii. 9-11, Jer. xviii. 1 f., xxxi. 3, Hos. ii. 20, Mal. i. 2, 3). There was no element in the religious consciousness of Israel more poignantly realized, as there was no element in the instruction they had received more insisted on, than that they owed their separation from the peoples of the earth to be the Lord's inheritance, and all the blessings they had as such received from Jehovah, not to any claim upon Him which they could urge, but to His own gracious love faithfully persisted in in spite of every conceivable obstacle.

In one word, the sovereignty of the Divine will as the principle of all that comes to pass, is a primary postulate of the whole religious life, as well as of the entire world-view of the

Old Testament. It is implicated in its very idea of God, its whole conception of the relation of God to the world and to the changes which take place, whether in nature or history, among the nations or in the life-fortunes of the individual; and also in its entire scheme of religion, whether national or personal. It lies at the basis of all the religious emotions, and lays the foundation of the specific type of religious character built up in Israel.

COSMICAL PREDESTINATION

The specific teaching of the Old Testament as to predestination naturally revolves around the two foci of that idea which may be designated general and special, or, more properly, cosmical and soteriological predestination; or, in other words, around the doctrines of the Divine Decree and the Divine Election. The former, as was to be expected, is comparatively seldom adverted to—for the Old Testament is fundamentally a soteriological book, a revelation of the grace of God to sinners; and it is only at a somewhat late period that it is made the subject of speculative discussion. But as it is implied in the primordial idea of God as an Almighty Person, it is postulated from the beginning and continually finds more or less clear expression. Throughout the Old Testament, behind the processes of nature, the march of history and the fortunes of each individual life alike, there is steadily kept in view the governing hand of God working out His preconceived plan—a plan broad enough to embrace the whole universe of things, minute enough to concern itself with the smallest details, and actualizing itself with inevitable certainty in every event that comes to pass.

Naturally, there is in the narrative portions but little formal enunciation of this pervasive and all-controlling Divine teleology. But despite occasional anthropomorphisms of rather startling character (as, e.g., that which ascribes 'repentance' to God, Gen. vi. 6, Joel ii. 13, Jon. iv. 2, Jer. xviii. 8, 10, xxvi. 3, 13), or rather, let us say, just because of the strictly anthropomorphic mould in which the Old Testament conception of God is run, according to which He is ever thought of as a personal spirit, acting with purpose like other personal spirits, but with a wisdom and in a sovereignty unlike that of others because infinitely perfect, these narrative portions of the Old Testament also bear continual witness to the universal Old Testament teleology. There is no explicit statement in the narrative of the creation, for example, that the mighty Maker of the world was in this process operating on a preconceived plan; but the teleology of creation lies latent in the orderly sequence of its parts, culminating in man for whose advent all that precedes is obviously a preparation, and is all but expressed in the Divine satisfaction at each of its stages, as a manifestation of His perfections (cf. Ps. civ. 31). Similarly, the whole narrative of the Book of Genesis is so ordered—in the succession of creation, fall, promise, and the several steps in the inauguration of the kingdom of God—as to throw into a very clear light the teleology of the whole world-history, here written from the Divine standpoint and made to centre around the developing Kingdom. In the detailed accounts of the lives of the patriarchs, in like manner, behind the external occurrences recorded there always lies a Divine ordering which provides the real plot of the story in its advance to the predetermined issue. It was not accident, for example, that brought Rebecca to the well to welcome Abraham's servant (Gen. xxiv), or that sent Joseph into Egypt (Gen. xlv. 8, l. 20; 'God meant [חשׁב] it for good'), or guided Pharaoh's daughter to the ark among the flags (Ex. ii.), or that, later, directed the millstone that crushed Abimelech's head (Judg. ix. 53), or winged the arrow shot at a venture to smite the king in the joints of the harness (I Kings xxii. 34). Every historical event is rather treated as an item in the orderly carrying out of an underlying Divine purpose; and the historian is continually aware of the presence in history of Him who gives even to the lightning a charge to strike the mark (Job xxxvi. 32).

In the Psalmists and Prophets there emerges into view a more abstract statement of the government of all things according to the good-pleasure of God (Ps. xxxiii. 11, Jer. x. 12, li. 15). All that He wills He does (Ps. cxv. 3, cxxxv. 6), and all that comes to pass has pre-existed in His purpose from the indefinite past of eternity ('long ago' Isa. xxii. 11, 'of ancient times' Isa. xxxvii. 26 = II Kings xix. 25), and it is only because it so pre-existed in purpose that it now comes to pass (Isa. xiv. 24, 27, xlvi. 11, Zech. i. 6, Job xlii. 2, Jer. xxiii. 20, Jon. i. 14, Isa. xl. 10). Every day has its ordained events (Job xiv. 5, Ps. cxxxix. 16). The plan of God is universal in its reach, and orders all that takes place in the interests of Israel—the Old Testament coun-terpart to the New Testament declaration that all things work together for good to those that love God. Nor is it merely for the national good of Israel that God's plan has made provision; He exercises a special care over every one of His people (Job v. 15 f., Ps. xci, cxxi, lxv. 3, xxxvii, xxvii. 10, 11, cxxxix. 16, Jon. iii. 5, Isa. iv. 3, Dan. xii. 1). Isaiah especially is never weary of emphasizing the universal teleology of the Divine operations and the surety of the realization of His eternal pur-pose, despite the opposition of every foe (xiv. 24-27, xxxi. 2, xl. 13, lviii. 8-11)—whence he has justly earned the name of the prophet of the Divine sovereignty, and has been spoken of as the Paul, the Augustine, the Calvin of the Old Testament.

It is, however, especially in connexion with the Old Testa-ment doctrine of the Wisdom (חָכְמָה) of God, the chief depository of which is the so-called *Hokhmah* literature, that the idea of the all-inclusive Divine purpose (עֵצָה and מַחֲשָׁבוֹת) in which lies predetermined the whole course of events—including every par-ticular in the life of the world (Amos iii. 7) and in the life of every individual as well (Ps. cxxxix. 14-16, Judg. i. 2)—is specu-latively wrought out. According to this developed conception, God, acting under the guidance of all His ethical perfections, has, by virtue of His eternal wisdom, which He 'possessed in the beginning of his way' (Prov. viii. 22), framed 'from ever-lasting, from the beginning,' an all-inclusive plan embracing all that is to come to pass; in accordance with which plan He now governs His universe, down to the least particular, so as to subserve His perfect and unchanging purpose. Everything that God has brought into being, therefore, He has made for its specific end (Prov. xvi. 4, cf. iii. 19, 20, Job xxviii. 23, xxxviii, xli, Isa. xl. 12 f., Jer. x. 12, 13); and He so governs it that it shall

attain its end,—no chance can escape (Prov. xvi. 33), no might
or subtlety defeat His direction (Prov. xxi. 30, 31, xix. 21, xvi. 9,
cf. Isa. xiv. 24, 27, Jer. x. 23), which leads straight to the goal
appointed by God from the beginning and kept steadily in view
by Him, but often hidden from the actors themselves (Prov.
xx. 24, cf. iii. 6, xvi. 1-9, xix. 21, Job xxxviii. 2, xlii. 3, Jer. x. 23),
who naturally in their weakness cannot comprehend the sweep
of the Divine plan or understand the place within it of the
details brought to their observation—a fact in which the Old
Testament sages constantly find their theodicy. No different
doctrine is enunciated here from that which meets us in the
Prophets and Psalmists,—only it is approached from a philo-
sophical-religious rather than from a national-religious view-
point. To prophet and sage alike the entire world—inanimate,
animate, moral—is embraced in a unitary teleological world-
order (Ps. xxxiii. 6, civ. 24, cxlviii. 8, Job ix. 4, xii. 13, xxxvii);
and to both alike the central place in this comprehensive world-
order is taken by God's redemptive purpose, of which Israel is
at once the object and the instrument, while the savour of its
saltness is the piety of the individual saint. The classical term
for this all-inclusive Divine purpose (עֵצָה) is accordingly found
in the usage alike of prophet, psalmist, and sage,—now used
absolutely of the universal plan on which the whole world is
ordered (Job xxxviii. 2, xlii. 3, cf. Delitzsch and Budde, *in loc.*),
now, with the addition of 'of Jehovah,' of the all-comprehending
purpose, embracing all human actions (Prov. xix. 21 and parallels; cf. Toy, *in loc.*), now with explicit mention of Israel as the
centre around which its provisions revolve (Ps. xxxiii. 11, cvii.
11, cf. Delitzsch, *in loc.;* Isa. xiv. 26, xxv. 1, xlvi. 10, 11), and
anon with more immediate concern with some of the details
(Ps. cvi. 13, Isa. v. 19, xix. 17, Jer. xlix. 20, l. 45, Mic. iv. 12).

There seems no reason why a Platonizing colouring should
be given to this simple attributing to the eternal God of an
eternal plan in which is predetermined every event that comes
to pass. This used to be done, e.g., by Delitzsch (see, e.g., on
Job xxviii. 25-28, Isa. xxii. 11; "Biblical Psychology," I. ii.),
who was wont to attribute to the Biblical writers, especially of

the "Hokhmah" and the latter portion of Isaiah, a doctrine of the pre-existence of all things in an ideal world, conceived as standing eternally before God at least as a pattern if not even as a quasi-objective mould imposing their forms on all His creatures, which smacked more of the Greek Academics than of the Hebrew sages. As a matter of course, the Divine mind was conceived by the Hebrew sages as eternally contemplating all possibilities, and we should not do them injustice in supposing them to think of its 'ideas' as the *causa exemplaris* of all that occurs, and of the Divine intellect as the *principium dirigens* of every Divine operation. But it is more to the point to note that the conceptions of the Old Testament writers in regard to the Divine decree run rather into the moulds of 'purpose' than of 'ideas,' and that the roots of their teaching are planted not in an abstract idea of the Godhead, but in the purity of their concrete theism. It is because they think of God as a person, like other persons purposeful in His acts, but unlike other persons all-wise in His planning and all-powerful in His performing, that they think of Him as predetermining all that shall come to pass in the universe, which is in all its elements the product of His free activity, and which must in its form and all its history, down to the least detail, correspond with His purpose in making it. It is easy, on the other hand, to attribute too little 'philosophy' to the Biblical writers. The conception of God in His relation to the world which they develop is beyond question anthropomorphic; but it is no unreflecting anthropomorphism that they give us. Apart from all question of revelation, they were not children prattling on subjects on which they had expended no thought; and the world-view they commend to us certainly does not lack in profundity. The subtleties of language of a developed scholasticism were foreign to their purposes and modes of composition, but they tell us as clearly as, say, Spanheim himself ("Decad. Theol." vi. § 5), that they are dealing with a purposing mind exalted so far above ours that we can follow its movements only with halting steps,— whose thoughts are not as our thoughts, and whose ways are not as our ways (Isa. lv. 8; cf. xl. 13, 28, xxviii. 29, Job xi. 7 f.,

Ps. xcii. 5, cxxxix. 14 f., cxlvii. 5, Eccl. iii. 11). Least of all in such a theme as this were they liable to forget that infinite exaltation of God which constituted the basis on which their whole conception of God rested.

Nor may they be thought to have been indifferent to the relations of the high doctrine of the Divine purpose they were teaching. There is no scholastic determination here either; but certainly they write without embarrassment as men who have attained a firm grasp upon their fundamental thought and have pursued it with clearness of thinking, no less in its relations than in itself; nor need we go astray in apprehending the outlines of their construction. It is quite plain, for example, that they felt no confusion with respect to the relation of the Divine purpose to the Divine foreknowledge. The notion that the almighty and all-wise God, by whom all things were created, and through whose irresistible control all that occurs fulfils the appointment of His primal plan, could govern Himself according to a foreknowledge of things which—perhaps apart from His original purpose of present guidance—*might haply* come to pass, would have been quite contradictory to their most fundamental conception of God as the almighty and all-sovereign Ruler of the universe, and, indeed, also of the whole Old Testament idea of the Divine foreknowledge itself, which is ever thought of in its due relation of dependence on the Divine purpose. According to the Old Testament conception, God foreknows only because He has pre-determined, and it is therefore also that He brings it to pass; His foreknowledge, in other words, is at bottom a knowledge of His own will, and His works of providence are merely the execution of His all-embracing plan. This is the truth that underlies the somewhat incongruous form of statement of late becoming rather frequent, to the effect that God's foreknowledge is conceived in the Old Testament as 'productive.' Dillmann, for example, says ("Handbuch der alttestamentlichen Theologie," p. 251): 'His foreknowledge of the future is a productive one; of an otiose foreknowledge or of a *prœscientia media* . . . there is no suggestion.' In the thought of the Old Testament writers, however, it is not God's foreknowledge that produces the events of the future; it is His irresistible providential government of the world He has created for Himself: and His foreknowledge of what is yet to be rests on His pre-arranged plan of government. His 'productive fore-knowledge' is but a transcript of His will, which has already determined not only the general plan of the world, but every particular that enters into the whole course of its development (Amos iii. 7, Job xxviii. 26, 27), and every detail in the life of every individual that comes into being (Jer. i. 5, Ps. cxxxix. 14-16, Job xxiii. 13, 14).

That the acts of free agents are included in this 'productive foreknowledge,' or rather in this all-inclusive plan of the life of the universe, created for the Old Testament writers apparently not the least embarrassment. This is not because they did not believe man to be free,—throughout the whole Old Testament there is never the least doubt expressed of the freedom or moral responsibility of man,—but because they did believe God to be free, whether in His works of creation or of providence, and could not believe He was hampered or limited in the attainment of His ends by the creatures of His own hands. How God governs the acts of free agents in the pursuance of His plan there is little in the Old Testament to inform us; but that He governs them in even their most intimate thoughts and feelings and impulses is its unvarying assumption: He is not only the creator of the hearts of men in the first instance, and knows them altogether, but He fashions the hearts of all in all the changing circumstances of life (Ps. xxxiii. 15); forms the spirit of man within him in all its motions (Zech. xii. 1); keeps the hearts of men in His hands, turning them whithersoever He will (Prov. xxi. 1); so that it is even said that man knows what is in his own mind only as the Lord reveals it to him (Amos iv. 13). The discussion of any antinomy that may be thought to arise from such a joint assertion of the absolute rule of God in the sphere of the spirit and the freedom of the creaturely will, falls obviously under the topic of Providential Government rather than under that of the Decree: it requires to be adverted to here only that we may clearly note the fact that the Old Testament teachers, as they did not hesitate to affirm the absolute sway of God over the thoughts and intents of the human heart, could feel no embarrassment in the inclusion of the acts of free agents within the all-embracing plan of God, the outworking of which His providential government supplies.

Nor does the moral quality of these acts present any apparent difficulty to the Old Testament construction. We are never permitted to imagine, to be sure, that God is the author of sin, either in the world at large or in any individual soul—that He is in any way implicated in the sinfulness of the acts performed by the perverse misuse of creaturely freedom. In all God's working He shows Himself pre-eminently the Holy One, and prosecutes His holy will, His righteous way, His all-wise plan: the blame for all sinful deeds rests exclusively on the creaturely actors (Ex. ix. 27, x. 16), who recognize their own guilt (II Sam. xxiv. 10, 17) and receive its punishment (Eccl. xi. 9 compared with xi. 5). But neither is God's relation to the sinful acts of His creatures ever represented as purely passive: the details of the doctrine of *concursus* were left, no doubt, to later ages speculatively to work out, but its assumption underlies the entire Old Testament representation of the Divine modes of working. That anything—good or evil—occurs in God's universe finds its account, according to the Old Testament conception, in His positive ordering and active concurrence; while the moral quality of the deed, considered in itself, is rooted in the moral character of the subordinate agent, acting in the circumstances and under the motives operative in each instance. It is certainly going beyond the Old Testament warrant to speak of the 'all-productivity of God,' as if He were the only efficient cause in nature and the sphere of the free spirit alike; it is the very delirium of misconception to say that in the Old Testament God and Satan are insufficiently discriminated, and deeds appropriate to the latter are assigned to the former. Nevertheless, it remains true that even the evil acts of the creature are so far carried back to God that they too are affirmed to be included in His all-embracing decree, and to be brought about, bounded and utilized in His providential government. It is He that hardens the heart of the sinner that persists in his sin (Ex. iv. 21, vii. 3, x. 1, 27, xiv. 4, 8, Deut. ii. 30, Jos. xi. 20, Isa. lxiii. 17); it is from Him that the evil spirits proceed that trouble sinners (I Sam. xvi. 14, Judg. ix. 23, I Kings xxii, Job i.); it is of Him that the evil impulses that rise in sinners' hearts take this or that specific form (II Sam. xxiv. 1). The philosophy that lies behind such representations, however, is not the pantheism which looks upon God as the immediate cause of all that comes to pass; much less the pandaimonism which admits no distinction between good and evil; there is not even involved a conception of God entangled in an undeveloped ethical discrimination. It is the philosophy that is expressed in Isa. xlv. 5 f., 'I am the LORD, and there is none else; beside me there is no God. . . . I am the LORD, and there is none else. I form the light and create darkness; I make peace and create evil; I am the LORD that doeth all these things'; it is the philosophy that is expressed in Prov. xvi. 4, 'The LORD hath made everything for its own end, yea, even the wicked for the day of evil.' Because, over against all dualistic conceptions, there is but one God, and He is indeed GOD; and because, over against all cosmotheistic conceptions, this God is a PERSON who acts purposefully; there is nothing that is, and nothing that comes to pass, that He has not first decreed and then brought to pass by His creation or providence. Thus all things find their unity in His eternal plan; and not their unity merely, but their justification as well; even the evil, though retaining its quality as evil and hateful to the holy God, and certain to be dealt with as hateful, yet does not occur apart from His provision or against His will, but appears in the world which He has made only as the instrument by means of which He works the higher good.

This sublime philosophy of the decree is immanent in every page of the Old Testament. Its metaphysics never come to explicit discussion, to be sure; but its elements are in a practical way postulated consistently throughout. The ultimate end in view in the Divine plan is ever represented as found in God alone: all that He has made He has made for Himself, to set forth His praise; the heavens themseives with all their splendid furniture exist but to illustrate His glory; the earth and all that is in it, and all that happens in it, to declare His majesty; the whole course of history is but the theatre of His self-manifestation, and the events of every individual life indicate His nature and perfections. Men may be unable to understand the place which the incidents, as they unroll themselves before their eyes, take in the developing plot of the great drama: they may, nay, must, therefore stand astonished and confounded before this or that which befalls them or befalls the world. Hence arise to them problems—the problem of the petty, the problem of the inexplicable, the problem of suffering, the problem of sin (e.g., Eccl. xi. 5). But, in the infinite wisdom of the Lord of all the earth, each event falls with exact precision into its proper place in the unfolding of His eternal plan; nothing, however small, however strange, occurs without His ordering, or without its peculiar fitness for its place in the working out of His purpose; and the end of all shall be the manifestation of His glory, and the accumulation of His praise. This is the Old Testament philosophy of the universe—a world-view which attains concrete unity in an absolute Divine teleology, in the compactness of an eternal decree, or purpose, or plan, of which all that comes to pass is the development in time.

Soteriological Predestination

Special or Soteriological Predestination finds a natural place in the Old Testament system as but a particular instance of the more general fact, and may be looked upon as only the general Old Testament doctrine of predestination applied to the specific case of the salvation of sinners. But as the Old Testament is a distinctively religious book, or, more precisely, a distinctively soteriological book, that is to say, a record of the gracious dealings and purposes of God with sinners, soteriological predestination naturally takes a more prominent place in it than the general doctrine itself, of which it is a particular application. Indeed, God's saving work is thrown out into such prominence, the Old Testament is so specially a record of the establishment of the kingdom of God in the world, that we easily get the impression in reading it that the core of God's general decree is His decree of salvation, and that His whole plan for the government of the universe is subordinated to His purpose to recover sinful man to Himself. Of course there is some slight illusion of perspective here, the materials for correcting which the Old Testament itself provides, not only in more or less specific declarations of the relative unimportance of what befalls man, whether the individual, or Israel, or the race at large, in comparison with the attainment of the Divine end; and of the wonder of the Divine grace concerning itself with the fortunes of man at all (Job xxii. 3 f., xxxv. 6 f., xxxviii, Ps. viii. 4): but also in the general disposition of the entire record, which places the complete history of sinful man, including alike his fall into sin and all the provisions for his recovery, within the larger history of the creative work of God, as but one incident in the greater whole, governed, of course, like all its other parts, by its general teleology. Relatively to the Old Testament record, nevertheless, as indeed to the Biblical record as a whole, which is concerned directly only with God's dealings with humanity, and that, especially, a sinful humanity (Gen. iii. 9, vi. 5, viii. 21, Lev. xviii. 24, Deut. ix. 4, I Kings viii. 46, Ps. xiv. 1, li. 5, cxxx. 3, cxliii. 2, Prov. xx. 9, Eccl. vii. 20, Isa. i. 4, Hos. iv. 1, Job xv. 14, xxv. 4, xiv. 4), soteriological predestination is the prime matter of importance; and the doctrine of election is accordingly thrown into relief, and the general doctrine of the decree more incidentally adverted to. It would be impossible, however, that the doctrine of election taught in the Old Testament should follow other lines than those laid down in the general doctrine of the decree,—or, in other words, that God should be conceived as working in the sphere of grace in a manner that would be out of accord with the fundamental conception entertained by these writers of the nature of God and His relations to the universe.

Accordingly, there is nothing concerning the Divine election more sharply or more steadily emphasized than its graciousness, in the highest sense of that word, or, in other terms,

its absolute sovereignty. This is plainly enough exhibited even
in the course of the patriarchal history, and that from the beginning. In the very hour of man's first sin, God intervenes
sua sponte with a gratuitous promise of deliverance; and at
every stage afterwards the sovereign initiation of the grace of
God—the Lord of the whole earth (Ex. xix. 5)—is strongly
marked, as God's universal counsel of salvation is more and
more unfolded through the separation and training of a people
for Himself, in whom the whole world should be blessed (Gen.
xii. 3, xviii. 18, xxii. 18, xxvi. 4, xxviii. 14): for from the beginning it is plainly indicated that the whole history of the world
is ordered with reference to the establishment of the kingdom
of God (Deut. xxxii. 8, where the reference seems to be to
Gen. xi). Already in the opposing lines of Seth and Cain (Gen.
iv. 25, 26) a discrimination is made; Noah is selected as the
head of a new race, and among his sons the preference is given
to Shem (Gen. ix. 25), from whose line Abraham is taken. Every
fancy that Abraham owed his calling to his own desert is carefully excluded,—he was 'known' of God only that in him God
might establish His kingdom (Gen. xviii. 19); and the very
acme of sovereignty is exhibited (as St. Paul points out) in the
subsequent choice of Isaac and Jacob, and exclusion of Ishmael
and Esau; while the whole Divine dealing with the patriarchs—
their separation from their kindred, removal into a strange land,
and the like—is evidently understood as intended to cast them
back on the grace of God alone. Similarly, the covenant made
with Israel (Ex. xix-xxiv) is constantly assigned to the sole
initiative of Divine grace, and the fact of election is therefore
appropriately set at the head of the Decalogue (Ex. xx. 2; cf.
xxxiv. 6, 7); and Israel is repeatedly warned that there was
nothing in it which moved or could move God to favour it
(e.g., Deut. iv. 37, vii. 7, viii. 17, ix. 4, x. 11, Ezk. xvi. 1 f., Amos
ix. 7). It has already been pointed out by what energetic figures
this fundamental lesson was impressed on the Israelitish consciousness, and it is only true to say that no means are left
unused to drive home the fact that God's gracious election of
Israel is an absolutely sovereign one, founded solely in His

unmerited love, and looking to nothing ultimately but the gratification of His own holy and loving impulses, and the manifestation of His grace through the formation of a heritage for Himself out of the mass of sinful men, by means of whom His saving mercy should advance to the whole world (Isa. xl, xlii, lx, Mic. iv. 1, Amos iv. 13, v. 8, Jer. xxxi. 37, Ezk. xvii. 22, xxxvi. 21, Joel ii. 28). The simple terms that are employed to express this Divine selection—'know' (יָדַע), 'choose' (בָּחַר) —are either used in a pregnant sense, or acquire a pregnant sense by their use in this connexion. The deeper meaning of the former term is apparently not specifically Hebrew, but more widely Semitic (it occurs also in Assyrian; see the *Dictionaries* of Delitzsch and Muss-Arnolt *sub. voc.*, and especially Haupt in "Beiträge zur Assyriologie," i. 14, 15), and it can create no surprise, therefore, when it meets us in such passages as Gen. xviii. 19 (cf. Ps. xxxvii. 18 and also i. 6, xxxi. 8; cf. Baethgen and Delitzsch *in loc.*), Hos. xiii. 5 (cf. Wünsche *in loc.*) in something of the sense expressed by the scholastic phrase, *nosse cum affectu et effectu;* while in the great declaration of Amos iii. 2 (cf. Baur and Gunning *in loc.*), 'You only have I known away from all the peoples of the earth,' what is thrown prominently forward is clearly the elective love which has singled Israel out for special care. More commonly, however, it is בָּחַר that is employed to express God's sovereign election of Israel: the classical passage is, of course, Deut. vii. 6, 7 (see Driver *in loc.*, as also, of the love underlying the 'choice,' at iv. 37, vii. 8), where it is carefully explained that it is in contrast with the treatment accorded to all the other peoples of the earth that Israel has been honoured with the Divine choice, and that the choice rests solely on the unmerited love of God, and finds no foundation in Israel itself. These declarations are elsewhere constantly enforced (e. g., iv. 37, x. 15, xiv. 2), with the effect of throwing the strongest possible emphasis on the complete sovereignty of God's choice of His people, who owe their 'separation' unto Jehovah (Lev. xx. 24, 26, I Kings viii. 33) wholly to the wonderful love of God, in which He has from the beginning taken knowledge of and chosen them.

It is useless to seek to escape the profound meaning of this fundamental Old Testament teaching by recalling the undeveloped state of the doctrine of a future life in Israel, and the national scope of its election,—as if the sovereign choice which is so insisted on could thus be confined to the choice of a people as a whole to certain purely earthly blessings, without any reference whatever to the eternal destiny of the individuals concerned. We are here treading very close to the abyss of confusing progress in the delivery of doctrine with the reality of God's saving activities. The cardinal question, after all, does not concern the extent of the knowledge possessed by the Old Testament saints of the nature of the blessedness that belongs to the people of God; nor yet the relation borne by the election within the election, by the real Israel forming the heart of the Israel after the flesh, to the external Israel: it concerns the existence of a real kingdom of God in the Old Testament dispensation, and the methods by which God introduced man into it. It is true enough that the theocracy was an earthly kingdom, and that a prominent place was given to the promises of the life that now is in the blessings assured to Israel; and it is in this engrossment with earthly happiness and the close connexion of the friendship of God with the enjoyment of worldly goods that the undeveloped state of the Old Testament doctrine of salvation is especially apparent. But it should not be forgotten that the promise of earthly gain to the people of God is not entirely alien to the New Testament idea of salvation (Matt. vi. 33, I Tim. iv. 8), and that it is in no sense true that in the Old Testament teaching, in any of its stages, the blessings of the kingdom were summed up in worldly happiness. The covenant blessing is rather declared to be *life*, inclusive of all that that comprehensive word is fitted to convey (Deut. xxx. 15; cf. iv. 1, viii. 1, Prov. xii. 28, viii. 35); and it found its best expression in the high conception of 'the favour of God' (Lev. xxvi. 11, Ps. iv. 8, xvi. 2, 5, lxiii. 4); while it concerned itself with earthly prosperity only as and so far as that is a pledge of the Divine favour. It is no false testimony to the Old Testament saints when they are described as looking for the city that has the foundations and as enduring as seeing the Invisible One: if their hearts were not absorbed in the contemplation of the eternal future, they were absorbed in the contemplation of the Eternal Lord, which certainly is something even better; and the representation that they found their supreme blessedness in outward things runs so grossly athwart their own testimony that it fairly deserves Calvin's terrible invective, that thus the Israel-itish people are thought of not otherwise than as a 'sort of herd of swine which (so, forsooth, it is pretended) the Lord was fattening in the pen of this world' ("Inst." II. x. 1). And, on the other hand, though Israel as a nation constituted the chosen people of God (I Chron. xvi. 13, Ps. lxxxix. 4, cv. 6, 13, cvi. 5), yet we must not lose from sight the fact that the nation as such was rather the symbolical than the real people of God, and was His people at all, indeed, only so far as it was, ideally or actually, identified with the inner body of the really 'chosen'—that people whom Jehovah formed for Himself that they might set forth His praise (Isa. xliii. 20, lxv. 9, 15, 22), and who constituted the real people of His choice, the 'remnant of Jacob' (Isa. vi. 13, Amos ix. 8-10, Mal. iii. 10; cf. I Kings xix. 18, Isa. viii. 18). Nor are we left in doubt as to how this inner core of actual people of God was constituted; we see the process in the call of Abraham, and the discrimination between Isaac and Ishmael, between Jacob and Esau, and it is no false testimony that it was ever a 'remnant according to the election of grace' that God preserved to Himself as the salt of His people Israel. In every aspect of it alike, it is the sovereignty of the Divine choice that is emphasized, whether the reference be to the segregation of Israel as a nation to enjoy the earthly favour of God as a symbol of the true entrance into rest, or the choice of a remnant out of Israel to enter into that real communion with Him which was the joy of His saints,—of Enoch who walked with God (Gen. v. 22), of Abraham who found in Him his exceeding great reward (Gen. xv. 1), or of David who saw no good beyond Him, and sought in Him alone his inheritance and his cup. Later times may have enjoyed fuller knowledge of what the grace of God had in store for His saints—whether in this world or that which is to come; later times may have possessed a clearer apprehension of the distinction between the children of the flesh and the children of the promise: but no later teaching has a stronger emphasis for the central fact that it is of the free grace of God alone that any enter in any degree into the participation of His favour. The kingdom of God, according to the Old Testament, in every circle of its meaning, is above and before all else a stone cut out of the mountain 'without hands' (Dan. ii. 34, 44, 45).

II. PREDESTINATION AMONG THE JEWS

The profound religious conception of the relation of God to the works of His hands that pervades the whole Old Testament was too deeply engraved on the Jewish consciousness to be easily erased, even after growing legalism had measurably corroded the religion of the people. As, however, the idea of law more and more absorbed the whole sphere of religious thought, and piety came to be conceived more and more as right conduct before God instead of living communion with God, men grew naturally to think of God more and more as abstract unapproachableness, and to think of themselves more and more as their own saviours. The post-canonical Jewish writings, while retaining fervent expressions of dependence on God as the Lord of all, by whose wise counsel all things exist and work out their ends, and over against whom the whole world, with every creature in it, is but the instrument of His will of good to Israel, nevertheless threw an entirely new emphasis on the autocracy of the human will. This emphasis increases until in the later Judaism the extremity of heathen self-sufficiency is reproduced, and the whole sphere of the moral life is expressly reserved from Divine determination. Meanwhile also heathen terminology was intruding into Jewish speech. The Platonic $\pi\rho\acute{o}\nuo\iota\alpha$, $\pi\rhoo\nuo\epsilon\hat{\iota}\nu$, for example, coming in doubtless through the medium of the Stoa, is found not only in Philo ($\pi\epsilon\rho\grave{\iota}\ \pi\rhoo\nuo\acute{\iota}\alpha\varsigma$), but also in the Apocryphal books (Wis. vi. 7, xiv. 3, xvii. 2, III Mac. iv. 21, v. 30, IV Mac. ix. 24, xiii. 18, xvii. 22; cf. also Dan. vi. 18, Septuagint 19); the perhaps even more precise as well as earlier ἐφορᾶν occurs in Josephus (*BJ* II. viii. 14), and indeed also in the Septuagint, though here doubtless in a weakened sense (II Mac. xii. 22, xv. 2, cf. III Mac. ii. 21, as also Job xxxiv. 24, xxviii. 24, xxii. 12, cf. xxi. 16; also Zech. ix. 1); while even the fatalistic term εἱμαρμένη is employed by Josephus (*BJ* II. viii. 14; *Ant.* XIII. v. 9, XVIII. i. 3) to describe Jewish views of predestination. With the terms there came in, doubtless, more or less of the conceptions connoted by them.

Whatever may have been the influences under which it was wrought, however, the tendency of post-canonical Judaism was towards setting aside the Biblical doctrine of predestination to a greater or less extent, or in a larger or smaller sphere, in order to make room for the autocracy of the human will, the רשות, as it was significantly called by the Rabbis (*Bereshith Rabba*, c. 22). This disintegrating process is little apparent perhaps in the Book of Wisdom, in which the sense of the almightiness of God comes to very strong expression (xi. 22, xii. 8-12). Or even in Philo, whose predestinarianism (*de Legg. Allegor.* i. 15, iii. 24, 27, 28) closely follows, while his assertion of human freedom (*Quod Deus sit immut.* 10) does not pass beyond that of the Bible: man is separated from the animals and assimilated to God by the gift of 'the power of voluntary motion' and suitable emancipation from necessity, and is accordingly properly praised or blamed for his intentional acts; but it is of the grace of God only that anything exists, and the creature is not giver but receiver in all things; especially does it belong to God alone to plant and build up virtues, and it is impious for the mind, therefore, to say 'I plant'; the call of Abraham, Isaac, Jacob was of pure grace without any merit, and God exercises the right to 'dispose excellently,' prior to all actual deeds. But the process is already apparent in so early a book as Sirach. The book at large is indeed distinctly predestinarian, and such passages as xvi. 26-30, xxiii. 20, xxxiii. 11-13, xxxix. 20, 21 echo the teachings of the canonical books on this subject. But, while this is its general character, another element is also present: an assertion of human autocracy, for example, which is without parallel in the canonical books, is introduced at xv. 11-20, which culminates in the precise declaration that 'man has been committed to the hand of his own counsel' to choose for himself life or death. The same phenomena meet us in the Pharisaic Psalms of Solomon (B.C. 70-40). Here there is a general recognition of God as the great and mighty King (ii. 34, 36) who has appointed the course of nature (xviii. 12) and directs the development of history (ii. 34, ix. 4, xvii. 4), ruling over the whole and determining the lot of each (v. 6, 18), on whom alone, therefore, can the hope of Israel be stayed (vii. 3, xvii. 3), and to whom alone can the individual look for good. But, alongside of this expression of general dependence on God, there occurs the strongest assertion of the moral autocracy of the human will: 'O God, our works are in our own souls' election and control, to do righteousness or iniquity in the works of our hand' (ix. 7).

It is quite credible, therefore, when Josephus tells us that the Jewish parties of his day were divided, as on other matters, so on the question of the Divine predestination—the Essenes affirming that fate (εἱμαρμένη, Josephus' affected Græcizing expression for predestination) is the mistress of all, and nothing occurs to men which is not in accordance with its destination; the Sadducees taking away 'fate' altogether, and considering that there is no such thing, and that human affairs are not directed according to it, but all actions are in our own power, so that we are ourselves the causes of what is good, and receive what is evil from our own folly; while the Pharisees, seeking a middle ground, said that some actions, but not all, are the work of 'fate,' and some are in our own power as to whether they are done or not (*Ant.* xiii. v. 9). The distribution of the several views among the parties follows the general lines of what might have been anticipated—the Essenic system being pre-eminently supranaturalistic, and the Sadducean rationalistic, while there was retained among the Pharisees a deep leaven of religious earnestness tempered, but not altogether destroyed (except in the extremest circles), by their ingrained legalism. The middle ground, moreover, which Josephus ascribes to the Pharisees in their attempt to distribute the control of human action between 'fate' and 'free will,' reflects not badly the state of opinion pre-supposed in the documents we have already quoted. In his remarks elsewhere (*BJ* II. viii. 14; *Ant.* XVIII. i. 3) he appears to ascribe to the Pharisees some kind of a doctrine of *concursus* also—a κρᾶσις between 'fate' and the human will by which both co-operate in the effect: but his language is obscure, and is coloured doubtless by reminiscences of Stoic teaching, with which philosophical sect he compares the Pharisees as he compares the Essenes with the Epicureans.

But whatever may have been the traditional belief of the Pharisees, in proportion as the legalistic spirit which constituted the nerve of the movement became prominent, the sense of dependence on God, which is the vital breath of the doctrine of predestination, gave way. The Jews possessed the Old Testament Scriptures in which the Divine lordship is a cardinal doctrine, and the trials of persecution cast them continually back upon God; they could not, therefore, wholly forget the Biblical doctrine of the Divine decree, and throughout their whole history we meet with its echoes on their lips. The laws of nature, the course of history, the varying fortunes of individuals, are ever attributed to the Divine predestination. Nevertheless, it was ever more and more sharply disallowed that man's moral actions fell under the same predetermination. Sometimes it was said that while the decrees of God were sure, they applied only so long as man remained in the condition in which he was contemplated when they were formed; he could escape all pre-determined evil by a change in his moral character. Hence such sayings as, 'The righteous destroy what God decrees' (*Tanchuma* on דברים;('Repentance, prayer, and charity ward off every evil decree' (*Rosh-hashana*). In any event, the entire domain of the moral life was more and more withdrawn from the intrusion of the decree; and Cicero's famous declaration, which Harnack says might be inscribed as a motto over Pelagianism, might with equal right be accepted as the working hypothesis of the later Judaism: 'For gold, land, and all the blessings of life we have to return thanks to God; but no one ever returned thanks to God for virtue' (*de Nat. Deorum,* iii. 36). We read that the Holy One determines prior to birth all that every one is to be—whether male or female, weak or strong, poor or rich, wise or silly; but one thing He does not determine—whether he is to be righteous or unrighteous; according to Deut. xxx. 15 this is committed to one's own hands. Accordingly, it is said that 'neither evil nor good comes from God; both are the results of our deeds' (*Midrash rab*, on ראה, and *Jalkut* there); and again, 'All is in the hands of God except the fear of God' (*Megilla* 25*a*); so that it is even somewhat cynically said, 'Man is led in the way in which he wishes to go' (*Maccoth* 10); 'If you teach him right, his God will make him know' (Isa. xxviii. 26; Jerusalem *Challah* i. 1). Thus the deep sense of dependence on God for all goods, and especially the goods of the soul, which forms the very core of the religious consciousness of the writers of the Old Testament, gradually vanished from the later Judaism, and was superseded by a self-assertiveness which hung all good on the self-determination of the human spirit, on which the purposes of God waited, or to which they were subservient.

III. Predestination in the New Testament

The New Testament teaching starts from the plane of the Old Testament revelation, and in its doctrines of God, Providence, Faith, and the Kingdom of God repeats or develops in a right line the fundamental deliverances of the Old Testament, while in its doctrines of the Decree and of Election only such advance in statement is made as the progressive execution of the plan of salvation required.

The Teaching of Our Lord

In the teaching of our Lord, as recorded in the Synoptic Gospels, for example, though there is certainly a new emphasis thrown on the Fatherhood of God, this is by no means at the expense of His infinite majesty and might, but provides only a more profound revelation of the character of 'the great King' (Matt. v. 35), the 'Lord of heaven and earth' (Matt. xi. 25, Luke x. 21), according to whose good pleasure all that is comes to pass. He is spoken of, therefore, specifically as the 'heavenly Father' (Matt. v. 48, vi. 14, 26, 32, xv. 13, xviii. 35, xxiii. 9, cf. v. 16, 45, vi. 1, 9, vii. 11, 21, x. 32, 33, xii. 50, xvi. 17, xviii. 14, 19, Mark xi. 25, 26, Luke xi. 13) whose throne is in the heavens (Matt. v. 34, xxiii. 22), while the earth is but the footstool under His feet. There is no limitation admitted to the reach of His power, whether on the score of difficulty in the task, or insignificance in the object: the category of the impossible has no existence to Him 'with whom all things are possible' (Matt. xix. 26, Mark x. 27, Luke xviii. 27, Matt. xxii. 29, Mark xii. 24, xiv. 36), and the minutest occurrences are as directly controlled by Him as the greatest (Matt. x. 29, 30, Luke xii. 7). It is from Him that the sunshine and rain come (Matt. v. 45); it is He that clothes with beauty the flowers of the field (Matt. vi. 28), and who feeds the birds of the air (Matt. vi. 26); not a sparrow falls to the ground without Him, and the very hairs of our heads are numbered, and not one of them is forgotten by God (Matt. x. 29, Luke xii. 6). There is, of course, no denial, nor neglect, of the mechanism of nature implied here; there is only clear perception of the providence of God guiding nature in all its operations, and not nature only, but the life of the free spirit as well (Matt. vi. 6, viii. 13, xxiv. 22, vii. 7, Mark xi. 23). Much less, however, is the care of God thought of as mechanical and purposeless. It was not simply of sparrows that our Lord was thinking when He adverted to the care of the heavenly Father for them, as it was not simply for oxen that God was caring when He forbade them to be muzzled as they trod out the corn (I Cor. ix. 9); it was that they who are of more value than sparrows might learn with what confidence they might depend on the Father's hand. Thus a hierarchy of providence is uncovered for us, circle rising above circle,—first the wide order of nature, next the moral order of the world, lastly the order of salvation or of the kingdom of God,—a preformation of the dogmatic, *schema* of *providentia generalis, specialis,* and *specialissima.* All these work together for the one end of advancing the whole world-fabric to its goal; for the care of the heavenly Father over the works of His hand is not merely to prevent the world that He has made from falling into pieces, and not merely to preserve His servants from oppression by the evil of this world, but to lead the whole world and all that is in it onwards to the end which He has appointed for it,—to that παλιγγενεσία of heaven and earth to which, under His guiding hand, the whole creation tends (Matt. xix. 28, Luke xx. 34).

In this divinely-led movement of 'this world' towards 'the world that is to come,' in which every element of the world's life has part, the central place is naturally taken by the spiritual preparation, or, in other words, by the development of the Kingdom of God which reaches its consummation in the 'regeneration.' This Kingdom, our Lord explains, is the heritage of those blessed ones for whom it has been prepared from the foundations of the world (Matt. xxv. 34, cf. xx. 23). It is built up on earth through a 'call' (Matt. ix. 13, Mark ii. 17, Luke v. 32), which, however, as mere invitation is inoperative (Matt. xxii. 2-14, Luke xiv. 16-23), and is made effective only by the exertion of a certain 'constraint' on God's part (Luke xiv. 23),— so that a distinction emerges between the merely 'called' and the really 'chosen' (Matt. xxii. 14). The author of this 'choice' is God (Mark xiii. 20), who has chosen His elect (Luke xviii. 7, Matt. xxiv. 22, 24, 31, Mark xiii. 20-22) before the world, in accordance with His own pleasure, distributing as He will of what is His own (Matt. x. 14, 15); so that the effect of the call is already predetermined (Matt. xiii), all providence is ordered for the benefit of the elect (Matt. xxiv. 22), and they are guarded from falling away (Matt. xxiv. 24), and, at the last day, are separated to their inheritance prepared for them from all eternity (Matt. xxv. 34). That, in all this process, the initiative is at every point taken by God, and no question can be entertained of precedent merit on the part of the recipients of the blessings, results not less from the whole underlying conception of God in His relation to the course of providence than from the details of the teaching itself. Every means is utilized, however, to enhance the sense of the free sovereignty of God in the bestowment of His Kingdom; it is 'the lost' whom Jesus comes to seek (Luke xix. 10), and 'sinners' whom He came to call

(Mark ii. 17); His truth is revealed only to 'babes' (Matt. xi. 25, Luke x. 21), and He gives His teaching a special form just that it may be veiled from them to whom it is not directed (Mark iv. 11), distributing His benefits, independently of merit (Matt. xx. 1-16), to those who had been chosen by God therefor (Mark xiii. 20).

In the discourses recorded by St. John the same essential spirit rules. Although, in accordance with the deeper theological apprehension of their reporter, the more metaphysical elements of Jesus' doctrine of God come here to fuller expression, it is nevertheless fundamentally the same doctrine of God that is displayed. Despite the even stronger emphasis thrown here on His Fatherhood, there is not the slightest obscuration of His infinite exaltation: Jesus lifts His eyes up when He would seek Him (xi. 41, xvii. 1); it is in heaven that His house is to be found (xiv. 2); and thence proceeds all that comes from Him (i. 51, iii. 13, vi. 31, 32, 33, 38, 41, 49, 50, 58); so that God and heaven come to be almost equivalent terms. Nor is there any obscuration of His ceaseless activity in governing the world (v. 17), although the stress is naturally thrown, in accordance with the whole character of this Gospel, on the moral and spiritual side of this government. But the very essence of the message of the Johannine Jesus is that the will ($\theta\acute{\epsilon}\lambda\eta\mu\alpha$) of the Father (iv. 34, v. 30, vi. 38, 39, 40, vii. 17, ix. 31, cf. iii. 8, v. 21, xvii. 24, xxi. 22, 23) is the principle of all things; and more especially, of course, of the introduction of eternal life into this world of darkness and death. The conception of the world as lying in the evil one and therefore judged already (iii. 18), so that upon those who are not removed from the evil of the world the wrath of God is not so much to be poured out as simply abides (iii. 36, cf. I John iii. 14), is fundamental to this whole presentation. It is therefore, on the one hand, that Jesus represents Himself as having come not to condemn the world, but to save the world (iii. 17, viii. 12, ix. 5, xii. 47, cf. iv. 42), and all that He does as having for its end the introduction of life into the world (vi. 33, 51); the already condemned world needed no further condemnation, it needed saving. And it is for the same reason, on the other hand, that He represents the wicked world as incapable of coming to Him that it might have life (viii. 43, 21, xiv. 17, x. 33), and as requiring first of all a 'drawing' from the Father to enable it to come (vi. 44, 65); so that only those hear or believe on Him who are 'of God' (viii. 47, cf. xv. 19, xvii. 14), who are 'of his sheep' (x. 26).

There is undoubtedly a strong emphasis thrown on the universality of Christ's mission of salvation; He has been sent into the world not merely to save some out of the world, but to save the world itself (iii. 16, vi. 51, xii. 47, xvii. 21, cf. i. 29, I John iv. 14, ii. 2). But this universality of destination and effect by which it is 'the world' that is saved, does not imply the salvation of each and every individual in the world, even in the earlier stages of the developing salvation. On the contrary, the saving work is a process (xvii. 20); and, meanwhile, the coming of the Son into the world introduces a crisis, a sifting by which those who, because they are 'of God,' 'of his sheep,' are in the world, but not of it (xv. 19, xvii. 14), are separated from those who are of the world, that is, of their father the devil (viii. 44), who is the Prince of this world (xii. 31, xiv. 30, xvi. 11). Obviously, the difference between men that is thus manifested is not thought of as inhering, after a dualistic or semi-Gnostic fashion, in their very natures as such, or as instituted by their own self-framed or accidentally received dispositions, much less by their own conduct in the world, which is rather the result of it,—but, as already pointed out, as the effect of an act of God. All goes back to the will of God, to accomplish which, the Son, as the Sent One, has come; and therefore also to the consentient will of the Son, who gives life, accordingly, to whom He will (v. 21). As no one can come to Him out of the evil world, except it be given him of the Father (vi. 65, cf. vi. 44), so all that the Father gives Him (vi. 37, 39) and only such (vi. 65), come to Him, being drawn thereunto by the Father (vi. 44). Thus the Son has 'his own in the world' (xiii. 1), His 'chosen ones' (xiii. 18, xv. 16, 19), whom by His choice He has taken out of the world (xv. 19, xvii. 6, 14, 16); and for these only is His high-priestly intercession offered (xvii. 9), as to them only is eternal life communicated (x. 28, xvii. 2, also iii. 15, 36, v. 24, vi. 40, 54, viii. 12). Thus, what the dogmatists call *gratia præveniens* is very strikingly taught; and especial point is given to this teaching in the great declarations as to the new birth recorded in John iii, from which we learn that the recreating Spirit comes, like the wind, without observation, and as He lists (iii. 8), the mode of action by which the Father 'draws' men being thus uncovered for us. Of course this drawing is not to be thought of as proceeding in a manner out of accord with man's nature as a psychic being; it naturally comes to its manifestation in an act of voluntary choice on man's own part, and in this sense it is 'psychological' and not 'physical'; accordingly, though it be God that 'draws,' it is man that 'comes' (iii. 21, vi. 35, 41, xiv. 6). There is no occasion for stumbling therefore in the ascription of 'will' and 'responsibility' to man, or for puzzling over the designation of 'faith,' in which the 'coming' takes effect, as a 'work' of man's (vi. 29). Man is, of course, conceived as acting humanly, after the fashion of an intelligent and voluntary agent; but behind all his action there is ever postulated the all-determining hand of God, to whose sovereign operation even the blindness of the unbelieving is attributed by the evangelist (xii. 39 f.), while the receptivity to the light of those who believe is repeatedly in the most emphatic way ascribed by Jesus Himself to God alone. Although with little use of the terminology in which we have been accustomed to expect to see the doctrines of the decree and of election expressed, the substance of these doctrines is here set out in the most impressive way.

From the two sets of data provided by the Synoptists and St. John, it is possible to attain quite a clear insight into the conception of predestination as it lay in our Lord's teaching. It is quite certain, for example, that there is no place in this teaching for a 'predestination' that is carefully adjusted to the foreseen performances of the creature; and as little for a 'decree' which may be frustrated by creaturely action, or an 'election' which is given effect only by the creaturely choice: to our Lord the Father is the omnipotent Lord of heaven and earth, according to whose pleasure all things are ordered, and who gives the Kingdom to whom He will (Luke xii. 32, Mark xi. 26, Luke x. 21). Certainly it is the very heart of our Lord's teaching that the Father's good-pleasure is a *good* pleasure, ethically right, and the issue of infinite love; the very name of Father as the name of God by preference on His lips is full of this conception; but the very nerve of this teaching is, that the Father's will is all-embracing and omnipotent. It is only therefore that His children need be careful for nothing, that the little flock need not fear, that His elect may be assured that none of them shall be lost, but all that the Father has given Him shall be raised up at the last day. And if thus the elective purpose of the Father cannot fail of its end, neither is it possible to find this end in anything less than 'salvation' in the highest sense, than entrance into that eternal life to communicate which to dying men our Lord came into the world. There are elections to other ends, to be sure, spoken of: notably there is the election of the apostles to their office (Luke vi. 13, John vi. 70); and Christ Himself is conceived as especially God's elect one, because no one has the service to render which He has (Luke ix. 35, xxiii. 35). But the elect, by way of eminence; 'the elect whom God elected,' for whose sake He governs all history (Mark xiii. 20); the elect of whom it was the will of Him who sent the Son, that of all that He gave Him He should lose nothing, but should raise it up at the last day (John vi. 39); the elect whom the Son of Man shall at the last day gather from the four winds, from the uttermost parts of the earth to the uttermost part of heaven (Mark xiii. 27): it would be inadequate to suppose that these are elected merely to opportunities or the means of grace, on their free cultivation of which shall depend their undecided destiny; or merely to the service of their fellow-men, as agents in God's beneficent plan for the salvation of the race. Of course this election is to privileges and means of grace; and without these the great end of the election would not be attained: for the 'election' is given effect only by the 'call,' and manifests itself only in faith and the holy life. Equally of course the elect are 'the salt of the earth' and 'the light of the world,' the few through whom the many are blessed; the eternal life to which they are elected does not consist in or with the silence and coldness of death, but only in and with the intensest activities of the conquering people of God. But the prime end of their election does not lie in these things, and to place exclusive stress upon them is certainly to gather in the mint and anise and cummin of the doctrine. That to which God's elect are elected is, according to the teaching of Jesus, all that is included in the idea of the Kingdom of God, in the idea of eternal life, in the idea of fellowship with Christ, in the idea of participation in the glory which the Father has given His Son. Their choice, and the whole development of their history, according to our Lord's teaching, is the loving work of the Father: and in His keeping also is the consummation of their bliss. Their segregation, of course, leaves others not elected, to whom none of their privileges are granted; from whom none of their services are expected; with whom their glorious destiny is not shared. This, too, is of God. But this side of the matter, in accordance with Jesus' mission in the world as Saviour rather than as Judge, is less dwelt upon. In the case of neither class, that of the elect as little as that of those that are without, are the purposes of God wrought out without the co-operation of the activities of the subjects; but in neither case is the decisive factor supplied by these, but is discoverable solely in the will of God and the consonant will of the Son. The 'even so, Father; for so it seemed good in thy sight' (Matt. xi. 26, Luke x. 21), is to our Lord, at least, an all-sufficient theodicy in the face of all God's diverse dealings with men.

THE TEACHING OF THE PRIMITIVE DISCIPLES

The disciples of Jesus continue His teaching in all its elements. We are conscious, for example, of entering no new atmosphere when we pass to the *Epistle of James*. St. James, too, finds his starting-point in a profound apprehension of the exaltation and perfection of God,—defining God's nature, indeed, with a phrase that merely repeats in other words the penetrating declaration that 'God is light' (I John i. 5), which, reflecting our Lord's teaching, sound the keynote of the beloved disciple's thought of God (Jas. i. 17),—and particularly in a keen sense of dependence on God (iv. 15, v. 7), to which it was an axiom that every good thing is a gift from Him (i. 17). Accordingly, salvation, the pre-eminent good, comes purely as His gift, and can be ascribed only to His will (i. 18); and its exclusively Divine origin is indicated by the choice that is made of those who receive it—not the rich and prosperous, who have somewhat perhaps which might command consideration, but the poor and miserable (ii. 5). So little does this Divine choice rest on even faith, that it is rather in order to faith (ii. 5), and introduces its recipients into the Kingdom as firstfruits of a great harvest to be reaped by God in the world (i. 18).

Similarly, in the *Book of Acts*, the whole stress in the matter of salvation is laid on the grace of God (xi. 23, xiii. 43, xiv. 3, 26, xv. 40, xviii. 27); and to it, in the most pointed way, the inception of faith itself is assigned (xviii. 27). It is only slightly varied language when the increase in the Church is ascribed to the hand of the Lord (xi. 21), or the direct act of God (xiv. 27, xviii. 10). The explicit declaration of ii. 47 presents, therefore, nothing peculiar, and we are fully prepared for the philosophy of the redemptive history expressed in xiii. 48, that only those 'ordained to eternal life' believed—the believing that comes by the grace of God (xviii. 27), to whom it belongs to open the heart to give heed to the gospel (xvi. 14), being thus referred to the counsel of eternity, of which the events of time are only the outworking.

The general philosophy of history thus suggested is implicit in the very idea of a promissory system, and in the recognition of a predictive element in prophecy, and is written large on the pages of the *historical books* of the New Testament. It is given expression in every declaration that this or that event came to pass 'that it might be fulfilled which was spoken by the prophets,'—a form of statement in which our Lord had Himself betrayed His teleological view of history, not only as respects details (John xv. 25, xvii. 12), but with the widest reference (Luke xxi. 22), and which was taken up cordially by His followers, particularly by Matthew (i. 22, ii. 15, 23, iv. 14, viii. 17,

xii. 17, xiii. 35, xxi. 4, xxvi. 56, John xii. 38, xviii. 9, xix. 24, 28, 36). Alongside of this phrase occurs the equally significant 'δεῖ of the Divine decree,' as it has been appropriately called, by which is suggested the necessity which rules over historical sequences. It is used with a view now to Jesus' own plan of redemption (by Jesus Himself, Luke ii. 49, iv. 43, ix. 22, xiii. 33, xvii. 25, xxiv. 7, John iii. 14, x. 16, xii. 34; by the evangelist, Matt. xvi. 21), now to the underlying plan of God (by Jesus, Matt. xxiv. 6, Mark xiii. 7, 10, Luke xxi. 9; by the writer, Matt. xvii. 10, Mark ix. 11, Acts iii. 21, ix. 16), anon to the prophetic declaration as an indication of the underlying plan (by Jesus, Matt. xxvi. 56, Luke xxii. 37, xxiv. 26, 44; by the writer, John xx. 9, Acts i. 16, xvii. 3). This appeal, in either form, served an important apologetic purpose in the first proclamation of the gospel; but its fundamental significance is rooted, of course, in the conception of a Divine ordering of the whole course of history to the veriest detail.

Such a teleological conception of the history of the Kingdom is manifested strikingly in the speech of St. Stephen (Acts vii.), in which the developing plan of God is rapidly sketched. But it is in such declarations as those of St. Peter recorded in Acts ii. 23, iv. 28 that the wider philosophy of history comes to its clearest expression. In them everything that had befallen Jesus is represented as merely the emerging into fact of what had stood beforehand prepared for in 'the determinate counsel and foreknowledge of God,' so that nothing had been accomplished, by whatever agents, except what 'his hand and his counsel has foreordained to come to pass.' It would not be easy to frame language which should more explicitly proclaim the conception of an all-determining decree of God governing the entire sequence of events in time. Elsewhere in *the Petrine discourses* of Acts the speech is coloured by the same ideas: we note in the immediate context of these culminating passages the high terms in which the exaltation of God is expressed (iv. 24 f.), the sharpness with which His sovereignty in the 'call' (προσκαλέομαι) is declared (ii. 39), and elsewhere the repeated emergence of the idea of the necessary correspondence of the events of time with the predictions of Scripture (i. 16, ii. 24, iii. 21). The same doctrine of predestination meets us in the pages of *St. Peter's Epistles.* He does, indeed, speak of the members of the Christian community as God's elect (I i. 1, ii. 9, v. 13, II i. 10), in accordance with the apostolic habit of assuming the reality implied in the manifestation; but this is so far from importing that election hangs on the act of man that St. Peter refers it directly to the elective foreknowledge of God (I i. 2), and seeks its confirmation in sanctification (II i. 10),—even as the stumbling of the disobedient, on the other hand, is presented as a confirmation of their appointment to disbelief (I ii. 8). The pregnant use of the terms 'foreknow' ($\pi\rho o\gamma\iota\nu\dot\omega\sigma\kappa\omega$) and 'foreknowledge' ($\pi\rho\dot o\gamma\nu\omega\sigma\iota\varsigma$) by St. Peter brought to our attention in these passages (Acts ii. 23, I Pet. i. 2, 20), where they certainly convey the sense of a loving, distinguishing regard which assimilates them to the idea of election, is worthy of note as another of the traits common to him and St. Paul (Rom. viii. 29, xi. 2, only in the New Testament). The usage might be explained, indeed, as the development of a purely Greek sense of the words, but it is much more probably rooted in a Semitic usage, which, as we have seen, is not without example in the Old Testament. A simple comparison of the passages will exhibit the impossibility of reading the terms of mere prevision (cf. Cremer *sub voc.,* and especially the full discussion in K. Müller's "Die Göttliche Zuvorersehung und Erwählung," etc. pp. 38 f., 81 f.; also Gennrich, "Theol. Studien und Kritiken," 1898, 382-395; Pfleiderer, "Urchristenthum," 289, "Paulinismus," 268; and Lorenz, "Lehrsystem," etc. 94).

The *teaching of St. John* in Gospel and Epistle is not distinguishable from that which he reports from his Master's lips, and need not here be reverted to afresh. The same fundamental view-points meet us also in the Apocalypse. The emphasis there placed on the omnipotence of God rises indeed to a climax. There only in the New Testament (except II Cor. vi. 18), for example, is the epithet $\pi\alpha\nu\tau o\kappa\rho\dot\alpha\tau\omega\rho$ ascribed to Him (i. 8, iv. 8, xi. 17, xv. 3, xvi. 7, 14, xix. 6, 15, xxi. 22, cf. xv. 3, vi. 10); and the whole purport of the book is the portrayal of the Divine guidance of history, and the very essence of its message that, despite all surface appearances, it is the hand of God that really directs all occurrences, and all things are hastening to the end of His determining. Salvation is ascribed unvaryingly to the grace of God, and declared to be His work (xii. 10, xix. 1). The elect people of God are His by the Divine choice alone: their names are from the foundation of the world written in the Lamb's Book of Life (xiii. 8, xvii. 8, xx. 12-15, xxi. 27), which is certainly a symbol of Divine appointment to eternal life revealed in and realized through Christ; nor shall they ever be blotted out of it (iii. 5). It is difficult to doubt that the destination here asserted is to a complete salvation (xix. 9), that it is individual, and that it is but a single instance of the completeness of the Divine government to which the world is subject by the Lord of lords and King of kings, the Ruler of the earth and King of the nations, whose control of all the occurrences of time in accordance with His holy purposes it is the supreme object of this book to portray.

Perhaps less is directly said about the purpose of God in the *Epistle to the Hebrews* than in any other portion of the New Testament of equal length. The technical phraseology of the subject is conspicuously absent. Nevertheless, the conception of the Divine counsel and will underlying all that comes to pass (ii. 10), and especially the entire course of the purchase (vi. 17, cf. x. 5-10, ii. 9) and application (xi. 39, 31, ix. 15) of salvation, is fundamental to the whole thought of the Epistle; and echoes of the modes in which this conception is elsewhere expressed meet us on every hand. Thus we read of God's eternal counsel ($\beta o \upsilon \lambda \acute{\eta}$, vi. 17) and of His precedent will ($\theta \acute{\epsilon} \lambda \eta \mu a$, x. 10) as underlying His redemptive acts; of the enrolment of the names of His children in heaven (xii. 23); of the origin in the energy of God of all that is good in us (xiii. 21); and, above all, of a 'heavenly call' as the source of the whole renewed life of the Christian (iii. 1, cf. ix. 15).

When our Lord spoke of 'calling' ($\kappa a \lambda \acute{\epsilon} \omega$, Matt. ix. 13, Mark ii. 17, Luke v. 32, and, parabolically, Matt. xxii. 3, 4, 8, 9, Luke

xiv. 8, 9, 10, 12, 13, 16, 17, 24; κλητός, Matt. xxii. 14 [xx. 16])
the term was used in the ordinary sense of 'invitation,' and
refers therefore to a much broader circle than the 'elect' (Matt.
xxii. 14); and this fundamental sense of 'bidding' may continue
to cling to the term in the hands of the evangelists (Matt. iv. 21,
Mark i. 20, cf. Luke xiv. 7, John ii. 2), while the depth of meaning which might be attached to it, even in such a connotation,
may be revealed by such a passage as Rev. xix. 9 'Blessed are
they which are bidden to the marriage supper of the Lamb.' On
the lips of the apostolic writers, however, the term in its application to the call of God to salvation took on deeper meanings,
doubtless out of consideration of the author of the call, who
has but to speak and it is done (cf. Rom. iv. 17). It occurs in
these writers, when it occurs at all, as the synonym no longer
of 'invitation,' but rather of 'election' itself; or, more precisely,
as expressive of the temporal act of the Divine efficiency by
which effect is given to the electing decree. In this profounder
sense it is practically confined to the writings of St. Paul and
St. Peter and the *Epistle to the Hebrews,* occurring elsewhere
only in Jude 1, Rev. xvii. 14, where the children of God are
designated the 'called,' just as they are (in various collocations
of the term with the idea of election) in Rom. i. 6, 7, I Cor. i.
2, Rom. viii. 28, I Cor. i. 24 (cf. Rom. i. 1, I Cor. i. 1). Κλητός,
as used in these passages, does not occur in the *Epistle to the
Hebrews,* but in iii. 1 κλῆσις occurs in a sense indistinguishable
from that which it bears in St. Paul (Rom. xi. 29, I Cor. i. 26,
Eph. i. 18, iv. 1, 4, Phil. iii. 14, II Thes. i. 11, II Tim. i. 9) and
St. Peter (II Pet. i. 10); and in ix. 15 (cf. special applications
of the same general idea, v. 4, xi. 8), καλέω bears the same deep
sense expressed by it in St. Paul (Rom. viii. 30 twice, ix. 11, 24,
I Cor. i. 9, vii. 15, 17, 18 twice, 20, 21, 22 twice, 24, Gal. i. 6, 15,
v. 8, 13, Eph. iv. 1, 4, Col. iii. 15, I Thes. ii. 12, iv. 7, v. 24,
II Thes. ii. 14, II Tim. i. 9) and in St. Peter (I i. 15, ii. 9, 21, iii.
9, v. 10, II i. 3, cf. προσκαλέω, Acts ii. 39, and in the language
of St. Luke, Acts xiii. 2, xvi. 10). The contrast into which the
'called' (iii. 1) are brought in this Epistle with the 'evangel-
ized' (iv. 2, 6), repeating in other terms the contrast which our

Saviour institutes between the 'elect' and 'called' (Matt. xxii. 14), exhibits the height of the meaning to which the idea of the 'call' has climbed. It no longer denotes the mere invitation,—that notion is now given in 'evangelize,'—but the actual ushering into salvation of the heirs of the promise, who are made partakers of the heavenly calling, and are called to the everlasting inheritance just because they have been destined thereunto by God (i. 14), and are enrolled in heaven as the children given to the Son of God (ii. 13).

The Teaching of Paul

It was reserved, however, to the Apostle Paul to give to the fact of predestination its fullest New Testament presentation. This was not because St. Paul exceeded his fellows in the strength or clearness of his convictions, but because, in the prosecution of the special task which was committed to him in the general work of establishing Christianity in the world, the complete expression of the common doctrine of predestination fell in his way, and became a necessity of his argument. With him, too, the roots of his doctrine of predestination were set in his general doctrine of God, and it was fundamentally because St. Paul was a theist of a clear and consistent type, living and thinking under the influence of the profound consciousness of a personal God who is the author of all that is and, as well, the upholder and powerful governor of all that He has made, according to whose will, therefore, all that comes to pass must be ordered, that he was a predestinarian; and more particularly he too was a predestinarian because of his general doctrine of salvation, in every step of which the initiative must be taken by God's unmerited grace, just because man is a sinner, and, as a sinner, rests under the Divine condemnation, with no right of so much as access to God, and without means to seek, much less to secure, His favour. But although possessing no other sense of the infinite majesty of the almighty Person in whose hands all things lie, or of the issue of all saving acts from His free grace, than his companion apostles, the course of the special work in which St. Paul was engaged, and the exigencies of the special controversies in which he was involved, forced him to a fuller expression of all that is implied in these convictions. As he cleared the whole field of Christian faith from the presence of any remaining confidence in human works; as he laid beneath the hope of Christians a righteousness not self-wrought but provided by God alone; as he consistently offered this God-provided righteousness to sinners of all classes without regard to anything in them by which they might fancy God could be moved to accept their persons,—he was inevitably driven to an especially pervasive reference of salvation in each of its elements to the free grace of God, and to an especially full exposition on the one hand of the course of Divine grace in the several acts which enter into the saving work, and on the other to the firm rooting of the whole process in the pure will of the God of grace. From the beginning to the end of his ministry, accordingly, St. Paul conceived himself, above everything else, as the bearer of a message of undeserved grace to lost sinners, not even directing his own footsteps to carry the glad tidings to whom he would (Rom. i. 10, I Cor. iv. 19, II Cor. ii. 12), but rather led by God in triumphal procession through the world, that through him might be made manifest the savour of the knowledge of Christ in every place—a savour from life unto life in them that are saved, and from death unto death in them that are lost (II Cor. ii. 15, 16). By the 'word of the cross' proclaimed by him the essential character of his hearers was thus brought into manifestation,—to the lost it was foolishness, to the saved the power of God (I Cor. i. 18): not as if this essential character belonged to them by nature or was the product of their own activities, least of all of their choice at the moment of the proclamation, by which rather it was only revealed; but as finding an explanation only in an act of God, in accordance with the working of Him to whom all differences among men are to be ascribed (I Cor. iv. 7)—for God alone is the Lord of the harvest, and all the increase, however diligently man may plant and water, is to be accredited to Him alone (I Cor. iii. 5 f.).

It is naturally the soteriological interest that determines in the main St. Paul's allusions to the all-determining hand of God,—the letters that we have from him come from Paul the evangelist,—but it is not merely a soteriological conception that he is expressing in them, but the most fundamental postulate of his religious consciousness; and he is accordingly constantly correlating his doctrine of election with his general doctrine of the decree or counsel of God. No man ever had an intenser or more vital sense of God,—the eternal (Rom. xvi. 26) and incorruptible (i. 23) One, the only wise One (xvi. 27), who does all things according to His good-pleasure (I Cor. xv. 38, xii. 18, Col. i. 19), and whose ways are past tracing out (Rom. xi. 33); before whom men should therefore bow in the humility of absolute dependence, recognizing in Him the one moulding power as well in history as in the life of the individual (Rom. ix.). Of Him and through Him and unto Him, he fervently exclaims, are all things (Rom. xi. 36, cf. I Cor. viii. 6); He is over all and through all and in all (Eph. iv. 6, cf. Col. i. 16); He worketh all things according to the counsel of His will (Eph. i. 11): all that is, in a word, owes its existence and persistence and its action and issue to Him. The whole course of history is, therefore, of His ordering (Acts xiv. 16, xvii. 26, Rom. i. 18 f., iii. 25, ix-xi, Gal. iii. iv.), and every event that befalls is under His control, and must be estimated from the view-point of His purposes of good to His people (Rom. viii. 28, I Thes. v. 17, 18), for whose benefit the whole world is governed (Eph. i. 22, I Cor. ii. 7, Col. i. 18). The figure that is employed in Rom. ix. 22 with a somewhat narrower reference, would fairly express St. Paul's world-view in its relation to the Divine activity: God is the potter, and the whole world with all its contents but as the plastic clay which He moulds to His own ends; so that whatsoever comes into being, and whatsoever uses are served by the things that exist, are all alike of Him. In accordance with this world-view St. Paul's doctrine of salvation must necessarily be interpreted; and, in very fact, he gives it its accordant expression in every instance in which he speaks of it.

There are especially *three chief passages* in which the

apostle so fully expounds his fundamental teaching as to the relation of salvation to the purpose of God, that they may fairly claim our primary attention.

(*a*) The first of these—Rom. viii. 29, 30—emerges as part of the encouragement which the apostle offers to his readers in the sad state in which they find themselves in this world, afflicted with fears within and fightings without. He reminds them that they are not left to their weakness, but the Spirit comes to their aid: 'and we know,' adds the apostle,—it is no matter of conjecture, but of assured knowledge,—'that with them that love God, God co-operates with respect to all things for good, since they are indeed the called according to [His] purpose.' The appeal is obviously primarily to the universal government of God: nothing takes place save by His direction, and even what seems to be grievous comes from the Father's hand. Secondarily, the appeal is to the assured position of his readers within the fatherly care of God: they have not come into this blessed relation with God accidentally or by the force of their own choice; they have been 'called' into it by Himself, and that by no thoughtless, inadvertent, meaningless, or changeable call; it was a call 'according to purpose,'—where the anarthrousness of the noun throws stress on the purposiveness of the call. What has been denominated 'the golden chain of salvation' that is attached to this declaration by the particle 'because' can therefore have no other end than more fully to develop and more firmly to ground the assurance thus quickened in the hearts of the readers: it accordingly enumerates the steps of the saving process in the purpose of God, and carries it thus successively through the stages of appropriating foreknowledge,—for 'foreknow' is undoubtedly used here in that pregnant sense we have already seen it to bear in similar connexions in the New Testament,—predestination to conformity with the image of God's Son, calling, justifying, glorifying; all of which are cast in the past tense of a purpose in principle executed when formed, and are bound together as mutually implicative, so that, where one is present, all are in principle present with it. It accordingly follows that, in St.

Paul's conception, glorification rests on justification, which in turn rests on vocation, while vocation comes only to those who had previously been predestinated to conformity with God's Son, and this predestination to character and destiny only to those afore chosen by God's loving regard. It is obviously a strict doctrine of predestination that is taught. This conclusion can be avoided only by assigning a sense to the 'foreknowing' that lies at the root of the whole process, which is certainly out of accord not merely with its ordinary import in similar connexions in the New Testament, nor merely with the context, but with the very purpose for which the declaration is made, namely, to enhearten the struggling saint by assuring him that he is not committed to his own power, or rather weakness, but is in the sure hands of the Almighty Father. It would seem little short of absurd to hang on the merely contemplative foresight of God a declaration adduced to support the assertion that the lovers of God are something deeper and finer than even lovers of God, namely, 'the called according to *purpose*,' and itself educing the joyful cry, 'If God is for us, who is against us?' and grounding a confident claim upon the gift of all things from His hands.

(*b*) The even more famous section, Rom. ix, x, xi, following closely upon this strong affirmation of the suspension of the whole saving process on the predetermination of God, offers, on the face of it, a yet sharper assertion of predestination, raising it, moreover, out of the circle of the merely individual salvation into the broader region of the historical development of the kingdom of God. The problem which St. Paul here faces grew so directly out of his fundamental doctrine of justification by faith alone, with complete disregard of all question of merit or vested privilege, that it must have often forced itself upon his attention,—himself a Jew with a high estimate of a Jew's privileges and a passionate love for his people. He could not but have pondered it frequently and deeply, and least of all could he have failed to give it treatment in an Epistle like this, which undertakes to provide a somewhat formal exposition of his whole doctrine of justification.

Having shown the necessity of such a method of salvation as he proclaimed, if sinful men were to be saved at all (i. 18-iii. 20), and then expounded its nature and evidence (iii. 21-v. 21), and afterwards discussed its intensive effects (vi. 1-viii. 39), he could not fail further to explain its extensive effects—especially when they appeared to be of so portentous a character as to imply a reversal of what was widely believed to have been God's mode of working heretofore, the rejection of His people whom He foreknew, and the substitution of the alien in their place. St. Paul's solution of the problem is, briefly, that the situation has been gravely misconceived by those who so represent it; that nothing of the sort thus described has happened or will happen; that what has happened is merely that in the constitution of that people whom He has chosen to Himself and is fashioning to His will, God has again exercised that sovereignty which He had previously often exercised, and which He had always expressly reserved to Himself and frequently proclaimed as the principle of His dealings with the people emphatically of His choice. In his exposition of this solution St. Paul first defends the propriety of God's action (ix. 6-24), then turns to stop the mouth of the objecting Jew by exposing the manifested unfitness of the Jewish people for the kingdom (ix. 30-x. 21), and finally expounds with great richness the ameliorating circumstances in the whole transaction (xi. 1-36). In the course of his defence of God's rejection of the mass of contemporary Israel, he sets forth the sovereignty of God in the whole matter of salvation—'that the purpose of God according to election might stand, not of works, but of Him that calleth'—with a sharpness of assertion and a clearness of illustration which leave nothing to be added in order to throw it out in the full strength of its conception. We are pointed illustratively to the sovereign acceptance of Isaac and rejection of Ishmael, and to the choice of Jacob and not of Esau before their birth and therefore before either had done good or bad; we are explicitly told that in the matter of salvation it is not of him that will, or of him that runs, but of God that shows mercy, and that has mercy on whom He wills, and whom He wills He hardens; we are pointedly directed to behold in God the potter who makes the vessels which proceed from His hand each for an end of His appointment, that He may work out His will upon them. It is safe to say that language cannot be chosen better adapted to teach predestination at its height.

We are exhorted, indeed, not to read this language in isolation, but to remember that the ninth chapter must be interpreted in the light of the eleventh. Not to dwell on the equally important consideration that the eleventh chapter must likewise be interpreted only in the light of the ninth, there seems here to exhibit itself some forgetfulness of the inherent continuity of St. Paul's thought, and, indeed, some misconception of the progress of the argument through the section, which is a compact whole and must express a much pondered line of thought, constantly present to the apostle's mind. We must not permit to fall out of sight the fact that the whole extremity of assertion of the ninth chapter is repeated in the eleventh (xi. 4-10); so that there is no change of conception or lapse of consecution observable as the argument develops, and we do not escape from the doctrine of predestination of the ninth chapter in fleeing to the eleventh. This is true even if we go at once to the great closing declaration of xi. 32, to which we are often directed as to the key of the whole section—which, indeed, it very much is: 'For God hath shut up all unto disobedience, that he might have mercy upon all.' On the face of it there could not readily be framed a more explicit assertion of the Divine control and the Divine initiative than this; it is only another declaration that He has mercy on whom He will have mercy, and after the manner and in the order that He will. And it certainly is not possible to read it as a declaration of universal salvation, and thus reduce the whole preceding exposition to a mere tracing of the varying pathways along which the common Father leads each individual of the race severally to the common goal. Needless to point out that thus the whole argument would be stultified, and the apostle convicted of gross exaggeration in tone and language where otherwise we find only impressive solemnity, rising at times into natural anguish. It is enough to observe that the verse cannot bear this sense in its context. Nothing is clearer than that its purpose is not to minimize but to magnify the sense of absolute dependence on the Divine mercy, and to quicken apprehension of the mystery of God's righteously loving ways; and nothing is clearer than that the reference of the double 'all' is exhausted by the two classes discussed in the immediate context,—so that they are not to be taken individualistically but, so to speak, racially. The intrusion of the individualistic-universalistic sentiment, so dominant in the modern consciousness, into the interpretation of this section, indeed, is to throw the whole into inextricable confusion. Nothing could be further from the nationalistic-universalistic point of view from which it was written, and from which alone St. Paul can be understood when he represents that in rejecting the mass of contemporary Jews God has not cast off His people, but, acting only as He had frequently done in former ages, is fulfilling His promise to the kernel while shelling off the husk. Throughout the whole process of pruning and ingrafting which he traces in the dealings of God with the olive-tree which He has once for all planted, St. Paul sees God, in accordance with His promise, saving His people. The continuity of its stream of life he perceives preserved throughout all its present experience of rejection (xi. 1-10); the gracious purpose of the present confinement of its channel, he traces with eager hand (xi. 11-15); he predicts with confidence the attainment in the end of the full breadth of the promise (xi. 15-32),—all to the praise of the glory of God's grace (xi. 33-36). There is undoubtedly a universalism of salvation proclaimed here; but it is an eschatological, not an individualistic universalism. The day is certainly to come when the whole world—inclusive of all the Jews and Gentiles alike, then dwelling on the globe—shall know and serve the Lord; and God in all His strange work of distributing salvation is leading the course of events to that great goal; but meanwhile the principle of His action is free, sovereign grace, to which alone it is to be attributed that any who are saved in the meantime enter into their inheritance, and through which alone shall the final goal of the race itself be attained. The central thought of the whole discussion, in a word, is that Israel does not owe the promise to the fact that it is Israel, but conversely owes the fact that it is Israel to the promise,— that 'it is not the children of the flesh that are the children of God, but the children of the promise that are reckoned for a seed' (ix. 8). In these words we hold the real key to the whole section; and if we approach it with this key in hand we shall have little difficulty in apprehending that, from its beginning to its end, St. Paul has no higher object than to make clear that the inclusion of any individual within the kingdom of God finds its sole cause in the sovereign grace of the choosing God, and cannot in any way or degree depend upon his own merit, privilege, or act.

Neither, with this key in our hand, will it be possible to raise a question whether the election here expounded is to eternal life or not rather merely to prior privilege or higher service. These too, no doubt, are included. But by what right is this long section intruded here as a substantive part of this Epistle, busied as a whole with the exposition of 'the power of God unto salvation to every one that believeth, to the Jew first and also to the Greek,' if it has no direct concern with this salvation? By what chance has it attached itself to that noble grounding of a Christian's hope and assurance with which the eighth chapter closes? By what course of thought does it reach its own culmination in that burst of praise to God, on whom all things depend, with which it concludes? By what accident is it itself filled with the most unequivocal references to the saving grace of God 'which hath been poured out on the vessels of his mercy which he afore prepared for glory, even on us whom he also called, not from the Jews only, but also from the Gentiles'? If such language has no reference to salvation, there is no language in the New Testament that need be interpreted of final destiny. Beyond question this section does explain to us some of the grounds of the mode of God's action in gathering a people to Himself out of the world; and in doing this, it does reveal to us some of the ways in which the distri-

bution of His electing grace serves the purposes of His kingdom on earth; reading it, we certainly do learn that God has
many ends to serve in His gracious dealings with the children
of men, and that we, in our ignorance of His multifarious purposes, are not fitted to be His counsellors. But by all this, the
fact is in no wise obscured that it is primarily to salvation that
He calls His elect, and that whatever other ends their election
may subserve, this fundamental end will never fail; that in
this, too, the gifts and calling of God are not repented of, and
will surely lead on to their goal. The difficulty which is felt by
some in following the apostle's argument here, we may suspect,
has its roots in part in a shrinking from what appears to them
an arbitrary assignment of men to diverse destinies without
consideration of their desert. Certainly St. Paul as explicitly
affirms the sovereignty of reprobation as of election,—if these
twin ideas are, indeed, separable even in thought: if he represents God as sovereignly loving Jacob, he represents Him
equally as sovereignly hating Esau; if he declares that He has
mercy on whom He will, he equally declares that He hardens
whom He will. Doubtless the difficulty often felt here is, in
part, an outgrowth of an insufficient realization of St. Paul's
basal conception of the state of men at large as condemned
sinners before an angry God. It is with a world of lost sinners
that he is representing God as dealing; and out of that world
building up a Kingdom of Grace. Were not all men sinners,
there might still be an election, as sovereign as now; and there
being an election, there would still be as sovereign a rejection:
but the rejection would not be a rejection to punishment, to
destruction, to eternal death, but to some other destiny consonant to the state in which those passed by should be left.
It is not indeed, then, because men are sinners that men are
left unelected; election is free, and its obverse of rejection must
be equally free: but it is solely because men are sinners that
what they are left to is destruction. And it is in this universalism of ruin rather than in a universalism of salvation that St.
Paul really roots his theodicy. When all deserve death it is a
marvel of pure grace that any receive life; and who shall gain-

say the right of Him who shows this miraculous mercy, to have mercy on whom He will, and whom He will to harden?

(c) In Eph. i. 1-12 there is, if possible, an even higher note struck. Here, too, St. Paul is dealing primarily with the blessings bestowed on his readers, in Christ, all of which he ascribes to the free grace of God; but he so speaks of these blessings as to correlate the gracious purpose of God in salvation, not merely with the plan of operation which He prosecutes in establishing and perfecting His kingdom on earth, but also with the all-embracing decree that underlies His total cosmical activity. In opening this circular letter, addressed to no particular community whose special circumstances might suggest the theme of the thanksgiving with which he customarily begins his letters, St. Paul is thrown back on what is common to Christians; and it is probably to this circumstance that we owe the magnificent description of the salvation in Christ with which the Epistle opens, and in which this salvation is traced consecutively in its preparation (vv. 4, 5), its execution (6, 7), its publication (8-10), and its application (11-14), both to Jews (11, 12) and to Gentiles (13, 14). Thus, at all events, we have brought before us the whole ideal history of salvation in Christ from eternity to eternity—from the eternal purpose as it lay in the loving heart of the Father, to the eternal consummation, when all things in heaven and earth shall be summed up in Christ. Even the incredible profusion of the blessings which we receive in Christ, described with an accumulation of phrases that almost defies exposition, is less noticeable here than the emphasis and reiteration with which the apostle carries back their bestowment on us to that primal purpose of God in which all things are afore prepared ere they are set in the way of accomplishment. All this accumulation of blessings, he tells his readers, has come to them and him only in fulfilment of an eternal purpose—only because they had been chosen by God out of the mass of sinful men, in Christ, before the foundation of the world, to be holy and blameless before Him, and had been lovingly predestinated unto adoption through Jesus Christ to Him, in accordance with the good-pleasure of His will, to the praise of the glory of His grace. It is therefore, he further explains, that to them in the abundance of God's grace there has been brought the knowledge of the salvation in Christ, described here as the knowledge of the mystery of the Divine will, according to His good-pleasure, which He purposed in Himself with reference to the dispensation of the fulness of the times, to sum up all things in the universe in Christ,—by which phrases the plan of salvation is clearly exhibited as but one element in the cosmical purpose of God. And thus it is, the apostle proceeds to explain, only in pursuance of this all-embracing cosmical purpose that Christians, whether Jews or Gentiles, have been called into participation of these blessings, to the praise of the glory of God's grace,—and of the former class, he pauses to assert anew that their call rests on a predestination according to the purpose of Him that works all things according to the counsel of His will. Throughout this elevated passage, the resources of language are strained to the utmost to give utterance to the depth and fervour of St. Paul's conviction of the absoluteness of the dominion which the God, whom he describes as Him that works all things according to the counsel of His will, exercises over the entire universe, and of his sense of the all-inclusive perfection of the plan on which He is exercising His world-wide government—into which world-wide government His administration of His grace, in the salvation of Christ, works as one element. Thus there is kept steadily before our eyes the wheel within wheel of the all-comprehending decree of God: first of all, the inclusive cosmical purpose in accordance with which the universe is governed as it is led to its destined end; within this, the purpose relative to the kingdom of God, a substantive part, and, in some sort, the hinge of the world-purpose itself; and still within this, the purpose of grace relative to the individual, by virtue of which he is called into the Kingdom and made sharer in its blessings: the common element with them all being that they are and come to pass only in accordance with the good-pleasure of His will, according to His purposed good-pleasure, according to the purpose of Him who works all things in accordance with the counsel of His will; and therefore all alike redound solely to His praise.

In these outstanding passages, however, there are only expounded, though with special richness, ideas which govern the Pauline literature, and which come now and again to clear expression in each group of St. Paul's letters. The whole doctrine of election, for instance, lies as truly in the declaration of II Thes. ii. 13 or that of II Tim. i. 9 (cf. II Tim. ii. 19, Tit. iii. 5) as in the passages we have considered from Romans (cf. I Cor. i. 26-31) and Ephesians (cf. Eph. ii. 10, Col. i. 27, iii. 12, 15, Phil. iv. 3). It may be possible to trace minor distinctions through the several groups of letters in forms of statement or modes of relating the doctrine to other conceptions; but from the beginning to the end of St. Paul's activity as a Christian teacher his fundamental teaching as to the Christian calling and life is fairly summed up in the declaration that those that are saved are God's 'workmanship created in Christ Jesus unto good works, which God afore prepared that they should walk in them' (Eph. ii. 10).

The most striking impression made upon us by a survey of the whole material is probably the intensity of St. Paul's practical interest in the doctrine—a matter fairly illustrated by the passage just quoted (Eph. ii. 10). Nothing is more noticeable than his zeal in enforcing its two chief practical contents —the assurance it should bring to believers of their eternal safety in the faithful hands of God, and the ethical energy it should arouse within them to live worthily of their vocation. It is one of St. Paul's most persistent exhortations, that believers should remember that their salvation is not committed to their own weak hands, but rests securely on the faithfulness of the God who has called them according to His purpose (e.g., I Thes. v. 24, I Cor. i. 8 f., x. 13, Phil. i. 6). Though the appropriation of their salvation begins in an act of faith on their own part, which is consequent on the hearing of the gospel, their appointment to salvation itself does not depend on this act of faith, nor on any fitness discoverable in them on the foresight of which God's choice of them might be supposed to be based, but (as I Thes. ii. 13 already indicates) both the preaching of the gospel and the exercise of faith consistently appear as steps in the carrying out of an election not conditioned on their occurrence, but embracing them as means to the end set by the free purpose of God. The case is precisely the same with all subsequent acts of the Christian life. So far is St. Paul from supposing that election to life should operate to enervate moral endeavour, that it is precisely from the fact that the willing and doing of man rest on an energizing willing and doing of God, which in turn rest on His eternal purpose, that the apostle derives his most powerful and most frequently urged motive for ethical action. That tremendous 'therefore,' with which at the opening of the twelfth chapter of Romans he passes from the doctrinal to the ethical part of the Epistle,—from a doctrinal exposition the very heart of which is salvation by pure grace apart from all works, and which has just closed with the fullest discussion of the effects of election to be found in all his writings, to the rich exhortations to high moral effort with which the closing chapters of this Epistle are filled,—may justly be taken as the normal illation of his whole ethical teaching. His Epistles, in fact, are sown (as indeed is the whole New Testament) with particular instances of the same appeal (e.g., I Thes. ii. 12, II Thes. ii. 13-15, Rom. vi, II Cor. v. 14, Col. i. 10, Phil. i. 21, ii. 12, 13, II Tim. ii. 19). In Phil. ii. 12, 13 it attains, perhaps, its sharpest expression: here the saint is exhorted to work out his own salvation with fear and trembling, just because it is God who is working in him both the willing and the doing because of His 'good-pleasure'—obviously but another way of saying, 'If God is for us, who can be against us?'

There is certainly presented in this a problem for those who wish to operate in this matter with an irreconcilable 'either, or,' and who can conceive of no freedom of man which is under the control of God. St. Paul's theism was, however, of too pure a quality to tolerate in the realm of creation any force beyond the sway of Him who, as he says, is over all, and through all, and in all (Eph. iv. 6), working all things according to the counsel of His will (Eph. i. 11). And it must be confessed that it is more facile than satisfactory to set his theistic world-view summarily aside as a 'merely religious view,' which stands in conflict with a truly ethical conception of the world—perhaps even with a repetition of Fritzsche's jibe that St. Paul would have reasoned better on the high themes of 'fate, free-will, and providence' had he sat at the feet of Aristotle rather than at those of Gamaliel. Antiquity produced, however, no ethical genius equal to St. Paul, and even as a teacher of the foundations of ethics Aristotle himself might well be content to sit rather at his feet; and it does not at once appear why a so-called 'religious' conception may not have as valid a ground in human nature, and as valid a right to determine human conviction, as a so-called 'ethical' one. It can serve no good purpose even to proclaim an insoluble antinomy here: such an antinomy St. Paul assuredly did not feel, as he urged the predestination of God not more as a ground of assurance of salvation than as the highest motive of moral effort; and it does not seem impossible for even us weaker thinkers to follow him some little way at least in looking upon those twin bases of religion and morality—the ineradicable feelings of dependence and responsibility—not as antagonistic sentiments of a hopelessly divided heart, but as fundamentally the same profound conviction operating in a double sphere. At all events, St. Paul's pure theistic view-point, which conceived God as in His providential *concursus* working all things according to the counsel of His will (Eph. i. 11) in entire consistency with the action of second causes, necessary and free, the proximate producers of events, supplied him with a very real point of departure for his conception of the same God, in the operations of His grace, working the willing and the doing of Christian men, without the least infringement of the integrity of the free determination by which each grace is proximately attained. It does not belong to our present task to expound the nature of that Divine act by which St. Paul represents God as 'calling' sinners 'into communion with his Son,' itself the first step in the realization in their lives of that conformity to His image to which they are predestinated in the counsels of eternity, and of which the first manifestation is that faith in the Redeemer of God's elect out of which the whole Christian life unfolds. Let it only be observed in passing that he obviously conceives it as an act of God's almighty power, removing old inabilities and creating new abilities of living, loving action. It is enough for our present purpose to perceive that even in this act St. Paul did not conceive God as dehumanizing man, but rather as energizing man in a new direction of his powers; while in all his subsequent activities the analogy of the *concursus* of Providence is express. In his own view, his strenuous assertion of the predetermination in God's purpose of all the acts of saint and sinner alike in the matter of salvation, by which the discrimination of men into saved and lost is carried back to the free counsel of God's will, as little involves violence to the ethical spontaneity of their activities on the one side, as on the other it involves unrighteousness in God's dealings with His creatures. He does not speculatively discuss the methods of the Divine providence; but the fact of its universality—over all beings and actions alike—forms one of his most primary presuppositions; and naturally he finds no difficulty in postulating the inclusion in the prior intention of God of what is subsequently evolved in the course of His providential government.

IV. THE BIBLE DOCTRINE OF PREDESTINATION

A survey of the whole material thus cursorily brought before us exhibits the existence of a consistent Bible doctrine of predestination, which, because rooted in, and indeed only a logical outcome of, the fundamental Biblical theism, is taught in all its essential elements from the beginning of the Biblical revelation, and is only more fully unfolded in detail as the more developed religious consciousness and the course of the history of redemption required.

The *subject* of the DECREE is uniformly conceived as God in the fulnes of His moral personality. It is not to chance, nor to necessity, nor yet to an abstract or arbitrary will,—to God acting inadvertently, inconsiderately, or by any necessity of nature,—but specifically to the almighty, all-wise, all-holy, all-righteous, faithful, loving God, to the Father of our Lord and Saviour Jesus Christ, that is ascribed the predetermination of the course of events. Naturally, the contemplation of the plan in accordance with which all events come to pass calls out primarily a sense of the unsearchable wisdom of Him who framed it, and of the illimitable power of Him who executes it; and these attributes are accordingly much dwelt upon when the Divine predestination is adverted to. But the moral attributes are no less emphasized, and the Biblical writers find their comfort continually in the assurance that it is the righteous, holy, faithful, loving God in whose hands rests the determination of the sequence of events and all their issues. Just because it is the determination of God, and represents Him in all His fulness, the decree is ever set forth further as in its *nature* eternal, absolute, and immutable. And it is only an explication of these qualities when it is further insisted upon, as it is throughout the Bible, that it is essentially one single composite purpose, into which are worked all the details included in it, each in its appropriate place; that it is the pure determination of the Divine will—that is, not to be confounded on the one hand with an act of the Divine intellect on which it rests, nor on the other with its execution by His power in the works of creation and providence; that it is free and unconditional— that is, not the product of compulsion from without nor of necessity of nature from within, nor based or conditioned on any occurrence outside itself, foreseen or unforeseen; and that it is certainly efficacious, or rather constitutes the unchanging norm according to which He who is the King over all administers His government over the universe. Nor is it to pass beyond the necessary implications of the fundamental idea when it is further taught, as it is always taught throughout the Scriptures, that the *object* of the decree is the whole universe of things and all their activities, so that nothing comes to pass, whether in the sphere of necessary or free causation, whether good or bad, save in accordance with the provisions of the primal plan, or more precisely save as the outworking in fact of what had lain in the Divine mind as purpose from all eternity, and is now only unfolded into actuality as the fulfilment of His all-determining will. Finally, it is equally unvaryingly represented that the *end* which the decreeing God had in view in framing His purpose is to be sought not without but within Himself, and may be shortly declared as His own praise, or, as we now commonly say, the glory of God. Since it antedates the existence of all things outside of God and provides for their coming into being, they all without exception must be ranked as means to its end, which can be discovered only in the glory of the Divine purposer Himself. The whole Bible doctrine of the decree revolves, in a word, around the simple idea of purpose. Since God is a Person, the very mark of His being is purpose. Since He is an infinite Person, His purpose is eternal and independent, all-inclusive and effective. Since He is a moral Person, His purpose is the perfect exposition of all His infinite moral perfections. Since He is the personal creator of all that exists, His purpose can find its final cause only in Himself.

Against this general doctrine of the decree, the Bible doctrine of ELECTION is thrown out into special prominence, being, as it is, only a particular application of the general doctrine of the decree to the matter of the dealings of God with a sinful race. In its fundamental characteristics it therefore partakes of all the elements of the general doctrine of the decree. It, too, is necessarily an act of God in His completeness as an infinite moral Person, and is therefore eternal, absolute, immutable— the independent, free, unconditional, effective determination by the Divine will of the objects of His saving operations. In the development of the idea, however, there are certain elements which receive a special stress. There is nothing that is more constantly emphasized than the absolute *sovereignty* of the elective choice. The very essence of the doctrine is made, indeed, to consist in the fact that, in the whole administration of His grace, God is moved by no consideration derived from the special recipients of His saving mercy, but the entire account of its distribution is to be found hidden in the free counsels of His own will. That it is not of him that runs, nor of him that wills, but of God that shows mercy, that the sinner obtains salvation, is the steadfast witness of the whole body of Scripture, urged with such reiteration and in such varied connexions as to exclude the possibility that there may lurk behind the act of election considerations of foreseen characters or acts or circumstances—all of which appear rather as results of election as wrought out in fact by the *providentia specialissima* of the electing God. It is with no less constancy of emphasis that the roots of the Divine election are planted in His unsearchable love, by which it appears as *the supreme act of grace*. Contemplation of the general plan of God, including in its provisions every event which comes to pass in the whole universe of being during all the ages, must redound in the first instance to the praise of the infinite wisdom which has devised it all; or as our appreciation of its provisions is deepened, of the glorious righteousness by which it is informed. Contemplation of the particular element in His purpose which provides for the rescue of lost sinners from the destruction due to their guilt, and their restoration to right and to God, on the other hand draws our thoughts at once to His inconceivable love, and must redound, as the Scriptures delight to phrase it, to the praise of His glorious grace. It is ever, therefore, specifically to the love of God that the Scriptures ascribe His elective decree, and they are never weary of raising our eyes from the act itself to its source in the Divine compassion. A similar emphasis is also everywhere cast on the *particularity* of the Divine election. So little is it the designation of a mere class to be filled up by undetermined individuals in the exercise of their own determination; or of mere conditions, or characters, or qualities, to be fulfilled or attained by the undetermined activities of individuals, foreseen or unforeseen; that the Biblical writers take special pains to carry home to the heart of each individual believer the assurance that he himself has been from all eternity the particular object of the Divine choice, and that he owes it to this Divine choice alone that he is a member of the class of the chosen ones, that he is able to fulfil the conditions of salvation, that he can hope to attain the character on which alone God can look with complacency, that he can look forward to an eternity of bliss as his own possession. It is the very nerve of the Biblical doctrine that each individual of that enormous multitude that constitutes the great host of the people of God, and that is illustrating the character of Christ in the new life now lived in the strength of the Son of God, has from all eternity been the particular object of the Divine regard, and is only now fulfilling the high destiny designed for him from the foundation of the world.

The Biblical writers are as far as possible from obscuring the doctrine of election because of any seemingly unpleasant corollaries that flow from it. On the contrary, they expressly draw the corollaries which have often been so designated, and make them a part of their explicit teaching. Their doctrine of election, they are free to tell us, for example, does certainly involve a corresponding *doctrine of preterition*. The very term adopted in the New Testament to express it—ἐκλέγομαι, which, as Meyer justly says (Eph. i. 4), 'always has, and must *of logical necessity* have, a reference to *others* to whom the chosen would, without the ἐκλογή, still belong'—embodies a declaration of the fact that in their election others are passed by and left without the gift of salvation; the whole presentation of the doctrine is such as either to imply or openly to assert, on its every emergence, the removal of the elect by the pure grace of God, not merely from a state of condemnation, but out of the company of the condemned—a company on whom the grace of God has no saving effect, and who are therefore left without hope in their sins; and the positive just reprobation of the impenitent for their sins is repeatedly explicitly taught in sharp contrast with the gratuitous salvation of the elect despite their sins. But, on the other hand, it is ever taught that, as the body out of which believers are chosen by God's unsearchable grace is the mass of justly condemned sinners, so the destruction to which those that are passed by are left is the righteous recompense of their guilt. Thus the discrimination between men in the matter of eternal destiny is distinctly set forth as taking place in the interests of mercy and for the sake of salvation: from the fate which justly hangs over all, God is represented as in His infinite compassion rescuing those chosen to this end in His

inscrutable counsels of mercy to the praise of the glory of
His grace; while those that are left in their sins perish most
deservedly, as the justice of God demands. And as the broader
lines of God's gracious dealings with the world lying in its
iniquity are more and more fully drawn for us, we are enabled
ultimately to perceive that the Father of spirits has not distributed His elective grace with niggard hand, but from the
beginning has had in view the restoration to Himself of the
whole world; and through whatever slow approaches (as men
count slowness) He has made thereto—first in the segregation
of the Jews for the keeping of the service of God alive in the
midst of an evil world, and then in their rejection in order that
the fulness of the Gentiles might be gathered in, and finally
through them Israel in turn may all be saved—has ever been
conducting the world in His loving wisdom and His wise love
to its destined goal of salvation,—now and again, indeed, shut-
ting up this or that element of it unto disobedience, but never
merely in order that it might fall, but that in the end He might
have mercy upon all. Thus the Biblical writers bid us raise our
eyes, not only from the justly condemned lost, that we may
with deeper feeling contemplate the marvels of the Divine love
in the saving of sinners not better than they and with no greater
claims on the Divine mercy; but from the relatively insignificant
body of the lost, as but the prunings gathered beneath the
branches of the olive-tree planted by the Lord's own hand, to
fix them on the thrifty stock itself and the crown of luxuriant
leafage and ever more richly ripening fruit, as under the loving
pruning and grafting of the great Husbandman it grows and
flourishes and puts forth its boughs until it shall shade the
whole earth. This, according to the Biblical writers, is the end
of election; and this is nothing other than the salvation of the
world. Though in the process of the ages the goal is not attained
without prunings and fires of burning,—though all the wild-
olive twigs are not throughout the centuries grafted in,—yet
the goal of a saved world shall at the end be gloriously realized.
Meanwhile, the hope of the world, the hope of the Church, and
the hope of the individual alike, is cast solely on the mercy of

a freely electing God, in whose hands are all things, and not least the care of the advance of His saving grace in the world. And it is undeniable that whenever, as the years have passed by, the currents of religious feeling have run deep, and the higher ascents of religious thinking have been scaled, it has ever been on the free might of Divine grace that Christians have been found to cast their hopes for the salvation alike of the world, the Church, and the individual; and whenever they have thus turned in trust to the pure grace of God, they have spontaneously given expression to their faith in terms of the Divine election.

APPENDIX

The Biblical Terminology of Predestination

The words 'predestine,' 'predestinate,' 'predestination' seem not to have been domiciled in English literary use until the later period of Middle English (they are all three found in Chaucer: "Troylous and Cryseyde," 966; "Orisoune to the Holy Virgin," 69; translation of "Boëthius," b. 1, pr. 6, 1. 3844; the Old English equivalent seems to have been 'fore-stihtian,' as in Ælfric's "Homilies," ii. 364, 366, in renderings of Rom. i. 4, viii. 30). 'Predestine,' 'predestination' were doubtless taken over from the French, while 'predestinate' probably owes its form directly to the Latin original of them all. The noun has never had a place in the English Bible, but the verb in the form 'predestinate' occurs in every one of its issues from Tindale to the Authorized Version. Its history in the English versions is a somewhat curious one. It goes back, of course, ultimately to the Latin 'prædestino' (a good classical but not pre-Augustan word; while the noun 'prædestinatio' seems to be of Patristic origin), which was adopted by the Vulgate as its regular rendering of the Greek προορίζω, and occurs, with the sole exception of Acts iv. 28 (Vulgate *decerno*), wherever the Latin translators found that verb in their text

(Rom. i. 4, viii. 29, 30, I Cor. ii. 7, Eph. i. 5, 11). But the Wy-
clifite versions did not carry 'predestinate' over into English
in a single instance, but rendered in every case by 'before
ordain' (Acts iv. 28 'deemed'). It was thus left to Tindale to
give the word a place in the English Bible. This he did, however, in only one passage, Eph. i. 11, doubtless under the influence of the Vulgate. His ordinary rendering of προορίζω is
'ordain before' (Rom. viii. 29, Eph. i. 5; cf. I Cor. ii. 7, where
the 'before' is omitted apparently only on account of the succeeding preposition into which it may be thought, therefore,
to coalesce), varied in Rom. viii. 30 to 'appoint before'; while,
reverting to the Greek, he has 'determined before' at Acts iv.
28 and, following the better reading, has 'declared' at Rom.
i. 4. The succeeding English versions follow Tindale very
closely, though the Genevan omits 'before' in Acts iv. 28 and,
doubtless in order to assimilate it to the neighbouring Eph.
i. 11, reads 'did predestinate' in Eph. i. 5. The larger use of
the word was due to the Rhemish version, which naturally
reverts to the Vulgate and reproduces its prœdestino regularly
in 'predestinate' (Rom. i. 4, viii. 29, 30, I Cor. ii. 7, Eph. i. 5,
11; but Acts iv. 28 'decreed'). Under this influence the Authorized Version adopted 'predestinate' as its ordinary rendering
of προορίζω (Rom. viii. 29, 30, Eph. i. 5, 11), while continuing
to follow Tindale at Acts iv. 28 'determined before,' I Cor.
ii. 7 'ordained,' as well as at Rom. i. 4 'declared,' in margin
'Greek determined.' Thus the word, tentatively introduced
into a single passage by Tindale, seemed to have intrenched
itself as the stated English representative of an important
Greek term. The Revised Version has, however, dismissed it
altogether from the English Bible and adopted in its stead the
hybrid compound 'foreordained' as its invariable representative of προορίζω (Acts iv. 28, Rom. viii. 29, 30, I Cor. ii. 7,
Eph. i. 5, 11),—in this recurring substantially to the language
of Wyclif and the preferred rendering of Tindale. None other
than a literary interest, however, can attach to the change
thus introduced: 'foreordain' and 'predestinate' are exact
synonyms, the choice between which can be determined only

by taste. The somewhat widespread notion that the seven-teenth century theology distinguished between them, rests on a misapprehension of the evidently carefully-adjusted usage of them in the Westminster Confession, iii. 3 ff. This is not, however, the result of the attribution to the one word of a 'stronger' or to the other of a 'harsher' sense than that borne by its fellow, but a simple sequence of a current employment of 'predestination' as the precise synonym of 'election,' and a resultant hesitation to apply a term of such precious associa-tions to the foreordination to death. Since then the tables have been quite turned, and it is questionable whether in popular speech the word 'predestinate' does not now bear an unpleasant suggestion.

That neither word occurs in the English Old Testament is due to the genius of the Hebrew language, which does not admit of such compound terms. Their place is taken in the Old Testament, therefore, by simple words expressive of pur-posing, determining, ordaining, with more or less contextual indication of previousness of action. These represent a variety of Hebrew words, the most explicit of which is perhaps יָצַר (Ps. cxxxix. 16, Isa. xxii. 11, xxxvii. 26, xlvi. 11), by the side of which must be placed, however, יָעַץ (Isa. xiv. 24, 26, 27, xix. 12, xix. 17, xxiii. 9, Jer. xlix. 20, l. 45), whose substantival derivative עֵצָה (Job xxxviii. 2, xlii. 3, Jer. xxiii. 19, Prov. xix. 21, Ps. xxxiii. 11, cvii. 11, Isa. xiv. 26, xlvi. 10, 11, Ps. cvi. 13, Isa. v. 19, xix. 17, Jer. xlix. 20, l. 45, Mic. iv. 12) is doubtless the most precise Hebrew term for the Divine plan or purpose, al-though there occurs along with it in much the same sense the term מַחֲשָׁבָה (Jer. xviii. 11, xxix. 11, xlix. 30, l. 45, Isa. lv. 8, Jer. li. 29, Mic. iv. 12, Ps. xcii. 6, a derivative of חָשַׁב (Gen. l. 20, Mic. ii. 3, Jer. xviii. 11, xxvi. 3, xxix. 11, xxxvi. 3, xlix. 50, l. 45, Lam. ii. 8). In the Aramaic portion of Daniel (iv. 14 (17), 21 (24) the common later Hebrew designation of the Divine decree (used especially in an evil sense) גְּזֵרָה occurs: and חק is occasionally used with much the same meaning (Ps. ii. 7, Zeph. ii. 2, Ps. cv. 10 = I Chron. xvi. 17, Job xxiii. 14). Other words of similar import are זָמַם (Jer. iv. 28, li. 12, Lam. ii. 19,

Zec. i. 6, viii. 14, 15) with its substantive מְזִמָּה (Job xlii. 2,
Jer. xxiii. 20, xxx. 24, li. 11); חָפֵץ (Ps. cxv. 3, cxxxv. 6, Prov.
xxi. 1, Isa. lv. 11, Jon. i. 14, Judg. xiii. 23, Isa. ii. 25, Isa. liii. 10)
with its substantive חֵפֶץ (Isa. xlvi. 10, xliv. 28, xlviii. 14, liii.
10); חָרַץ (Job xiv. 5, Isa. x. 22, 23, xxviii. 22, Dan. ix. 26, 27,
xi. 36); חָתַךְ (Dan. ix. 24); הוֹאִיל (I Sam. xii. 22, I Chron. xvii.
27, II Sam. vii. 29). To express that special act of predestination
which we know as 'election,' the Hebrews commonly utilized
the word בָּחַר (of Israel, Deut. iv. 37, vii. 6, 7, x. 15, xiv. 2, Isa.
xli. 8, 9, xliii. 10, 30, xliv. 1, 2, Jer. xxxiii. 24; and of the future,
Isa. xiv. 1, lxv. 9, 15, 22; of Jehovah's servant, xlii. 1, xlix. 7;
of Jerusalem, Deut. xii. 14, 18, 26, xiv. 25, xv. 20, xvi. 7, 15, 16,
xvii. 8, 10, xviii. 6, xxxi. 11, Jos. ix. 27, I Kings viii. 44, 48, xi.
13, 32, 36, xiv. 21, II Kings xxi. 7, xxiii. 27) with its substantive
בָּחִיר (exclusively used of Jehovah's 'elect,' II Sam. xxi. 6, I
Chron. xvi. 13, Ps. lxxxix. 4, cv. 6, 43, cvi. 5, 23, Isa. xlii. 1, xliii.
20, xlv. 4, lxv. 9, 15, 22), and occasionally the word יָדַע in a pregnant sense (Gen. xviii. 19, Amos iii. 2, Hos. xiii. 5, cf. Ps. i. 6,
xxxi. 8(7), xxxvii. 18, Isa. lviii. 3); while it is rather the execution of this previous choice in an act of separation that is
expressed by הִבְדִּיל (Lev. xx. 24, xx. 26, I Kings viii. 53).

In the Greek of the New Testament the precise term
προορίζω (Acts iv. 28, I Cor. ii. 7, Rom. viii. 29, 30, Eph. i. 5,
11) is supplemented by a number of similar compounds, such
as προτάσσω (Acts xvii. 26); προτίθημι (Eph. i. 9) with its
more frequently occurring substantive, πρόθεσις (Rom. viii.
28, ix. 11, Eph. i. 11, iii. 11, II Tim. i. 9); προετοιμάζω (Rom.
ix. 23, Eph. ii. 10) and perhaps προβλέπω in a similar sense of
providential pre-arrangement (Heb. xi. 40), with which may
be compared also προεῖδον (Acts ii. 31, Gal. iii. 8); προγιγ-
νώσκω (Rom. viii. 29, xi. 2, I Pet. i. 20) and its substantive
πρόγνωσις (I Pet. i. 2, Acts ii. 23); προχειρίζω (Acts xxii. 14,
iii. 20) and προχειροτονέω (Acts iv. 41). Something of the same
idea is, moreover, also occasionally expressed by the simple
ὁρίζω (Luke xxii. 22, Acts xvii. 26, 31, ii. 23, Heb. iv. 7, Acts
x. 42), or through the medium of terms designating the will,
wish, or good-pleasure of God, such as βουλή (Luke vii. 30,

Acts ii. 23, iv. 28, xiii. 36, xx. 27, Eph. i. 11, Heb. vi. 17, cf. βούλημα Rom. ix. 19 and βούλομαι Heb. vi. 17, Jas. i. 18, II Pet. iii. 9), θέλημα (e.g., Eph. i. 5, 9, 11, Heb. x. 7, cf. θέλησις Heb. ii. 4, θέλω, e.g., Rom. ix. 18, 22), εὐδοκία (Luke ii. 14, Eph. i. 5, 9, Phil. ii. 13, cf. εὐδοκέω Luke xii. 32, Col. i. 19, Gal. i. 15, I Cor. i. 21). The standing terms in the New Testament for God's sovereign choice of His people are ἐκλέγεσθαι, in which both the composition and voice are significant (Eph. i. 4, Mark xiii. 20, John xv. 16 twice, 19, I Cor. i. 27 twice, Jas. ii. 5; of Israel, Acts xiii. 17; of Christ, Luke ix. 35; of the disciples, Luke vi. 13, John vi. 70, xiii. 18, Acts i. 2; of others, Acts i. 24, xv. 7), ἐκλεκτός (Matt. [xx. 16] xxii. 14, xxvi. 22, 24, 31, Mark xiii. 20, 22, 27, Luke xviii. 7, Rom. viii. 33, Col. iii. 12, II Tim. ii. 10, Tit. i. 1, I Pet. i. 1, [ii. 9], Rev. xvii. 14; of individuals, Rom. xvi. 13, II John i. 13; of Christ, Luke xxiii. 35, John xiii. 18; of angels, I Tim. v. 21), ἐκλογή Acts ix. 15, Rom. ix. 11. xi. 5, 7, 28, I Thes. i. 4, II Pet. i. 10),—words which had been prepared for this New Testament use by their employment in the Septuagint—the two former to translate בָּחַר and בָּחִיר. In II Thes. ii. 13 αἱρέομαι is used similarly.

CHAPTER XII

ARE THEY FEW THAT BE SAVED?*

THE *paucitas salvandorum* has long ranked among a wide circle of theologians as an established dogma. To cite only a couple of examples from the great Lutheran systematists of the seventeenth century, John Gerhard (1621) and John Andrew Quenstedt (1685), uncle and nephew, both teach it without misgiving. Speaking of what he calls "the object of eternal life," "Gerhard remarks,[1] that so far as sinners of the human race are concerned, they are first of all "few." "No doubt," he adds in the wish to do justice to the whole subject, "if the elect are considered *in themselves* and *absolutely,* their number is sufficiently large (Rev. 7:9: 'After these things I saw and behold a great multitude which no man could number out of every nation, and of all tribes and peoples and tongues, standing before the throne and before the Lamb, in white robes and palms in their hands'). But if they are considered *comparatively,* that is in comparison with the company of the lost, they are and are said to be few. Without any contradiction, therefore, the Scriptures assert that 'many shall come from the east and the west, and shall sit down with Abraham and Isaac and Jacob in the kingdom of heaven' (Matt. 18:11), and that 'there are few that be saved' (Lk. 13:23), that 'the gate is narrow and the way straitened that leadeth unto life, and few are they that find it' (Mat. 7:14; Lk. 13:24), that 'many are called but few chosen' (Mat. 20:16; 22:14)." Similarly, Quenstedt, in enumerating the "attributes" of the elect and of the reprobate—synonyms of the saved and the lost—gives the primary place in the two instances respectively to "fewness" and "multitudinousness." "The attributes of the elect," says he,[2] "are (1). *Fewness,*

* *Lutheran Church Review,* 1915, pp. 42-58.
[1] Loci Communes, Ed. Cotta, 1781, Vol. XX, p. 518.
[2] Theologia Didactica-Polemica, 1715, tom. II. col. 30.

as is taught in Mat. 20:16; 22:14 and elsewhere. 'Many are called but few chosen.' Here ὀλίγοι 'few' are opposed to τοῖς πολλοῖς, 'many,' or πασῖν, 'all,' as is shown by the lucid contrast made by Christ. But Christ contrasts, not *election* and *vocation,* but the number of the *elect* and of the *called.* If it be asked why the lesser part of men are elected and the larger part repro- bated, the answer is that, according to the counsel of God, *believers* who are few are the elect, and *unbelievers* who are many are the reprobate. Because there are few that believe, there are also few who are elected." And again[3]: "The attributes of the reprobate are (1) *multitudinousness.* For, because many are unbelieving, therefore also many are reprobated. It is there- fore said, 'Few are chosen' (Mat. 20:16), in comparison, that is, with the far greater multitude of the reprobate. The Saviour intimates the same thing in Mat. 7:13 f., saying: 'Enter in by the narrow gate, for wide is the gate and broad is the way that leadeth unto destruction; and many are they that enter in thereby. For narrow is the gate and straitened the way that leadeth unto life, and few are they that find it.' Observe, the gates are wide and narrow, and the two ways are broad and strait. The broad way leads to death, the strait to life; the former is trodden by many, the latter is found by few."[4]

The firmness with which this dogma is held could scarcely receive a more striking illustration than is afforded by the neces- sity under which Abraham Kuyper seems to feel that he rests,

---

[3] Col. 34.

[4] We add in a note a parallel example from a Reformed divine of the same general standing. John Henry Heidegger, Corpus Theologiae Christianae, 1700, Vol. I, p. 109 (Locus, V. §4), writes as follows: "Not only did God not elect all, but not even most, but a few. For, although the elect are, absolutely, suffi- ciently many, πολλοί. 'Many shall come from the east and the west, and shall sit down with Abraham, Isaac and Jacob in the Kingdom of heaven' (Mat. 8: 11), 'To the general assembly and church of the first born which are written in heaven' (Heb. 12: 23), 'A great multitude which no man can number out of every nation and tribe, and people and tongue' (Rev. 7: 9); yet, comparatively to those who are not elect, the elect are said to be few, 'Many are called, ὀλίγοι, few, are chosen' (Mat. 20: 16), 'Narrow and straitened is the way which leads to life and ὀλίγοι, few, are those who find it' (Mat. 16: 9), 'Fear not μικρὸν ποίμνιον, little flock, for it is the Father's good pleasure to give you the King- dom' (Lu. 12: 32)."

of bringing into harmony with it the great fact on which he has repeatedly and very fruitfully insisted, that it is "mankind as an organic whole which is saved" and the lost are accordingly only individuals who have been cut off from the stem of humanity.[5] "Ask," he finely says, on one occasion,[6] "whether God has deserted since the fall this, His splendid creation, this human race with all its treasure of His image,—in a word, *this His world,* in order that, casting it aside, He may create *an entirely new somewhat* out of and for the elect. And the answer of the Scriptures is a decided negative. . . . If we liken mankind, thus, as it has grown up out of Adam, to a tree, then the elect are not leaves which have been plucked off from the tree that there may be braided from them a wreath for God's glory, while the tree itself is to be felled, rooted up and cast into the fire; but precisely the contrary, the lost are the branches, twigs and leaves which have fallen away from the stem of mankind, while the elect alone remain attached to it. Not the stem itself goes to destruction, leaving only a few golden leaflets strewn on the fields of eternal light, but, on the contrary, the stem, the tree, the race abides, and what is lost is broken from the stem and loses its organic connection." Nevertheless he conceives him-

---

[5] Encyclopedia of Sacred Theology, E. T., pp. 283-4. It is worth observing that Robert J. Breckinridge from an apparently opposite standpoint (verbally at least) would not feel it impossible to adjust himself to the view that the greater part of the race are saved. "The human race," he says (The Knowledge of God, Objectively Considered, 1869, p. 513), "is not a restored race, out of which a certain number are lost; but it is a fallen race out of which a certain number are saved. It is logically immaterial what the proportions of the lost and saved to the whole race, and to each other, may be; but the question as to the mode is vital as regards the possibility of any salvation at all. . . . The race is lost, with a portion of it—far the greater portion it may be—saved through the free, sovereign, efficacious, spiritual grace of God." So far as Dr. Breckinridge is contending that the human race as a whole has not been first redeemed, and out of the redeemed race subsequently some are lost, Dr. Kuyper would agree with him; and so far as he thinks that this is best expressed by saying that saved humanity (however large in number) is not the human race, but something else created out of the salvage of the human race, Dr. Kuyper would disagree with him.

[6] E Voto Dordraceno, Vol. II, pp. 176-178; cf. De Gemeene Gratie, Vol. II, pp. 91-92; Uit het Woord, pp. 237 ff; College-Dictaat: De Peccato, p. 130, and De Ecclesia, pp. 18 ff.

self bound to explain that the tree of humanity which abides
may be, and in point of fact is, less in actual mass than the
branches which are broken off for the burning. It is of the very
nature of an organic as distinguished from a mechanical object,
he argues, that it can suffer changes—even such as contract and
curtail it—without losing its identity. "The human race," he
explains,[7] "is thus to be compared to a tree which has been
pruned and now again shoots up in a smaller size. The ruin of
the *genus humanum* is not restored in its entirety; it becomes
in its reconstitution an organism of smaller proportions. The
Church, thus, conceived as the reconstitution of the human
race, forms an organism of smaller compass, but the organism
itself undergoes no change from this. Taken thus relatively, in
comparison with the compass which the organism had earlier,
the Church is a little flock. Taken absolutely, on the other hand,
it is a great host which no man can number. The idea of some
Christians that the whole of Europe is sometime to be Christianized, and after a while the entirety of the human race is to
bow the knee to Jesus, cannot be maintained. The Holy Scriptures contradict this erroneous idea: Mat. 20:16, 'For many are
called, but few chosen,' Mat. 7:14; Lk. 13:23."

The *dicta probantia,* relied upon for the establishment of
this dogma of the fewness of the saved, are, as will have been
observed from the instances cited, ordinarily[8] these four: Mat.

[7] College-Dictaat, Locus De Ecclesia, p. 36. Herman Bavinck, Gereformeerde Dogmatiek, Edition 2, Vol. IV, 1911, p. 84, thinks we can know nothing
of the relative number of the saved and lost, but is sure that the organism is
preserved. "Though many may fall away, however that may disturb us, nevertheless the communion, humanity, the world is saved by Christ. The organism
of the creation is restored. Sinners are consumed out of the earth (Ps. 104: 35),
they are cast out (Jno. 12: 31; 15: 6; Rev. 22: 15). But all things, in heaven
and on earth, are summed up in Christ (Eph. 1: 10). All things have been
created through Him and unto Him (Col. 1: 16)."

[8] We may take it as a proof of the fixity of this tradition of proof texts what
a writer so far removed from the general current of orthodox tradition as
S. Hoekstra, Christelijke Geloofsleer, 1898, Vol. II, p. 338, says simply: "According to the Gospels (Mat. 7:13; cf. 20:16; 22:14; Luk. 13:23) the greater
number are lost." Jonathan Edwards, "Original Sin," I, i, 7 (four volumes ed.
Works, New York, 1856, II, p. 343) appeals to the same four passages (to
which some Old Testament passages are added subsidiarily) for the more

7:14 f.; Luke 13:23 f.; Mat. 20:16; 22:14. As Mat. 20:16, a mere repetition in any event of Mat. 22:14, is spurious, the proof texts reduce to the three following, which we reproduce from the American Revised Version. "And one said unto him, Lord, are they few that are saved? And He said unto them, Strive to enter in by the narrow door: for many, I say unto you, shall seek to enter in, and shall not be able." (Luke 13: 23 f.) "Enter ye in by the narrow gate: for wide is the gate, and broad is the way that leadeth to destruction, and many are they that enter in thereby. For narrow is the gate and straitened the way that leadeth into life, and few are they that find it." (Mat. 7:13 f.) "For many are called, but few chosen." (Mat. 22:14.)

A scrutiny of these passages will make it sufficiently apparent that they do not form an adequate basis for the tremendous conclusion which has been founded on them. In all of them alike our Lord's purpose is rather ethical impression than prophetic disclosure. Spoken out of the immediate circumstances of the time to the immediate needs of those about Him, His words supply valid motives to action to all who find themselves with similar needs in like circumstances; but they cannot be read as assurances that the circumstances intimated or implied are necessarily constant and must remain forever unchanged. What He says is directed to inciting His hearers to strenuous effort to make their calling and election sure, rather than to revealing to them the final issue of His saving work in the world. When we read His words in the latter sense, we, therefore, do a certain violence to them; in deflecting them from their purpose we distort also their meaning and confuse their implications. We can always learn from these passages that salvation is difficult and that it is our duty to address ourselves to obtaining it with diligence and earnest effort. We can never learn from them how many are saved.

With respect to Luke 13:23, 24, this is obvious on the face

---

legitimate purpose of showing that the world is not full of good men,—"the exceeding smallness of the number of the saints compared with the whole world."

of it.[9] The mere fact that Luke has introduced this question and its answer immediately after his record of the two parables of the mustard seed and the leaven in the meal (13:18-21) is evidence enough that he at least saw no intimation in our Lord's declaration that the number of the saved would be few. Theodor Zahn even goes the length of supposing that Luke was led to introduce this question and answer at this point, precisely by his record of these parables. The recognition in them that the Kingdom of God was in its beginnings small and insignificant suggested to him to record the question which these small and insignificant beginnings raised in the mind of one of Jesus' followers and Jesus' response to it.[10] However that may be, it surely would in any event have been impossible for Luke thus to bring simply into immediate conjunction words of our Lord which announce the complete conquest of the world by His Kingdom and words of our Lord which declare that only a few shall be saved.

Meanwhile it is clear that the questioner in our passage spoke under the oppression of the pitiful weakness of the Kingdom as it presented itself to his observation. Certainly Jesus had attracted to His person only a "little flock," and to them He had distinctly promised the Kingdom (12:32). He had been intimating, moreover, ever more and more clearly of late, the exclusion from the Kingdom of the great mass of the people. And His face was now set towards Jerusalem (verse 22).[11] We

[9] "But He said to them, Strive to go in by the narrow door, for many, I say to you, shall try to go in and shall not have power" (or "shall not prevail"). Note the plain directness of the language.

[10] Das Evangelium des Lucas ausgelegt, 1913, p. 533: "Since a historical connection between the question directed to Jesus (verse 23), whether only a few are to be saved, and what precedes is indicated by nothing, Luke is led to annex the question with Jesus' response here by the connection between the idea expressed in the parables (verses 18-20) and that expressed in the question of His adherent (verse 23). Jesus had fully recognized in these two parables the fact that the Kingdom of God was at the time a small and insignificant thing. . . ."

[11] Calvin, Harmony of the Evangelists. E. T., Vol. I, p. 358, already finds the occasion of the question in the small number of disciples that Jesus had as yet collected and the apparent rejection by Him of the whole nation. "A similar doubt steals upon us," he adds, applying the matter, according to his wont, to

may fancy the questioner either as deeply troubled by the puzzling situation,[12] or as rather pluming himself on belonging to so exclusive a circle.[13] But whether speaking out of a heavy heart or out of a light head,[14] the question he put was a natural one in the circumstances.

Our Lord, however, gives no direct response to the question put to Him. He only makes it the occasion of addressing to those about Him[15] (among whom the questioner is, of course, included) an exhortation and a warning. They are to "strive to go in by the narrow door"—that is the exhortation. And the warning is: "Because many shall try to go in and shall not have the power." The important thing for them is not, to know whether few or many are saved, but, to address themselves strenuously to their own salvation. There is no revelation here accordingly that only a few are saved; there is a solemn declaration that many of those who seek to be saved fail. It is, in other words, not the number of the saved that is announced, but the difficulty of salvation. The point of the remark is that salvation is not to be assumed by any one as a matter of course, but is to be sought with earnest and persistent effort.[16] We must fight[17] if we would win; it is in its due application true of all, everywhere and always, that they must enter into the Kingdom of God through many tribulations (Acts 14:22).

The meaning of Mat. 7:13-14, though somewhat more complicated, is scarcely less clear[18] than that of Luke 13:23, 24.

ourselves, "when we look at the melancholy condition of the world." Christ, he says, withdraws His people "from a foolish curiosity" "as if they were unwilling to be saved but in a crowd," and bids believers "to give their earnest attention" to obtaining life for themselves.

[12] So apparently Zahn.

[13] So Hahn.

[14] Zahn's language.

[15] Contrast: "And one said unto Him" with "And He said unto them."

[16] A. B. Bruce in loc.: "In the interpretation, the one point to be insisted on is: be in earnest."

[17] ἀγωνίζεσθε.

[18] "Go in by the narrow gate: for broad and roomy is the way that leads off to destruction, and many are those who go in by it; for narrow is the gate and straitened the way that leads off to life, and few are those who find it." Note the fulness and vividness of the language.

The chief formal difference between the two passages is that what is only implied in Luke—the wide door contrasting with the narrow, the two ways leading respectively to the two doors —is brought into open view in Matthew, and the whole scene is painted in detail for us. The characteristic of Matthew's account is, indeed, picturesque vividness, and we shall understand it best if we will visualize it as a picture; if we will summon up in our imagination the broad and roomy road running off on the one side, crowded with passengers, and the hemmed in and constricted pathway passing through its narrow gate on the other, with only a sparse traveller on it here and there; and hear our Lord say as He points the two out, This leads off to destruction, that to life: go in by the narrow gate! It is nevertheless just Luke's "Strive to go in by the narrow door" over again, presented more vividly and drawn out more fully. The lesson is the same; the exhortation is the same; and though the motive adduced is less explicit than in Luke, it, too, is the same. The specialty of Luke's account is the emphasis with which it throws up the difficulty of the task: the exhortation is to strenuous endeavor, "strive"; and the motive adduced is the failure of many to compass the task, "for many, I say to you, shall try to go in and shall not prevail." In Matthew's account, the difficulty of the task is no less the underlying motive of the exhortation, but it is not so openly asserted. It is left to be implied by the contrast between the wideness and roominess of the road that leads off to destruction, and the narrowness of the gate and the constriction of the way that lead off to life; and the consequent populousness of the one road and the fewness of those by whom the other is discovered.[19] A. B. Bruce says, quite erroneously: "The passage itself contains no clue to the right way except that it is the way of *the few*." The mark of the right way, on the contrary, is presented as that, in contrast with the broad, ample and smooth road which leads to destruction, it is

[19] Observe the "find," as if it had to be looked for to be discovered. The Glossa Ordinaria says significantly of the broad road on the other hand: "This, though they do not seek it, all nevertheless find, because they are born in it." This is certainly true, but perhaps not perfectly apposite to the similitude: say, rather, "because it appeals to their natural dispositions."

narrow and constricted and hard to travel.[20] That there are many who enter in by the one road and few who find the other is presented as merely the result of the difference in the roads themselves,—that the one is inviting and easy, the other repellent and difficult. The lesson that is taught, therefore, is not that there are few that are saved but that the way of life is hard. It is, therefore, that the fundamental exhortation was not "Go with the few!" but "Go in by the narrow gate!"[21]

No doubt in the picture presented to our gaze the broad and roomy road is represented as crowded with journeyers and the straitened way as followed only by a few. A contrast is thus drawn between those who enter through the broad and roomy road as many, and those who find the narrow gate and straitened way as few. It is not unnatural to read this as intended to teach that the number of the saved in general is inconsiderable, at least in comparison with the number of the lost. Nevertheless it would be wrong thus to transmute this vivid transcript of a phase of life into a didactic assertion of the ultimate proportions of the saved and lost. We should be warned against such mechanical dealings with our Lord's similitudes by a remembrance of parallel instances. There is no more reason to suppose that this similitude teaches that the saved shall be fewer than the lost than there is to suppose that the parable of the Ten Virgins (Mat. 25:1 ff.) teaches that they shall be precisely equal in number: and there is far less reason to suppose that this similitude teaches that the saved shall be few comparatively to the lost than there is to suppose that the parable of the Tares in

---

[20] Cf. Zahn, Des Evangelium des Matthaeus ausgelegt, 1903, p. 310: "In verses 13 ff. a new mark is given by which the disciples may recognize whether they are in the right way. The emphasis lies . . . as the reason assigned shows, on the choice of the narrow gate. . . . We must go through the narrow gate, because only the gateway which leads to destruction is broad and roomy. As a natural consequence of this it appears that many choose this way. . . ."

[21] Certainly our Lord could not in any case be supposed to lay it down as a universal rule of life: "Go with the few!" There seems no reason, however, why we may not suppose that by the introduction of this mark of the way of life—that few travel it—He may have had the secondary purpose in view of (besides emphasizing the difficulty of the road) protecting His followers from the inference that their cause is bad because few embrace it.

the Wheat (Mat. 13:24 ff.) teaches that the lost shall be inconsiderable in number in comparison with the saved—for that,
indeed, is an important part of the teaching of that parable.
What we have in our present similitude is merely a vivid picture
of life, true to the life that lay before the eyes of those our
Saviour was addressing; true, no doubt, too, to the life that lies
still before our eyes after two thousand years have passed; and
therefore carrying home to their consciences and to ours with
poignancy and effect the fundamental teaching of the similitude—that the way of life is hard and it is our first duty to
address ourselves with vigor to walking firmly in it. But why
must we say that this similitude must be equally true to life
always and everywhere? Can there be no community—has there
never been a community, is there no community today—however small, in which, happily, the majority of the inhabitants
have deserted the broad and ample road that leads to destruction and are pursuing the straitened way through the narrow
gate that leads to life? And as the years and centuries and ages
flow on, can it never be—is it not to be—that the proportions
following "the two ways" shall be reversed? There is nothing in
this vivid picture of the life of man as falling under the observation of our Lord's hearers—and our own—to forbid the hope—
or expectation—of such a reversal.[22] That could be only if it
were didactically asserted that in the ultimate distribution of
the awards of human life, few are to be found among the saved,
many among the lost. That is so far from the case here, however,
that the proportions of travellers on the two ways are introduced only incidentally and for the purpose of giving point to
another lesson,—the difficulty of salvation and the consequent
duty of effort in seeking it. If there be any intimation elsewhere
in the Scriptures that the proportions of the travellers on the

22 Cf. A. Tholuck, Commentary on the Sermon on the Mount, E. T., p. 417:
"Here He describes simply the actual facts of the case at the time when He
spoke, and neither generally of the present αἰών nor of that which is to come
(Mat. 12:32)." Also A. H. Strong (quoting Alvah Hovey, Biblical Eschatology,
p. 167), Systematic Theology, ed. 2, p. 599; last ed., p. 1054: "It seems to be
intended to describe the conduct of men then living, rather than to foreshadow
the two opposite currents of human life to the end of time."

two roads may be altered as time goes on, there is no reason why we should insist, on the basis of this passage, that there must always be few following the narrow way and many the wide—with the result that the sum in the one case shall to the end remain small and in the other shall by the end become enormous. And when we have said that we have already said that the passage supplies in no case any real ground for such an assumption.

There is no more reason to suppose that our Lord intends to sum up the whole history of redemption in the words of Matt. 22:14.[23] The parable of which these words form the concluding clause is no doubt historical in its teaching; it pictures the offering of the Kingdom of God to the Jews by the prophets and the apostles and their rejection of it; and then the turning to the Gentiles and the gathering of the mixed body of the external church. It is with His eye on the rejection of the invitation of the Kingdom by the Jews and the sifting out of the unworthy among the Gentiles, symbolized by the single figure of verses 12 and 13, that our Lord sums up the results of this history in the words rendered in our English versions, "For many are called but few chosen."[24] For a right estimate of the meaning of these words it is important to determine whether

[23] James Moffat, The New Testament, etc., 1913, renders: "For many are invited, but few are chosen." Perhaps we may even translate: "For many are bidden, but few accepted." Crisp conciseness is the characteristic of the clause.

[24] There is no doubt a difficulty in interpreting these words in their relation to the parable, arising from the circumstance that the parable itself does not obviously suggest that the proportion of the bidden and the accepted is that of many and few. If the whole body of those first bidden scorned the invitation, their place seems to have been fully supplied by their successors: "The wedding was filled with guests." And only a single one of these guests was found without a wedding garment. A. Jülicher Die Gleichnisreden Jesu, Vol. II, 1899, p. 427, makes use of this circumstance to argue a composite origin for the parable as it stands. The final clause, for instance, though a genuine gnome of Jesus', does not belong to this parable, but has been attached to it by Matthew. We are at least warned not to put too much pressure on details of representation; and we may, as Jülicher indeed suggests, fairly suppose that the single man represented as without a wedding garment may be only a symbol of what might more numerously occur.

they form part of the parable itself, the closing words of the king, or (cf. Matt. 18:35) are an addition by our Lord in His own person, summing up the teaching of the parable.[25] In the latter case the terms employed in the saying need not be and probably are not, but in the former case—which seems assuredly the true case[26]—they cannot be and certainly are not, technical theological terms, analogous to, though not identical in signification with, the terms "called," "elect," which meet us in the didactic portions of the New Testament; but must find their explanation in the foregoing narrative. As this narrative is told, there had been many bidden to the marriage feast, and comparatively few, perhaps, approved; and it must be presumed that it is this experience which the king sums up in his closing words—if they be his. If they be, on the other hand, our Lord's own words summing up the teaching of His parable, it is still most natural to suppose that He confines Himself in His summing up to the bit of history which He had recited and speaks from the standpoint of the moment rather than that of the distant Judgment Day. The bit of history which the parable portrays, however, relates only the contemptuous and ultimately violent rejection of the Kingdom of God by the Jews and the consequent turning to the Gentiles with the result of attracting to it a mixed multitude. This situation is very fairly summarized in the words: "Many are bidden, but few accepted." It would in any event be incredibly harsh to take the word "called" here with any other reference than that in which "call," "called" are repeatedly used in the earlier portion of the parable. Whether, then, we assign the words to the king or to Jesus Himself, speaking outside the limits of the parable, their reference seems confined to the historical experience re-

25 Jülicher considers this matter unimportant. The words mean the same thing in either case and it is indifferent whether they are represented as spoken by the King who stands for God or by Jesus who is the Son of God. But this seems scarcely to allow for the increased certainty in the former case that the terms employed are not technical terms.

26 So e.g. James Moffat.

lated in the parable, and that is as much as to say to the days of the founding of the Church.[27]

It is therefore that Calvin in his comment on the passage contents himself with saying: "I do not enter into a searching discussion here of the eternal election of God, because the words of Christ have no other meaning than that an external profession of faith is not at all a sufficient proof that God will acknowledge as His own all who appear to have accepted His invitation."[28] That, of course, is spoken on the supposition that the reference of the words is only to the immediately preceding verses, which describe the casting out of the man who had not on a wedding garment. If the reference be broadened, as it would seem that it should be, to the whole series of invitations described in the parable and their results,[29] the lesson must be correspondingly broadened to something like—if we may borrow Jülicher's words without attaching ourselves too closely to his meaning—"The enjoyment of the Kingdom of God is connected with quite other conditions than merely having been invited."[30] Perhaps we may say that the meaning is simply that there are many who have been invited to the gospel feast who do not really belong there; and that our Lord's ethical intention —always a foremost thing in our Lord's teaching—is, like that of Mat. 7:13 f., Luke 13:23 f., to incite His hearers to see to it that they both respond to the invitation of the Gospel and live according to it. This is finely brought out by Melanchthon[31] in the intimation that the declaration contains for us a consolation and a warning: a consolation—by reminding us, when we see so many hypocrites in the church, that, after all, there is a true

[27] Cf. A. Loisy, Les Synoptiques, Vol. II, p. 329: "It is difficult to say whether the sentence, 'Many are called but few chosen' which forms the conclusion of the parable is to be put on the lips of the King or on those of Jesus. It is self-evident that this sentence does not concern the theological question of predestination, and does not refer to the absolute relation of vocation to election. . . ." Cf. also Zahn in loc., p. 631.

[28] Calvini Opera. Ed. Baum, Cunitz and Reuss, Vol. XIV, p. 402; E. T. Harmony of the Evangelists, Vol. II, p. 175.

[29] So Zahn.

[30] P. 427.

[31] Corpus Operum, Vol. IX, p. 951 f.

church within the church; and a warning, for ourselves to make our calling and election sure.

The weakness of the basis for a dogma of *paucitas salvandorum* supplied by these passages cannot be buttressed by the adduction of other passages of similar nature. Passages of similar nature are somewhat difficult to discover; and they naturally rest under similar disabilities. Perhaps the most notable of those which readily suggest themselves is I Peter 3:20. There we are told that "a few, that is eight souls," escaped in the ark through the water, and this is presented as a type of Christians passing through the water of baptism to safety.[32] The express mention of the fewness of those saved in the ark is certainly noticeable, and suggests that Peter was writing out of a keen sense of the fewness of those whom he saw typified by this escape.[33] This being granted, however, we are scarcely justified in going on and seeing here an assertion of the fewness of the saved as the ultimate fact of all Christian development. Why may we not rather see here the reflection in Peter's consciousness of his own experience of the first proclamation of Christianity? Unquestionably it was in very small beginnings that the Kingdom of God began; or, perhaps, the right form of statement is that the Kingdom of God has begun—for is not this church of the twentieth century still the primitive church?"[34]

[32] In this mode of statement we are following Charles Bigg, *in loc.* It is more common to take "through the water" instrumentally.

[33] Cf. J. E. Huther *in loc.*: "The antithesis which exists between ὑμᾶς and the preceding ὀλίγοι indicates that the proportion saved by baptism to the unbelieving is but small. ὀλίγοι has accordingly a typical significance." Cf. also E. H. Plumtre, *in loc.*: "In the stress laid upon the 'few' that were thus saved, we may legitimately recognize the impression made by our Lord's answer to the question: Are there few that be saved? (Lu. 13:23.) The apostle looked round him and saw that those who were in the way of salvation were few in number. He looked back upon the earliest records of the work of a preaching of repentance and found that there also few only were delivered." C. Bigg also thinks that ὀλίγοι may be a reminiscence of Lu. 13:23.

[34] A truth much too often forgotten, which has its application to our subject, too, is enunciated by William Temple, Foundations, 1913, p. 340 note: "The earth will in all probability be habitable for myriads of years yet. If Christianity is the final religion, the church is still in its infancy. Two thousand years are as two days. The appeal to the 'primitive church' is misleading; we are the

To our Lord, to His apostles, to His followers up to today the Kingdom of God has been like the mustard seed, "which indeed is less than all seeds," or like a mere speck of leaven which is lost in the meal in which it is buried. (Mat. 13:31-35.) E. H. Plumtre is not without a measure of justification, therefore, when he writes: "The sad contrast between the many and the few runs through all our Lord's teaching. He came to 'save the world,' and yet those whom He chooses out of the world are but a 'little flock.' The picture is a dark one; and yet it represents but too faithfully the impression made—I do not say on Calvinist or even Christian, but on any ethical teacher—by the actual state of mankind around us." What saves the picture from being as dark as it is painted is that the contrast between the many and the few is not the only contrast which runs through our Lord's teaching and the teaching of His apostles. Side by side with it is the contrast between the present and the future. These small beginnings are to give way to great expansions. The grain of mustard seed when sowed in the field (which is the world) is not to remain less than all seeds: it is to become a tree in the branches of which the birds of heaven lodge. The speck of leaven is not to remain hidden in the mass of meal: it is to work through the meal until the *whole*[35] of it is leavened. The presence of this class of representations side by side with those which speak of few being saved necessarily confines the reference of the latter to the initial stages of the kingdom, and opens out the widest prospect for the reach of the saving process as time flows on; so wide a prospect as quite to reverse the

'primitive church.' " Contrast the unhappy pessimism as to the future of the church of R. A. Knox, Some Loose Stones, 1913, pp. 111 f. Cf. James Adderley, The Hibbert Journal, July, 1914 (XII: 4), p. 765: "But we must remember that Christianity is a very young religion, and that we are only at the beginning of Christian history even now."

[35] Jülicher, as cited, p. 578: ὅλον totally (ganz und gar), viz., the three measures, cf. Lu. 11:34-36"—where ὅλον is defined as meaning without the omission of any part. Cf. R. C. Trench, Notes on the Parables of our Lord, New York, 1878, p. 119: "Nor can we consider these words, 'Till the whole is leavened,' as less than a promise of the final complete triumph of the Gospel—that it will diffuse itself through all nations and purify and ennoble all life."

implications with respect to the ultimate proportions of the saved and the lost.

It does not fall within the scope of this discussion to adduce the positive evidence that the number of the saved shall in the end be not small but large, and not merely absolutely but comparatively large; that, to speak plainly, it shall embrace the immensely greater part of the human race. Its purpose has been fulfilled if it has shown that the foundation on which has been erected the contrary opinion, that the number of the saved shall be comparatively few, far the smaller part of the race, crumbles when subjected to scrutiny. For the rest it will suffice simply to remark in passing that it is the constant teaching of Scripture that Christ must reign until He shall have put all His enemies under His feet—by which assuredly spiritual, not physical, conquest is intimated; that it is inherent in the very idea of the salvation of Christ, who came as Saviour of the world, in order to save the world, that nothing less than the world shall be saved by Him; and that redemption as a remedy for sin cannot be supposed to reach its final issue until the injury inflicted by sin on the creation of God is repaired, and mankind as such is brought to the destiny originally designed for it by its creator. We must judge, therefore, that those theologians have the right of it who not merely refuse to repeat the dogma that only a few are saved, but are ready to declare with Alvah Hovey, as he brings his little book on *Biblical Eschatology*[36] to a close with a reference "to the vast preponderance of good over evil as the fruit of redemption," that "not only will order be restored throughout the universe, but the good will far outnumber the bad; the saved will be many times more than the lost."

These theologians include—to go no further afield—such honored names among prophets of our own as Charles Hodge,

[36] Pp. 167 ff. Dr. Hovey outlines a comprehensive argument for his position, throwing particular emphasis on such expressions as Eph. 1:10, 22, 23; Col. 1:11. He lays stress (with Dr. Hodge) on the salvation of all who died in infancy, and, though as less to the point (with Dr. Shedd), on the salvation of many heathen; he also (more tellingly) brings into view (like Dr. Dabney) "the duration and character" of the so-called "millennium"—which, however, he erroneously connects with Rev. 20.

Robert L. Dabney and William G. T. Shedd. "We have reason to believe," writes Charles Hodge,[37] ". . . that the number finally lost in comparison with the whole number of the saved will be very inconsiderable. Our blessed Lord, when surrounded by the innumerable company of the redeemed, will be hailed as the 'Salvator Hominum,' the Saviour of men, as the Lamb that bore the sins of the world." Robert L. Dabney, expressing regret that the fact has been "too little pressed" "that ultimately the vast majority of the whole mass of humanity, including all generations, will be actually redeemed by Christ," adds:[38] "There is to be a time, blessed be God, when literally all the then world will be saved by Christ, when the world will be finally, completely and wholly lifted by Christ out of the gulf, to sink no more. So that there is a sense, most legitimate, in which Christ is the prospective Saviour of the world." "Two errors, therefore," remarks W. G. T. Shedd,[39] "are to be avoided: First, that all men are saved; secondly, that only a few men are saved. . . . Some . . . have represented the number of the reprobated as greater than that of the elect, or equal to it. They found this upon the word of Christ, 'Many are called, but few are chosen.' But this describes the situation at the time when our Lord spake, and not the final result of His redemptive work. But when Christ shall have 'seen of the travail of His soul' and been 'satisfied' with what He has seen; when the whole course of the Gospel shall be complete, and shall be surveyed from beginning to end, it will be found that God's elect, or church, is 'a great multitude which no man can number, out of *all* nations, and kindreds, and peoples, and tongues,' and that their voice is as the voice of many waters, and as the voice of mighty thunderings, saying, 'Hallelujah, for the Lord God omnipotent reigneth.' Rev. 7:9; 19:6."

[37] Systematic Theology, Vol. III, 1876, pp. 879-880. Dr. Hodge interpreted Mat. 7:13, 14 as referring to adults only (Vol. 1, p. 26, cf. Vol. II, p. 648) and was led to throw the weight of his doctrine too heavily on the salvation of those that die in infancy.

[38] Syllabus and Notes, etc., 3d ed., 1885, p. 525.

[39] Dogmatic Theology, 1888, Vol. II, p. 712. We need not concern ourselves with Dr. Shedd's connection of this true idea with the erroneous opinion that men may be saved apart from the Gospel.

CHAPTER XIII

ON THE BIBLICAL NOTION OF "RENEWAL"[1]

THE TERMS "renew," "renewing," are not of frequent occurrence in our English Bible. In the New Testament they do not occur at all in the Gospels, but only in the Epistles (Paul and Hebrews), where they stand, respectively, for the Greek terms ἀνακαινόω (II Cor. iv. 16, Col. iii. 10) with its cognates, ἀνακαινίζω (Heb. vi. 6) and ἀνανεόομαι (Eph. iv. 23), and ἀνακαίνωσις (Rom. xii. 2, Tit. iii. 5). If we leave to one side II Cor. iv. 16 and Heb. vi. 6, which are of somewhat doubtful interpretation, it becomes at once evident that a definite theological conception is embodied in these terms. This conception is that salvation in Christ involves a radical and complete transformation wrought in the soul (Rom. xii. 2, Eph. iv. 23) by God the Holy Spirit (Tit. iii. 5, Eph. iv. 24), by virtue of which we become "new men" (Eph. iv. 24, Col. iii. 10), no longer conformed to this world (Rom. xii. 2, Eph. iv. 22, Col. iii. 9), but in knowledge and holiness of the truth created after the image of God (Eph. iv. 24, Col. iii. 10, Rom. xii. 2). The conception, it will be seen, is a wide one, inclusive of all that is comprehended in what we now technically speak of as regeneration, renovation and sanctification. It embraces, in fact, the entire subjective side of salvation, which it represents as a work of God, issuing in a wholly new creation (II Cor. v. 17, Gal. vi. 15, Eph. ii. 10). What is indicated is, therefore, the need of such a subjective salvation by sinful man, and the provision for this need made in Christ (Eph. iv. 20, Col. iii. 11, Tit. iii. 6).

The absence of the terms in question from the Gospels does not in the least argue the absence from the teaching of the Gospels of the thing expressed by them. This thing is so of the essence of the religion of revelation that it could not be absent from any stage of its proclamation. That it should be absent

[1] From *The Princeton Theological Review*, v. ix, 1911, pp. 242-267; also from *Biblical Doctrines*, pp. 439-462.

would require that sin should be conceived to have wrought no subjective injury to man, so that he would need for his recovery from sin only an objective cancelling of his guilt and reinstatement in the favor of God. This is certainly not the conception of the Scriptures in any of their parts. It is uniformly taught in Scripture that by his sin man has not merely incurred the divine condemnation but also corrupted his own heart; that sin, in other words, is not merely guilt but depravity: and that there is needed for man's recovery from sin, therefore, not merely atonement but renewal; that salvation, that is to say, consists not merely in pardon but in purification. Great as is the stress laid in the Scriptures on the forgiveness of sins as the root of salvation, no less stress is laid throughout the Scriptures on the cleansing of the heart as the fruit of salvation. Nowhere is the sinner permitted to rest satisfied with pardon as the end of salvation; everywhere he is made poignantly to feel that salvation is realized only in a clean heart and a right spirit.

In the Old Testament, for example, sin is not set forth in its origin as a purely objective act with no subjective effects, or in its manifestation as a series of purely objective acts out of all relation to the subjective condition. On the contrary, the sin of our first parents is represented as no less corrupting than inculpating; shame is as immediate a fruit of it as fear (Gen. iii. 7). And, on the principle that no clean thing can come out of what is unclean (Job xiv. 4), all that are born of woman are declared "abominable and corrupt," to whose nature iniquity alone is attractive (Job xv. 14-16). Accordingly, to become sinful, men do not wait until the age of accountable action arrives. Rather, they are apostate from the womb, and as soon as they are born go astray, speaking lies (Ps. lviii. 3): they are even shapen in iniquity and conceived in sin (Ps. li. 5). The propensity (יֵצֶר) of their heart is evil from their youth (Gen. viii. 21), and it is out of the heart that all the issues of life proceed (Prov. iv. 23, xx. 11). Acts of sin are therefore but the expression of the natural heart, which is deceitful above all things and desperately sick (Jer. xvii. 9). The only hope of an amendment of the life, lies accordingly in a change of heart; and this change of heart is the desire of God for His people (Deut. v. 29) and the passionate longing of the saints for themselves (Ps. li. 10). It is, indeed, wholly beyond man's own power to achieve it. As well might the Ethiopian hope to change his skin and the leopard his spots as he who is wonted to evil to correct his ways (Jer. xiii. 23); and when it is a matter of cleansing not of hands but of heart—who can declare that he has made his heart clean and is pure from sin (Prov. xx. 9)? Men may be exhorted to circumcise their hearts (Deut. x. 16, Jer. iv. 4), and to make themselves new hearts and new spirits (Ezek. xviii. 31); but the background of such appeals is rather the promise of God than the ability of man (Deut. v. 29, Ezek. xi. 19, cf. Keil *in loc.*). It is God alone who can "turn" a man "a new heart" (I Sam. x. 9), and the cry of the saint who has come to understand what his sin means, and therefore what cleansing from it involves, is ever, "Create (בָּרָא) in me a new heart, O God, and renew (חָדַשׁ) a steadfast spirit within me" (Ps. li. 10[12]). The express warrant for so great a prayer is afforded by the promise of God who, knowing the incapacity of the flesh, has Himself engaged to perfect His people. He will circumcise their hearts, that they may love the Lord their God with all their heart and with all their soul; and so may live (Deut. xxx. 6). He will give them a heart to know Him that He is the Lord; that so they may really be His people and He their God (Jer. xxiv. 7). He will put His law in their inward parts and write it in their heart so that all shall know Him (Jer. xxxi. 33, cf. xxxii. 39). He will take the stony heart out of their flesh and give them a heart of flesh, that they may walk in His statutes and keep His ordinances and do them, and so be His people and He their God (Ezek. xi. 19). He will give them a new heart and take away the stony heart out of their flesh; and put His Spirit within them and cause them to walk in His statutes and keep His judgments and do them: that so they may be His people and He their God (Ezek. xxxvi. 26, cf. xxxvii. 14). Thus the expectation of a new heart was made a substantial part of the Messianic promise, in which was embodied the whole hope of Israel.

It does not seem open to doubt that in these great declarations we have the proclamation of man's need of "renewal" and of the divine provision for it as an essential element in salvation.[2] We must not be misled by the emphasis placed in the Old Testament on the forgiveness of sins as the constitutive fact of salvation, into explaining away all allusions to the cleansing of the heart as but figurative expressions for pardon. Pardon is no doubt frequently set forth under the figure or symbol of washing or cleansing: but expressions such as those which have been adduced go beyond this. When, then, it is suggested[3] that Psalm li, for example, "contains only a single prayer, namely, that for forgiveness"; and that "the cry, 'Create in me a clean heart' is not a prayer for what we call renewal" but only for "forgiving grace," we cannot help thinking the contention an extravagance,—an extravagance, moreover, out of keeping with its author's language elsewhere, and indeed in this very context where he speaks quite simply of the pollution as well as the guilt of sin as included in the scope of the confession made in this psalm.[4] The word "create" is a strong one and appears to invoke from God the exertion of His almighty power for the production of a new subjective state of things: and it does not seem easy to confine the word "heart" to the signification "conscience" as if the prayer were merely that the con-

[2] "The necessity of a change of disposition for the reception of salvation is indicated (Jer. xxxi. 33, Ezek. xxxvi. 35)"—König, "Offenbarungsbegriff d.A.T.," II, p. 398, note. "Indications are not wholly lacking that some of the prophets, at least, believed man unable to make himself acceptable before God. . . . It is God who cleanses the heart and life by purging away the dross (Isa. i. 25, vi. 7, Jer. xxxi. 31-34, xxxiii. 8)"—J. M. P. Smith, "Biblical Ideas of Atonement," 1909, p. 28. "Ezekiel is even so bold as to declare that we amend our lives because God gives us a new heart and a new spirit (xi. 19)"—*Expository Times*, Feb. 1908, p. 240.

[3] Cf. A. B. Davidson, "Theology of the O. T.," p. 232.

[4] P. 234; cf. in general p. 244: There is, therefore, both guilt and pollution to be removed in the realization in Israel of the life of God. Similarly Delitzsch *in loc.*: "the prayer for justification is followed by the prayer for renewing."

science might be relieved from its sense of guilt. Moreover, the parallel clause, "Renew a steadfast spirit within me," does not readily lend itself to the purely objective interpretation.[5] That the transformation of the heart promised in the great prophetic passages must also mean more than the production of a clear conscience, is equally undeniable and indeed is not denied. When Jeremiah (xxxi. 31-33), for example, represents God as declaring that what shall characterize the New Covenant which He will make with the House of Israel, is that He will put His law in the inward parts of His people and write it in their hearts, he surely means to say that God promises to work a subjective effect in the hearts of Israel, by virtue of which their very instincts and most intimate impulses shall be on the side of the law, obedience to which shall therefore be but the spontaneous expression of their own natures.[6]

It is equally important to guard against lowering the conception of the Divine holiness in the Old Testament until the demand of God that His people shall be holy as He is holy,[7]

[5] Baethgen's comment on the verse runs: "The singer knows that for the steadfastness of heart sought in verse 8, there is needed a new creation, a rebirth. בָּרָא in the Kal is always used only of the divine production. The heart is the central organ of the whole religious moral life; the parallel רוּחַ is its synonym. Steadfast (נָכוֹן) the spirit is called so far as it does not hesitate between good and evil."

[6] Cf. e.g., A. B. Davidson, "Hastings' B.D.," i, pp. 514 sq.: "Jehovah will make a new covenant with Israel, that is, forgive their sins and write His law on their hearts—the one in His free grace, the other by His creative act"; also iv, p. 119 a, and the fine exposition of Ezek. xxxvi. 17-38 in the "Theology of the O. T.," p. 343. On the other hand Giesebrecht, "Handkom. Jer.," p. 171 thinks "Jeremiah has not yet advanced to the 'new heart' (Ezek. xi. 19, xxxvi. 26 sq., Ps. li. 12); what he is thinking of is an inner influence on the heart by divine power, so that it attains a new attitude to the contents of the law." But this divine power is certainly conceived as creative. "The prophets," says Gunkel, "Die Wirkungen des heiligen Geistes," 1909, p. 77, "were convinced that God Himself must interfere in order to produce the ideal condition which He demands. The ideal kingdom in which dwell piety and righteousness cannot, therefore, be a result of the natural development of the people, but it can come into existence only by an act of God, by a miracle, by the outpouring of the divine Spirit."

[7] Cf. Dillmann, "Alttest. Theologie," pp. 421-422.

and the provisions of His Grace to make them holy by an inner creative act, are robbed of more or less of their deeper ethical meaning. Here, too, some recent writers are at fault, speaking at times almost as if holiness in God were merely a sort of fastidiousness, over against which is set not so much all sin as uncleanness, as all uncleanness, as in this sense sin.[8] The idea is that what this somewhat squeamish God did not find agreeable those who served Him would discover it well to avoid; rather than that all sin is necessarily abominable to the holy God and He will not abide it in His servants. This lowered view is sometimes even pushed to the extreme of suggesting[9] that "it is nowhere intimated that there is any danger to the sinner because of his uncleanness"; if he is "cut off" that is solely on account of his disobedience in not cleansing himself, not on account of the uncleanness itself. The extremity of this contention is its sufficient refutation. When the sage declares that no one can say "I have made my heart clean, I am pure from sin" (Prov. xx. 9), he clearly means to intimate that an unclean heart is itself sinful. The Psalmist in bewailing his inborn sinfulness and expressing his longing for truth in the inward parts and wisdom in the hidden parts, certainly conceived his unclean heart as properly sinful in the sight of God (Ps. li). The prophet abject before the holy God (Isa. vi) beyond question looked upon his uncleanness as itself iniquity requiring to be taken away by expiatory purging. It would seem unquestionable that throughout the Old Testament the uncleanness which is offensive to Jehovah is sin considered as pollution, and that salvation from sin involves therefore a process of purification as well as expiation.

The agent by whom the cleansing of the heart is effected is in the Old Testament uniformly represented as God Himself, or, rarely, more specifically as the Spirit of God, which is the Old Testament name for God in His effective activity. It has, indeed, been denied that the Spirit of God is ever regarded in

---

[8] E.g., A. B. Davidson, "Theology of O. T.," pp. 348 *sq.*
[9] *Ibid.*, pp. 352-353, against Riehm.

the Old Testament as the worker of holiness.[10] But this extreme position cannot be maintained.[11] It is true enough that the Spirit of God comes before us in the Old Testament chiefly as the Theocratic Spirit endowing men as servants of the Kingdom, and after that as the Cosmical Spirit, the principle of all world-processes; and only occasionally as the creator of new ethical life in the individual soul.[12] But it can scarcely be doubted that in Ps. li. 11 [13] God's Holy Spirit, or the Spirit of God's holiness, is conceived in that precise manner, and the same is true of Psalm cxliii. 10 (cf. Isa. lxiii. 10, 11 and see Gen. vi. 3, Neh. ix. 20, I Sam. x. 6, 9).[13] It is chiefly, however, in promises of the future that this aspect of the Spirit's work is dwelt upon.[14] The recreative activity of the Spirit of God is even made the crowning Messianic blessing (Isa. xxxii. 15, xxxiv. 16, xliv. 3, on the latter of which see Giesebrecht, "Die Berufsbegabung," etc., p. 144, lix. 21, Ezek. xi. 19, xviii. 31, xxxvi. 27, xxxvii. 14, xxxix. 29, Zech. xii. 10); and this is as much

10 Cf. e.g., Beversluis, "De heilige Geest en zijne Werkingen," 1896, p. 38: "Although the spirit of God may, no doubt, be brought into connection with a moral renewing (in Ezek. xxxvi. 27) nevertheless an ethical operation of the Spirit of God is nowhere taught in the Old Testament."

11 Cf. e.g., Swete, "Hastings' B.D.," ii., pp. 403-404; and Davidson, *ibid.*, iv, p. 119 a: "Later prophets perceive that man's spirit must be determined by an operation of God who will write His law on it (Jer. xxxi. 33), or who will put His own Spirit within him as the impulsive principle of his life (Isa. xxxii. 15, Ezek. xxxvi. 26 ff.)."

12 Cf. *The Presbyterian Reformed Review*, Oct. 1895, pp. 669 *sq.*

13 As even Gunkel allows, "Die Wirkungen, &c².," p. 77: "On the other hand the Spirit appears as the principle of religion and morality in Ezek. xxxvi. 27; Isa. xxviii. 6; xxxii. 15 *sq.*, with which Zech. xii. 10 may be compared. To these may be added the passages, not cited by Wendt, Isa. xi. 2 and Ps. li. 13; cxliii. 10, the two last of which have far the most significance for our problem, because they present the doctrine of the Spirit in its relation to the life of pious individuals" (cf. pp. 78 and 79). Delitzsch, on Ps. li. 12, 13, thinks it nevertheless a mistake to take "the Holy Spirit" here as "the Spirit of grace" as distinct from the "Spirit of office." David, he says, is thinking of himself as king, as Israelite, and as man, without distinguishing between them: the Spirit in his mind is that with which he was anointed (I Sam. xvi. 13); and he speaks of His total effects without differentiation.

14 Cf. Gunkel, as cited, p. 78, and Delitzsch on Ps. li. 12, 13; also Dalman, "Words of Jesus," p. 296: "Jeremiah and Ezekiel recognized a miraculous transformation in the heart of the people of the future."

as to say that the promised Messianic salvation included in it provision for the renewal of men's hearts as well as for the expiation of their guilt.[15]

It would be distinctly a retrogression from the Old Testament standpoint, therefore, if our Lord—Himself, in accordance with Old Testament prophecy (e.g., Isa. xi. 1, xlii. 1, lxi. 1), endowed with the Spirit (Mt. iii. 16, iv. 1, xii. 18, 28, Mk. i. 10, 12, Lk. iii. 22, iv. 1, 14, 18, x. 21, Jno. i. 32, 33) above measure (Jno. iii. 34)[16]—had neglected the Messianic promise of spiritual renewal. In point of fact, He began His ministry as the dispenser of the Spirit (Mt. iii. 11, Mk. i. 8, Lk. iii. 16, Jno. i. 33). And the purpose for which He dispensed the Spirit is unmistakably represented as the cleansing of the heart. The distinction of Jesus is, indeed, made to lie precisely in this,— that whereas John could baptise only with water, Jesus baptised with the Holy Spirit: the repentance which was symbolized by the one was wrought by the other. And this repentance ($\mu\epsilon\tau\acute{a}\nu o\iota a$) was no mere vain regret for an ill-spent past ($\mu\epsilon\tau a\mu\acute{\epsilon}\lambda\epsilon\iota a$), or surface modification of conduct, but a radical transformation of the mind which issues indeed in "fruits worthy of repentance" (Lk. iii. 8) but itself consists in an inward reversal of mental attitude.

There is little subsequent reference in the Synoptic Gospels, to be sure, to the Holy Spirit as the renovator of hearts. It is made clear, indeed, that He is the best of gifts and that the Father will not withhold Him from those that ask Him (Lk. xi. 13), and that He abides in the followers of Jesus and works in and through them (Mt. x. 20, Mk. xiii. 11, Lk. xii. 12); and it is made equally clear that He is the very principle of holiness, so that to confuse His activity with that of unclean spirits argues absolute perversion (Mt. xii. 31, Mk. iii. 29, Lk. xii. 10). But these two things do not happen to be brought together in these Gospels.[17]

[15] Cf. in general, *The Presbyterian and Reformed Review*, Oct. 1895, art. "The Spirit of God in the O. T.," pp. 679 ff.

[16] For on the whole it seems best so to understand this verse.

[17] See in general, however, Bruce, "The Kingdom of God," p. 259.

In the Gospel of John, on the other hand, the testimony of the Baptist is followed up by the record of the searching conversation of our Lord with Nicodemus, in which Nicodemus is rebuked for not knowing—though "the teacher of Israel"—that the Kingdom of God is not for the children of the flesh but only for the children of the Spirit (cf. Mt. iii. 9). Nicodemus had come to our Lord as to a teacher, widely recognized as having a mission from God. Jesus repels this approach as falling far below recognizing Him for what He really was and for what He had really come to do. As a divinely sent teacher He solemnly assures Nicodemus that something much more effective than teaching is needed: "Verily, verily, I say unto thee, except a man be born anew he cannot see the Kingdom of God" (iii. 3). And then, when Nicodemus, oppressed by the sense of the profundity of the change which must indeed be wrought in man if he is to be fitted for the Kingdom of God, despairingly inquires "How can this be?" our Lord explains equally solemnly that it is only by a sovereign, recreating work of the Holy Spirit, that so great an effect can be wrought: "Verily, verily, I say unto thee, except a man be born of water and the Spirit he cannot enter into the Kingdom of God" (iii. 5). Nor, he adds, ought such a declaration to cause surprise: what is born of the flesh can be nothing but flesh; only what is born of the Spirit is spirit. He closes the discussion with a reference to the sovereignty of the action of the Spirit in regenerating men: as with the wind which blows where it lists, we know nothing of the Spirit's coming except Lo, it is here! (iii. 8). About the phrase, "Born of water and the Spirit" much debate has been had; and various explanations of it have been offered. The one thing which seems certain is that there can be no reference to an external act, performed by men, of their own will: for in that case the product would not be spirit but flesh, neither would it come without observation. Is it fanciful to see here a reference back to the Baptist's, "I indeed baptise with water; He baptises with the Holy Spirit"? The meaning then would be that entrance into the Kingdom of God requires, if we cannot quite say not only repentance but also regeneration, yet at least we may say both repentance and regeneration. In any event it is very pungently taught here that the precondition of entrance into the Kingdom of God is a radical transformation wrought by the Spirit of God Himself.[18]

Beyond this fundamental passage there is little said in John's Gospel of the renovating activities of the Spirit. The communication of the Spirit of xx. 22 seems to be an official endowment; and although in vii. 39 the allusion appears to be to the gift of the Spirit to believers at large, the stress seems to fall rather on the blessing they bring to others by virtue of this endowment, than on that they receive themselves. There remains only the great promise of the Paraclete. It would probably be impossible to attribute more depth or breadth of meaning than rightfully belongs to them, to the passages which embody this promise (xiv. 16, 26, xv. 26, xvi. 7, 13). But the emphasis appears to be laid in them upon the illuminating (cf. also Lk. i. 15, 41, 67, ii. 25, 26; Mt. xxii. 43) more than upon the sanctifying influences of the Spirit, although assuredly the latter are not wholly absent (xvi. 7-11).

Elsewhere in John, although apart from any specific reference to the Spirit as the agent, repeated expression is given to the fundamental conception of renewal. Men lie dead in their sins and require to be raised from the dead if they are to live (xi. 25, 26); it is the prerogative of the Son to quicken whom He will (v. 21); it is impossible for men to come to the Son, unless they be drawn by the Father (vi. 44); being in the Son it is only of the Father that they can bear fruit (xv. 1). Similarly in the Synoptics there is lacking nothing to this teaching, except the specific reference of the effects to the Holy Spirit. What is required of men is nothing less than perfection even as the heavenly Father is perfect (Mt. v. 48—the New Testament form of the Old Testament "Ye shall be holy for I am holy, Jehovah

---

[18] Cf. Wendt, "The Teaching of Jesus," E. T., ii, 91: "Jesus here at the outset declares, in the only passage in the Fourth Gospel where the conception of the Kingdom of God is directly mentioned, that a complete new birth, taking place from the commencement, and, indeed, a birth from the Spirit of God, is indispensably necessary in order both to seeing (that is, experiencing) and to entering the Kingdom of God (vss. 3 and 5)."

your God," Lev. xix. 2). And this perfection is not a matter of external conduct but of internal disposition. One of the objects of the "Sermon on the Mount" is to deepen the conception of righteousness and to carry back both sin and righteousness into the heart itself (Mt. v. 20). Accordingly, the external righteousness of the Scribes and Pharisees is pronounced just no righteousness at all; it is the cleansing merely of the outside of the cup and of the platter (Mt. xxiii. 25), and they are therefore but as whited sepulchres, which outwardly appear beautiful but inwardly are full of dead men's bones (Mt. xxiii. 27, 28). True cleansing must begin from within; and this inward cleansing will cleanse the outside also (Mt. xxiii. 26, xv. 11). The fundamental principle is that every tree brings forth fruit according to its nature, whether good or bad; and therefore the tree must be made good and its fruit good, or else the tree corrupt and its fruit corrupt (Mt. vii. 17, xii. 33, xv. 11, Mk. vii. 15, Lk. vi. 43, xi. 34). So invariable and all-inclusive is this principle in its working, that it applies even to the idle words which men speak, by which they may therefore be justly judged: none that are evil can speak good things, "for it is out of the abundance of the heart that the mouth speaketh" (Mt. xii. 34). Half-measures are therefore unavailing (Mt. vi. 21); a radical change alone will suffice—no mere patching of the new on the old, no pouring of new wine into old bottles (Mt. ix. 16, 17, Mk. ii. 21, 22, Lk. v. 36, 39). He who has not a wedding-garment—the gift of the host—even though he be called shall not be chosen (Mt. xxii. 11, 12).

Accordingly when—in the Synoptic parallel to the conversation with Nicodemus—the rich young ruler came to Jesus with his heart set on purchase (as a rich man's heart is apt to be set), pleading his morality, Jesus repelled him and took occasion to pronounce upon not the difficulty only but the impossibility of entrance into the Kingdom of heaven on such terms (Mt. xix. 23, Mk. x. 23, Lk. xviii. 24). The possibility of salvation, He explains, just because it involves something far deeper than this, rests in the hands of God alone (Mt. xix. 26, Mk. x. 27, Lk. xviii. 27). Man himself brings nothing to it;

the Kingdom is received in naked helplessness (Mt. xix. 21 ||).
It is not without significance that, in all the Synoptics, the
conversation with the rich young ruler is made to follow immediately upon the incident of the blessing of the little children
(Mt. xix. 13 ||). When our Lord says, with reference to these
children (they were mere babies, Lk. xviii. 15),[19] that, "Of such
is the kingdom of heaven," he means just to say that the
kingdom of heaven is never purchased by any quality whatever,
to say nothing now of deed: whosoever enters it enters it as a
child enters the world,—he is born into it by the power of God.
In these two incidents, of the child set in the midst and of the
rich young ruler, we have, in effect, acted parables of the new
birth; they exhibit to us how men enter the kingdom and set the
declaration made to Nicodemus (Jno. iii. 1 *sq.*) before us in
vivid object-lesson. And if the kingdom can be entered thus only
in nakedness as a child comes into the world, all stand before it
in like case and it can come only to those selected therefor by
God Himself: where none have a claim upon it the law of its
bestowment can only be the Divine will (Mt. xi. 27, xx. 15).[20]

The broad treatment characteristic of the Gospels only
partly gives way as we pass to the Epistles. Discriminations of
aspects and stages, however, begin to become evident; and with
the increased material before us we easily perceive lines of
demarcation which perhaps we should not have noted with the
Gospels only in view. In particular we observe two groups of
terms standing over against one another, describing, respectively, from the manward and from the Godward side, the
great change experienced by him who is translated from the
power of darkness into the kingdom of the Son of God's love
(Col. i. 13). And within the limits of each of these groups, we
observe also certain distinctions in the usage of the several
terms which make it up. In the one group are such terms as
μετανοεῖν with its substantive μετάνοια, and its cognate μεταμέλεσθαι, and ἐπιστρέφειν and its substantive ἐπιστροφή. These
tell us what part man takes in the change. The other group in-

[19] Cf. "Hastings' DCG.," art "Children."
[20] Cf. Wendt, as cited, p. 54-55 note.

cludes such terms as γεννηθῆναι ἄνωθεν or ἐκ τοῦ θεοῦ or ἐκ τοῦ πνεύματος, παλινγενεσία, ἀναγεννᾶν, ἀποκυεῖσθαι, ανανεοῦσθαι, ἀνακαινοῦσθαι, ἀνακαίνωσις. These tell what part God takes in the change. Man repents, makes amendment, and turns to God. But it is by God that men are renewed, brought forth, born again into newness of life. The transformation which to human vision manifests itself as a change of life (ἐπιστροφή) resting upon a radical change of mind (μετάνοια), to Him who searches the heart and understands all the movements of the human soul is known to be a creation (κτίζειν) of God, beginning in a new birth from the Spirit (γεννηθῆναι ἄνωθεν ἐκ τοῦ πνεύματος) and issuing in a new divine product (ποίημα), created in Christ Jesus, into good works prepared by God beforehand that they may be walked in (Eph. ii. 10).

There is certainly synergism here; but it is a synergism of such character that not only is the initiative taken by God (for "all things are of God," II Cor. v. 18, cf. Heb. vi. 6), but the Divine action is in the exceeding greatness of God's power, according to the working of the strength of His might which He wrought in Christ when He raised Him from the dead (Eph. i. 19). The "new man" which is the result of this change is therefore one who can be described no otherwise than as "created" (κτισθέντα) in righteousness and holiness of truth (Eph. iv. 24), after the image of God significantly described as "He who created him" (τοῦ κτίσαντος αὐτόν, Col. iii. 10),—that is not He who made him a man, but He who has made him by an equally creative efflux of power this new man which he has become.[21] The exhortation that we shall "put on" this new man (Eph. iv. 24, cf. iii. 9, 10), therefore does not imply that either the initiation or the completion of the process by which the "new creation" (καινὴ κτίσις; II Cor. v. 17, Gal. vi. 15) is wrought lies in our own power; but only urges us to that diligent coöperation with God in the work of our salvation, to which He calls us in all departments of life (I Cor. iii. 9), and the classical expression of which in this particular department

21 Cf. Lightfoot in loc.

is found in the great exhortation of Phil. ii. 12, 13 where we
are encouraged to work out our own salvation thoroughly to
the end, with fear and trembling, on the express ground that
it is God who works in us both the willing and doing for His good
pleasure. The express inclusion of "renewal" in the exhortation
(Eph. iv. 23 ἀνανεοῦσθαι; Rom. xii. μεταμορφοῦσθε τῇ ἀνακαινώ-
σει) is indication enough that this "renewal" is a process wide
enough to include in itself the whole synergistic "working out"
of salvation (κατεργάζεσθε, Phil. ii. 12). But it has no tendency
to throw doubt upon the underlying fact that this "working out"
is both set in motion (τὸ θέλειν) and given effect (τὸ ἐνεργεῖν),
only by the energizing of God (ὅ ἐνεργῶν ἐν ὑμῖν), so that
all (τὰ πάντα) is from God (ἐκ τοῦ θεοῦ, II Cor. v. 18). Its effect
is merely to bring "renewal" (ἀνακαίνωσις) into close parallelism with "repentance" (μετάνοια)—which itself is a gift of
God (II Tim. ii. 25, cf. Acts v. 31, xi. 18) as well as a work of
man—as two names for the same great transaction, viewed
now from the Divine, and now from the human point of sight.

It will not be without interest to observe the development
of μετανοεῖν, μετάνοια into the technical term to denote the
great change by which man passes from death in sin into life in
Christ.[22] Among the heathen writers, the two terms μεταμέλεσθαι, μεταμέλεια and μετανοεῖν, μετάνοια, although no doubt affected in their coloring by their differing etymological suggestions, and although μετανοεῖν, μετάνοια seems always to have
been the nobler term, were practically synonymous. Both were
used of the dissatisfaction which is felt in reviewing an unworthy deed; both of the amendment which may grow out of
this dissatisfaction. Something of this undiscriminating usage
extends into the New Testament. In the only three instances
in which μεταμέλεσθαι occurs in the Gospels (Mt. xxi. 29, 32,
xxvii. 3, cf. Heb. vii. 21 from Old Testament), it is used of a

---

[22] Cf. Trench, "Synonyms of the N. T.," § lxix. Also Effie Freeman Thomp-
son, Ph.D., "ΜΕΤΑΝΟΕΩ and ΜΕΤΑΜΕΛΕΙ in Greek Literature until 100 A. D.,"
1908, p. 29 especially the summary of New Testament usage pp. 28-29:
μετανοεῖν is not used in the New Testament of the intellect or sensibilities but
always of voluntative action; and prevailingly not of specific but of generic
choice.

repentance which issued in the amended act; while in Lk. xvii. 3, 4 (but there only) μετανοεῖν may very well be understood of a repentance which expended itself in regret. Elsewhere in the New Testament μεταμέλεσθαι is used in a single instance only (except Heb. vii. 21 from Old Testament) and then it is brought into contrast with μετάνοια as the emotion of regret is contrasted with a revolution of mind (II Cor. vii. 8 sq.). The Apostle had grieved the Corinthians with a letter and had regretted it (μετεμελόμην); he had, however, ceased to regret it (μεταμέλομαι), because he had come to perceive that their grief had led the Corinthians to repent of their sin (μετάνοια), and certainly the salvation to which such a repentance tends is not to be regretted (ἀμεταμέλητον). Here μεταμέλεσθαι is the painful review of the past; but so little is μετάνοια this, that it is presented as a result of sorrow,—a total revolution of mind traced by the Apostle through the several stages of its formation in a delicate analysis remarkable for its insight into the working of a human soul under the influence of a strong revulsion (verse 11). Its roots were planted in godly sorrow, its issue was amendment of life, its essence consisted in a radical change of mind and heart towards sin. In this particular instance it was a particular sin which was in view; and in heathen writers the word is commonly employed of a specific repentance of a specific fault. In the New Testament this, however, is the rarer usage.[23] Here it prevailingly stands for that fundamental change of mind by which the back is turned not upon one sin or some sins, but upon all sin, and the face definitely turned to God and to His service,—of which therefore a transformed life (ἐπιστροφή) is the outworking.[24] It is not itself this transformed life, into which it issues, any more than it is the painful regret out of which it issues. No doubt, it may spread its skirts so widely as to include

[23] Lk. xvii. 3, 4, Acts viii. 22, II Cor. vii. 9, 10, xii. 21, Heb. xii. 17; cf. also Rev. ii. 5, 5, 16, 21, 22, iii, 3, 19.

[24] Mt. iii. 2, iv. 17, xi. 20, 21, xii. 41, Mk. i. 15, vi. 12, Lk. x. 13, xi. 32, xiii. 3, 5, xv. 7, 10, xvi. 30, Acts ii. 38, iii. 19, xvii. 30, xxvi. 20, Mt. iii. 8, 11, Mk. i. 4, Lk. iii. 3, 8, v. 32, xv. 7, xxiv. 47, Acts v. 31, xi. 18, xiii. 24, xix. 4, xxvi. 20, Rom. ii. 4, II Tim. ii. 25, Heb. vi. 1, 6, II Pet. iii. 9, Rev. ix. 20, 21, xvi. 9, 11, cf. ii. 5, 5, 16, 21, 22, iii. 3, 19.

on this side the sorrow for sin and on that the amendment of life; but what it precisely is, and what in all cases it emphasizes, is the inner change of mind which regret induces and which itself induces a reformed life. Godly sorrow works repentance (II Cor. vii. 10): when we "turn" to God we are doing works worthy of repentance (Acts iii. 19, xxvi. 20, cf. Lk. iii. 8).

It is in this, its deepest and broadest sense, that μετάνοια corresponds from the human side to what from the divine point of sight is called ἀνακαίνωσις; or, rather, to be more precise, that μετάνοια is the psychological manifestation of ἀνακαίνωσις. This "renewal" (ἀνακαινοῦσθαι, ἀνακαίνωσις, ἀνανεοῦσθαι) is the broad term of its own group. It may be, to be sure, that παλινγενεσία should take its place by its side in this respect. In one of the only two passages in which it occurs in the New Testament (Mt. xix. 28) it refers to the repristination not of the individual, but of the universe, which is to take place at "the end": and this usage tends to stamp upon the word the broad sense of a complete and thoroughgoing restoration. If in Tit. iii. 5 it is applied to the individual in such a broad sense, it would be closely coextensive in meaning with the ἀνακαίνωσις by the side of which it stands in that passage, and would differ from it only as a highly figurative differs from a more literal expression of the same idea.[25] Our salvation, the Apostle would in that case say, is not an attainment of our own, but is wrought by God in His great mercy, by means of a regenerating washing, to wit, a renewal by the Holy Spirit.

The difficulty we experience in confidently determining the scope of παλινγενεσία, arising from lack of a sufficiently copious usage to form the basis of our induction, attends us also with the other terms of its class. Nevertheless it seems tolerably clear that over against the broader "renewal" expressed by ἀνακαινοῦσθαι and its cognates and perhaps also by παλινγενεσία, ἀναγεννᾶν (I Pet. i. 23) and with it, its synonym ἀποκυεῖσθαι (James i. 18) are of narrower connotation. We have, says Peter, in God's great mercy been rebegotten, not of corruptible seed,

---

[25] So e.g., Weiss *in loc.*

but of incorruptible, by means of the Word of the living and abiding God. It is in accordance with His own determination, says James, that we have been brought forth by the Father of Lights, from whom every good gift and every perfect boon comes, by means of the Word of truth. We have here an effect, the efficient agent in working which is God in His unbounded mercy, while the instrument by means of which it is wrought is "the word of good-tidings which has been preached" to us, that is to say, briefly, the Gospel of Jesus Christ. The issue is, equally briefly, just salvation. This salvation is characteristically described by Peter as awaiting its consummation in the future, while yet it is entered upon here and now not only (verse 4 *sq.*) as a "living hope" which shall not be put to shame (because it is reserved in heaven for us, and we meanwhile are guarded through faith for it by the power of God), but also in an accordant life of purity as children of obedience who would fain be like their Father and as He is holy be also ourselves holy in all manner of living. James intimates that those who have been thus brought forth by the will of God may justly be called "first fruits of His creatures," where the reference assuredly is not to the first but to the second creation, that is to say, they who have already been brought forth by the word of truth are themselves the product of God's creative energy and are the promise of the completed new creation when all that is shall be delivered from the bondage of corruption into the liberty of the glory of the children of God (Rom. viii. 19 *sq.*, Mt. xix. 28).

The new birth thus brought before us is related to the broader idea of "renewal" (ἀνακαίνωσις) as the initial stage to the whole process. The conception is not far from that embodied by our old Divines in the term "effectual calling" which they explained to be "by the Word and Spirit"; it is nowadays perhaps more commonly but certainly both less Scripturally and less descriptively spoken of as "conversion." It finds its further explanation in the Scriptures accordingly not under the terms ἐπιστρέφειν, ἐπιστροφή, which describe to us that in which it issues, but under the terms καλέω, κλῆσις[26] which describe to us precisely what it is. By these terms, which are practically confined to Paul and Peter, the follower of Christ is said to owe his introduction into the new life to a "call" from God—a call distinguished from the call of mere invitation (Mt. xxii. 14), as "the call according to purpose" (Rom. viii. 28), a call which cannot fail of its appropriate effect, because there works in it the very power of God. The notion of the new birth is confined even more closely still to its initial step in our Lord's discourse to Nicodemus, recorded in the opening verses of the third chapter of John's Gospel. Here the whole emphasis is thrown upon the necessity of the new birth and its provision by the Holy Spirit. No one can see the Kingdom of God unless he be born again; and this new birth is wrought by the Spirit. Its advent into the soul is unobserved; its process is inscrutable; its reality is altogether an inference from its effects. There is no question here of means. That the ἐξ ὕδατος of verse 5 is to be taken as presenting the external act of baptism as the proper means by which the effect is brought about, is, as we have already pointed out, very unlikely. The axiom announced in verse 6 that all that is born of flesh is flesh and only what is born of the Spirit is spirit seems directly to negative such an interpretation by telling us flatly that we cannot obtain a spiritual effect from a physical action. The explanation of verse 8 that like the wind, the Spirit visits whom He will and we can only observe the effect and say Lo, it is here! seems inconsistent with supposing that it always attends the act of baptism and therefore can always be controlled by the human will. The new birth appears to be brought before us in this discussion in the purity of its conception; and we are made to perceive that at the root of the whole process of "renewal" there lies an immediate act of God the Holy Spirit upon the soul by virtue of which it is that the renewed man bears the great name of Son of God. Begotten not of blood, nor of the will of the flesh, nor of the will of man, but of God (Jno. i. 13), his new life will necessarily bear the

---

[26] Cf. "Hastings' B. D.," iv, 57 b.

lineaments of his new parentage (I Jno. iii. 9, 10; v. 4, 18):
kept by Him who was in an even higher sense still begotten of
God, he overcomes the world by faith, defies the evil one (who
cannot touch him), and manifests in his righteousness and love
the heritage which is his (I Jno. ii. 29, iv. 7, v. 1). Undoubtedly
the Spirit is active throughout the whole process of "renewal";
but it is doubtless the peculiarly immediate and radical nature
of his operation at this initial point which gives to the product
of His renewing activities its best right to be called a new
creation (II Cor. v. 17, Gal. vi. 15), a quickening (Jno. v. 21,
Eph. ii. 5), a making alive from the dead (Gal. iii. 21).

We perceive, then, that the Scriptural phraseology lays before us, as its account of the great change which the man experiences who is translated from what the Scriptures call darkness
to what they call God's marvellous light (Eph. v. 8, Col. i. 13,
I Pet. ii. 9, I Jno. ii. 8) a process; and a process which has two
sides. It is on the one side a change of the mind and heart,
issuing in a new life. It is on the other side a renewing from on
high issuing in a new creation. But the initiative is taken by
God: man is renewed unto repentance: he does not repent that
he may be renewed (cf. Heb. vi. 6). He can work out his salvation with fear and trembling only because God works in him
both the willing and the doing. At the basis of all there lies an
enabling act from God, by virtue of which alone the spiritual
activities of man are liberated for their work (Rom. vi. 22,
viii. 2). From that moment of the first divine contact the work
of the Spirit never ceases: while man is changing his mind and
reforming his life, it is ever God who is renewing him in true
righteousness. Considered from man's side the new dispositions
of mind and heart manifest themselves in a new course of life.
Considered from God's side the renewal of the Holy Spirit
results in the production of a new creature, God's workmanship, with new activities newly directed. We obtain thus a
regular series. At the root of all lies an act seen by God alone,
and mediated by nothing, a direct creative act of the Spirit,
the new birth. This new birth pushes itself into man's own
consciousness through the call of the Word, responded to under

the persuasive movements of the Spirit; his conscious possession of it is thus mediated by the Word. It becomes visible to his fellow-men only in a turning to God in external obedience, under the constant leading of the indwelling Spirit (Rom. viii. 14). A man must be born again by the Spirit to become God's son. He must be born again by the Spirit and Word to become consciously God's son. He must manifest his new spiritual life in Spirit-led activities accordant with the new heart which he has received and which is ever renewed afresh by the Spirit, to be recognized by his fellow-men as God's son. It is the entirety of this process, viewed as the work of God on the soul, which the Scriptures designate "renewal."

It must not be supposed that it is only in these semi-technical terms, however, that the process of "renewal" is spoken of in the Epistles of the New Testament any more than in the Gospels. There is, on the contrary, the richest and most varied employment of language, literal and figurative, to describe it in its source, or its nature, or its effects. It is sometimes suggested, for example, under the image of a change of vesture (Eph. iv. 24, Col. iii. 9, 10, cf. Gal. iii. 27, Rom. xiii. 14): the old man is laid aside like soiled clothing, and the new man put on like clean raiment. Sometimes it is represented, in accordance with its nature, less figuratively, as a metamorphosis (Rom. xii. 2): by the renewing of our minds we become transformed beings, able to free ourselves from the fashion of this world and prove what is the will of God, good and acceptable and perfect. Sometimes it is more searchingly set forth as to its nature as a reanimation (Jno. v. 21, Eph. ii. 4-6, Col. ii. 12, 13, Rom. vi. 3, 4): we are dead through our trespasses and the uncircumcision of our flesh; God raises us from this death and makes us sit in the heavenly places with Christ. Sometimes with less of figure and with more distinct reference to the method of the divine working, it is spoken of as a recreation (Eph. ii. 10, iv. 24, Col. iii. 10), and its product, therefore, as a new creature (II Cor. v. 17, Gal. vi. 15): we emerge from it as the workmanship of God, created in Christ Jesus unto good works. Sometimes with more particular reference to the nature and effects of the transaction, it is defined rather as a sanctification, a making holy (ἁγιάζω, I Thess. v. 23, Rom. xv. 16, Rev. xxii. 11; ἁγνίζω, I Pet. i. 22; ἁγιασμός, I Thess. iv. 3, 7, Rom. vi. 19, 22, Heb. xii. 14, II Thess. ii. 13, I Pet. i. 2; cf. Ellicott, on I Thess. iv. 3, iii. 13): and those who are the subjects of the change are, therefore, called "saints" (ἅγιοι, e.g., Rom. viii. 27, I Cor. vi. 1, 2, Col. i. 12). Sometimes again, with more distinct reference to its sources, it is spoken of as the "living" (Gal. ii. 20, Rom. vi. 9, 10, Eph. iii. 17) or "forming" (Gal. iv. 19, cf. Eph. iii. 17, I Cor. ii. 16, II Cor. iii. 8) of Christ in us, or more significantly (Rom. viii. 9, 10, Gal. iv. 6) as the indwelling of Christ or the Spirit in us, or with greater precision as the leading of the Spirit (Rom. viii. 14, Gal. v. 18): and its subjects are accordingly signalized as Spiritual men, that is, Spirit-determined, Spirit-led men (πνευματικοί, I Cor. ii. 15, iii. 1, Gal. vi. 1, cf. I Pet. ii. 5), as distinguished from carnal men, that is, men under the dominance of their own weak, vicious selves (ψυχικοί, I Cor. ii. 14, Jude 19, σαρκικοί, I Cor. iii. 3). None of these modes of representation more clearly define the action than the last mentioned. For the essence of the New Testament representation certainly is that the renewal which is wrought upon him who is by faith in Christ, is the work of the Spirit of Christ, who dwells within His children as a power not themselves making for righteousness, and gradually but surely transforms after the image of God, not the stream of their activities merely, but themselves in the very centre of their being.

The process by which this great metamorphosis is accomplished is laid bare to our observation with wonderful clearness in Paul's poignant description of it, in the seventh chapter of Romans. We are there permitted to look in upon a heart into which the Spirit of God has intruded with His transforming power. Whatever peace it may have enjoyed is broken up. All its ingrained tendencies to evil are up in arms against the intruded power for good. The force of evil habit is so great that the Apostle, in its revelation to him, is almost tempted to despair. "O wretched man that I am," he cries, "who shall

deliver me out of the body of this death?" Certainly not himself. None knows better than he that with man this is impossible. But he bethinks himself that the Spirit of the most high
God is more powerful than even ingrained sin; and with a
great revulsion of heart he turns at once to cry his thanks to
God through Jesus Christ our Lord. This conflict he sees within
him, he sees now to bear in it the promise and potency of victory; because it is the result of the Spirit's working within him,
and where the Spirit works, there is emancipation from the
law of sin and death. The process may be hard—a labor, a
struggle, a fight; but the end is assured. No matter how far
from perfect we yet may be, we are not in the flesh but in the
Spirit if the Spirit of God dwells in us; and we may take heart
of faith from that circumstance to mortify the deeds of the
body and to enter upon our heritage as children of God. Here
in brief compass is the Apostle's whole doctrine of renewal.
Without holiness we certainly shall not see the Lord: but he in
whom the Holy Spirit dwells, is already potentially holy; and
though we see not yet what we shall be, we know that the work
that is begun within us shall be completed to the end. The very
presence of strife within us is the sign of life and the promise of
victory.

The church has retained, on the whole, with very considerable constancy the essential elements of this Biblical doctrine
of "renewal." In the main stream of Christian thought, at all
events, there has been little tendency to neglect, much less to
deny it, at least theoretically. In all accredited types of Christian teaching it is largely insisted upon that salvation consists
in its substance of a radical subjective change wrought by the
Holy Spirit, by virtue of which the native tendencies to evil are
progressively eradicated and holy dispositions are implanted,
nourished and perfected.

The most direct contradiction which this teaching has received in the history of Christian thought was that given it by
Pelagius at the opening of the fifth century. Under the stress
of a one-sided doctrine of human freedom, in pursuance of
which he passionately asserted the inalienable ability of the

will to do all righteousness, Pelagius was led to deny the need and therefore the reality of subjective operations of God on the soul ("grace" in the inner sense) to secure its perfection; and this carried with it as its necessary presupposition the denial also of all subjective injury wrought on man by sin. The vigorous reassertion of the necessity of subjective grace by Augustine put pure Pelagianism once for all outside the pale of recognized Christian teaching; although in more or less modified or attenuated forms, it has remained as a widely spread tendency in the churches, conditioning the purity of the supernaturalism of salvation which is confessed.

The strong emphasis laid by the Reformers upon the objective side of salvation, in the enthusiasm of their rediscovery of the fundamental doctrine of justification, left its subjective side, which was not in dispute between them and their nearest opponents, in danger of falling temporarily somewhat out of sight. From the comparative infrequency with which it was in the first stress of conflict insisted on, occasion, if not given, was at least taken, to represent that it was neglected if not denied. Already in the first generation of the Reformation movement, men of mystical tendencies like Osiander arraigned the Protestant teaching as providing only for a purely external salvation. The reproach was eminently unjust, and although it continues to be repeated up to today, it remains eminently unjust. Only among a few Moravian enthusiasts, and still fewer Antinomians, and, in recent times, in the case of certain of the Neo-Kohlbrüggian party, can a genuine tendency to neglect the subjective side of salvation be detected. With all the emphasis which Protestant theology lays on justification by faith as the root of salvation, it has never failed to lay equal emphasis on sanctification by the Spirit as its substance. Least of all can the Reformed theology with its distinctive insistence upon "irresistible grace"—which is the very heart of the doctrine of "renewal"—be justly charged with failure to accord its rights to the great truth of supernatural sanctification. The debate at this point does not turn on the reality or necessity of sanctification, but on the relation of sanctification to justification.

In clear accord with the teaching of Scripture, Protestant theology insists that justification underlies sanctification, and not *vice versa*. But it has never imagined that the sinner could get along with justification alone. It has rather ever insisted that sanctification is so involved in justification that the justification cannot be real unless it be followed by sanctification. There has never been a time when it could not recognize the truth in and (when taken out of its somewhat compromising context) make heartily its own such an admirable statement of the state of the case as the following:[27]—"However far off it may be from us or we from it, we cannot and ought not to think of our salvation as anything less than our own perfected and completed sinlessness and holiness. We may be, to the depths of our souls, grateful and happy to be sinners pardoned and forgiven by divine grace. But surely God would not have us satisfied with that as the end and substance of the salvation He gives us in His Son. Jesus Christ is the power of God in us unto salvation. It does not require an exercise of divine power to extend pardon; it does require it to endow and enable us with all the qualities, energies, and activities that make for, and that make holiness and life. See how St. Paul speaks of it when he prays, That we may know the exceeding greatness of God's power to usward who believe, according to that working of the strength of His might which He wrought in Christ when He raised Him from the dead."

[27] W. P. Du Bose, "The Gospel in the Gospels," p. 175.

CHAPTER XIV

ON FAITH IN ITS PSYCHOLOGICAL ASPECTS[1]

THE English word "faith" came into the language under the influence of the French, and is but a modification of the Latin "fides," which is itself cognate with the Greek πίστις. Its root-meaning seems to be that of "binding." Whatever we discover to be "binding" on us, is the object of "faith."[2] The corresponding Germanic term, represented by the English word "believe" (and the German "glauben"), goes back to a root meaning "to be agreeable" (represented by our English "lief"), and seems to present the object of belief as something which we "esteem"—which we have "estimated" or "weighed" and "approved." The notion of "constraint" is perhaps less prominent in "belief" than in "faith," its place being taken in "belief" by that of "approval." We "believe" in what we find worthy of our confidence; we "have faith" in what compels our confidence. But it would be easy to press this too far, and it is likely that the two terms "faith," "belief" really express much the same idea.[3] In the natural use of language, therefore, which is normally controlled by what we call etymology, that is, by the intrinsic connotation of the terms, when we say "faith," "belief," our minds are preoccupied with the grounds of the conviction expressed: we are speaking of a mental act or state to which we feel constrained by considerations objective to ourselves, or at

[1] Reprinted from *The Princeton Theological Review*, ix. 1911, pp. 537-566; also from *Studies in Theology*, pp. 313-342.

[2] The Hebrew האמין, אמונה go back to the idea of "holding": we believe in what "holds." In both the sacred languages, therefore, the fundamental meaning of faith is "surety." Cf. Latin "credo."

[3] Cf. M. Heyne's German Dictionary, *sub voc.* "Glaube": "*Glaube* is confiding acceptance of a truth. At the basis of the word is the root *lub*, which, with the general meaning of agreeing with and of approving, appears also in *erlauben* and *loben*."

375

least to the act or state in question. The conception embodied in the terms "belief," "faith," in other words, is not that of an arbitrary act of the subject's; it is that of a mental state or act which is determined by sufficient reasons.

In their fundamental connotation, thus, these terms are very broad. There seems nothing in the terms themselves, indeed, to forbid their employment in so wide a sense as to cover the whole field of "sureness," "conviction." Whatever we accept as true or real, we may very properly be said to "believe," to "have faith in"; all that we are convinced of may be said to be matter of "belief," "faith." So the terms are, accordingly, very often employed. Thus, for example, Professor J. M. Baldwin defines "belief" simply as "mental endorsement or acceptance of something thought of, as real"; and remarks of "conviction," that it "is a loose term whose connotation, so far as exact, is near to that here given to belief."[4] He even adds—we think with less exactness—that "judgment" is merely "the logical or formal side of the same state of mind" which, on the psychological side, is called "belief." To us, "judgment" appears a broader term than "belief," expressing a mental act which underlies belief indeed, but cannot be identified with it.[5]

Meanwhile we note with satisfaction that Professor Baldwin recognizes the element of constraint ("bindingness") in "belief," and distinguishes it clearly from acts of the will, thereby setting aside the definition of it—quite commonly given—which finds the differentia of beliefs, among convictions, in this—that they are "voluntary convictions." "There is," he says,[6] "a distinct difference in consciousness between the consent of belief and the consent of will. The consent of belief is in a measure a forced consent: it attaches to what is—to what stands in the order of things whether I consent or no. The consent of will is a forceful consent—a consent to what shall be through me."

[4] Baldwin and Stout, "Dictionary of Philosophy and Psychology," i. 1901, pp. 110 and 112.

[5] Professor Baldwin does not allow any psychological distinction between "belief" and "knowledge." See sub voc. "Knowledge."

[6] Ibid., p. 112. The passage is quoted from Baldwin, "Handbook of Psychology: Feeling and Will," 1891, p. 171.

That is to say, with respect to belief, it is a mental recognition of what is before the mind, as objectively true and real, and therefore depends on the evidence that a thing is true and real and is determined by this evidence; it is the response of the mind to this evidence and cannot arise apart from it. It is, therefore, impossible that belief should be the product of a volition; volitions look to the future and represent our desires; beliefs look to the present and represent our findings.

Professor Baldwin does not recognize this, however, in its entirety, as is already apparent from the qualification inserted into his description of "belief." It is, says he, *"in a measure a forced consent."* He wishes, after all, to leave room for "voluntary beliefs." Accordingly, he proceeds: "In cases in which belief is brought about by desire and will, there is a subtle consciousness of inadequate evidence, until by repetition the item desired and willed no longer needs volition to give it a place in the series deemed objective: then it is for the first time belief, but then it is no longer will." "Beliefs," then, according to Professor Baldwin, although not to be confounded with acts of the will, may yet be produced by the action of the will, even while the "evidence" on which they should more properly rest, is recognized by the mind willing them to be insufficient.

We cannot help suspecting this suggestion to rest on a defective analysis of what actually goes on in the mind in the instances commented on. These appear to us to be cases in which we determine to act on suppositions recognized as lacking sufficient evidence to establish them in our minds as accordant with reality and therefore not accepted as accordant with reality, that is to say, as "beliefs." If they pass, as Dr. Baldwin suggests, gradually into "beliefs," when repeatedly so acted upon—is that not because the mind derives from such repeated action, resulting successfully, additional evidence that the suppositions in question do represent reality and may be safely acted on as such? Would not the thing acted on in such cases be more precisely stated as the belief that these suppositions may be accordant with reality, not that they are? The consciousness that the evidence is inadequate which accompanies such action (though Dr. Baldwin calls it "subtle")—is it not in fact just the witness of consciousness that it does not assert these suppositions to be accordant with reality, and does not recognize them as "beliefs," though it is willing to act on them on the hypothesis that they may prove to be accordant with reality and thus make good their aspirations to become beliefs? And can any number of repetitions (repetitions of what, by the way?) make this testimony of consciousness void? Apparently what we repeat is simply volitions founded on the possibility or probability of the suppositions in question being in accordance with reality; and it is difficult to see how the repetition of such volitions can elevate the suppositions in question into the rank of beliefs except by eliminating doubt as to their accordance with reality by creating evidence for them through their "working well." The repetition of a volition to treat a given proposition as true—especially if it is accompanied by a consciousness (however subtle) that there is no sufficient evidence that it is true—can certainly not result in making it true; and can scarcely of itself result in producing an insufficiently grounded conviction in the mind (always at least subtly conscious that it rests on insufficient evidence) that it is true, and so in giving it "a place in the series deemed objective." A habit of treating a given proposition as correspondent to reality may indeed be formed; and as this habit is formed, the accompanying consciousness that it is in point of fact grounded in insufficient evidence, may no doubt drop into the background, or even wholly out of sight; thus we may come to act—instinctively, shall we say? or inadvertently?—on the supposition of the truth of the proposition in question. But this does not seem to carry with it as inevitable implication that "beliefs" may be created by the action of the will. It may only show that more or less probable, or more or less improbable, suppositions, more or less clearly envisaged as such, may enter into the complex of conditions which influence action, and that the human mind in the processes of its ordinary activity does not always keep before it in perfect clearness the lines of demarcation which separate the two classes of its beliefs and its conjectures, but may sometimes rub off the labels which serve to mark its convictions off from its suppositions and to keep each in its proper place.

It would seem to be fairly clear that "belief" is always the product of evidence and that it cannot be created by volitions, whether singly or in any number of repetitions. The interaction of belief and volition is, questionless, most intimate and most varied, but one cannot be successfully transmuted into the other, nor one be mistaken for the other. The consent of belief is in its very nature and must always be what Dr. Baldwin calls "forced consent," that is to say, determined by evidence, not by volition; and when the consent of will is secured by a supposition, recognized by consciousness as inadequately based in evidence, this consent of will has no tendency to act as evidence and raise the supposition into a belief—its tendency is only to give to a supposition the place of a belief in the ordering of life.

We may infer from this state of the case that "preparedness to act" is scarcely a satisfactory definition of the state of mind which is properly called "faith," "belief." This was the definition suggested by Dr. Alexander Bain. "Faith," "belief" certainly expresses a state of preparedness to act; and it may be very fairly contended that "preparedness to act" supplies a very good test of the genuineness of "faith," "belief." A so-called "faith," "belief" on which we are not prepared to act is near to no real "faith," "belief" at all. What we are convinced of, we should certainly confide in; and what we are unwilling to confide in we seem not quite sure of—we do not appear thoroughly to believe, to have faith in. But though all "faith," "belief" is preparedness to act, it does not follow that all preparedness to act is "faith," "belief." We may be prepared to act, on some other ground than "faith," "belief"; on "knowledge," say—if knowledge may be distinguished from belief—or, as we have already suggested, on "supposition"—on a probability or even a possibility. To be sure, as we have already noted, the real ground of our action in such cases may be stated in terms of "faith," "belief." Our preparedness to act may be said to be our belief—our conviction—that, if the supposition in question is not yet shown to be in conformity to reality, it yet may be so. Meanwhile, it is clear that the supposition in question is not a thing believed to be in accordance with fact, and is therefore not a belief but a "supposition"; not a "conviction" but a conjecture. "Belief," "faith" is the consent of the mind to the reality of the thing in question; and when the mind withholds its consent to the reality, "belief," "faith" is not present. These terms are not properly employed except when a state of conviction is present; they designate the response of the mind to evidence in a consent to the adequacy of the evidence.

It, of course, does not follow that all our "beliefs," "faiths" correspond with reality. Our convictions are not infallible. When we say that "belief," "faith" is the product of evidence and is in that sense a compelled consent, this is not the same as saying that consent is produced only by compelling evidence, that is, evidence which is objectively adequate. Objective adequacy and subjective effect are not exactly correlated. The amount, degree, and quality of evidence which will secure consent varies from mind to mind and in the same mind from state to state. Some minds, or all minds in some states, will respond to very weak evidence with full consent; some minds or all minds in some states, will resist very strong evidence. There is no "faith," "belief" possible without evidence or what the mind takes for evidence; "faith," "belief" is a state of mind grounded in evidence and impossible without it. But the fullest "faith," "belief" may ground itself in very weak evidence—if the mind mistakes it for strong evidence. "Faith," "belief" does not follow the evidence itself, in other words, but the judgment of the intellect on the evidence. And the judgment of the intellect naturally will vary endlessly, as intellect differs from intellect or as the states of the same intellect differ from one another.

From this circumstance has been taken an attempt to define "faith," "belief" more closely than merely mental endorsement of something as true—as, broadly, the synonym of "conviction" —and to distinguish it as a specific form of conviction from other forms of conviction. "Faith," "belief," it is said (e.g. by Kant), is conviction founded on evidence which is subjectively adequate. "Knowledge" is conviction founded on evidence which is objectively adequate. That "faith" and "knowledge" do differ from one another, we all doubtless feel; but it is not easy to believe that their specific difference is found in this formula. It is of course plain enough that every act of "faith," "belief" rests on evidence which is subjectively adequate. But it is far from plain that this evidence must be objectively inadequate on pain of the mental response ceasing to be "faith," "belief" and becoming "knowledge." Are all "beliefs," "faiths," specifically such, in their very nature inadequately established convictions; convictions, indeed—matters of which we feel sure—but of which we feel sure on inadequate grounds—grounds either consciously recognized by us as inadequate, or, if supposed by us to be adequate, yet really inadequate?

No doubt there is a usage of the terms current—especially when they are set in contrast with one another—which does conceive them after this fashion; a legitimate enough usage, because it is founded on a real distinction in the connotation of the two terms. We do sometimes say, "I do not *know* this or that to be true, but I fully *believe* it"—meaning that though we are altogether persuaded of it we are conscious that the grounds for believing it fall short of complete objective coerciveness. But this special usage of the terms ought not to deceive us as to their essential meaning. And it surely requires little consideration to assure us that it cannot be of the essence of "faith," "belief" that the grounds on which it rests are—consciously or unconsciously—objectively inadequate. Faith must not be distinguished from knowledge only that it may be confounded with conjecture. And how, in any case, shall the proposed criterion of faith be applied? To believe on grounds of the inadequacy of which we are conscious, is on the face of it an impossibility. The moment we perceive the objective inadequacy of the grounds on which we pronounce the reality of anything, they become subjectively inadequate also. And so long as they appear to us subjectively adequate, the resulting conviction will be indistinguishable from "knowledge." To say that "knowledge" is a justified recognition of reality and "faith," "belief" is an unjustified recognition of reality, is to erect a distinction which can have no possible psychological basis. The recognizing mind makes and can make no such distinction between the soundness and unsoundness of its own recognitions of reality. An outside observer might certainly distribute into two such categories the "convictions" of a mind brought under his contemplation; but the distribution would represent the outside observer's judgment upon the grounds of these convictions, not that of the subject himself. The moment the mind observed itself introducing such a distribution among its "convictions" it would remove the whole class of "convictions" to which it assigned an inadequate grounding out of the category of "convictions" altogether. To become conscious that some of its convictions were unjustified would be to abolish them at once as convictions, and to remove them into the category at best of conjectures, at worst of erroneous judgments. We accord with Dr. Baldwin, therefore, when he declares of this distinction that it is "not psychological."[7] The mind knows and can know nothing of objectively and subjectively adequate grounds in forming its convictions. All it is conscious of is the adequacy or inadequacy of the grounds on which its convictions are based. If they appeal to it as adequate, the mind is convinced; if they do not, it remains unconvinced. Faith, belief, is to consciousness just an act or state of conviction, of being sure; and therefore cannot be explained as something less than a conviction, something less than being sure, or as a conviction indeed, but a conviction which differs from other convictions by being, if not ungrounded, yet not adequately grounded. That were all one with saying it is a conviction, no doubt, but nevertheless not quite a conviction—a manifest contradiction in terms.

The failure of this special attempt to distinguish between faith and knowledge need not argue, however, that there is

---

[7] "Dictionary of Philosophy and Psychology," i. 1901, p. 603.

no distinction between the two. Faith may not be inadequately grounded conviction any more than it is voluntary conviction—the two come to much the same thing—and yet be a specific mode of conviction over against knowledge as a distinct mode of conviction. The persistence with which it is set over against knowledge in our popular usage of the words as well as in the definitions of philosophers may be taken as an indication that there is some cognizable distinction between the two, could we but fasten upon it. And the persistence with which this distinction is sought in the nature of the grounds on which faith in distinction from knowledge rests is equally notable. Thus we find Dr. Alexander T. Ormond[8] defining "faith" as "the personal acceptance of something as true or real, but—the distinguishing mark—on grounds that, in whole or part, are different from those of theoretic certitude." Here faith is distinguished from other forms of conviction—"knowledge" being apparently in mind as the other term of the contrast. And the distinguishing mark of "faith" is found in the nature of the grounds on which it rests. The nature of these grounds, however, is expressed only negatively. We are not told what they are but only that they are (in whole or in part) different to "those of theoretic certitude." The effect of the definition as it stands is therefore only to declare that the term "faith" does not express all forms of conviction, but one form only; and that this form of conviction differs from the form which is given the name of "theoretic certitude"—that is to say, doubtless, "knowledge"—in the grounds on which it rests. But what the positive distinguishing mark of the grounds on which the mode of conviction which we call "faith" rests is, we are not told. Dr. Ormond does, indeed, go on to say that "the moment of will enters into the assent of faith," and that "in the form of some subjective interest or consideration of value." From this it might be inferred that the positive differentia of faith, unexpressed in the definition, would be that it is voluntary conviction, conviction determined not by the evidence of reality present to our minds, but by our desire

8 Baldwin's "Dictionary of Philosophy and Psychology," i. 1901, p. 369.

or will that it should be true—this desire or will expressing "some subjective interest or consideration of value."[9]

Put baldly, this might be interpreted as meaning that we "know" what is established to us as true, we "believe" what we think we should be advantaged by if true; we "know" what we perceive to be real, we "believe" what we should like to be real. To put it so baldly may no doubt press Dr. Ormond's remark beyond his intention. He recognizes that "some faith-judgments are translatable into judgments of knowledge." But he does not believe that all are; and he suggests that "the final test of validity" of these latter must lie in "the sphere of the practical rather than in that of theoretical truth." The meaning is not throughout perfectly clear. But the upshot seems to be that in Dr. Ormond's opinion, that class of convictions which we designate "faith" differs from that class of convictions which we designate "knowledge" by the fact that they rest (in whole or in part) not on "theoretical" but on "practical" grounds—that is to say, not on evidence but on considerations of value. And that appears ultimately to mean that we know a thing which is proved to us to be true or real; but we believe a thing which we would fain should prove to be true or real. Some of the things which we thus believe may be reduced to "knowledge" because there may be proofs of their reality available which were not, or not fully, present to our minds "when we believed." Others of them may be incapable of such reduction either because no such proofs of their truth or reality exist, or because those proofs are not accessible to us. But our acceptance of them all alike as true rests, not on evidence that they are true, but (in whole or in part) on "some subjective interest" or "consideration of value." Failing "knowledge" we may take these things "on faith"—because we perceive that it would be well if they were true, and we cannot believe that that at least

---

[9] In his fuller discussion in his "Foundations of Knowledge," 1900, Part iii. chap. 1, Dr. Ormond tells us that what positively characterizes belief as over against knowledge is, subjectively, that "the volitional motive begins to dominate the epistemological" (p. 306), and, objectively, that the quality of "coerciveness" (p. 307) is lacking. The two criteria come very much to the same thing.

is not true of which it is clear to us that it would be in the highest degree well if it were true.

It is not necessary to deny that many things are accepted by men as true and accordant with reality on grounds of subjective interest or considerations of value; or that men may be properly moved to the acceptance of many things as true and real by such considerations. Considerations of value may be powerful arguments—they may even constitute proofs—of truth and reality. But it appears obvious enough that all of those convictions which we know as "beliefs," "faiths" do not rest on "subjective interest or considerations of value"—either wholly or even in part. Indeed, it would be truer to say that none of them rest on subjective interests or considerations of value as such, but whenever such considerations enter into their grounds they enter in as evidences of reality or as factors of mental movement lending vividness and vitality to elements of proper evidence before the mind. Men do not mean by their "faiths," "beliefs" things they would fain were true; they mean things they are convinced are true. Their minds are not resting on considerations of value, but on what they take to be evidences of reality. The employment of these terms to designate "acceptances as true and real" on the ground of subjective interest or of considerations of value represents, therefore, no general usage but is purely an affair of the schools, or rather of a school. And it does violence not only to the general convictions of men but also to the underlying idea of the terms. No terms, in fact, lend themselves more reluctantly to the expression of a "voluntary acceptance," in any form, than these. As we have already seen, they carry with them the underlying idea of bindingness, worthiness of acceptance; they express, in Dr. Baldwin's phrase, a "forced consent"; and whenever we employ them there is present to the mind a consciousness of grounds on which they firmly rest as expressive of reality. Whatever may be the differentia of "belief," "faith" as a specific form of conviction, we may be sure, therefore, that desire or will cannot be the determining element of the grounds on which this conviction rests. What we gain from Dr. Ormond's definition then is only the assurance that by "faith" is denoted not all forms of conviction, but a specific form—that this specific form is differentiated from other forms by the nature of the grounds on which the conviction called "faith" rests—and that the grounds on which this form of conviction rests are not those of theoretic certitude. The form of conviction which rests on grounds adapted to give "theoretic certitude" we call "knowledge." What the special character of the grounds on which the form of conviction we call "faith" rests remains yet to seek.

This gain, although we may speak of it as, for the main matter, only negative, is not therefore unimportant. To have learned that in addition to the general usage of "faith," "belief," in which it expresses all "mental endorsement or acceptance" of anything "as real," and is equipollent with the parallel term "conviction," there is a more confined usage of it expressing a specific form of "conviction" in contrast with the form of conviction called "knowledge," is itself an important gain. And to learn further that the specific character of the form of conviction which we call "knowledge" is that it rests on grounds which give "theoretic certitude," is an important aid, by way of elimination, in fixing on the specific characteristic of the form of conviction which in contrast to "knowledge" we call "faith." "Faith" we know now is a form of conviction which arises differently to "theoretic certitude"; and if certain bases for its affirmation of reality which have been suggested have been excluded in the discussion—such as that it rests on a volition or a series of volitions, on considerations of value rather than of reality, on evidence only subjectively but not objectively adequate—the way seems pretty well cleared for a positive determination of precisely what it is that it does rest on. We have at least learned that while distinguishing it from "knowledge," which is conviction of the order of "theoretic certitude," we must find some basis for "faith," "belief" which will preserve its full character as "conviction" and not sublimate it into a wish or a will, a conjectural hypothesis or a mistake.

It was long ago suggested that what we call "faith," "belief," as contradistinguished from "knowledge," is conviction grounded in authority, as distinguished from conviction grounded in reason. "We *know*," says Augustine, "what rests upon *reason; we believe* what rests upon *authority*"; and Sir William Hamilton pronounces this "accurately" said.[10] It is not intended of course to represent "faith," "belief" as irrational, any more than it is intended to represent "knowledge" as free from all dependence on taking-on-trust. It was fully recognized by Augustine—as by Sir William Hamilton— that an activity of reason underlies all "faith," and an act of "faith" underlies all knowledge. "But reason itself," says Sir William Hamilton, expounding Augustine's dictum,[11] "must rest at last upon authority; for the original data of reason do not rest on reason, but are necessarily accepted by reason on the authority of what is beyond itself. These data are, therefore, in rigid propriety, *Beliefs* or *Trusts*. Thus it is, that in the last resort, we must, perforce, philosophically admit, that *belief* is the primary condition of reason, and not reason the ultimate ground of *belief*." With equal frankness Augustine allows that reason underlies all acts of faith. That mental act which we call "faith," he remarks, is one possible only to rational creatures, and of course we act as rational beings in performing it;[12] and we never believe anything until we have found it worthy of our belief.[13] As we cannot accord faith, then, without perceiving good grounds for according it, reason as truly underlies faith as faith reason. It is with no intention, then, of denying or even obscuring this interaction of faith and knowledge—what may be justly called their interdependence—that they are distinguished from one another in their secondary applications as designating two distinguishable modes of conviction, the one resting on reason, the other on authority. What is intended is to discriminate the proximate grounds on which the mental consent designated by the one and the other rests. When the

10 "The Works of Thomas Reid," ed. 2, 1849, p. 760 (Note A, § v.).

11 *Loc. cit.*

12 Ep. 120, [i.] 3 ("Opera Omnia," Paris, ii. 1836, col. 518): "we should not be able to believe if we did not have rational minds."

13 "De prædestinatione sanctorum," [ii.] 5 ("Opera Omnia," X. i. 1838, col. 1349).

proximate ground of our conviction is reason, we call it "knowledge"; when it is authority we call it "faith," "belief." Or to put it in other but equivalent terms, we know what we are convinced of on the ground of perception: we believe what we are convinced of on the ground of testimony. "With respect to things we have seen or see," says Augustine,[14] "we are our own witnesses; but with respect to those we believe, we are moved to faith by other witnesses." We cannot believe, any more than we can know, without adequate grounds; it is not faith but "credulity" to accord credit to insufficient evidence; and an unreasonable faith is no faith at all. But we are moved to this act of conviction by the evidence of testimony, by the force of authority—rationally determined to be trustworthy—and not by the immediate perception of our own rational understandings.[15] In a word, while both knowing and believing are states of conviction, sureness—and the surety may be equally strong—they rest proximately on different grounds. Knowledge is seeing, faith is crediting.[16]

[14] Ep. 147, [iii.] 8 ("Opera Omnia," ii. 1836, col. 709).

[15] On Augustine's doctrine of Faith and Reason see *The Princeton Theological Review*, v. 1907, pp. 389 ff. (or B. B. Warfield, "Studies in Tertullian and Augustine," 1930, pp. 170 ff.).

[16] This conception of "faith" naturally became traditional. Thus e.g. Reginald Pecock (middle of the fifteenth century) defines faith as "a knowyng wherbi we assenten to eny thing as to trouth, for as mych as we have sure evydencis gretter than to the contrarie that it is toold and affermid to us to be trewe, bi him of whom we have sure evydencis, or notable likli evydencis, gretter than to the contrarie, that therinne he not lied" ("The Folewer to the Donet," f. 28, cited in J. L. Morison's "Reginald Pecock's Book of Faith," 1909, p. 85). Here we have "faith" resting on evidence; and the specific evidence on which it rests, testimony. Accordingly he defines Christian faith thus: "that feith, of which we speken now, into which we ben bounde, and which is oon of the foundementis of Cristen religioun, is thilke kinde or spice of knowyng, which a man gendrith and getith into his undirstonding, principali bi the telling or denouncing of another persoone, which may not lie, or which is God" ("The Booke of Faith," I. i. f. 9a, Morison's edition, p. 123). At the end of the discussion (f. 10a) Pecock plainly adds: "and bi this maner of his geting and gendring, feith is dyvers from other kindis and spicis of kunnyngis, which a man gendrith and getith into his undirstonding bi bisynes and labour of his natural resoun, bi biholding upon the causis or effectis or circumstancis in nature of the conclusioun or trouthe, and withoute eny attendaunce maad to eny sure teller or denouncer, that thilk conclusioun is a trouthe."

It powerfully commends this conception of the distinction between faith and knowledge, that it employs these terms to designate a distinction which is undoubtedly real. Whatever we choose to call these two classes of convictions, these two classes of convictions unquestionably exist. As Augustine puts it, "no one doubts that we are impelled to the acquisition of knowledge by a double impulse—of authority and of reason."[17] We do possess convictions which are grounded in our own rational apprehension; and we do possess convictions which are grounded in our recognition of authority. We are erecting no artificial categories, then, when we distinguish between these two classes of convictions and label them respectively "knowledges" and "beliefs," "faiths." At the worst we are only applying to real distinctions artificial labels. It may possibly be said that there is no reason in the fitness of things why we should call those convictions which are of the order of "theoretical certitude," knowledge; and those which represent the certitude born of approved testimony, faith. But it cannot be said that no two such categories exist. It is patent to all of us, that some of our convictions rest on our own rational perception of reality, and that others of them rest on the authority exercised over us by tested testimony. The only question which can arise is whether "knowledge," "faith" are appropriate designations by which to call these two classes of convictions.

No one, of course, would think of denying that the two terms "knowledge," and "faith," "belief" are frequently employed as wholly equivalent—each designating simply a conviction, without respect to the nature of its grounds. Augustine already recognized this broad use of both terms to cover the whole ground of convictions.[18] But neither can it be denied that they are often brought into contrast with one another as expressive each of a particular class of convictions, distinguishable from one another. The distinction indicated, no doubt, is often a distinction not in the nature of the evidence on which the

[17] "Contra academicos," iii. [xx.] 43 ("Opera Omnia," Paris, i. 1836, col. 488). Cf. "De ordine," ii. [ix.] 26 ("Opera Omnia," i. coll. 568 f.).
[18] "Retractationes," I. xiv. 3 ("Opera Omnia," i. coll. 52 f.).

several classes of conviction rest but in—shall we say the firmness, the clearness, the force of the conviction? The difficulty of finding the exact word to employ here may perhaps be instructive. When we say, for example, "I do not *know* it—but I fully *believe* it," is it entirely clear that we are using "knowledge" merely of a higher degree of conviction than "faith" expresses? No doubt such a higher degree of conviction is intimated when, for example, to express the force of our conviction of a matter which nevertheless we are assured of only by testimony, we say emphatically, "I do not merely *believe* it; I *know* it." But may it not be that it would be more precise to say that "knowledge" even here expresses primarily rather a more direct and immediate grounding of conviction, and "faith," "belief," a more remote and mediate grounding of it—and that it is out of this primary meaning of the two terms that a secondary usage of them has arisen to express what on the surface appears as differing grades of convictions, but in the ultimate analysis is really differing relations of immediacy of the evidence on which the conviction rests? It adds not a little to the commendation of the distinction between "knowledge" and "faith" under discussion, at all events, that it provides a starting-point on the assumption of which other current usages of the terms may find ready and significant explanations.

When we come to inquire after the special appropriateness of the employment of the terms "faith," "belief" to designate those convictions which rest on authority or testimony, in distinction from those which rest on our immediate perception (physical or mental), attention should be directed to an element in "faith," "belief" of which we have as yet spoken little but which seems always present and indeed characteristic. This is the element of trust. There is an element of trust lying at the bottom of all our convictions, even those which we designate "knowledge," because, as we say, they are of the order of "theoretic certitude," or "rational assurance." "The original data of reason," says Sir William Hamilton truly, "do not rest on reason, but are necessarily accepted by reason on the authority of what is beyond itself." "These data," he adds, "are, therefore, in rigid propriety, *Beliefs* or *Trusts*." The collocation of the terms here, "beliefs or trusts," should be observed; it betrays the propinquity of the two ideas. To say that an element of trust underlies all our knowledge is therefore equivalent to saying that our knowledge rests on belief. The conceptions of believing and trusting go, then, together; and what we have now to suggest is that it is this open implication of "trust" in the conception of "belief," "faith" which rules the usage of these terms.

There is, we have said, an element of trust in all our convictions, and therefore "faith," "belief" may be employed of them all. And when convictions are distinguished from convictions, the convictions in which the element of trust is most prominent tend to draw to themselves the designations of "faith," "belief." It is not purely arbitrary, therefore, that those convictions which rest on our rational perceptions are called "knowledge," while those which rest on "authority" or "testimony" receive the name of "belief," "faith." It is because the element of trust is, not indeed more really, but more prominently, present in the latter than in the former. We perceive and feel the element of trust in according our mental assent to facts brought to us by the testimony of others and accepted as facts on their authority as we do not in the findings of our own rational understandings. And therefore we designate the former matters of faith, belief, and the latter matters of knowledge. Knowing, we then say, is seeing; believing is crediting. And that is only another way of saying that "knowledge" is the appropriate designation of those convictions which rest on our own mental perceptions, while "faith," "belief" is the appropriate designation of those convictions which rest on testimony or authority. While we may use either term broadly for all convictions, we naturally employ them with this discrimination when they are brought in contrast with one another.

It appears, therefore, not only that we are here in the presence of two classes of convictions—the difference between which is real—but that when these two classes are designated respectively by the terms "knowledge" and "faith," "belief" they are appropriately designated. These designations suggest the real difference which exists between the two classes of convictions. Matters of faith, matters of belief are different from matters of knowledge—not as convictions less clear, firm, or well-grounded, not as convictions resting on grounds less objectively valid, not as convictions determined rather by desire, will, than by evidence—but as convictions resting on grounds less direct and immediate to the soul, and therefore involving a more prominent element of trust, in a word, as convictions grounded in authority, testimony as distinguished from convictions grounded in rational proof. The two classes of convictions are psychologically just convictions; they are alike, in Dr. Baldwin's phrase, "forced consents"; they rest equally on evidence and are equally the product of evidence; they may be equally clear, firm, and assured; but they rest on differing kinds of evidence and differ, therefore, in accordance with this difference of kind in the evidence on which they rest. In "knowledge" as the mental response to rational considerations, the movement of the intellect is prominent to the obscuration of all else. Of course the whole man is active in "knowledge" too—for it is the man in his complex presentation who is the subject of the knowledge. But it is "reason" which is prominent in the activity which assures itself of reality on grounds of mental perception. In "faith," on the other hand, as the mental response to testimony, authority, the movement of the sensibility in the form of trust is what is thrust forward to observation. Of course, every other faculty is involved in the act of belief—and particularly the intellectual faculties to which the act of "crediting" belongs; but what attracts the attention of the subject is the prominence in this act of crediting, of the element of trust which has retired into the background in those other acts of assent which we know as "knowledge." "Faith" then emerges as the appropriate name of those acts of mental consent in which the element of trust is prominent. Knowledge is seeing; faith, belief, is trusting.

In what we call religious faith this prominent implication of trust reaches its height. Religious belief may differ from other belief only in the nature of its objects; religious beliefs are beliefs which have religious conceptions as their contents. But the complex of emotions which accompany acts of assent to propositions of religious content, and form the concrete state of mind of the believer, is of course indefinitely different from that which accompanies any other act of believing. What is prominent in this state of mind is precisely trust. Trust is the active expression of that sense of dependence in which religion largely consists, and it is its presence in these acts of faith, belief, which communicates to them their religious quality and raises them from mere beliefs of propositions, the contents of which happen to be of religious purport, to acts possessed of religious character. It is the nature of trust to seek a personal object on which to repose, and it is only natural, therefore, that what we call religious faith does not reach its height in assent to propositions of whatever religious content and however well fitted to call out religious trust, but comes to its rights only when it rests with adoring trust on a person. The extension of the terms "faith," "belief" to express an attitude of mind towards a person, does not wait, of course, on their religious application. We speak familiarly of believing in, or having faith in, persons in common life; and we perceive at once that our justificaton in doing so rests on the strong implication of trust resident in the terms. It has been suggested not without justice, that the terms show everywhere a tendency to gravitate towards such an application.[19] This element at all events becomes so prominent in the culminating act of religious faith when it rests on the person of God our benefactor, or of Christ our Saviour, as to absorb the prior implication of crediting almost altogether. Faith in God, and above all, faith in Jesus Christ, is just trust in Him in its purity. Thus in its higher applications the element of trust which is present in faith in all its applications, grows

[19] "It is the nature and tendency of the word," says Bishop Moule, "to go out towards a person. . . . When we speak of having Faith we habitually direct the notion either towards a veritable person, or towards something which we personify in the mind. . . . I do not attempt to explain the fact, as fact I think it is. Perhaps we may trace in it a far-off echo of that primeval Sanskrit word whose meaning is 'to bind' . . ." ("Faith: its Nature and its Work," 1909, pp. 10-11).

more and more prominent until it finishes by becoming well-nigh the entire connotation of the term; and "to believe in," "to have faith in" comes to mean simply "entrust yourself to." When "faith" can come thus to mean just "trust" we cannot wonder that it is the implication of "trust" in the term which rules its usage and determines its applications throughout the whole course of its development.

The justification of the application of the terms "believing," "faith" to these high religious acts of entrusting oneself to a person does not rest, however, entirely upon the circumstance that the element of trust which in these acts absorbs attention is present in all other acts of faith and only here comes into full prominence. It rests also on the circumstance that all the other constituent elements of acts of faith, belief, in the general connotation of these terms, are present in these acts of religious faith. The more general acts of faith, belief and the culminating acts of religious belief, faith, that is, differ from one another only in the relative prominence in each of elements common to both. For example, religious faith at its height—the act by which we turn trustingly to a Being conceived as our Righteous Governor, in whose hands is our destiny, or to a Being conceived as our Divine Saviour, through whom we may be restored from our sin, and entrust ourselves to Him—is as little a matter of "the will" and as truly a "forced" consent as in any other act called faith, belief. The engagement of the whole man in the act —involving the response of all the elements of his nature—is no doubt more observable in these highest acts of faith than in the lower, as it is altogether natural it should be from the mere fact that they are the highest exercises of faith. But the determination of the response by the appropriate evidence—its dependence on evidence as its ground—is no less stringent or plain. Whenever we obtain a clear conception of the rise in the human soul of religious faith as exercised thus at its apex as saving trust in Christ we perceive with perfect plainness that it rests on evidence as its ground.

It is not unusual for writers who wish to represent religious faith in the form of saving trust in Christ as an act of the will to present the case in the form of a strict alternative. This faith, they say, is an exercise not of the intellect but of the heart. And then they proceed to develop an argument, aiming at a *reductio ad absurdum* of the notion that saving faith can possibly be conceived as a mere assent of the intellect. A simple assent of the mind, we are told, "always depends upon the nature and amount of proof" presented, and is in a true sense "involuntary." When a proposition is presented and sufficiently supported by proof "a mind in a situation to appreciate the proof believes inevitably." "If the proposition or doctrine is not supported by proof, or if the mind is incapable, from any cause, of appreciating proof, unbelief or doubt is equally certain." "Such a theory of faith would, therefore, suspend our belief or unbelief, and consequently our salvation or damnation, upon the manner in which truth is presented to our minds, or our intellectual capability of its appreciation." "To express the whole matter briefly," concludes the writer whose argument we have been following, "it excludes the exercise of the will, and makes faith or unbelief a matter of necessity."[20]

It is not necessary to pause to examine this argument in detail. What it is at the moment important to point out is that the fullest agreement that saving faith is a matter not of the intellect but of the heart, that it is "confidence" rather than "conviction," does not exclude the element of intelligent assent from it altogether, or escape the necessity of recognizing that it rests upon evidence. Is the "confidence" which faith in this its highest exercise has become, an ungrounded confidence? A blind and capricious act of the soul's due to a purely arbitrary determination of the will? Must it not rest on a perceived—that is to say a well-grounded—trustworthiness in the object on which it reposes? In a word, it is clear enough that a conviction lies beneath this confidence, a conviction of the trustworthiness of the object; and that this conviction is produced like other convictions, just by evidence. Is it not still true, then, that the confidence in which saving faith consists is inevitable if the proof

[20] Dr. Richard Beard, "Lectures on Theology," ii. 1871, pp. 362-363,

of the trustworthiness of the object on which it reposes is sufficient—or as we truly phrase it, "compelling"—and the mind is in a situation to appreciate this proof; and doubt is inevitable if the proof is insufficient or the mind is incapable from any cause of appreciating the proof? Is not the confidence which is the faith of the heart, therefore, in any case, as truly as the conviction which is the faith of the intellect, suspended "upon the manner in which truth is presented," or our "capability of its appreciation"? In a word, is it not clear that the assent of the intelligence is an inamissible element of faith even in its highest exercises, and it never comes to be an arbitrary "matter of choice," in which I may do "as I choose"?[21] For the exercise of this faith must there not then always be present to the mind, (1) the object on which it is to repose in confidence; (2) adequate grounds for the exercise of this confidence in the object? And must not the mind be in a situation to appreciate these grounds? Here, too, faith is, in Dr. Baldwin's phrase, a "forced consent," and is the product of evidence.

The impulse of the writer whose views we have just been considering to make "saving faith" a so-called "act of free volition" is derived from the notion that only thus can man be responsible for his faith. It is a sufficiently odd notion, however, that if our faith be determined by reasons and these reasons are good, we are not responsible for it, because forsooth, we then "believe inevitably" and our faith is "a matter of necessity." Are we to hold that responsibility attaches to faith only when it does not rest on good reasons, or in other words is ungrounded, or insufficiently grounded, and is therefore arbitrary? In point of fact, we are responsible for our volitions only because our volitions are never arbitrary acts of a faculty within us called "will," but the determined acts of our whole selves, and therefore represent us. And we are responsible for our faith in precisely the same way because it is *our* faith, and represents us. For it is to be borne in mind that faith, though resting on evidence and thus in a true sense, as Professor Baldwin calls it,

[21] Dr. Beard, as cited, p. 364.

a "forced consent," is not in such a sense the result of evidence that the mind is passive in believing—that the evidence when adequate objectively is always adequate subjectively, or vice versa, quite independently of the state of the mind that believes. Faith is an act of the mind, and can come into being only by an act of the mind, expressive of its own state. There are two factors in the production of faith. On the one hand, there is the evidence on the ground of which the faith is yielded. On the other hand, there is the subjective condition by virtue of which the evidence can take effect in the appropriate act of faith. There can be no belief, faith without evidence; it is on evidence that the mental exercise which we call belief, faith rests; and this exercise or state of mind cannot exist apart from its ground in evidence. But evidence cannot produce belief, faith, except in a mind open to this evidence, and capable of receiving, weighing, and responding to it. A mathematical demonstration is demonstrative proof of the proposition demonstrated. But even such a demonstration cannot produce conviction in a mind incapable of following the demonstration. Where musical taste is lacking, no evidence which derives its force from considerations of melody can work conviction. No conviction, whether of the order of what we call knowledge or of faith, can be produced by considerations to which the mind to be convinced is inhabile.

Something more, then, is needed to produce belief, faith, besides the evidence which constitutes its ground. The evidence may be objectively sufficient, adequate, overwhelming. The subjective effect of belief, faith is not produced unless this evidence is also adapted to the mind, and to the present state of that mind, which is to be convinced. The mind, itself, therefore—and the varying states of the mind—have their parts to play in the production of belief, faith; and the effect which is so designated is not the mechanical result of the adduction of the evidence. No faith without evidence; but not, no evidence without faith. There may stand in the way of the proper and objectively inevitable effect of the evidence, the subjective nature or condition to which the evidence is addressed. This is the ground of responsibility for belief, faith; it is not merely a question of evidence but of subjectivity; and subjectivity is the other name for personality. Our action under evidence is the touchstone by which is determined what we are. If evidence which is objectively adequate is not subjectively adequate the fault is in us. If we are not accessible to musical evidence, then we are by nature unmusical, or in a present state of unmusicalness. If we are not accessible to moral evidence, then we are either unmoral, or, being moral beings, immoral. The evidence to which we are accessible is irresistible if adequate, and irresistibly produces belief, faith. And no belief, faith can arise except on the ground of evidence duly apprehended, appreciated, weighed. We may cherish opinions without evidence, or with inadequate evidence; but not possess faith any more than knowledge. All convictions of whatever order are the products of evidence in a mind accessible to the evidence appropriate to these particular convictions.

These things being so, it is easy to see that the sinful heart—which is enmity towards God—is incapable of that supreme act of trust in God—or rather of entrusting itself to God, its Saviour —which has absorbed into itself the term "faith" in its Christian connotation. And it is to avoid this conclusion that many have been tempted to make faith not a rational act of conviction passing into confidence, resting on adequate grounds in testimony, but an arbitrary act of sheer will, produced no one knows how. This is not, however, the solution of the difficulty offered by the Christian revelation. The solution it offers is frankly to allow the impossibility of "faith" to the sinful heart and to attribute it, therefore, to the gift of God. Not, of course, as if this gift were communicated to man in some mechanical manner, which would ignore or do violence to his psychological constitution or to the psychological nature of the act of faith. The mode of the divine giving of faith is represented rather as involving the creation by God the Holy Spirit of a capacity for faith under the evidence submitted. It proceeds by the divine illumination of the understanding, softening of the heart, and quickening of the will, so that the man so affected may freely

and must inevitably perceive the force and yield to the compelling power of the evidence of the trustworthiness of Jesus
Christ as Saviour submitted to him in the gospel. In one word
the capacity for faith and the inevitable emergence in the heart
of faith are attributed by the Christian revelation to that great
act of God the Holy Spirit which has come in Christian theology
to be called by the significant name of Regeneration. If sinful
man as such is incapable of the act of faith, because he is
inhabile to the evidence on which alone such an act of confident
resting on God the Saviour can repose, renewed man is equally
incapable of not responding to this evidence, which is objectively compelling, by an act of sincere faith. In this its highest
exercise faith thus, though in a true sense the gift of God, is in
an equally true sense man's own act, and bears all the character
of faith as it is exercised by unrenewed man in its lower
manifestations.

It may conduce to a better apprehension of the essential
nature of faith and its relation to the evidence in which it is
grounded, if we endeavor to form some notion of the effect of
this evidence on the minds of men in the three great stages of
their life on earth—as sinless in Paradise, as sinful, as regenerated by the Spirit of God into newness of life. Like every other
creature, man is of course absolutely dependent on God. But
unlike many other creatures, man, because in his very nature
self-conscious, is conscious of his dependence on God; his relation of dependence on God is not merely a fact but a fact of
his self-consciousness. This dependence is not confined to any
one element of human nature but runs through the whole of
man's nature; and as self-conscious being man is conscious of
his absolute dependence on God, physically, psychically, mor-
ally, spiritually. It is this comprehensive consciousness of dependence on God for and in all the elements of his nature and
life, which is the fundamental basis in humanity of faith, in its
general religious sense. This faith is but the active aspect of the
consciousness of dependence, which, therefore, is the passive
aspect of faith. In this sense no man exists, or ever has existed

or ever will exist, who has not "faith." But this "faith" takes very different characters in man as unfallen and as fallen and as renewed.

In unfallen man, the consciousness of dependence on God is far from a bare recognition of a fact; it has a rich emotional result in the heart. This emotional product of course includes fear, in the sense of awe and reverence. But its peculiar quality is just active and loving trust. Sinless man delights to be dependent on God and trusts Him wholly. He perceives God as his creator, upholder, governor, and bountiful benefactor, and finds his joy in living, moving, and having his being in Him. All the currents of his life turn to Him for direction and control. In this spontaneous trust of sinless man we have faith at its purest.

Now when man fell, the relation in which he stood to God was fundamentally altered. Not as if he ceased to be dependent on God, in every sphere of his being and activity. Nor even as if he ceased to be conscious of this his comprehensive dependence on God. Even as sinner man cannot but believe in God; the very devils believe and tremble. He cannot escape the knowledge that he is utterly dependent on God for all that he is and does. But his consciousness of dependence on God no longer takes the form of glad and loving trust. Precisely what sin has done to him is to render this trust impossible. Sin has destroyed the natural relation between God and His creature in which the creature trusts God, and has instituted a new relation, which conditions all his immanent as well as transient activities Godward. The sinner is at enmity with God and can look to God only for punishment. He knows himself absolutely dependent on God, but in knowing this, he knows himself absolutely in the power of his enemy. A fearful looking forward to judgment conditions all his thought of God. Faith has accordingly been transformed into unfaith; trust into distrust. He expects evil and only evil from God. Knowing himself to be dependent on God he seeks to be as independent of Him as he can. As he thinks of God, misery and fear and hatred take the place of joy and trust and love. Instinctively and by his very nature the sinner, not being able to escape from his belief in God, yet cannot possibly have faith in God, that is trust Him, entrust himself to Him.

The reëstablishment of *this* faith in the sinner must be the act not of the sinner himself but of God. This because the sinner has no power to render God gracious, which is the objective root, or to look to God for favor, which is the subjective root of faith in the fiducial sense. Before he can thus believe there must intervene the atoning work of Christ canceling the guilt by which the sinner is kept under the wrath of God, and the recreative work of the Holy Spirit by which the sinner's heart is renewed in the love of God. There is not required a creation of something entirely new, but only a restoration of an old relation and a renewal therewith of an old disposition. Accordingly, although faith in the renewed man bears a different character from faith in unfallen man, inasmuch as it is trust in God not merely for general goodness but for the specific blessing of salvation—that is to say it is soteriological—it yet remains essentially the same thing as in unfallen man. It is in the one case as in the other just trust—that trust which belongs of nature to man as man in relation to his God. And, therefore, though in renewed man it is a gift of God's grace, it does not come to him as something alien to his nature. It is beyond the powers of his nature as sinful man; but it is something which belongs to human nature as such, which has been lost through sin and which can be restored only by the power of God. In this sense faith remains natural even in the renewed sinner, and the peculiar character which belongs to it as the act of a sinner, namely its soteriological reference, only conditions and does not essentially alter it. Because man is a sinner his faith terminates not immediately on God, but immediately on the mediator, and only through His mediation on God; and it is proximately trust in this mediator for salvation—relief from the guilt and corruption of sin—and only mediately through this relief for other goods. But it makes its way through these intermediating elements to terminate ultimately on God Himself and to rest on Him for all goods. And thus it manifests its fundamental and universal character as trust in God, recognized by the renewed sinner, as by the unfallen creature, as the inexhaustible fountain to His creatures of all blessedness, in whom to live and move and have his being is the creature's highest felicity.

In accordance with the nature of this faith the Protestant theologians have generally explained that faith includes in itself the three elements of *notitia, assensus, fiducia.* Their primary object has been, no doubt, to protest against the Romish conception which limits faith to the assent of the understanding. The stress of the Protestant definition lies therefore upon the fiducial element. This stress has not led Protestant theologians generally, however, to eliminate from the conception of faith the elements of understanding and assent. No doubt this has been done by some, and it is perhaps not rare even today to hear it asserted that faith is so purely trust that there is no element of assent in it at all. And no doubt theologians have differed among themselves as to whether all these elements are to be counted as included in faith, or some of them treated rather as preliminary steps to faith or effects of faith. But speaking broadly Protestant theologians have reckoned all these elements as embraced within the mental movement we call faith itself; and they have obviously been right in so doing. Indeed, we may go further and affirm that all three of these elements are always present in faith—not only in that culminating form of faith which was in the mind of the theologians in question—saving faith in Christ—but in every movement of faith whatever, from the lowest to the highest instances of its exercise. No true faith has arisen unless there has been a perception of the object to be believed or believed in, an assent to its worthiness to be believed or believed in, and a commitment of ourselves to it as true and trustworthy. We cannot be said to believe or to trust in a thing or person of which we have no knowledge; "implicit faith" in this sense is an absurdity. Of course we cannot be said to believe or to trust the thing or person to whose worthiness of our belief or trust assent has not been obtained. And equally we cannot be said to believe that which we distrust too much to commit ourselves to it. In every movement of faith, therefore, from the lowest to the highest, there is an intellectual, an emotional, and a voluntary element, though naturally these elements vary in their relative prominence in the several movements of faith. This is only as much as to say that it is the man who believes, who is the subject of faith, and the man in the entirety of his being as man. The central movement in all faith is no doubt the element of assent; it is that which constitutes the mental movement so called a movement of conviction. But the movement of assent must depend, as it always does depend, on a movement, not specifically of the will, but of the intellect; the *assensus* issues from the *notitia*. The movement of the sensibilities which we call "trust," is on the contrary the product of the assent. And it is in this movement of the sensibilities that faith fulfills itself, and it is by it that, as specifically "faith," it is "formed."

CHAPTER XV

FAITH[1]

I. THE HISTORICAL PRESENTATION

IT LIES on the very surface of the New Testament that its writers were not conscious of a chasm between the fundamental principle of the religious life of the saints of the old covenant and the faith by which they themselves lived. To them, too, Abraham is the typical example of a true believer (Rom. iv., Gal. iii., Heb. xi., Jas. ii); and in their apprehension 'those who are of faith,' that is, 'Christians,' are by that very fact constituted Abraham's sons (Gal. iii. 7, Rom. iv. 16), and receive their blessing only along with that 'believer' (Gal. iii. 9) in the steps of whose faith it is that they are walking (Rom. iv. 12) when they believe on Him who raised Jesus our Lord from the dead (Rom. iv. 24). And not only Abraham, but the whole series of Old Testament heroes are conceived by them to be examples of the same faith which was required of them 'unto the gaining of the soul' (Heb. xi.). Wrought in them by the same Spirit (II Cor. iv. 13), it produced in them the same fruits, and constituted them a 'cloud of witnesses' by whose testimony we should be stimulated to run our own race with like patience in dependence on Jesus, 'the author and finisher of our faith' (Heb. xii. 2). Nowhere is the demand of faith treated as a novelty of the new covenant, or is there a distinction drawn between the faith of the two covenants; everywhere the sense of continuity is prominent (Jn. v. 24, 46, xii. 38, 39, 44, I Pet. ii. 6), and the 'proclamation of faith' (Gal. iii. 2, 5, Rom. x. 16) is conceived as essentially one in both dispensations, under both of which the law reigns that 'the just shall live by his faith' (Hab. ii. 4, Rom. i. 17, Gal. iii. 11, Heb. x. 38). Nor do we need to

[1] Article "Faith," from "A Dictionary of the Bible," ed. by James Hastings, v. i, pp. 827-838. Pub. N. Y. 1905, by Charles Scribner's Sons; also from *Biblical Doctrines*, pp. 467-507.

penetrate beneath the surface of the Old Testament to perceive
the justice of this New Testament view. Despite the infrequency of the occurrence on its pages of the terms 'faith,' 'to
believe,' the religion of the Old Testament is obviously as fundamentally a religion of faith as is that of the New Testament.
There is a sense, to be sure, in which all religion presupposes
faith (Heb. xi. 6), and in this broad sense the religion of Israel,
too, necessarily rested on faith. But the religion of Israel was a
religion of faith in a far more specific sense than this; and that
not merely because faith was more consciously its foundation,
but because its very essence consisted in faith, and this faith
was the same radical self-commitment to God, not merely as
the highest good of the holy soul, but as the gracious Saviour
of the sinner, which meets us as the characteristic feature of
the religion of the New Testament. Between the faith of the
two Testaments there exists, indeed, no further difference than
that which the progress of the historical working out of redemption brought with it.

The hinge of Old Testament religion from the very beginning turns on the facts of man's sin (Gen. iii.) and consequent
unworthiness (Gen. iii. 2-10), and of God's grace (Gen. iii. 15)
and consequent saving activity (Gen. iii. 4, iv. 5, vi. 8, 13 f.).
This saving activity presents itself from the very beginning also
under the form of promise or covenant, the radical idea of
which is naturally faithfulness on the part of the promising God
with the answering attitude of faith on the part of the receptive
people. Face to face with a holy God, the sinner has no hope
except in the free mercy of God, and can be authorized to trust
in that mercy only by express assurance. Accordingly, the only
cause of salvation is from the first the pitying love of God (Gen.
iii. 15, viii. 21), which freely grants benefits to man; while on
man's part there is never question of merit or of a strength by
which he may prevail (I Sam. ii. 9), but rather a constant sense
of unworthiness (Gen. xxxii. 10), by virtue of which humility
appears from the first as the keynote of Old Testament piety.
In the earlier portions of the Old Testament, to be sure, there
is little abstract statement of the ideas which ruled the hearts

and lives of the servants of God. The essence of patriarchal religion is rather exhibited to us in action. But from the very beginning the distinctive feature of the life of the pious is that it
is a life of faith, that its regulative principle is drawn, not from
the earth but from above. Thus the first recorded human acts
after the Fall—the naming of Eve, and the birth and naming
of Cain—are expressive of trust in God's promise that, though
men should die for their sins, yet man should not perish from
the earth, but should triumph over the tempter; in a word, in
the great promise of the Seed (Gen. iii. 15). Similarly, the whole
story of the Flood is so ordered as to throw into relief, on the
one hand, the free grace of God in His dealings with Noah
(Gen. vi. 8, 18, viii. 1, 21, ix. 8), and, on the other, the determination of Noah's whole life by trust in God and His promises
(Gen. vi. 22, vii. 5, ix. 20). The open declaration of the faith-
principle of Abraham's life (Gen. xv. 6) only puts into words,
in the case of him who stands at the root of Israel's whole national and religious existence, what not only might also be said
of all the patriarchs, but what actually is most distinctly said
both of Abraham and of them through the medium of their
recorded history. The entire patriarchal narrative is set forth
with the design and effect of exhibiting the life of the servants
of God as a life of faith, and it is just by the fact of their implicit
self-commitment to God that throughout the narrative the servants of God are differentiated from others. This does not mean,
of course, that with them faith took the place of obedience: an
entire self-commitment to God which did not show itself in
obedience to Him would be self-contradictory, and the testing
of faith by obedience is therefore a marked feature of the patriarchal narrative. But it does mean that faith was with them the
precondition of all obedience. The patriarchal religion is essentially a religion, not of law but of promise, and therefore not
primarily of obedience but of trust; the holy walk is characteristic of God's servants (Gen. v. 22, 24, vi. 9, xvii. 1, xxiv. 40,
xlviii. 15), but it is characteristically described as a walk 'with
God'; its peculiarity consisted precisely in the ordering of life
by entire trust in God, and it expressed itself in conduct grow-

ing out of this trust (Gen. iii. 20, iv. 1, vi. 22, vii. 5, viii. 18, xii. 4, xvii. 23, xxi. 12, 16, xxii.). The righteousness of the patriarchal age was thus but the manifestation in life of an entire self-commitment to God, in unwavering trust in His promises.

The piety of the Old Testament thus began with faith. And though, when the stage of the law was reached, the emphasis might seem to be thrown rather on the obedience of faith, what has been called 'faith in action,' yet the giving of the law does not mark a fundamental change in the religion of Israel, but only a new stage in its orderly development. The law-giving was not a setting aside of the religion of promise, but an incident in its history; and the law given was not a code of jurisprudence for the world's government, but a body of household ordinances for the regulation of God's family. It is therefore itself grounded upon the promise, and it grounds the whole religious life of Israel in the grace of the covenant God (Ex. xx. 2). It is only because Israel are the children of God, and God has sanctified them unto Himself and chosen them to be a peculiar people unto Him (Deut. xiv. 1), that He proceeds to frame them by His law for His especial treasure (Ex. xix. 5; cf. Tit. ii. 14). Faith, therefore, does not appear as one of the precepts of the law, nor as a virtue superior to its precepts, nor yet as a substitute for keeping them; it rather lies behind the law as its presupposition. Accordingly, in the history of the giving of the law, faith is expressly emphasized as the presupposition of the whole relation existing between Israel and Jehovah. The signs by which Moses was accredited, and all Jehovah's deeds of power, had as their design (Ex. iii. 12, iv. 1, 5, 8, 9, xix. 4, 9) and their effect (Ex. iv. 31, xii. 28, 34, xiv. 31, xxiv. 3, 7, Ps. cvi. 12) the working of faith in the people; and their subsequent unbelief is treated as the deepest crime they could commit (Num. xiv. 11, Deut. i. 32, ix. 23, Ps. lxxviii. 22, 32, cvi. 24), as is even momentary failure of faith on the part of their leaders (Num. xx. 12). It is only as a consequent of the relation of the people to Him, instituted by grace on His part and by faith on theirs, that Jehovah proceeds to carry out His gracious purposes for them, delivering them from bondage, giving them a law for the regulation of their lives, and framing them in the promised land into a kingdom of priests and a holy nation. In other words, it is a precondition of the law that Israel's life is not of the earth, but is hid with God, and is therefore to be ordered by His precepts. Its design was, therefore, not to provide a means by which man might come into relation with Jehovah, but to publish the mode of life incumbent on those who stand in the relation of children to Jehovah; and it is therefore that the book of the law was commanded to be put by the side of the ark of the covenant of the LORD, that it might be a witness against the transgressions of Israel (Deut. xxxi. 26).

The effect of the law was consonant with its design. Many, no doubt, looked upon it in a purely legalistic spirit, and sought, by scrupulous fulfilment of it as a body of external precepts, to lay the foundation of a claim on God in behalf of the nation or the individual, or to realize through it, as a present possession, that salvation which was ever represented as something future. But, just in proportion as its spirituality and inwardness were felt, it operated to deepen in Israel the sense of shortcoming and sin, and to sharpen the conviction that from the grace of God alone could salvation be expected. This humble frame of conscious dependence on God was met by a twofold proclamation. On the one hand, the eyes of God's people were directed more longingly towards the future, and, in contrast with the present failure of Israel to realize the ordinances of life which had been given it, a new dispensation of grace was promised in which the law of God's kingdom should be written upon the heart, and should become therefore the instinctive law of life of His people (Jer. xxiv. 7, xxxi. 11 f., Ezek. xxxvi. 25 f.; cf. Ezek. xvi. 60, Joel iii., Jos. ii. 9 f.). It lay in the very nature of the Old Testament dispensation, in which the revelation of God was always incomplete, the still unsolved enigmas of life numerous, the work of redemption unfinished, and the consummation of the kingdom ever yet to come, that the eyes of the saints should be set upon the future; and these deficiencies were felt very early. But it also lay, in the nature of the case, that the sense of them should increase as time passed and the perfecting of Israel was delayed, and especially as the whole national and religious existence of Israel was more and more put in jeopardy by assaults from without and corruption from within. The essence of piety came thus to be ever more plainly proclaimed as consisting in such a confident trust in the God of salvation as could not be confounded either by the unrighteousness which reigned in Israel or by Jehovah's judgments on Israel's sins,—such a confidence as even in the face of the destruction of the theocracy itself, could preserve, in enduring hope, the assurance of the ultimate realization of God's purposes of good to Israel and the establishment of the everlasting kingdom. Thus hopeful waiting upon Jehovah became more and more the centre of Israelitish piety, and Jehovah became before all 'the Hope of Israel' (Jer. xiv. 8, xvii. 13, l. 7, cf. Ps. lxxi. 5). On the other hand, while thus waiting for the salvation of Israel, the saint must needs stay himself on God (Isa. xxvi. 3, l. 10), fixing his heart on Jehovah as the Rock of the heart (Ps. lxxiii. 26), His people's strength (Ps. xlvi. 1) and trust (Ps. xl. 4, lxv. 5, lxxi. 5, Jer. xvii. 7). Freed from all illusion of earthly help, and most of all from all self-confidence, he is meanwhile to live by faith (Hab. ii. 4). Thus, along with an ever more richly expressed corporate hope, there is found also an ever more richly expressed individual trust, which finds natural utterance through an ample body of synonyms bringing out severally the various sides of that perfect commitment to God that constitutes the essence of faith. Thus we read much of trusting in, on, to God, or in His word, His name, His mercy, His salvation (בָּטַח), of seeking and finding refuge in God or in the shadow of His wings (חָסָה), of committing ourselves to God (גָּלַל), setting confidence (כָּסַל) in Him, looking to Him (הִבִּיט), relying upon Him (נִשְׁעַן), staying upon Him (נִסְמַךְ), setting or fixing the heart upon Him (הֵכִין לֵב), binding our love on Him (חָשַׁק), cleaving to Him (דָּבַק). So, on the hopeful side of faith, we read much of hoping in God (קִוָּה), waiting on God (יִחַל), of longing for Him (חִכָּה), patiently waiting for Him (הִתְחוֹלֵל), and the like.

By the aid of such expressions, it becomes possible to form

a somewhat clear notion of the attitude towards Him which was required by Jehovah of His believing people, and which is summed up in the term "faith." It is a reverential (Ex. xiv. 31, Num. xiv. 11, xx. 12) and loving faith, which rests on the strong basis of firm and unshaken conviction of the might and grace of the covenant God and of the trustworthiness of all His words, and exhibits itself in confident trust in Jehovah and unwavering expectation of the fulfilment of, no doubt, all His promises, but more especially of His promise of salvation, and in consequent faithful and exclusive adherence to Him. In one word, it consists in an utter commitment of oneself to Jehovah, with confident trust in Him as guide and saviour, and assured expectation of His promised salvation. It therefore stands in contrast, on the one hand, with trust in self or other human help, and on the other with doubt and unbelief, despondency and unfaithfulness. From Jehovah alone is salvation to be looked for, and it comes from His free grace alone (Deut. vii. 7, viii. 18, ix. 5, Amos iii. 2, Hos. xiii. 5, Ezek. xx. 6, Jer. xxxix. 18, Mal. i. 2), and to those only who look solely to Him for it (Isa. xxxi. 1, lvii. 13, xxviii. 16, xxx. 15, Jer. xvii. 5, xxxix. 18, Ps. cxviii. 8, cxlvi. 3, xx. 7, I Sam. xvii. 45, Job xxxi. 24, Ps. lii. 9). The reference of faith is accordingly in the Old Testament always distinctly soteriological; its end the Messianic salvation; and its essence a trusting, or rather an entrusting of oneself to the God of salvation, with full assurance of the fulfilment of His gracious purposes and the ultimate realization of His promise of salvation for the people and the individual. Such an attitude towards the God of salvation is identical with the faith of the New Testament, and is not essentially changed by the fuller revelation of God the Redeemer in the person of the promised Messiah. That it is comparatively seldom designated in the Old Testament by the names of 'faith,' 'believing,' seems to be due, as has been often pointed out, to the special place of the Old Testament in the history of revelation, and the adaptation of its whole contents and language to the particular task in the establishment of the kingdom of God which fell to its writers. This task turned on the special temptations and difficulties of the Old Testament stage of development, and required emphasis to be laid on the majesty and jealousy of Jehovah and on the duties of reverence, sincerity, and patience. Meanwhile, the faith in Him which underlies these duties is continually implied in their enforcement, and comes to open expression in frequent paraphrase and synonym, and as often in its own proper terms as is natural in the circumstances. Especially in the great crises of the history of redemption (Gen. xv., Ex. iv. 5, xix. 9, Isa. vii.) is the fundamental requirement of faith rendered explicit and prominent.

On the coming of God to His people in the person of His Son, the promised Messianic King, bringing the salvation, the hope of which had for so many ages been their support and stay, it naturally became the primary task of the vehicles of revelation to attract and attach God's people to the person of their Redeemer. And this task was the more pressing in proportion as the form of the fulfilment did not obviously correspond with the promise, and especially with the expectations which had grown up on the faith of the promise. This fundamental function dominates the whole New Testament, and accounts at once for the great prominence in its pages of the demand for faith, by which a gulf seems to be opened between it and the Old Testament. The demand for faith in Jesus as the Redeemer so long hoped for, did indeed create so wide a cleft in the consciousness of the times that the term faith came rapidly to be appropriated to Christianity and 'to believe' to mean to become a Christian; so that the old covenant and the new were discriminated from each other as the ages before and after the 'coming of faith' (Gal. iii. 23, 25). But all this does not imply that faith now for the first time became the foundation of the religion of Jehovah, but only suggests how fully, in the new circumstances induced by the coming of the promised Redeemer, the demand for faith absorbed the whole proclamation of the gospel. In this primary concern for faith the New Testament books all necessarily share; but, for the rest, they differ among themselves in the prominence given to it and in the aspects in which it is presented, in accordance with the place of each in the historical development of the new life; and that is as much as to say in accordance with the historical occasion out of which each arose and the special object to subserve which each was written.

Indeed, the word 'to believe' first appears on the pages of the New Testament in quite Old Testament conditions. We are conscious of no distinction even in atmosphere between the commendation of faith and rebuke of unbelief in Exodus or the Psalms and the same commendation and rebuke in the days just before the 'coming of faith' (Lk. i. 20, 45); these are but specific applications of the thesis of prophetism, expressed positively in II Chron. xx. 20 and negatively in Isa. vii. 9. Already, however, the dawn of the new day has coloured the proclamation of the Baptist, the essence of which Paul sums up for us as a demand for faith in the Coming One (Acts xix. 4), and which John reports to us (Jn. iii. 36). In the synoptic report of the teaching of Jesus, the same purpose is the dominant note. All that Jesus did and taught was directed to drawing faith to Himself. Up to the end, indeed, He repelled the unbelieving demand that He should 'declare plainly' the authority by which He acted and who He really was (Mt. xxi. 23, Lk. xxii. 67): but this was only that He might, in His own way, the more decidedly confound unbelief and assert His divine majesty. Even when He spoke of general faith in God (Mk. xi. 22), and that confident trust which becomes men approaching the Almighty in prayer (Mt. xxi. 22 || Mk. ix. 24, Lk. xviii. 8), He did it in a way which inevitably directed attention to His own person as the representative of God on earth. And this accounts for the prevalence, in the synoptic report of His allusions to faith, of a reference to that exercise of faith which has sometimes been somewhat sharply divided from saving faith under the name of 'miracle faith' (Mt. viii. 10, 13 || Lk. vii. 9; Mt. ix. 2; Mt. ix. 22 || Mk. v. 34, Lk. viii. 48; Mt. ix. 28, 29; Mt. xv. 28; Mt. xvii. 20 || Mk. ix. 20; Mt. xxi. 21, 22, cf. Lk. xvii. 6; Mk. iv. 40; Mk. v. 36 || Lk. viii. 50; Mk. x. 52 || Lk. xviii. 42; Lk. vii. 9). That in these instances we have not a generically distinct order of faith, directed to its own peculiar end, but only a specific movement of that entire trust in Himself which Jesus would arouse in all, seems clear from the manner in which He dealt with it,—now praising its exercise as a specially great exhibition of faith quite generally spoken of (Lk. vii. 9), now pointing to it as a manifestation of that believing to which 'all things are possible' (Mk. ix. 23), now connecting with it not merely the healing of the body but the forgiveness of sins (Mt. ix. 2), and everywhere using it as a means of attaching the confidence of men to His person as the source of all good. Having come to His own, in other words, Jesus took men upon the plane on which He found them, and sought to lead them through the needs which they felt, and the relief of which they sought in Him, up to a recognition of their greater needs and of His ability to give relief to them also. That word of power, 'Thy faith hath saved thee,' spoken indifferently of bodily wants and of the deeper needs of the soul (Lk. vii. 50), not only resulted, but was intended to result, in focusing all eyes on Himself as the one physician of both body and soul (Mt. viii. 17). Explicit references to these higher results of faith are, to be sure, not very frequent in the synoptic discourses, but there are quite enough of them to exhibit Jesus' specific claim to be the proper object of faith for these effects also (Lk. viii. 12, 13, xxii. 32, Mt. xviii. 6 || Mk. ix. 42, Lk. vii. 50), and to prepare the way for His rebuke, after His resurrection, of the lagging minds of His followers, that they did not understand all these things (Lk. xxiv. 25, 45), and for His great commission to Paul to go and open men's eyes that they might receive 'remission of sins and an inheritance among the sanctified by faith in Him' (Acts xxvi. 18).

It is very natural that a much fuller account of Jesus' teaching as to faith should be given in the more intimate discourses which are preserved by John. But in these discourses, too, His primary task is to bind men to Him by faith. The chief difference is that here, consonantly with the nature of the discourses recorded, much more prevailing stress is laid upon the higher aspects of faith, and we see Jesus striving specially to attract to Himself a faith consciously set upon eternal good. In a number of instances we find ourselves in much the same atmosphere as in the Synoptics (iv. 21 *sq.*, 48 *sq.*, ix. 35); and the method of Jesus is the same throughout. Everywhere He offers Himself as the object of faith, and claims faith in Himself for the highest concerns of the soul. But everywhere He begins at the level at which He finds His hearers, and leads them upward to these higher things. It is so that He deals with Nathanael (i. 51) and Nicodemus (iii. 12); and it is so that He deals constantly with the Jews, everywhere requiring faith in Himself for eternal life (v. 24, 25, 38, vi. 35, 40, 47, vii. 38, viii. 24, x. 25, 36, xii. 44, 46), declaring that faith in Him is the certain outcome of faith in their own Scriptures (v. 46, 47), is demanded by the witness borne Him by God in His mighty works (x. 25, 36, 37), is involved in and is indeed identical with faith in God (v. 25, 38, vi. 40, 45, viii. 47, xii. 44), and is the one thing which God requires of them (vi. 29), and the failure of which will bring them eternal ruin (iii. 18, v. 38, vi. 64, viii. 24). When dealing with His followers, His primary care was to build up their faith in Him. Witness especially His solicitude for their faith in the last hours of His intercourse with them. For the faith they had reposed in Him He returns thanks to God (xvii. 8), but He is still nursing their faith (xvi. 31), preparing for its increase through the events to come (xiii. 19, xvi. 29), and with almost passionate eagerness claiming it at their hands (xiv. 1, 10, 11, 12). Even after His resurrection we find Him restoring the faith of the waverer (xx. 29) with words which pronounce a special blessing on those who should hereafter believe on less compelling evidence—words whose point is not fully caught until we realize that they contain an intimation of the work of the apostles as, like His own, summed up in bringing men to faith in Him (xvii. 20, 21).

The record in Acts of the apostolic proclamation testifies to the faithfulness with which this office was prosecuted by Jesus' delegates (Acts iii. 22, 23). The task undertaken by them was, by persuading men (Acts xvii. 4, xxviii. 24), to bring them unto obedience to the faith that is in Jesus (Acts vi. 7, Rom. i. 5, xvi. 26, cf. II Thess. i. 8, II Cor. x. 5). And by such 'testifying faith towards our Lord Jesus Christ' (Acts xx. 21, cf. x. 43) there was quickly gathered together a community of 'believers' (Acts ii. 44, iv. 4, 32), that is, of believers in the Lord Jesus

Christ (Acts v. 14, ix. 42, xi. 17, xiv. 23), and that not only in Jerusalem but beyond (viii. 12, ix. 42, x. 45, xi. 21, xiii. 48, xiv. 1), and not only of Jews (x. 45, xv. 1, xxi. 20) but of Gentiles (xi. 21, xiii. 48, xiv. 1, xv. 7, xvii. 12, 34, xviii. 27, xix. 18, xxi. 25). The enucleation of this community of believers brought to the apostolic teachers the new task of preserving the idea of faith, which was the formative principle of the new community, and to propagate which in the world, pure and living and sound, was its chief office. It was inevitable that those who were called into the faith of Christ should bring into the infant Church with them many old tendencies of thinking, and that within the new community the fermentation of ideas should be very great. The task of instructing and disciplining the new community soon became unavoidably one of the heaviest of apostolic duties; and its progress is naturally reflected in their letters. Thus certain differences in their modes of dealing with faith emerge among New Testament writers, according as one lays stress on the deadness and profitlessness of a faith which produces no fruit in the life, and another on the valuelessness of a faith which does not emancipate from the bondage of the law; or as one lays stress on the perfection of the object of faith and the necessity of keeping the heart set upon it, and another on the necessity of preserving in its purity that subjective attitude towards the unseen and future which constitutes the very essence of faith; or as one lays stress on the reaching out of faith to the future in confident hope, and another on the present enjoyment by faith of all the blessings of salvation.

It was to James that it fell to rebuke the Jewish tendency to conceive of the faith which was pleasing to Jehovah as a mere intellectual acquiescence in His being and claims, when imported into the Church and made to do duty as 'the faith of our Lord Jesus Christ, the Glory' (ii. 1). He has sometimes been misread as if he were depreciating faith, or at least the place of faith in salvation. But it is perfectly clear that with James, as truly as with any other New Testament writer, a sound faith in the Lord Jesus Christ as the manifested God (ii. 1) lies at the very basis of the Christian life (i. 3), and is the condition of all acceptable approach to God (i. 6, v. 15). It is not faith as he conceives it which he depreciates, but that professed faith (λέγη, ii. 14) which cannot be shown to be real by appropriate works (ii. 18), and so differs by a whole diameter alike from the faith of Abraham that was reckoned unto him for righteousness (ii. 23), and from the faith of Christians as James understood it (ii. 1, i. 3, cf. i. 22). The impression which is easily taken from the last half of the second chapter of James, that his teaching and that of Paul stand in some polemic relation, is, nevertheless, a delusion, and arises from an insufficient realization of the place occupied by faith in the discussions of the Jewish schools, reflections of which have naturally found their way into the language of both Paul and James. And so far are we from needing to suppose some reference, direct or indirect, to Pauline teaching to account for James' entrance upon the question which he discusses, that this was a matter upon which an earnest teacher could not fail to touch in the presence of a tendency common among the Jews at the advent of Christianity (cf. Mt. iii. 9, vii. 21, xiii. 3, Rom. ii. 17), and certain to pass over into Jewish-Christian circles: and James' treatment of it finds, indeed, its entire presupposition in the state of things underlying the exhortation of i. 22. When read from his own historical standpoint, James' teachings are free from any disaccord with those of Paul, who as strongly as James denies all value to a faith which does not work by love (Gal. v. 6, I Cor. xiii. 2, I Thess. i. 3). In short, James is not depreciating faith: with him, too, it is faith that is reckoned unto righteousness (ii. 23), though only such a faith as shows itself in works can be so reckoned, because a faith which does not come to fruitage in works is dead, non-existent. He is rather deepening the idea of faith, and insisting that it includes in its very conception something more than an otiose intellectual assent.

It was a far more serious task which was laid upon Paul. As apostle to the Gentiles he was called upon to make good in all its depth of meaning the fundamental principle of the religion of grace, that the righteous shall live by faith, as over-against what had come to be the ingrained legalism of Jewish thought now intruded into the Christian Church. It was not, indeed, doubted that faith was requisite for obtaining salvation. But he that had been born a Jew and was conscious of the privileges of the children of the promise, found it hard to think that faith was all that was requisite. What, then, was the advantage of the Jew? In defence of the rights of the Gentiles, Paul was forced in the most uncompromising way to validate the great proposition that, in the matter of salvation, there is no distinction between Jew and Gentile,—that the Jew has no other righteousness than that which comes through faith in Jesus Christ (Gal. ii. 15 *sq.*), and that the Gentile fully possesses this righteousness from faith alone (Gal. iii. 7 *sq.*); in a word, that the one God, who is God of the Gentiles also, 'shall justify the circumcision by faith, and the uncircumcision through faith' (Rom. iii. 30). Thus was it made clear not only that 'no man is justified by the law' (Gal. ii. 16, iii. 11, Rom. iii. 20), but also that a man is justified by faith apart from law-works (Rom. iii. 28). The splendid vigour and thoroughness of Paul's dialectic development of the absolute contrast between the ideas of faith and works, by virtue of which one peremptorily excludes the other, left no hiding-place for a work-righteousness of any kind or degree, but cast all men solely upon the righteousness of God, which is apart from the law and comes through faith unto all that believe (Rom. iii. 21, 22). Thus, in vindicating the place of faith as the only instrument of salvation, Paul necessarily dwelt much upon the object of faith, not as if he were formally teaching what the object is on which faith savingly lays hold, but as a natural result of his effort to show from its object the all-sufficiency of faith. It is because faith lays hold of Jesus Christ, who was delivered up for our trespasses and was raised for our justification (Rom. iv. 25), and makes us possessors of the righteousness provided by God through Him, that there is no room for any righteousness of our own in the ground of our salvation (Rom. x. 3, Eph. ii. 8). This is the reason of that full development of the object of faith in Paul's writings, and especially of the specific connexion between faith and the righteousness of God proclaimed in Christ, by which the doctrine of

Paul is sometimes said to be distinguished from the more general conception of faith which is characteristic of the Epistle to the Hebrews. This more general conception of faith is not, however, the peculiar property of that epistle, but is the fundamental conception of the whole body of biblical writers in the Old Testament and in the New Testament (cf. Mt. vi. 25, xvi. 23, Jn. xx. 29, 31, I Pet. i. 8), including Paul himself (II Cor. iv. 18, v. 7, Rom. iv. 16-22, viii. 24); while, on the other hand, the Epistle to the Hebrews, no less than Paul, teaches that there is no righteousness except through faith (x. 38, xi. 7, cf. xi. 4).

That in the Epistle to the Hebrews it is the general idea of faith, or, to be more exact, the subjective nature of faith, that is dwelt upon, rather than its specific object, is not due to a peculiar conception of what faith lays hold upon, but to the particular task which fell to its writer in the work of planting Christianity in the world. With him, too, the person and work of Christ are the specific object of faith (xiii. 7, 8, iii. 14, x. 22). But the danger against which, in the providence of God, he was called upon to guard the infant flock, was not that it should fall away from faith to works, but that it should fall away from faith into despair. His readers were threatened not with legalism but with 'shrinking back' (x. 39), and he needed, therefore, to emphasize not so much the object of faith as the duty of faith. Accordingly, it is not so much on the righteousness of faith as on its perfecting that he insists; it is not so much its contrast with works as its contrast with impatience that he impresses on his readers' consciences; it is not so much to faith specifically in Christ and in Him alone that he exhorts them as to an attitude of faith—an attitude which could rise above the seen to the unseen, the present to the future, the temporal to the eternal, and which in the midst of sufferings could retain patience, in the midst of disappointments could preserve hope. This is the key to the whole treatment of faith in the Epistle to the Hebrews—its definition as the assurance of things hoped for, the conviction of things not seen (xi. 1); its illustration and enforcement by the example of the heroes of faith in the past, a list chosen and treated with the utmost skill for the end in view (xi.); its constant attachment to the promises (iv. 1, 2, vi. 12, x. 36, 38, xi. 9); its connexion with the faithfulness (xi. 11, cf. x. 23), almightiness (xi. 19), and the rewards of God (xi. 6, 26); and its association with such virtues as boldness (iii. 6, iv. 16, x. 19, 35), confidence (iii. 14, xi. 1), patience (x. 36, xii. 1), hope (iii. 6, vi. 11, 18, x. 23).

With much that is similar to the situation implied in Hebrews, that which underlies the Epistle of Peter differs from it in the essential particular that their prevailingly Gentile readers were not in imminent danger of falling back into Judaism. There is, accordingly, much in the aspect in which faith is presented in these epistles which reminds us of what we find in Hebrews, as, for example, the close connexion into which it is brought with obedience (I Pet. i. 2, 22, ii. 7, iii. 1, iv. 17), its prevailing reference to what is unseen and future (I Pet. i. 5, 7-10, 21), and its consequent demand for steadfastness (v. 9, cf. i. 7), and especially for hope (i. 21, cf. i. 3, 13, iii. 5, 15). Yet there is a noteworthy difference in the whole tone of the commendation of faith, which was rooted, no doubt, in the character of Peter, as the tone of his speeches recorded in Acts shows, but which also grew out of the nature of the task set before him in these letters. There is no hint of despair lying in the near background, but the buoyancy of assured hope rings throughout these epistles. Having hearkened to the prophet like unto Moses (Deut. xviii. 15, 19, Acts iii. 22, 23), Christians are the children of obedience (I Pet. i. 14), and through their precious faith (I Pet. i. 7, II Pet. i. 1) possessors of the preciousness of the promises (I Pet. ii. 7). As they have obeyed the voice of God and kept His covenant, they have become His peculiar treasure, a kingdom of priests and a holy nation (Ex. xix. 5, I Pet. ii. 9). Naturally, the duty rests upon them of living, while here below, in accordance with their high hopes (I Pet. i. 13, II Pet. i. 5). But in any event they are but sojourners and pilgrims here (I Pet. ii. 11, i. 1, 17), and have a sure inheritance reserved for them in heaven (i. 4), unto which they are guarded through faith by

the power of God (i. 5). The reference of faith in Peter is therefore characteristically to the completion rather than to the inception of salvation (i. 5, 9, ii. 6, cf. Acts xv. 11). Of course this
does not imply that he does not share the common biblical conception of faith: he is conscious of no difference of view from
that of the Old Testament (I Pet. ii. 6); and, no less than with
James, with him faith is the fountain of all good works (I Pet.
i. 7, 21, v. 9, II Pet. i. 5); and, no less than with Paul, with him
faith lays hold of the righteousness of Christ (II Pet. i. 1). It
only means that in the circumstances of his writing he is led to
lay special emphasis on the reference of faith to the consummated salvation, in order to quicken in his readers that hope
which would sustain them in their persecutions, and to keep
their eyes set, not on their present trials, but, in accordance
with faith's very nature, on the unseen and eternal glory.

In the entirely different circumstances in which he wrote,
John wished to lay stress on the very opposite aspect of faith.
For what is characteristic of John's treatment of faith is insistence not so much on the certainty and glory of the future
inheritance which it secures, as on the fulness of the present
enjoyment of salvation which it brings. There was pressing
into the Church a false emphasis on knowledge, which affected
to despise simple faith. This John met, on the one hand, by
deepening the idea of knowledge to the knowledge of experience, and, on the other, by insisting upon the immediate
entrance of every believer into the possession of salvation. It is
not to be supposed, of course, that he was ready to neglect or
deny that out-reaching of faith to the future on which Peter lays
such stress: he is zealous that Christians shall know that they
are children of God from the moment of believing, and from
that instant possessors of the new life of the Spirit; but he does
not forget the greater glory of the future, and he knows how to
use this Christian hope also as an incitement to holy living
(I Jn. iii. 2). Nor are we to suppose that, in his anti-Gnostic
insistence on the element of conviction in faith, he would lose
sight of that central element of surrendering trust which is the

heart of faith in other portions of the Scriptures: he would
indeed have believers know what they believe, and who He is
in whom they put their trust, and what He has done for them,
and is doing, and will do, in and through them; but this is not
that they may know these things simply as intellectual propositions, but that they may rest on them in faith and know them
in personal experience. Least of all the New Testament writers
could John confine faith to a merely intellectual act: his whole
doctrine of faith is rather a protest against the intellectualism
of Gnosticism. His fundamental conception of faith differs in
nothing from that of the other New Testament writers; with
him, too, it is a trustful appropriation of Christ and surrender
of self to His salvation. Eternal life has been manifested by
Christ (Jn. i. 4, I Jn. i. 1, 2, v. 11), and he, and he only, who
has the Son has the life (I Jn. v. 12). But in the conflict in
which he was engaged he required to throw the strongest emphasis possible upon the immediate entrance of believers into
this life. This insistence had manifold applications to the circumstances of his readers. It had, for example, a negative application to the antinomian tendency of Gnostic teaching, which
John does not fail to press (I Jn. i. 5, ii. 4, 15, iii. 6): 'whosoever
believeth that Jesus is the Christ is begotten of God' (I Jn.
v. 1), and 'whosoever is begotten of God doeth no sin' (I Jn.
iii. 9). It had also a positive application to their own encouragement: the simple believer was placed on a plane of life to which
no knowledge could attain; the new life received by faith gave
the victory over the world; and John boldly challenges experience to point to any who have overcome the world but he that
believes that Jesus is the Son of God (I Jn. v. 4, 5). Accordingly,
it is characteristic of John to announce that 'he that believeth
hath eternal life' (Jn. iii. 36, v. 24, vi. 47, 54, I Jn. iii. 14, 15,
v. 11, 12, 13). He even declares the purpose of his writing to
be, in the Gospel, that his readers 'may believe that Jesus is the
Christ, the Son of God, and that, believing, they may have life
in his name' (xx. 31); and in the First Epistle, that they that
believe in the name of the Son of God 'may know that they
have eternal life' (I Jn. v. 13).

II. THE BIBLICAL CONCEPTION

By means of the providentially mediated diversity of emphasis of the New Testament writers on the several aspects of faith, the outlines of the biblical conception of faith are thrown into very high relief.

Of its *subjective nature* we have what is almost a formal definition in the description of it as an 'assurance of things hoped for, a conviction of things not seen' (Heb. xi. 1). It obviously contains in it, therefore, an element of knowledge (Heb. xi. 6), and it as obviously issues in conduct (Heb. xi. 8, cf. v. 9, I Pet. i. 22). But it consists neither in assent nor in obedience, but in a reliant trust in the invisible Author of all good (Heb. xi. 27), in which the mind is set upon the things that are above and not on the things that are upon the earth (Col. iii. 2, cf. II Cor. iv. 16-18, Mt. vi. 25). The examples cited in Heb. xi are themselves enough to show that the faith there commended is not a mere belief in God's existence and justice and goodness, or crediting of His word and promises, but a practical counting of Him faithful (xi. 11), with a trust so profound that no trial can shake it (xi. 35), and so absolute that it survives the loss of even its own pledge (xi. 17). So little is faith in its biblical conception merely a conviction of the understanding, that, when that is called faith, the true idea of faith needs to be built up above this word (Jas. ii. 14 ff.). It is a movement of the whole inner man (Rom. x. 9, 10), and is set in contrast with an unbelief that is akin, not to ignorance but to disobedience (Heb. iii. 18, 19, Jn. iii. 36, Rom. xi. 20, 30, xv. 31, I Thess. i. 8, Heb. iv. 2, 6, I Pet. i. 7, 8, iii. 1, 20, iv. 18, Acts xiv. 2, xix. 9), and that grows out of, not lack of information, but that aversion of the heart from God (Heb. iii. 12) which takes pleasure in unrighteousness (II Thess. ii. 12), and is so unsparingly exposed by our Lord (Jn. iii. 19, v. 44, viii. 47, x. 26). In the breadth of its idea, it is thus the going out of the heart from itself and its resting on God in confident trust for all good. But the scriptural revelation has to do with, and is directed to the needs of, not man in the abstract, but sinful man; and for sinful man this hearty reliance on God necessarily becomes humble trust in Him for the fundamental need of the sinner— forgiveness of sins and reception into favour. In response to the revelations of His grace and the provisions of His mercy, it commits itself without reserve and with abnegation of all self-dependence, to Him as its sole and sufficient Saviour, and thus, in one act, empties itself of all claim on God and casts itself upon His grace alone for salvation.

It is, accordingly, solely from its *object* that faith derives its value. This object is uniformly the God of grace, whether conceived of broadly as the source of all life, light, and blessing, on whom man in his creaturely weakness is entirely dependent, or, whenever sin and the eternal welfare of the soul are in view, as the Author of salvation in whom alone the hope of unworthy man can be placed. This one object of saving faith never varies from the beginning to the end of the scriptural revelation; though, naturally, there is an immense difference between its earlier and later stages in fulness of knowledge as to the nature of the redemptive work by which the salvation intrusted to God shall be accomplished; and as naturally there occurs a very great variety of forms of statement in which trust in the God of salvation receives expression. Already, however, at the gate of Eden, the God in whom the trust of our first parents is reposed is the God of the gracious promise of the retrieval of the injury inflicted by the serpent; and from that beginning of knowledge the progress is steady, until, what is implied in the primal promise having become express in the accomplished work of redemption, the trust of sinners is explicitly placed in the God who was in Christ reconciling the world unto Himself (II Cor. v. 19). Such a faith, again, could not fail to embrace with humble confidence all the gracious promises of the God of salvation, from which indeed it draws its life and strength; nor could it fail to lay hold with strong conviction on all those revealed truths concerning Him which constitute, indeed, in the varied circumstances in which it has been called upon to persist throughout the ages, the very grounds in view of which it has been able to rest upon Him with steadfast trust. These truths, in which the 'Gospel' or glad-tidings to God's people has been from time to time embodied, run all the way from such simple facts as that it was the very God of their fathers that had appeared unto Moses for their deliverance (Ex. iv. 5), to such stupendous facts, lying at the root of the very work of salvation itself, as that Jesus is the Christ, the Son of God sent of God to save the world (Jn. vi. 69, viii. 24, xi. 42, xiii. 19, xvi. 27, 30, xvii. 8, 21, xx. 31, I Jn. v. 15), that God has raised Him from the dead (Rom. x. 9, I Thess. iv. 14), and that as His children we shall live with Him (Rom. vi. 8). But in believing this variously presented Gospel, faith has ever terminated with trustful reliance, not on the promise but on the Promiser,—not on the propositions which declare God's grace and willingness to save, or Christ's divine nature and power, or the reality and perfection of His saving work, but on the Saviour upon whom, because of these great facts, it could securely rest as on One able to save to the uttermost. Jesus Christ, God the Redeemer, is accordingly the one object of saving faith, presented to its embrace at first implicitly and in promise, and ever more and more openly until at last it is entirely explicit and we read that 'a man is not justified save through faith in Jesus Christ' (Gal. ii. 16). If, with even greater explicitness still, faith is sometimes said to rest upon some element in the saving work of Christ, as, for example, upon His blood or His righteousness (Rom. iii. 25, II Pet. i. 1), obviously such a singling out of the very thing in His work on which faith takes hold, in no way derogates from its repose upon Him, and Him only, as the sole and sufficient Saviour.

The *saving power* of faith resides thus not in itself, but in the Almighty Saviour on whom it rests. It is never on account of its formal nature as a psychic act that faith is conceived in Scripture to be saving,—as if this frame of mind or attitude of heart were itself a virtue with claims on God for reward, or at least especially pleasing to Him (either in its nature or as an act of obedience) and thus predisposing Him to favour, or as if it brought the soul into an attitude of receptivity or of sympathy with God, or opened a channel of communication from Him.

It is not faith that saves, but faith in Jesus Christ: faith in any other saviour, or in this or that philosophy or human conceit (Col. ii. 16, 18, I Tim. iv. 1), or in any other gospel than that of Jesus Christ and Him as crucified (Gal. i. 8, 9), brings not salvation but a curse. It is not, strictly speaking, even faith in Christ that saves, but Christ that saves through faith. The saving power resides exclusively, not in the act of faith or the attitude of faith or the nature of faith, but in the object of faith; and in this the whole biblical representation centres, so that we could not more radically misconceive it than by transferring to faith even the smallest fraction of that saving energy which is attributed in the Scriptures solely to Christ Himself. This purely mediatory function of faith is very clearly indicated in the regimens in which it stands, which ordinarily express simple instrumentality. It is most frequently joined to its verb as the dative of means or instrument (Acts xv. 9, xxvi. 18, Rom. iii. 28, iv. 20, v. 2, xi. 20, II Cor. i. 24, Heb. xi. 3, 4, 5, 7, 8, 9, 11, 17, 20, 21, 23, 24 || 27, 28, 29, 30, 31); and the relationship intended is further explained by the use to express it of the prepositions $\dot{\epsilon}\kappa$ (Rom. i. 17, 17, iii. 26, 30, iv. 16, 16, v. 1, ix. 30, 32, x. 6, xiv. 23, 23, Gal. ii. 16, iii. 7, 8, 9, 11, 12, 27, 28, v. 5, I Tim. i. 5, Heb. x. 38, Jas. ii. 24) and $\delta\iota\acute{a}$ (with the genitive, never with the accusative, Rom. iii. 22, 25, 30, II Cor. v. 7, Gal. ii. 16, iii. 14, 26, II Tim. iii. 15, Heb. vi. 12, xi. 33, 39, I Pet. i. 5),— the fundamental idea of the former construction being that of source or origin, and of the latter that of mediation or instrumentality, though they are used together in the same context, apparently with no distinction of meaning (Rom. iii. 25, 26, 30, Gal. ii. 16). It is not necessary to discover an essentially different implication in the exceptional usage of the prepositions $\dot{\epsilon}\pi\acute{\iota}$ (Acts iii: 16, Phil. iii. 9) and $\kappa\alpha\tau\acute{a}$ (Heb. xi. 7, 13, cf. Mt. ix. 29) in this connexion: $\dot{\epsilon}\pi\acute{\iota}$ is apparently to be taken in a quasi-temporal sense, 'on faith,' giving the occasion of the divine act, and $\kappa\alpha\tau\acute{a}$ very similarly in the sense of conformability, 'in conformity with faith.' Not infrequently we meet also with a construction with the preposition $\dot{\epsilon}\nu$ which properly designates the sphere, but which in passages like Gal. ii. 20, Col. ii. 7, II

Thess. ii. 13 appears to pass over into the conception of instru-mentality.

So little indeed is faith conceived as containing in itself the energy or ground of salvation, that it is consistently represented as, in its *origin*, itself a gratuity from God in the prosecution of His saving work. It comes, not of one's own strength or virtue, but only to those who are chosen of God for its reception (II Thess. ii. 13), and hence is His gift (Eph. vi. 23, cf. ii. 8, 9, Phil. i. 29), through Christ (Acts iii. 16, Phil. i. 29, I Pet. i. 21, cf. Heb. xii. 2), by the Spirit (II Cor. iv. 13, Gal. v. 5), by means of the preached word (Rom. x. 17, Gal. iii. 2, 5); and as it is thus obtained from God (II Pet. i. 1, Jude 3, I Pet. i. 21), thanks are to be returned to God for it (Col. i. 4, II Thess. i. 3). Thus, even here all boasting is excluded, and salvation is conceived in all its elements as the pure product of unalloyed grace, issuing not from, but in, good works (Eph. ii. 8-12). The place of faith in the process of salvation, as biblically conceived, could scarcely, therefore, be better described than by the use of the scholastic term 'instrumental cause.' Not in one portion of the Scriptures alone, but throughout their whole extent, it is conceived as a boon from above which comes to men, no doubt through the channels of their own activities, but not as if it were an effect of their energies, but rather, as it has been finely phrased, as a gift which God lays in the lap of the soul. 'With the heart,' indeed, 'man believeth unto righteousness'; but this believing does not arise of itself out of any heart indifferently, nor is it grounded in the heart's own potencies; it is grounded rather in the freely-giving goodness of God, and comes to man as a bene-faction out of heaven.

The *effects* of faith, not being the immediate product of faith itself but of that energy of God which was exhibited in raising Jesus from the dead and on which dependence is now placed for raising us with Him into newness of life (Col. ii. 12), would seem to depend directly only on the fact of faith, leaving questions of its strength, quality, and the like more or less to one side. We find a proportion, indeed, suggested between faith and its effects (Mt. ix. 29, viii. 13, cf. viii. 10, xv. 28, xvii. 20, Lk.

vii. 9, xvii. 6). Certainly there is a fatal doubt, which vitiates with its double-mindedness every approach to God (Jas. i. 6-8, cf. iv. 8, Mt. xxi. 21, Mk. xi. 23, Rom. iv. 20, xiv. 23, Jude 22). But Jesus deals with notable tenderness with those of 'little faith,' and His apostles imitated Him in this (Mt. vi. 30 f., 20, xiv. 31, xvi. 8, xvii. 20, Lk. xii. 28, Mk. ix. 24, Lk. xvii. 5, cf. Rom. xiv. 1, 2, I Cor. viii. 7). The effects of faith may possibly vary also with the end for which the trust is exercised (cf. Mk. x. 51 ἵνα ἀναβλέψω with Gal. ii. 16 ἐπιστεύσαμεν ἵνα δικαιωθῶμεν). But he who humbly but confidently casts himself on the God of salvation has the assurance that he shall not be put to shame (Rom. xi. 11, ix. 33), but shall receive the end of his faith, even the salvation of his soul (I Pet. i. 9). This salvation is no doubt, in its idea, received all at once (Jn. iii. 36, I Jn. v. 12); but it is in its very nature a process, and its stages come, each in its order. First of all, the believer, renouncing by the very act of faith his own righteousness which is out of the law, receives that 'righteousness which is through faith in Christ, the righteousness which is from God on faith' (Phil. iii. 9, cf. Rom. iii. 22, iv. 11, ix. 30, x. 3, 10, II Cor. v. 21, Gal. v. 5, Heb. xi. 7, II Pet. i. 1). On the ground of this righteousness, which in its origin is the 'righteous act' of Christ, constituted by His 'obedience' (Rom. v. 18, 19), and comes to the believer as a 'gift' (Rom. v. 17), being reckoned to him apart from works (Rom. iv. 6), he that believes in Christ is justified in God's sight, received into His favour, and made the recipient of the Holy Spirit (Jn. vii. 39, cf. Acts v. 32), by whose indwelling men are constituted the sons of God (Rom. viii. 13). And if children, then are they heirs (Rom. viii. 17), assured of an incorruptible, undefiled, and unfading inheritance, reserved in heaven for them; and meanwhile they are guarded by the power of God through faith unto this gloriously complete salvation (I Pet. i. 4, 5). Thus, though the immediate effect of faith is only to make the believer possessor before the judgment-seat of God of the alien righteousness wrought out by Christ, through this one effect it draws in its train the whole series of saving acts of God, and of saving effects on the soul. Being justified by faith, the enmity which has existed between the sinner and God has been abolished, and he has been introduced into the very family of God, and made sharer in all the blessings of His house (Eph. ii. 13 f.). Being justified by faith, he has peace with God, and rejoices in the hope of the glory of God, and is enabled to meet the trials of life, not merely with patience but with joy (Rom. v. 1 f.). Being justified by faith, he has already working within him the life which the Son has brought into the world, and by which, through the operations of the Spirit which those who believe in Him receive (Jn. vii. 39), he is enabled to overcome the world lying in the evil one, and, kept by God from the evil one, to sin not (I Jn. v. 19). In a word, because we are justified by faith, we are, through faith, endowed with all the privileges and supplied with all the graces of the children of God.

APPENDIX

THE PHILOLOGICAL EXPRESSION OF FAITH

THE verb 'to believe' in the Authorized Version of the Old Testament uniformly represents the Hebrew הֶאֱמִין, Hiphil of אָמַן, except, of course, in Dan. vi. 23 where it represents the corresponding Aramaic form. The root, which is widely spread among the Semitic tongues, and which in the word 'Amen' has been adopted into every language spoken by Christian, Jew, or Mohammedan, seems everywhere to convey the fundamental ideas of 'fixedness, stability, steadfastness, reliability.' What the ultimate conception is which underlies these ideas remains somewhat doubtful, but it would appear to be rather that of 'holding' than that of 'supporting' (although this last is the sense adopted in "Oxf. Heb. Lex."). In the simple species the verb receives both transitive and intransitive vocalization. With intransitive vocalization it means 'to be firm,' 'to be secure,' 'to be faithful,' and occurs in biblical Hebrew only in the past participle, designating those who are 'faithful' (II Sam. xx. 19, Ps. xii. 1, xxxi. 23). Wth transitive vocalization it occurs in

biblical Hebrew only in a very specialized application, conveying the idea, whether as participle or verbal noun, of 'care-
taking' or 'nursing' (II Kings x. 1, 5, Est. ii. 7, Ru. iv. 16, II Sam.
iv. 4, Num. xi. 12, Isa. xlix. 23, Lam. iv. 5; cf. II Kings xviii. 16
'pillars' and [the Niphal] Isa. lx. 4), the implication in which
seems to be that of 'holding,' 'bearing,' 'carrying.' The Niphal
occurs once as the passive of transitive Qal (Isa. lx. 4): elsewhere it is formed from intransitive Qal, and is used very much
in the same sense. Whatever holds, is steady, or can be depended upon, whether a wall which securely holds a nail (Isa.
xxii. 23, 25), or a brook which does not fail (Jer. xv. 18), or a
kingdom which is firmly established (II Sam. vii. 16), or an
assertion which has been verified (Gen. xlii. 20), or a covenant
which endures for ever (Ps. lxxxix. 28), or a heart found faithful
(Neh. ix. 8), or a man who can be trusted (Neh. xiii. 13), or
God Himself who keeps covenant (Deut. vii. 9), is נֶאֱמָן. The
Hiphil occurs in one passage in the primary physical sense of
the root (Job xxxix. 24). Elsewhere it bears constantly the sense
of 'to trust,' weakening down to the simple 'to believe' (Ex. iv.
31, Ps. cxvi. 10, Isa. vii. 9, xxviii. 16, Hab. i. 5). Obviously it is
a subjective causative, and expresses the acquisition or exhibi-
tion of the firmness, security, reliability, faithfulness which lies
in the root-meaning of the verb, in or with respect to its object.
The מַאֲמִין is therefore one whose state of mind is free from
faintheartedness (Isa. vii. 9) and anxious haste (Isa. xxviii. 16),
and who stays himself upon the object of his contemplation
with confidence and trust. The implication seems to be, not so
much that of a passive dependence as of a vigorous active commitment. He who, in the Hebrew sense, exercises faith, is secure,
assured, confident (Deut. xxviii. 66, Job xxiv. 22, Ps. xxvii. 13),
and lays hold of the object of his confidence with firm trust.

The most common construction of הֶאֱמִין is with the preposition בְּ, and in this construction its fundamental meaning seems
to be most fully expressed. It is probably never safe to represent
this phrase by the simple 'believe'; the preposition rather introduces the person or thing in which one believes, or on which one
believingly rests as on firm ground. This is true even when the

object of the affection is a thing, whether divine words, commandments, or works (Ps. cvi. 12, cxix. 66, lxxviii. 32), or some earthly force or good (Job xxxix. 12, xv. 31, xxiv. 22, Deut. xxviii. 66). It is no less true when the object is a person, human (I Sam. xxvii. 12, Prov. xxvi. 25, Jer. xii. 6, Mic. vii. 5) or superhuman (Job iv. 18, xv. 15), or the representative of God, in whom therefore men should place their confidence (Ex. xix. 9, II Chron. xx. 20). It is above all true, however, when the object of the affection is God Himself, and that indifferently whether or not the special exercise of faith adverted to is rooted in a specific occasion (Gen. xv. 6, Ex. xiv. 31, Num. xiv. 11, xx. 12, Deut. i. 32, II Kings xvii. 14, II Chron. xx. 20, Ps. lxxviii. 22, Jon. iii. 5). The weaker conception of 'believing' seems, on the other hand, to lie in the construction with the preposition ל, which appears to introduce the person or thing, not on which one confidingly rests, but to the testimony of which one assentingly turns. This credence may be given by the simple to every untested word (Prov. xiv. 15); it may be withheld until seeing takes the place of believing (I Kings x. 7, II Chron. ix. 6); it is due to words of the Lord and of His messengers, as well as to the signs wrought by them (Ps. cvi. 24, Isa. liii. 1, Ex. iv. 8, 9). It may also be withheld from any human speaker (Gen. xlv. 26, Ex. iv. 1, 8, Jer. xl. 14, II Chron. xxxii. 15), but is the right of God when He bears witness to His majesty or makes promises to His people (Isa. xliii. 10, Deut. ix. 23). In this weakened sense of the word the proposition believed is sometimes attached to it by the conjunction כִּי (Ex. iv. 5, Job ix. 16, Lam. iv. 12). In its construction with the infinitive, however, its deeper meaning comes out more strongly (Judg. xi. 20, Job xv. 22, Ps. xxvii. 13), and the same is true when the verb is used absolutely (Ex. iv. 31, Isa. vii. 9, xxviii. 16, Ps. cxvi. 10, Job xxix. 24, Hab. i. 5). In these constructions faith is evidently the assurance of things hoped for, the conviction of things not seen.

No hiphilate noun from this root occurs in the Old Testament. This circumstance need not in itself possess significance; the notions of 'faith' and 'faithfulness' lie close to one another, and are not uncommonly expressed by a single term (so πίστις, *fides*, faith). As a matter of fact, however, 'faith,' in its active sense, can barely be accounted an Old Testament term. It occurs in the Authorized Version of the Old Testament only twice: Deut. xxxii. 20 where it represents the Hebrew אֵמֻן and Hab. ii. 4 where it stands for the Hebrew אֱמוּנָה; and it would seem to be really demanded in no passage but Hab. ii. 4. The very point of this passage, however, is the sharp contrast which is drawn between arrogant self-sufficiency and faithful dependence on God. The purpose of the verse is to give a reply to the prophet's inquiry as to God's righteous dealings with the Chaldæans. Since it is by faith that the righteous man lives, the arrogant Chaldæan, whose soul is puffed up and not straight within him, cannot but be destined to destruction. The whole drift of the broader context bears out this meaning; for throughout this prophecy the Chaldæan is ever exhibited as the type of insolent self-assertion (i. 7, 11, 16), in contrast with which the righteous appear, certainly not as men of integrity and steadfast faithfulness, but as men who look in faith to God and trustingly depend upon His arm. The obvious reminiscence of Gen. xv. 6 throws its weight into the same scale, to which may be added the consent of the Jewish expositors of the passage. Here we have, therefore, thrown into a clear light the contrasting characteristics of the wicked, typified by the Chaldæan, and of the righteous: of the one the fundamental trait is self-sufficiency; of the other, faith. This faith, which forms the distinctive feature of the righteous man, and by which he obtains life, is obviously no mere assent. It is a profound and abiding disposition, an ingrained attitude of mind and heart towards God which affects and gives character to all the activities. Here only the term occurs in the Old Testament; but on this its sole occurrence it rises to the full height of its most pregnant meaning.

The extreme rarity of the noun 'faith' in the Old Testament may prepare us to note that even the verb 'to believe' is far from common in it. In a religious application it occurs in only some thirteen Old Testament books, and less than a score and a half times. The thing believed is sometimes a specific word or

work of God (Lam. iv. 12, Hab. i. 5), the fact of a divine revelation (Ex. iv. 5, Job ix. 16), or the words or commandments
of God in general (with ב Ps. cvi. 12, cxix. 66). In Ex. xix. 9
and II Chron. xx. 20 God's prophets are the object of His
people's confidence. God Himself is the object to which they
believingly turn, or on whom they rest in assured trust, in
some eleven cases. In two of these it is to Him as a faithful
witness that faith believingly turns (Deut. ix. 23, Isa. xliii. 10).
In the remainder of them it is upon His very person that faith
rests in assured confidence (Gen. xv. 6, Ex. xiv. 31, Num. xiv.
11, xx. 12, Deut. i. 32, II Kings xvii. 14, II Chron. xx. 20, Ps.
lxxviii. 22, Jon. iii. 5). It is in these instances, in which the construction is with ב, together with those in which the word is
used absolutely (Ex. iv. 31, Isa. vii. 9, xxviii. 16, Ps. cxvi. 10),
to which may be added Ps. xxvii. 13 where it is construed with
the infinitive, that the conception of religious believing comes
to its rights. The typical instance is, of course, the great word
of Gen. xv. 6, 'And Abram believed in the LORD, and he
counted it to him for righteousness'; in which all subsequent
believers, Jewish and Christian alike, have found the primary
example of faith. The object of Abram's faith, as here set forth,
was not the promise which appears as the occasion of its exercise; what it rested on was God Himself, and that not merely as
the giver of the promise here recorded, but as His servant's
shield and exceeding great reward (xv. 1). It is therefore not
the assentive but the fiducial element of faith which is here
emphasized; in a word, the faith which Abram gave Jehovah
when he 'put his trust in God' (ἐπίστευσεν τῷ θεῷ LXX), was
the same faith which later He sought in vain at the hands of
His people (Num. xiv. 11, cf. Deut. i. 32, II Kings xvii. 14),
and the notion of which the Psalmist explains in the parallel,
'They believed not in God, and trusted not in his salvation'
(Ps. lxxviii. 22). To believe in God, in the Old Testament sense,
is thus not merely to assent to His word, but with firm and unwavering confidence to rest in security and trustfulness upon
Him.

In the Greek of the Septuagint πιστεύειν takes its place as

the regular rendering of הֶאֱמִין and is very rarely set aside in favour of another word expressing trust (Prov. xxvi. 25 πείθεσ-θαι). In a few cases, however, it is strengthened by composition with a preposition (Deut. i. 32, Judg. xi. 20, II Chron. xx. 20, cf. Sir. i. 15, ii. 10 etc., I Macc. i. 30, vii. 16, etc., ἐμπιστεύειν; Mic. vii. 5, καταπιστεύειν); and in a few others it is construed with prepositions (ἔν τινι, Jer. xii. 6, Ps. lxxviii. 22, Dan. vi. 23, I Sam. xxvii. 12, II Chron. xx. 20, Mic. vii. 5, Sir. xxxv. 21; ἐπί τινα, Isa. xxviii. 16 (?), III Macc. ii. 7; ἐπί τινι, Wis. xii. 2; εἰς τινα, Sir. xxxviii. 31; κατά τινα, Job iv. 18, xv. 15, xxiv. 22).

It was by being thus made the vehicle for expressing the high religious faith of the Old Testament that the word was prepared for its New Testament use. For it had the slightest possible connection with religious faith in classical speech. Resting ultimately on a root with the fundamental sense of 'binding,' and standing in classical Greek as the common term for 'trusting,' 'putting faith in,' 'relying upon,' shading down into 'believing,' it was rather too strong a term for ordinary use of that ungenial relation to the gods which was character-istic of Greek thought, and which was substantively expressed by πίστις—the proper acknowledgment in thought and act of their existence and rights. For this νομίζειν was the usual term, and the relative strength of the two terms may be observed in their use in the opening sections of Xenophon's "Memorabilia" (I. i. 1 and 5), where Socrates is charged with not believing in the gods whom the city owned (νομίζειν τοὺς θεούς), but is affirmed to have stood in a much more intimate relation to them, to have trusted in them (πιστεύειν τοῖς θεοῖς). Something of the same depth of meaning may lurk in the exhortation of the Epinomis (980 C), Πιστεύσας τοῖς θεοῖς εὔχου. But ordi-narily πιστεύειν τοῖς θεοῖς appears as the synonym of νομίζειν τοὺς θεούς, and imports merely the denial of atheism (Plut. "de Superst.," ii.; Arist. "Rhet.," ii. 17). It was only by its adoption by the writers of the Septuagint to express the faith of the Old Testament that it was fitted to take its place in the New Testament as the standing designation of the attitude of the man of faith towards God.

This service the Septuagint could not perform for πίστις also, owing to the almost complete absence of the noun 'faith' in the active sense from the Old Testament; but it was due to a Hellenistic development on the basis of the Old Testament religion, and certainly not without influence from Gen. xv. 6 and Hab. ii. 4 that this term, too, was prepared for New Testament use. In classical Greek πίστις is applied to belief in the gods chiefly as implying that such belief rests rather on trust than on sight (Plut. "Mor.," 756 B). Though there is no suggestion in this of weakness of conviction (for πίστις expresses a strong conviction, and is therefore used in contrast with 'impressions'), yet the word, when referring to the gods, very rarely rises above intellectual conviction into its naturally more congenial region of moral trust (Soph. "Oed. Rex," 1445). That this, its fuller and more characteristic meaning, should come to its rights in the religious sphere, it was necessary that it should be transferred into a new religious atmosphere. The usage of Philo bears witness that it thus came to its rights on the lips of the Greek-speaking Jews. It is going too far, to be sure, to say that Philo's usage of 'faith' is scarcely distinguishable from that of New Testament writers. The gulf that separates the two is very wide, and has not been inaptly described by saying that with Philo, faith, as the queen of the virtues, is the righteousness of the righteous man, while with St. Paul, as the abnegation of all claim to virtue, it is the righteousness of the unrighteous. But it is of the utmost significance that, in the pages of Philo, the conception is filled with a content which far transcends any usage of the word in heathen Greek, and which is a refraction of the religious conceptions of the Old Testament. Fundamental to his idea of it as the crowning virtue of the godly man, to be attained only with the supremest difficulty, especially by creatures akin to mortal things, is his conception of it as essentially a changeless, unwavering 'standing by God' (Deut. v. 31),— binding us to God, to the exclusion of every other object of desire, and making us one with Him. It has lost that soteriological content which is the very heart of faith in the Old Testament; though there does not absolutely fail an occasional reference to God as Saviour, it is, with Philo, rather the Divinity, τὸ ὄν, upon which faith rests, than the God of grace and salvation; and it therefore stands with him, not at the beginning but at the end of the religious life. But we can perceive in the usage of Philo a development on Jewish ground of a use of the word πίστις to describe that complete detachment from earthly things, and that firm conviction of the reality and supreme significance of the things not seen, which underlies its whole New Testament use.

The disparity in the use of the terms 'faith' and 'believe' in the two Testaments is certainly in a formal aspect very great. In contrast with their extreme rarity in the Old Testament, they are both, though somewhat unevenly distributed and varying in relative frequency, distinctly characteristic of the whole New Testament language, and oddly enough occur about equally often (about 240 times each). The verb is lacking only in Col., Philem., II Pet., II and III Jn., and the Apocalypse; the noun only in the Gospel of John and II and III Jn.: both fail only in II and III Jn. The noun predominates not only in the epistles of St. Paul, where the proportion is about three to one, and in St. James (about five to one), but very markedly in the Epistle to the Hebrews (about sixteen to one). In St. John, on the other hand, the verb is very frequent, while the noun occurs only once in I Jn. and four times in the Apocalypse. In the other books the proportion between the two is less noteworthy, and may fairly be accounted accidental. In the Old Testament, again, 'faith' occurs in the active sense in but a single passage; in the New Testament it is the passive sense which is rare. In the Old Testament in only about half the instances of its occurrence is the verb 'to believe' used in a religious sense; in the New Testament it has become so clearly a technical religious term, that it occurs very rarely in any other sense. The transitive usage, in which it expresses entrusting something to someone, occurs a few times both in the active (Lk. xvi. 11, Jn. ii. 24) and the passive (I Cor. ix. 17, Gal. ii. 7, I Thess. ii. 4, I Tim. i. 11, Tit. i. 3); but besides this special case there are very few instances in which the word does not express religious believing, possibly only the following: Jn. ix. 18, Acts ix. 26, I Cor. xi. 18, Mt. xxiv. 23, 26, Mk. xiii. 21, II Thess. ii. 11, cf. Acts xiii. 41, xv. 11, Jn. iv. 21, I Jn. iv. 1. The classical construction with the simple dative which prevails in the Septuagint retires in the New Testament in favour of constructions with prepositions and the absolute use of the verb; the construction with the dative occurs about forty-five times, while that with prepositions occurs some sixty-three times, and the verb is used absolutely some ninety-three times.

When construed with the dative, πιστεύειν in the New Testament prevailingly expresses believing assent, though ordinarily in a somewhat pregnant sense. When its object is a thing, it is usually the spoken (Lk. i. 20, Jn. iv. 50, v. 47, xii. 38, Rom. x. 16, cf. II Thess. ii. 11) or written (Jn. ii. 22, v. 47, Acts xxiv. 14, xxvi. 27) word of God; once it is divine works which should convince the onlooker of the divine mission of the worker (Jn. x. 38). When its object is a person it is rarely another than God or Jesus (Mt. xxi. 25, 32, Mk. xi. 31, Lk. xx. 5, Jn. v. 46, Acts viii. 12, I Jn. iv. 1), and more rarely God (Jn. v. 24, Acts xvi. 34, xxvii. 25, Rom. iv. 3 (17), Gal. iii. 6, Tit. iii. 8, Jas. ii. 23, I Jn. v. 10) than Jesus (Jn. iv. 21, v. 38, 46, vi. 30, viii. 31, 45, 46, x. 37, 38, xiv. 11, Acts xviii. 8, II Tim. i. 12). Among these passages there are not lacking some, both when the object is a person and when it is a thing, in which the higher sense of devoted, believing trust is conveyed. In I Jn. iii. 23, for example, we are obviously to translate, not 'believe the name,' but 'believe in the name of his Son, Jesus Christ,' for in this is summed up the whole Godward side of Christian duty. So there is no reason to question that the words of Gen. xv. 6 are adduced in Rom. iv. 3, Gal. iii. 6, Jas. ii. 23 in the deep sense which they bear in the Old Testament text; and this deeper religious faith can scarcely be excluded from the belief in God adverted to in Acts xvi. 34, Tit. iii. 8 (cf. Jn. v. 24), or from the belief in Jesus adverted to in II Tim. i. 12 (cf. Jn. v. 38, vi. 30), and is obviously the prominent conception in the faith of Crispus declared in Acts xviii. 8. The passive form of this construction occurs only twice—once of believing assent (II Thess. i. 10), and once with the highest implications of confiding trust (I Tim. iii. 16). The few passages in which the construction is with the accusative (Jn. xi. 26, Acts xiii. 41, I Cor. xi. 18, xiii. 7, I Jn. iv. 16) take their natural place along with the commoner usage with the dative, and need not express more than crediting, although over one or two of them there floats a shadow of a deeper implication. The same may be said of the cases of attraction in Rom. iv. 17 and x. 14. And with these weaker constructions must be ranged also the passages, twenty in all (fourteen of which occur in the writings of St. John), in which what is believed is joined to the verb by the conjunction ὅτι. In a couple of these the matter believed scarcely rises into the religious sphere (Jn. ix. 18, Acts ix. 26); in a couple more there is specific reference to prayer (Mk. xi. 23, 24); in yet a couple more it is general faith in God which is in mind (Heb. xi. 6, Jas. ii. 19). In the rest, what is believed is of immediately soteriological import—now the possession by Jesus of a special power (Mt. ix. 28), now the central fact of His saving work (Rom. x. 9, I Thess. iv. 14), now the very hinge of the Christian hope (Rom. vi. 8), but prevailingly the divine mission and personality of Jesus Himself (Jn. vi. 69, viii. 24, xi. 27, 42, xiii. 19, xiv. 10, xvi. 27, 30, xvii. 8, 21, xx. 31, I Jn. v. 1, 5). By their side we may recall also the rare construction with the infinitive (Acts xv. 11, Rom. xiv. 2).

When we advance to the constructions with prepositions, we enter a region in which the deeper sense of the word—that of firm, trustful reliance—comes to its full rights. The construction with ἐν, which is the most frequent of the constructions with prepositions in the Septuagint, retires almost out of use in the New Testament; it occurs with certainty only in Mk. i. 15, where the object of faith is 'the gospel,' though Jn. iii. 15, Eph. i. 13 may also be instances of it, where the object would be Christ. The implication of this construction would seem to be firm fixedness of confidence in its object. Scarcely more common is the parallel construction of ἐπί with the dative, expressive of steady, resting repose, reliance upon the object. Besides the quotation from Isa. xxviii. 16, which appears alike in Rom. ix. 33, x. 11, I Pet. ii. 6, this construction occurs only twice: Lk.

xxiv. 25, where Jesus rebukes His followers for not 'believing on,' relying implicitly upon, all that the prophets have spoken; and I Tim. i. 16, where we are declared to 'believe on' Jesus Christ unto salvation, i.e., to obtain salvation by relying upon Him for it. The constructions with prepositions governing the accusative, which involve an implication of 'moral motion, mental direction towards,' are more frequently used. That with ἐπί, indeed, occurs only seven times (four of which are in Acts). In two instances in Rom. iv. where the reminiscence of the faith of Abraham gives colour to the language, the object on which faith is thus said relyingly to lay hold is God, described, however, as savingly working through Christ—as He that justifies the ungodly, He that raised Jesus our Lord from the dead. Elsewhere its object is Christ Himself. In Mt. xxvii. 42 the Jewish leaders declare the terms on which they will become 'believers on' Jesus; in Acts xvi. 31 this is the form that is given to the proclamation of salvation by faith in Christ—'turn with confident trust to Jesus Christ,' and appropriately, therefore, it is in this form of expression that those are designated who have savingly believed on Christ (Acts ix. 42, xi. 17, xxii. 19). The special New Testament construction, however, is that with εἰς, which occurs some forty-nine times, about four-fifths of which are Johannine and the remainder more or less Pauline. The object towards which faith is thus said to be reliantly directed is in one unique instance 'the witness which God hath witnessed concerning his Son' (I Jn. v. 10), where we may well believe that 'belief in the truth of the witness is carried on to personal belief in the object of the witness, that is, the Incarnate Son Himself.' Elsewhere the object believed on, in this construction, is always a person, and that very rarely God (Jn. xiv. 1, cf. I Jn. v. 10, and also I Pet. i. 21, where, however, the true reading is probably πιστοὺς εἰς θεόν), and most commonly Christ (Mt. xviii. 6, Jn. ii. 11, iii. 16, 18, 36, iv. 39, vi. 29, 35, 40, vii. 5, 31, 38, 39, 48, viii. 30, ix. 35, 36, x. 42, xi. 25, 26, 45, 48, xii. 11, 37, 42, 44, 44, 46, xiv. 1, 12, xvi. 9, xvii. 20, Acts x. 43, xiv. 23, xix. 4, Rom. x. 14, 14, Gal. ii. 16, Phil. i. 29, I Pet. i. 8, I Jn. v. 10, cf. Jn. xii. 36, i. 12, ii. 23, iii. 18, I Jn. v. 13). A glance over these passages will bring clearly out the pregnancy of the meaning conveyed. It may be more of a question wherein the pregnancy resides. It is probably sufficient to find it in the sense conveyed by the verb itself, while the preposition adjoins only the person towards whom the strong feeling expressed by the verb is directed. In any event, what these passages express is 'an absolute transference of trust from ourselves to another,' a complete self-surrender to Christ.

Some confirmation of this explanation of the strong meaning of the phrase πιστεύειν εἰς may be derived from the very rich use of the verb absolutely, in a sense in no way inferior. Its absolute use is pretty evenly distributed through the New Testament occurring 29 times in John, 23 times in Paul, 22 times in Acts, 15 times in the Synoptics, and once each in Hebrews, James, I Peter, and Jude; it is placed on the lips of Jesus some 18 times. In surprisingly few of these instances is it used of a non-religious act of crediting,—apparently only in our Lord's warning to His followers not to believe when men say ' "Lo, here is the Christ," or "here" ' (Mt. xxiv. 23, 26, Mk. xiii. 21). In equally surprisingly few instances is it used of specific acts of faith in the religious sphere. Once it is used of assent given to a specific doctrine—that of the unity of God (Jas. ii. 19). Once it is used of believing prayer (Mt. xxi. 22). Four times in a single chapter of John it is used of belief in a specific fact—the great fact central to Christianity of the resurrection of Christ (Jn. xx. 8, 25, 29, 29). It is used occasionally of belief in God's announced word (Lk. i. 45, Acts xxvi. 27), and occasionally also of the credit given to specific testimonies of Jesus, whether with reference to earthly or heavenly things (Jn. iii. 12, 12, i. 50, Lk. xxii. 67), passing thence to general faith in the word of salvation (Lk. viii. 12, 13). Twice it is used of general soteriological faith in God (Jude 5, Rom. iv. 18), and a few times, with the same pregnancy of implication, where the reference, whether to God or Christ, is more or less uncertain (Jn. i. 7, Rom. iv. 11, II Cor. iv. 13, 13). Ordinarily, however, it expresses soteriological faith directed to the person of Christ. In a few instances, to be sure, the immediate trust expressed is in the extraordinary power of Jesus for the performance of earthly effects (the so-called 'miracle faith'), as in Mt. viii. 13, Mk. v. 36, ix. 23, 24, Lk. viii. 50, Jn. iv. 48, xi. 40; but the essential relation in which this faith stands to 'saving faith' is clearly exhibited in Jn. iv. 48 compared with v. 53 and ix. 38, and Jn. xi. 40 compared with v. 15 and xii. 39; and, in any case, these passages are insignificant in number when compared with the great array in which the reference is distinctly to saving faith in Christ (Mk. ix. 42, xv. 32 [Jn. iii. 15], Jn. iii. 18, iv. 41, 42, 53, v. 44, vi. 36, 47, 64, 64, ix. 38, x. 25, 26, xi. 15, xii. 39, xiv. 29, xvi. 31, xix. 35, xx. 31, Acts ii. 44, iv. 4, 32, v. 14, viii. 13, xi. 21, xiii. 12, 39, 48, xiv. 1, xv. 5, 7, xvii. 12, 34, xviii. 8, 27, xix. 2, 18, xxi. 20, 25, Rom. i. 16, iii. 22, x. 4, 10, xiii. 11, xv. 13, I Cor. i. 21, iii. 5, xiv. 22, xv. 2, 11, Gal. iii. 22, Eph. i. 13, 19, I Thess. i. 7, ii. 10, 13, II Thess. i. 10, Heb. iv. 3, I Pet. ii. 7). A survey of these passages will show very clearly that in the New Testament 'to believe' is a technical term to express reliance on Christ for salvation. In a number of them, to be sure, the object of the believing spoken of is sufficiently defined by the context, but, without contextual indication of the object, enough remain to bear out this suggestion. Accordingly, a tendency is betrayed to use the simple participle very much as a verbal noun, with the meaning of 'Christian': in Mk. ix. 42, Acts xi. 21, I Cor. i. 21, Eph. i. 13, 19, I Thess. i. 7, ii. 10, 13 the participial construction is evident; it may be doubted, however, whether οἱ πιστεύσαντες is not used as a noun in such passages as Acts ii. 44, iv. 32, II Thess. i. 10, Heb. iv. 3; and in Acts v. 14 πιστεύοντες is perhaps generally recognized as used substantively. Before the disciples were called 'Christians' (Acts xi. 26, cf. xxvi. 28, I Pet. iv. 16) it would seem, then, that they were called 'believers,'—those who had turned to Christ in trusting reliance (οἱ πιστεύσαντες), or those who were resting on Christ in trusting reliance (οἱ πιστεύοντες); and that the undefined 'to believe' had come to mean to become or to be a Christian, that is, to turn to or rest on Christ in reliant trust. The occasional use of οἱ πιστοί in an equivalent sense (Acts x. 45, Eph. i. 1, I Tim. iv. 3, 12, I Pet. i. 21, Rev. xvii. 14), for which the way was prepared by the comparatively frequent use of this adjective in the classically rare active sense (Jn. xx. 27, Acts xvi. 1, I Cor. vii. 14, II Cor. vi. 15, Gal. iii. 9, I Tim. iv. 10, v. 16, vi. 2, Tit. i. 6), adds weight to this conclusion; as do also the use of ἄπιστοι of 'unbelievers,' whether in the simple (I Cor. vi. 6, vii. 12-15, x. 27, xiv. 22-24, I Tim. v. 8) or deepened sense (II Cor. iv. 4, vi. 14 f., Tit. i. 15, cf. Jn. xx. 27, Mt. xvii. 17, Mk. ix. 19, Lk. ix. 41), and the related usage of the words ἀπιστία (Mk. ix. 24 (xvi. 14), Mt. xiii. 58, Mk. vi. 6, Rom. iv. 20, xi. 20, 23, I Tim. i. 13, Heb. iii. 12, 19), ἀπιστέω (Mk. xvi. 11 (16), Lk. xxiv. 11, 41, Acts xxviii. 24, I Pet. ii. 7), and ὀλιγόπιστος (Mt. vi. 30, viii. 26, xiv. 31, xvi. 8, Lk. xii. 28), ὀλιγοπιστία (Mt. xvii. 20).

The impression which is thus derived from the usage of πιστεύειν is only deepened by attending to that of πίστις. As already intimated, πίστις occurs in the New Testament very rarely in its passive sense of 'faithfulness,' 'integrity' (Rom. iii. 3 of God; Mt. xxiii. 23, Gal. v. 22, Tit. ii. 10, of men; cf. I Tim. v. 12 'a pledge'; Acts xvii. 31 'assurance'; others add I Tim. vi. 11, II Tim. ii. 22, iii. 10, Philem. 5). And nowhere in the multitude of its occurrences in its active sense is it applied to man's faith in man, but always to the religious trust that reposes on God, or Christ, or divine things. The specific object on which the trust rests is but seldom explicitly expressed. In some six of these instances it is a thing, but always something of the fullest soteriological significance—the gospel of Christ (Phil. i. 27), the saving truth of God (II Thess. ii. 13), the working of God who raised Jesus from the dead (Col. ii. 12, cf. Acts xiv. 9, iii. 16), the name of Jesus (Acts iii. 16), the blood of Jesus (Rom. iii. 25), the righteousness of Jesus (II Pet. i. 1). In as many more the object is God, and the conception is prevailingly that of general trust in God (Mk. xi. 22, Rom. xiv. 22, I Thess. i. 8, Heb. vi. 1, I Pet. i. 21, cf. Col. ii. 12). In most instances, however, the object is specified as Christ, and the faith is very pointedly soteriological (Acts xx. 21, xxiv. 24, xxvi. 18, Gal. ii. 16, 16, 20, Rom. iii. 22, 26, Gal. iii. 22, 26, Eph. i. 15, iii. 12, iv. 13, Phil. iii. 9, Col. i. 4, ii. 5, I Tim. i. 14, iii. 13, 15, II Tim. i. 13, iii. 15, Philem. 5, Jas. ii. 1, Rev. ii. 13, xiv. 12). Its object is most frequently joined to πίστις as an objective genitive, a construction occurring some seventeen times, twelve of which fall in the writings of Paul. In four of them the genitive is that of the thing, namely in Phil. i. 27 the gospel, in II Thess. ii. 13 the saving truth, in Col. ii. 12 the almighty working of God, and in Acts iii. 16 the name of Jesus. In one of them it is God (Mk. xi. 22). The certainty that the genitive is that of object in these cases is decisive with reference to its nature in the remaining cases, in which Jesus Christ is set forth as the object on which faith rests (Rom. iii. 22, 26, Gal. ii. 16, 16, 20, iii. 22, Eph. iii. 12, iv. 13, Phil. iii. 9, Jas. ii. 1, Rev. ii. 13, xiv. 12). Next most frequently its object is joined to faith by means of the preposition ἐν (9 times), by which it is set forth as the basis on which faith rests, or the sphere of its operation. In two of these instances the object is a thing—the blood or righteousness of Jesus (Rom. iii. 25, II Pet. i. 1); in the rest it is Christ Himself who is presented as the ground of faith (Gal. iii. 26, Eph. i. 15, Col. i. 4, I Tim. i. 14, iii. 13, II Tim. i. 13, iii. 15). Somewhat less frequently (5 times) its object is joined to πίστις by means of the preposition εἰς, designating, apparently, merely the object with reference to which faith is exercised (cf. especially Acts xx. 21); the object thus specified for faith is in one instance God (I Pet. i. 21), and in the others Christ (Acts xx. 21, xxiv. 24, xxvi. 18, Col. ii. 5). By the side of this construction should doubtless be placed the two instances in which the preposition πρός is used, by which faith is said to look and adhere to God (I Thess. i. 8) or to Christ (Philem. 5). And it is practically in the same sense that in a single instance God is joined to πίστις by means of the preposition ἐπί as the object to which it restingly turns. It would seem that the pregnant sense of πίστις as self-abandoning trust was so fixed in Christian speech that little was left to be expressed by the mode of its adjunction to its object.

Accordingly, the use of the word without specified object is vastly preponderant. In a few of such instances we may see a specific reference to the general confidence which informs believing prayer (Lk. xviii. 8, Jas. i. 6, v. 15). In a somewhat greater number there is special reference to faith in Jesus as

a worker of wonders—the so-called 'miracle faith' (Mt. viii.
10, ix. 2, 22, 29, xv. 28 [xvii. 20] [xxi. 21], Mk. ii. 5, iv. 40, v.
34, x. 52, Lk. v. 20, vii. 9, viii. 25, 48, xvii. 19, xviii. 42, Acts iii.
16, xiv. 9)—although how little this faith can be regarded as
non-soteriological the language of Mt. ix. 2, Mk. ii. 5, Lk. v. 20
shows, as well as the parallelism between Lk. vii. 50 (cf. viii.
48, xvii. 19) and Mt. ix. 22, Mk. v. 34. The immense mass of
the passages in which the undefined πίστις occurs, however, are
distinctly soteriological, and that indifferently whether its implied object be God or Christ. Its implied reference is indeed
often extremely difficult to fix; though the passages in which it
may, with some confidence, be referred to Christ are in number about double those in which it may, with like confidence, be
referred to God. The degree of clearness with which an implied
object is pointed to in the context varies, naturally, very greatly;
but in a number of cases there is no direct hint of object in the
context, but this is left to be supplied by the general knowledge
of the reader. And this is as much as to say that πίστις is so used
as to imply that it had already become a Christian technical
term, which needed no further definition that it might convey
its full sense of saving faith in Jesus Christ to the mind of every
reader. This tendency to use it as practically a synonym for
'Christianity' comes out sharply in such a phrase as οἱ ἐκ πίστεως
(Gal. iii. 7, 9), which is obviously a paraphrase for 'believers.'
A transitional form of the phrase meets us in Rom. iii. 26,
τὸν ἐκ πίστεως Ἰησοῦ; that the Ἰησοῦ could fall away and leave
the simple οἱ ἐκ πίστεως standing for the whole idea, is full of
implications as to the sense which the simple undefined πίστις
had acquired in the circles which looked to Jesus for salvation.
The same implications underlie the so-called objective use of
πίστις in the New Testament. That in such passages as Acts vi.
7, Gal. i. 23, iii. 23, vi. 10, Phil. i. 25, Jude 3, 20 it conveys the
idea of 'the Christian religion' appears plain on the face of the
passages; and by their side can be placed such others as the
following, which seem transitional to them, namely: Acts xvi.
5, I Cor. xvi. 13, Col. i. 23, I Tim. i. 19, iv. 1, 6, v. 8, Tit. i. 13,
and, at a slightly further remove, such others as Acts xiii. 8,

Rom. i. 5, xvi. 26, Phil. i. 25, I Tim. iii. 9, vi. 10, 12, II Tim. iii. 8, iv. 7, Tit. i. 4, iii. 15, I Pet. v. 9 It is not necessary to suppose that πίστις is used in any of these passages as *doctrina fidei*; it seems possible to carry through them all the conception of 'subjective faith conceived of *objectively* as a power,'—even through those in Jude and I Timothy, which are more commonly than any others interpreted as meaning *doctrina fidei*. But this generally admitted objectivizing of subjective faith makes πίστις, as truly as if it were understood as *doctrina fidei*, on the verge of which it in any case trembles, a synonym for 'the Christian religion.' It is only a question whether 'the Christian religion' is designated in it from the side of doctrine or life; though it be from the point of view of life, still 'the faith' has become a synonym for 'Christianity,' 'believers' for 'Christians,' 'to believe' for 'to become a Christian,' and we may trace a development by means of which πίστις has come to mean the religion which is marked by and consists essentially in 'believing.' That this development so rapidly took place is significant of much, and supplies a ready explanation of such passages as Gal. iii. 23, 25, in which the phrases 'before the faith came' and 'now that faith is come' probably mean little more than before and after the advent of 'Christianity' into the world. On the ground of such a usage, we may at least re-affirm with increased confidence that the idea of 'faith' is conceived of in the New Testament as the characteristic idea of Christianity, and that it does not import mere 'belief' in an intellectual sense, but all that enters into an entire self-commitment of the soul to Jesus as the Son of God, the Saviour of the world.

Chapter XVI

MYSTICISM AND CHRISTIANITY[1]

RELIGION is, shortly, the reaction of the human soul in the presence of God. As God is as much a part of the environment of man as the earth on which he stands, no man can escape from religion any more than he can escape from gravitation. But though every man necessarily reacts to God, men react of course diversely, each according to his nature, or perhaps we would better say, each according to his temperament. Thus, broadly speaking, three main types of religion arise, corresponding to the three main varieties of the activity of the human spirit, intellectual, emotional, and voluntary. According as the intellect, sensibility, or will is dominant in him, each man produces for himself a religion prevailingly of the intellect, sensibility, or active will; and all the religions which men have made for themselves find places somewhere among these three types, as they produce themselves more or less purely, or variously intermingle with one another.

We say advisedly, all the religions which men have made for themselves. For there is an even more fundamental division among religions than that which is supplied by these varieties. This is the division between man-made and God-made religions. Besides the religions which man has made for himself, God has made a religion for man. We call this revealed religion; and the most fundamental division which separates between religions is that which divides revealed religion from unrevealed religions. Of course, we do not mean to deny that there is an element of revelation in all religions. God is a person, and persons are known only as they make themselves known—reveal themselves. The term revelation is used in this distinction,

---

[1] Reprinted from *The Biblical Review*, ii. 1917, pp. 169-191 (published by The Biblical Seminary in New York; copyrighted); also from *Studies in Theology*, pp. 649-666.

therefore, in a pregnant sense. In the unrevealed religions God is known only as He has revealed Himself in His acts of the creation and government of the world, as every person must reveal himself in his acts if he acts at all. In the one revealed religion God has revealed Himself also in acts of special grace, among which is included the open Word.

There is an element in revealed religion, therefore, which is not found in any unrevealed religion. This is the element of authority. Revealed religion comes to man from without; it is imposed upon him from a source superior to his own spirit. The unrevealed religions, on the other hand, flow from no higher source than the human spirit itself. However much they may differ among themselves in the relative prominence given in each to the functioning of the intellect, sensibility, or will, they have this fundamental thing in common. They are all, in other words, natural religions in contradistinction to the one super- natural religion which God has made.

There is a true sense, then, in which it may be said that the unrevealed religions are "religions of the spirit" and re- vealed religion is the "religion of authority." Authority is the correlate of revelation, and wherever revelation is—and only where revelation is—is there authority. Just because we do not see in revelation man reaching up lame hands toward God and feeling fumblingly after Him if haply he may find Him, but God graciously reaching strong hands down to man, bringing him help in his need, we see in it a gift from God, not a creation of man's. On the other hand, the characteristic of all unrevealed religions is that they are distinctly man-made. They have no authority to appeal to, they rest solely on the deliverances of the human spirit. As Rudyard Kipling shrewdly makes his "Tommy" declare:

> The 'eathen in 'is blindness bows down to wood and stone,
> 'E don't obey no orders unless they is 'is own.

Naturally it makes no difference in this respect whether it is the rational, emotional, or volitional element in the activities of the human spirit to which appeal is chiefly made. In no case are the foundations sunk deeper than the human spirit itself, and nothing appears in the structure that is raised which the human spirit does not supply. The preponderance of one or another of these activities in the structure does, however, make an immense difference in the aspect of that structure. Mysticism is the name which is given to the particular one of these structures, the predominant place in which is taken by the sensibility. It is characteristic of mysticism that it makes its appeal to the feelings as the sole, or at least as the normative, source of knowledge of divine things. That is to say, it is the religious sentiment which constitutes for it the source of religious knowledge. Of course mystics differ with one another in the consistency with which they apply their principle. And of course they differ with one another in the account they give of this religious sentiment to which they make their appeal. There are, therefore, many varieties of mystics, pure and impure, consistent and inconsistent, naturalistic and supernaturalistic, pantheistic and theistic—even Christian. What is common to them all, and what makes them all mystics, is that they all rest on the religious sentiment as the source of knowledge of divine things.

The great variety of the accounts which mystics give of the feeling to which they make their appeal arises from the very nature of the case. There is a deeper reason for a mystic being "mute"—that is what the name imports—than that he wishes to make a mystery of his discoveries. He is "mute" because, as a mystic, he has nothing to say. When he sinks within himself he finds feelings, not conceptions; his is an emotional, not a conceptional, religion; and feelings, emotions, though not inaudible, are not articulate. As a mystic, he has no conceptional language in which to express what he feels. If he attempts to describe it he must make use of terms derived from the religious or philosophical thought in vogue about him, that is to say, of non-mystical language. His hands may be the hands of Esau, but his voice is the voice of Jacob. The language in which he describes the reality which he finds within him does not in the least indicate, then, what it is; it is merely a concession to the necessity of communicating with the external world or with his own more external self. What he finds within him is just to his apprehension an "unutterable abyss." And Synesius does himself and his fellow mystics no injustice when he declares that "the mystic mind says this and that, gyrating around the unutterable abyss."

On the brink of this abyss the mystic may stand in awe, and, standing in awe upon its brink, he may deify it. Then he calls it indifferently Brahm or Zeus, Allah or the Holy Spirit, according as men about him speak of God. He explains its meaning, in other words, in terms of the conception of the universe which he has brought with him, or, as it is more fashionable now to phrase it, each in accordance with his own world-view. Those who are held in the grasp of a naturalistic conception of the world will naturally speak of the religious feeling of which they have become acutely conscious as only one of the multitudinous natural movements of the human soul, and will seek merely, by a logical analysis of its presuppositions and implications, to draw out its full meaning. Those who are sunk in a pantheistic world-view will speak of its movements as motions of the subliminal consciousness, and will interpret them as the surgings within us of the divine ground of all things, in listening to which they conceive themselves to be sinking beneath the waves that fret the surface of the ocean of being and penetrating to its profounder depths. If, on the other hand, the mystic chances to be a theist, he may look upon the movements of his religious feelings as effects in his soul wrought by the voluntary actions of the God whom he acknowledges; and if he should happen to be a Christian, he may interpret these movements, in accordance with the teachings of the Scriptures, as the leadings of the Holy Spirit or as the manifestations within him of the Christ within us the hope of glory.

This Christian mysticism, now, obviously differs in no essential respect from the parallel phenomena which are observable in other religions. It is only general mysticism manifesting itself on Christian ground and interpreting itself accordingly in the forms of Christian thought. It is mysticism which has learned to speak in Christian language. The phenomena themselves are universal. There has never been an age of the world, or a form of religion, in which they have not been in evidence. There are always everywhere some men who stand out among their fellows as listeners to the inner voice, and who, refusing the warning which Thoas gives to Iphigenia in Goethe's play, "There speaks no God: thy heart alone 'tis speaks," respond like Iphigenia with passionate conviction, " 'Tis only through our hearts the gods e'er speak." But these common phenomena are, naturally, interpreted in each instance, according to the general presuppositions of each several subject or observer of them. Thus, for example, they are treated as the intrusion of God into the soul (Ribet), or as the involuntary intrusion of the unconscious into consciousness (Hartmann), or as the intrusion of the subconscious into the consciousness (Du Prel), or as the intrusion of feeling, strong and overmastering, into the operations of the intellect (Goethe).

According to these varying interpretations we get different types of mysticism, differing from one another not in intrinsic character so much as in the explanations given of the common phenomena. Many attempts have been made to arrange these types in logical schemes which shall embrace all varieties and present them in an intelligible order. Thus, for example, from the point of view of the ends sought, R. A. Vaughan distinguishes between theopathic, theosophic, and theurgic mysticism, the first of which is content with feeling, while the second aspires to knowledge, and the third seeks power. The same classes may perhaps be called more simply emotional, intellectual, and thelematic mysticism. From the point of view of the inquiry into the sources of religious knowledge four well-marked varieties present themselves, which have been given the names of naturalistic, supernaturalistic, theosophical, and pantheistic mysticism.

The common element in all these varieties of mysticism is that they all seek all, or most, or the normative or at least a substantial part, of the knowledge of God in human feelings, which they look upon as the sole or at least the most trust-worthy or the most direct source of the knowledge of God. The differences between them turn on the diverging concep-tions which they entertain of the origin of the religious feel-ings thus appealed to. Naturalistic mysticism conceives them as merely "the natural religious consciousness of men, as ex-cited and influenced by the circumstances of the individual." Supernaturalistic, as the effects of operations of the divine Spirit in the heart, the human spirit moving only as it is moved upon by the divine. Theosophical mysticism goes a step further and regards the religious feelings as the footprints of Deity moving in the soul, and as, therefore, immediate sources of knowledge of God, which is to be obtained by simple quiescence and rapt contemplation of these His movements. Pantheistic mysticism advances to the complete identification of the soul with God, who is therefore to be known by applying oneself to the simple axiom: "Know thyself."

Clearly it is the type which has been called supernaturalistic that has the closest affinity with Christianity. Christian mys-ticism accordingly, at its best, takes this form and passes in-sensibly from it into evangelical Christianity, to which the indwelling of the Holy Ghost—the Christ within—is funda-mental, and which rejoices in such spiritual experiences as are summed up in the old categories of regeneration and sanctifi-cation—the rebegetting of the soul into newness of life and the leading of the new-created soul along the pathway of holy living. From these experiences, of course, much may be in-ferred not only of the modes of God's working in the salvation of men but also of the nature and character of God the worker.

The distinction between mysticism of this type and evan-gelical Christianity, from the point of view which is now occupying our attention, is nevertheless clear. Evangelical Christianity interprets all religious experience by the norma-tive revelation of God recorded for us in the Holy Scriptures, and guides, directs, and corrects it from these Scriptures, and thus molds it into harmony with what God in His revealed Word lays down as the normal Christian life. The mystic, on the other hand, tends to substitute his religious experience for the objective revelation of God recorded in the written Word, as the source from which he derives his knowledge of God, or at least to subordinate the expressly revealed Word as the less direct and convincing source of knowledge of God to his own religious experience. The result is that the external revelation is relatively depressed in value, if not totally set aside.

In the history of Christian thought mysticism appears accordingly as that tendency among professing Christians which looks within, that is, to the religious feelings, in its search for God. It supposes itself to contemplate within the soul the movements of the divine Spirit, and finds in them either the sole sources of trustworthy knowledge of God, or the most immediate and convincing sources of that knowledge, or, at least, a coördinate source of it alongside of the written Word. The characteristic of Christian mysticism, from the point of view of religious knowledge, is therefore its appeal to the "inner light," or "the internal word," either to the exclusion of the external or written Word, or as superior to it and normative for its interpretation, or at least as coördinate authority with it, this "inner light" or "internal word" being conceived not as the rational understanding but as the immediate deliverance of the religious sentiment. As a mere matter of fact, now, we lack all criteria, apart from the written Word, to distinguish between those motions of the heart which are created within us by the Spirit of God and those which arise out of the natural functioning of the religious consciousness. This substitution of our religious experience—or "Christian consciousness," as it is sometimes called—for the objective Word as the proper source of our religious knowledge ends therefore either in betraying us into purely rationalistic mysticism, or is rescued from that by the postulation of a relation of the soul to God which strongly tends toward pantheizing mysticism.

In point of fact, mysticism in the Church is found to gravitate, with pretty general regularity, either toward rationalism or toward pantheism. In effect, indeed, it appears to differ from rationalism chiefly in temperament, if we may not even say in temperature. The two have it in common that they appeal for knowledge of God only to what is internal to man; and to what, internal to man, men make their actual appeal, seems to be determined very much by their temperaments, or, as has been said, by their temperatures. The human soul is a small thing at best; it is not divided into water-tight compartments; the streams of feeling which are flowing up and down in it and the judgments of the understanding which are incessantly being framed in it are constantly acting and reacting on one another. It is not always easy for it to be perfectly clear, as it turns within itself and gazes upon its complex movements, of the real source, rational or emotional, of the impressions which it observes to be crystallizing within it into convictions. It has often been observed in the progress of history, accordingly, that men who have deserted the guidance of external revelation have become mystics or rationalists largely according as their religious life was warm or cold. In periods of religious fervor or in periods of fervid religious reactions they are mystics; in periods of religious decline they are rationalists. The same person, indeed, sometimes vibrates between the two points of view with the utmost facility.

It is, however, with pantheism that mysticism stands in the closest association. It would not be untrue, in fact, to say that as a historical phenomenon mysticism is just pantheism reduced to a religion, that is to say, with its postulates transformed into ends. Defenses of mysticism against the inevitable (and true) charge of pantheizing usually, indeed, stop with the announcement of this damaging fact. "Lasson," remarks Dean Inge as if that were the conclusion of the matter instead of, as it is, the confesssion of judgment, "says well, in his book on Meister Eckhart, 'Mysticism views everything from the standpoint of teleology, while pantheism generally stops at causality.' " What it is of importance to observe is that it is precisely what pantheism, being a philosophy, postulates as conditions of being that mysticism, being a religion, proposes as objects of attainment. Mysticism is simply, therefore, pantheism expressed in the terms of religious aspiration.

This is as true within the Christian Church as without it. All forms of mysticism have no doubt from time to time found a place for themselves within the Church. Or perhaps we should rather say that they have always existed in it, and have from time to time manifested their presence there. This must be said even of naturalistic mysticism. There are those who call themselves Christians who yet conceive of Christianity as merely the natural religious sentiment excited into action by contact with the religious impulse set in motion by Jesus Christ and transmitted down the ages by the natural laws of motion, as motion is transmitted, say, through a row of billiard balls in contact with one another. Yet it would only be true to say that mysticism as a phenomenon in the history of the Church has commonly arisen in the wake of the dominating influence in the contemporary world of a pantheizing philosophy. It is the product of a pantheizing manner of thinking impinging on the religious nature, or, if we prefer to phrase it from the opposite point of view, of religious thought seeking to assimilate and to express itself in terms of a pantheizing philosophy.

The fullest stream of mystical thought which has entered the Church finds its origin in the Neoplatonic philosophy. It is to the writings of the Pseudo-Dionysius that its naturalization in the Eastern Church is usually broadly ascribed. The sluice-gates of the Western Church were opened for it, in the same broad sense, by John Scotus Erigena. It has flowed strongly down through all the subsequent centuries, widening here and there into lakelets. The form of mysticism which is most widely disturbing the modern Protestant churches comes, however, from a different source. It takes its origin from the movement inaugurated in the first third of the nineteenth century by Friedrich Schleiermacher, with the ostensible purpose of rescuing Christianity from the assaults of rationalism by vindicating for religion its own independent right of existence, in a region "beyond reason." The result of this attempt to separate religion from reason has been, of course, merely to render religion unreasonable; even Plotinus warned us long ago that "he who would rise above reason falls outside of it." But what we are immediately concerned to observe is the very widespread rejection of all "external authority," which has been one of the results of this movement, and the consequent casting of men back upon their "religious experience," corporate or individual, as their sole trustworthy ground of religious convictions. This is, of course, only "the inner light" of an earlier form of mysticism under a new and (so it has been hoped) more inoffensive name; and it is naturally, therefore, burdened with all the evils which inhere in the mystical attitude. These evils do not affect extreme forms of mysticism only; they are intrinsic in the two common principles which give to all its forms their fundamental character— the misprision of "external authority," and the attempt to discover in the movements of the sensibilities the ground or norm of all the religious truth which will be acknowledged.

"Mystics," says George Tyrrell, "think they touch the divine when they have only blurred the human form with a cloud of words." The astonishing thing about this judgment is not the judgment itself but the source from which it comes. For Tyrrell himself as a "Modernist" held with our "experientialists," and when he cast his eye into the future could see nothing but mysticism as the last refuge for religion. "Houtin and Loisy are right," he writes; "the Christianity of the future will consist of mysticism and charity, and possibly the eucharist in its primitive form as the outward bond. I desire no more." The plain fact is that this "religious experience," to which we are referred for our religious knowledge, can speak to us only in the language of religious thought; and where there is no religious thought to give it a tongue it is dumb. And above all, it must be punctually noted, it cannot speak to us in a Christian tongue unless that Christian tongue is lent it by the Christian revelation. The rejection of "external authority" and our relegation to "religious experience" for our religious knowledge is nothing more nor less, then, than the definitive abolition of Christianity and the substitution for it of natural religion. Tyrrell perfectly understood this, and that is what he means when he speaks of the Christianity of the future as reduced to "mysticism and charity." All the puzzling facts of Christianity (this is his view)

—the incarnation and resurrection of the Son of God and all the puzzling doctrines of Christianity—the atonement in Christ's blood, the renewal through the Spirit, the resurrection of the body— all, all will be gone. For all this rests on "external authority." And men will content themselves, will be compelled to content themselves, with the motions of their own religious sensibilities—and (let us hope) with charity.

There is nothing more important in the age in which we live than to bear constantly in mind that all the Christianity of Christianity rests precisely on "external authority." Religion, of course, we can have without "external authority," for a man is a religious animal and will function religiously always and everywhere. But Christianity, no. Christianity rests on "external authority," and that for the very good reason that it is not the product of man's religious sentiment but is a gift from God. To ask us to set aside "external authority" and throw ourselves back on what we can find within us alone—call it by whatever name you choose, "religious experience," "the Christian consciousness," "the inner light," "the immanent Divine"—is to ask us to discard Christianity and revert to natural religion. Natural religion is of course good—in its own proper place and for its own proper purposes. Nobody doubts—or nobody ought to doubt—that men are by nature religious and will have a religion in any event. The *sensus divinitatis* implanted in us—to employ Calvin's phrases—functions inevitably as a *semen religionis*.

Of course Christianity does not abolish or supersede this natural religion; it vitalizes it, and confirms it, and fills it with richer content. But it does so much more than this that, great as this is, it is pardonable that it should now and then be overlooked. It supplements it, and, in supplementing it, it transforms it, and makes it, with its supplements, a religion fitted for and adequate to the needs of sinful man. There is nothing "soteriological" in natural religion. It grows out of the recognized relations of creature and Maker; it is the creature's response to the perception of its Lord, in feelings of dependence and responsibility. It knows nothing of salvation. When the creature has become a sinner, and the relations proper to it as creature to its Lord have been superseded by relations proper to the criminal to its judge, natural religion is dumb. It fails just because it is natural religion and is unequal to unnatural conditions. Of course we do not say that it is suspended; we say only that it has become inadequate. It requires to be supplemented by elements which are proper to the relation of the offending creature to the offended Lord. This is what Christianity brings, and it is because this is what Christianity brings that it so supplements and transforms natural religion as to make it a religion for sinners. It does not supersede natural religion; it takes it up in its entirety unto itself, expanding it and developing it on new sides to meet new needs and supplementing it where it is insufficient for these new needs.

We have touched here the elements of truth in George Tyrrell's contention, otherwise bizarre enough, that Christianity builds not on Judaism but on paganism. The antithesis is unfortunate. Although in very different senses, Christianity builds both on Judaism and on paganism; it is the completion of the supernatural religion begun in Judaism, and it is the supernatural supplement to the natural religion which lies beneath all the horrible perversions of paganism. Tyrrell, viewing everything from the point of view of his Catholicism and dealing in historical as much as in theological judgments, puts his contention in this form: "That Catholicism is Christianized paganism or world-religion and not the Christianized Judaism of the New Testament." The idea he wishes to express is that Catholicism is the only tenable form of Christianity because it alone is founded, not on Judaism, but on "world-religion." What is worthy of our notice is that he says "world-religion," not "world-religions." He is thinking not of the infinite variety of pagan religions—many of them gross enough, none of them worthy of humanity ("man's worst crimes are his religions," says Dr. Faunce somewhere, most strikingly)—but of the underlying religion which sustains and gives whatever value they possess to them all.

Now mysticism is just this world-religion; that is to say,

it is the expression of the ineradicable religiosity of the human race. So far as it is this, and nothing but this, it is valid religion, and eternal religion. No man can do without it, not even the Christian man. But it is not adequate religion for sinners. And when it pushes itself forward as an adequate religion for sinners it presses beyond its mark and becomes, in the poet's phrase, "procuress to the lords of hell." As vitalized and informed, supplemented and transformed by Christianity, as supplying to Christianity the natural foundation for its supernatural structure, it is valid religion. As a substitute for Christianity it is not merely a return to the beggarly elements of the world, but inevitably rots down to something far worse. Confining himself to what he can find in himself, man naturally cannot rise above himself, and unfortunately the self above which he cannot rise is a sinful self.

The pride which is inherent in the self-poised, self-contained attitude which will acknowledge no truth that is not found within oneself is already an unlovely trait, and a dangerous one as well, since pride is unhappily a thing which grows by what it feeds on. The history of mysticism only too clearly shows that he who begins by seeking God within himself may end by confusing himself with God. We may conceivably think that Mr. G. K. Chesterton might have chosen his language with a little more delicacy of feeling, but what he says in the following telling way much needs to be said in this generation in words which will command a hearing. He had seen some such observation as that which we have quoted from Tyrrell, to the effect that the Christianity of the future is to be mere mysticism. This is the way he deals with it:

Only the other day I saw in an excellent weekly paper of Puritan tone this remark, that Christianity when stripped of its armor of dogma (as who should speak of a man stripped of his armor of bones) turned out to be nothing but the Quaker doctrine of the Inner Light. Now, if I were to say that Christianity came into the world specially to destroy the doctrine of the Inner Light, that would be an exaggeration. But it would be very much nearer the truth. . . . Of all the conceivable forms of enlightenment, the worst is what these people call the Inner Light. Of all horrible religions the most horrible is the worship of the God within. Anyone who knows anybody knows how it would work; anyone who knows anyone from the Higher Thought Center knows how it does work. That Jones should worship the God within him turns out ultimately to mean that Jones shall worship Jones. Let Jones worship the sun or moon, anything rather than the Inner Light; let Jones worship cats or crocodiles, if he can find any in his street, but not the God within. Christianity came into the world firstly in order to assert with violence that a man had not only to look inward, but to look outward, to behold with astonishment and enthusiasm a divine company and a divine captain. The only fun of being a Christian was that a man was not left alone with the Inner Light, but definitely recognized an outer light, fair as the sun, clear as the moon, terrible as an army with banners.

Certainly, valuable as the inner light is—adequate as it might be for men who were not sinners—there is no fate which could be more terrible for a sinner than to be left alone with it. And we must not blink the fact that it is just that, in the full terribleness of its meaning, which mysticism means. Above all other elements of Christianity, Christ and what Christ stands for, with the cross at the center, come to us solely by "external authority." No "external authority," no Christ, and no cross of Christ. For Christ is history, and Christ's cross is history, and mysticism which lives solely on what is within can have nothing to do with history; mysticism which seeks solely eternal verities can have nothing to do with time and that which has occurred in time. Accordingly a whole series of recent mystical devotional writers sublimate the entire body of those historical facts, which we do not say merely lie at the basis of Christianity —we say rather, which constitute the very substance of Christianity—into a mere set of symbols, a dramatization of psychological experiences succeeding one another in the soul. Christ Himself becomes but an external sign of an inward grace. Read but the writings of John Cordelier. Not even the most reluctant mystic, however, can altogether escape some such process of elimination of the external Christ; by virtue of the very fact that he will not have anything in his religion which he does not find within himself he must sooner or later "pass beyond Christ."

We do not like Wilhelm Herrmann's rationalism any better than we like mysticism, and we would as soon have no Christ at all as the Christ Herrmann gives us. But Herrmann tells the exact truth when he explains in well-chosen words that "the piety of the mystic is such that at the highest point to which it leads Christ must vanish from the soul along with all else that is external." "When he has found God," he explains again, "the mystic has left Christ behind." At the best, Christ can be to the mystic but the model mystic, not Himself the Way as He declared of Himself, but only a traveler along with us upon the common way. So Miss Underhill elaborately depicts Him, but not she alone. Söderblom says of von Hügel that Jesus is to him "merely a high point in the religious development to which man must aspire." "He has no eye," he adds, "for the unique personal power which His figure exercises on man." This applies to the whole class. But much more than this needs to be said. Christ may be the mystic's brother. He may possibly even be his exemplar and leader, although He is not always recognized as such. What He cannot by any possibility be is his Saviour. Is not God within him? And has he not merely to sink within himself to sink himself into God? He has no need of "salvation" and allows no place for it.

We hear much of the revolt of mysticism against the forensic theory of the atonement and imputed righteousness. This is a mere euphemism for its revolt against all "atonement" and all "justification." The whole external side of the Christian salvation simply falls away. In the same euphemistic language Miss Underhill declares that "nothing done for us, or exhibited to us, can have the significance of that which is done *in* us." She means that it has no significance for us at all. Even a William Law can say: "Christ given *for* us is neither more nor less than Christ given *into* us. He is in no other sense our full, perfect, and sufficient Atonement, than as His nature and spirit are born and formed in us." The cross and all that the cross stands for are abolished; it becomes at best but a symbol of a general law—*per aspera ad astra.* "There is but one salvation for all mankind," says Law, "and the way to it is one; and that is the desire of the soul turned to God. This desire brings the soul to God and God into the soul: it unites with God, it coöperates with God, and is one life with God." If Christ is still spoken of, and His death and resurrection and ascension, and all the currents of religious feeling still turn to Him, that is because Christians must so speak and feel. The same experiences may be had under other skies and will under them express themselves in other terms appropriate to the traditions of those other times and places. That Christian mysticism is Christ mysticism, seeking and finding Christ within and referring all its ecstasies to Him, is thus only an accident. And even the functions of this Christ within us, which alone it knows, are degraded far below those of the Christ within us of the Christian revelation.

The great thing about the indwelling Christ of the Christian revelation is that He comes to us in His Spirit with creative power. *Veni, creator Spiritus,* we sing, and we look to be new creatures, created in Christ Jesus into newness of life. The mystic will allow, not a resurrection from the dead, but only an awakening from sleep. Christ enters the heart not to produce something new but to arouse what was dormant, what has belonged to man as man from the beginning and only needs to be set to work. "If Christ was to raise a new life like His own in every man," writes Law, "then every man must have had originally in the inmost spirit of his life a seed of Christ, or Christ as a seed of heaven, lying there in a state of insensibility, out of which it could not arise but by the mediatorial power of Christ." He cannot conceive of Christ bringing anything new; what Christ seems to bring he really finds already there. "The Word of God," he says, "is the hidden treasure of every human soul, immured under flesh and blood, till as a day-star it arises in our hearts and changes the son of an earthly Adam into a son of God." Nothing is brought to us; what is already in us is only "brought out," and what is already in us—in every man—is "the Word of God." This is Christ mysticism; that is to say, it is the mysticism in which the divinity which is in every man by nature is called Christ—rather than, say, Brahm or Allah, or what not.

Even in such a movement as that represented by Bishop Chandler's Cult of the Passing Moment, the disintegrating operation of mysticism on historical Christianity—which is all the Christianity there is—is seen at work. Bishop Chandler himself, we are thankful to say, exalts the cross and thinks of it as a creative influence in the lives of men. But this only exemplifies the want of logical consistency, which indeed is the boast of the school which he represents. If our one rule of life is to be the spiritual improvement of the impressions of the moment, and we are to follow these blindly whithersoever they lead with no steadying, not to say guidance, derived from the great Revelation of the past, there can be but one issue. We are simply substituting our own passing impulses, interpreted as inspirations, for the one final revelation of God as the guide of life; that God has spoken once for all for the guidance of His people is forgotten; His great corporate provision for His people is cast aside; and we are adrift upon the billows of merely subjective feeling.

We see that it is not merely Christ and His cross, then, which may be neglected, as external things belonging to time and space. God Himself, speaking in His Word, may be forgotten— in "the cult of the passing moment." We are reminded that there have been mystics who have not scrupled openly to contrast even the God without them with the God within, and to speak in such fashion as to be understood (or misunderstood) as counseling divesting ourselves of God Himself and turning only to the inwardly shining light. No doubt they did not mean all that their words may be pressed into seeming to say. Nevertheless, their words may stand for us as a kind of symbol of the whole mystical conception, with the exaggerated value which it sets upon the personal feelings and its contempt for all that is external to the individual's spirit, even though it must be allowed that this excludes all that makes Christianity the religion of salvation for a lost world—the cross, Christ

Himself, and the God and Father of our Lord and Saviour Jesus Christ who in His love gave His Son to die for sinners.

The issue which mysticism creates is thus just the issue of Christianity. The question which it raises is, whether we need, whether we have, a provision in the blood of Christ for our sins; or whether we, each of us, possess within ourselves all that can be required for time and for eternity. Both of these things cannot be true, and obviously *tertium non datur*. We may be mystics, or we may be Christians. We cannot be both. And the pretension of being both usually merely veils defection from Christianity. Mysticism baptized with the name of Christianity is not thereby made Christianity. A rose by any other name will smell as sweet. But it does not follow that whatever we choose to call a rose will possess the rose's fragrance.

CHAPTER XVII

THE PROPHECIES OF ST. PAUL[1]

I. — I AND II THESSALONIANS

THE whole teaching, whether oral or written, of the Apostles of the New Testament, was essentially prophetic. St. Paul, in entire harmony with the Old Testament conception, defines a prophet to be one who "knows mysteries and knowledge" (I Cor. xiii. 2) and "speaks to men edification and exhortation and consolation" (I Cor. xiv. 3). This is a fair description of his own work; his Epistles are full of mysteries and knowledge, and speak to men edification, strengthening, and comfort. Among the mysteries which they declare—the word, we must remember, does not denote something inherently inscrutable, but only something as yet unknown and needing to be revealed—there are not lacking some that have to do with the future. We may properly speak, therefore, of Paul's prophecies, even in that narrow sense in which the word is popularly used, and which makes it synonymous with predictions. It is in this sense, indeed, although under a mild protest, that we use it in these papers. Our purpose is to study the predictions of Paul.

We begin with his earliest writings, the Epistles to the Thessalonians, which were written at Cornith in A.D. 52 and 53. As is well known to every careful reader of the New Testament, these Epistles are also the richest in predictions of all Paul's writings. It is not too much to say that their main burden is the Coming of the Lord. To explanations concerning this, their only didactic portions are given; and, in the first Epistle at least, a constant allusion to it is woven like a golden thread throughout its whole texture, and each section, whatever its subject, is sure to reach its climax in a reference to it (i. 10; ii. 19; iii. 13; v. 23). This seems strange to some. And it has been

[1] From *The Expositor*, 3d ser. v. iv, 1886, pp. 30-44, 131-148, 439-452; also from *Biblical Doctrines*, pp. 601-640.

suggested, either that the Apostle in his early ministry made more of the Second Advent in his teaching than growing wisdom permitted him to do later; or else, that at this particular period, amid the special trials of his work—the persecutions in Macedonia, the chill indifference at Athens, the discouragements that met him at Cornith—he had his heart turned more than was usual with him to the blessed consolation of a Christian's expectation of the coming glory. Both of these explanations are entirely gratuitous. A sufficient reason for this marked peculiarity lies at the hand of all in that other fact that distinguishes these letters from all their fellows—they are the only letters that have come down to us, which were addressed to an infant community just emerged from heathenism.

For it is undeniable that the staple of Paul's preaching to the Gentiles was God and the Judgment. When addressing Jews he could appeal to prophecy, and he preached Jesus to them as Him whom all the prophets pointed unto, the Messiah whom God had graciously promised. But with Gentiles he could appeal only to conscience; and he preached Jesus to them as Him through whom God would judge the world in righteousness, whereof He hath given assurance to all men in that He hath raised Him from the dead. The address on the Areopagus, which was delivered only a few months before I Thessalonians was written, admirably illustrates how the Apostle tried to reach the consciences of his heathen hearers; and the totality of the message delivered in it was God (Acts xvii. 24-29) and the Judgment (Acts xvii. 30, 31). But if Christ coming for judgment was thus the very centre and substance of Paul's proclamation to the Gentiles, it would not be strange if he had dwelt upon it to the Thessalonians also. And that he had preached just in this strain to them, when, so shortly before writing this letter, he was with them, he tells us himself (I Thess. i. 9, 10). For, what he chiefly thanks God for in their case is that they "turned unto God from idols" in order to do two things:—"serve the living and true God," and "await patiently His Son from the heavens, whom He raised from the dead, Jesus, our deliverer from the coming wrath." The parallel

with the speech on Mars' Hill is precise; it almost looks as if
the Apostle had repeated at Athens the sermon that had been
so effective at Thessalonica.

But we not only learn thus how it happens that Paul dwells
so much on the Second Advent when writing to the Thessalonians, but we learn also what is much more important,—how
he himself thought of the Advent and in what aspect he proclaimed it. Plainly to him it was above all things else the Judgment. It was the Judgment Day that he announced in its proclamation; and this was the lever with which he prized at
Gentile consciences. "The day in which God will judge the
world in righteousness" was what he proclaimed to the Athenians, and that it was just this that was in mind in I Thess. i.
10 is evident from the office assigned to the expected Jesus,—
"the Deliverer from the coming wrath." In harmony with this,
every passage in which the Second Advent is adverted to in
these Epistles conceives of it pointedly as the Judgment Day.
The Apostle's eager desire for the purity and sanctification of
his readers is always referred to the Advent: he wishes to have
them to boast of before the Lord Jesus at His coming (I Thess.
ii. 19),—he prays that their hearts may be established unblame-
worthy in holiness before God at the coming of our Lord Jesus
(I Thess. iii. 13),— he beseeches the God of peace to preserve
them in their whole being and all their faculties blameless, at
the coming of our Lord Jesus Christ (I Thess. v. 23),—he declares that the Day of the Lord will bring sudden destruction
upon the wicked (I Thess. v. 3), and will draw a sharp line in
justice between the good and bad (II Thess. i. 9). He speaks of
the Advent freely as the "Day of the Lord" (I Thess. v. 2, 4;
II Thess. i. 10), a term which from Joel down had stood in all
prophecy as the synonym of the final judgment.

The most important passage in this point of view is II Thess.
i. 6-10, where the matter is not only treated at large, but the
statements are explicit. Here the declaration is distinctly made
that "at the revelation of the Lord Jesus from heaven (ἐν τῇ
ἀποκαλύψει) together with the angels of His power, in a fire
of flame," God will justly recompense affliction to those who

persecuted the Thessalonians, and rest or relief to them. Both the statement of what is to occur and the definition of the time when it is to occur are to be here observed; and as the one can refer to nothing else than the distribution of rewards and punishments for the deeds done in the body, so the other can have no other reference than to the act of the coming of Christ. Both matters are made even plainer by what follows. The Apostle proceeds to declare broadly that this revelation of Jesus of which he is speaking is as one giving vengeance to those ignorant of God and those disobedient to the gospel—a vengeance that comes in the way of justice, and consists in eternal destruction away from the face of the Lord and from the glory of His might. And so closely and even carefully is the time defined, that to the exact statement that all this occurs at the revelation of Christ from heaven, it is added at the end, that this "eternal destruction" takes place whenever (ὅταν) the Lord gloriously comes,—"at that day." Unless the Apostle is here representing the persecutors of the Thessalonians as partakers in the horrors of the punitive side of the Second Advent because he expected and here asserts that the Advent was to come before that generation passed away—and this will not satisfy the general representation of verses 8 *seq.*—it is certain that he here thinks of the Advent, considered as an act and not as a state, as the last judgment itself, when

"Nil inultum remanebit."

In this case it would presuppose a general resurrection.

That Paul had a resurrection in mind as accompanying the Second Advent is certain from another important passage (I Thess. iv. 13-18). The Thessalonians did not doubt that Jesus had risen from the dead (v. 14); but they had not realized even in thought all the consequents of this great fact. Like certain at a somewhat later date at Cornith, they did not understand that all men that die rise again by virtue of Christ's conquest of death. And thus, as they saw one and another of their own number "fall on sleep," they sorrowed inordinately over them, like the rest that have no hope. It is not exactly clear what they thought of the state of the dead,—whether they conceived of them as with Christ indeed, in Paradise, but condemned to an eternity of shade existence, separated from the body for ever, which seems to have been the case with their Corinthian fellow-errorists,—or whether they fancied that with the cessation of bodily activity, the whole life went out, as may be hinted in the sad words that they sorrowed as the rest who have no hope (v. 13). In either case the Apostle brings them quick consolation in the glad announcement that the resurrection of Christ implies that of those who have fallen asleep; and that, raised through Jesus, God will bring them with Him at His coming (v. 14). With this assurance he makes Christ's coming doubly precious to them. Then proceeding to more minute details, he declares that those who are alive and are left unto the coming of the Lord shall in no wise be beforehand with those who have fallen asleep; for the Lord will come with a shout, and with an archangel's voice, and with a blast of the trumphet of God, which will pierce even into the grave. Thus the rising of Christ's dead is secured before He reaches the earth; and only after they have joined the throng, are the living along with them to be caught up in (or on) clouds unto His meeting,—into the air, to "swell the trumph of His train." "So," adds the Apostle, "we shall be always with the Lord" (v. 17). Dire, then, as the coming will be to those who know not God and who obey not the gospel, it will be bliss unspeakable to those in Christ; and as the results, on the one side, are "eternal destruction away from the face of the Lord and from the glory of His might" (II Thess. i. 9); so on the other they will be eternal dwelling with the Lord (I Thess. iv. 17). It goes without saying that the Apostle has the believing dead only in his mind in our present passage (iv. 16). How could he in such a passage speak of any other? But is not the parallel too close for us not to suspect that, as in the one case both the living and dead in Christ shall partake in the bliss and the living shall not precede the dead, so in the other the living

who are left unto the Coming shall not precede those who
have passed away, in receiving the terrible doom, and that the
blare of the trumphet of God veritably

"Coget omnes ante thronum"?

Or is it more probable that Paul believed and taught that
the Lord would certainly come before that generation passed
away? There is no room to doubt that the Thessalonians expected the Advent in their own time. Their feelings towards
death (I Thess. iv. 13 *seq.*) would be otherwise inexplicable.
And it is worthy of note that the Apostle does not correct them
in this belief. He points out to them that to fall asleep was not
to miss the glory of the Advent, but that whether they waked
or slept they should live together with their Lord (I Thess. v.
10). But he says no word that would declare them mistaken in
expecting to live until "that day." On the contrary, he expresses
himself in terms that left the possibility open that the Lord
might come while they were still alive and left on the earth (I
Thess. iv. 15, 17). This was far from asserting that the Lord
would come in that generation; but, in the connexion in which
the words stand, they would have been impossible had the
Apostle felt justified in asserting that He would not come. And
this appears to be the exact difference between the attitude of
the Thessalonians and that of Paul; they confidently expected
the Lord in their own day—he was in complete uncertainty
when He would come. That He would assuredly come, to bring
sudden destruction (I Thess. v. 3) upon all appointed unto
wrath (v. 9) and rest and salvation to those in Christ, he was
sure; but the times and seasons he knew perfectly were hidden
in the Father's power (I Thess. v. 1). He might come soon—
when He did come, it would be, he knew, with the unexpected-
ness of a thief in the night (I Thess. v. 2). But meanwhile,
whether it found him waking or sleeping was of no moment; and
though it became him to watch (I Thess. v. 6), yet the watch
was to be not a nervous expectancy, but a quiet and patient
waiting (I Thess. i. 10, ἀναμένειν, cf. Judith viii. 17). But if, just
because the "when" was unknown, the Apostle could not confidently expect the Lord in his own time, the categorical asser-

tion that the Advent would bring "eternal destruction away from the face of the Lord" (II Thess. i. 9) to the special persecutors of the Thessalonians, rests on his view of the Advent as synchronous with the final judgment and presupposes a general resurrection.

The very moderation of the Apostle's attitude made it difficult for the excited Thessalonians to yield themselves to his leading. Certainly his first letter did not allay their fanaticism. Things went rather from bad to worse, and so certain were they that the Lord was coming at once, that they fell an easy prey to every one who should cry "Lo, here!" or "Lo, there!" and even, apparently from this cause, began to neglect their daily business and became mere busybodies, refusing to work, and eating the bread of others. The Apostle sternly rebukes their disorder, and commands that they work with quietness; and with a view to preserving them from sudden agitation whenever any one chose to declare "the day of the Lord is upon us!" he points out certain events that must come before the Lord. That this practical, ethical purpose was the occasion of the important revelation in II Thess. ii. 1-12, the Apostle tells us himself (ii. 2). And a simple glance at his words is enough to expose the almost ludicrous inappropriateness of the contention of some that the error of the Thessalonians was not feverish expectancy of the Lord's coming, but the belief that the day of the Lord had already come and had brought none of the blessings they had expected from it,—not the Lord Himself, nor their resurrected friends,—nothing of all that the Apostle had taught and they had hoped.[2] What the Apostle says is that he wishes to

---

[2] This curious misinterpretation is founded on a pressure of the verb ἐνέστηκεν, ii. 2, in forgetfulness of three things. (1) That this verb is a compound of ἵστημι, not of εἰμί, and means, not "is in progress," but "is upon us," in the two senses of "to threaten," and "to be actual" (especially in the participle). While it may mean "to be present," therefore, it need not mean it, and is not likely to in such a case. (2) That the clause "either by spirit or by word, or by letter as if from us," is an essential part of the context, the omission of which falsifies the text. What the Apostle says is not "be not troubled—as that the day of the Lord," etc. but "be not troubled by any statement as that the day of the Lord is upon us!"—something essentially different, which excludes the above interpretation. (3) That the broad context renders this explanation impossible and meaningless.

save them from being suddenly shaken from their senses or troubled by any statement from any quarter, as that the day of the Lord was upon them. The passage is parallel to and probably founded upon the words of our Lord in His warning to His disciples not to be led astray or deceived by any "who should say, 'Lo, here is the Christ!' or 'Here!'" (Mt. xxiv. 23), and is already a valuable indication that throughout this whole section Paul has the great apocalyptic discourse of Jesus in mind and is to be interpreted from it.

The impression has become very widespread that, owing to the lack on our part of the previous information to which Paul alludes as given by him on a former occasion to the Thessalonians (verses 5 and 6), the interpretation of this prophecy must remain for all time a sealed riddle to us. That two important events, called by Paul "the apostasy," and "the revelation of the man of sin," the latter of which was at the time deterred by something else mysteriously designated "the restraint," or "the restrainer," were to take place before the coming of the Lord—this, we are told, is all that we can know, and any effort to obtain any defined outlines for the misty shapes thus barely named to us only succeeds in bringing the dense darkness in which they are steeped into tangibility and visibility. We find it difficult to believe the matter so hopeless. On the contrary, the broad outlines, at least, of the prophecy appear to us sufficiently clear; and we believe that a sound method of study will give the humble student who is willing to put a stern check on his imagination and follow the leading of the exegetical hints alone, an adequately exact understanding of its chief details.

First of all, we must try to keep fresh in our minds the great principle that all prophecy is ethical in its purpose, and that this ethical end controls not only what shall be revealed in general, but also the details of it and the very form which it takes. Next, we must not fail to observe that our present prophecy is not independent of previous ones,—that its roots are in Daniel, and from beginning to end it is full of allusions to our Lord's great apocalyptic discourse. Still again, we must bear in mind that it comes from a hand which throughout these

Epistles preserves an attitude of uncertainty of the "times and seasons," and so expresses himself as to imply that he believed that the Lord might come, in despite of all these preliminary events, in his own day.

If, holding fast to these principles, we approach the prophecy itself, we observe first of all, that although the three things— the Apostasy, the Revelation of the Man of Sin, and the Coming of the Lord—are brought together, they are not declared to be closely connected, or immediately consecutive to one another. The mere "and" of verse 3 reveals nothing beyond the simple fact that both of those events must come to pass before the Lord comes. So too for all that the prophecy tells us, both of these evil developments might come and pass away, and be succeeded by ages on ages which in turn might pass away, and yet men be able to say, "Where is the promise of His coming?" To point to the declaration in verse 8, that "the Lord Jesus shall destroy" the lawless one—almost, "blow him away"— "with the breath of His mouth and abolish him with the manifestation of His presence," as proving that he will still be lording it on earth when the Lord comes to his destruction, is to neglect the apparent indications of the context. For this assertion does not go, in either vividness or literality of expression, beyond what is stated just before of the generation then living (II Thess. i. 7, 9); and it is inserted here not as a chronological detail—and is out of place (cf. verses 9, *seq.*) if considered a chronological detail—but as part of the description of the lawless one, and for the ethical purpose of keeping in the mind of the reader his judgment by God and his final fate. In a word, this statement only declares of the Man of Sin what was just before declared of the lesser enemies of the Gospel, and what was in I Thess. v. 3 *seq.* declared of all to whom wrath is appointed— that he shall meet with destruction at the Second Coming of the Lord. The revelation of the Man of Sin is not, then, necessarily to be sought at the end of time: we know of it, only that it will succeed the removal of the "restraint," and precede, by how much we are not told, the coming of the Lord.

We cannot fail to observe, however, next, that in his de-

scription of the Man of Sin, the Apostle has a contemporary, or
nearly contemporary phenomenon in mind. The withholding
power is already present. Although the Man of Sin is not yet
revealed, as a mystery his essential "lawlessness" is already
working—"only until the present restrainer be removed from
the midst." He expects him to sit in "the temple of God," which
perhaps most naturally refers to the literal temple in Jerusalem,
although the Apostle knew that the out-pouring of God's wrath
on the Jews was close at hand (I Thess. ii. 16). And if we compare the description which the Apostle gives of him with our
Lord's address on the Mount of Olives (Mt. xxiv.), to which,
as we have already hinted, Paul makes obvious allusion, it becomes at once in the highest degree probable that in the words,
"he that exalteth himself against all that is called God, or is
worshipped, so that he sitteth in the sanctuary of God showing
himself that he is God," Paul can have nothing else in view than
what our Lord described as "the abomination of desolation
which was spoken of by Daniel the prophet, standing in the
holy place" (Mt. xxiv. 15); and this our Lord connects immediately with the beleaguering of Jerusalem (cf. Luke xxi.
20). This obvious parallel, however, not only places the revelation of the Man of Sin in the near future, but goes far towards
leading us to his exact identification. Our Lord's words not only
connect him with the siege of Jerusalem, but place him distinctly among the besiegers; and, led by the implication of the
original setting of the phrase (in Dan. xi. 36) which Paul uses,
we cannot go far wrong in identifying him with the Roman
emperor.

Whether a single emperor was thought of or the line of
emperors, is a more difficult question. The latter hypothesis
will best satisfy the conditions of the problem; and we believe
that the line of emperors, considered as the embodiment of
persecuting power, is the revelation of iniquity hidden under
the name of the Man of Sin. With this is connected in the description certain other traits of Roman imperialism—more especially the rage for deification, which, in the person of Calig-
ula, had already given a foretaste of what was to come. It was

Nero, then, the first persecutor of the Church,—and Vespasian the miracle-worker,[3]—and Titus, who introduced his divine-self and his idolatrous insignia into the Holy of Holies, perhaps with a directly anti-Christian intent,[4]—and Domitian,—and the whole line of human monsters whom the world was worshipping as gods, on which, as a nerve-cord of evil, these hideous ganglia gathered,—these and such as these it was that Paul had in mind when he penned this hideous description of the son of perdition, every item of which was fulfilled in the terrible story of the emperors of Rome.

The restraining power, on this hypothesis, appears to be the Jewish state. For the continued existence of the Jewish state was both graciously and naturally a protection to Christianity, and hence a restraint on the revelation of the persecuting power. Graciously, it was God's plan to develop Christianity under the protection of Judaism for a short set time, with the double purpose of keeping the door of salvation open to the Jews until all of their elect of that generation should be gathered in and the apostasy of the nation should be rendered doubly and trebly without excuse, and of hiding the tender infancy of the Church within the canopy of a protecting sheath until it should grow strong enough to withstand all storms. Naturally, the effect of the continuance of Judaism was to conceal Christianity from notice through a confusion of it with Judaism—to save it thus from being declared an illicit religion—and to enable it to grow strong under the protection accorded to Jewish worship. So soon as the Jewish apostasy was complete and Jerusalem given over to the Gentiles—God deserting the temple which was no longer His temple to the fury of the enemies, of those who were now His enemies—the separation of Christianity from Judaism, which had already begun, became evident to every eye; the conflict between the new faith and heathenism culminating in and now alive almost only in the Emperor-worship, became intense; and the persecuting power of the empire was inevitably let loose. Thus the continued existence of Juda-

3 Tac., "Hist.," iv. 82; Suet., "Vesp.," 7; Dio Cass., lxvi. 8.
4 Sulp. Sev., "Sacr. Hist.," ii. 30, §§ 6. 7.

ism was in the truest sense a restraint on the persecution of Christians, and its destruction gave the signal for the lawless one to be revealed in his time.

If the masculine form of "the restrainer" in verse 7 demands interpretation as a person—which we more than doubt—it might possibly be referred without too great pressure to James of Jerusalem, God's chosen instrument in keeping the door of Christianity open for the Jews and by so doing continuing and completing their probation. Thus he may be said to have been the upholder of the restraining power, the savour of the salt that preserved the Christians from persecution, and so in a high sense the restrainer.

Finally, in this interpretation, the apostasy is obviously the great apostasy of the Jews, gradually filling up all these years and hastening to its completion in their destruction. That the Apostle certainly had this rapidly completing apostasy in his mind in the severe arraignment that he makes of the Jews in I Thess. ii. 14-16, which reached its climax in the declaration that they were continually filling up more and more full the measure of their sins, until already the measure of God's wrath was prematurely ($\check{\epsilon}\phi\theta a\sigma\epsilon\nu$) filled up against them and was hanging over them like some laden thunder-cloud ready to burst and overwhelm them,—adds an additional reason for supposing his reference to be to this apostasy—above all others, "the" apostasy—in this passage.

We venture to think that the core of this interpretation may be accounted very probable,—so much of it as this: that the Apostle had in view in this prophecy a development in the immediate future closely connected with the Jewish war and the destruction of Jerusalem, although not as if that were the coming of Christ for which he was patiently waiting, but rather in full recognition of its being only the culmination of the Jewish apostasy and the falling of God's wrath upon them to the uttermost. When he declares that these events must precede the coming of Christ, this no doubt was clear evidence that the Advent was not to be looked for immediately; but was in no wise inconsistent with uncertainty whether it would come during that generation or not. As a matter of mere fact the growing apostasy of the Jews was completed—the abomination of desolation had been set up in the sanctuary—Jerusalem and the temple, and the Jewish state were in ruins—Christianity stood naked before her enemies—and the persecuting sword of Divus Cæsar was unsheathed and Paul had himself felt its keenness: all the prophecy had been fulfilled before two decades had passed away.

Let us gather up for the close, in brief recapitulation, the events which Paul predicts in these two Epistles. First of all, and most persistently of all, he predicts the coming of the Lord from heaven unto judgment, with its glorious accompaniments of hosts of angels, the shout, the voice of the archangel and the blast of the trumpet of God that awake the dead. Thus, he predicts the resurrection of Christ's dead to partake in the glory of His coming. Then, he foretells the results of the judgment—eternal destruction from the face of God for the wicked, and everlasting presence with the Lord for His own. Of the time of the Advent the Apostle professes ignorance; he only knows that it will come unexpectedly. But he does know that before it the apostasy of the Jews must be completed, and the persecuting power of the Roman state be revealed. This apostasy and its punishment he sees is immediately ready for completion (I Thess. ii. 16). Finally, he mentions having previously foretold the persecutions under which the Thessalonians were already suffering (I Thess. iii. 4).

II. The Epistles to the Galatians, Corinthians, and Romans

When we pass from the Epistles to the Thessalonians to the next group of letters—those to the Galatians, Corinthians and Romans, all four of which were written in the course of a single year, some five years later (A.D. 57-58)—we are at once aware of a great diminution in the allusions to the future. Galatians contains rather more matter than both letters to the Thessalonians, but does not contain a single prediction; and the much longer letter to the Romans, while alluding now and then to what the future was to bring forth, contains no explicit mention of the Second Advent. The first letter to the Corinthians is three times as long as both letters to the Thessalonians, but contains rather less predictive matter. We should not be far wrong if we estimated that these four letters, in about nine times the space, give us about as much eschatological matter as the two letters to the Thessalonians.

The contrast exists in nothing else, however, except the mere matter of amount. The two groups of letters are thoroughly at one in their teaching as to the future—at one, but not mere repetitions of one another. This group is continually supplying what almost seems to be explanations and extensions of the revelations in Thessalonians, so that it exhibits as great an advance in what is revealed as decrease in the relative amount of space given to revelations. So clear is it that the Apostle's preaching to all heathen communities was in essence the same, and that all grew up to the stature of manhood in Christ through practically the same stages, that we may look upon the Thessalonian letters as if they had been addressed to the infancy of every Church, and treat those at present before us as if they were intended to supplement them. This is probably the true account of the very strong appearance of being supplementary and explanatory to those in the letters to Thessalonica, which the predictions in this group of letters are continually presenting.

In these as in those, the Second Advent is represented primarily and most prominently in the aspect of judgment—as the last judgment. Here, too, the desire for moral perfection is referred constantly to it, as for example in I Cor. i. 8 cf. 7, where the actual moment in mind is that of the revelation of the Lord Jesus Christ. The mutual glorying of the Apostle and his readers in each other is to be "in the day of our Lord Jesus" (I Cor. i. 8). This is the day of punishment also: the incestuous man is delivered now unto Satan to be punished in the flesh in order that his spirit may be saved in the day of the Lord (I Cor. v. 5); and in exactly similar wise, those who are visited with bodily ills for unworthy partaking of the Lord's Supper, receive this chastening that they may not be condemned with the world (I Cor. xi. 32). The sanction of the anathema pronounced against all who do not love the Lord is Maranatha—"the Lord cometh!" (I Cor. xvi. 22). His coming is indeed so sharply defined as the time of judging, in the mind of Paul, that he advises his readers to "judge nothing before the time, until the Lord come" (I Cor. iv. 5). The connotation of "the day of the Lord" was to him so entirely judgment, that the word "day" had come to mean judgment to him, and he actually uses it as its synonym, speaking of a "human day," for "human judgment" (I Cor. iv. 3). Of like import is the representation of the second coming as the great day of revelation of character. Of the builders on the edifice of God's Church it is declared that "each man's work shall be made manifest by 'the day.'" "For the day is revealed in fire, and each man's work, of what sort it is,—the fire itself shall test." "If any man's work abideth, he shall receive reward; if any man's work is burned up, he shall be mulcted, but himself shall be saved, but so as through fire" (I Cor. iii. 13-15). It is scarcely an extension of this teaching to declare openly that when the Lord comes, He "will both bring to light the hidden things of darkness, and make manifest the counsels of the hearts; and then shall his praise come to each from God" (I Cor. iv. 5).

In the light of this it is evident what time the Apostle has in mind when he declares that "all of us must needs be made manifest[5] before the judgment-seat of Christ, that each may receive the things [done] through the body according to what he practised, whether good or bad" (II Cor. v. 10); and which day to him was "the day when God shall judge the secrets of men according to my gospel, by Jesus Christ"—"the day of wrath and revelation of the righteous judgment of God" (Rom. ii. 16, 5). Yet, in this last passage it is beyond all question that the Apostle has in mind the final judgment, when God "will render to every man according to his works," and the two verses which have been adduced are respectively the opening and

---

[5] φανερωθῆναι, cf. φανερόν, I Cor. iii. 13; φανερώσει, I Cor. iv. 5.

closing verse of the splendid passage in which Paul gives us his fullest description of the nature and standards of the awful trial to which all men, whether Jews or Gentiles, whether those who have law or those who have no law, are summoned "in the day when God shall judge the secrets of men according to my gospel through Christ Jesus." Elsewhere in Romans, where judgment necessarily holds an important place in the general argument, the wrath of God is kept hanging over ungodliness and unrighteousness (i. 18; iii. 5; v. 9) and the coming judgment is held before the eyes of the reader (iii. 6; xiv. 10).

For the realization of such a judgment scene (Rom. ii. 5-16; II Cor. v. 10; Rom. xiv. 10), a resurrection is presupposed, and the reference of the Apostle is obvious when he expresses his confidence that "He who raised up Jesus shall raise up us also with Jesus, and shall present us with you" (II Cor. iv. 14; cf. v. 10; also I Cor. vi. 14). In this compressed sentence, there is pointed out the relation of our resurrection both to the judgment ($\pi\alpha\rho\alpha\sigma\tau\hat{\eta}\sigma\epsilon\iota$, cf. Col. i. 22) as preceding and in order to it, and to the resurrection of Christ ($\sigma\grave{\upsilon}\nu$ Ἰησοῦ, cf. the use of $\sigma\upsilon\nu\epsilon\gamma\epsilon\acute{\iota}\rho\omega$ in Col. ii. 12; iii. 1) as included in it as a necessary result and part of it. The latter matter is made very plain by the remarkably simple way in which Jesus is declared in Rom. i. 4 to have been marked out as the Son of God "by the resurrection of the dead"—a phrase which has no meaning except on the presupposition that the raising of Jesus was the beginning of the resurrection of the dead and part and parcel of it (cf. also Rom. vi. 4; viii. 11, etc.).

At this point our attention is claimed by that magnificent combined argument and revelation contained in the 15th chapter of I Corinthians, which has been the instruction and consolation of the saints through all Christian ages. The occasion which called it forth was singularly like and singularly unlike that which gave rise to the parallel revelation in I Thessalonians. As in the one Church so in the other, there were those who failed to grasp the great truth of the Resurrection, and laid their dead away without hope of their rising again. But in Thessalonica this was due to sorrowing ignorance; in Corinth, to philosophizing pride of intellect. And in the one case, the Apostle meets it with loving instruction; in the other, with a brilliant refutation which confounds opposition, and which, although carrying a tender purpose buried in its bosom, as all the world has felt, yet flashes with argument and even here and there burns with sarcasm. The Corinthian errorists appear to have been spiritualistic philosophizers, perhaps of the Platonic school, who, convinced of the immortality of the soul, thought of the future life as a spiritual one in which men attained perfection apart from, perhaps largely because separate from, the body. They looked for and desired no resurrection; and their formula, perhaps somewhat scoffingly and certainly somewhat magisterially pronounced, was: "There is no rising again of dead men." It is instructive to observe how the Apostle meets their assertion. They did not deny the resurrection of Christ (I Cor. xv. 2, 11)—probably explaining it as a miracle like the reanimation of Lazarus. Yet the Apostle begins by laying firm the proofs of Christ's resurrection (xv. 1-11), and doing this in such a way as to suggest that they needed primary instruction. He "makes known to them," rather than reminds them of the Gospel which he and all the Apostles preached and all Christians believed. With this opening sarcasm, he closes the way of retreat through a denial of the resurrection of Christ, and then presses as his sole argument the admitted fact that Christ had risen. How could they deny that dead men rise, when Christ, who was a dead man, had risen? If there is no resurrection of dead men, then not even is Christ risen. It is plain that their whole position rested on the assertion of the impossibility of resurrection; to which it was a conclusive reply that they confessed it in one case. Having uncovered their logical inconsistency, Paul leaves at once the question of fact and presses at length the hideous corollaries that flow from their denial of the possibility of dead men rising, through its involved denial that Jesus, the dead man, had risen—aiming, no doubt, at arousing a revulsion against a doctrine fruitful of such consequences (xv. 14-34).

Having thus moved his readers to shame, he proceeds to

meet squarely their real objection to the resurrection, by a full explanation of the nature of the resurrection-body (xv. 35-50), to which he adjoins a revelation concerning the occurrences of the last day (xv. 51-58). To each of these we should give a moment's attention.

The intimate connexion of our resurrection with that of Christ, which we have seen Paul everywhere insisting upon, would justify the inference that the nature of our resurrection-bodies was revealed to men in His resurrection-body, that was seen and handled of men for forty days. This is necessarily implied in the assumption that underlies the argument at I Cor. xv. 12 *sq.*, and is almost openly declared at verse 49; II Cor. iv. 14; Rom. viii. 11. In our present passage, however, the Apostle reserves this for the last, and begins by setting forth from natural analogies the possibility of a body being truly one's own body and yet differing largely from that which has hitherto been borne. This is an assertion of sameness and difference. At verse 42 he proceeds to explain the differences in detail. As the change in the form of expression advises us, the enumeration divides itself into two parts at the end of verse 43—the former portion describing in threefold contrast, the physical, and the latter in a single pregnant phrase the moral difference. On the one hand the new bodies that God will give us will no longer be liable to corruption, dishonour or weakness. On the other, they will no longer be under the power of the only partially sanctified human nature, but rather will be wholly informed, determined and led by the Holy Ghost (verse 44). That this is the meaning of the much disputed phrase: "It is sown a natural (psychic) body, it is raised a spiritual (pneumatic) body," is demonstrable from the usage of the words employed. It is plain matter of fact that "psychic" in the New Testament naturally means and is uniformly used to express "self-led" in contrast to "God-led," and therefore, unconverted or unsanctified; while "pneumatic" never sinks in the New Testament so low in its connotation as the human spirit, but always (with the single exception of Eph. vi. 12, where superhuman evil spirits are in mind) refers to "Spirit" in its highest sense,—the Holy

Ghost.[6] In this compressed phrase, thus, the Apostle declares that in this life believers do not attain to complete sanctification (Rom. vii. 14-viii. 11), but groan in spirit awaiting the redemption of the body (Rom. viii. 23, vii. 24); while in the heavenly life even their bodies will no longer retain remainders of sin, but will be framed by (Rom. viii. 11), filled with, and led by the Holy Ghost. The incomparable importance of this moral distinction over the merely physical ones is illustrated by the Apostle's leaving them to devote the next five verses to the justification of this, closing (verse 50) with a chiasmic recapitulation in which he pointedly puts the moral difference first: "Now this I say, brethren, that flesh and blood cannot inherit the kingdom of God, neither doth corruption inherit incorruption." For, that "flesh and blood" must here be understood ethically and not physically is already evident from the preceding context and is put beyond question by the settled ethical sense of the phrase—which is, of course, used in the New Testament also only in its established ethical sense, and could not be used otherwise without misleading the reader. All crass inferences that have been drawn from it, therefore, in a physical sense are illegitimate to start with, and are negatived to end with by the analogy of Christ's resurrection-body, which we have seen Paul to understand to be a case under the rule, and which certainly had flesh and bones (Luke xxiv. 39). Paul does not deny to our resurrection-body, therefore, materiality, which

[6] This is gradually becoming recognized by the best expositors. Compare the satisfactory article on πνευματικός in the *third* edition of Cremer's "Biblico-Theological Lexicon of N. T. Greek," with the very unsatisfactory one in the second edition. He now tells us that the word is used "in profane Greek only in a physical or physiological sense, commonly the former;—in biblical Greek only in a religious, that is religio- or soteriologico-psychological sense = belonging to the Holy Ghost or determined by the Holy Ghost," p. 675, cf. p. 676. (The reader needs to be warned that he will find no hint of Cremer's entire rewriting of this article, in the *Supplement* to their edition of Cremer's Lexicon issued by T. & T. Clark this year.) So Meyer's latest view (to which he did not correct the Commentary throughout) is given in his Com. on I Cor., E. T., p. 298, *note:* "Πνευματικός" is nowhere "in the New Testament the opposite of *material,* but of *natural* (I Pet. ii. 5 not excluded); and the πνεῦμα to which πνευματικός refers is always (except Eph. vi. 12, where it is the *diabolic* spirit-world that is spoken of) the *Divine* πνεῦμα." The italics are his own.

would be a *contradictio in adjecto;* he does not deny "flesh" to it,—which he hints, rather, will be its material, though of "another" kind than we are used to (verse 39); he denies to it "fleshliness" in any, even the smallest degree, and weakness of any and every sort. In a word, he leaves it human but makes it perfect.

After so full an explanation of the nature of the resurrection-body, it was inevitable that deeper questions should arise concerning the fate of those found by the advent still clothed in their bodies of humiliation. Hence a further revelation was necessary beyond what had been given to the Thessalonians, and the Apostle adds to that, that those found living shall be the subjects of an instantaneous change which will make them fit companions for the perfected saints that have slept. For when the trumpet sounds and the dead are raised incorruptible, they too in the twinkling of an eye shall be "changed." And the change is for them as for the dead a putting on of incorruption and of immortality. The spectacle of these multitudes, untouched by death, receiving their perfect and immortal bodies is the great pageant of the conquest of death, and the Apostle on witnessing it in spirit cannot restrain his shout of victory over that whilom enemy of the race, whose victory is now reversed and the sinews of whose fatal sting wherewith it had been wont to slay men are now cut. So complete is Christ's conquest that it looses its hold over its former victims and the men still living cannot die. The rapidity of action on "the great day" is also worth notice. The last trump sounds—the dead spring forth from the grave—the living in the twinkling of an eye are changed—and all together are caught up into the air to His meeting,—or ever the rushing train of angels that surround their Lord and ours can reach the confines of the earth. Truly events stay not, when the Lord comes.

Important as these revelations are, they become almost secondary when compared with the contents of that wonderful passage I Cor. xv. 20-28, the exceeding richness of which is partially accounted for by the occasion of its utterance. It comes in the midst of Paul's effort to move his readers by painting the terrible consequences of denial of the possibility of resurrection, involving denial of the fact that Christ has risen. He feels the revulsion he would beget in them, and relieves his overburdened heart by suddenly turning to rest a moment on the certainty of Christ's rising, and to sweep his eye over all the future, noting the effects of that precious fact up to the end. He begins by reasserting the inclusion of our resurrection in that of Christ, who was but the first-fruits of those asleep, and then justifies it by an appeal to the parallel of Adam's work of destruction, declaring, apparently, that as physical death came upon all men through Adam's sin, so all men shall be rescued from its bondage by Christ's work of redemption. The context apparently confines the word "death" in these verses to its simple physical sense, while on the contrary the "all" of both clauses seems unlimited, and the context appears to furnish nothing to narrow its meaning to a class. They thus assert the resurrection of all men without distinction as dependent on and the result of Christ's work, just as all men, even the redeemed, taste of death as the result of Adam's sin. "But," the Apostle adds, returning to the Christian dead, "this resurrection though certain, is not immediate; each rises in his own place in the ranks—Christ is the first-fruits, then His own rise at His coming; then is the end" (verses 23, 24). The interminable debates that have played around the meaning of this statement are the outgrowth of strange misconceptions. Because the resurrection of the wicked is not mentioned it does not at all follow that it is excluded; the whole section has nothing to do with the resurrection of the wicked (which is only incidentally included and not openly stated in the semi-parenthetic explanations of verses 21 and 22), but, like the parallel passage in I Thessalonians, confines itself to the Christian dead. Nor is it exegetically possible to read the resurrection of the wicked into the passage as a third event to take place at a different time from that of the good, as if the Apostle had said: "Each shall rise in his own order; Christ the first-fruits,—then Christ's dead at His coming, —then, the end of the resurrection, namely, of the wicked." The term, "the end," is a perfectly definite one with a set and distinct

meaning, and from Matthew (e.g., xxiv. 6, cf. 14) throughout
the New Testament, and in these very epistles (I Cor. i. 8;
II Cor. i. 13, 14), is the standing designation of the "end of
the ages," or the "end of the world." It is illegitimate to press it
into any other groove here. Relief is not however got by varying the third term, so as to make it say that "then comes the
end, accompanied by the resurrection of the wicked," for this
is importing into the passage what there is absolutely nothing
in it to suggest. The word τάγμα does not in the least imply
succession; but means "order" only in the sense of that word
in such phrases as "orders of society." Neither does the "they
that are Christ's" prepare the mind to expect a statement as to
"those who are not Christ's," any more than in Rom. ix. 6,
when we hear of "Israel," and "those of Israel," we expect
immediately to hear of "those not of Israel." The contrast is
entirely absorbed by the "Christ" of the preceding clause, and
only the clumsiness of our English gives a different impression.
Not only, however, is there no exegetical basis for this exposition in this passage; the whole theory of a resurrection of the
wicked at a later time than the resurrection of the just is
excluded by this passage. Briefly, this follows from the statement that after the coming of Christ, "then comes the end"
(verse 24). No doubt the mere word "then" (εἶτα) does not
assert immediateness, and for ought necessarily said in it, "the
end" might be only the next event mentioned by the Apostle,
although the intervening interval should be vast and crowded
with important events. But the context here necessarily limits
this "then" to immediate subsequence.

Exegetically this follows, indeed, from the relation of verse
28 to 23 *b*, for the long delay asserted in which it assigns the
reason: Christ's children rise not with Him, because death is
the last enemy to be conquered by Him, and their release from
death cannot, therefore, come until all His conquests are completed. The matter can be reduced, however, to the stringency
of a syllogism. "The end" is declared to take place "whenever
Christ giveth over (the immediateness is asserted by the present) the kingdom to God"; and this occurs "whenever He shall

have conquered" all His enemies, the last of which to be conquered is death (verse 26). Shortly, then, the end comes so soon
as death is conquered. But death is already conquered when it
is forced to loose its hold on Christ's children; and that is at
the Parousia (ver. 23). If any should think to escape this, as if
it were an inference, it would be worth while to glance at verse
54, where it is, as we have seen, asserted that the victory over
death is complete and his sting destroyed at the Second Advent,
and that the rising of Christ's dead is a result of this completed
conquest. The end then is synchronous with the victory over
death, which itself is synchronous with the second coming, and
if the wicked rise at all (which verses 21, 22 assert), it is all one
whether we say they rise at the Advent or at the end, since these
two are but two names for the same event. Of this, indeed,
Paul's language elsewhere should have convinced us: "who
shall also confirm you unto the end, unaccusable in the day of
our Lord Jesus Christ" (I Cor. i. 8), "I hope ye will acknowledge unto the end, . . . that we are your glorying even as ye are
also ours, in the day of our Lord Jesus" (II Cor. i. 14). So, then,
the Second Advent is represented to be itself "THE END."

With the emergence of this fact, the importance of our
present passage is revealed. It is immediately seen to open to
us the nature of the whole dispensation in which we are living,
and which stretches from the First to the Second Advent, as a
period of advancing conquest on the part of Christ. During its
course He is to conquer "every rulership and every authority
and power" (verse 24), and "to place all His enemies under
His feet" (verse 25), and it ends when His conquests complete
themselves by the subjugation of the "last enemy," death. We
purposely say, period of "conquest," rather than of "conflict,"
for the essence of Paul's representation is not that Christ is
striving against evil, but progressively ($\check{\epsilon}\sigma\chi\alpha\tau\sigma$ς, verse 26) over-
coming evil, throughout this period. A precious passage in the
Epistle to the Romans (xi. 25 sq., cf. verse 15) draws the veil
aside to gladden our eyes with a nearer view of some of these
victories; telling us that "the fulness of the Gentiles shall be
brought into" the Church, and after that "all Israel shall be

saved," and by their salvation great blessings,—such a spiritual awakening as can only be compared to "life from the dead" —shall be brought to all God's people. There may be some doubt as to the exact meaning of these phrases. The "fulness of the Gentiles," however, in accordance with the usual sense of the genitive with "pleroma," and the almost compulsion of the context, should mean, not the Gentile contingent to the elect, but the whole body of the Gentiles.[7] And "Israel" almost certainly means not the true but the fleshly "Israel." In this case, the prophecy promises the universal Christianization of the world,—at least the nominal conversion of all the Gentiles and the real salvation of all the Jews. In any understanding of it, it promises the widest practicable extension of Christianity, and reveals to us Christ going forth to victory. But in this, which seems to us the true understanding, it gives us a glimpse of the completion of His conquest over spiritual wickedness, and allows us to see in the spirit the fulfilment of the prayer, "Thy kingdom come, Thy will be done in earth even as it is in heaven." It is natural to think that such a victory cannot be wrought until the end is hastening—that with its completion nothing will remain to be conquered but death itself. But the

---

[7] The exegetical question really turns on the sense to be given to Ἰσραήλ in xi. 26. If τὸ πλήρωμα τῶν ἐθνῶν in verse 25 means "those of the Gentiles who go towards filling up the kingdom," then πᾶς Ἰσραήλ of verse 26 must of necessity be the spiritual Israel, distinguished from Ἰσραήλ of verse 25, by the inclusive πᾶς. Then the sense would be that "hardening has befallen Israel" temporarily— viz. until the Gentile contingent comes in,—and thus ("in this way," the most natural sense of οὕτως), ALL Israel shall be saved;—not part only, but all. So that the passage continues to justify the temporary rejection of Israel by its gracious purpose, viz. that thus the Gentiles receive their calling, and all God's children, out of every nation, are saved. On the other hand if, as is most natural and usual, τῶν ἐθνῶν is genitive of what is filled up, so that the phrase means, the whole body of the Gentiles, then there is no thought to carry over from it to condition πᾶς Ἰσραήλ in verse 26, and it naturally follows in sense the Ἰσραήλ of verse 25. The sense then is that which is suggested in the text. That Ἰσραήλ of verse 26 is the fleshly Israel seems to follow from the succeeding context, as well as from the difficulty of taking the words in two different senses in so narrow a context. But if so, this carries the meaning of the "fulness of the Gentiles" with it, and the interpretation given in the text is the only admissible one.

Apostle does not tell us this,[8] and we know not from him how long the converted earth is to await its coming Lord.

An even more important fact faces us in the wonderful revelation we have been considering (I Cor. xv. 20-28): the period between the two advents is the period of Christ's kingdom, and when He comes again it is not to institute His kingdom, but to lay it down (verses 24, 28). The completion of His conquest, which is marked by conquering "the last enemy," death (verse 28), which in turn is manifest when the just arise and Christ comes (verses 54, 23), marks also the end of His reign (verse 25) and the delivery of the kingdom to God, even the Father (verse 24). This is indubitably Paul's assertion here, and it is in perfect harmony with the uniform representation of the New Testament, which everywhere places Christ's kingdom before and God's after the Second Advent. The contrast in Mt. xiii. 41 and 43 is not accidental. We cannot enter into the many deep questions that press for discussion when this ineffable prediction is even approached. Suffice it to say that when we are told that Jesus holds the kingship for a purpose (verse 25), namely, the completion of His mediatorial work, and that when it is accomplished He will restore it to Him who gave it to Him (verse 28), and thus the Father will again become "all relations among all creations,"—nothing is in the remotest way suggested inconsistent with the co-equal Deity of the Son with the Father and His eternal co-regnancy with Him over the universe. Manifestly we must distinguish between the mediatorial kingship which Jesus exercises by appointment of His Father, and the eternal kingship which is His by virtue of His nature, and which is one with God's own.

As to the duration of Christ's kingdom—or in other words the length of time that was to elapse before the Lord came—Paul says nothing in this passage. Nor does he anywhere in these Epistles speak more certainly about it than in those to

---

[8] I shall not deny that the ζωὴ ἐκ νεκρῶν of ver. 15 *may* mean the general resurrection, but it is an unexampled phrase for this conception and cannot be asserted to mean it. Nor in this context is it natural to so understand it.

the Thessalonians (I Cor. i. 7; xi. 26). He so expresses himself as to leave the possibility open that the Lord might come in his own time (I Cor. xv. 51); but he makes it a matter for experience to decide whether He will or not (II Cor. v. 1, ἐάν with the subjunctive, cf. verse 3 sq). It is only through misunderstanding that passages have been adduced as asserting a brief life for the world. When (I Cor. x. 11) the "ends of the ages" are said to have already come, a technical term is used which declares that after this present inter-adventual period there remains no further earthly dispensation, but nothing is implied as to the duration of these "last times" (acharith hayyamin). So, when (I Cor. vii. 25-29) the Corinthians are advised to refrain from earthly entanglements because of "the impending distress," which should shortly tear asunder every human tie, there is nothing to show that the Apostle had the Second Advent in mind, and everything that the Neronian persecution and the wars of succession and the succeeding trials to Christians fully satisfy the prediction.[9] The very difficult passage at Rom. xiii. 11-14 appears also to have been misapplied to the advent by the modern exegesis. Its obvious parallels are Eph. v. 1-14 and I Thess. v. 1-11. The whole gist of the passage turns on moral awaking; and the word "salvation" appears to refer to the consummation of salvation in a subjective rather than objective sense (Rom. x. 10; II Thess. ii. 13); while the aorist, "When we believed," seems not easily to lend itself to furnishing a terminus a quo for the calculation of time, but rather to express the act by which their salvation was brought closer. So that the meaning of the passage would seem to be: "Fulfil the law of love, I say. I appeal to you for renewed efforts by your knowledge of the time: that it is high time for you at length to awake out of sleep. Long ago when you believed, you professed to have come out of darkness into light, and to have shaken

---

[9] The reference of the phrase, "for the fashion of this world passeth away" (verse 31) is not to the broad but the narrow context, justifying the immediately preceding statement, that those who use the world should be as those not using it. It is but equivalent to the line, "This world is all a fleeting show," and is parallel to I John ii. 17. Although it may have some reference to the Second Advent, as the day of renovation, it does not affect verses 20 and 29.

yourselves free from the inertia as well as deeds of the night. Now salvation is closer to us than it was when we made that step. Having begun, we have advanced somewhat towards the goal. The night of sin in which the call for repentance found us is passing away. Let us take off at length our night-clothes, and buckle on the armour for the good fight—yea, let us rid ourselves of all that belongs to the night, and put on the Lord Jesus Himself." If this understanding is correct, the Apostle does not count the days and assert that the time that had elapsed since his conversion had nearly run the sands of all time out, but rather appeals to his readers to renew their strenuous and hearty working out of their salvation by the encouragement that they had already progressed somewhat on the road, and could more easily and hopefully take a second step.

There remain two very interesting passages (II Cor. v. 1-10; Rom. viii. 18-25) which give us an insight as no others do into the Apostle's personal feelings towards this life, death, and the Advent. Nowhere else are the trials under which he suffered life so clearly revealed to us as in the opening chapters of II Corinthians. Amid them all, the very allusions to which, lightly touched as they are, appal us, the Apostle is upheld by the greatness of his ministry and the greatness of his hope. Though his outward man is worn away—what then? He need not faint, for his inward man is renewed day by day, and this affliction is light compared with the eternal weight of glory in store for him. He longs for the rest of the future life (cf. also Rom. vii. 25); but he shrinks from death. He could desire rather to be alive when the Lord comes, and that he might put on "the house from God, the dwelling not made with hands, eternal in the heavens," over this "earthly tent-dwelling" which he now inhabits. He only desires—does not expect this; he does not at all know whether he shall be found not naked when the putting-on time comes. But he longs for relief from the burdens of life, that somehow this mortality may be swallowed up of life. And when he bethinks him that to be at home in the body is to be abroad from the Lord, the other world is so glorious to him that he is not only willing but even desires ("rather," verse 8) to enter it even "naked"—he is well pleased to go abroad from the body and go home to the Lord. Like Bunyan and the sweet singer, Paul, looking beyond the confines of earth, can only say, "Would God that I were there!" This longing for relief from earthly life is repeated in Romans (vii. 25), and the groaning expectation of the consummation as the swallowing up of corruption in incorruption is attributed in the wonderful words of Romans viii. 18 *sq.* to the whole of the lower creation. All nature, says Paul, travails in the same longing. And the consummation brings not only relief to Christ's children, who have received the firstfruits of the Spirit, in the redemption of the body, but also deliverance and renovation to all nature as well. This noble conception was implied already in the teaching of the Old Testament, not only in its declaration that the world was cursed for man's sake (Rom. viii. 20), but in the prediction of a new heavens and a new earth (verse 21). Paul here simply takes his position in the company of the prophets.

The glories of the future world find comparative expression again in I Cor. xiii. 10-13 as not only spiritual but eternal and perfect. There are besides two rapid allusions to future glories which are so slightly touched on in contexts of stinging satire as not fully to explain themselves. The one reminds the saints that they shall judge the world and angels (I Cor. vi. 2, 3), and the other assumes that at some time or other, they are to come to a kingship (I Cor. iv. 8). Out of our present epistles alone the time and circumstances when these promises shall be fulfilled can scarcely be confidently asserted. We can only say that if the reigning of the saints refers to a co-reigning with Christ (cf. II Tim. ii. 12), it must be fulfilled before Christ lays down His kingdom. And in like manner the judging must come before the Advent, unless it refers only to the part the saints take in the last judgment scene (cf. Mt. xix. 28; xxv. 31). The Apostle expects his readers to understand his allusions out of knowledge obtained elsewhere than in these epistles. Perhaps he has in mind such "words of the Lord" as are recorded in Luke xxii. 29, 30. For us, the whole matter may rest for the present *sub judice*.

III. THE LATER EPISTLES

The distribution of predictive passages through the letters written by St. Paul during his first imprisonment,—Ephesians, Colossians, Philemon and Philippians (A.D. 62 and 63),—is analogous to what we have observed in the preceding group. In the more theological and polemical letters, as there, so here, such passages are few, while in the more practical and personal letters they are comparatively numerous. The Second Advent is not directly mentioned at all in Ephesians, and only once, and then very incidentally, in Colossians; while, although the brief and purely occasional letter to Philemon naturally enough contains no allusions to the future, the Epistle to the Philippians, which resembles in general manner and contents the letters to the Corinthians and Thessalonians, like them too is full of them. The nature of the eschatological matter which is found in each epistle is in striking harmony with its purpose and general character: in Ephesians and Colossians it is confined to allusions, sometimes somewhat obscure, to eschatological facts which are introduced usually with a theological or polemic object; in Philippians, where Paul pours out his heart, it is free and rich, and usually has a direct personal design of encouragement or consolation. In all these epistles alike, however, it is introduced only incidentally—no section has it as its chief end to record the future; but in Philippians it is more fully and lovingly dwelt upon, in Ephesians and Colossians more allusively touched. It is not surprising, under such circumstances, that very little is revealed to us concerning the future in these epistles beyond what was already contained in the earlier letters, the teaching of which most commonly furnishes the full statement of the facts here briefly referred to. Now and then, however, they cast a ray of light on points or sides of the truth which were not before fully illuminated, and thus enable us to count distinct gains from their possession. Nowhere are they out of harmony with what the earlier epistles have revealed.

The eschatological contents of the twin letters, Ephesians

and Colossians, will illustrate all this very sharply. Much is made in them of an inheritance of hope laid up in heaven for the saints in light (Eph. i. 14, cf. ii. 7; Col. i. 12, i. 5: cf. iii. 24). The time of its realization is when Christ our life shall be manifested, at which time we also shall be manifested with Him in glory (Col. iii. 4). It is clearly presupposed that the reception of the inheritance is conditioned on a previous judgment. We must be made meet for it by the Father, by a deliverance from the power of darkness and translation into the kingdom of Him by whom we have redemption, the forgiveness of our sins (Col. i. 12). Whatsoever good thing each one does, the same he shall certainly receive from the Lord (Eph. vi. 8). The inheritance itself is thus a recompense for our service here (Col. iii. 24). Judgment again is implied in the constant undertone of allusion to a presentation of us by God or Christ, pure and blameless and unaccusable at once before Christ and in Christ (Eph. i. 22; Col. i. 22, 28). But if Christ is thus the judge, we naturally enough are to live our life here in His fear (Eph. v. 21). The resurrection of the saints is implied now and then (Col. ii. 12, 13; cf. Eph. v. 23), and once asserted in the declaration that Christ has become "the first-born from the dead, that in all things He might have the pre-eminence" (Col. i. 18). The nature of this inter-adventual period is explained with apparent reference to some such teaching as is given in I Cor. xv. 25, to be a period of conflict (Eph. vi. 12), and its opening days are hence said to be evil (Eph. v. 16), though, no doubt, the evil will decrease as conflict passes into victory. The enemies of the Lord are named as principalities and powers, and their subjugation was potentially completed at His death and resurrection (Col. ii. 15). The actual completion of the victory and subjection of all things to the Son is briefly re-stated in each epistle. In the one it is declared that God has purposed with reference to the dispensation of the fulness of the times (i.e. this present dispensation of the ends of the ages, I Cor. x. 11) to gather again all things as under one head in Christ, the things in the heavens and the things upon earth (Eph. i. 10). In the other it is said that it was the Father's good pleasure that all the fulness should dwell in the Son, and that through Him all things should be reconciled to Him, whether things upon the earth or things in the heavens, and that this reconciliation should be wrought by His blood outpoured on the cross (Col. i. 19). The only difference between such statements and such a one as II Cor. v. 19 is that these deal with the universe, while that treats only of man, and hence these presuppose the full teaching implied in I Cor. xv. 10-28 and Rom. viii. 18-25, and sum up in a single pregnant sentence the full effects of the Saviour's work. The method of Christ's attack on the principalities and powers and world-rulers of this darkness and spiritual hosts of wickedness, and the means by which He will work His victory, are declared at Eph. vi. 12; from which we learn—as we might have guessed from Rom. xi. 25, *sq.*—that Christians are His soldiers in this holy war, and it is through our victory that His victory is known. It is easy to see that there is nothing new in all this, and yet there is much that has the appearance of being new. We see everything from a different angle; the light drops upon it from a new point, and the effect is to bring out new relations in the old truths and give us a feeling of its substantialness. We become more conscious that we are looking at solid facts, with fronts and backs and sides, standing each in due and fixed relations to all.

The Epistle to the Philippians differs from the others of its group only in dwelling more lingeringly on the matters it mentions, and thus transporting us back into the full atmosphere of Corinthians and Thessalonians. Here, too, Paul thinks of the advent chiefly in the aspect of the judgment at which we are to receive our eternal approval and reward or disapproval and rejection. He is sure that He who began a good work in His readers will perfect it, until the day of Jesus Christ (i. 6); he prays that they may be pure and void of offence against the day of Christ (i. 10); he desires them to complete their Christian life that he may have whereof to glory in the day of Christ that he did not run in vain, neither labour in vain (ii. 16). These sentences might have come from any of the earlier epistles. The events of the day of the Lord are detailed quite in the spirit of the earlier epistles in iii. 20, 21. Our real home, the commonwealth in which is our citizenship, is heaven, from whence we patiently await a Saviour, the Lord Jesus Christ, who shall fashion anew the body of our humiliation so that it shall be conformed to the body of His glory, according to the working whereby He is able to subdue all things unto Himself. These two verses compress within their narrow compass most of the essential features of Paul's eschatology: Christ's present enthronement as King of the state in which our citizenship is, in heaven, from whence we are to expect Him to return in due time; our resurrection and the nature of our new bodies on the one side as no longer bodies of humiliation, on the other as like Christ's resurrection body, and hence glorious; Christ's conquest of all things to Himself, and last of all of death, in our resurrection, of which, therefore, all His other conquests are a guerdon.

The description of our resurrection bodies as conformed to Christ's glorified body is important in itself, and all the more so as it helps us to catch the meaning of the almost immediately preceding statement (iii. 10 *sq.*) of Paul's deep desire "to know Christ and the power of His resurrection and the fellowship of His suffering, becoming conformed unto His death, if by any means he may attain to the resurrection of the dead." It has become somewhat common to see in this passage a hint that Paul knew only of a resurrection of the redeemed, and himself expected to rise only in case he was savingly united to Christ. This exposition receives, no doubt, some colour from the phraseology used; but when we observe the intensely moral nature of the longing, as expressed in the immediately subsequent context, we cannot help limiting the term "resurrection from the dead" here, by the added idea of resurrection to glory, and the full statement of verse 21 inevitably throws back its light upon it. It is not mere resurrection that Paul longs for; he gladly becomes conformed to Christ in His death that he may be conformed to Him in His resurrection also, and the gist of the whole passage is bound up in this idea of conformity to Christ, with which it opens (verse 10) and with which it closes (verse 21).

To think of two separate resurrections here—of the just and the unjust—in the former of which Paul desires to rise, is to cut the knot, not untie it. Nothing in the language suggests it—the "resurrection from the dead" is as unlimited[10] as the "death" that precedes it. Nothing in the context demands or even allows it. Nothing anywhere in Paul's writings justifies it. It is inconsistent with what we have found Paul saying about the Second Advent and its relation to the end, at I Cor. xv. 20-28. And finally it is contradicted by his explicit statements concerning the general resurrection, in the discourses in Acts which are closest in time to the date of these letters, and which ought to be considered along with them, especially Acts xxiv. 15, where in so many words the resurrection is made to include both the just and unjust (cf. xxiii. 6; xxvi. 8, 23; xxviii. 20). The limitation which the context supplies in our present passage is not that of class, much less that of time, but that of result; Paul longs to be conformed to Christ in resurrection as in death—he is glad to suffer with Him that he may be also glorified together with Him. Yea, he counts his sufferings but refuse, if he may gain Christ and *be found in Him,* clothed in the righteousness which is by faith. This is the ruling thought which conditions the statements of verse 11, and is openly returned to at verse 21.

The mention of the subjection of all things to Christ in verse 21, which recalls the teaching of I Cor. xv. 20-28 again, was already prepared for by the account of the glory which God gave the Son as a reward for His work of suffering, in ii. 9-11. There His supreme exaltation is stated to have been given Him of God for a purpose—that all creation should be subjected to Him, should bow the knee to His Name and confess Him to be Lord to the glory of God the Father. The completion of this purpose Paul here (iii. 21) asserts Christ to have the power to bring about, but nothing is implied in either passage as to the rapidity of its actual realization.

Some have thought, however, that in this epistle also Paul

[10] On ἐξανάστασις, see Meyer *in loc.*

expresses his confidence that all should be fulfilled in his own time. Plainly, however, the reference of the completion of our moral probation, or of our victory over the present humiliation, to the Second Advent goes no further than to leave the possibility of its coming in our generation open (i. 6; iii. 21), and the latter at least is conditioned by the desire for a good resurrection, which is earnestly expressed immediately before. "The Lord is at hand" (iv. 5) would be more to the point, if its reference to time and the Second Advent were plainer. But although it was early so understood (e.g., by Barnabas), it can hardly be properly so taken. It is, indeed, scarcely congruous to speak of a person as near in time; we speak of events or actions, times or seasons as near, meaning it temporally; but when we say a person is near, we mean it inevitably of a space-relation. And the connexion of the present verse points even more strongly in the same direction. Whether we construe it with what goes before, or with what comes after—whether we read "Let your gentleness be known to all men, [for] the Lord is near," or "The Lord is near, [therefore] be anxious for nothing, but in everything . . . let your requests be made known unto God," —the reference to God's continual nearness to the soul for help is preferable to that to the Second Advent. And if, as seems likely, the latter connexion be the intended one, the contextual argument is pressing. The fact that the same phrase occurs in the Psalter in the space-sense, and must have been therefore in familiar use in this sense by Paul and his readers alike, while the asyndetic, proverbial way in which it is introduced here gives it the appearance of a quotation, adds all that was needed to render this interpretation of it here certain.

The Apostle's real feelings towards the future life are clearly exposed to us in the touching words of i. 21 *sq.*, the close resemblance of which to II Cor. v. 1-10 is patent. Here he does not refer in the remotest way to a hope of living to see the advent, but begins where he ended in II Corinthians, with the assertion of his personal preference for death rather than life, because death brought the gain of being with Christ, "which is far bet-

ter." Even the "naked" intermediate state of the soul, between
death and resurrection, is thus in Paul's view to be chosen
rather than a life at home in the body but abroad from the Lord.
Yet he does not therefore choose to die: "but what if to live in
the flesh—this means fruit of my work?" he pauses to ask himself, and can but answer that he is in a strait betwixt the two,
and finally that since to die is advantageous to himself alone,
while to live is more needful for his converts, he knows he
shall abide still a while in this world. To him, too, man here
is but

> "a hasty traveller
> Posting between the present and the future,
> That baits awhile in this dull fleshly tavern";

and yet, though this tent-dwelling is seen by him in all its
insufficiency and inefficiency, like the good Samaritan he is
willing to prolong his stay in even so humble a caravanserai
(iii. 21) for the succouring of his fellows—nay, like the Lord
Himself, he counts the glory of the heavenly life not a thing to
be graspingly seized, so long as by humbling himself to the
form of a tenant here he may save the more. The spirit that was
in Christ dwelt within him.

The eschatology of the Pastoral Epistles—I Timothy, Titus,
and II Timothy (A.D. 67, 68)—the richest depository of which
is the Second Epistle to Timothy, is indistinguishable from
that of the other Pauline letters. In these letters again the
Second Advent is primarily and most prominently conceived as
the closing act of the world, the final judgment of men, and
therefore the goal of all their moral endeavours. Timothy is
strenuously exhorted "to keep the commandment," that is, the
evangelical rule of life, "spotless and irreproachable until the
appearing of our Lord Jesus Christ" (I Tim. vi. 14). All of
Paul's confidence is based on his persuasion that Jesus Christ,
the abolisher of death and bringer of life and incorruption to
light through the Gospel, is able to guard his deposit[11] "against

11 τὴν παραθήκην μου = "what I have entrusted to him."

that day" (II Tim. i. 12), and that there is laid up for him the crown of righteousness which the Lord, the righteous Judge, shall give him at that day (II Tim. iv. 8). "And not to me only," he adds, as if to guard against his confidence seeming one personal to himself, "but also to all them that have loved His appearing." Though at that day the Lord will render to Alexander according to his works (II Tim. iv. 14), he will grant mercy to Onesiphorus (II Tim. i. 16); and in general he will attach to godliness the promise both of the life that now is and that which is to come (I Tim. iv. 8).

It follows, therefore, that for all those in Christ the Second Advent is a blessed hope to be waited for with patience, but also with loving desire and longing. Christians are described as those that love Christ's appearing (II Tim. iv. 8), and the hope of it is blessed (Titus ii. 13) because it is the epiphany of the glory of our great God and Saviour Jesus Christ, even as the former coming was the epiphany of His grace (Titus ii. 13, cf. 11). It is implied that as the grace so the glory is for Christ's children. What this glory consists in is not, however, very sharply defined. It is the deposit of life and incorruption that the Saviour holds in trust for His children (II Tim. i. 12). It is the crown of righteousness which the righteous Judge will bestow upon them (II Tim. iv. 8). It is freedom from all iniquity (Titus ii. 14). It is the actual inheritance of the eternal life now hoped for (Titus iii. 7). But all this is description rather than definition. Nothing is said of resurrection except that they gravely err who think it already past (II Tim. ii. 18), nothing of the new bodies to be given to the saints, or of any of the glories that accompany the final triumph. What is said describes only the full realization of what is already enjoyed in its first fruits here or what comes in some abundance in the imperfect intermediate state.

For the glories of the advent do not blind Paul to the bliss of a Christian's hope in "this world," whether in the body or out of the body. In the fervid music of a Christian hymn the Apostle assures his son Timothy of his own steadfast faith in the faithful saying (II Tim. ii. 11-13):—

"If we died with Him, we shall also live with Him;
    If we endure we shall also reign with Him;
    If we shall deny Him, He will also deny us;
    If we are faithless—He abideth faithful,
    For He cannot deny Himself."

And death itself, he says, can but "save him into Christ's heavenly kingdom" (II Tim. iv. 18). The partaking in Christ's death and life in this passage seems to be meant ethically; and the co-regnancy with the Lord that is promised to the suffering believer apparently concerns the being with Christ in the heavenly kingdom,—whether in the body or abroad from the body. Thus the Apostle is not here contemplating the glories of the advent, but comforting and strengthening himself with the profitableness of godliness in its promise of the life that now is, under the epiphany of God's grace, when we can be but looking for the epiphany of His glory. That he expects death (for now he was sure of death, II Tim. iv. 6) to introduce him into Christ's heavenly kingdom advertises to us that that kingdom is now in progress, and II Tim. iv. 1 is in harmony with this just because it tells us nothing at all of the time of the kingdom.[12]

About Christ's reign and work as king—in other words, concerning the nature of this period in which we live—these epistles are somewhat rich in teaching. These "latter times" or "last days"[13]—for these are, according to the fixed usage of the times, the designations under which the Apostle speaks of the dispensation of the Spirit,—are not to be an age of idleness or of sloth among Christians; but, in harmony with the statements of the earlier letters, which represented it as a time of conflict with and conquest of evil, it is here pictured as a time in which apostasies shall occur (I Tim. iv. 1), and false doctrines flourish along with evil practices (II Tim. iii. 1, sq.), when the just shall

---

12 Notice that the correct translation is: "I charge thee before God and Christ Jesus who shall judge the quick and the dead, and by His appearing and by His kingdom." Each item is adduced entirely separately; the Apostle is accumulating the incitements to action, not giving a chronological list, which, in any case, the passage does not furnish.

13 ἐν ὑστέροις καιροῖς, I Tim. iv. 1; ἐν ἐσχάταις ἡμέραις, II Tim. iii. 1.

suffer persecution, and evil men and impostors wax worse and worse (II Tim. iii. 13), and, even in the Church, men shall not endure sound doctrine, but shall introduce teachers after their own lusts (II Tim. iv. 3 *sq.*). It would be manifestly illegitimate to understand these descriptions as necessarily covering the life of the whole dispensation on the earliest verge of which the prophet was standing. Some of these evils had already broken out in his own times, others were pushing up the ground preparatory to appearing above it themselves. It is historically plain to us, no doubt, that they suitably describe the state of affairs up to at least our own day. But we must remember that all the indications are that Paul had the first stages of "the latter times" in mind, and actually says nothing to imply either that the evil should long predominate over the good, or that the whole period should be marked by such disorders.

When the Lord should come, he indeed keeps as uncertain in these epistles as in all his former ones. In II Timothy he expects his own death immediately, and he contemplates it with patience and even joy, no longer with the shrinking expressed in II Corinthians. It is all the more gratuitous to insist here that the natural reference of Timothy's keeping the faith to the advent as the judgment (I Tim. vi. 14), implies that he confidently expected that great closing event at once or very soon. On the contrary it is reiterated in the same context that God alone knows the times and seasons, in the assertion that God would show the epiphany of our Lord Jesus Christ "in His own times." Beyond this the Apostle never goes; and it is appropriate that in his earliest and latest epistles especially he should categorically assert the absolute uncertainty of the time of the consummation (I Thess. v. 1; I Tim. vi. 15). Surely an intense personal conviction that the times and seasons were entirely out of his knowledge can alone account for so consistent an attitude of complete uncertainty.

IV. SUMMARY

It appears to be legitimate to affirm in the light of the preceding pages that it is clear that there is such a thing as a Pauline eschatology; a consistent teaching on the last things which runs through the whole mass of his writings, not filling them, indeed, as some would have us believe, but appearing on their surface like daisies in a meadow—here in tolerable profusion, there in quite a mass, there scattered one by one at intervals of some distance—everywhere woven into it as constituent parts of the turf carpeting. The main outlines of this eschatology are repeated over and over again, and exhibited from many separate points of view, until we know them from every side and are confident of their contour and exact nature. Details are added to the general picture by nearly every letter; and each detail falls so readily into its place in the outline as to prove both that the Apostle held a developed scheme of truth on this subject, and that we are correctly understanding it. A general recapitulation of the broadest features of his doctrine will alone be necessary in closing.

Paul, then, teaches that as Jesus has once come in humiliation, bringing grace into the world, and God has raised Him to high exaltation and universal dominion in reward for His sufferings and in order to the completion of His work of redemption; so when He shall have put all His enemies under His feet, He shall come again to judgment in an epiphany of glory, to close the dispensation of grace and usher in the heavenly blessedness. The enemies to be conquered are principalities and powers and world-rulers of this darkness and spiritual hosts of wickedness; this whole period is the period of advancing conquest and will end with the victory over the last enemy, death, and the consequent resurrection of the dead. In this advancing conquest Christ's elect are His soldiers, and the conversion of the world—first of the Gentiles, then of the Jews—marks the culminating victory over the powers of evil. How long this conflict continues before it is crowned with complete victory, how long the supreme and sole kingship of Christ endures before He restores the restored realm to His father, the Apostle leaves in complete uncertainty. He predicts the evil days of the opening battle, the glad days of the victory; and leaves all questions of times and seasons to Him whose own times they are. At the end, however, are the general resurrection and the general judgment, when the eternal rewards and punishments are awarded by Christ as judge, and then, all things having been duly gathered together thus again under one head by Him, he subjects them all to God that He may once more become "all relations among all creations." That the blessed dead may be fitted to remain for ever with the Lord, He gives them each his own body, glorified and purified and rendered the willing organ of the Holy Ghost. Christ's living, though they die not, are "changed" to a like glory. Not only man, but all creation feels the renovation and shares in the revelation of the sons of God, and there is a new heaven and a new earth. And thus the work of the Redeemer is completed, the end has come, and it is visible to men and angels that through Him in whom it was His pleasure that all the fulness should dwell, God has at length reconciled all things unto Himself, having made peace through the blood of His cross—through Him, whether things upon the earth or things in the heavens—yea, even us, who were in times past alienated and enemies, hath He reconciled in the body of His flesh through death, to present us holy and without blemish and unreproachable before Him.

SUPPLEMENT

SERMONS

I

GOD'S IMMEASURABLE LOVE[1]

JOHN iii. 16:—For God so loved the world, that He gave His only begotten Son, that whosoever believeth on Him should not perish, but have eternal life.

To WHOM we owe this great declaration of the love of God, it is somewhat difficult to determine; whether to our Lord Himself, or to that disciple who had lain upon His bosom and had imbibed so much of His spirit that he thenceforth spoke with his Master's voice and in his Master's words. Happily it is a matter of no substantial importance. For what difference does it make to you and me whether the Lord speaks to us through His own lips, or through those of His servant, the Apostle, to whom He had promised, and to whom He had given, His Holy Spirit to teach him all the truth? What concerns us is not the instrumentality through which the message comes, but the message itself. And what a great message it is,—the message of the greatness of the love of God! Let us see to it that, as the words sound in our ears, it is this great revelation that fills our hearts, fills them so full as to flood all their being and wash into all their recesses. The greatness of the love of God, the immeasurable greatness of the love of God!

This exhortation is not altogether superfluous. Strange as it may sound, it is true, that many—perhaps the majority—of those who feed their souls on this great declaration, seem to have trained themselves to think, when it falls upon their ears, in the first instance at least, not so much of how great, how immeasurably great, God's love is, as rather of how great the world is. It is the world that God loves, they say,—the world: and forthwith they fall to thinking how great the world is, and how, nevertheless, God loves it all. Think, they cry, of the multitudes

[1] From the volume of sermons entitled *The Saviour of the World*, pp. 103-130.

of men that swarm over the face of the earth; and have swarmed over it through all the countless generations from the beginning; and will swarm over it in ever-increasing numbers through perhaps even more countless generations yet to come, until the end: and God loves them all, each and every one of them, from the least to the greatest; so loves them that He has given His only begotten Son to die for them, for each and every one of them—and for each and every one of them with the same intent, —the intent, namely, that he may be saved. O how great the love of God must be to embrace in its compass these uncounted multitudes of men; and so to embrace them that every individual that enters as a constituent unit into the mass of mankind receives his full share of it, or rather is inundated by its undivided and undiminished flood!

Certainly this is a great conception. But it is just as certainly not a great enough conception to meet the requirements of our text. For, look you, will you measure the immeasurable greatness of God's love by the measure of man? All these multitudes of men that have lived, do live, or shall live, from the beginning to the end of the world's entire span,—what is their finite sum to the infinitude of God? Lo, the world, and all that is in the world,—and all that has ever been in the world or can ever be in the world,—lies as nothing in the sight of the Infinite. One, floats as an evanescent particle in His eternal vision. How can we exalt our conception of the greatness of the divine love by thinking of it as great enough to embrace all this? Can we praise the blacksmith's brawn by declaring it capable of supporting a mustard-seed on an outstretched palm? This standard is too small: we cannot compute such masses in terms of it. Conceive the world as vastly as you may, it remains ever incommeasurable with the immeasurable love of God.

And what warrant does the text offer for conceiving so greatly of the world, or indeed for thinking of it at all under the category of extension, as if it were its size that was oppressing the imagination of the speaker, and its parts—down to the last analysis—that were engaging his wondering attention? Evidently the text envisages the world, of which it speaks in the concrete, as a whole. This world is made up of parts, no doubt, and the differing destinies that await the individuals which compose it are adverted to. But the emphasis does not fall upon its component elements, as if their number, for example, could form the ground of the divine love, or explain the wonder of its greatness. Distribution of it into its elements and engagement with the individuals which compose it, is merely the result of the false start made when the mind falls away from contemplating the immensity of the love of God with which the text is freighted, to absorb itself rather in wonder over the greatness of the world which is loved.

And having begun with this false step it is not surprising if the wandering mind finds itself shortly lost in admiration not even of the greatness of the world, but rather of the greatness of the individual soul. These souls of men, each and every one of which God loves so deeply that He has given His Son to die for it,—what great, what noble, what glorious things they must be! O what value each of us should place upon this precious soul of ours that God so highly esteemed as to give His Son to die for it! A great and inspiring thought, again, beyond all doubt: but, again, obviously not great enough to be the thought of the text. Clearly, what the text invites us to think of is the greatness of the love of God, not the greatness of the human soul.

And how can we fancy that we can measure the love of God by what He has done for each and every human soul? Persist in reading the text thus distributively, making "the world" mean each and every man that lives on the earth, and what, after all, does it declare that the love of God has done for them? Just open a way of salvation before men, give them an opportunity to save themselves. For, what, in that contingency, does the text assert? Just this: that "God so loved the world"—that is, each and every man that has lived, does live, or shall live in this world,—"that He gave His only begotten Son, that *whosoever believeth on Him* should not perish, but have eternal life." "Whosoever believeth on Him,"—those only. Is this, then, the measure of the immeasurable love of God—that He barely opens a pathway to salvation before sinful men, and stops right there; does nothing further for them—leaving it to their own unassisted initiation whether they will walk in it or not? Surely this cannot be the teaching of the text; and that, for many reasons,—primary among which is this: that we all know that the love of God has done much more than this for multitudes of the children of men, namely, has not merely opened a way of salvation before them, but has actually saved them. Nor is our text silent on this point. It is not in this mere opening of a way of salvation before each and every man that the love of God for the world is declared by it to issue, but in the actual saving of the world. We read the next verse and we discover it asserting that God sent His Son into the world for this specific end, that the world should be "saved by Him." God did not then only so love the world as to give it a bare chance of salvation: He so loved the world that He saved the world. And surely this is something far better: and provides a much higher standard by which to estimate the greatness of God's love.

We discover, then, that the distribution of the term "world" in our text into "each and every man" in the world not only begins with the obvious misstep of directing our attention at once rather to the greatness of the world than to the greatness of God's love and only infers the latter from the former; but ends by positively belittling the love of God, as if it could content itself with half-measures,—nay, in numerous instances, with what is practically no measure at all. For if it is satisfied with merely opening a way of salvation and leaving men to walk in this way or not as they list, the hard facts of life force us to add that it is satisfied with merely opening a way of salvation for multitudes to whom it should never be made known that a way of salvation lay open before them, although their sole hope lies in their walking in it. And why dwell on special cases? Shall we not recognize frankly that so meagre a provision would be operative in no case? For even when it is made known to men that a way of salvation is opened before them—can they being sinners, walk in it? Let our passage itself tell us. Does it not explicitly declare that every one that doeth ill hateth the light and cometh not to the light? And who of us does not know that he, at least,—if not every man,—doeth ill? Does the love of God expend itself then in inoperative manifestations? Surely not so can be measured the love of God, of which the Scriptures tell us that its height and depth, and length and breadth pass knowledge: of which Paul declares that nothing can separate us from it, not death, nor life, nor angels, nor principalities, nor things present, nor things to come, nor powers, nor height, nor depth, nor any other creature: of which he openly asserts, that if it avails to reconcile us with God, through the death of His Son, much more shall it avail to bring us into the fruition of salvation by His life.

Obviously, then, the distribution of the notion "world" in our text into "each and every man" in the world, does less than justice to the infinitude of the love of God which it is plainly the object of the text to exalt in our thought. Reacting from the ineptitudes of this interpretation, and determined at all costs to take the conception of the love of God at the height of its idea, men of deeper insight have therefore suggested that it is not the world at large that is in question in the text, but God's people, the chosen of God in the world. Surely, it is God's seeking, nay, God's finding love that is celebrated here, they argue; the love which goes out to its object with a vigour which no obstacle can withstand, and, despite every difficulty, brings it safely into the shelter of its arms. The "world" that God so loved that He gave His Son for it,—surely that is not the "world" that He loved so little as to leave it to take or leave the Son so given, as its own wayward heart might dictate; but the "world" that He loved enough, after giving His Son for it, prevalently to move upon with His quickening Spirit and graciously to lead into the offered salvation. The "world" of believers, in a word, as they are called in the following clause; or, as they are called elsewhere in Scripture, the "world" of God's elect. It was these whom God loved before the foundations of the world with a love beyond all expression great and strong, constant and prevailing, a love which was not and could not be defeated, just because it was *love*, the very characteristic of which, Paul tells us, is that it suffereth long, is not provoked, taketh no account of evil, beareth all things, endureth all things, yea, never faileth: and therefore was not and could not be satisfied until it had brought its objects home.

It is very clear that this interpretation has the inestimable advantage over the one formerly suggested, that it penetrates into the heart of the matter and refuses to evacuate the text of its manifest purport. The text is given to enhance in our hearts the conception of the love of God to sinners: to make us to know somewhat of the height and depth and length and breadth of it, though truly it passes knowledge. It will not do, then, as we read it to throw limitations around this love, as if it could not accomplish that whereto it is set. Beyond all question the love which is celebrated is the saving love of God; and the "world" which is declared to be the object of this love is a "world" that is—not merely given an opportunity of salvation— but actually saved. As none but believers—or if you choose to look at them *sub specie æternitatis,* none but the elect—attain salvation, so it seems but an identical proposition to say that it is just the world of believers, or the world of the elect, that is embraced in the love of God here celebrated. When the text declares, therefore, that God so loved the world that He gave His only begotten Son for it, is not what is meant, and what must be meant, just the elect scattered throughout the world? It may seem strange to us, indeed, to speak of the elect as "the world." But is not that largely because, in the changed times in which we live, we do not sufficiently poignantly appreciate or deal seriously enough with the universalism of Christianity, in contrast with the nationalism of the old dispensation? In this universalistic and anti-Jewish Gospel of John, especially, what more natural than to find the "world" brought into contrast with Jewish exclusivism? In fine, is not the meaning of our text just this: that Jesus Christ came to make propitiation for the sins not of Jews only, but of the whole world, that is to say, not of course for each and every man that lives in the world, but in any event for men living throughout the world, heirs of the world's life and partakers in the world's fortunes? Certainly it is difficult for us to appreciate the greatness of the revolution wrought in the religious consciousness of men like John, bred in the exclusivism of Judaism and accustomed to think of the Messiah as the peculiar property of Israel, when the world-wide mission of Christianity was brought home to their minds and hearts. To John and men like John its universalism was no doubt well-nigh the most astonishing fact about Christianity. And the declaration that God so loved the world—not Israel merely, but the world—that He gave His only begotten Son, that whosoever—from every nation, not from the Jews merely—should believe on Him should have eternal life: this great declaration must have struck upon their hearts with a revelation of the wideness of God's mercy and the unfathomable profundities of His love, such as we can scarcely appreciate in our days of age-long familiarity with the great fact. Is not this, then, the real meaning of the immense declaration of the text: that Jesus Christ is the world-wide Saviour, that now the middle-wall of partition has been broken down and God has called to Himself a people out of all the nations of the earth, and has so loved this His people gathered thus from the whole world, that He has given His only begotten Son to die for them? And is not this a truth big with consequences, worthy of such a record as is given it in our text, and capable of awakening in our hearts a most profound response?

Assuredly no one will doubt the value and inspiration of such suggestions. The truth that lies in them, who can gainsay? But it is difficult to feel that they quite exhaust the meaning of the great words of the text. In their effort to do justice to the conception of the love of God, do they not do something less than justice to the conception embodied in the term "the world"? In identifying "the world" with believers, do they not neglect, if we may not quite say the contrast of the two things, yet at least the distinction between the two notions which the text seems to institute? "God so loved the world," we read, "that He gave His only begotten Son, that whosoever believeth on Him should not perish, but have eternal life." Certainly here "the world" and "believers" do not seem to be quite equipollent terms: there seems, surely, something conveyed by the one which is not wholly taken up in the other. How, then, shall we say that "the world" means just "the world of believers," just those scattered through the world, who, being the elect of God, shall believe in His Son and so have eternal life? There is obviously much truth in this idea: and the main difficulty which it faces may, no doubt, be avoided by saying that what is taught is that God's love of the world is shown by His saving so great a multitude as He does save out of the world. The wicked world deserved at His hands only total destruction. But He saves out of it a multitude which no man can number, out of every nation, and of all tribes and peoples and tongues. How much must, then, God love the world! This interpretation, beyond question, reproduces the fundamental meaning of the text. But does it completely satisfy all its suggestions? Does there not lie in the text some more subtle sequence of thought than is explicated by it? Is there not implied in it some profounder and yet more glorious truth than even the world-wide reach of God's love, manifested in the Great Commission, and issuing in the multitude of the saved, the voice of whose praise ascends to heaven as the voice of many waters and as the voice of mighty thunders?

Neither of the more common interpretations of the text, therefore, appears to bring out quite fully its real significance. The one fails to rise to the height of the conception of the love of God embodied in it; the other appears to do something less than full justice to the conception of the world which God is said by it to love. The difficulty in both cases seems to arise from a certain unwillingness to go deeply enough: a surface meaning, possible to impose upon the text, seems to be seized upon, while its profundities are left unexplored. If we would make our own the great revelation of the love of God here given us, we must be more patient. Renouncing the easy imposition upon it of meanings of our own devising, we must just permit the text to speak its own language to our hearts. Its prime intention is to convey some conception of the immeasurable greatness of the love of God. The method it employs to do this is to declare the love of God for the world so great that

He gave His Son to save it. The central affirmation obviously, then, is this,—and it is a sufficiently great one to absorb our entire attention—that God loved the world. "God," "loved," "the world"—we must deal seriously with this great assertion, and with every element of it. We must first of all, then, thoroughly enter into the meaning of the three great terms here brought together: "God," "loved," "the world."

We shall not make the slightest step forward in understanding our text, for instance, so long as we permit ourselves to treat the great term "God" merely as the subject of a sentence. We must endeavour rather to rise as nearly as may be to its fullest significance. When we pronounce the word we must see to it that our minds are flooded with some wondering sense of God's infinitude, of His majesty, of His ineffable exaltation; of His holiness, of His righteousness, of His flaming purity and stainless perfection. This is the Lord God Almighty whom the heaven of heavens cannot contain, to whom the earth is less than the small dust on the balance. He has no need of aught, nor can His unsullied blessedness be in any way affected— whether by way of increase or decrease—by any act of the creatures of His hands. What we call infinite space is but a speck on the horizon of His contemplation: what we call infinite time is in His sight but as yesterday when it is past. Serene in His unapproachable glory, His will is the resistless law of all existences to which their every motion conforms. Apparelled in majesty and girded with strength, righteousness and judgment are the foundations of His throne. He sits in the heavens and does whatsoever He pleases. It is this God, a God of whom to say that He is the Lord of all the earth is to say so little that it is to say nothing at all, of whom our text speaks. And if we are ever to catch its meaning we must bear this fully in mind.

Now the text tells us of this God—of *this* God, remember,— that He loves. In itself, before we proceed a step further, this is a marvellous declaration. The metaphysicians have not yet plumbed it and still protest inability to construe the Absolute in terms of love. We shall not stop to dwell upon this somewhat abstract discussion. Enough for us that a God without emotional life would be a God without all that lends its highest dignity to personal spirit whose very being is movement; and that is as much as to say no God at all. And more than enough for us that our text assures us that God loves, nay, that He is Love. What it concerns us now to note, however, is not the mere fact that He loves, but what it is that He is declared to love. For therein lies the climax of the great proclamation. This is nothing other than "the world." For this is the unimaginable declaration of the text: "God so loved the world." It is just in this that lies the mystery of the greatness of His love.

For what is this "world" which we are so strangely told that God loves? We must not throw the reins on the neck of our fancy and seek a response that will suit our ideas of the right or the fitting. We must just let the Scriptures themselves tell us, and primarily that Apostle to whom we owe this great declaration. Nor does he fail to tell us; and that without the slightest ambiguity. The "world," he tells us, is just the synonym of all that is evil and noisome and disgusting. There is nothing in it that can attract God's love,—nay, that can justify the love of any good man. It is a thing not to be dallied with, or acquiesced in: they that are of it, are by that very fact not of God; and what the Christian has to do with it is just to overcome it; for everything that is begotten of God manifests that great fact precisely by this—that he overcomes the world. "Love not the world, neither the things that are in the world," is John's insistent exhortation. And the reason for it he states very pungently: because "if any man love the world, the love of the Father is not in him." God and the world, then, are precise contradictions. "Nothing that is in the world is of the Father," we are told; or, as it is put elsewhere in direct positive form: "The whole world lieth in the evil one." "The world, the flesh and the devil"—this is the pregnant combination in which we have learned from Scripture to express the baleful forces that war against the soul: and the three terms are thus cast together because they are essentially synonyms. See, then, whither we are brought. When we are told that God loves the world, it is much as if we were told that He loves the flesh and the devil. And we may, indeed, take courage from our text and say it boldly: God does love the world and the flesh and the devil. Therein indeed is the ground of all our comfort and all our hope: for we—you and I—are of the world and of the flesh and of the devil. Only,—we must punctually note it,—the love wherewith God loves the world, the flesh and the devil—therefore, us—is not a love of complacency, as if He the Holy One and the Good could take pleasure in what is worldly, fleshly, devilish: but that love of benevolence which would fain save us from our worldliness, fleshliness and devilishness.

That indeed is precisely what the text goes on at once to say: "For God so loved the world, that He gave His only begotten Son, that whosoever believeth on Him should not perish, but have eternal life." The world then was perishing: and it was to save it that God gave His Son. The text is, then, you see, in principle an account of the coming of the Son of God into the world. There were but two things for which He, being what He was as the Son of God, could come into the world, being what it was: to judge the world or to save the world. It was for the latter that He came. "For," the next verse runs on, "God sent not His Son into the world to judge the world, but that the world through Him should be saved." Not wrath, then, though wrath were due, but love was the impelling cause of the coming of the Son of God into this wicked world of ours. "For God so loved the world, that He gave His only begotten Son." The intensity of the love is what is emphasized: it was so intense that it was not deterred even by the sinfulness of its objects. You will perceive that what we have here then is, in effect, but the Johannean way of saying what Paul says when he tells us that "God commendeth His own love towards us, in that while we were yet sinners, Christ died for us." The marvel, in other words, which the text brings before us is just that marvel above all other marvels in this marvellous world of ours—the marvel of God's love for sinners. And this is the measure by which we are invited to measure the greatness of the love of God. It is not that it is so great that it is able to extend over the whole of a big world: it is so great that it is able to prevail over the Holy God's hatred and abhorrence of sin. For herein is love, that *God* could love the *world*—the world that lies in the evil one: that God who is all-holy and just and good, could so love this world that He gave His only begotten Son for it,—that He might not judge it, but that it might be saved.

The key to the passage lies, therefore, you see, in the significance of the term "world." It is not here a term of extension so much as a term of intensity. Its primary connotation is ethical, and the point of its employment is not to suggest that the world is so big that it takes a great deal of love to embrace it all, but that the world is so bad that it takes a great kind of love to love it at all, and much more to love it as God has loved it when He gave His son for it. The whole debate as to whether the love here celebrated distributes itself to each and every man that enters into the composition of the world, or terminates on the elect alone chosen out of the world, lies thus outside the immediate scope of the passage and does not supply any key to its interpretation. The passage was not intended to teach, and certainly does not teach, that God loves all men alike and visits each and every one alike with the same manifestations of His love: and as little was it intended to teach or does it teach that His love is confined to a few especially chosen individuals selected out of the world. What it is intended to do is to arouse in our hearts a wondering sense of the marvel and the mystery of the love of God for the sinful world—conceived, here, not quantitatively but qualitatively as, in its very distinguishing characteristic, sinful. And search the universe through and through—in all its recesses and through all its historical development—and you will find no marvel so great, no mystery so unfathomable, as this, that the great and good God, whose perfect righteousness flames in indignation at the sight of every iniquity and whose absolute holiness recoils in abhorrence in the presence of every impurity, yet loves this sinful world,—yes, has so loved it that He has given His only begotten Son to die for it. It is this marvel and this mystery that our text would fain carry home to our hearts, and we would be wise if we would permit them to be absorbed in its contemplation.

At the same time, however, although we cannot permit the passage to be interpreted in the terms of the debate in question, it would not be quite true to say it has no bearing upon that debate.

One thing, for instance, which the passage tells us, and tells us with great emphasis, is that the love which it celebrates is a saving love; not a love which merely tends towards salvation, and may—perhaps easily—be defeated in its aim by, say, the unwillingness of its objects. The very point of the passage lies, on the one side, in the mightiness of the love of God; and on the other in the unwillingness not of some but of all its objects. The love here celebrated is, we must remember, the love of *God*—of the Lord God Almighty: and it is love to the *world*— which altogether "lies in the evil one." It is a love which is great, and powerful, and all-conquering; which attains its end, and will not stand helpless before any obstacle. It is the precise purpose of the passage to teach us this, to raise our hearts to some apprehension of the inconceivable greatness of the love of God, set as it is upon saving the wicked world. It would be possible to believe that such a love as this terminates equally and with the same intent upon each and every man who is in "the world," only if we may at the same time believe that it works out its end completely and with full effect on each and every man. But this the passage explicitly forbids us to believe, proceeding at once to divide the "world" into two classes, those that perish and those that have eternal life. The almighty, all-conquering love of God, therefore, certainly does not pour itself equally and with the same intent upon each and every man in the world. In the sovereignty that belongs of necessity to His love as to all love, He rather visits with it whom He will.

But neither will the text allow us to suppose that God grants this His immeasurable love only to a few, abstracted from the world, while the world itself He permits to fall away to its destruction. The declaration is, not that God has loved some out of the world, but that He has loved the world. And we must rise to the height of this divine universalism. It is the world that God has loved with His deathless love, this sinful world of ours: and it is the world, this sinful world of ours, that He has given His Son to die for: and it is the world that through the sacrifice of His dear Son, He has saved, this very sinful world of ours. "God sent not His Son into the world," we read, "to judge the world, but that the world should be saved by Him": that is to say, God did not send His Son into the world for the purpose of judging the world, but for the purpose of saving the world: a declaration which could not be true if, despite His coming, the world were lost and only a select few saved out of it. The purposes of God do not fail.

You must not fancy, then, that God sits helplessly by while the world, which He has created for Himself, hurtles hopelessly to destruction, and He is able only to snatch with difficulty here and there a brand from the universal burning. The world does not govern Him in a single one of His acts: He governs it and leads it steadily onward to the end which, from the beginning, or ever a beam of it had been laid, He had determined for it. As it was created for His glory, so shall it show forth His praise: and this human race on which He has impressed His image shall reflect that image in the beauty of the holiness which is its supreme trait. The elect—they are not the residuum of the great conflagration, the ashes, so to speak, of the burnt-up world, gathered sadly together by the Creator, after the catastrophe is over, that He may make a new and perhaps better beginning with them and build from them, perchance, a new structure, to replace that which has been lost. Nay, they are themselves "the world"; not the world as it is in its sin, lying in the evil one; but the world in its promise and potency of renewed life. Through all the years one increasing purpose runs, one *increasing* purpose: the kingdoms of the earth become ever more and more the kingdom of our God and His Christ. The process may be slow; the progress may appear to our impatient eyes to lag. But it is God who is building: and under His hands the structure rises as steadily as it does slowly, and in due time the capstone shall be set into its place, and to our astonished eyes shall be revealed nothing less than a saved world.

Meanwhile, we who live in the midst of the process see not yet the end. These are days of incompleteness, and it is only by faith that we can perceive the issue. The kingdom of God is as yet only in the making; and the "world" is not yet saved. So, there appear about us two classes: there are those that perish as well as those that have eternal life. With the absoluteness which characterizes the writer of this Gospel, these two classes are set before us in the text and in the paragraph of which it forms a part, in their intrinsic antagonism. They are believers and unbelievers in the Son of God: and they are believers and unbelievers in the Son of God, because they are in their essential natures good or bad, lovers of light or lovers of darkness. "For every one that doeth evil hateth the light and cometh not to the light; but he that doeth the truth cometh to the light." Throughout the whole process of the world's development, therefore, the Light that has come into the world draws to Itself those that are of the light: He, that is, who through love of the world came into the world to save the world,—yea, and who shall save the world—in the meantime attaches to Himself in every generation those who in their essential nature belong to Him. How they come to be His, and therefore to be attracted to Him, and therefore to enter into the life that is life indeed— to become portions no longer of the world that lies in the evil one, but of the reconstructed world that abides in Him—the paragraph in which our text is set leaves us much uninformed. Accordingly some rash expositors wish to insist that to it the division of men into the essentially good and the essentially bad is an ultimate fact. They speak therefore much of the ineradicable dualism of Jesus' conception, not staying to consider the confusion thus wrought in the whole paragraph. For in that case how could there be talk of the Son of God coming into the world to *save* the world? Obviously, to the text, those that belong to the Son themselves require saving; that is to say, no less than the lost themselves, they belong by nature to the "evil one," in whom the whole world—not a part of it only—we are told explicitly "lieth."

And if we will but attend to the context in which our paragraph is set, we will perceive that we are not left without guidance to its proper understanding. For we must remember that this paragraph is not an isolated document standing off to itself and complete in itself, but is a comment upon the discourse of our Lord to Nicodemus. It necessarily receives its colour and explanation, therefore, from that discourse of which it is either a substantive part or upon which it is at least a reflection. And what does that discourse teach us except this: that all that is born of flesh is flesh, and only what is reborn of Spirit is Spirit; that no man can enter the Kingdom of God, therefore, except he be born again of God; and that this birth is not at the command of men, but is the gift of a Spirit which is like the wind that bloweth where it listeth, the sound whereof we hear though we know not whence it cometh and whither it goeth—but can say of it only, Lo, it is here! Here then is the explanation of the essential difference in men revealed in the varying reception they give to the Son of God. It is not due to accident of birth or to diversity of experience in the world, least of all to inherent qualities of goodness or badness belonging to each by nature. It is due solely to this,—whether or not they have been born again by the Spirit and so are of the light and come spontaneously to the light when it dawns upon their waiting eyes. The sequence in this great process of salvation, then, according to our passage, when taken in its context, is this: the gift of the Son of God to save the world; the preparation of the hearts of men to receive the Son of God in vital faith: the attraction of these "children of the light" to the Light of the world; and the gradual rebuilding of the fabric of the world along the lines of God's choosing into that kingdom of light which is thus progressively prepared for its perfect revelation at the last day.

Thus, thus, then, it is that God is saving the world—the world, mind you, and not merely some individuals out of the world: by a process which involves not supplanting but reformation, recreation. We look for new heavens and a new earth, it is true; but these new heavens and new earth are not another heaven and another earth, but the old heaven and old earth renewed; or as the Scriptures phrase it "regenerated." For not the individual merely but the world-fabric itself is to be regenerated in that "regeneration when the Son of Man is to sit on the throne of His glory." During the process there may be much that is discarded: but when the process is completed, then also shall be completed the task which the Son of Man has taken upon Himself, and the "world" shall be saved—this wicked world of sinful men transformed into a world of righteousness.

Surely, we shall not wish to measure the saving work of God by what has been already accomplished in these unripe days in which our lot is cast. The sands of time have not yet run out. And before us stretch, not merely the reaches of the ages, but the infinitely resourceful reaches of the promise of God. Are not the saints to inherit the earth? Is not the recreated earth theirs? Are not the kingdoms of the world to become the Kingdom of God? Is not the knowledge of the glory of God to cover the earth as the waters cover the sea? Shall not the day dawn when no man need say to his neighbour, "Know the Lord," for all shall know Him from the least unto the greatest? O raise your eyes, raise your eyes, I beseech you, to the far horizon: let them rest nowhere short of the extreme limit of the divine purpose of grace. And tell me what you see there. Is it not the supreme, the glorious, issue of that love of God which loved, not one here and there only in the world, but the world in its organic completeness; and gave His Son, not to judge the world, but that the world through Him should be saved? And He said unto me, "Come hither, I will shew thee the bride, the wife of the Lamb. And he . . . shewed me the holy city Jerusalem, coming down out of heaven from God, having the glory of God. . . . And the city hath no need of the sun, neither of the moon, to shine upon it: for the glory of God did lighten it, and the Lamb, the lamp thereof. And the nations shall walk amidst the light thereof; and the kings of the earth do bring their glory into it. And the gates thereof shall in no wise be shut by day (for there shall be no night there): and they shall bring the glory and the honour of the nations into it: and there shall in no wise enter into it anything unclean, or he that maketh an abomination and a lie; but only they which are written in the Lamb's book of life." Only those written in the Lamb's book of life, and yet all the nations! It is the vision of the saved world. "For God so loved the world, that He gave His only begotten Son, that whosoever believeth on Him should not perish, but have eternal life." It is the vision of the consummated purpose of the immeasurable love of God.

II

THE PRODIGAL SON[1]

LUKE XV. 11-32:— And he said, A certain man had two sons: and the younger of them said to his father, Father, give me the portion of thy substance that falleth to me. And he divided unto them his living. And not many days after the younger son gathered all together, and took his journey into a far country; and there he wasted his substance with riotous living. And when he had spent all, there arose a mighty famine in that country; and he began to be in want. And he went and joined himself to one of the citizens of that country; and he sent him into his fields to feed swine. And he would fain have been filled with the husks that the swine did eat: and no man gave unto him. But when he came to himself he said, How many hired servants of my father's have bread enough and to spare, and I perish here with hunger! I will arise and go to my father, and will say unto him, Father, I have sinned against heaven, and in thy sight: I am no more worthy to be called thy son: make me as one of thy hired servants. And he arose, and came to his father. But while he was yet afar off, his father saw him, and was moved with compassion, and ran, and fell on his neck, and kissed him. And the son said unto him, Father, I have sinned against heaven, and in thy sight: I am no more worthy to be called thy son. But the father said to his servants, Bring forth quickly the best robe, and put it on him; and put a ring on his hand, and shoes on his feet: and bring the fatted calf, and kill it, and let us eat, and make merry: for this my son was dead, and is alive again; he was lost, and is found. And they began to be merry. Now his elder son was in the field: and as he came and drew nigh to the house, he heard music and dancing. And he called to him one of the servants, and inquired what these things might be. And he said unto him, Thy brother is come; and thy father hath killed the fatted calf, because he hath received him safe and sound. But he was angry, and would not go in: and his father came out, and intreated him. But he answered and said to his father, Lo, these many years do I

[1] From the volume of sermons entitled *The Saviour of the World*, pp. 3-33.

serve thee, and I never transgressed a commandment of thine: and yet thou never gavest me a kid, that I might make merry with my friends: but when this thy son came, which hath devoured thy living with harlots, thou killedst for him the fatted calf. And he said unto him, Son, thou art ever with me, and all that is mine is thine. But it was meet to make merry and be glad: for this thy brother was dead, and is alive again; and was lost, and is found.

I WISH to speak to you today of the parable of the prodigal son, or, as it is becoming very common to call it, perhaps with greater exactness, the parable of the lost son. Probably no passage of the Scriptures is more widely known or more universally admired. The conversation and literature of devotion are full of allusions to it. And in the conversation and literature of the world it has far from an unhonoured place.

It owes the high appreciation it has won, no doubt, in large part to the exquisiteness of its literary form. From this point of view it fully deserves not only the measured praise of a Grotius, but the enthusiastic exclamations of a Trench. It is "the finest of Christ's parables, filled with true feeling, and painted in the most beautiful colours." It is "the pearl and crown of all the parables of Scripture." Nothing could exceed the chaste perfection of the narrative, the picturesque truth of its portraiture, the psychological delicacy of its analysis. Here is a gem of story-telling, which must be pronounced nothing less than artistically perfect, whether viewed in its general impression, or in the elaboration of its details. We must add to its literary beauty, however, the preciousness of the lesson it conveys before we account for the place it has won for itself in the hearts of men. In this setting of fretted gold, a marvel of the artificer, there lies a priceless jewel; and this jewel is displayed to such advantage by its setting that men cannot choose but see and admire.

Indeed, we may even say that the universal admiration the parable commands has finished by becoming in some quarters a little excessive. The message which the parable brings us is certainly a great one. To lost sinners like you and me, assuredly few messages could appeal with more overwhelming force. Our hearts are wrung within us as we are made to realize that our Father in heaven will receive our wandering souls back with the joy with which this father in the parable received back his errant son. But it is an exaggeration to represent this message as all the Gospel, or even as the core of the Gospel; and to speak of this parable therefore, as it has become widely common to speak of it, as "the Gospel in the Gospel," or even as the summation of the Gospel. It is not that. There are many truths which it has no power to teach us that are essential to the integrity of the Gospel: nay, the very heart of the Gospel is not in it. And, therefore, precious as this parable is to us, and priceless as is its message, there are many other passages of Scripture more precious still, because their message enters more deeply into the substance of the Gospel. Take this passage for example: "For God so loved the world, that He gave His only begotten Son, that whosoever believeth on Him should not perish, but have everlasting life." Or this passage: "God, being rich in mercy, for His great love wherewith He loved us, even when we were dead through our trespasses, quickened us together with Christ (by grace have ye been saved), and raised us up with Him and made us sit with Him in the heavenly places with Christ Jesus." Or even this short passage: "For the Son of Man came to seek and to save that which was lost." All these are more precious passages than the parable of the lost son, not merely because they tell us more fully what is contained in the Gospel, but because they uncover to us, as it does not, what lies at the heart of the Gospel.

It is important that we should recognize this. For the exaggerated estimate which has been put upon this parable has borne bitter fruit in the world. Beginning with an effort to read into it all the Gospel, or at least the essence of the Gospel, it has ended by reading out of the Gospel all that is not in the parable. And thus this parable, the vehicle of a priceless message, has been transformed into the instrument of a great wrong. The worst things are often the corruption of the best: and the attempt to make the parable of the lost son the norm of the Gospel has resulted, I will not say merely in the curtailment

of the Gospel,—I will say rather in the evisceration of the
Gospel. On this platform there take their stand today a growing multitude the entire tendency and effect of all of whose
efforts it is to eliminate from Christianity all that gives it value
in the world, all that makes it that religion whch has saved the
world, and to reduce it to the level of a merely natural religion.
"The Christianity of the prodigal son is enough for us," they
declare: and they declare this with gusto because, to put it
briefly, they do not like the Christianity of the Bible or the
Christianity of Christ, and are happy not to find them in the
parable of the lost son.

Now, let us recognize frankly at the outset, that the reason
why these new teachers of an unchristian Christianity do not
find Christianity in the parable of the lost son is, briefly, because
this parable does not set forth Christianity, but only a small
fragment of Christian teaching. The turn they have given to
affairs is therefore merely the nemesis that treads on the heels
of the mistaken attempts to read a full Christianity into this
parable. The parable was not given to teach us Christianity, in
its essence or its sum. lt was given to teach us one single truth:
a truth of the utmost value, not only full of emotional power,
but, when placed in its relation to other truths, of the highest
doctrinal significance; but not in itself sufficient to constitute
Christianity, or even to embody its essence. How little what this
parable teaches us can be conceived as of itself Christianity may
easily be made plain by simply enumerating some of the fundamental elements of Christianity which receive no expression in
it: and this negative task seems to be made incumbent on us at
the outset of any study of the parable by the circumstance of its
perversion to the uses of the propaganda of unbelief.

We observe, then, in the first place, that there is no atonement in this parable. And indeed it is precisely because there is
no atonement in this parable that it has been seized upon by the
modern tendency to which we have alluded, as the norm of the
only Christianity it will profess. For nothing is more characteristic of this new type of Christianity than that it knows and will

know nothing of an atonement. The old Socinians were quick to perceive this feature of the parable, and to make use of it in their assault upon the doctrine of Christ's satisfaction for sin. See, they cried, the father in the parable asks no satisfaction before he will receive back his son: he rather sees him afar off and runs to meet him and gives him a free and royal welcome. The response is no doubt just that other Scriptures clearly teach the atonement of which no hint is given here; and that we have no "right to expect that every passage in Scripture, and least of all these parables, which exist under necessary limitations in their power of setting forth the truth, shall contain the whole circle of Christian doctrine." This answer is sufficient against the Socinian who appealed to Scripture as a whole and required to be reminded that we "must consider not what one Scripture says, but what all." But it scarcely avails against our modern enthusiast who either professedly or practically would fain make this parable the embodiment of all the Christianity he will profess. For him, Christianity must do without an atonement, because it is quite obvious that there is no atonement in this parable.

Nor is that more than the beginning of the matter. It must do without a Christ as well. For, we must observe, the parable has as little of Christ in it as it has of an atonement. The Socinians neglected to take note of this. In their zeal to point out that there is no trace in the parable of a satisfaction offered to the Father by which alone He might be enabled to receive back the sinner, they failed to note that neither is there trace in it of any mission of a Son at all—even merely to plead with the wanderer, make known the Father's continued love to him, and win him back to his right relation to the Father. That much of a mission of Christ they themselves confessed. But it is as absent from the parable as is the expiating Christ of the Evangelicals. In truth, there is in the parable no trace whatsoever of a Christ, in any form of mission. From all that appears from the narrative, the errant son was left absolutely alone in his sin, until, wholly of his own motion, he conceived the idea of returning to the

Father. If its teaching is to be the one exclusive source of our Christianity we must content ourselves therefore with a Christianity without Christ.

Nor is even this by any means all. For, as has no doubt been noted already, there is as little trace of the saving work of the Holy Spirit in the parable as of that of Christ. The old Pelagians were as quick to see this as were the Socinians later to observe the absence of any hint of a sacrificial atonement. See, they said, the prodigal moves wholly of his own power: there is no efficient grace here, no effectual calling, no regeneration of the Spirit. And there is not. If this parable is to constitute our Christianity, then our Christianity must do without these things.

And doing without these things, it must do without a Holy Spirit altogether. For there is not the slightest hint of a Holy Spirit in any conceivable activity he may be thought to employ in the whole parable. Reduce the mode and effect of His operation to the most attenuated possible. Allow Him merely to plead with men from without the penetralium of their personality, to exercise influences upon them only of the nature of persuasion, such as men can exercise upon one another—still there is no hint of such influences here. From all that appears, the prodigal *suo motu* turned to the Father and owed to no one so much as a suggestion, much less assistance, in his resolve or its execution. If our Christianity is to be derived from this parable only, we shall have to get along without any Holy Spirit.

And even this is only the beginning. We shall have to get along also without any God the Father. What! you say,—the whole parable concerns the father! But what a father is this? It is certainly not the Father of the Christian revelation and not the Father of the Christian heart. He permits his son to depart from him without apparent emotion; and so far as appears he endures the absence of his son without a pang,—making not the slightest endeavor to establish or maintain communication with him or to recover him either to good or to himself. If he manifests joy at the happy return of the son after so many days, there is not the least evidence that in all the intervening time he had expended upon him so much as a single message, much less brought to bear upon him the smallest inducement to return. In other words, what we know as the "seeking love of God" is absolutely absent from the dealing of the father with the son as here depicted: that is, the love of God which most nearly concerns you and me as sinners is conspicuous only by its absence. In this respect the parable stands in its suggestions below the companion parables of the lost sheep and the lost coin. When the shepherd lost his sheep, he left the ninety and nine in the wilderness and went after the lost one until he found it. When the woman lost her coin, she lit a candle and swept the house and sought diligently until she found it. But in the parable of the lost son, the father is not pictured as doing anything of the sort. The son leaves him and the son returns to him; and meanwhile the father, so far as appears, goes about his own affairs and leaves the son to go about his. So clear is it that this parable was not intended to embody the whole Gospel and does not contain even its essence. For what is the essence of the Gospel if it is not the seeking love of God?

The commentators, of course, have not left it so. Determined to get the Gospel out of the parable, they diligently go to work first to put it in. Thus one, in depicting the father's state of mind, grows eloquent in his description of his yearning love. "He has not forgotten his son, though he has forgotten him. He has been thinking of him during the long period of his absence. Probably he often cast glances along the road to see if perchance the erring one was returning, thinking he saw him in every stranger who made his appearance. He has continued looking, longing, till hope deferred has made the heart sick and weary to despair." Now no doubt the father felt all this. Only the parable does not tell us so. And it would not have omitted to tell us so, if this state of mind on the father's part entered into the essence of its teaching. The fact is that this commentator is rewriting the parable. He is not expounding the parable we have, but composing another parable, a different parable with different lessons. Our Lord, with His exquisitely nice adjustment of every detail of this parable to His purpose, we may be sure, has omitted nothing needed for the most poignant conveyance of the meaning He intended it to convey. That the expositor feels it necessary to insert all this merely proves that he is bent on making the parable teach something foreign to it as it stands. What he has especially in mind to make it teach proves, as we read on, to be the autonomy of the human will. The lost thing, in the case of this parable, is a man: and because he is a man, and no lifeless thing nor an unthinking beast, we are told, he cannot, like the coin and the sheep, be sought. He must be left alone, to return, if return he ever does, wholly of his own motion and accord. Therefore, forsooth, the father's solicitude can only take the form of a waiting! *Seeking* love can be expended on a coin or a sheep, but not, it seems, on a man. In the case of a man, *waiting* love is all that is in place, or is possible. Is this the Gospel? Is this the Gospel even of these three parables? When we were told of the shepherd seeking his sheep, of the woman searching for her coin, was it of sheep and coins that the Master would have His hearers think? Does God care for oxen, or was it not altogether for our sakes that these parables too were spoken?

Into such self-contradictions, to say nothing of oppositions to the very *cor cordis* of the Gospel, do we fall when we refuse to be led by the text and begin to twist it like a nose of wax to the teaching of our own lessons. The fact is, the parable teaches us none of these things and we must not bend or break it in a vain effort to make it teach them. Even when another commentator more modestly tells us that the two earlier parables—those of the lost sheep and the lost coin—set forth mainly the seeking love of God; while the third—that of the lost son—"describes rather the rise and growth, responsive to that love, of repentance in the heart of man"; he has gone far beyond his warrant. Why say this parable teaches the rise and growth of repentance "responsive to the seeking love of God"? There is no seeking love of God in the parable's picture of the relation of the father to the lost son, as indeed had just been allowed, in the assignment of the teaching as to that to the preceding parables. But why say even that it describes "the rise and growth of repentance"? It does of course describe the path which one repentant sinner's feet trod as he returned to his father: and so far as the case of one may be the case of all, we may therefore be said to have here, so far as the narrative goes, a typical instance. But there is no evidence that this description was intended as normative, and certainly no ground for finding in this the purpose of the parable. That purpose the text itself places elsewhere; and our wisdom certainly lies in refusing to turn the parable into allegory, reading into it all sorts of lessons which we fancy we may see lurking in its language here and there. We are safest in strictly confining ourselves to reading out of it the lesson it was designed to teach. This lesson was certainly not "the growth and course of sin" and "the growth and course of repentance"; but simply that "there is joy in heaven over one sinner that repenteth." The exquisite surety of our Lord's touch as He paints the career of the unhappy man whose fortunes He employs to point His moral may tempt us to look upon the vivid picture He draws as the normative instance of sin and repentance: and surely there is no reason why we should not recognize that the picture thus brought before us corresponds with remarkable closeness to the great drama of human sin and repentance. But one must be on his guard against being led astray here. After all, the descriptions and analyses in the parable are determined directly by the requirements of the story, not by those of the history of the sinful soul over against its God; and we must beware of treating the parable as if its details belonged less to the picture than to something else which it seems to us adapted to illustrate. The only safe course is strictly to confine ourselves to the lesson the parable was framed to teach.

This is not to say, however, that this lesson is so single and simple that we can derive no teaching from the parable beyond what is compressible into a single proposition. It undoubtedly has its main lesson; but it could not well teach that lesson without teaching along with it certain subsidiary ones, closely connected with it as corollaries and supports, or at least implicated in the manner in which it is taught. Only, we must be very wary that we do not either on the one hand confuse these subsidiary things with the main lesson of the parable, or on the other read into it lessons of our own, fancifully derived from its mere forms of expression. We may perhaps illustrate what we mean and at the same time gather the teaching we may legitimately derive from the parable by asking ourselves now seriously what we do really learn from it.

And here, beginning at the extreme circumference of what we may really affirm we learn from this parable, I think we may say that we may derive from it, in the first place,—in its context, in the way it is introduced and in its relation to the fellow-parables coupled with it—one of those subtle evidences of the deity of our Lord which are strewn through the Synoptic Gospels. Although it leads us away from our main course, it behoves us to pause and take note of this, in view of the tendency lingering in some quarters to deny to the Synoptic Gospels a doctrine of the deity of Christ, and especially to the Jesus of the Synoptics any real divine consciousness. It would seem impossible for the unprejudiced reader to glance over these parables in their setting without feeling that both the evangelist and the Master as reported by him speak here out of an underlying consciousness of His divine claims and estate. For, note the occasion out of which these parables arose and the immediate end to which they are directed. The publicans and sinners were flocking to the gracious preaching of Jesus, and Jesus was so far from repelling them, that He welcomed them to Him and mixed in intimate intercourse with them. This the Pharisees and Scribes made the subject of unpleasant remark among themselves. And our Lord spoke these parables in defence of Himself against their attack. But now note how He defends Himself. By parables of a good shepherd seeking his lost sheep; of a distressed woman seeking her lost coin; of a deserted father receiving back his wayward child. We surely do not need to argue that the good shepherd, the distressed woman, the deserted father stands in each instance for God. Jesus Himself tells us this in His application: "I say unto you" (and we must not miss here the slight but majestic intimation of the dignity of His person) "that there shall be joy in heaven";

"Likewise, I say unto you there is joy before the angels of God."
Yet these parables are spoken to vindicate not God's, but Jesus'
reception of sinners. The underlying assumption that Jesus'
action and God's action are one and the same thing is unmistakable: and no reader fails tacitly to recognize Jesus Himself
under the good shepherd and the distressed woman and the deserted father. In Him and His action men may see how things
are looked upon in heaven. The lost, when they come to Him,
are received because this is heaven's way; and since this is
heaven's way, how could *He* do otherwise? This is not a mere
appeal, as some have supposed, to the sympathy of heaven: as
if He would say to the objector, "I have not your sympathy in
this, but heaven is on my side!" Nor is it a mere appeal to a
future vindication: as if He would say, "Now you condemn, but
you will see it differently after a while." It is a defence of His
conduct by reference of it to its true category. These publicans
and sinners—why, they are His lost ones: and does not in every
sphere of life he who loses what he values welcome its recovery
with joy? Throughout the whole discussion there throbs thus
the open implication that He bears the same relation to these
sinners that the shepherd does to the sheep lost from the flock,
the woman does to a coin lost from her store, the father does
to a wandering child. And what is this but an equally open
implication that He is in some mysterious way that Divine Being
against whom all sin is committed, away from whose smile all
sinners have turned, and back to whom they come when, re-
penting of their sin, they are recovered to good and to God?

In these parables, then, we see Jesus teaching with authority.
And His divine voice is heard in them also rebuking sin. For the
next thing, perhaps, which it behoves us to take notice of is the
rebuke that sounds in them of the sin of spiritual pride and
jealousy. This rebuke of course culminates in the portrait of the
elder son and his unsympathetic attitude towards the rejoicing
over his brother's return home, which occupies the latter part of
the parable of the lost son. This episode has given the expositors
much trouble; but this has been occasioned solely by their failure to apprehend aright the purpose of the parable. It is in truth

an integral part of the parable, without which the parable would be incomplete.

In the former two parables—those of the lost sheep and the lost coin—Jesus was directly justifying Himself for "receiving sinners and eating with them." His justification is, shortly, that it is precisely the lost who require His attention: He came to seek and to save the *lost*. But these parables run up into a higher declaration: the declaration that there is joy in heaven over one sinner that repents rather than over ninety and nine just persons who need no repentance. This high note then becomes the dominant note of the discourse: and it is to illustrate it and to give it vividness and force on the consciousness of His hearers that the third parable—that of the lost son—is spoken. This third parable has not precisely the same direct apologetic purpose, therefore, which dominates the other two. It becomes more didactic and as such more of a mirror to reflect the entire situation and to carry home to the questioners the whole involved truth. Its incidents are drawn from a higher plane of experience and the action becomes more complex, by which a more varied play of emotion is allowed and a more complicated series of lessons is suggested. It is, therefore, not content, like the former parables, merely to illustrate the bare fact that joy accompanies the finding of the lost, with the implication that as sinners are what is lost to God, it is their recovery which causes Him joy. It undertakes to take up this fact, already established by the preceding parables, and to fix it in the heart as well as in the mind by summoning to its support the deepest emotions of the human soul, relieving at the same time the free play of these emotions from all interference from the side of a scrupulous sense of justice.

It is this latter function which the episode of the elder brother subserves; and it appears therefore not as an excrescence upon the parable, but as an essential element in it. Its object is to hold up the mirror of fact to the Pharisaic objectors that they may see their conduct and attitude of mind in their true light. Their moving principle was not, as they fancied, a zeal for righteousness which would not have sin condoned, but just a mean-spirited jealousy which was incapable of the natural response of the human spirit in the presence of a great blessing. They are like some crusty elder brother, says our Lord, who, when the long-lost wanderer comes contritely home, is filled with bitter jealousy of the joyful reception he receives rather than with the generous delight that moves all human hearts at the recovery of the lost.

The effect, you see, is to place the Pharisaic objectors themselves in the category of sinners, side by side with the outcasts they had despised; to probe their hard hearts until they recognized their lost estate also; and so to bring them as themselves prodigals back in repentance to the Father's house. That they came back the parable does not say. It leaves them in the midst of bitter controversy with the Father because He is good. And here emerges a wonderful thing. That "seeking love" which is not signalized in the parable with reference to the lost—the confessedly lost—son, is brought before us in all its beautiful appeal with reference to these yet unrepentant elder brothers. For, you will observe, the father does not wait for the elder brother to come into the house to him; he goes out to him. He speaks soothing words to him in response to his outpouring of bitterness and disrespect. When, in outrageous words, this son celebrates his own righteousness and accuses the father of hardness and neglect, refusing indeed in his wrath to recognize his relationship either with him or his: the father responds with mild entreaties, addressing him tenderly as "child," proffering unbroken intercourse with him, endowing him with all his possessions,—in a word, pleading with him as only a loving father can. Did the elder son hearken to these soft reproofs and yield to this endearing appeal? It was for the Pharisees to answer that question. Our Lord leaves it there. And the effect of the whole is to show them that, contrary to their assumption, the Father in heaven has no righteous children on earth; that His grace is needed for all, and most of all for those who dream they have no need of it. By thus skilfully dissecting, under the cover of the sour elder brother, the state of mind of the Pharisaic objectors, our Lord breaks down the artificial distinction by which they had separated themselves from their sinful brethren, and in doing so breaks down also the barriers which held their sympathies back and opens the way to full appreciation by them of the joy He would have them feel in the recovery of the lost. Was there one among them with heart yet open to the appeal of the seeking God, surely he smote his breast as he heard these poignant closing words of the parable and cried, no longer in the voice of a Pharisee, but in the voice of the publican, "God be merciful to me a sinner!" Surely, like one of their own number only a few years later, the scales fell from his eyes and he confessed himself not only a sinner, but even the chief of sinners.

It would not be quite exact perhaps to say that the parable rebukes spiritual pride and jealousy as well as proclaims the joy in heaven over the recovery of the lost. Its lesson is one; and its one lesson is only thrown into a clearer light by the revelation of the dreadfulness of its contrast in jealousy of the good fortune of the saved. When all are in equal need of salvation, where is there room for censorious complaint of the goodness of God? This levelling effect of the parable raises the question whether there is not contained in it some hint of the universalism of the Gospel. Surely through and through its structure sounds the note of, "For there is no difference!" No difference between the publicans and sinners on the one side, and the Pharisees and the Scribes on the other. The Pharisees themselves being judges, this were equivalent to no difference between Jew and Gentile. Were not the publicans to them as heathen men? And was not "sinners" just the name by which they designated the Gentiles? If their scrupulous attention to the law did not raise them above all commerce or comparison with sinners, what profit was there in being a Jew? We certainly do not purpose to say with some that Jesus was teaching a universal religion without knowing it: and we certainly do not discover here the germ of a universal religion in this—that Jesus meant to teach that nothing lies between the sinner and his recovery to God but an act of the sinner's own will, an act to which every sinner is ever competent, at all times and in all circumstances. And yet it seems not improper to perceive in the leveling effect of the implied inclusion of the Pharisees themselves in the one great class of sinners a hint of that universalism which Jesus gave His Gospel when He proclaimed Himself the Saviour of all who believe on Him.

But, however this may be, we approach nearer to the great lesson of the parable when we note that there is certainly imbedded in its teaching that great and inexpressibly moving truth that there is no depth of degradation, return from which will not be welcomed by God. A sinner may be too vile for any and every thing else; but he cannot be too vile for salvation. We observe at any rate that our Lord does not hold His hand when He comes to paint the degradation of sinners, through His picture of the degradation into which the lost son had sunk. No depths are left beneath the depths which He here portrays for us. This man had dealt with his inheritance with the utmost recklessness. He had wasted the whole of it until he was left stripped bare of all that he had brought from his father's house. Nor was there anything to take its place. The country in which he had elected to dwell was smitten, throughout its whole extent, with a biting famine. In all its length and breadth there was nothing on which a man might live. The prodigal was reduced to "bend and pray and fawn" at the feet of a certain citizen of that dread land; and was sent by him out into the barren fields—to feed swine! To a Jew, degradation could not be more poignantly depicted. Yes, it could: there was one stage worse and that stage was reached. The lost son not only herded the swine; he herded with them. "He was fain to fill his belly from the husks that the swine did eat." Not with the same quality of food, observe, but from the swine's own store—for "no man gave unto him." In this terrible description of extreme degradation there may be a side glance at the actual state of the publicans, our Lord's reception of and association with whom was such an offence to the Jewish consciousness. For did not they not merely serve against their own people those swines of Gentiles, but actually feed themselves at their trough? But however this may be, it is clear that our Lord means to paint degradation in its depths. He does not spare the sinners with whom He consorted. His defence for receiving them does not turn upon any failure to recognize or feel their true quality; any representation of them as not so bad after all; as if they had been painted blacker than they were, and were nice enough people to associate with if only we were not so fastidious. He says rather that they are bad past expression and past belief. His defence is that they can be saved; and that He is here to save them. Lost? Yes, they are lost; and there is no reason why we should not take the word at the top—or rather at the bottom—of its meaning: this is the parable of the *lost* son. But Jesus is the Saviour of the lost; and there is none so lost that he may not be found by Him, and, being found by Him, be also found in Him. Oh, no! Jesus does not rejoice in sinners: it is not sin He loves nor sinners as sinners. What He rejoices in is the rescue of sinners from their sin. And the deeper the sin the greater the rescue and the greater the joy. "I say unto you, there is joy before the angels of God over one sinner that repenteth." "I say unto you, there shall be joy in heaven over one sinner that repenteth, rather than over ninety and nine just persons, such as have no need of repentance."

It is in this great declaration that the real purport of the parable is expressed. This parable was spoken to teach us, to put it briefly, that God in heaven rejoices over the repentance of every sinner that repents. It is a commentary therefore on those great passages which tell us that God would have no man perish, but all to come to Him and live; and it is more than a commentary on these passages, inasmuch as it throws the emphasis upon the positive side and tells us of the joy that God feels at the repentance of every sinner who repents. To the carrying of this great message home to our hearts all the art of the parable is directed, and it is our wisdom to read it simply to this end. We need not puzzle ourselves over the significance, then, of this detail or that, as if we were bound or indeed permitted to discover, allegorically, some spiritual meaning in each turn of the story. The most of these find their account in the demands of the story itself and enter into its lesson only as con-

.ributory details, adding vividness and truth to the illustration.

Thus, for instance, if we ask why there are only two sons in the parable, while there were ten pieces of silver in the preceding one, and a hundred sheep in the first one; the answer is that just two sons were needed to serve Jesus' purpose of illustrating the contrast between the Pharisees and Scribes on the one side and the publicans and sinners on the other; His purpose not being at all to indicate proportion of numbers, but difference in status and conduct. In the former parables the suggestion of comparative insignificance was requisite to bring out the full lesson; in this, the contrast of character serves His purpose. If again it is asked why it is the younger son who becomes a prodigal, the answer is that the propriety of the story demands it. It would be inconceivable that the older son, who according to custom was the co-possessor and heir of the fundamental estate, should have asked or received an inheritance apart from it. But the thing was not unnatural, and doubtless not unusual, in a younger son, who was to be portioned off in any event in the end, and was only asking that he might not wait on his father's death, but might be permitted to "set up for himself" at once. We cannot therefore with confidence discover the beginnings of the prodigal's downfall in his request that his inheritance might be told off to him, or wonder overmuch why the father so readily granted this request. It is tempting, no doubt, to see in the wish of the son to "set up for himself" a hint of a heart already little at one with the law and custom of the father's house. But such allegorizing is dangerous, especially when not suggested by any hint in the language of the narrative or necessarily contained in the situation depicted. It is customary to speak of the younger son as a young man. It may be so. But the narrative does not say so. He may have been in middle life; and it may well have seemed to all concerned that a desire on his part to begin to build up his own house was altogether right and fitting. The separation of his goods from his father's at all events appears in the parable only as the precedent condition of his spending them, not as the beginning of his downfall.

We need not go further, however, into detail. Enough that

the story has a single point. And that point is the joy of the father at the return of the son, a joy which is the expression, not of the natural love of the father for a son, but of the overwhelming emotion of mingled relief and thankfulness and overmastering rapture which fills the heart of a father on the recovery of a lost son. The point of the narrative is not, then, that this prodigal is a son, though that underlies and gives its verisimilitude to the picture. The point is that this son is a prodigal. It is because he has been lost and is now found that the joy of the father is so great. The elder son is a son too; and the father loves him also. Let him who doubts it read again the exquisite narrative of the father's tender and patient dealings with him. There is not in all literature a more beautiful picture of parental affection pleading with unfilial passion. This father knew perfectly how to fulfil the injunction later laid down by the apostle Paul: "And ye fathers, provoke not your children to wrath; but nurture them in the chastening and admonition of the Lord." From this point of view that soothing admonition, "Child, *thou*" (the emphasis on the "thou" must not be neglected) "art always with me; and all that is mine is thine; but it was meet to make merry and be glad, because this thy brother was dead and is alive, and was lost and is found"—is simply perfect. So clear is it that the lesson of the parable does not turn on the prodigal's being a son, but on this son being a prodigal.

In other words, its lesson is not that God loves His children, but that God loves sinners. And thus this parable is seen ranging with the preceding ones. The lost sheep, the lost coin, the lost son, have only this one thing in common, that they are lost; and the three parables unite in commending the one common lesson to us, that as men rejoice in the recovery of what is lost, so God rejoices in the recovery of sinners—since sinners are the things that to Him are lost. We must not, then, use this parable to prove that God is a father, or draw inferences from it as if that were its fundamental teaching. It does not teach that. What it teaches is that God will receive the returning sinner with the same joy that the father in the parable received the returning prodigal; because as this son was to that father's heart above all other things that he had lost, his lost one, and his return was therefore above all other things that might have been returned to him his recovery; so sinners are above all else that God has lost in the world His lost ones, and their return to Him above all other restorations that may be made to Him His recovery. The vivid picture of the father not staying to receive the returning son, but, moved with compassion as he spied him yet a great way off, running out to meet him and falling on his neck and kissing him in his ecstasy again and again; cutting short his words of confession with the command that the best robe be brought to clothe him, and shoes for his blistered feet, and a ring for his finger, and the order that the fatted calf be killed and the feast be spread, and the music and the dance be prepared—because, as he says, "This my son was dead and is alive, was lost and is found"—all this in the picture is meant to quicken our hearts to some apprehension of the joy that fills God's heart at the return of sinners to Him.

O brethren, our minds are dulled with much repetition, and refuse to take the impression our Lord would make on them. But even we—can we fail to be moved with wonder today at this great message, that God in heaven rejoices—exults in joy like this human father receiving back his son—when sinners repent and turn to Him? On less assurance than that of Jesus Christ Himself the thing were perhaps incredible. But on that assurance shall we not take its comfort to our hearts? We are sinners. And our only hope is in one who loves sinners; and has come into the world to die for sinners. Marvel, marvel beyond our conception; but, blessed be God, as true as marvellous. And when we know Him better, perhaps it may more and more cease to be a marvel. At least, one of those who have known Him best and served Him most richly in our generation, has taught us to sing thus of His wondrous death for us:

> That He should leave His place on high,
> And come for sinful man to die,
> You count it strange?—so do not I,
>   Since I have known my Saviour.

> Nay, had there been in all this wide
> Wide world no other soul beside
> But only mine, then He had died
>   That He might be its Saviour;
>
> Then had He left His Father's throne,
> The joy untold, the love unknown,
> And for that soul had given His own,
>   That He might be its Saviour!

Is that too high a flight for us—that passion of appropriation by which the love of Jesus for me—my own personal soul—is appreciated so fully that it seems natural to us that He, moved by that great love that was in Him for me—even me—should leave His throne that He might die for me,—just me,—even were there none else beside? At least we may assent to the dispassionate recognition that in the depths of our parable is hidden the revelation of that fundamental characteristic of Jesus Christ by virtue of which He did become the Saviour at least of sinners. And seeing this and knowing ourselves to be sinners, we may acknowledge Him afresh today as our Saviour, and at least gratefully join in our passionate sinner's prayer:

> And oh! that He fulfilled may see
> The travail of His soul in me,
> And with His work contented be,
>   As I am with my Saviour!
>
> Yea, living, dying, let me bring
> My strength, my solace from this spring,
> That He who lives to be my King,
>   Once died to be my Saviour!

III

THE LEADING OF THE SPIRIT[1]

"For as many as are led by the Spirit of God, these are sons of God."—Rom. viii. 14. (R. V.)

THESE words constitute the classical passage in the New Testament on the great subject of the "leading of the Holy Spirit." They stand, indeed, almost without strict parallel in the New Testament. We read, no doubt, in that great discourse of our Lord's which John has preserved for us, in which, as He was about to leave His disciples, He comforts their hearts with the promise of the Spirit, that "when He, the Spirit of truth, is come, He shall guide you into all the truth." But this "guidance into truth" by the Holy Spirit is something very different from the "leading of the Spirit" spoken of in our present text; and it is appropriately expressed by a different term. We read also in Luke's account of our Lord's temptation that He was "led by the Spirit in the wilderness during forty days, being tempted of the devil," where our own term is used. But though undoubtedly this passage throws light upon the mode of the Spirit's operation described in our text, it can scarcely be looked upon as a parallel passage to it. The only other passage, indeed, which speaks distinctly of the "leading of the Spirit" in the sense of our text is Gal. v. 18, where in a context very closely similar Paul again employs the same phrase: "But if ye are led by the Spirit, ye are not under the law." It is from these two passages primarily that we must obtain our conception of what the Scriptures mean by "the leading of the Holy Spirit."

There is certainly abundant reason why we should seek to learn what the Scriptures mean by "spiritual leading." There

[1] From volume of sermons entitled *The Power of God Unto Salvation*, pp. 151-179.

are few subjects so intimately related to the Christian life, of which Christians appear to have formed, in general, conceptions so inadequate, where they are not even positively erroneous. The sober-minded seem often to look upon it as a mystery into which it would be well not to inquire too closely. And we can scarcely expect those who are not gifted with sobriety to guide us in such a manner into the pure truth of God. The consequence is that the very phrase, "the leading of the Spirit," has come to bear, to many, a flavor of fanaticism. Many of the best Christians would shrink with something like distaste from affirming themselves to be "led by the Spirit of God"; and would receive with suspicion such an averment on the part of others, as indicatory of an unbalanced religious mind. It is one of the saddest effects of extravagance in spiritual claims that, in reaction from them, the simple-minded people of God are often deterred from entering into their privileges. It is surely enough, however, to recall us to a careful searching of Scripture in order to learn what it is to be "lead by the Spirit of God," simply to read the solemn words of our text: "As many as are led by the Spirit of God, these are sons of God." If the case be so, surely it behooves all who would fain believe themselves to be God's children to know what the leading of the Spirit is.

Let us, then, commit ourselves to the teaching of Paul, and seek to learn from him what is the meaning of this high privilege. And may the Spirit of truth here too be with us and guide us into the truth.

Approaching the text in this serious mood, the first thing that strikes us is that the leading of the Spirit of God of which it speaks is not something peculiar to eminent saints, but something common to all God's children, the universal possession of the people of God.

"As many as are led by the Spirit of God," says the apostle, "these are sons of God." We have here in effect a definition of the sons of God. The primary purpose of the sentence is not, indeed, to give this definition. But the statement is so framed as to equate its two members, and even to throw a stress upon the co-extensiveness of the two designations. "As many as are led by the Spirit of God, these and these only are sons of God." Thus, the leading of the Spirit is presented as the very characteristic of the children of God. This is what differentiates them from all others. All who are led by the Spirit of God are thereby constituted the sons of God; and none can claim the high title of sons of God who are not led by the Spirit of God. The leading of the Spirit thus appears as the constitutive fact of sonship. And we dare not deny that we are led by God's Spirit lest we therewith repudiate our part in the hopes of a Christian life. In this aspect of it our text is the exact parallel of the immediately preceding declaration, which it thus takes up and repeats: "But if any one hath not the Spirit of Christ, that one is not His."

It is obviously a mistake, therefore, to look upon the claim to be led by God's Spirit as an evidence of spiritual pride. It is rather a mark of spiritual humility. This leading of the Spirit is not some peculiar gift reserved for special sanctity and granted as the reward of high merit alone. It is the common gift poured out on all God's children to meet their common need, and is the evidence, therefore, of their common weakness and their common unworthiness. It is not the reward of special spiritual attainment; it is the condition af all spiritual attainment. In its absence we should remain hopelessly the children of the devil; by its presence alone are we constituted the children of God. It is only because of the Spirit of God shed abroad in our hearts that we are able to cry, Abba, Father.

We observe, therefore, next that the end in view in the spiritual leading of which Paul speaks is not to enable us to escape the difficulties, dangers, trials or sufferings of this life, but specifically to enable us to conquer sin.

Had the former been its object, it might indeed have been a special grace granted to a select few of God's children, and its possession might have separated them from among their brethren as the peculiar favorites of the Deity. Since, however, the latter is its object, it is the appropriate gift of all those who are sinners, and is the condition of their conquest over the least of their sins. In the preceding context Paul discovers to us our inherent sin in all its festering rottenness. But he discovers to us also the Spirit of God as dwelling in us and forming the principle of a new life. It is by the presence of the Spirit within us alone that the bondage in which we are by nature held to sin is broken; that we are emancipated from sin and are no longer debtors to live according to the flesh. This new principle of life reveals itself in our consciousness as a power claiming regulative influence over our actions; leading us, in a word, into holiness.

If we consider our life of new obedience from the point of view of our own activities, we may speak of ourselves as fighting the good fight of faith; a deeper view reveals it as the work of God in us by His Spirit. When we consider this Divine work within our souls with reference to the end of the whole process we call it sanctification; when we consider it with reference to the process itself, as we struggle on day by day in the somewhat devious and always thorny pathway of life, we call it spiritual leading. Thus the "leading of the Holy Spirit" is revealed to us as simply a synonym for sanctification when looked at from the point of view of the pathway itself, through which we are led by the Spirit as we more and more advance toward that conformity to the image of His Son, which God has placed before us as our great goal.

It is obvious at once then how grossly it is misconceived when it is looked upon as a peculiar guidance granted by God to His eminent servants in order to insure their worldly safety, worldly comfort, even worldly profit. The leading of the Holy Spirit is always for good; but it is not for all goods, but specifically for spiritual and eternal good. I do not say that the good man may not, by virtue of his very goodness, be saved from many of the sufferings of this life and from many of the failures of this life. How many of the evils and trials of life are rooted in specific sins we can never know. How often even failure in business may be traced directly to lack of business integrity rather than to pressure of circumstances or business incompetency is mercifully hidden from us. Nor do I say that the gracious Lord has no care for the secular life of His people. But it surely is obvious that the leading of the Spirit spoken of in the text is not in order to guide men into secular goods; and it is not to be inferred to be absent when trials come—sufferings, losses, despair of this world. It is specifically in order to guide them into eternal good; to make them not prosperous, not free from care or suffering, but holy, free from sin. It is not given us to save us from the consequences of our business carelessnesses or incompetences, to take the place of ordinary prudence in the conduct of our affairs. It is not given us to preserve us from the necessity of strenuous preparation for the tasks before us or from the trouble of rendering decision in the difficult crises of life. It is given specifically to save us from sinning; to lead us in the paths of holiness and truth.

Accordingly, we observe next that the spiritual leading of which Paul speaks is not something sporadic, given only on occasion of some special need of supernatural direction, but something continuous, affecting all the operations of a Christian man's activities throughout every moment of his life.

It has but one end in view, the saving from sin, the leading into holiness; but it affects every single activity of every kind—physical, intellectual, and spiritual—bending it toward that end. Were it directed toward other ends, we might indeed expect it to be more sporadic. Were it simply the omniscience of God placed at the disposal of His favorites, which they might avail themselves of in times of perplexity and doubt, it might well be occasional and temporary. But since it is nothing other than the power of God unto salvation, it must needs abide with the sinner, work constantly upon him, enter into all his acts, condition all his doings, and lead him thus steadily onward toward the one great goal.

It is easy to estimate, then, what a perversion it is of the "leading of the Spirit" when this great saving energy of God, working continually in the sinner, is forgotten, and the name is accorded to some fancied sporadic supernatural direction in the common offices of life. Let us not forget, indeed, the reality of providential guidance, or imagine that God's greatness makes Him careless of the least concerns of His children. But let us much more not forget that the great evil under which we are suffering is sin, and that the great promise which has been given us is that we shall not be left to wander, self-directed, in the paths of sin into which our feet have strayed, but that the Spirit of holiness shall dwell within us, breaking our bondage and leading us into that other pathway of good works, which God has afore prepared that we should walk in them.

All of this will be powerfully supported and the subject perhaps somewhat further elucidated if we will seek now to penetrate a little deeper into the inmost nature of the work of the Holy Spirit which Paul calls here a "leading," by attending more closely to the term which he has chosen to designate it when he calls it by this name. This term, as those skilled in such things tell us, is one which throws emphasis on three matters: on the extraneousness of the influence under which the movement suggested takes place; on the completeness of the control which this influence exerts over the action of the subject led; and on the pathway over which the resultant progress is made. Let us glance at each of these matters in turn.

One is not led when he goes his own way. It is only when an influence distinct from ourselves determines our movements that we can properly be said to be led. When Paul, therefore, declares that the sons of God are "led by the Spirit of God," he emphasizes, first of all, the distinction between the leading Spirit and the led sons of God. As much as this he declares with great emphasis—that there is a power within us, not ourselves, that makes for righteousness. And he identifies this extraneous power with the Spirit of God. The whole preceding context accentuates this distinction, inasmuch as its entire drift is to paint the conflict which is going on within us between our native impulses which make for sin, and the intruded power which makes for righteousness. Before all else, then, spiritual leading consists in an influence over our actions of a power which is not to be identified with ourselves—either as by nature or as renewed—but which is declared by the apostle Paul to be none other than the Spirit of God Himself.

We thoroughly misconceive it, therefore, if we think of spiritual leading as only a conquest of our lower impulses by our higher nature, or even as a conquest by our regenerated nature of the remnants of the old man lingering in our members. Both of these conquests are realities of the Christian life. The child of God will never be content to be the slave of his lower impulses, but will ever strive, and with ultimate success, to live on the plane of his higher endowments. The regenerated soul will never abide the remnants of sin that vex his members, but will have no rest until he eradicates them to the last shred. But these victories of our nobler selves—natural or gracious— over what is unworthy within us, do not so much constitute the essence of spiritual leading as they are to be counted among its fruits. Spiritual leading itself is not a leading of ourselves by ourselves, but a leading of us by the Holy Ghost. The declaration of its reality is the declaration of the reality of the indwelling of the Holy Spirit in the heart, and of the subjection of the activities of the Christian heart and life to the control of this extraneous power. He that is led by the Spirit of God is not led by himself or by any element of his own nature, native or acquired, but is led by the Holy Ghost. He has ceased to be what the Scriptures call a "natural man," and has become what they call a "spiritual man"; that is, to translate these terms accurately, he has ceased to be a self-led man and has become a Spirit-led man—a man led and determined in all his activities by the Holy Ghost. It is this extraneousness of the source of these activities which Paul emphasizes first of all when he declares that the sons of God are led by the Spirit of God.

The second matter which is emphasized by his declaration is the controlling power of the influence exerted on the activities of God's children by the Holy Spirit. One is not led, in the sense of our text, when he is merely directed in the way he should go, guided, as we may say, by one who points out the path and leads only by going before in it; or when he is merely upheld while he himself finds or directs himself to the goal.

The Greek language possesses words which precisely express these ideas, but the apostle passes over these and selects a term which expresses determining control over our actions. Some of these other terms are used elsewhere in the Scriptures to set forth appropriate actions of the Spirit with reference to the people of God. For example, our Lord promised His disciples that when the Spirit of Truth should come, He should guide them into all the truth. Here a term is employed which does not express controlling leading, but what we may perhaps call suggestive leading. It is used frequently in the Greek Old Testament of God's guidance of His people, and once, at least, of the Holy Spirit: "Teach us to do Thy will, for Thou art my God; let Thy good Spirit guide us in the land of uprightness." But the term which Paul employs in our text is a much stronger one than this. It is not the proper word to use of a guide who goes before and shows the way, or even of a commanding general, say, who leads an army. It has stamped upon it rather the conception of the exertion of a power of control over the actions of its subject, which the strength of the led one is insufficient to withstand.

This is the proper word to use, for example, when speaking of leading animals, as when our Lord sent His disciples to find the ass and her colt and commanded them "to loose them and lead them to Him" (Matt. xxi. 2); or as when Isaiah declares in the Scripture which was being read by the Eunuch of Ethiopia whom Philip was sent to meet in the desert, "He was led as a sheep to the slaughter." It is applied to the conveying of sick folk—as men who are not in a condition to control their own movements; as, for example, when the good Samaritan set the wounded traveler on his own beast and led him to an inn and took care of him (Luke x. 34); or when Christ commanded the blind man of Jericho "to be led unto Him" (Luke xviii. 40). It is most commonly used of the enforced movements of prisoners; as when we are told that they led Jesus to Caiaphas to the palace (John xviii. 28); or when we are told that they seized Stephen and led him into the council (Acts vi. 12); or that Paul was provided with letters to Damascus unto the synagogues, "that if he found any that were of the Way, he might lead them bound to Jerusalem" (Acts ix. 2). In a word, though the term may, of course, sometimes be used when the idea of force retires somewhat into the background, and is commonly so used when it is transferred from external compulsion to internal influence—as, for example, when we are told that Barnabas took Paul and led him to the apostles (Acts ix. 2), and that Andrew led Simon unto Jesus (John i. 42)—yet the proper meaning of the word includes the idea of control, and the implication of prevailing determination of action never wholly leaves it.

Its use by Paul on the present occasion must be held, therefore, to emphasize the controlling influence which the Holy Spirit exercises over the activities of the children of God in His leading of them. That extraneous power which has come into our hearts making for righteousness, has not come into them merely to suggest to us what we should do—merely to point out to us from within the way in which we ought to walk—merely to rouse within us and keep before our minds certain considerations and inducements toward righteousness. It has come within us to take the helm and to direct the motion of our frail barks on the troubled sea of life. It has taken hold of us as a man seizes the halter of an ox to lead it in the way which he would have it go; as an attendant conducts the sick in leading him to the physician; as the jailer grasps the prisoner to lead him to trial or to the jail. We were slaves to sin; a new power has entered into us to break that bondage—but not that we should be set, rudderless, adrift on the ocean of life; but that we should be powerfully directed on a better course, leading to a better harbor.

Accordingly Paul, when he declares that we have been emancipated from the law of sin and of death by the advent of the law of the Spirit of life in Christ Jesus into our hearts, does not leave it so, as if emancipation were all. He adds, "Accordingly then, we are bound." Though emancipated, still

bound! We are bound; but no longer to the flesh, to live after
the flesh, but to the Spirit, to live after the Spirit. He hastens,
indeed, to point out that this is no hard bondage, but a happy
one; that sons is a name better fitted to express its circumstances
than "slaves"—that it includes childship and heirship to God
and with Christ. But all this blessed assurance operates to
exhibit the happy estate of the service into which we have been
brought, rather than to alter the nature of it as service. The
essence of the new relation is that it also is one of control,
though a control by a beneficent and not a cruel power. We do
not at all catch Paul's meaning therefore, unless we perceive
the strong emphasis which lies on this fact—that those who are
led by the Spirit of God are under the control of the Spirit of
God. The extraneous power which has come into us, making
for righteousness, comes as a controlling power. The children
of God are not the directors of their own activities; there is One
that dwells in them who is not merely their guide, but their
governor and strong regulator. They go, not where they would,
but where He would; they do not what they might wish, but
what He determines. This it is to be led by the Spirit of God.

It is to be observed, however, on the other hand, that
although Paul uses a term here which emphasizes the controlling influence of the Spirit of God over the activities of God's
children, he does not represent the action of the Spirit as a
substitute for their activities. If one is not led, in the sense of
our text, when he is merely guided, it is equally true that one
is not led when he is carried. The animal that is led by the
attendant, the blind man that is led to Christ, the prisoner that
is led to jail—each is indeed under the control of his leader,
who alone determines the goal and the pathway; but each also
proceeds on that pathway and to that goal by virtue of his own
powers of locomotion.

There was a word lying at the apostle's hand by which he
could have expressed the idea that God's children are borne by
the Spirit's power to their appointed goal of holiness, apart
from any activities of their own, had He elected to do so. It is

employed by Peter when he would inform us how God gave His message of old to His prophets. "For no prophecy," he tells us, "ever came by the will of man: but men spake from God, being borne by the Holy Ghost." This term, "borne," emphasizes, as its fundamental thought, the fact that all the power productive of the motion suggested is inherent in, and belongs entirely to, the mover. Had Paul intended to say that God's children are taken up as it were in the Spirit's arms and borne, without effort on their own part, to their destined goal, he would have used this word. That he has passed over it and made use of the word "led" instead, indicates that, in his teaching, the Holy Spirit leads and does not carry God's children to their destined goal of holiness; that while the Spirit determines both the end and the way toward it, His will controlling their action, yet it is by their effort that they advance to the determined end.

Here, therefore, there emerges an interesting indication of the difference between the Spirit's action in dealing with the prophet of God in imparting through him God's message to men, and the action of the same Spirit in dealing with the children of God in bringing them into their proper holiness of life. The prophet is "borne" of the Spirit; the child of God is "led." The prophet's attitude in receiving a revelation from God is passive, purely receptive; he has no part in it, adds nothing to it, is only the organ through which the Spirit delivers it to men; he is taken up by the Spirit, as it were, and borne along by Him by virtue of the power that resides in the Spirit, which is natural to Him, and which, in its exercise, supersedes the natural activities of the man. Such is the import of the term used by Peter to express it. On the other hand, the son of God is not purely passive in the hands of the sanctifying Spirit; he is not borne, but led—that is, his own efforts enter into the progress made under the controlling direction of the Spirit; he supplies, in fact, the force exerted in attaining the progress, while yet the controlling Spirit supplies the entire directing impulse. Such is the import of the term used by Paul to express it. Therefore no prophet could be exhorted to work out his own message with fear and trembling; it is not left to him to work it out—the Holy

Spirit works it out for him and communicates it in all its rich completeness to and through him. But the children of God are exhorted to work out their own salvation in fear and trembling because they know the Spirit is working in them both the willing and the doing according to His own good pleasure.

In order to appreciate this element of the apostle's teaching at its full value it is perhaps worth while to observe still further that in his choice of a term to express the nature of the Spirit's action in leading God's children the apostle avoids all terms which would attribute to the Spirit the power employed in making progress along the chosen road. Not only does he not represent us as being carried by the Spirit; he does not even declare that we are drawn by Him. There was a term in common use which the apostle could have used had he intended to express the idea that the Spirit drags, by physical force as it were, the children of God onward in the direction in which He would have them go. This term is actually used when the Saviour declares that no man can come unto Him except the Father draw him (John vi. 44)—which is as much as to say that men in the first instance do not and cannot come to Christ by virtue of any powers native to themselves, but require the action upon them of a power from without, coming to them, drawing their inert, passive weight to Christ, if they are to be brought to Him at all. We can identify this act of drawing—"dragging" would perhaps express the sense of the Greek term none too strongly— with that act which we call, in our theological analysis, regeneration, and which we explain in accordance with the import of this term, as the monergistic act of God, impinging on a sinner who is and remains, as far as this act is concerned, purely passive, and therefore does not move, but is moved.

Such, however, is not the method of the Spirit's leading of which Paul speaks in our text. This is not a drawing or dragging of a passive weight toward a goal which is attained, if attained at all, only by virtue of the power residing in the moving Spirit; but a leading of an active agent to an end determined indeed by the Spirit, and along a course which is marked out by the Spirit, but over which the soul is carried by virtue of its own power of action and through its own strenuous efforts. If we are not borne by the Spirit out of our sin into holiness with a smooth and easy movement, almost unnoted by us or noted only with the languid pleasure with which a child resting peacefully on its mother's breast may note its progress up some rough mountain road, so neither are we dragged by the Spirit as a passive weight over the steep and rugged path. We are led. We are under His control and walk in the path in which He sets our feet. It is His part to keep us in the path and to bring us at length to the goal. But it is we who tread every step of the way; our limbs that grow weary with the labor; our hearts that faint, our courage that fails—our faith that revives our sinking strength, our hope that instills new courage into our souls—as we toil on over the steep ascent.

And thus it is most natural that the third matter to which Paul's declaration that we are led by the Spirit of God directs our attention concerns the pathway over which our progress is made.

One is not led who is unconscious of the road over which he advances; such a one is rather carried. He who is led treads the road himself, is aware of its roughness and its steepness, pants with the effort which he expends, is appalled by the prospect of the difficulties that open out before him, rejoices in the progress made, and is filled with exultant hope as each danger and obstacle is safely surmounted. He who is led is in the hands of an extraneous power, of a power which controls his actions; but the pathway over which he is thus led is trodden by his own efforts—by his own struggles it may be—and the goal that is attained is attained at the cost of his own labor.

When Paul chooses this particular term, therefore, and declares that the sons of God are led by the Spirit, he is in no way forgetful of the arduous nature of the road over which they are to advance, or of the strenuous exertion on their own part by which alone they may accomplish it. He strengthens and comforts them with the assurance that they are not to tread the path alone; but he does not lull them into inertness by suggesting that they are not to tread it. The term he employs avouches to them the constant and continuous presence with them of the leading Spirit, not merely setting them in the right path, but keeping them in it and leading them through it; for it designates not an impulse which merely initiates a movement in a given direction, but a continuous influence unbrokenly determining a movement to its very goal. But his language does not promise them relief from the weariness of the journey, alleviation of the roughness of the road, freedom from difficulty or danger in its course, or emancipation from the labor of travel. That they have been placed in the right path, that they will be kept continuously in it, that they will attain the goal—of this he assures them; for this it is to be led of the Spirit of God, a power not ourselves controlling our actions, prevalently directing our movement to an end of His choice. But He does not encourage us to relax our own endeavors; for he who is led, even though it be by the Spirit of God, advances by virtue of his own powers and his own efforts. In a word, Paul chooses language to express the action of the Spirit on the sons of God which is in perfect harmony with his exhortation to the children of God to which we have already alluded—to work out their own salvation with fear and trembling because they know it is God that is working in them both the willing and the doing according to His own good pleasure.

What a strong consolation for us is found in this gracious assurance—poor, weak children of men as we are! To our frightened ears the text may come at first as with the solemnity of a warning: "As many as are led by the Spirit of God, these and these only are sons of God." Is there not a declaration here that we are not God's children unless we are led by God's Spirit? Knowing ourselves, and contemplating the course of our lives and the character of our ambitions, dare we claim to be led by the Spirit of God? Is this life—this life that I am living in the flesh—is this the product of the Spirit's leading? Shall not despair close in upon me as I pass the dreadful judgment on myself that I am not led by God's Spirit, and that I am, therefore, not one of His sons? Let us hasten to remind ourselves, then, that such is not the purport nor the purpose of the text. It stands here not in order to drive us to despair, because we see we have sin within us; but to kindle within us a great fire of hope and confidence because we perceive we have the Holy Spirit within us.

Paul, as we have seen, does not forget the sin within us. Who has painted it and its baleful power with more vigorous touch? But neither would he have us forget that we have the Holy Spirit within us, and what that blessed fact, above all blessed facts, means. He would not have us reason that because sin is in us we cannot be God's children; but in happy contradiction to this, that because the Holy Spirit is in us we cannot but be God's children. Sin is great and powerful; it is too great and too powerful for us; but the Holy Ghost is greater and more powerful than even sin. The discovery of sin in us might bring us to despair did not Paul discern the Holy Spirit in us—who is greater than sin—that he may quicken our hope.

This declaration that frightens us is not written, then, to frighten, but to console and to enhearten. It stands here for the express purpose of comforting those who would despair at the sight of their sin. Is there a conflict of sin and holiness in you? asks Paul. This very fact that there is conflict in you is the charter of your salvation. Where the Holy Spirit is not, there conflict is not; sin rules undisputed lord over the life. That there is conflict in you, that you do not rest in complacency in your sin, is a proof that the Spirit of God is within you, leading you to holiness. And all who are led by the Spirit of God are the children of God; and if children, then heirs, heirs of God and joint heirs with Christ Jesus. This is the purport of the message of the text to us. Paul points us not to the victory of good over evil, but to the conflict of good with evil—not to the end but to the process—as the proof of childship to God. The note of the passage is, thus, not one of fear and despair, but one of hope and triumph. "If God be for us who can be against us?"—that is the query the apostle would have ring in our hearts. Sin has a dreadful grasp upon us; we have no power to withstand it. But there enters our hearts a power not ourselves making for righteousness. This power is the Spirit of the most high God. "If God be for us who can be against us?" Let our hearts repeat this cry of victory today.

And as we repeat it, let us go onward, in hope and triumph, in our holy efforts. Let our slack knees be strengthened and new vigor enter our every nerve. The victory is assured. The Holy Spirit within us cannot fail us. The way may be rough; the path may climb the dizzy ascent with a rapidity too great for our faltering feet; dangers, pitfalls are on every side. But the Holy Spirit is leading us. Surely, in that assurance, despite dangers and weakness, and panting chest and swimming head, we can find strength to go ever forward.

In these days, when the gloom of doubt if not even the blackness of despair, has settled down on so many souls, there is surely profit and strength in the certainty that there is a portal of such glory before us, and in the assurance that our feet shall press its threshold at the last. In this assurance we shall no longer beat our disheartened way through life in dumb despondency, and find expression for our passionate but hope-less longings only in the wail of the dreary poet of pessimism:—

"But if from boundless spaces no answering voice shall start,
Except the barren echo of our ever yearning heart—
Farewell, then, empty deserts, where beat our aimless wings,
Farewell, then, dream sublime of uncompassable things."

We are not, indeed, relieved from the necessity for healthful effort, but we can no longer speak of "vain hopes." The way may be hard, but we can no longer talk of "the unfruitful road which bruises our naked feet." Strenuous endeavor may be required of us, but we can no longer feel that we are "beating aimless wings," and can expect no further response from the infinite expanse than "a sterile echo of our own eternal longings." No, no—the language of despair falls at once from off our souls. Henceforth our accents will be borrowed rather from a nobler "poet of faith," and the blessing of Asher will seem to be spoken to us also:—

"Thy shoes shall be iron and brass,
And as thy days, so shall thy strength be.
There is none like unto God, O Jeshurun,
Who rideth upon the heavens for thy help,
And in His excellency on the skies.
The eternal God is thy dwelling-place,
And underneath are the everlasting arms."

IV

FALSE RELIGIONS AND THE TRUE[1]

"What therefore ye worship in ignorance, this set I forth unto you."—Acts xvii. 23. (R. V.)

THESE words give the gist of Paul's justly famous address at Athens before the court of the Areopagus. The substance of that address was, to be sure, just what the substance of all his primary proclamations to Gentile hearers was, namely, God and the judgment. The necessities of the case compelled him to approach the heathen along the avenue of an awakened conscience. They had not been prepared for the preaching of Jesus by a training under the old covenant, and no appeals to prophecy and its fulfillment could be made to them. God and the judgment necessarily constituted, therefore, the staple of his proclamation to them; and so typical an instance as this address to the Areopagus could not fail to exhibit the characteristics of its class with especial purity.

Nevertheless, the peculiar circumstances in which it was delivered have imprinted on this address also a particular character of its own. Paul spoke it under a specially poignant sense of the depths of heathen ignorance and of the greatness of heathen need. The whole address palpitates with his profound feeling of the darkness in which the heathen world is immersed, and his eager longing to communicate to it the light intrusted to his care. All that goes before the words selected for the text and all that comes after serve but to enhance their great declaration—build for it, as it were, but a lofty platform upon which it is raised to fix the gaze of men. Out of it all Paul fairly shouts this one essential message to the whole unbeliev-

[1] From the volume of sermons entitled *The Power of God Unto Salvation*, pp. 219-254.

ing world: "What therefore ye worship in ignorance, this set I forth unto you."

Let us consider for a little while the circumstances in which the address was delivered. Summoned by a supernatural vision, Paul had crossed the sea and brought the gospel into Europe. Landing in Macedonia, he had preached in its chief cities, meeting on the one hand with great acceptance, and arousing on the other the intensest opposition. He had been driven from city to city until the brethren had at last fled with him to the sea and, hurrying him upon a ship, had conveyed him far to the south and, at last, landed him at Athens. There they left him—alone but in safety—and returned to Macedonia to send his companions to him.

Meanwhile Paul awaited their coming at Athens. Athens! mother of wisdom, mistress of art; but famous, perhaps, above all its wisdom and above all its art for the intensity of its devotion to the gods. Paul had had a missionary's experience with idolatry, in its grosser and more refined forms alike; he had been forced into contact with it throughout his Asian work. Even so, Athens seems to have been a revelation to him—a revelation which brought him nothing less than a shock. Here he was literally in the thick of it. No other nation was so given over to idolatry as the Athenians. One writer tells us that it was easier to find a god in populous Athens than a man; another, scarcely exaggerating, declares that the whole city was one great altar, one great sacrifice, one great votive offering. The place seemed to Paul studded with idols, and the sight of it all brought him a paroxysm of grief and concern.

He was in Athens, as it were, in hiding. But he could not keep silence. He went to the synagogue on the Sabbath and there preached to the Jews and those devout inquirers who were accustomed to visit the synagogues of the Jews in every city. But this did not satisfy his aroused zeal. He went also to the market place—that agora which the public teachers of the city had been wont to frequent for the propagation of their views—and there, like them, every day, he argued with all

whom he chanced to meet. Among these he very naturally en-
countered certain adherents of the types of philosophy then
dominant—the Epicurean and Stoic—and in conflict with them
he began to attract attention.

He was preaching, as was his wont, "Jesus" and the "resurrection"—doubtless much as he preached them in his recorded
address, to which all this led up. Some turned with light contempt away from him and called him a mere smatterer; others,
with perhaps no less contempt, nevertheless took him more
seriously and anxiously asked if he were not "a proclaimer of
alien divinities." This was an offense in Athens; and so they
brought him to the Areopagus. He was not formally arraigned
for trial—there was only set on foot something like a preliminary official inquiry; and the question put to him is oddly
compounded of courteous suggestion and authoritative demand. They said: "May we be allowed to know what this new
teaching is that is talked of by thee? For thou dost bring certain strange things to our ears; and it is our wish to know what
these things may be." The hand is gloved, but you see the iron
showing through. It was to Paul, however, only another opportunity; and in the conscious authority of his great mission he
stood forth in the midst of the court and began to speak.

We must bear in mind that Paul was put to the question on
the general charge that he was "a proclaimer of strange deities."
He had no intention whatever of denying this general allegation. He was rather firmly determined to seize this opportunity
yet once more to proclaim a Deity evidently unknown to the
Athenians. And this, in fact, he proceeded at once to do. But
he did it after a fashion which disarmed the complaint; which
enlisted the Athenians themselves as unwilling indeed, but
nevertheless real, worshipers of the God he proclaimed; and
which powerfully pried at their consciences as well as appealed
to their intelligences and even their national pride to give wings
to his proclamation.

The hinge on which the whole speech turns is obviously
Paul's deep sense of the darkness of heathen ignorance. As our

Saviour said to the Samaritan woman, so Paul, in effect, says to the Athenian jurists and philosophers, "You worship you know not what." The altar at Athens which he signalizes as especially significant of heathen worship is precisely the altar inscribed "To a Not-known God." The whole course of their heathen development he characterizes as a seeking of God, if by any chance—"in the possible hope at least that"—they may touch Him as a blind man touches with his hands fumblingly what he cannot see—and so doubtfully find Him; nay, shortly and crisply, as "times of ignorance." The very purpose of his proclamation of his gospel among them is to bring light into this darkness, to make them to know the true nature and the real modes of working, the all-inclusive plan and the decisive purpose of the one true God. Therefore it is simply true to say that the hinge on which the whole speech turns is the declaration that the heathen are steeped in ignorance and require, above all things, the light of divine instruction.

But when we have said this we have not said all. After all, it is not quite a blank ignorance that Paul ascribes to the Athenians. He institutes a certain connection between what they worship and the God he was commending to them. He does not wholly scoff at their religion, though he certainly sharply reprobates and deeply despises the modes in which it expresses itself. He does not entirely condemn their worship even of a not-known god; he rather makes it a point of attachment for proclaiming the higher worship of the known God of heaven and earth which he is recommending to them. There is, in a word, a certain amount of recognition accorded by him to their religious feelings and aspirations.

It is accordingly not all a scoff when he tells them that he perceives that they are apparently "very religious." The word he employs is no doubt sometimes used in a bad sense, and accordingly is frequently translated here by the ill-savored word "superstitious." So our English version translates it: "I perceive that in all things ye are too superstitious" or "somewhat superstitious," as the Revised Version puts it. But it is scarcely possible to believe that Paul uses it in this evil sense

here. It means in itself nothing but "divinity-fearing"—not exactly "God-fearing," though generally equivalent to that, because it has a hint in it of the gods many and lords many of
the heathen. It easily, therefore, lends itself to a bad sense,
and is often, as we have seen, so used. But as often it is used
in a perfectly good sense, as equivalent simply to "religious,"
and surely it is so used here. Paul is not charging his hearers
with superstition; he is recognizing in them a religious disposition. He chooses a term, indeed, of somewhat non-committal
character—which would not say too much—which might be
taken perhaps as bearing a subtle implication of incomplete
approval: but a word by which he expresses at least no active
disapproval and even a certain measure of active approval.
Paul, in fine, commends the religiousness of the Athenians.

The forms in which this religiousness expressed itself he
does not commend. The sight of them, indeed, threw him into
a paroxysm of distress, if not of indignation. He could not view
without disgust and horror the degradation of their worship.
In one sense we may say that it reached its lowest level in this
altar, "To a Not-known God." For what could be worse than
the superstitious dread which, after cramming every corner of
the city with altars to every conceivable divinity, was not yet
satisfied, but must needs feel blindly out after still some other
power of earth or air or sky to which to immolate victims or
before which to cringe in unintelligent fear? But in another aspect it may even have seemed to Paul that in this altar might
rather be seen the least degraded expression of the religious
aspirations of the Athenians. Where every definite trait given
to their conceptions of divinity was but a new degradation of
the idea of the divine, there is a certain advantage attaching to
vagueness. At least no distinctive foulness was attributed to a
god confessedly unknown. Perhaps just because of its undif-
ferentiation and indefiniteness it might therefore seem a purer
symbol of that seeking after God for which God had destined
all nations when He appointed to them the ordained times and
limits of their habitation, if by any chance they might feel

Him and so find Him. Surely the forms they gave to the gods they more definitely conceived, the characters they ascribed to them, the functions they assigned them, and the legendary stories of their activities which they wove around them, sufficiently evinced that in them the Athenians had not so much as fumblingly touched God, much less found Him. A worship offered to "an unknown god" was at least free from the horror of definitely conceiving God as corruptible men and birds and fourfooted beasts and creeping things.

In any event, behind the worship, however ill conceived, Paul sees and recognizes the working of that which he does not shame to call religion. Enshrined within his general condemnation of the heathenism of the Athenians there lies thus a recognition of something not to be condemned—something worthy of commendation rather—fit even on his lips to bear the name of "religion." All this is implied in the words we have chosen as our text, and it is therefore that we have said of them that they give us the gist of the whole address. "What ye thus not knowing adore," says Paul, "that it is that I am proclaiming to you." It will repay us, probably, to probe the matter a little in the way of its wider applications.

First, then, we say there is given in the apostolic teaching a certain recognition to the religion of the heathen.

We do not say, mark you, that a recognition is given to the heathen religions. That is something very different. The heathen religions are uniformly treated as degrading to man and insulting to God. The language of a recent writer which declares that man's "most unfortunate things" are his religions—nay, that man's religions are "among his worst crimes"—is thoroughly justified by the apostolic attitude toward them. Read but the account given at the end of the first chapter of Romans of the origin of these religions in the progressive degradation of man's thought of God, as man's repeated withdrawals from God and God's repeated judicial blindings of man interwork to the steady destruction of all religious insight and all moral perception alike, and from this observe how the writers of the New Testament conceived of the religions which men have in the procession of the ages formed for themselves.

Nor is it to be imagined that only the more degraded of the popular superstitions were in the apostle's mind when he painted this dreadful picture of the fruits of human religious thinking. In an almost contemporary epistle he calmly passes his similar judgment on all the philosophies of the world. Not by all its wisdom, he tells us, has the world come to know God, but in these higher elaborations also, becoming vain in its imaginations, its foolish heart has only become darkened. In a somewhat later epistle he sums up his terrible estimate of the religious condition of the Gentiles in that dreadful declaration that "they walk in the vanity of their mind, being darkened in their understanding, alienated from the life of God, because of the ignorance that is in them, because of the hardening of their heart."

This is what the apostle thought—not of some heathen, but of heathen as such, in their religious life—not of the degraded bushmen of Australia or Africa or New Guinea, but of the philosophic minds of Greece and Rome in the palmiest days of their intellectual development and ethical and æsthetic culture; of the Socrateses and Platos and Aristotles and Epictetuses and Marcus Aureliuses of that ancient world, which some would have us look upon as so fully to have found God as veritably to have taken heaven by storm and to have entered it by force of its own attainments. To him it was, on the contrary, in his briefest phrase, "without hope and without God."

Nevertheless, alongside of and in the very midst of this sweeping and unmitigated condemnation of the total religious manifestation of heathendom there exists an equally constant and distinct recognition of the reality and value of religion even among the heathen. It does not seem ever to have occurred to the writers of the New Testament to doubt that religion is as universal as intelligence itself; or to question the reality or value of this universal religiousness. To them man, as such, appears to be esteemed no more a reasonable creature than a religious animal; and they appeal to his religious instinct and build upon it expectations of a response to their appeal, with the same confidence which they show when they make their appeal to his logical faculty. They apparently no more expect to find a man without religion than they expect to find a man without understanding, and they seem to attach the same fundamental value to his inherent religiousness as to his inherent rationality.

In this the passage that is more particularly before us today is thoroughly representative of the whole New Testament. Paul, it is seen at once, does not here in any way question the fact that the Athenians are religious, any more than he questions that they are human beings. He notes, rather, with satisfaction that they are very especially religious. "I perceive that ye are in all things exceedingly divinity-fearing." There is a note of commendation in that which is unmistakable. Nor does he betray any impulse to denounce their religious sentiment as intrinsically evil. On the contrary, he takes it frankly as the basis of his appeal to them. In effect, he essays merely to direct and guide its functioning, and in so doing recognizes it as the foundation of all the religious life which he would, as the teacher of Christianity to them, fain see developed in and by them. In the same spirit he always deals with what we may call the inherent religiousness of humanity. Man, as such, in his view is truly and fundamentally religious.

Now this frank recognition, or, we might better say, this emphatic assertion of the inherent religiousness of humanity, constitutes a fact of the first importance in the biblical revelation. It puts the seal of divine revelation on the great fundamental doctrine that there exists in man a *notitia Dei insita*— a natural knowledge of God, which man can no more escape than he can escape from his own humanity. Endowed with an ineradicable sense of dependence and of responsibility, man knows that Other on which he depends and to whom he is responsible in the very same act by which he knows himself. As he can never know himself save as dependent and responsible, he can never know himself without a consciousness of that Other Not-self, on whom he is dependent and to whom he is responsible; and in this co-knowledge of self and Over-not-self is rooted the whole body of his religious conceptions, religious feelings, and religious actions—which are just as inevitable functionings of his intellect, sensibility, and will as any actions of those faculties, the most intimate and immediate we can conceive of. Thus man cannot help being religious; God is implicated in his very first act of self-consciousness, and he can avoid thinking of God, feeling toward Him, acting with respect to Him, only by avoiding thinking, feeling, and acting with respect to self.

How he shall conceive God—what notion he shall form, that is, of that Over-not-self in contrast with which he is conscious of dependence and responsibility; how he shall feel toward God—that is, toward that Over-not-self, conceived after this fashion or that; how he shall comport himself toward God— that is, over against that Over-not-self, so and not otherwise conceived, and so and not otherwise felt toward: these questions, it is obvious, raise additional problems, the solution of which must wait upon accurate knowledge of the whole body of conditions and circumstances in which the faculties of intellect, feeling, and will function in each given case. But that in his very first act of consciousness of self as a dependent and responsible and not as a self-centered and self-sufficient being, man is brought into contact with the Over-not-self on which he is dependent and to which he is responsible; and must therefore form some conception of it, feel in some way toward it, and act in some manner with respect to it, is as certain as that he will think and feel and act at all.

That man is a religious being, therefore, and will certainly have a religion, is rooted in his very nature, and is as inevitable as it is that man will everywhere and always be man. But what religion man will have is no more subject to exact *a priori* determination than is the product of the action of his faculties along any other line of their functioning. Religion exists and must exist everywhere where man lives and thinks and feels and acts; but the religions that exist will be as varied as the idiosyncrasies of men, the conditions in which their faculties work, the influences that play on them and determine the character of their thoughts and feelings and deeds.

Bearing this in mind, we shall not be surprised to note that along with the recognition of the religiousness of man embodied in the apostolic teaching, there is equally prominent in it, as we have said, the unwavering assertion of the absolute necessity of religious instruction for the proper religious development of man.

The whole mission of the apostle is founded upon, or, more properly speaking, is the appropriate expression of, this point of sight. Nor could he be untrue to it on an occasion like that which is more particularly engaging our attention today. We observe, then, as we have already pointed out, that though he commends the Athenians for their God-fearingness and finds in their altar to a "not-known god" a point of attachment for his proclamation of the true God; he does not for a moment suggest that their native religiousness could be left safely to itself to blossom into a fitting religious life; or that his proclamation of the known God of heaven and earth possessed only a relative necessity for them.

Clearly he presents the necessity rather as absolute. God had for a time, no doubt, left the nations of the world to the guidance of their own religious nature, that they might seek after Him in the possible expectation at least of finding Him. But on God's part this was intended rather as a demonstration of their incapacity than as a hopeful opportunity afforded them; and in its results it provides an empirical proof of the absolute necessity of His interference with direct guidance. Accordingly the apostle roundly characterizes the issue of all heathen religious development, inclusive of that in Athens itself, the seat of the highest heathen thinking on divine things, as just bald ignorance. That the world by its wisdom knows not God and lies perishing in its ignorance is the most fixed element of his whole religious philosophy.

What is involved here is, of course, the whole question of the necessity of "special revelation." It is a question which has been repeatedly fought out during the course of Christian history. In the eighteenth century, for example, it was this very issue that was raised in the sharpest possible form by the deistic controversy. A coterie of religious philosophers, possessing an eye for little in man beyond his logical understanding, undertook to formulate what they called the "natural religion." This they then set over against the supernatural religion, which Christianity professed to be, as the religion of nature in contrast with the religion of authority—authority being prejudged to be in this sphere altogether illegitimate. The result was certainly instructive. Bernard Pünger is not a jot too severe when he remarks of this boasted "natural religion" of the Deists, that it deserves neither element of its designation. "It is," he declares, "neither religion nor natural, but only an extremely artificial abstraction of theologians and philosophers. It is no religion, for nowhere, in no spot, in either the old or new world, has there ever existed even the smallest community which recognized this 'natural religion.' And it is not natural; for no simple man ever arrived of himself at the ideas of this 'natural religion.' "

And when it was thus at last formulated by the philosophers of the eighteenth century, it proved no religion even to them. A meager body of primary abstract truth concerning God and His necessary relations to man was the entire result. This formed, indeed, an admirable witness to the rational rooting of these special truths concerning God and our relations to Him in the very nature of man as a dependent and responsible being; and this the Christian thinker may well view with satisfaction. It may be taken as supplying him also with a demonstration, once for all, that an adequate body of religious truth can never be obtained by the artificial process of abstracting from all the religions of the world the elements held in common by them all, and labeling this "natural religion." Neither in religion nor in any other sphere of life can the maxim be safely adopted that the least well-endowed member of a coterie shall be crowned king over all. Yet obviously that is the result of proceeding by what is called "the consensus method" in seeking a norm of religious truth.

Taught wisdom by experience like this, our more modern world has found a new method of ridding itself of the necessity of revelation. The way was pointed out to it by no less a genius than Friedrich Schleiermacher himself. Led no doubt by the laudable motive of seeking a place for religion unassailable on the shallow ground of intellectualistic criticism, he relegated it in its origin exclusively to the region of feeling. In essence he said, religion is the immediate feeling of absolute dependence.

He calls it an "immediate feeling" or an "immediate self-consciousness" just in order to eliminate from it every intellectual element. That is to say, he wishes to distinguish between two forms of self-consciousness or feeling, the one mediated by the perception of an object and the other not so mediated, but consisting in an immediate and direct sensation, abstracted from every intellectual representation or idea; and in this latter class of feelings he places that feeling of absolute dependence with which he identifies religion. Religion, therefore, it is argued, is entirely independent of every intellectual conception; it is rooted in a pure feeling or immediate consciousness which enters into and affects all of our intellectual exercises, but is itself absolutely independent of them all, and persists the same through whatever intellectual conceptions we may form of the object of our worship or through whatever actions we may judge appropriate to the service of that object thus or otherwise conceived.

Upon the basis of this mode of conceiving religion we have been treated of late to innumerable pæans to religion as a primal force running through all the religions; and are being constantly exhorted to recognize as absolutely immaterial what forms it takes in its several manifestations, and to greet it as subsisting equally valid and equally noble beneath all its forms of manifestation indifferently, because in itself independent of them all. It is thus only the common cry that echoes all around us which Père Hyacinthe repeats in his passionate declaration: "It is not true that all religions are false except one only."

Only a few years ago when a professor was being inducted into a new chair of the History of Religion established in one of the oldest of the Reformed schools, he took up the same cry with much the same passion, and professed himself able to feel brotherhood with every form of religion—except that perhaps which arrogated to itself to be the only legitimate form. "When the history of religions," he eloquently said, "places in our hands the religious archives of humanity it is surely our duty rather to garner these treasures than to proclaim Christianity the only good, the only true one among the religions of men. 'We also, we also are the offspring of God,' the poet Aratus cried three centuries before Christ. Let us pause before this cry of the human soul and let us contemplate with attention the luminous web in which the history of this divine sonship has been woven by universal worship. When we have opened, with the same respect which we demand for our own, the sacred books of other peoples, when we have observed them clinging, as to their most holy possessions, to their sublime traditions, in which are enshrined the mother-thoughts of all true religion—lavishing their genius in exalting them, sacrificing their fortunes in defending them, exiling themselves to the most distant lands and sinking into the burning sands in propagating them, accepting death itself in order to preserve them— our hearts, moved with surprise and brotherly sympathy, will repudiate for ever the Pharisaic pride which treats as heathen or as uncircumcised all God's creatures which are without the sacred pale of the elect." "Men of all nations," he tells us, "and of all tongues—whether savage or civilized, whether ignorant or instructed, whether Parsi or Christian—though God may have been revealed to them diversely, though they may be looking up to Him through variously-colored glasses—are yet all looking nevertheless up to the same God, by whatever liturgical name He may be known to them—and it is to Him that all their prayers alike are ascending. And to all of them," he adds, "I feel myself a brother—except to the hypocrite."

"No one," he concludes, "who has ever felt echoing in his heart the murmur of this universal worship will ever be able to return to the sectarian apologetics with which the unhappiness of the times inspired the Jews after the exile, and which from Judaism has passed into the Church of Christ."

I have not thus adverted to this eloquent address because it is especially extreme in its assertions. It is not. Rather, let it be said, it enunciates with unusual balance and moderation views common to a large part of the modern world. It is on this very account that I have adduced its presentation of this very widespread conception—because it affords us a very favorable opportunity to observe it at its best, touched with fervor and announced with winning eloquence of speech. Even in it, however, we may perceive the portentous results to which the whole conception of religion as an "immediate feeling" may take us—nay, must inevitably carry us. If what it tells us be true, it obviously is of no importance whatever with what conceptions religion may be connected. So only the religious sentiment be present, all that enters into the essence of religion is there; and one may call himself Brahmin or Mohammedan, Parsi or Christian, and may see God through whatever spectacles and name Him by whatever designation he will, and yet be and remain alike, and alike, validly, religious. We may justly look upon this inevitable result of the identification of religion with an "immediate feeling" as its sufficient refutation.

In no event could it be thought difficult, however, to exhibit the untenability of this entire conception. We should probably only need to ask, How could an abstract feeling of dependence, with no implication whatever of the object on which the dependence leans, possess any distinctively religious quality whatever? It would appear too clear to require arguing that the whole religious quality of a feeling of dependence, recognized as religious, must be derived necessarily from the nature of the object depended upon—viz., God. If we conceive that object as something other than God, then the feeling of dependence ceases to be in any intelligible sense religious. It is assuredly only on God that a specifically religious feeling can rest.

Schleiermacher himself appears to have felt this. And accordingly he distinguished between the feeling of dependence in general and the feeling of absolute dependence in particular; and on the supposition that absolute dependence can be felt only toward the Absolute, confined the religious feeling to it. Here there appears to be a subintroduction of the idea of God; and therefore a veiled admission that we have in this "feeling of absolute dependence" not an "immediate feeling," but a feeling mediated by an idea, to wit, the idea of God. Thus the whole contention is, in principle, yielded; and we revert to the more natural and only valid ground—that all their quality is supplied to feelings by the objects to which they are directed, and that, therefore, the nature of our conceptions so far from having nothing, has everything, to do with religion.

I recall with great vividness of memory a striking picture I once saw, painted by that weird Russo-German genius Sasha Schneider, in order to illustrate religion conceived as the feeling of absolute dependence, and at the same time to express the artist's repugnance to it and scorn of it. It has seemed to me to provide us with a most striking parable. He figures a man stripped naked and laden down with chains, head bowed, in every trait dejection, every fiber of every muscle relaxed, every line a line of hopelessness and despair. The ground on which he stands is the earth itself, fashioned, however, into the hideous presentment of a monstrous form, so painted as to give it the texture of hard, black, iron-like stone. The horizon that stretches around the figure and seems to bend in upon him consists of two great iron-like arms ending in dreadfully protuberant fingers, which appear about to close in on his limbs; while just before him heavy shoulders rise slightly into a low forbidding hillock, and between them thrusts forward the hard mound of a scarce-distinguishable head, lit by two malevolent eyes, like low volcano-fires glaring up upon their victim. Thus is set forth the artist's conception of religious sentiment as the "feeling of absolute dependence."

Yes—but we then must add, there are two points that require criticism in the conception presented. First, in this figure of a despondent man, the artist has, after all, painted not the feeling of dependence, but rather the feeling of helplessness. These are very different things. And in their difference we touch, as I think, the very heart of the error we are seeking to unmask. A feeling of dependence, properly so-called, necessarily implies an object: helplessness—yes, that may exist without an object, but not dependence. He that depends must needs have somewhat on which to depend. A feeling of dependence is unthinkable apart from the object on which the dependence rests. In picturing for us abject "helplessness," then, the artist has not at all pictured for us "dependence." The former is passive, the latter is active, and the abjectness that belongs to the one is not at all inherent in the other. Secondly, even so, the artist has not been able to get along without an object. He has painted this dejected man: there he stands before us the very picture of helplessness. But the artistic sense is not satisfied: and so he throws around him these hideous encircling arms; he sets upon him this baleful gaze. He must suggest, after all, an object toward which the feeling of dependence he is endeavoring to depict turns. But why this hideous object? Only to justify the abjectness of the figure he has painted. From which we may learn at once that the character of the feeling—all that gives quality and meaning to it—is, after all, necessarily dependent on the nature of the object to which it is referred.

And so, if we mistake not, Sasha Schneider's picture is itself the sufficient refutation of the whole conception of religion we are discussing. Given no object, the figure of helplessness remains inexplicable and meaningless and will result in nothing. Given a monstrous object, it develops at once into a figure of abject misery. Given a glorious object—a God of righteousness and goodness—and only then does it develop into a figure of that dependence which we call religion. And if we require an earthly image of this feeling of dependence, let us find it in an infant on its mother's bosom, looking up in confidence and trust into a face on which it perceives the smiles of goodness and love. Even the heathen poet tells us that the happy infant laughs as it sees the smile of love on the mother's countenance. It is in such scenes as this that the true earthly portrait of the absolute dependence, which is religion is to be found.

But it is neither to logical analysis nor to the artistic instinct of a Sasha Schneider that we need to turn today to assure ourselves that this whole construction of religion as independent of knowledge is impossible. For surely it is obvious that it is the very antipodes of Paul's view of the matter. This we have already sufficiently pointed out, and need only now to remind ourselves of it.

Perhaps it is enough for this purpose simply to ask afresh how Paul dealt with the religiousness of the Athenians, notable as they were among all nations for their religiousness. Assuredly he did not withhold due recognition from it. "O men of Athens," he cried, "I perceive that in all things ye are exceedingly religious." But did he account this exceeding religiousness enough for their needs? As he went about the streets of Athens and beheld the great city studded with idols—one great sanctuary, as it were—did he reason within himself that the forms of manifestation were of no importance, that through and beneath them we should rather perceive that pure impulse to worship which sustained and gave vitality and value to them all; and, observing in it the essence of all religions alike, recognize it as enough?

Our text gives us the emphatic answer: "What ye, thus, in ignorance adore, that it is that I declare unto you." The whole justification of his mission hangs on the value he attaches to knowledge as the informing principle of all right, of all valid, of all availing religion. And if we care to follow Paul we must for our part also, once and for all, renounce with the strongest emphasis all attempts to conceive the native religious impulse as capable in sinful man of producing religious phenomena which can be recognized as well pleasing in the sight of God.

No doubt we shall be under manifold temptations to do otherwise. Our modern atmosphere is charged to saturation with temptations to do otherwise. Let us all the more carefully arm ourselves against them. In warning us against this over-estimate of natural religions Paul may perhaps be allowed to give us also a name for it, by the employment of which we may possibly be able to put a new point on our self-admonitions. He calls it, as we have seen, in the case of the Athenians, by a term of somewhat peculiar flavor. "Divinity-fearing" we bunglingly translate it—that is, so to say, "generally Divinity-fearing," without too close inquisition into which divinity it is that we fear or what is the character of the service that we render it. "Deisidaimonism" is the Greek term he makes use of. It is an uncouth term. But, then, it is not a very lovely thing it designates. And perhaps, in the absence of a good translation, we may profitably adopt the Greek term today, with all its uncouthness of sound and its unlovely association, and so enable ourselves to make a recognizable distinction between that general natural religiosity and its fruits which we may call "deisidaimonism" and true religion, which is the product of the saving truth of God operating upon our native religious instincts and producing through them phenomena which owe all their value to the truth that gives them form.

Ah, brethren, let us avoid "deisidaimonism" in all its manifestations! As you look out over the heathen world with its lords many and gods many, and see working in every form of faith the same religious impulses, the same religious aspirations, producing in varying measure indeed, but yet everywhere, to some extent, the same civilizing and moralizing effects—are you perhaps sometimes tempted to pronounce it enough; possibly adding something about the special adaptation of the several faiths to the several peoples, or even something about the essential truth underlying all religions? This is "deisidaimonism." And on its basis the whole missionary work of the Church is an impertinence, the whole history of the Church a gigantic error; the great commission itself a crime against humanity—launching the Christian world upon a fool's errand, every step of which has dripped with wasted blood. Surely the proclamation of the gospel is made, then, mere folly and the blood of the martyrs becomes only the measure of the narrow fanaticism of earlier and less enlightened times.

It is possible, however, that your temptation does not come to you in such a crass shape. Perhaps it may whisper to you only something about the narrowness of sectarianism within the limits of Christianity—of the folly of contentions over what we may at the moment be happening to call "the truth." Look, it may say—do you not see that under every faith the religious life flourishes? Why lay stress then on creed? Creeds are divisive things; away with them! Or at least let us prune all their distinctive features away, and give ourselves a genial and unpolemic Christianity, a Christianity in which all the stress is laid on life, not dogma, the life of the spirit in its aspirations toward God, or perchance, even the life of external activities in the busy fulfillment of the duties of life. This too, you observe, is "deisidaimonism." Embark once on that pathway and there is no logical and—oh, the misfortune of it!—no practical stopping-point until you have evaporated all recognizable Christianity away altogether and reduced all religion to the level of man's natural religiosity. A really "undogmatic Christianity" is just no Christianity at all.

Let us not for an instant suppose, to be sure, that religion is a matter of the intellect alone or chiefly. But in avoiding the Scylla of intellectualism let us not run into the Charybdis of mere naturalism. All that makes the religion we profess distinctively Christian is enshrined in its doctrinal system. It is therefore that it is a religion that can be taught, and is to be taught—that is propagated by what otherwise would be surely, in the most literal sense, the foolishness of preaching. Mere knowledge, indeed, does not edify; it only puffs up. But neither without knowledge can there be any edification; and the purer the knowledge that is propagated by any church the purer, the deeper, the more vital and the more vitalizing will be the Christianity that is built up under that church's teaching. Let us renounce, then, in this sphere, too, all "deisidaimonism," and demand that our church shall be the church of a creed and that that creed shall be the pure truth of God—all of it and nothing but it. Only so can we be truly, purely, and vitally Christian.

And what shall we say of "deisidaimonism" in the personal religious life? Ah, brethren, there is where its temptations are the most subtle and its assaults the most destructive! How easy it is to mistake the currents of mere natural religious feeling, that flow up and down in the soul, for signs that it is well with us in the sight of God! Happy the man who is born with a deep and sensitive religious nature! But shall that purely natural endowment save him? There are many who have cried, Lord, Lord, who shall never enter into the kingdom of heaven. Not because you are sensitive and easily moved to devotion; not because your sense of divine things is profound or lofty; not because you are like the Athenians, by nature "divinity-fearing"; but because, when the word of the Lord is brought to you, and Jesus Christ is revealed in your soul, under the prevailing influence of the Holy Ghost, you embrace Him with a hearty faith—cast yourself upon His almighty grace for salvation, and turning from your sins, enter into a life of obedience to Him— can you judge yourself a Christian. Religious you may be, and deeply religious, and yet not a Christian. How instructive that when Paul himself preached in "deisidaimonistic" Athens, where religiosity ran riot, no church seems to have been founded. We have only the meager result recorded that "there were some men that clave unto him and believed, among whom also was Dionysius, the Areopagite, and a woman named Damaris, and others along with them." The natively religious are not, therefore, nearer to the kingdom of God.

But, thank God, the contrary is also true. Those who have no special native religious endowments are not, therefore, excluded from the kingdom of God. We may rightly bewail our coldness: we may rightly blame ourselves that there is so little response in our hearts to the sight of the glory of God in the face of Jesus Christ, or even to the manifestation of His unspeakable love in the death of His Son. Oh, wretched men that we are to see that bleeding love and not be set on fire with a flame of devotion! But we may be all the more thankful that it is not in our frames and feelings that we are to put our trust. Let us abase ourselves that we so little respond to these great spectacles of the everlasting and unspeakable love of God. But let us ever remember that it is on the love of God and not on our appreciation of it that we are to build our confidence. Jesus our Priest and our Sacrifice, let us keep our eyes set on Him! And though our poor sinful hearts so little know how to yield to that great spectacle the homage of a suitable response, His blood will yet avail even for us.

> "Nothing in my hand I bring,
> Simply to Thy cross I cling"—

here—and let us bless God for it—here is the essence of Christianity. It is all of God and nothing of ourselves.